THE VEGETARIAN
FLAVOR
BIBLE

BOOKS BY KAREN PAGE AND ANDREW DORNENBURG

THE VEGETARIAN FLAVOR BIBLE

THE ESSENTIAL GUIDE TO CULINARY CREATIVITY WITH VEGETABLES, FRUITS, GRAINS, LEGUMES, NUTS, SEEDS, AND MORE, BASED ON THE WISDOM OF LEADING AMERICAN CHEFS

KAREN PAGE

PHOTOGRAPHS BY ANDREW DORNENBURG

LITTLE, BROWN AND COMPANY
NEW YORK | BOSTON | LONDON

Little, Brown and Company
Hachette Book Group
1290 Avenue of the Americas, New York, NY 10104
littlebrown.com

First Edition: October 2014

Little, Brown and Company is a division of Hachette Book Group, Inc. The Little, Brown name and logo are trademarks of Hachette Book Group, Inc.

The publisher is not responsible for websites (or their content) that are not owned by the publisher.

This book should not take the place of personalized medical care or treatment. This book contains the opinions and ideas of its author and is intended to provide useful information on its subject matter. It is sold with the understanding that the author and publisher are not engaged in rendering professional services via this book. The author and publisher disclaim all liability in connection with the use of this book.

ISBN 978-0-316-24418-3
Library of Congress Control Number: 2014939697
10 9 8 7 6 5 4 3 2 1
IM
Printed in Italy

"And God said, See, I have given you every herb that yields seed which is upon the face of all the earth, and every tree whose fruit yields seed; to you it shall be for food."
—Genesis 1:29, New King James Bible

"It is my view that a vegetarian manner of living . . . would most beneficially influence the lot of mankind."
—Albert Einstein, in a letter to Hermann Huth (December 27, 1930)

"The weight of evidence at this point in time . . . is so overwhelming. . . . Nothing else . . . can begin to compete with the evidence available for the whole food, plant-based diets in terms of promoting human health."
—T. Colin Campbell, author of *The China Study*

For Andrew,

who — even after twenty-nine years — still continues to surprise me

CONTENTS

INTRODUCTION

ix

INTRODUCTION

"Over half of Americans [52 percent] believe it is easier to figure out their income taxes than to figure out what they should and shouldn't eat to be healthier."
—THE 2012 FOOD & HEALTH SURVEY: CONSUMER ATTITUDES TOWARD FOOD SAFETY, NUTRITION & HEALTH, COMMISSIONED BY THE INTERNATIONAL FOOD INFORMATION COUNCIL FOUNDATION

"In all my interviews with nutrition experts, the benefits of a plant-based diet provided the only point of universal consensus."
—MICHAEL POLLAN, *IN DEFENSE OF FOOD* (2008)

This book started with a problem: I didn't know what to eat.

In two decades of writing about food, I've have had the pleasure and privilege of interviewing many of the world's greatest chefs while studying their secrets for making food taste great. My work-related eating (including wine-tasting lunches and dinners) often took me to the dining rooms of DANIEL, Le Bernardin, and Per Se — or, during a year spent eating at chefs' favorite restaurants from coast to coast, sampling In-N-Out burgers, pork-and-crab soup dumplings, and both Pat's and Geno's cheese steaks. My life included an endless pursuit of deliciousness, and I was always thrilled to discover what I'd learn from the next bite. But as more and more headlines trumpeted the relationship between nutrition and wellness, it dawned on me that for someone who ate for a living, I'd thought surprisingly little about what to put in my body to keep myself healthy when I wasn't busy eating for professional reasons.

After I lost both my father and stepmother to cancer between 2006 and 2009, I couldn't help thinking about my own half-century birthday looming on the horizon. It finally occurred to me, for the first time in my life, that I might want to start including healthfulness as a criterion for choosing what to eat.

After poring over dozens of books and websites on food and nutrition, I found myself confused by varying (and often contradictory) nutritional advice. If I — a graduate of Northwestern and Harvard and longtime culinary professional — was having a tough time figuring out what makes a healthful diet, what about everyone else? I was not surprised, then, to discover that in a 2012 poll, over half of Americans polled said they found it easier to *do their taxes* than to figure out what to eat to keep themselves healthy. Now *that's* frustration.

The general public's lack of nutritional knowledge is tragic, because it turns out that **the leading cause of death in this country is nutritionally controllable diseases**, such as cancer, heart disease, and diabetes. Diets that forego animal protein in favor of plant protein are associated with a lower risk of all three.

I eventually did find this common thread among what I learned to be the best-respected authorities: their advice to **eat a plant-based diet**, especially plentiful vegetables. The corollary was to avoid processed "junk" foods with empty calories (especially from fat and sugar) and to instead **opt for whole foods** as much as possible.

When I finally decided to experiment with virtually full-time vegetarianism in May 2012, I kept quiet about it — because having grown up in the heart of the Midwest, eating meat at least two and often three times a day, I had serious doubts that I could stick with a meatless diet for even a week or two.

My husband, Andrew — who had cooked professionally at some of the best restaurants in Boston and New York City, and who bravely joined me in my experiment in meatless eating — typically did our grocery shopping and most of the cooking. I provided "help" by giving him a list of what *not* to buy: Junk foods. Soft drinks. White flour, white sugar, white rice. Anything with hydrogenated vegetable oil. Trans fats. GMOs. Every news report seemed to add a new no-no to the list.

Over time, my "what-*not*-to-buy" list got so long that he grumbled, "Maybe you could make a list of what you'd *like* me to buy."

A light bulb went off. I realized that avoiding certain foods — whether meats or white foods — was only one part of the picture. I decided to start a list of the healthiest ingredients that would provide us with the biggest nutritional bang for the calorie — "superfoods" that we could easily enjoy at home: Black beans. Blueberries. Broccoli. Kale. Lemons. Quinoa. Spinach. Then I started researching compatible flavors and flavor affinities for each, for ease in creating dishes. Then dish ideas themselves were added, often inspired by my research on the cookbooks, restaurants, and signature dishes of America's best vegetarian and vegan chefs, dozens of whom I eventually interviewed. Although I started without any intention other than eating healthier at home, the project eventually evolved into this book and the lists you'll find in Chapter 3.

Months later, we were both surprised to find that we didn't miss meat at all. Instead, we were thrilled by all of the new flavor discoveries we were making about an exciting new repertoire of ingredients. We also noticed that when dining out, others were showing more interest in the meatless dishes we were being served than we had in those they were served. Andrew and I have been eating 99 percent vegetarian ever since.

When I finally started to mention this to others, I was asked time and time again by well-meaning friends and colleagues what I've since learned is the Number One question asked of vegetarians and vegans: *"But how do you get your protein?"*

My desire to make certain that the vegetarian diet I was embracing was indeed healthful — and to have well-informed, intelligent answers to such questions — led me to earn a certificate in plant-based nutrition from Cornell in conjunction with the T. Colin Campbell Foundation. The certificate program was created by the author of *The China Study*, the most groundbreaking, far-reaching nutritional study ever published. This is the education that helped inform my subsequent research for this book, which addresses three primary questions: what to eat (and in what quantities), how to make it healthful, and how to make it so delicious that its meatlessness is completely beside the point!

MAKING IT HEALTHFUL

"Let food be thy medicine."

—HIPPOCRATES

Hippocrates was right. Each of us can play a role in solving our nation's health crisis by taking the responsibility for choosing and administering our own "medicine," an average of three times a day. As many doctors receive little or no training in nutrition, it's up to each of us to learn the basics so we can eat to keep ourselves in good health and our immune systems strong. Happily, more Americans are finally understanding the health risks posed by animal protein and are reducing or eliminating it from their diets. Per capita meat consumption in the U.S. has fallen for the last five years and is forecasted to keep falling.

However, even when following a vegetarian diet, what you eat is just as important as what you

PROTEIN: IT'S WHAT'S FOR DINNER (AND LUNCH AND BREAKFAST) — EVEN WHEN YOU'RE EATING PLANTS

Here's a typical conversation I've had after admitting to eating vegetarian, a version of which I first wrote as a class assignment for Cornell:

"Hey, Karen — did I hear you're a vegetarian now? How are you getting enough protein if you're not eating meat anymore? You don't seem like the tofu and 'wheat meat' type!"

"Hi, Pat — actually, I've had some really delicious dishes made with tofu and seitan and even tempeh, but I don't eat them very often. I probably get my protein from many of the same foods you do."

"You mean you're sneaking a cheeseburger here and there?"

"No, I mean I ran into you at the bagel place around the corner the other morning. A medium-sized bagel contains 10 grams of protein."

"No kidding — I thought I was carbo-loading then!"

"Well, you got protein along with your carbs. I had my bagel that morning with a couple of tablespoons of peanut butter, which added another 8 grams of protein. And that night for dinner, Andrew made pasta primavera — with 8 grams of protein from the cup of pasta and another 9 grams of protein from the cup each of broccoli and spinach he added. It was delicious!"

"Guess I thought you had to eat meat to get protein. What other foods have it?"

"Lots of plant-based whole foods have protein, including legumes, such as beans, lentils, and peas — and chickpeas, which I know you like because I saw you eating that hummus wrap the other week. Plus whole grains, nuts, and seeds. . . . The list is long."

"And you get as much protein from them as you would from a cheeseburger?"

"You can easily get enough protein from a balanced plant-based diet — but with a lot less fat. And because of the health risks — including cancer and heart disease — you definitely *don't* want to be eating *too much* protein."

"Wow — I didn't know. . . . I thought protein was good for you."

"It is — it's essential. But many people are unaware that it can actually be very risky to eat too much animal protein — which might just explain why there are so many sick people in the U.S., despite the fact that we spend more on healthcare than any other country."

don't eat. After all, a soy burger on a white bun with corn chips and a soft drink may not contain meat, but few would argue that it's a healthful meal.

On a visit several years ago to one of the top-rated vegetarian restaurants in the New York City *Zagat Survey,* I was struck by how many dishes were deep-fried and how "heavy" I felt afterward. The lesson hit home that it's also important to favor dishes made via water-based cooking techniques (e.g., boiling, poaching, steaming) over fat-based cooking techniques (e.g., deep-fat frying, sautéing).

In addition, you'll want to make sure your diet emphasizes foods that are the most nutritionally dense, delivering the most nutrients for the fewest calories. Dr. Joel Fuhrman, the bestselling author of *Eat to Live,* has developed a useful system called ANDI (Aggregate Nutrient Density Index), which Whole Foods shoppers might already be familiar with, as it's used throughout the stores. Various foods are rated for nutrient content on a scale of 0–1000, so you can minimize foods at the lower end of the scale (e.g., cola and corn chips, which score a 1 and a 7, respectively) and seek out those at the higher end of the scale (e.g., greens such as collard, kale, and watercress, all of which score a perfect 1000). Other systems such as Dr. David Katz's NuVal (featured at grocers like Kroger and Lowes) similarly score foods based on their nutrition. In Chapter 3, you'll find many foods color-coded to help you find those that are more nutritionally dense (i.e., those with dark green and green dots) and exercise judgment when it comes to others (i.e., those with orange and red dots). As a rule of thumb,

● Dark Green   Most green vegetables (and many herbs and spices)
● Green   Most nongreen vegetables, fresh fruits, and legumes
● Yellow   Most dried or sweeter fruits, grains, nuts, and seeds
● Orange   Most dairy products (e.g., cheese, full-fat milk and yogurt)
● Red   Most oils and sweeteners

But opting for kale 100 percent of the time to fulfill your vegetable quotient doesn't make for a healthful diet, either, despite its status as a nutritional powerhouse. You need vitamins, minerals, and other nutrients that can come only from eating a wide *variety* of vegetables. My own strategy is to eat "in a different country" most days of the week, which presents me with a broad range of vegetables over the course of a week or two. For example:

Chinese:	bok choy, broccoli, eggplant, long beans, mushrooms, snow peas
Ethiopian:	beets, collard greens, green beans, lentils, onions
French:	carrots, celery root, eggplant, French lentils, leeks, onions
Greek:	chickpeas, eggplant, gigante beans, romaine lettuce, spinach
Indian:	cauliflower, chickpeas, eggplant, jackfruit, lentils, spinach
Italian:	arugula, broccoli rabe, tomatoes, white beans, zucchini

Japanese:	edamame, mushrooms, sea vegetables (e.g., kelp, wakame), spinach
Mexican:	avocados, beans, chayote, chiles, corn, tomatillos, tomatoes
Moroccan:	cabbage, carrots, chickpeas, sweet potatoes, turnips, zucchini
Spanish:	green or white asparagus, piquillo peppers, potatoes
Thai:	bamboo shoots, bell peppers, eggplant, green beans, onions
Vietnamese:	cabbage, cucumbers, lettuce, mushrooms, taro, watercress

Variety is just as important when it comes to the rest of your diet — namely, fruits, grains, legumes, nuts, and seeds — which helps to ensure you're taking in the variety of nutrients your body needs. Dr. Fuhrman even came up with the useful acronym "G-BOMBS" as a reminder of the most nutritionally dense foods he believes should be a part of a healthful daily diet: **g**reens, **b**eans, **o**nions, **m**ushrooms, **b**erries, and **s**eeds, which he has found to be "extremely effective at preventing chronic disease and promoting health and longevity."

I love rules of thumb because they're straightforward and useful. One of the easiest to remember is Michael Pollan's seven-word mantra: "Eat food. Mostly plants. Not too much." By advising us to "eat food," Pollan refers to whole foods — meaning we should avoid processed foods. "Mostly plants" means we should make sure that the majority of our diet consists of vegetables, fruits, whole grains and whole-grain products, legumes, nuts, and seeds. And "not too much" warns against overconsuming food in such quantities that we become overweight or obese and put ourselves at greater risk of heart disease, hypertension, and diabetes.

ChooseMyPlate.gov offers "Tips for Vegetarians," suggesting that they may need to give special attention to their intake of "protein, iron, calcium, zinc, and vitamin B12." I address the (non-)issue of getting sufficient nutrients such as protein and calcium later in this chapter, but it's worth covering the others here briefly. Vegetarians who eat eggs and/or dairy shouldn't have a problem getting enough **vitamin B12**. Vegans sometimes sprinkle cheesy-tasting nutritional yeast (a great source of B12) on their popcorn and tofu scrambles or take B12 supplements.

However, both **iron** (in beans, black-eyed peas, blackstrap molasses, broccoli, chard, chickpeas, collard greens, lentils, spinach, tempeh, tofu) and **zinc** (in almonds, beans, cashews, chickpeas, green peas, oatmeal, pumpkin seeds, wheat germ) are readily available via plant-based sources. Since I started to eat vegetarian, my blood tests haven't indicated any nutritional deficiencies; in addition, my hair and skin (which now feel amazingly moisturized from the inside out) both have a new glow, and perhaps most tellingly, I feel better than ever.

A nutrient-rich, whole-food plant-based diet is the answer to so many health concerns — from protecting our bones, brains, eyes, hearts, and kidneys, to preventing or sometimes even reversing autoimmune diseases, cancer, diabetes, heart disease, and more. And if you're seeking any additional reasons to consider a vegetarian or even vegan diet, you're likely to find them in Chapter 1.

WHAT TO EAT (AND HOW MUCH)

"Vegetarian diets can meet all the recommendations for nutrients. The key is to consume a variety of foods and the right amount of foods to meet your calorie needs."
—CHOOSEMYPLATE.GOV, "TIPS FOR VEGETARIANS"

"Go with plants. Eating a plant-based diet is healthiest. Make your plate vegetables and fruits (potatoes and French fries don't count as vegetables). . . . Get most or all of your protein from beans, nuts and seeds, or tofu."
—THE NUTRITION SOURCE, HARVARD SCHOOL OF PUBLIC HEALTH (HSPH.HARVARD.EDU)

Food is composed of one or more of three macronutrients: **protein**, **carbohydrates**, and **fat**. All three are essential to a healthful diet, so you'll want to choose foods that provide you with sufficient quantities of each — but not too much of any, especially protein and fat, which correlate with increased rates of disease when they are overconsumed. But what *is* the right proportion? Based on all I've learned, I'll give a short answer and a long answer.

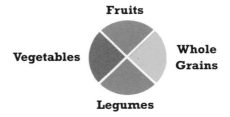

The Short Answer: A healthful meatless diet consists *primarily* of roughly equal proportions of **vegetables**, **fruits**, **legumes**, and **whole grains** (accented by nuts and seeds). If you picture yourself filling your plate with some of each at every meal, making sure to eat a wide variety of whole, unprocessed foods from every category over the course of every week (to ensure that you're getting a variety of vitamins, minerals, and other nutrients), and *not* overeating (i.e., not consuming too many calories, particularly from protein or fat), generally speaking, you don't need to worry about counting calories, grams of protein, or anything else.

The Long Answer: Opinions differ on exactly what proportions of total calories you should get from each macronutrient. For benchmarks, I'll share what the U.S. government recommends via its 2010 ChooseMyPlate.gov program — which many have argued overemphasizes meat and dairy as a result of those industries' enormous economic and political clout — and contrast that with recommendations from other respected sources such as *The China Study*. Each of us needs to decide for ourselves what to eat, and those decisions are, ideally, well informed and appropriate to our personal circumstances (e.g., younger and healthy, versus older and trying to reverse heart disease). For what it's worth, I'll also share what I personally choose to eat, based on what I've learned.

PROTEIN

The 2010 Dietary Guidelines for Americans recommends that 10 to 35 percent of total daily calories come from protein.

However, in *The China Study*, T. Colin Campbell recommends that **less than 10 percent of total daily calories** come from healthful protein (sufficient to meet the body's need for 5 to 6 percent dietary protein to replace that which the body regularly excretes, yet insufficient to trigger the onset of disease), which translates into just 50 to 60 grams of protein per day. The average American typically consumes 70 to 100 grams per day, primarily from animal-based sources (e.g., meats, poultry, seafood), a level of overconsumption that correlates with a higher risk of diseases such as heart disease and certain cancers. Because 50 to 60 grams of protein a day can easily be provided by a plant-based diet, *The China Study* recommends avoiding meat, poultry, eggs, and dairy.

"Dietary protein within the range of 10 – 20 percent is associated with a broad array of health problems [e.g., higher blood cholesterol levels, higher risks of atherosclerosis, cancer, osteoporosis, Alzheimer's disease, and kidney stones], especially when most of the protein is from animal sources."
—T. COLIN CAMPBELL, *THE CHINA STUDY*

PROTEIN FOODS

ChooseMyPlate.gov recommends 5 to 6½ ounces or "ounce equivalents" of protein per day for adults.

What counts? A wide variety of vegetarian foods provide protein.

Sample choices: beans (e.g., black, kidney, navy, pinto, white), eggs (e.g., frittatas, omelets), *falafel,* legumes (e.g., black-eyed peas, chickpeas, lentils, split peas), nuts and nut butters (e.g., almonds, cashews, hazelnuts, peanuts, pecans, pistachios, walnuts), seeds (e.g., chia, hemp, pumpkin, sesame, sunflower), seitan, *soups* (e.g., bean, lentil, split pea), soybeans and soy products, tempeh, texturized vegetable protein (TVP), tofu, *vegetarian chili* made with beans, some *veggie burgers* (e.g., those made with beans or other legumes or soy), not to mention many other foods that contain protein (e.g., grains, such as kamut and quinoa; or vegetables such as broccoli, cauliflower, kale, spinach, and watercress, as more than 40 percent of their calories are from protein).

One "ounce equivalent" is about ¼ cup cooked beans, 1 egg, 1 tablespoon of peanut butter, or ½ ounce of nuts or seeds. Or, if you'd rather count grams of protein to make sure you're not getting too much, here are some examples of **the number of grams of protein in common servings**:

1 large egg = 6 grams
½ cup black beans = 7.5 grams

½ cup black-eyed peas = 6.5 grams
½ cup chickpeas = 7.5 grams
½ cup lentils = 9 grams
1 ounce almonds = 6 grams
1 ounce peanut butter = 7 grams
1 ounce tempeh = 5 grams
¼ cup firm (raw) tofu = 10 grams
1 Burger King veggie burger = 14 grams
1 Shake Shack 'Shroom (vegetarian) burger = 18 grams

Don't forget that vegetarian protein sources also include **vegetables** and **grains**! Here are a few examples of **other foods with protein content:**

1 medium artichoke = 3 grams
1 cup asparagus = 4 grams
1 cup pureed avocado = 5 grams
½ large bagel = 7 grams
1 cup broccoli = 4 grams
1 cup Brussels sprouts = 4 grams
1 medium potato = 5 grams
½ cup quinoa = 4 grams
1 cup spinach = 5 grams
½ cup sun-dried tomatoes = 4 grams

By the way, contrary to popular belief, the idea that you have to combine certain proteins (e.g., beans and rice) at the same meal has been disproven. Given reports of the myth's persistence as of this writing, this finding seems to bear repeating.

"Protein is found in most plant foods as well as animal foods. Your body will make its own complete protein if a variety of foods and enough calories are eaten during the day."
—ACADEMY OF NUTRITION AND DIETETICS (EATRIGHT.ORG)

T. Colin Campbell, author of *The China Study*, recommends that you avoid meat, poultry, dairy, and eggs; eat all you want (while getting lots of variety) of any whole, unrefined plant-based foods (e.g., legumes, nuts, etc.).

Dr. Caldwell Esselstyn, author of the bestselling book *Prevent and Reverse Heart Disease*, recommends "not eating anything with a mother or a face (no meat, poultry, or fish)."

What I do: I aim to consume less than 10 percent of my total calories from protein — and to get the protein from plants. *A few tips:* I typically eat one half-cup to one cup of legumes daily. For breakfast, I sometimes spread peanut butter on apple slices or whole-grain toast or make a tofu scramble. I love adding beans or chickpeas to soups and even green or grain salads, and low-fat hummus is one food you'll always find in our refrigerator. For Chinese or Thai meals, I add cubes of tofu to brown rice dishes and curries.

CARBOHYDRATES

The 2010 Dietary Guidelines for Americans **recommends that 45 to 65 percent of total daily calories come from carbohydrates.**

Dr. Campbell recommends that **at least 80 percent of total daily calories** come from healthful carbohydrates.

The primary sources of carbohydrates are vegetables, fruits, grains/cereals, and legumes. Legumes (primarily peas and beans) are also a significant source of protein, so vegetarians can count them as either carbohydrates (vegetables) or protein.

"The USDA Food Patterns classify beans and peas as a subgroup of the Vegetable Group. The USDA Food Patterns also indicate that beans and peas may be counted as part of the Protein Foods Group. Individuals can count beans and peas as either a vegetable or a protein food. Green peas, green lima beans, and green (string) beans are not considered to be part of the beans and peas subgroup. Green peas and green lima beans are similar to other starchy vegetables and are grouped with them. Green beans are grouped with other vegetables such as onions, lettuce, celery, and cabbage because their nutrient content is similar to those foods."
—CHOOSEMYPLATE.GOV

VEGETABLES

ChooseMyPlate.gov recommends 2 to 3 cups daily for adults.

What counts? Whole, cut, or mashed vegetables (fresh, frozen, dehydrated, or canned, served either raw or cooked), or 100 percent vegetable juice.

Sample choices: A variety from among the five sub-groups of vegetables, each of which provides a different mix of nutrients.

- **Dark green:** beet greens, bok choy, broccoli, chard, collard greens, dark green lettuce, endive, escarole, kale, mustard greens, romaine, spinach, turnip greens, watercress

Know Your Nutrition
If you'd like to analyze the nutritional content of various foods, visit the USDA's National Nutrient Database for Standard Reference at **ndb.nal.usda.gov** or the more user-friendly site based on its data at **nutritiondata.self.com.**

To analyze the nutritional content of a recipe or your diet, visit a website such as **caloriecount.about.com,** which also provides "Nutrition Grades" for specific foods.

- **Red and orange:** acorn squash, butternut squash, carrots, Hubbard squash, pumpkin, red bell peppers, sweet potatoes, tomatoes and tomato juice
- **Starchy:** black-eyed peas, corn, green peas, green plantains, Jerusalem artichokes, lima beans, parsnips, plantains, potatoes, pumpkin, sweet potatoes, taro, water chestnuts, winter squash, yams (Note that starchy vegetables, which are calorically dense, should be eaten in moderation, especially by those seeking to lose weight.)
- **Peas and beans:** black beans, black-eyed peas, chickpeas, kidney beans, lentils, navy beans, pinto beans, soybeans, split peas, white beans (These also contain significant amounts of protein.)
- **Other:** artichokes, asparagus, avocados, beets, Brussels sprouts, cabbage, cauliflower, celery, cucumbers, eggplant, green beans, green bell peppers, iceberg lettuce, mushrooms, okra, onions, sea vegetables, sprouts (e.g., bean), summer squash, turnips, zucchini

Dr. Campbell recommends that you eat all you want, while getting lots of variety, of any whole, unrefined plant-based food such as vegetables.

What I do: I eat as many vegetables as possible every day — about half raw (e.g., in salads, or in juices and smoothies) and half cooked. I shoot for two or three green leafy vegetables, and one or two cruciferous vegetables (e.g., broccoli, cabbage, cauliflower) among them. *Tips:* I eat a salad with lots of raw veggies at lunch and/or dinner. I also try to eat one or two vegetables at every meal (e.g., a banana-and-kale smoothie, a veggie omelet, or veggie-tofu scramble at breakfast; a vegetable-based soup at lunch or dinner, as well as vegetables in a main course, such as a burrito, farrotto/risotto, noodle or rice bowl, pasta, pizza, stir-fry, etc.). Knowing the importance of having two or three green leafy vegetables (e.g., collard greens, kale, spinach) every day, I've discovered that a glass of green juice gives me a great natural pick-me-up — better than caffeine! — so I've traded in my former 4:00 p.m. coffee break for an afternoon green juice break.

FRUITS
ChooseMyPlate.gov recommends 1½ to 2 cups daily for adults.

What counts? Whole, cut, or pureed fruit, or 100 percent fruit juice (e.g., apple, grape, grapefruit, orange). Because of its concentration of nutrients and fiber, a half-cup of dried fruit, such as prunes or raisins, counts as a one-cup serving.

Sample choices: apples and applesauce, apricots, bananas, berries (e.g., blackberries, blueberries, raspberries, strawberries), cherries, citrus fruits (e.g., grapefruits, lemons, limes, oranges), grapes, kiwis, mangoes, melons (e.g., cantaloupes, honeydews, watermelons), nectarines, peaches, pears, papayas, pineapples, plums, tangerines

Dr. Campbell recommends eating all you want, while getting lots of variety, of any whole, unrefined plant-based food such as fruits.

What I do: I aim for an average of three servings of raw, fresh fruit daily. *Tips:* I have fruit on top of my morning oatmeal, as part of a fruit or green salad, or in a smoothie. I love freezing bananas and putting them through a Champion juicer for a softserve-like dessert.

GRAINS / CEREALS

ChooseMyPlate.gov recommends 5 – 8 ounces or "ounce equivalents" daily for adults, with more than 50 percent coming from whole grains.

What counts? Whole-grain foods include breads, cereals such as granola or muesli, crackers, pastas, tortillas, etc., made from whole grains or whole "pseudo-grains" (which are not technically grains but are commonly grouped with them), e.g., amaranth, barley, brown rice, buckwheat, bulgur, corn and whole-grain corn-meal, farro, kamut, kasha, millet, oats (including rolled oats and oatmeal), pop-corn, quinoa, rice, rye berries, sorghum, spelt, teff, triticale, wheat berries, wild rice, or another cereal grain.

Sample choices: One "ounce equivalent" is about ¼ large bagel, 1 slice of bread, ½ English muffin, ½ cup cooked grain (e.g., bulgur, oats), pasta, or rice; 2 three-inch pancakes, 3 cups of popcorn, 1 cup of prepared cereal, or 1 six-inch tortilla.

Dr. Campbell recommends eating all you want, while getting lots of variety, of any whole, unrefined plant-based foods such as whole grains (e.g., in breads, pastas, etc.).

What I do: I limit my grains to three to five servings daily. *Tips:* I sometimes make myself oatmeal or another whole grain as a hot breakfast cereal and have a sandwich on a slice or two of whole-grain bread or pita for lunch, while dinner sometimes revolves around brown rice or another whole grain (e.g., farro, wheat berries) served risotto-style, whole-grain pasta or pizza dough, or whole-grain torti-llas. Most of the time, I try to avoid refined grains (i.e., white rice or anything made from white flour, including white bread) altogether, and to opt for whole-grain ver-sions of rice noodles, cornbread, corn tortillas, and couscous.

FAT

The 2010 Dietary Guidelines for Americans recommends that 20 to 35 percent of total daily calories come from fat.

Dr. Campbell recommends that **less than 10 percent of total daily calories** come from fat.

OILS / FATS

ChooseMyPlate.gov suggests an allowance of 5 to 7 teaspoons of oils daily for adults. One teaspoon of any oil or fat contains 40 calories. ChooseMyPlate.gov indicates that *no* added fats may be necessary, given that "some Americans consume enough oil in the foods they eat, such as nuts, [fish,] cooking oil, and salad dressings." The Standard American Diet (SAD) is close to 40 percent fat, so for many people, achieving a healthier target requires a dramatic lifestyle change — such as not making or ordering fried dishes, omitting the oil from stir-fries, or not slathering butter or oil on breads.

What counts? oils and oily foods (Note that solid fats — fats that are solid at room temperature, such as butter, margarine, and milk fat, along with coconut oil and palm oil — should be minimized or avoided in vegetarian diets aiming to lower cholesterol levels.)

Sample choices: oils (e.g., canola; corn; hazelnut; olive and other plant-based, organic, expeller-pressed, high-oleic oils; safflower; sesame; soybean; sunflower; walnut) and oily foods such as avocados, mayonnaise, nuts (e.g., almonds, cashews, hazelnuts, peanuts, walnuts) and nut butters, olives, seeds (e.g., flax, hemp, pumpkin, sesame, sunflower), some salad dressings

Dr. Campbell recommends minimizing added vegetable oils (e.g., corn oil, olive oil, peanut oil).

Dr. Esselstyn famously recommends "NO OIL!" at all. Zero. No avocados or nuts, either.

What I do: I avoid adding much, if any, oil to my diet (e.g., by cooking in vegetable stock instead of oil). I do sometimes add a little olive oil to certain salad dressings, but in less than the standard 1:3 ratio. *Tips:* Eat something every day for healthful omega-3 fats (e.g., canola oil, flaxseeds in smoothies, walnuts in granola or oatmeal). And I do love avocados as guacamole, added to salads, or whipped into salad dressings.

DAIRY

(**Note:** Whole milk is 50 percent fat, 30 percent carbs, and 20 percent protein, while cheese is 75 percent fat and 25 percent protein — which is why this food group is listed here. Note, however, that dairy is not listed as a fat at ChooseMyPlate.gov.)

ChooseMyPlate.gov recommends 3 cups or "cup equivalents" daily for adults, especially fat-free or low-fat options.

What counts? cheese, cream and ice cream, milk and ice milk, (calcium-fortified) soy milk, yogurt and frozen yogurt. (You'll also want to count foods like cream-based soups, milk-based coffee drinks, and yogurt-based dips or smoothies.)

Sample choices: One "cup equivalent" is about 2 cups cottage cheese, 1½ ounces hard cheese, 1½ cups ice cream, 1 cup milk or calcium-fortified soy milk, 1 cup milk-based pudding, ½ cup ricotta cheese, ⅓ cup shredded cheese, or 1 cup yogurt.

Dr. Campbell recommends avoiding dairy.

Dr. Esselstyn recommends avoiding dairy.

What I do: I am lactose intolerant. It's a trait I happen to share with 75 percent of the world's population, according to the Physicians Committee for Responsible Medicine, which also points out that the lot of us are starting to be referred to as "normal" and those who are able to digest lactose as "lactose persistent." I avoid milk, cream, and other dairy — and gag at the thought of ever trying to consume ChooseMyPlate's recommended 3 cups a day! I find some cheeses and yogurts somewhat easier to digest, but — given some indication of a correlation between high levels of full-fat dairy consumption and certain diseases such as breast cancer — I eat them only very rarely, such as to garnish pasta (e.g., Parmesan), Greek food (e.g., tzatziki), or Indian food (e.g., raita). *Tips:* I gave up my former daily cappuccino habit more than a decade ago, and I've happily switched to almond milk with my morning oatmeal or granola and love the way it enhances the flavor of both.

ChooseMyPlate.gov emphasizes that foods in the dairy group "provide nutrients that are vital for health and maintenance of your body," including protein (see above), calcium, potassium, and vitamin D. However, those of us who choose to largely or entirely avoid dairy can healthfully turn to other options for these nutrients:

- **Calcium:** beans (e.g., black, kidney, navy, pinto, white), black-eyed peas, blackstrap molasses, bok choy, broccoli, chickpeas, dark leafy greens (e.g., collard, mustard, turnip), fortified soy milk, kale, nuts and nut butters (e.g., almonds), sesame seeds and sesame paste, spinach, tempeh, tofu that is processed with calcium sulfate
- **Potassium:** avocados, beans (e.g., kidney, lima, pinto), chard, fruits (especially bananas) and fruit juices, lentils, papayas, potatoes, spinach
- **Vitamin D:** egg yolks, mushrooms (e.g., portobellos, shiitakes), or vitamin D–fortified foods such as cereals, juices, and milks (both dairy and non-dairy) — or simply spend 10 to 15 minutes in the sunshine every day or two, and your body will make its own vitamin D. If it's cloudy or you can't be outdoors enough, consider taking a supplement.

By the way, on the question of **what to drink** as a beverage instead of milk, I'll share that I typically drink hot tea at breakfast, water or iced tea at lunch (I'm particularly fond of caffeine-free SPORTea, which I was first introduced to at the Lodge at Woodloch in Pennsylvania), and one glass of wine at dinner (per the 2010 Dietary Guidelines for Americans, which allow two glasses of wine for men).

MAKING IT DELICIOUS

"I believe the future is vegetables and fruits. They are so much sexier than a piece of chicken. . . . You get a piece of meat and you put it in your mouth, you chew, the first five seconds, all the juices flow around your mouth, they're gone, and then you are twenty more seconds chewing something that is tasteless at this point. Something like this doesn't happen with a pineapple, an asparagus, or a green pea."

—CHEF JOSÉ ANDRÉS, IN AN INTERVIEW WITH ANDERSON COOPER ON *60 MINUTES* (APRIL 27, 2010)

Once you've committed to enjoying a whole foods, plant-based diet, this is where the real fun begins.

In Chapter 2, you'll find insights from some of the country's leading chefs on how to do so deliciously. In Chapter 3, you'll find a comprehensive A-to-Z list of fruits, vegetables, whole grains, legumes, nuts, seeds, and other ingredients, along with the herbs, spices, and other seasonings that best enhance their flavor — not to mention the techniques that best showcase their texture and flavor. You'll also find tips from leading chefs on how they work with these ingredients and how the ingredients are combined into signature dishes.

My pursuit of deliciousness never went away — it's merely changed direction over the past few years. If I hadn't discovered eating vegetarian to be so delicious, I'd never have lasted beyond that first meatless week. But as I've learned through the vegetarian and even vegan anniversary and birthday meals we've enjoyed at Blue Hill, DANIEL, Eleven Madison Park, the Inn at Little Washington, Mélisse, Per Se, Picholine, Zaytinya, and elsewhere — not to mention at America's diverse range of impressive vegetarian and vegan restaurants, which have been a revelation to experience, as well as ethnic and other vegetable-centric restaurants — eating this way offers the thrill of discovery of new avenues of flavor. In the pages that follow, I'm happy to share with you all I've had the pleasure of learning over the past several years, and I am confident you'll be as happy as I've been to find that this way of eating can be even more satisfying and delicious than you ever dreamed possible. Best of all, armed with this book, you'll be on the front line of creating new dishes and a whole new way of eating that's as healthful for others and for the planet as it is for you.

THE VEGETARIAN FLAVOR BIBLE

Chapter

1

FOR THE LOVE OF PLANTS:
VEGETARIANISM THROUGH THE AGES

*"The gods created certain kinds of beings to replenish our bodies . . .
the trees and the plants and the seeds."*
—PLATO

*"I do feel that spiritual progress does demand at some stage that we
should cease to kill our fellow creatures for the satisfaction of our
bodily wants."*
—MOHANDAS GANDHI

*"The average person doesn't have a clue that the meat they're eating is
causing all this havoc. They don't understand about the effects on the
environment or on human cells. The suffering of the animals they might
try to turn away from. So how to make them listen and understand is
difficult, but it's happening."*
—JANE GOODALL

For the first time in history, interest in vegetarianism is on its way to becoming mainstream. After being embraced by countless people over millennia, it is still not typical—with just 5 percent of American adults self-identifying as vegetarian (abstaining from all meat), and another 2 percent as vegan (abstaining from all meat, eggs, and dairy), according to a July 2012 Gallup poll—although these numbers are growing. However, when they are added to the more than 47 percent of adult Americans who acknowledge a wish to decrease their meat consumption (according to a 2011 *USA Today* report), one could argue that the desire to eat less or even no meat is finally becoming the norm. Four consecutive years of decline in U.S. meat consumption, from 2006 to 2010—the first on record—and USDA projections of further declines offer additional evidence that a profound shift is under way.

Eating vegetarian, and even vegan, is easier than ever before. The proliferation of dedicated vegetarian restaurants—from upscale Vedge in Philadelphia, which *GQ* named one of the best new restaurants of 2012, to fast-casual chains like Native Foods and Veggie Grill—not to mention vegetarian menu options everywhere from Chipotle and Subway to DANIEL and the French Laundry to countless independent Asian, Indian, Mediterranean, and other ethnic restaurants, makes vegetarian dining a no-brainer. At the same time, the rapid growth in farmers' markets, CSAs, and vegetarian cookbooks and media have been a boon to home cooks. Even veganism is less challenging, as evidenced by more widespread availability of nondairy milks (which saw U.S. sales topping $1.4 billion in 2013), nondairy butters (e.g., Earth Balance) and nondairy cheeses (e.g., Daiya), as well as eggless mayonnaises (e.g., Vegenaise).

No longer exclusively the domain of countercultural "hippies," vegetarianism and veganism are, well, hip, thanks to their endorsement by some of the most influential people of this era. Television personalities such as Ellen DeGeneres and Oprah Winfrey and popular entertainers including Kristen Bell, Russell Brand, Alan Cumming, Woody Harrelson, Anne Hathaway, Chrissie Hynde, Joan Jett, Jared Leto, Adam Levine, Jennifer Lopez, Tobey Maguire, Lea Michele, Morrissey, Natalie Portman, Prince, Alicia Silverstone, Carrie Underwood, and Forest Whitaker have thrust meatless diets into the media spotlight and helped to keep them there. Even *BusinessWeek* has profiled industry leaders who eschew meat, including Twitter cofounder Biz Stone and hotelier Steve Wynn, and perhaps most notably former President Bill Clinton, who lost 24 pounds after 2004 quadruple bypass surgery and 2010 stent surgery by switching to a vegan diet.

Vegetarianism has been around for as long as human beings themselves, and compelling arguments for abstaining from meat are numerous and timeless. A glance through history shows the various cultural, economic, environmental, ethical, global, medical, nutritional, patriotic, practical, religious, and other factors that have given rise to vegetarianism. On the heels of the teachings of world religions and Greek and Roman philosophers, an impressive number of history's greatest geniuses—including da Vinci, Einstein, and Gandhi—lived some or all of their adult lives as vegetarians.

The advent of nutritional science in the twentieth century has established the relationship between diet and health, as well as demonstrated a correlation between consuming too much animal protein and many chronic diseases, including heart disease, certain cancers, and obesity. Groundbreaking studies republished in bestselling books like *The China Study*, reinforced by other efforts such as the popular "Meatless Monday" campaign, have helped make common knowledge out of this information. Former Beatle Sir Paul McCartney famously quipped, "If slaughterhouses had glass walls, everyone would be vegetarian." Indeed, the Internet and YouTube have put just a click away horrifying video images of some of what goes on in the factory farms that supply 99 percent of the meat, eggs, and dairy products consumed in the United States, providing virtual "glass walls" that have been fueling the growing animal welfare movement. And facts, figures, and photos of what eating animals is doing to our most precious natural resources—our air, land, and water—make the reality too hard to ignore, leading even billionaire Bill Gates, who's investing in companies developing vegan meat and egg replacements, to advocate a move toward vegetarianism as a way to save the planet and avoid the looming global food shortage crisis.

With such powerful champions and arguments, why isn't *everyone* vegetarian yet? There are also powerful cultural, economic, and political forces underlying American society and its meat- and dairy-centric status quo. Turn on the TV, and you'll find a seemingly endless stream of ads promoting meaty, cheesy fast food, followed by another endless stream of ads for pharmaceuticals that promise relief from the ailments often correlated with overconsuming such products.

Government policy is arguably more supportive of big business that contributes mightily to the U.S. economy than of the health of its individual citizens (especially our children, whose obesity-driven diabetes epidemic is leading to tragic predictions of shorter lifespans). Commodity products like corn and soybeans that are fed to livestock are subsidized with taxpayer dollars, as are the meat and dairy industries themselves, which in 2011 benefited directly or indirectly from 63 percent of government agricultural subsidies, while fruit and vegetable producers received less than 1 percent. Over the past fifty years, those representing the interests of the meat and dairy industries have sometimes been the ones setting our country's nutritional policy guidelines (as a 2000 court ruling determined), despite the obvious conflicts of interest.

But it's becoming clearer every day that moving toward vegetarianism is better for your health, better for the health of other living beings, and better for the planet as a whole. While you don't have to be a full-time vegetarian to reap the benefits, I hope that you'll discover—as I have—that eating vegetarian is so delicious and makes you feel so much better, lighter, and more energetic, that you'll opt to maximize these benefits by eliminating as much meat as you choose. And I do believe it's important to emphasize that what you choose to eat is a *personal* decision — one best made by fully understanding how eating animals affects your personal health and well-being, that of your family and others, and that of our planet.

"If anyone wants to save the planet, all they have to do is stop eating meat."
—SIR PAUL MCCARTNEY

Choosing to not eat meat, or even to eat less of it, is a simple yet powerful way to be a part of the solution to some of the most pressing problems of today and tomorrow. Think of vegetarianism as presenting a spectrum of choices:

Vegetarianism: A Spectrum of Choices

Omnivore	Semi-Vegetarian or Flexitarian	Ovo-Lacto Vegetarian	Ovo-Vegetarian or Lacto-Vegetarian	Vegan
(46%)	(47%)		(5%)	(2%)

Fully 93 percent of the population does not self-identify as wholly vegetarian or vegan. Bestselling author Dr. John McDougall counts himself among that majority, even though he has espoused the health benefits of a low-fat vegan diet for decades while eating a 99+ percent meatless diet himself. He explains, "I do not want to be thought of as a vegetarian because so many people who call themselves vegetarians are unhealthy," citing a soy burger, French fries, and Coca-Cola as a vegetarian meal. I also count myself among that 93 percent, even though I have eaten a 99+ percent meatless diet since May 2012. I believe labels can be divisive, emphasizing differences rather than bringing people together—and bringing people together can be one of food's greatest benefits and pleasures.

Clearly, nonvegetarians fall along a broad spectrum representing a wide range of diets. Omnivores (people who eat everything, both animals and plants) can choose to limit the amount of meat they eat, making them "semi-vegetarians" or "flexitarians." Some eat no meat other than fish and are called "pescetarians." "Vegetarian" typically describes those who abstain from meat (including red meat, poultry, and seafood). "Lacto-vegetarians" are vegetarians who also abstain from eggs but not dairy, while "ovo-vegetarians" are vegetarians who abstain from dairy but not eggs. "Vegan" is used to describe vegetarians who abstain from both dairy and eggs (and, depending on one's personal definition, often other animal-derived products, such as gelatin and honey). As McDougall suggests, a healthful vegetarian or even vegan diet is about what you choose to eat as much as what you choose *not* to eat, which is why a "whole-food, plant-based diet" has become the catchphrase for this healthful approach to eating.

Ultimately, the decisions each of us makes throughout the day give us the opportunity to create the future of food—and the world—by voting with our forks. The 1960s taught us that "the personal is political" and that how we choose to live our lives is our statement of who we are. "We are what we eat" sums this up succinctly. Believing the dictum that "those who cannot remember the past are condemned to repeat it," this book begins with a broad-brush overview of the roots of vegetarianism and our fast-growing enjoyment of a plant-based diet, by way of a timeline highlighting some of the key influencers and organizations, classic books, notable events, and other milestones that have influenced this shift.

SOME NOTABLE EVENTS IN VEGETARIAN HISTORY

YEAR	EVENT

~3000–2000 BCE — One of the world's most ancient religions, **Hinduism**, teaches that humans should not inflict pain on other animals, leading to the peaceful and compassionate practice (or *sadhana*, which means "spiritual practice") of vegetarianism.

~500s BCE — Chinese sage **Lao Tzu** (c. 604–531 BCE) writes the classic Chinese text *Tao Te Ching*, which gives rise to **Taoism**, one of the three primary religions of China (along with Buddhism and Confucianism), which calls for doing no harm to any other life form.

Greek philosopher **Pythagoras** (c. 570–495 BCE), the man whose theorem $a^2 + b^2 = c^2$ rocked the field of geometry, leads what is thought to be the first community requiring a vegetarian diet and is described in Ovid's *Metamorphoses* as "the first to censure man for eating the flesh of animals." People who abstained from eating meat were often called "Pythagoreans" before the term "vegetarian" was coined in the late nineteenth century.

After forty-nine days of meditation, Siddhartha Gautama (c. 563–483 BCE) achieves enlightenment, becoming the **Buddha** and inspiring **Buddhism**, which forbids harming any living creature, and millions of Buddhist followers who practice vegetarianism. He encourages his followers to eat spinach.

Prince Vardhamana (Nigantha Nataputta), or **Mahavira** (c. 540–510 BCE), founds **Jainism**, one of India's primary religions, which values animal rights and forbids the taking of life (whether an insect or a root vegetable). Vegetarianism is mandatory for followers.

~400s BCE — In *The Laws*, Greek philosopher **Plato** (429–347 BCE) notes the relationship between one's diet and one's conduct. In *The Republic*, the character Socrates asserts that the ideal city would be vegetarian, saying that meat is a luxury that leads to decadence and war. He also questions the excessive amount of land needed to raise cattle.

8 CE — The Roman poet **Ovid** (c. 43 BCE–17 CE) writes *Metamorphoses*, which includes a speech in the voice of Pythagoras, urging abstinence from eating meat and the abandonment of animal sacrifice.

"For what sort of dinner is not costly, for which a living creature loses its life?"
—PLUTARCH

"Mortals, refrain from defiling your bodies with sinful feasting, for you have the fruits of the earth and of arbors, whose branches bow with their burden; for you the grapes ripen, for you the delicious greens are made tender by cooking; milk is permitted to you too, and thyme-scented honey. Earth is abundantly wealthy and freely provides you her gentle sustenance, offered without any bloodshed."
—THE CHARACTER OF PYTHAGORAS, IN OVID'S IN *METAMORPHOSES, BOOK XV* (8 CE)

~100 CE   Greek philosopher **Plutarch** (c. 46–120 CE), a vegetarian, writes a number of pro-vegetarian essays, including *On the Eating of Flesh*. In the nineteenth century, the Oxford graduate and Romantic poet **Percy Shelley** (1792–1822) will translate them into English and become a vegetarian himself.

~200s CE   The Greek philosopher **Porphyry** (233–304), a practicing vegetarian, revives interest in Plato's philosophy.

1400s   **Leonardo da Vinci** (1452–1519), widely considered history's greatest genius, is one of the first important ethical vegetarians since ancient times to oppose meat-eating on humanitarian grounds. He is said to have frequently bought live birds for sale as food at the market in Florence just to set them free.

> "You needn't be a genius to be a vegetarian, but many geniuses — including **Leonardo da Vinci**, Albert Einstein, Gandhi, and Nikola Tesla— endorsed vegetarianism. . . . Andrea Corsali, an Italian explorer, wrote a letter to his sponsor Giuliano de' Medici in which he noted the meatless diet of the [Indian] Gujurati peoples he observed in his travels. Corsali writes that in addition to avoiding meat, they do not 'permit among them any injury be done to any living thing,' and then he adds, 'like our Leonardo da Vinci.'"
> —MICHAEL GELB, AUTHOR OF *HOW TO THINK LIKE LEONARDO DA VINCI*

1699   **John Evelyn** (1620–1706) writes *Acetaria: A Discourse of Sallets*, advocating the eating of salads and providing what's been since called "the world's first A–Z of salad ingredients," classifying dozens of herbs by their appropriateness for cooking versus being served uncooked.

1732   German settlers in Pennsylvania, led by **Johann Conrad Beissel** (1691–1768), create the **Ephrata Cloister**, which advocates vegetarianism as a path to spiritual goals and which by its dissolution in 1813 has become the longest-lived commune in America. The physical site is still open for daily tours.

1790s   Massachusetts native John Chapman—better known as **Johnny Appleseed** (1774–1845)—begins his journey to sow apple seeds throughout the Midwest. A vegetarian follower of Christian mystic Emanuel Swedenborg, he is said to have subsisted mainly on foraged nuts and berries.

1809   The Reverend **William Cowherd** (1763–1816), founds the **Bible Christian Church** (BCC) near Manchester, England, and advocates for abstinence from eating meat. The BCC is now credited as the forerunner of modern vegetarianism.

1813   Inspired by *Return to Nature, or, A Defence of the Vegetable Regimen* by his friend **John Frank Newton** (1766–1837), **Percy Shelley** (1792–1822) makes the case for vegetarianism in his essay "A Vindication of Natural Diet," which argues against the waste of both animal life and valuable land.

1817   The Reverend **William Metcalfe** (1788–1862) and forty other pilgrims from Manchester's Bible Christian Church (BCC) sail to America to establish the vegetarian sect in Pennsylvania.

1821   **Martha Brotherton**—wife of Joseph, who was a preacher at the Bible Christian Church and a leader in the Vegetarian Society—writes **one of the first vegetarian cookbooks**, *A New System of Vegetable Cookery*.

1837   The first American book dedicated to the subject of bread, *A Treatise on Bread, and Bread-Making* by **Sylvester Graham** (1794–1851) is published. He travels to preach the virtues of whole wheat bread (arguing that to separate the bran from the rest of the wheat berry was "against the will of God") and vegetarianism, and is so persuasive that his followers become known as Grahamites. He is credited both with influencing *New York Tribune* founder **Horace Greeley** to become a vegetarian and with inspiring the creation of the whole wheat flour–based Graham cracker.

On March 7, in Boston, William Alcott and Sylvester Graham are among the founders of the **American Physiological Society** (APS). The organization's constitution states that "the farinaceous vegetables" are "the best food for man."

1838   **William Andrus Alcott** (1798–1859) writes *Vegetable Diet: As Sanctioned by Medical Men, and By Experience in All Ages*. This popular book, one of the first American books to espouse a vegetarian diet, includes the chapter "A Vegetable Diet Defended," which makes seven key arguments for vegetarianism: *"1) The **Anatomical** Argument, 2) The **Physiological** Argument, 3) The **Medical** Argument, 4) The **Political** Argument, 5) The **Economical** Argument, 6) The Argument from **Experience**, 7) The **Moral** Argument."* Alcott advo-

"The most fertile districts of the habitable globe are now actively cultivated by men for animals, at a delay and waste of aliment absolutely incapable of calculation."
—PERCY SHELLEY

"The **APS** also moved meat abstention away from religious doctrinal structures and placed dietary reform firmly within the realm of scientific study."
—ADAM D. SHPRINTZEN, IN *THE VEGETARIAN CRUSADE* (2013)

cates replacing meat-based breakfasts with grain-based dishes, such as brown bread (also known as Graham bread), boiled rice, or rye toast.

Alcott House, named after educational reformer **Bronson Alcott**, is established in England as a spiritual school embracing vegetarian principles. It thrives over the next several years, giving rise to the **first Vegetarian Society** in 1847.

1842 The word "vegetarian" is used in print for the first time (in *The Healthian,* a publication of Alcott House) to describe the consumption of only plants, in accordance with the common meaning of the word "vegetable" at that time, which included fruits and grains.

1843 **The British and Foreign Society for the Promotion of Humanity and Abstinence from Animal Food** is formed.

(Amos) Bronson Alcott (1799–1888), a relative and neighbor of William Alcott, and his family (including daughter Louisa May Alcott, the future author of *Little Women*) and followers found America's first vegetarian commune in Harvard, Massachusetts. The farm is named "Fruitlands."

1847 The first **Vegetarian Society** is formed on a September evening at a coastal hospital in England. Within a year, it grows from 150 to 265 members, ranging in age from fourteen to seventy-six. Before the end of the century, vegetarian societies form in many other countries, including the U.S. (1850), Germany (1867), Austria (1878), France (1879), Switzerland (1880), New Zealand (1882), Hungary (1884), Australia (1886), India (1889), Ireland (1890), Chile (1891), Netherlands (1894), Sweden (1895), Denmark (1896), Belgium (1897), and Italy (1899).

1850 During a time when most people believe illness to be a mystery or the will of God, on May 15 at Clinton Hall in New York City, the Presbyterian minister turned health reformer **Sylvester Graham** (1794–1851) co-founds the **American Vegetarian Society** with **Rev. William Metcalfe** (1788–1862) and **Dr. William Alcott** (1798–1859, who serves as its first president), with significant support from the Bible Christian Church (BCC).

1853   At a banquet held by the American Vegetarian Society, vegetarian suffragist **Susan B. Anthony** (1820–1906) raises a toast to both vegetarianism and women's rights.

1854   **Henry David Thoreau** (1817–1862)'s *Walden,* an account of his experiment in living in solitude on Walden Pond in Massachusetts, is published.

"I have no doubt that it is a part of the destiny of the human race, in its gradual improvement, to leave off eating animals."
—HENRY DAVID THOREAU

1860   **John Smith**, of Yorkshire, England, writes **The Principles and Practices of Vegetarian Cookery**, which includes a substantial amount of theory ("being an attempt to prove from history, anatomy, physiology, and chemistry, that the original, natural, and best diet of man is derived from the vegetable kingdom") as well as several hundred recipes.

1863   **Ellen G. White** (1827–1915), husband **James White**, and others found what is now known as the Seventh-day Adventist Church in Battle Creek, Michigan. In June, she reports visions from God inspiring her to promote a meatless diet. Three years later, the couple founds the Western Health Reform Institute, which later achieves world renown as the Battle Creek Sanitarium under the leadership of **John Harvey Kellogg**.

1868   Influenced by Sylvester Graham, **James Caleb Jackson** (1811–1895)'s **How to Treat the Sick Without Medicine** is published, promoting a fruit- and grain-based diet, such as the one served at Our Home on the Hillside, a Dansville, New York–based sanitarium where he invents the **first cold grain-based breakfast cereal**, which he dubs "Granula" (Latin for "little grains"), and which serves as an inspiration for the Whites' Battle Creek institute.

1881   **Anna Kingsford** (1846–1888), one of the first English women to earn a medical degree, writes about the benefits of vegetarianism in **The Perfect Way in Diet** and helps found the Food Reform Society. She travels throughout Europe to speak out about vegetarianism and against animal experimentation (which she notably managed to avoid in medical school).

1883   The first book of vegetarian history, **The Ethics of Diet**, is written by **Howard Williams** (1837–1931). It will influence vegetarians from Leo Tolstoy to Henry Salt to Mohandas Gandhi.

| 1888 | **The London Vegetarian Society** is formed, with its own publication, *The Vegetarian*. |

Late 1800s A Seventh-day Adventist for much of his life, **John Harvey Kellogg** (1852–1943) works during his youth as an errand runner for Ellen and James White, after which they sponsor his medical education at an Adventist-run school in New Jersey. Upon graduation, he is hired by—and later heads—the **Battle Creek Sanitarium** (originally the Western Health Reform Institute). During a time when a typical breakfast might feature sausage and whiskey, the noted surgeon develops for the sanitarium dozens of innovative meatless foods—most notably flaked and ready-to-eat breakfast cereals, which will revolutionize the morning meal within a decade. The sanitarium attracts leading celebrities of the day, including Amelia Earhart, Thomas Edison, Henry Ford, Mary Todd Lincoln, John D. Rockefeller, President Taft, Sojourner Truth, and Johnny Weissmuller. Kellogg becomes the leading promoter of vegetarianism in his time, and the success of the W. K. Kellogg Company (run by his brother Will Keith) inspires the founding of other national companies providing ready-to-eat cereals that often replace breakfast meats.

1890 After a St. Louis doctor suggests grinding peanuts as a source of protein for elderly patients unable to chew meat, George Bayle begins to sell **peanut butter** commercially. Five years later, Dr. John Harvey Kellogg registers the first patent for a peanut-based "Process of Preparing Nut Meal," which is served at the Battle Creek Sanitarium as a healthful meat substitute. By 1899, the U.S. is producing an estimated two million pounds. After being featured at the 1904 St. Louis World Fair, sales of peanut butter skyrocket to approximately 34 million pounds by 1907.

1892 **Leo Tolstoy** (1828–1910) writes his influential vegetarian essay **"The First Step"** as the preface to the Russian translation of *The Ethics of Diet*.

1893 **Ella Eaton Kellogg** (1853–1920), wife of Dr. John Harvey Kellogg, writes her first vegetarian cookbook, *Science in the Kitchen*.

1895 New York's first vegetarian restaurant—the aptly named **Vegetarian Restaurant Number 1**—is opened by the New York Vegetarian Society in the Hotel Byron on West 23rd Street. (By comparison, in 1897 there are thirteen vegetarian restaurants in

London.) Within five years, a chain of vegetarian cafes called **Pure Food** will also serve meatless meals in Manhattan. Within thirty-five years, a chain of three vegetarian restaurants called **Farmfood** will serve meatless meals on the west side of Manhattan.

1898 **The Vegetarians' Home and Teetotaller Café**, later renamed **Hiltl**, opens in Zurich. Said to be the world's oldest continuously-operating vegetarian restaurant, it still operates today, and the owners have added a chain of vegetarian fast food spots called **Tibits by Hiltl.**

1899 Influenced by poet Percy Shelley's poems and pamphlets, animal welfare activist **Henry Salt** (1851–1939) writes his classic book *The Logic of Vegetarianism*, which later influences Mohandas Gandhi to renew his commitment to vegetarianism. He also introduces Gandhi to the writings of Thoreau, including *Civil Disobedience*, which Gandhi cites as a major influence. Salt is considered the first writer to champion animals' rights, via his 1894 *Animals' Rights*, versus mere animal welfare reform.

1900 **Chicago's first vegetarian restaurant**, Pure Food Lunch Room, opens at 176 E. Madison in the Loop.

Noted scientist and inventor (a rival of Thomas Edison, he has been called "inventor of the electrical age") **Nikola Tesla** (1856–1943) writes an article titled "The Problem of Increasing Human Energy" for the June issue of *Century Illustrated*, in which he calls "want of healthful nutriment" the "chief evil," condemns the inefficiency of raising animals as food, and praises vegetarianism. Over his adult life, he shifts away from meat toward fish and then finally to a vegetarian diet.

01 The first **Vegetarian Society** is formed in **Russia**. After the 1917 revolution, vegetarianism will be declared illegal in Soviet Russia, leading to the closing of its vegetarian societies and restaurants.

02 Pulp publishing magnate **Bernarr Macfadden** (1868–1955) opens his first **Physical Culture vegetarian restaurant** in lower Manhattan. Within six years, it is a successful chain with locations in Boston, Buffalo, New York City, Philadelphia, Pittsburgh, and Chicago. He also writes more than one hundred books, espousing a diet made up mostly of fresh fruits, vegetables, and whole grains as vital to good health—a revolutionary concept at the time.

"It is certainly preferable to raise vegetables, and I think, therefore, that vegetarianism is a commendable departure from the established barbarous habit. That we can subsist on plant food and perform our work even to advantage is not a theory, but a well-demonstrated fact. Many races living almost exclusively on vegetables are of superior physique and strength. There is no doubt that some plant food, such as oatmeal, is more economical than meat, and superior to it in regard to both mechanical and mental performance. . . . In view of these facts every effort should be made to stop the wanton and cruel slaughter of animals, which must be destructive to our morals. To free ourselves from animal instincts and appetites, which keep us down, we should begin at the very root from which we spring: we should effect a radical reform in the character of the food."

—NIKOLA TESLA, "THE PROBLEM OF INCREASING HUMAN ENERGY"

1906   After a spate of stockyard scandals, the novel *The Jungle,* by **Upton Sinclair** (1878–1968), is published, revealing the revoltingly unsanitary conditions and inhumane labor practices at Chicago stockyards. It becomes an instant bestseller, and fuels both the growing vegetarian movement and the addition of meatless entrees (from omelets to pastas) on mainstream restaurant menus.

1907   On September 24, a *New York Times* article titled "**Cancer Increasing Among Meat Eaters** . . . on the Other Hand, Italians and Chinese, Practically Vegetarians, Show the Lowest Mortality of All" reports on Chicago-based Dr. G. Cooke Adams' seven-year study indicating higher cancer risk among those who eat meat, stating, "Dr. Adams has proved conclusively that diet is a most important factor in the increase in the disease and its death rate."

1908   The **International Vegetarian Union** is formed to unite vegetarian societies around the world and to organize a global conference in a different part of the world every two or three years.

The June issue of the Vegetarian Society of Great Britain's magazine *Vegetarian Messenger* reports that during a recent bout of mastoiditis, American inventor **Thomas Edison** (1847–1931) "ceased using meat and went for a thorough course of vegetarianism. Mr. Edison was so pleased with the change of diet that, now he has regained his normal health, he continues to renounce meat in all its forms."

1917   The United States enters World War I in April, leading head of the U.S. Food Administration **Herbert Hoover** to launch "**Meatless Mondays**" and "Wheatless Wednesdays" to inspire Americans to reduce their consumption of these staple foods to help increase exports to starving allies in Europe. More than 13 million American families—the majority—pledge their participation over the course of U.S. involvement (ending in November 1918). Millions also plant liberty and war gardens, which will later be called victory gardens.

1920s   Soy food products, such as soy bread, cereal, cheese, coffee, ice cream, milk, and nuts, are developed and promoted to a wider audience by Seventh-day Adventists such as **T. A. Van Gundy** (1874–1935) and **Jethro Kloss** (1863–1923).

1925   Irish playwright **George Bernard Shaw** (1856–1950), a vegetarian who in 1901 famously quipped, "I was a cannibal for twenty-five years. For the rest I have been a vegetarian," is awarded the Nobel Prize for Literature.

1929   A *Saturday Evening Post* article reports that as a result of "Meatless Monday" and other World War I dietary changes, "Americans began to look seriously into the question of what and how much they were eating. Lots of people discovered for the first time that they could eat less and feel no worse—frequently much better."

The stock market crash of October 29 sets off the **Great Depression**, a time when farmers are producing lots of food that few can afford to purchase—so Americans go hungry, and farmers start going out of business. This leads to the first **Farm Bill**, passed in 1933 as part of FDR's New Deal, and the updated Agricultural Adjustment Act of 1938, which stipulates that the Farm Bill be updated every five years, as it is to this day.

1930s   **Sadie Schildkraut** (1899–1981), known as the "mother of cooked vegetarian dishes," runs a chain of fifteen vegetarian restaurants throughout New York City. Yidisher Vegetarian Society of New York members, who view vegetarianism as a moral philosophy, dine on signature dishes such as mushroom cutlets, protose steak, and creamed beets.

1931   **Mohandas Gandhi** (1869–1948) helps to launch the vegan movement in London on November 20. He credits the writings of Leo Tolstoy and Henry David Thoreau with greatly influencing his philosophy of nonviolence. While other Indian students renounce their vegetarianism in carnivorous England, he is influenced by Henry Salt's *A Plea for Vegetarianism* to re-commit to it. After joining the London Vegetarian Society, he is elected to its executive committee and contributes articles to its newspaper.

1932–1934   In the U.K., the People's League of Health and the Gowland Hopkins Committee report **major problems with the safety of dairy,** with a minimum of 40 percent of tested dairy cows being infected with tuberculosis and chronically transmitting it to a huge portion of the country's human population. (In 1930, 58 percent of a sample of London children test positive for tuberculosis exposure.)

20246380

1934 Automaker **Henry Ford** (1863–1947), a vegetarian who believes in reincarnation and is a soybean fanatic, showcases soybean dishes (such as cookies and puree) at the Century of Progress Exposition in Chicago.

1939 **Jethro Kloss**'s book on herbal medicine, natural foods, and home remedies, titled *Back to Eden,* is published and goes on to sell more than four million copies and to help inspire the natural foods movement of the 1960s and 1970s.

1941 The United States enters World War II. Americans are encouraged to plant **"victory gardens"**—in back yards, front yards, vacant lots, and even public land, from the Boston Commons to San Francisco's Golden Gate Park (which at one point has eight hundred gardens)—to grow their own food. In 1943,  U.S. rations limit families to twenty-eight ounces of meat per week. Over the course of the war, more than 20 million such gardens cumulatively produce more than 40 percent of the fresh vegetables consumed in the U.S.

1942 **B&H Dairy** kosher vegetarian restaurant (mostly meatless, though lox is served) is opened by Abie Bergson and his partner Heller at 127 Second Avenue in New York City. Today, B&H still serves its housemade soups,  pierogi, and specialties like **vegetarian cutlet with kasha and mushroom gravy**, along with a "vegetarian liver" made from eggs, onions, soybeans, and a not-so-secret ingredient: "love."

1944 The term **"vegan"** is coined by **Donald Watson** (1910–2005), a woodworker in Britain, to describe vegetarians who do not consume dairy or eggs. He even specifies in his Vegan Society newsletter how it should be pronounced: "Veegan, not Veejan."

1945 *The New York Times Magazine* runs the story **"Heyday for the Vegetarians"** on vegetarians' efforts to convert meat eaters in the wake of meat shortages. Symon Gould, an editor of *American Vegetarian* magazine, classifies the hierarchy of vegetarians.

Post-WWII	The United States, which had built ten large-scale munitions factories by the end of the war, sees their production shift from bombs to fertilizers. **Agribusiness** is born as large-scale farming becomes a chemical-based process.
1948	**Dr. Catherine Nimmo** and **Rubin Abramowitz** found a **Vegan Society** in California, which continues to 1960.
	The **Framingham Heart Study** is established in Massachusetts to identify the factors contributing to cardiovascular disease. The half-century-plus study spurs the publication of 1,200 articles in leading medical journals on key risk factors such as obesity, smoking, high fat diet, high blood pressure, and diabetes.
1949	The **First American Vegetarian Convention** is held in August at Lake Geneva, Wisconsin.
Mid–1900s	The advent of **nutritional science** leads vegetarianism to be embraced as a healthful dietary option.
1958	After spending his young adult years growing his hair long and living off the land in California as one of about a dozen "Nature Boys," Robert Bootzin (1914–2004) — later known as **Gypsy Boots** — opens the first health-food restaurant in Los Angeles, known as the **Back to Nature Health Hut**, which attracts a celebrity clientele including Pat Boone, Red Buttons, Angie Dickinson, George Hamilton, and Gloria Swanson. Through more than twenty appearances on Steve Allen's popular talk show and several books, he introduces a wide American audience to the idea of a healthful vegetarian diet and edibles such as figs, garlic, wheatgrass, and "**smoothies**."
1960	**H. Jay Dinshah** (1933–2000) establishes the **American Vegan Society** in New Jersey. His wife, **Freya Dinshah**, will write *The Vegan Kitchen*, the first American book to use the word "vegan," in 1965, and will run the AVS after his death.
1961	An editorial in the ***Journal of the American Medical Association*** (JAMA) asserts that "a vegetarian diet can prevent 90 percent of our thrombo-embolic disease and 97 percent of our coronary occlusions." The statement is widely reported by vegetarian publications in subsequent years.

"If Americans adopted a **vegetarian** diet, the [heart disease epidemic responsible for the death of half of all Americans] would disappear."
—DR. WILLIAM CASTELLI, FORMER DIRECTOR OF THE FRAMINGHAM HEART STUDY, ON THE PBS/SCIENTIFIC AMERICAN *FRONTIERS* EPISODE "AFFAIRS OF THE HEART"

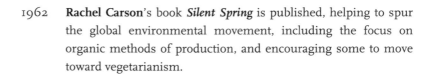

"In the diet in the average home, meats and any products derived from animal fats contain the heaviest residues of chlorinated hydrocarbons [i.e., pesticides]. This is because these chemicals are soluble in fat. Cooking does not destroy residues."

—RACHEL CARSON, IN *SILENT SPRING* (1962)

1962   **Rachel Carson**'s book *Silent Spring* is published, helping to spur the global environmental movement, including the focus on organic methods of production, and encouraging some to move toward vegetarianism.

1967   **The Tassajara Zen Mountain Center**, the first Zen training monastery outside of Asia, is established in the San Francisco Bay area, with **Edward Espé Brown** becoming the head cook. Three years later, he writes *The Tassajara Bread Book*, which features Buddhist vegetarian recipes and goes on to sell a million copies. In 1971, Brown is ordained as a Zen priest. In 1973, he comes out with his second cookbook, *Tassajara Cooking*. He will later be the subject of Doris Dörrie's 2007 documentary *How to Cook Your Life*.

1968   Manhattan socialite and radio host **Pegeen Fitzgerald** sees her book *Meatless Cooking: Pegeen's Vegetarian Recipes* published, and it proves popular with the two million listeners of the radio show that she and her husband co-host. Her 1989 *New York Times* obituary says she headed two animal welfare organizations and "believed deeply in antivivisection and ethical vegetarianism, refusing to eat meat or fish or to wear a fur coat 'because I don't want any living thing killed for my own use or pleasure.'"

Ten Talents, by nutritionist **Rosalie Hurd** and her physician husband **Frank Hurd**, is published, becoming one of the first few vegetarian/vegan resources available. (The 2012 edition of the Genesis 1:29–inspired cookbook is its forty-ninth printing.)

The Beatles study transcendental meditation in India. Afterward, **George Harrison**, **John Lennon**, **Paul McCartney**, and **Ringo Starr** declare their vegetarianism, inspiring others around the globe to follow suit. All but Lennon will remain lifelong vegetarians.

1969   On April 1, Silver Star–decorated Marine and World War II veteran **Jim Baker** (also known as "Father Yod") opens **The Source** on Sunset Boulevard, one of the first hugely popular vegetarian restaurants in Los Angeles. It features a menu of items (such as lentil-based veggie burgers) said to be "consciously prepared for the highest vibration" and attracts a celebrity clientele said to include Warren Beatty, Marlon Brando, Julie Christie, Jane Fonda, Goldie Hawn, Don Johnson, John Lennon, Steve McQueen, Carl Reiner, and Donald Sutherland. (In the 1977 film *Annie Hall*, Woody Allen's character Alvy Singer visits The Source, ordering "alfalfa

> "**Follow Your Heart** was a very different scene from **The Source** [another LA vegetarian restaurant of the day], which was run by a cult led by a real character. We were the opposite of that, preferring to think of everyone as a brother or sister, whether they wore a suit and tie or had long hair or no hair. Even stronger than our belief in vegetarianism was the belief that everyone should be welcomed like they would be when visiting a friend's home. We've never aimed to proselytize or get people to change. Number one, you can't — and number two, it's morally wrong, because it disrespects others' right to choose. We've always aimed to serve food that people would enjoy and simply said, 'Taste this — it's delicious!' In 1972, you could get a Love Plate — an avocado sandwich and a cup of soup — for 95 cents. It's still on the menu today — at $9.50. . . . Only about 20 to 25 percent of those dining at Follow Your Heart are vegetarian — which is not surprising if you think about what percentage of diners at any Chinese restaurant are Chinese. . . . When my generation embraced vegetarianism, it was considered radical. But it's an interesting dynamic that many of today's Millennials skip vegetarianism altogether and go right to veganism. . . . The ease with which you can find something to eat almost anywhere today is simply stunning. I know I live in Mecca, but it's just not difficult to be a vegetarian anymore. What excites me most is not only the dawning of wonderful meatless creativity [as exemplified by restaurants such as Dave Anderson's Madeleine Bistro and Tal Ronnen's Crossroads], but also the dawning of the recognition of the relationship between diet and health."
>
> —BOB GOLDBERG, CO-OWNER, FOLLOW YOUR HEART (CANOGA PARK, CALIFORNIA)

sprouts and mashed yeast.") The restaurant will become the subject of the 2007 book *The Source: The Untold Story of Father Yod, Ya Ho Wa 13, and the Source Family* by Isis Aquarian with Electricity Aquarian, upon which **Jodi Wille and Maria Demopoulos**'s 2013 documentary *The Source Family* is based.

1970   The first **Earth Day** is held on April 22, a bipartisan effort in support of a healthy, sustainable planet, marking the birth of the modern mainstream environmental movement.

Frances Moore Lappé writes a seventy-five-page pamphlet making the case for a vegetarian diet. An expanded version is published the following year as the revolutionary book *Diet for a Small Planet*

and goes on to sell more than three million copies. Arguing that "hunger is human made," Lappé's economic and environmental rationales against meat — such as that a cow had to be fed sixteen pounds of grain and soy to produce one pound of beef — merged with concerns about global hunger to spur vegetarians and activists to take up the cause in earnest.

A year after actor Johnny Weissmuller opens his American Natural Foods store in Los Angeles, **Bob Goldberg** and three friends (**Paul Lewin**, still a partner in 2013, and **Michael Besancon** and **Spencer Windbiel**, who will move on in 1985) take over its operations, which include a seven-seat juice and sandwich bar. They buy the store and transform the bar into a full-fledged vegetarian cafe, renaming it **Follow Your Heart**. After they discover their supplier of supposedly eggless mayonnaise to be fraudulent, they end up having to create their own — and the vegan mayonnaise **Vegenaise** is born. A popular national line of vegetarian salad dressings and **Vegan Gourmet** cheeses follows.

1971   **Alice Waters** founds **Chez Panisse** in Berkeley, California, where she launches a revolution by rejecting flavorless commercial produce and starting to create her own network of local farmers and other suppliers. While not vegetarian in mission, she is credited as the creator of an alternative food supply that inspires the improvement of the quality, purity, and flavor of vegetables served in the United States, which encourages more chefs to cook with them and more diners to order them.

> "During my years at **Chez Panisse**, Alice Waters had vegetable dishes that tasted so good, but they never had to shout that they were 'vegetarian' dishes. You'd see a dish of pizza with nettles and an egg on the menu, and you wouldn't be thinking, 'Oh, that's vegetarian' — you'd be thinking, 'Oh, that sounds delicious!' **Zuni Café** was like that, too. I think that approach was really important."
>
> —DEBORAH MADISON, FOUNDING CHEF OF GREENS RESTAURANT

1971 – 1976   During **Earl Butz**'s tenure as Secretary of Agriculture, he implements many broad-based changes to U.S. agricultural policy. Small farmers are told to "get big, or get out," and many family-run farms go under. Subsidies are instead given to big agriculture, which — aided by new chemical-based fertilizers and technology — has larger-than-ever harvests and produces an **unprecedented supply of food**. While Americans' food costs as a percentage of their income fall over the next three decades, health-care costs *rise* in similar proportion.

1972   **Alice Laden**, housekeeper and cook to 1925 Nobelist and long-time ethical vegetarian **George Bernard Shaw** (1856–1950), co-authors *The George Bernard Shaw Vegetarian Cookbook* with R. J. Minney, featuring dishes such as lentil curry and savory rice.

On May 12, UCLA graduate film student **Anna Thomas's** book *Vegetarian Epicure* is published by Knopf, followed by *Vegetarian Epicure – Book Two* six years later. The two books are translated into multiple languages and sell millions of copies.

The feminist collective (and mostly if not entirely vegetarian) restaurant **Mother Courage** is opened by Dolores Alexander and Jill Ward in New York City's Greenwich Village.

1973   **The Moosewood Collective** — a restaurant co-founded by **Mollie Katzen** and others — opens in January in Ithaca, New York, and specializes in healthful natural foods cuisine. It commits to a vegetarian menu the following year. Through its continuous operation for more than four decades and the publication of a dozen cookbooks, it becomes a driving force in creative vegetarian cuisine and is eventually named by *Bon Appétit* as "one of the 13 most influential restaurants of the 20th century." In 1977, *The Moosewood Cookbook* by Mollie Katzen is published, and it goes

"One of the biggest influences on my cuisine was my obsession with international ethnic folk music. I'd visit music festivals as a hobby, as it offered a full cultural immersion in not only the folk music but the food of places like Greece, Turkey, the Balkans, and Israel. It's how I first discovered tabbouleh, and how things like hummus became mainstream.... I had earned $2.25 an hour cooking at a vegetarian restaurant called the **Shandygaff** in San Francisco, so my brother and some friends recruited me to come back to Ithaca to help them put a restaurant together, and I ended up staying. When I wrote *The Moosewood Cookbook*, it was a homespun effort in every way. The original project was collated by hand; it was written in a very private voice for my siblings and cousins and something that I never imagined would become so very public."
—MOLLIE KATZEN, CO-FOUNDER, THE MOOSEWOOD COLLECTIVE

"All we had to do was find someone to eat this avalanche of cheap, low-quality food. In just two generations, **a nation wracked by hunger ate its way into obesity, diabetes, and all sorts of other problems**."
—DIRECTOR CHRISTOPHER TAYLOR'S 2008 DOCUMENTARY *FOOD FIGHT*

"I remember reading Anna Thomas's *Vegetarian Epicure*, and being very taken with how well-traveled she was and how well she conveyed the sensuality of food. It balanced the compelling politics of Frankie [Frances Moore Lappé]'s *Diet for a Small Planet*."
—AUTHOR MOLLIE KATZEN

"We visited **Mother Courage** restaurant many, many times in the 1970s. When we asked them for help with our plans to open Bloodroot, they opened their books and were enormously helpful to us."
—SELMA MIRIAM, FOUNDER OF BLOODROOT (BRIDGEPORT, CT)

on to be cited by *The New York Times* as one of the ten bestselling cookbooks of all time, with more than two million copies sold. Multiple editions of Katzen's book *The Enchanted Broccoli Forest* will cumulatively sell more than a million copies.

Deborah Santana (wife of musician Carlos Santana) and her sister **Kitsaun** open **Dipti Nivas**, one of the first vegetarian restaurants in San Francisco. Over the coming decade, it becomes renowned for its casseroles and veggie burgers at reasonable prices.

1974 The first issue of *Vegetarian Times* magazine is published by its founder and editor — twenty-three-year-old Chicago nurse **Paul Barrett Obis, Jr.** — who distributes it through health-food stores. By 1987, its paid circulation will grow to 133,000, and by its four-hundredth issue in January 2013, it will hit 315,000.

1975 United Nations Secretary-General **Kurt Waldheim** is quoted in *Vegetarian Voice* as describing **the food consumption of rich countries** (which typically eat more meat than other countries) as **one of the causes of global hunger**.

Wishing to introduce Americans to the pleasures of tofu, **William Shurtleff** and **Akiko Aoyagi** write *The Book of Tofu*, which goes on to sell hundreds of thousands of copies. They follow with *The Book of Miso* and *The Book of Tempeh*.

The Farm, a long-lived (to this day!) spiritual community founded in 1971 in Summertown, Tennessee, comes out with *The Farm Vegetarian Cookbook*, which plays a key role in popularizing tempeh, soy-based foods, and a vegan diet.

Animal Liberation by Australian philosopher **Peter Singer** is published, giving birth to the modern animal rights movement through condemning factory farming and medical research.

A *New York Times* headline reports "**Vegetarianism: Growing Way of Life, Especially Among the Young.**"

The biannual **World Vegetarian Congress** is held in Maine, drawing 1,500 vegetarians from across the United States and around the globe.

The medical journal *Cancer Research* publishes a study by **Professor Kenneth K. Carroll** summarizing other studies in multiple countries, all demonstrating that higher animal fat (but not plant fat) intake is correlated with increased breast cancer mortality.

1976   *Laurel's Kitchen* by **Laurel Robertson**, **Carol Flinders**, and **Bronwen Godfrey** is published. It goes on to sell more than one million copies and is considered one of the first classic American vegetarian cookbooks of this era.

Cornell Class of 1971 graduate **Julie Jordan** comes out with her first cookbook *Wings of Life: Vegetarian Cookery* (later to be followed by 1986's *Cabbagetown Café Cookbook,* and 1998's *A Taste of Julie Jordan*). From 1977 through 1991, she owns vegetarian **Cabbagetown Café** in Ithaca, New York, which is known for its cashew chili, enchilada del dia, and fresh-baked bread. After the café closes in 1993, its signature salad of greens, chickpeas, broccoli, brown rice, herbed tofu, olives, nuts, and cheeses lives on at Wegmans, where Jordan today oversees the development of the Northeast supermarket chain's meatless prepared dishes.

The organic vegetarian/vegan restaurant **Angelica Kitchen** opens in New York City. In 2000 its former executive chef (1992 – 1999) **Peter Berley** will come out with *The Modern Vegetarian Kitchen.* In 2003, then-owner **Leslie McEachern** will come out with *The Angelica Home Kitchen*, with recipes for signature dishes such as the Dragon Bowl.

1977   The **U.S. Senate Select Committee on Nutrition**, chaired by **Senator George McGovern**, recommends decreasing consumption of saturated fat and cholesterol while increasing that of fruits, vegetables, and whole-grain cereals. The "McGovern report" causes an uproar in the meat, egg, and dairy industries.

Bloodroot, a feminist collective vegetarian restaurant, is founded in Bridgeport, Connecticut. Two of the original collective members, **Selma Miriam** and **Noel Furie**, continue with the restaurant over three decades, writing two cookbooks (one vegetarian, one vegan).

"One of the many popular vegetarian cookbooks, *Laurel's Kitchen* (1976), written by disciples of Eknath Easwaran [an Indian spiritual teacher influenced by Gandhi], warned against 'speedy refueling.' "
—FROM THE TEN-VOLUME *SOCIAL HISTORY OF THE UNITED STATES* (2009)

"**Julie Jordan's** *Wings of Life* cookbook was our bible at the very beginning. . . . It was unsophisticated, but honest, and the recipes were for simple food with integrity and flavor."
—SELMA MIRIAM, FOUNDER OF BLOODROOT (BRIDGEPORT, CT)

"[Senator George] McGovern later told me that he took more pride in this work than in anything he had ever done, even if it had cost him and some of his colleagues in the Midwestern states their political careers. This was one of my first deeply troubling experiences with the politics of science."
—T. COLIN CAMPBELL, AUTHOR OF *THE CHINA STUDY*

1977   The **Natural Gourmet Institute** (NGI) is founded in New York City by **Dr. Annemarie Colbin** on the principle that "what we eat significantly affects our physical, mental, and spiritual well-being." While not vegetarian in mission, the institute hosts popular weekly Friday night vegetarian dinners showcasing its students' cooking and produces many influential vegetarian chefs, including **Amanda Cohen** of Dirt Candy, **Tal Ronnen** of Crossroads, and vegan cookbook author **Bryant Terry**.

With a huge peach surplus, California legislation prohibiting farmers from selling their produce outside commercial markets leaves tons of peaches to rot. Angry farmers dump them on the lawn of the State Capitol, leading **Governor Jerry Brown** to finally relax restrictions and allow farmers to sell produce at **farmers' markets,** which spurs their proliferation. By 1979, the farmers' market in Gardena becomes the first to open in southern California, and one of the first few in the state. By 2005, there will be nearly five hundred farmers' markets in California, and by 2009, five thousand farmers' markets in the United States. As of 2013, there are 8,144, according to the USDA.

> "I moved to New Mexico [in the 1990s] to open a restaurant, but there were some delays, so when one day I overheard someone say he needed help at the **Santa Fe Farmers Market**, I said, 'I have some time.' The next week, I was manager of the market. And it was the best thing I ever did — I met the most wonderful growers. . . . It's not easy to grow fruit in this climate — some years we have it, many years we don't — so it was mostly vegetables. Santa Fe has always been known for its chiles, but there's much more than chiles in the market. Today, we have heirloom corn that is ground for the most wonderful cornmeal, and by late July we have everything."
> —DEBORAH MADISON, AUTHOR, *VEGETARIAN COOKING FOR EVERYONE*

On October 1, the first **World Vegetarian Day** is held by the North American Vegetarian Society, becoming an annual tradition to kick off October as **Vegetarian Awareness Month**, which continues to this day. The following year, the **International Vegetarian Union** endorses October 1 as World Vegetarian Day.

The *American Journal of Clinical Nutrition* reports on a study of 24,000 Seventh-day Adventists, indicating that **males aged 35 to 64 eating a plant-based diet had three times less risk of heart disease** than nonvegetarians in that demographic.

A Conversation with Deborah Madison, Founding Chef of Greens Restaurant (1979–1983)

"I've never identified myself as vegetarian. When I was a student at the San Francisco Zen Center, we decided as a group that out of respect for the Buddhist principle of not taking life, we would be vegetarian within our community, so that was the way we ate. I took over the cooking for the Center from a good macrobiotic cook, but as we had visitors at our tables, we didn't want them to have to wonder what they were being served. The goal, for me, was to create food that would be familiar and bring people together at the table. My influences were very classic — *Escoffier, Larousse Gastronomique* — so it was kind of the reverse of what others are doing today: Instead of whole wheat pancakes, people wanted pancakes that would fluff up, so I switched to white flour. I added butter and cheese to the menu — as this was well before the vegan era.

"When Greens first opened, it was only open for lunch, and we had women [guests] who would say, 'I'm going to bring my husband!' And he'd get there at the end of a long day or week and want a steak. But we won husbands over with touches like bringing warm focaccia with rosemary to the table. We also set out roasted almonds wrapped in parchment paper, and it was like unwrapping a present! I got that idea from Elizabeth David's *Salt, Spices and Aromatics in the English Kitchen*. And we'd win them over with dishes like Many Layered Crepe Cake, which had layers of fresh tomato sauce or cheese between each crepe — it created a lot of physical drama at the table and gave focus that replaced the lack of meat.

"Greens in 1979 was a very stylish restaurant. I didn't want it to have any vegetarian clichés, so we didn't serve sprouts and there were no macramé hangings on the walls. In the early days, the food was pretty cheese-y. Of our early customers, there was only one who didn't eat dairy, which was so rare that he had his own nickname: Non-Dairy Jerry. Today, that part has really flipped.

"Today — finally — nobody has to make a big deal out of being vegetarian. And I have seen that many people are eating far less meat, and the meat they are eating is of higher quality. I do make it a point to tell people that I am not a vegetarian because I don't want people to not invite me over. But I do eat vegetarian a lot of the time, and when I'm out on book tour, I frequently order vegetarian dishes, especially if I'm not eating somewhere I trust the other ingredients."

1978   When **The Inn at Little Washington** opens in Washington, Virginia — 70 miles outside Washington, DC — few suppliers are willing to make deliveries. Chef-owner **Patrick O'Connell** sources produce from dozens of local farmers instead, and by January 2011 the restaurant's success will allow him to hire the Inn's own farmer-in-residence to grow specialty produce ranging from haricots verts to microgreens to sweet peas on the Inn's property to supplement that provided by more than 100 different suppliers, which are spotlighted on the Inn's vegetarian tasting menu, arguably America's finest.

1979   **Greens Restaurant** opens in San Francisco under the auspices of the San Francisco Zen Center, becoming America's first vegetarian fine dining restaurant under founding chef **Deborah Madison.** It showcases elegant preparations of produce from the Zen Center's organic Green Gulch Farm in Marin. In 1981, **Annie Somerville** is hired to assist Madison; she will take over as chef when Madison departs in 1983.

The Vegetarian Feast by **Martha Rose Shulman** is published, going on to win the Tastemaker Award in the Health and Special Diets category.

The Vegetarians by **Rynn Berry** (1945–2014) — which is based on interviews with famous vegetarians such as actors Marty Feldman, Cloris Leachman, and Dennis Weaver, and Nobel Prize–winning author Isaac Bashevis Singer — is published. Berry goes on to author or co-author other vegetarian books, including 1996's *Famous Vegetarians and Their Favorite Recipes: Lives and Lore from Buddha to the Beatles*; 1998's *Food for the Gods: Vegetarianism & the World's Religions*; 2004's *Hitler: Neither Vegetarian Nor Animal Lover*; and the annual *Vegan Guide to New York City*.

1980   Influenced in part by Peter Singer's book *Animal Liberation*, **Ingrid Newkirk,** with established animal rights activist **Alex Pacheco**, co-founds **People for the Ethical Treatment of Animals** (PETA), which organizes animal rights awareness campaigns.

The U.S. Departments of Health, Education and Welfare (now HHS) and Agriculture (USDA) jointly issue seven principles for a healthful diet, in response to the public's demand for guidelines on diet and health. The principles become **the first edition of *Nutrition and Your Health: Dietary Guidelines for Americans.***

They will be revisited every five years to reflect the latest scientific research, although they remain remarkably consistent.

1981   *Madhur Jaffrey's World-of-the-East Vegetarian Cooking* is published, which goes on to win a James Beard Book Award in the category of Natural Foods/Special Diet.

In their report "**The Causes of Cancer**: Quantitative Estimates of Avoidable Risks of Cancer in the United States Today," published by the *Journal of the National Cancer Institute,* **Sir Richard Doll** and **Sir Richard Peto** estimate that 35 percent of human cancers (with a "range of acceptable estimates" of 10–70 percent) may be attributed to diet. The results are summarized for the U.S. Congress.

Studies published in the journals *Cancer* and *Lancet* show that lung cancer among 14,000 smokers is substantially lower among those consuming beta-carotene-containing vegetables. **These ⸳lies suggest that increased consumption of plant-based foods ⸳reduce cancer risk.**

⸳ional Research Council releases its **Diet, Nutrition, and ⸳ort**, the first major report connecting diet, nutrition, ⸳'s major recommendations include reducing the con-⸳ts and increasing the consumption of fruits, veg-⸳'e-grain cereal products.

Cha⸳ and **Debra Wasserman** establish the organization Baltin⸳ Vegetarians. By 1990, it evolves into the **Vegetarian Resource Group**, reflecting the national demand for its research reports. The group publishes the *Vegetarian Journal* and a number of books, including 1991's *Simply Vegan*, which sells more than 50,000 copies, and 1997's *Conveniently Vegan.*

Actor **William Shatner** narrates *The Vegetarian World,* a thirty-minute documentary on vegetarianism, produced by **Jonathon Kay.** Even if Shatner's jogging suit seems quaintly passé, its major points are relevant to this day.

The *New York Times* publishes Marian Burros's article "**In Defense of Vegetarianism: Seven Yeas,**" based on conversations with seven well-known vegetarians, including actors Marty Feldman, Carol Kane, and Dennis Weaver. She writes, "Being a vegetarian in a largely carnivorous society has often meant second-class

"If, through some miracle, I decided to resort to a vegetable diet forever, this new book by **Madhur Jaffrey**, who is to my mind the finest authority on Indian cooking in America, would be my Bible. It is by far the most comprehensive, fascinating, and inspired book on vegetable cookery that I have encountered."
—CRAIG CLAIBORNE, WRITING OF MADHUR JAFFREY'S *WORLD-OF-THE-EAST VEGETARIAN COOKING* IN HIS MEMOIR *A FEAST MADE FOR LAUGHTER*

gastronomic citizenship. . . . But the situation has improved significantly in the last few years, say a number of well-known people who attempt to follow one version or another of a vegetarian diet. The improvement results, in part at least, from the increase in the number of people who call themselves vegetarians. There are now too many of them to be ignored. The Vegetarian Information Service, a nonprofit educational organization, puts the figure in this country at between seven and 12 million."

1983   Nikki and David Goldbeck's *American Wholefoods Cuisine: 1,300 Meatless Wholesome Recipes, from Short Order to Gourmet* is published, leading *Newsday* to characterize it as "the vegetarian *Joy of Cooking*" and *Vegetarian Times* as "a monumental work." It will be reissued in 2005.

In her *New York Times* article **"New Research on the Vegetarian Diet,"** **Jane Brody** argues that "the main question has become whether it is healthier to be a vegetarian than to be a meat eater," which her column answers in the affirmative.

The March issue of *Vegetarian Times* contains an interview with Nobel Prize–winning author and vegetarian **Isaac Bashevis Singer** (1904 – 1991), who is quoted as saying, "Vegetarianism for me is a protest . . . protesting against everything which is not just: about the fact that there is so much sickness, so much death, so much cruelty. **My vegetarianism is my religion**, and it's part of my protest against the conduct of the world."

Customer requests for the hearty soup recipes served at the popular Los Angeles vegetarian restaurant lead to the publication of *Follow Your Heart's Vegetarian Soup Cookbook* by Janice Cook Migliaccio. Co-owner Bob Goldberg recalls, "We serve three to five soups every day, including one dairy soup and one no-salt/no-oil soup, and have historically given out samples of each so customers could decide which to order. People loved them so much that they'd ask for the recipes, so it was a no-brainer to decide to do a cookbook. Of course, those recipes feature more butter and dairy than we use today."

Physician **John A. McDougall** writes *The McDougall Plan*, which embraces a starch-based diet (e.g., beans, bread, corn, lentils, pasta, potatoes, rice) incorporating vegetables and fruits and eschewing animal-based foods and added oils. It is the first book by a Western

"On the whole, vegetarians are less likely to be afflicted with the chronic diseases that are leading killers and cripplers in societies where meat is the centerpiece of the diet. . . . To glean the heart-saving benefits of vegetarianism, consumption of such foods as hard cheese, cream cheese, ice cream, and eggs should be moderate."

—JANE BRODY, *THE NEW YORK TIMES* (OCTOBER 12, 1983)

"Vegetables are my life. . . . Vegetables are much more generous and luxurious than any protein from an animal. . . . [They] are the portal to the treatment of all other foods."

—CHEF MICHEL BRAS, AS QUOTED ON GRUBSTREET.COM IN 2011

doctor suggesting that food combining to make "complete proteins" is unnecessary, debunking a myth that is still widespread. He goes on to write another dozen health-related books, which collectively sell more than a million copies.

Marshall "Mickey" Hornick and his partner (and, later, wife) "Chef Jo" Kaucher open The Chicago Diner in Chicago, which serves meatless versions of diner classics. Just after the restaurant's 20th anniversary, they release *The Chicago Diner Cookbook,* and on the restaurant's 30th anniversary in 2013, *The New Chicago Diner Cookbook.*

Chef Michel Bras cooks his first vegetable menu at restaurant Bras in Laguiole, France, and will earn his third Michelin star in 1999. His signature dish gargouillou [pronounced gar-goo-yoo] — gorgeous composed salads featuring dozens of seasonal young vegetables, herbs, leaves, and seeds — will inspire versions by other chefs around the world in the decades to come.

Soy foods pioneer Louise Hagler's book *Tofu Cookery* is published.

> "All large populations of trim, healthy people, throughout verifiable human history, have obtained the bulk of their calories from starch. Examples of once thriving people include Japanese, Chinese, and other Asians eating sweet potatoes, buckwheat, and/or rice; Incas in South America eating potatoes; Mayans and Aztecs in Central America eating corn; and Egyptians in the Middle East eating wheat."
> —DR. JOHN A. MCDOUGALL, IN HIS NEWSLETTER (FEBRUARY 2009)

> "Louise Hagler's 1983 book *Tofu Cookery* is one of the books that changed my life. After my mom brought it home, she and my sister and I — who all went vegetarian together — started cooking and eating from it, almost every day it seemed. As we'd never shopped or cooked together before, it was the cookbook that brought everyone together. For the time, it had cutting-edge food photography, and everything looked great. I still make the brownies and the barbecue tofu — I even make the tofu balls, which are flavored with peanut butter and soy sauce, every week."
> —ISA CHANDRA MOSKOWITZ, AUTHOR OF *ISA DOES IT* AND *VEGANOMICON*

1984   Bart Potenza purchases Sunny's, a health food store and juice bar on Manhattan's Upper East Side, and renames it the Healthy Candle in tribute to the prior owners' nightly lighting of candles as a blessing. Over time, it evolves into a full-service vegetarian café.

Chef Raymond Blanc opens Le Manoir aux Quat'Saisons in Oxfordshire, England, where he offers a vegetarian menu option. The restaurant goes on to earn two Michelin stars.

1985   Dr. Neal Barnard founds the Washington, DC–based nonprofit Physicians Committee for Responsible Medicine (PCRM), which grows into a nationwide group of physicians and other supporters

> "Now, more than ever, eating less meat and more vegetables represents a step toward a healthier lifestyle. This is the future of food."
> —CHEF RAYMOND BLANC

that promotes preventive medicine and addresses controversies in contemporary medicine, including efforts to reform federal dietary guidelines.

Classic Indian Vegetarian and Grain Cooking by **Julie Sahni** is published. It goes on to win the Glenfiddich Best Cookbook Award.

1986 **Gene Baur** and his then-wife **Lorri Houston** found **Farm Sanctuary** in Watkins Glen, New York, which gives rescued factory-farmed animals a place to live. The Sanctuary will expand to 175 acres in upstate New York and 300 acres in northern California.

Nutritionist **Marion Nestle** moves to Washington, DC, to serve as editor of the **Surgeon General's** *Report on Nutrition and Health*, a 700-page book released in the summer of 1988. She later reveals that she was told on her first day not to recommend eating less meat or less of any other food category.

Community Supported Agriculture (CSA), which got its start in Germany, Japan, and Switzerland, takes root in the United States. Its growth takes off, leading to CSAs in every state, with more than 12,500 farms participating in CSAs by 2007.

1987 **Yamuna Devi**, who had received world-class culinary training from Srila Prabhupada, writes the classic cookbook *Lord Krishna's Cuisine: The Art of Indian Vegetarian Cooking*. It becomes the first vegetarian cookbook to win the prestigious International Association of Culinary Professionals (IACP) Cookbook Award.

Diet for a New America by **John Robbins** (son of a founder of the ice cream chain Baskin-Robbins) is published, spotlighting the moral, economic, and emotional price we pay for the food we eat — and championing vegetarianism and even veganism as a cure for world hunger and the environment. The book becomes an instant classic, and Robbins continues to be an influential voice with books such as 1992's *May All Be Fed: Diet for a New World* and 2001's *The Food Revolution*, as well as at FoodRevolution.org.

The International Congress on Vegetarian Nutrition convenes in Washington, DC, with more than four hundred nutritional experts and researchers in attendance. It reconvenes every five years, and starting in 1997 it takes residence at Loma Linda University in southern California, its current home.

Deborah Madison, with **Edward Espé Brown**, writes *The Greens Cookbook: Extraordinary Vegetarian Cuisine from the Celebrated Restaurant*, which becomes a bestselling classic.

"Edward [Espé Brown] had written the *Tassajara Bread Book,* and [when I wanted to write my first book] the New York publishing community asked 'Who's Deborah Madison?' I couldn't get a book deal unless Edward's name was on it, too. So we co-authored *The Greens Cookbook*. . . . I caught up with him a few years back during a visit to Larkspur. He made biscuits, and I was so impressed to see his hands and how they worked the dough, and how very delicious the biscuits were."
—DEBORAH MADISON, FOUNDING CHEF OF GREENS RESTAURANT

1989   **Linda McCartney**'s *Home Cooking* is published, celebrating a vegetarian lifestyle shared with former Beatle **Paul McCartney**. Two years later, she founds her own line of vegetarian foods. After Linda's untimely death in 1998, McCartney will take up the vegetarian cause in earnest.

In September, *Connoisseur* magazine names the ten best restaurants in the world, noting that one of them — **Alain Ducasse**'s Le Louis XV in Monte Carlo, Monaco — features a vegetarian tasting menu.

At a meeting of the American Heart Association in New Orleans, the director of Sausalito, California's Preventative Medicine Research Institute, **Dr. Dean Ornish**, presents the findings of his groundbreaking study of the effects of a vegetarian diet and lifestyle modifications on preventing and even reversing heart disease. He writes several national bestsellers, including 1990's *Dr. Dean Ornish's Program for Reversing Heart Disease*; 1993's *Eat More, Weigh Less*; and 2007's *The Spectrum*.

"Life-Style Shift Can Unclog Ailing Arteries, Study Finds . . . [**Dr. Dean Ornish's**] study showed that a **vegetarian diet**, moderate exercise, and an hour a day of yoga and meditation could produce a reversal of atherosclerosis, a blockage of the arteries that can lead to a heart attack, in men and women who were strict in following the daily regimen. Experts say this is the first study to show that such blockage can be reversed without using cholesterol-lowering drugs or surgery."
—DANIEL GOLEMAN, *THE NEW YORK TIMES* (NOVEMBER 14, 1989)

1980s   A severe hailstorm wipes out the Ohio family farm of **Bob Jones, Sr.**, and his sons **Lee Jones** and **Bob Jones, Jr.** Celebrated chef Jean-Louis Palladin's request for squash blossoms grown organically leads to the family's radical decision to focus on chefs' needs for the highest quality, most flavorful produce as part of their rebuilding strategy. The result is **The Chef's Garden**, which today supplies some of the best chefs in America with specialty produce such as microgreens, micro herbs, heirloom vegetables, specialty lettuces, and edible flowers. Their nonprofit **Veggie U** supplies classroom garden kits and a five-week science program that has been taught in 4,700 elementary and special needs classes across thirty-two states and Washington, DC.

1990   **T. Colin Campbell** first announces the results of the **China-Cornell Study**, a groundbreaking work confirming the benefits of a plant-based diet. Jane Brody's May 8 *New York Times* article on the study is titled **"Huge Study of Diet Indicts Fat and Meat."**

The Savory Way, an illustrated vegetarian cookbook by former Greens Restaurant chef **Deborah Madison**, wins the IACP's Cookbook of the Year Award.

Sundays at Moosewood Restaurant by the Moosewood Collective is published.

Classically trained French chef **Jean-Georges Vongerichten**, then of the four-star restaurant Lafayette in New York City, comes out with his groundbreaking and influential cookbook *Simple Cuisine*, which eschews the use of meat stocks in favor of lighter vinaigrettes, flavored oils, and vegetable juices and broths.

1990–1991   Drafts of the **U.S. Department of Agriculture's** proposed **Food Pyramid** are reviewed.

1991   On January 13, Chicago chef **Charlie Trotter** prepares **a seven-course all-potato menu at the James Beard House** in New York City, which is thought to be the first meatless (and likely the first vegetarian) meal ever served there. Some of the dishes include a terrine of potato and sauerkraut with chèvre cream, new potato and sweetcorn risotto with corn consommé and crispy sweet potatoes, and potato-black truffle ice cream.

Dr. Caldwell Esselstyn, Jr., of the Cleveland Clinic presents his ground-breaking five-year longitudinal study of dramatically reduced advanced heart disease among eighteen seriously ill patients consuming a diet free of animal-based foods and added oils, at the first National Conference for the Elimination of Coronary Heart Disease, in Tucson.

"The quality of the produce that **The Chef's Garden** delivers is absolutely unbelievable. They're always turning us on to something special. . . . **Farmer Lee Jones** has been predicting that vegetables would become 'the next center of the plate item' for years."

—CHEF MARK LEVY, THE POINT (SARANAC LAKE, NY)

"Early findings from the most comprehensive large study ever undertaken of the relationship between diet and the risk of developing disease are challenging much of American dietary dogma. **The study, being conducted in China, paints a bold portrait of a plant-based eating plan** that is more likely to promote health than disease. The study can be considered the Grand Prix of epidemiology."

—JANE BRODY, *THE NEW YORK TIMES* (MAY 8, 1990)

"We do a vegetable degustation menu at the restaurant that now accounts for about 20 percent of our orders. . . . Many of the dishes we served on the potato menu were originally on the vegetable menu."

—CHARLIE TROTTER, AS QUOTED IN *NATION'S RESTAURANT NEWS* (FEBRUARY 25, 1991)

On April 8, **The Physicians Committee for Responsible Medicine** (PCRM) proposes replacing the USDA's long-time (since 1956) four food groups (meat, milk, fruits/vegetables, and breads/cereals) with their New Four Food Groups — whole grains, vegetables, legumes, and fruits — based on decades of peer-reviewed studies establishing the value of a plant-based diet.

On April 27, the U.S. Department of Agriculture (USDA) withdraws its proposed **Eating Right Pyramid Food Guide** under pressure from the meat and dairy industries, bringing to light the conflict of interest of its dual mandates to promote agriculture and to inform the public on nutrition.

 **Zen Palate**, a hip vegetarian restaurant, opens in Manhattan's theater district. Years later, it will be described as "the granddaddy of Pan-Asian vegetarian restaurants in New York City."

The Now and Zen Epicure: Gourmet Vegan Recipes for the Enlightened Palate by San Francisco's Now and Zen Bakery founder **Miyoko Nishimoto** (later **Schinner**) is published. She will follow it with 1999's vegetarian *Japanese Cooking,* as well as 2012's bestselling *Artisanal Vegan Cheese,* which spurs home cooks and professional chefs alike to experiment with vegan cheese-making.

Friendly Foods by **Brother Ron Pickarski**, a Franciscan monk, is published, focusing on whole grains, vegetables, legumes, sea vegetables, and various other so-called "friendly" foods that "do not bear the high environmental, economic, and nutritional costs of meat and processed foods."

The **National Restaurant Association** (NRA) commissions its first survey on meatless menu options, with "astounding" results. Twenty percent of American adults responded that they were "likely or very likely" to choose a restaurant with vegetarian options, based on health concerns and taste preferences.

1992   As interest in classic French restaurants slows, **Hubert Keller**'s renowned restaurant **Fleur de Lys** in San Francisco replaces butter and cream with vegetable stocks and purees and offers a five-course vegetarian tasting menu. Cardiologist Dr. Dean Ornish taps Keller for recipes to include in his heart-healthy cookbook *Eat More, Weigh Less.*

"This [April 27] incident also highlights the inherent conflict of interest in the Department of Agriculture's dual mandates to promote U.S. agricultural products and to advise the public about healthy food choices."
—MARION NESTLE, VIA AN ABSTRACT OF HER ARTICLE "FOOD LOBBIES, THE FOOD PYRAMID, AND U.S. NUTRITION POLICY" IN THE *INTERNATIONAL JOURNAL OF HEALTH SERVICES* (1993)

"**Zen Palate** is a rare and oddball treasure, a special taste — somewhere between loving Tom Waits' singing and eating rose petals for breakfast. And yet everyone I've taken there has seemed enchanted. . . . The food is eclectic, too, quite Chinese and a little Japanese with a hint of Indonesia, hometown healthful meets nouvelle cuisine."
—GAEL GREENE, IN HER MAY 28, 1991, *NEW YORK* MAGAZINE REVIEW, WHICH SHE RECALLS IN 2013 AS THE ONLY VEGETARIAN RESTAURANT SHE EVER REVIEWED IN MORE THAN FOUR DECADES AS A RESTAURANT CRITIC

"**Ann Gentry** [has come up with] a cuisine that is as interesting and delicious as it is healthful."

—BON APPÉTIT

In June, the U.S. Dept. of Agriculture introduces the **Food Pyramid** as the government's primary food group symbol representing a nutritious diet.

Recipes from an Ecological Kitchen by **Lorna Sass** is published. It is later reissued as *Lorna Sass's Complete Vegetarian Kitchen,* which Mollie Katzen characterizes as "the best vegan cookbook."

1993   Healthy Candle owner **Bart Potenza** and his nutritionist partner, **Joy Pierson**, play the lottery (using the numbers of both their birthdays) on Friday the 13th — winning $53,000. The proceeds are used to create **Candle Cafe** (1994) and, a decade later, **Candle 79** (2003), considered two of the very best fine-dining vegan restaurants in America.

In June, **Ann Gentry** opens the organic, plant-based restaurant **Real Food Daily** in Santa Monica. Additional locations in West Hollywood and Pasadena will follow.

1994   On the heels of the success of its sister restaurant Milly's in San Rafael, California, San Francisco's **Millennium** opens as a fine-dining vegetarian restaurant under executive chef **Eric Tucker.** In 1998, Tucker co-authors *The Millennium Cookbook* and in 2003, *The Artful Vegan.*

Chef **Tanya Petrovna** opens **Native Foods** in Palm Springs, California. In November/December 2009, *Vegetarian Times* will describe it as "the vegan restaurant with a global consciousness" which "has expanded into eight locations in Southern California, with plans to grow a dozen more branches reaching beyond the Golden State." In 2010, the vegan fast-casual chain will be acquired by a couple, **Andrea McGinty** and **Daniel Dolan**, who move the California company's national headquarters to Chicago and forecast 2011 sales at its multiple locations to be $15 million. In 2013, the company will project having forty-five locations operating in both existing and new markets (e.g., Baltimore, Dallas, and Philadelphia) by the end of 2014, and two hundred locations by 2017.

World Vegan Day's first annual celebration is held on November 1, to mark the fiftieth anniversary of the Vegan Society.

1995 The film *Babe*, starring twenty-year vegetarian **James Cromwell**, debuts. On the heels of the Oscar-nominated film's success, Cromwell campaigns against animal cruelty toward pigs.

1996 A fourth-generation dairy farmer and cattle rancher turned vegetarian and food-safety activist, **Howard Lyman** makes comments on *The Oprah Winfrey Show* that lead Oprah to publicly swear off hamburgers. The National Cattlemen's Beef Association sues Lyman and Winfrey, although both are found not guilty of any wrongdoing in 1998. Lyman comes out with a 1998 book on dangerous practices of the cattle and dairy industries entitled *Mad Cowboy: Plain Truth from the Cattle Rancher Who Won't Eat Meat.*

Joseph Connelly launches the Syracuse Area Vegetarian Education Society and a twenty-eight-page newspaper tabloid. Four years later, he teams with **Colleen Holland** to turn it into a glossy, four-color magazine called *VegNews.*

Husband-and-wife vegetarians **Jeff and Sabrina Nelson** found **VegSource.com**, which celebrates vegetarianism. Within five years, it will be ranked the number-one food-oriented site on the web.

Two years after the publication of his eponymous first cookbook, Chicago chef **Charlie Trotter** comes out with his book *Charlie Trotter's Vegetables.*

Seven-year-old **Ristorante Joia** restaurant in Milan becomes the **first vegetarian restaurant in Europe to win a Michelin star.**

1997 On May 23, **Didi Emmons**'s book *Vegetarian Planet* is published. It goes on to sell more than 200,000 copies.

Erik Marcus's book *Vegan: The New Ethics of Eating* is published. Eleven years later, he will run the website **Vegan.com**.

Vegetarian Cooking for Everyone by **Deborah Madison** is published. The following year, it is named "Cookbook of the Year" by the International Association of Culinary Professionals (IACP) and wins the James Beard Book Award for Best Vegetarian Cookbook, becoming one of the year's bestselling cookbooks.

"**Start with one meal a day,** then up it to one day a week, then one week a month. **Work your way into not consuming animals and animal products** and inform yourself. It doesn't take anything at all, and it's very easy to do. Then you start to think, 'What else?' This process begins your consciousness."
—VEGETARIAN ACTOR JAMES CROMWELL, WHO BECAME A VEGAN AFTER MAKING *BABE*

"I felt better knowing that there was one answer to many of the different ills afflicting both ourselves and our environment. Everything revolved around the fork."
—HOWARD LYMAN, IN *MAD COWBOY* (1998)

"**I have always considered vegetable cookery the most interesting part of cuisine.** Vegetables provide an incredible depth and complexity in both flavor and texture, not to mention an extraordinary range of colors and shapes. . . . I just happen to be in love with the experience of touching, cooking, and eating the multitude of vegetables, fruits, legumes, and grains. It is sincerely one of the most sensual joys of my life."
—CHARLIE TROTTER, IN *CHARLIE TROTTER'S VEGETABLES* (1996)

1998   In May, *Vegetarian Times* reports on the proliferation of **vegetarian tasting menus** at upscale restaurants across America. Restaurants cited as examples include **Aquavit** (NYC), **Cascabel** (NYC), **Chanterelles** (Philadelphia), **Charlie Trotter's** (Chicago), **Fleur de Lys** (San Francisco), **French Laundry** (Yountville, CA), **Jojo** (NYC), **La Grenouille** (NYC), **Lespinasse** (NYC), **Patina** (Los Angeles), **Restaurant DANIEL** (NYC), **Seeger's** (Atlanta), and **Verbena** (NYC).

1999   **Eric Brent** launches **HappyCow.com**, a worldwide database of vegetarian restaurants, which lists about 1000. That number will increase to 5,500 by early 2014 for the United States alone.

2000   For the first time in history, **the world experiences a net loss in farmland**. Acreage continues to fall annually, as the population continues to rise. Concerns about the logistical impossibility of feeding the world's population if such rates continue lead to growing worries about global hunger.

   In October, a court ruling determines that the **USDA** has violated federal law by withholding documents and hiding financial conflicts of interest. The USDA provides information showing **financial conflicts of interest for six Dietary Guidelines Committee members (out of eleven, or the majority), who had financial ties to the food industry**.

2001   Michelin three-star chef **Alain Passard** removes red meat and seafood from the menu of his Paris restaurant L'Arpège.

2002   On May 14 (the same day as the launch of his album *18*), musician **Moby** (a vegan since 1986) opens the vegan café **TeaNY** in New York City with his partner, **Kelly Tisdale**.

2003   The U.S. Centers for Disease Control and Prevention (CDC) reports that one in three children born in 2000 will develop type 2 diabetes during their lifetime, concluding that the increase in the incidence of diabetes is directly proportional to the increasing rates of obesity. The study also shows that diabetes significantly reduces life expectancy. **For the first time in U.S. history, a generation has a *shorter* life expectancy than its parents' generation.**

The "**Meatless Mondays**" campaign is relaunched — this time, not as a war effort, but as a way to help people decrease meat and saturated fats in their diet by about 15 percent (or one-seventh). The effort, led by health advocate and retired ad executive **Sid Lerner** in conjunction with the Johns Hopkins Bloomberg School of Public Health's Center for a Livable Future, creates awareness of the preventable illnesses associated with excessive consumption of meat. Within several years, it becomes a global campaign involving participants in twenty-three countries, led by **Peggy Neu**.

Dismayed by the lack of vegan cooking shows, 20-something vegetarians-since-sixteen **Isa Chandra Moskowitz** and **Terry Hope Romero** launch their own show, aired on community access television in Manhattan and Brooklyn, called "The Post-Punk Kitchen." While working to start a vegan 'zine called *Vegan with a Vengeance*, Moskowitz gets offered a book deal that leads her to instead publish her recipes as her first book in 2005, and it goes on to sell more than 50,000 copies in its first two years. Moskowitz and Romero co-author several subsequent books, including 2006's *Vegan Cupcakes Take Over the World* and 2007's *Veganomicon*, and the two also go on to author other books separately.

Candle 79 is founded in New York City; it will be considered the grande dame of upscale vegan restaurants.

Chicago chef **Charlie Trotter** and Larkspur, California, raw chef **Roxanne Klein** coauthor *Raw*, a coffee table-style book showcasing juiced, dehydrated, and blended fruits and vegetables.

The Chair of New York University's Department of Nutrition, Food Studies, and Public Health **Marion Nestle** comes out with her groundbreaking book *Food Politics: How the Food Industry Influences Nutrition and Health*, which goes on to win a number of major book awards. She will later write 2003's *Safe Food* and 2006's *What to Eat,* and in 2013, *Food Politics* will be reissued in an updated 10th anniversary edition.

Dr. Joel Fuhrman's *Eat to Live*: *The Amazing Nutrient-Rich Program for Fast and Sustained Weight Loss* is published, espousing the notion that health equals nutrients divided by calories — or nutrient density (later popularized by his ANDI ratings seen at

Whole Foods) — and advocates a six-week vegetarian diet to kick
off weight loss. The book becomes a *New York Times* number-one
bestseller and goes on to sell more than a million copies.

2004 The American Medical Association reverses its negative stance on
a vegan diet, citing many new scientific studies.

Karen Iacobbo and **Michael Iacobbo** write the first complete history of vegetarianism in the United States, *Vegetarian America:
A History*.

In March, **Terces and Matthew Engelhart** open their first organic,
local, sustainable (and meat-free) **Café Gratitude** in San Francisco.
Other locations will follow in the Bay Area as well as in Los Angeles
(2011), as will their organic, vegan, non-GMO Mexican restaurant
Gracias Madre in both San Francisco (2010) and Los Angeles
(2014). Their daughter Mollie will open LA-based **KindKreme**
(vegan ice cream) and **Sage** (vegan beer garden), and sons Ryland
and Cary will produce the food documentary *May I Be Frank?*

Then-partners **Matthew Kenney**
and **Sarma Melngailis** open
Pure Food and Wine, New York
City's first raw vegan fine dining restaurant. In 2005, they
co-author *Raw Food / Real World:
100 Recipes to Get the Glow. Forbes*
will name Pure one of its "All Star New York Eateries," and it will
also appear on *New York's* "Top 100 Restaurants" list.

After heading the kitchens at Trio in Evanston and his own sea-
food-focused restaurant, Spring, in Chicago, chef **Shawn McClain**
opens the upscale vegetarian restaurant **Green Zebra** in Chicago.
In 2006, McClain will be named Best Chef: Midwest by the James
Beard Foundation.

Forbes magazine reports that **vegetarian food sales have doubled
since 1998**, hitting $1.6 billion in 2003, with 61 percent growth
forecasted by 2008.

2005 Southern California-based **Veggie Grill** is founded by partners
Kevin Boylan and **T. K. Pillan**. By 2014, the fast-casual vegetarian

chain will have twenty-six locations in California, Oregon, and Washington State, with plans for continued expansion.

Cornell professor **T. Colin Campbell** and his son **Thomas M. Campbell II**'s book *The China Study: The Most Comprehensive Study of Nutrition Ever Conducted and the Startling Implications for Diet, Weight Loss and Long-Term Health* is published, and goes on to sell more than a million copies.

The new Dietary Guidelines mark **the first time the USDA acknowledges that not everyone can digest dairy**, with a comment about those who "don't or can't consume milk."

Dr. Walter Willett, chair of the Department of Nutrition at Harvard School of Public Health and author of *Eat, Drink and Be Healthy,* creates a score card to rank who benefits most from the **2005 Dietary Guidelines**. "Big dairy" wins with a score of 10 points, "Big beef" comes in second with eight points, while the public's health comes in third with six points.

In December, an irreverent vegan diet book co-authored by a former model and modeling agent is published. *Skinny Bitch* by **Rory Freedman** and **Kim Barnouin** sells more than 250,000 copies within two years. It goes on to be translated into multiple languages and, with more than three million copies in print, becomes the bestselling vegetarian diet book of all time.

2006 The **United Nations Food and Agriculture Organization** (FAO) reports that livestock farming generates 18 percent of the Earth's greenhouse gas emissions. In contrast, all the world's transportation systems (boats, cars, planes, trains, etc.) total just 13 percent.

Sublime, a vegan restaurant opened in 2003 by animal rights activist **Nanci Alexander,** which earmarks 100 percent of its profits for animal welfare, reopens after hurricane damage and a hiatus in Ft. Lauderdale, Florida.

On the heels of Horizons Café (1994 – 2005), **Rich Landau** and **Kate Jacoby** open **Horizons** in Philadelphia, which gains many followers in its subsequent five-year run. Staff go on to open their own vegan spots in Philadelphia (e.g., 2010's **Blackbird Pizza** and **Sprig and Vine**, 2012's **Hip City Veg** and **Miss Rachel's Pantry**).

2007 In an article titled "Got Beef? No, and They're Doing Fine, Thank You," the Associated Press reports that **vegetarian restaurants are growing in number and in popularity**, citing as examples **Candle 79** (New York), **Horizons** (Philadelphia), and **Sublime** (Ft. Lauderdale).

Dr. Caldwell B. Esselstyn, Jr., comes out with his book *Prevent and Reverse Heart Disease: The Revolutionary, Scientifically Proven, Nutrition-Based Cure*, which advocates a strict vegetarian diet. It becomes a huge bestseller.

On September 28, comedian, political commentator, and talk-show host **Bill Maher** takes on pharmaceutical companies in his "New Rules" rant, concluding, "The answer isn't another pill. The answer is spinach."

On the heels of the popularity of his bestselling book *How to Cook Everything*, author **Mark Bittman** comes out with *How to Cook Everything Vegetarian*. In 2013, he'll fuel the part-time vegan trend with his book *VB6: Eat Vegan Before 6:00 to Lose Weight and Restore Your Health . . . for Good*.

2008 Inspired by **Kathy Freston**'s new book *Quantum Wellness: A Practical and Spiritual Guide to Health and Happiness*, talk-show host **Oprah Winfrey** undertakes a three-week vegan cleanse. Her 21-Day Cleanse menu is created by chef **Tal Ronnen**.

Chef **Amanda Cohen** — who previously cooked at Pure Food and Wine and Moby's vegetarian restaurant TeaNY — opens her restaurant **Dirt Candy** in New York City's East Village. Four years  later, it will win a rave two-star review from the *New York Times* — only the second vegetarian restaurant in history (after Candle 79) to do so. In 2012, Cohen will come out with her popular memoir-cum-comic-book-cum-cookbook: *Dirt Candy: A Cookbook: Flavor-Forward Food from the Upstart New York City Vegetarian Restaurant*, of which Pete Wells writes in the *New York Times,* "Humor is so integral to [**Amanda**] **Cohen's** work that she may be the only chef in America who could publish her first cookbook in comic-book form and make the decision seem not just sensible but inevitable."

In April, *Vegetarian Times* publishes its study "**Vegetarianism in America**," which indicates that 7.3 million Americans are vegetarians and that an additional 22.8 million say they largely follow a vegetarian-inclined diet.

On July 15, Napa Valley vegetarian restaurant Ubuntu's chef **Jeremy Fox** and pastry chef **Deanie Fox** cook the first vegetarian dinner in nearly two decades at the **James Beard House** in New York City. The same year, Jeremy Fox is named one of *Food & Wine* magazine's "Best New Chefs."

"Wow. Sweet peas, tangy mint, crunchy macadamias and buttery white chocolate. Smooth coconut milk, floral Kaffir lime, peppery coriander and sugary watermelon. Creamy Anson Mills grits folded with a spinachy borage puree and a piquant nasturtium foam. **Last night I got to eat some of the most exciting, delicious combinations I've tasted anywhere, let alone at the James Beard House** . . . Jeremy Fox of Ubuntu in California's Napa Valley, an F&W Best New Chef 2008 pretty much knocked our socks off. And then his wife — Ubuntu's pastry chef, **Deanie** — knocked us all flat with her unbelievable vegan (vegan!) carrot cupcakes with teeny-tiny candied carrots on top."
—EMILY KAISER OF *FOOD & WINE*, IN A BLOG POST TITLED "**THE MOST EXCITING CHEFS IN AMERICA?**" (JULY 16, 2008)

On July 17, director **Mike Anderson** releases his documentary *Eating*. Two years later, hotelier Steve Wynn watches it on his yacht and immediately goes vegan, buying 10,000 copies of the film to distribute to his employees before bringing in consulting chef Tal Ronnen to help add vegan options to every one of his Las Vegas restaurants (including steakhouses).

"I was kind of intimidated to be brought in to consult with some of the celebrated restaurants at Wynn, one of which had two Michelin stars. I told them right off the bat that I wasn't there to teach them how to cook — just to show them a few tricks to help them accommodate their vegan diners, like substituting heavy cream with cashew cream, or butter with Earth Balance. It was definitely a collaborative process over two years to come up with vegan dishes that fit each restaurant's menu, from Italian to seafood."
—TAL RONNEN, CROSSROADS (LOS ANGELES)

"**We won't stop being sick until we stop making ourselves sick**. . . . The government isn't your nanny — they're your dealer, and they subsidize illness in America. They have to. There's too much money in it. You see, there's no money in healthy people. And there's no money in dead people. The money's in the middle: people who are alive, sort of, but with one or more chronic conditions that put them in need of [prescription medications]. . . . **The answer isn't another pill. The answer is spinach**."
—BILL MAHER (SEPTEMBER 28, 2007)

"The 2008 study also indicated that over half (53 percent) of current vegetarians eat a vegetarian diet to improve their overall health. Environmental concerns were cited by 47 percent; 39 percent cited 'natural approaches to wellness'; 31 percent cited food-safety concerns; 54 percent cited animal welfare; 25 percent cited weight loss; and 24 percent weight maintenance."
—*VEGETARIAN TIMES* (APRIL 2008)

2009

In January, PETA names the **Top 8 Vegetarian Restaurants in America** as **Candle 79** (NYC), **Dragonfly Neo-V** (Columbus, OH), **Green Zebra** (Chicago), **Horizons** (Philadelphia), **Madeleine Bistro** (LA), **Millennium** (San Francisco), **Sublime** (Ft. Lauderdale), and **VegiTerranean** (Akron, OH).

In February, Texas firefighter **Rip Esselstyn**'s book *The Engine-2 Diet* is published, which describes his putting his unit on a low-fat vegetarian diet, and how every single firefighter was inspired by the health benefits. The book becomes a *New York Times* bestseller.

Spearheaded by First Lady **Michelle Obama**, in March the **White House** breaks ground on the largest **vegetable garden** on its lawn in history, and the first since First Lady **Eleanor Roosevelt**'s victory garden during World War II. Its mission is educational: to teach children about the healthfulness of fresh, local fruits and vegetables and thereby intervene in the nation's childhood obesity and diabetes crisis.

Jonathan Safran Foer's *Eating Animals* is published, which vegetarian talk-show host Ellen DeGeneres describes as "one of the most important books I've ever read."

In July, the American Dietetic Association, known since 2012 as the **Academy of Nutrition and Dietetics**, issues its "Position on Vegetarianism," which states, "It is the position of the American Dietetic Association that **appropriately planned vegetarian diets, including total vegetarian or vegan diets, are healthful, nutritionally adequate, and may provide health benefits in the prevention and treatment of certain diseases.** . . . The results of an evidence-based review showed that a vegetarian diet is associated with a lower risk of death from ischemic heart disease. Vegetarians also appear to have lower low-density lipoprotein cholesterol levels, lower blood pressure, and lower rates of hypertension and type 2 diabetes than nonvegetarians. Furthermore, vegetarians tend to have a lower body mass index and lower overall cancer rates. **Features of a vegetarian diet that may reduce risk of chronic disease include lower intakes of saturated fat and cholesterol and higher intakes of fruits, vegetables, whole grains, nuts, soy products, fiber, and phytochemicals.**"

Actress, conservationist, and activist **Alicia Silverstone** comes out with *The Kind Diet: A Simple Guide to Feeling Great, Losing Weight,* *and Saving the Planet,* which advocates a vegan diet. It becomes an instant bestseller.

On November 3, chef **Rich Landau** and pastry chef **Kate Jacoby** (currently of Philadelphia's Vedge) cook **the first-ever vegan dinner at the James Beard House** in New York City. The menu includes portobello carpaccio with squash bread pudding; fennel-cauliflower bisque; celery root ravioli with charred Brussels sprouts, royal trumpet mushrooms, and a sage-mustard emulsion; salt-roasted beets with peppercorn-crusted tofu; and heirloom pumpkin cheesecake with quince jam and candied chestnut.

On November 19, cooking-show host **Martha Stewart** hosts a "Vegetarian Thanksgiving Special," with guests including Napa Valley vegetarian restaurant Ubuntu chef **Jeremy Fox**, *Eating Animals* author **Jonathan Safran Foer**, and *Food, Inc.* documentarian **Robert Kenner**. Stewart, whose daughter Alexis is a vegetarian, reveals her plans to attend a vegetarian Thanksgiving dinner.

2010 In January, **Dr. Joel Fuhrman** brings his ANDI (Aggregate Nutrient Density Index) scores, which measure foods' nutrients relative to their calorie counts, to **Whole Foods Markets'** customers via the chain's North America-wide "**Health Starts Here**" campaign, which emphasizes the healthy-eating principles of a plant-based diet: whole foods, low-fat (and the right fats: unsaturated and from plants), and nutrient dense (with high ANDI scores, e.g., vegetables — especially green ones — plus beans/legumes, fresh fruits, whole grains, and raw nuts and seeds).

On February 1, *The Oregonian*'s food editor **Grant Butler**, a lifelong carnivore, announces his conversion to veganism. The reasons? Butler acknowledges veganism as a fast-growing part of Portland's food culture, as offering a good challenge, as being a greener (as well as more compassionate and kind) way to eat, and as offering the prospect of kick-starting a little weight loss.

In her February 7 column in the *San Francisco Chronicle,* "**Vegan Diets Get Some Love,**" nutritionist Marion Nestle writes, "Why anyone would question the benefits of vegetarian diets, or diets that are largely vegetarian, is beyond me. **People who eat vegetarian diets are generally healthier than people who eat large amounts of meat.**"

"Yes, I have stayed vegan and love it. Greatest personal gift I've ever received."
—GRANT BUTLER, FOOD EDITOR, *THE OREGONIAN*, IN A PRIVATE EXCHANGE WITH THE AUTHOR (SEPTEMBER 9, 2013)

"Think about it: Entire civilizations — in ancient Egypt, China and Mexico, for examples — were based on wheat, rice, beans or corn as sources of protein. Nutritionists used to believe that vegetarians had to carefully combine plant foods (beans and corn, for example), but now know that variety and calories take care of protein needs."
—MARION NESTLE, *SAN FRANCISCO CHRONICLE* (FEBRUARY 7, 2010)

2010   In February, talk-show host **Ellen DeGeneres** is interviewed by **Katie Couric** on the reasons she became vegan. She cites the book *Skinny Bitch* and Sean Monson's 2005 documentary *Earthlings*, narrated by Oscar-nominated actor and vegetarian **Joaquin Phoenix**.

Long-time Howard Stern sidekick and new vegan **Robin Quivers** launches her own YouTube vegan cooking series called "Vegucating Robin." Three years later, it will spur her vegan memoir *The Vegucation of Robin: How Real Food Saved My Life*.

In a May 2 *60 Minutes* profile of the James Beard Award–winning chef, **José Andrés** describes meat to host **Anderson Cooper** as "overrated" and "slightly boring," adding, "I believe the future is vegetables and fruits. They are so much sexier than a piece of chicken."

On June 22, **Chloe Coscarelli** wins the Food Network's televised baking competition *Cupcake Wars* with four vegan cupcake flavors: Chocolate Strawberry Shortcake, Crème-filled Chocolate Orange with Candied Orange Peel, Ginger Nutmeg Spice with Date Caramel Drizzle, and Raspberry Tiramisu.

In August, chef **Mario Batali** announces **the world's first "vegetable butchers"** at Eataly, his Italian uber-market in New York City. The first, **Jennifer Rubell**, a graduate of both the Culinary Institute of America and Harvard, trains a team of butchers to peel, trim, chop, and/or slice customers' vegetables and otherwise prep them (free!) for easy cooking at home.

At the end of August, Dirt Candy chef-owner **Amanda Cohen** becomes the first vegetarian chef featured on the national TV show *Iron Chef* when she takes on Masaharu Morimoto for the title.

New York City Mayor Michael R. Bloomberg proclaims September 19–26 to be **official heirloom vegetable week**, and on September 23, Sotheby's holds its **first heirloom-vegetable auction**, which brings in $100,000-plus to benefit farmers and educational programs for children on farming and cooking.

On November 4, *BusinessWeek* magazine publishes "**The Rise of the Power Vegans**," spotlighting the growing number of prominent Americans who have adopted veganism, including former

President Bill Clinton, automotive scion Bill Ford, venture capitalist Joi Ito, Whole Foods CEO John Mackey, hip hop pioneer Russell Simmons, Twitter cofounder Biz Stone (who credits a 2000 visit to Farm Sanctuary in upstate New York with his conversion), boxer Mike Tyson, hotelier Steve Wynn, and media magnate Mort Zuckerman.

An article titled "Americans Do Not Meet Federal Dietary Recommendations," published in the *Journal of Nutrition*, reports that **nearly the entire U.S. population consumes a diet that does not meet federal dietary recommendations**. For example, 80 percent of Americans consume insufficient fruit, 90 percent consume insufficient vegetables, and 99 percent consume insufficient whole grains. At the same time, overconsumption of solid fats, added sugars, and alcoholic beverages (all representing "empty calories") is ubiquitous.

> "Among the food groups, **dark green vegetables**, **orange vegetables**, **legumes**, and **whole grains** had the poorest showing, with nearly everyone in each sex-age group failing to meet recommendations."
> —JOURNAL OF NUTRITION (2010)

2011   On February 1, talk-show host **Oprah Winfrey** and 378 of her staff members report the results of their going vegan for a week, which inspires many viewers to take on the show's Vegan Challenge.

In April, a **Physicians Committee for Responsible Medicine** (PCRM) report indicates conflicts between U.S. dietary guidelines (which recommend eating more fruits and vegetables and less meat and dairy) and its agricultural policy, which channels 63 percent of taxpayer dollars directly or indirectly into meat and dairy production, 15 percent into sugar/starch/oil/alcohol production, and less than 1 percent to fruit and vegetable production.

In June, **MyPlate** replaces MyPyramid as the U.S. government's primary food group symbol.

The National Restaurant Association's "**What's Hot in 2011**" survey of 1,500-plus professional chefs indicates that more than half consider **meatless/vegetarian entrées and vegan entrées** a "hot trend." Nearly one in four consider meatless/vegetarian entrées a "perennial favorite."

Sixty-five-year-old former **President William Jefferson Clinton** (b. 1946), whose love of foods ranging from barbecue to hamburgers during his presidency was well known and who had undergone quadruple bypass surgery in 2004 and stent surgery in 2010, speaks out about his veganism, saying that his vegan diet led to

> "As a physician, I urge you to shut down federal programs that pump billions of dollars into direct and indirect subsidies for meat, sugar, and other unhealthy products that are feeding record levels of obesity, type 2 diabetes and other health problems that kill and disable millions of Americans every year. Most taxpayers have no idea that they subsidize unhealthy foods."
> —DR. NEAL BARNARD, PRESIDENT OF THE **PHYSICIANS COMMITTEE FOR RESPONSIBLE MEDICINE**, IN A LETTER TO THE CHAIRS OF THE HOUSE AND SENATE AGRICULTURE COMMITTEES IN CONGRESS

"Ever since [**Dovetail**] chef **John Fraser** launched his Monday-night vegetable menu in March, the elegant Upper West Side joint has been fairly jumping on what is traditionally the deadest day of the week, all on account of such proven crowd-pleasers as turnips, parsnips, and salsify."

—ROBIN RAISFELD AND ROB PATRONITE IN "VEGETABLES ARE THE NEW MEAT," *NEW YORK* (NOVEMBER 7, 2011)

his dropping twenty-four pounds. On CNN, Clinton credits his conversion to a low-fat, plant-based diet with inspiration from a number of doctors, including **Dr. Dean Ornish**, one of Clinton's doctors for nearly two decades, and **Dr. Caldwell Esselstyn, Jr.,** both of whom have promoted the ability of a whole-food, plant-based diet to prevent and even reverse heart disease.

2011   Independent filmmaker **Lee Fulkerson**'s documentary *Forks Over Knives* is released, examining the profound claim that "Most, if not all, of the degenerative diseases that afflict us can be controlled, or even reversed, by rejecting our present menu of animal-based and processed foods." The film features the personal odysseys of **Dr. T. Colin Campbell** and **Dr. Caldwell Esselstyn**. (Long-time vegetarian actress **Kristen Bell** credits the film with her decision to go vegan, stating, *"Forks Over Knives* outlines an extremely compelling approach to the prevention of heart disease and cancer.") The following year, *Forks Over Knives: The Cookbook* by **Del Sroufe** is published.

"One of the more convincing, radical and politically volatile docus to come out of the burgeoning good-food genre, *Forks Over Knives* advocates quite convincingly for the adoption of a plant-based diet, the intent being the eradication of the diabetes, obesity and hypertension afflicting an increasing number of Americans."
—JOHN ANDERSON, *VARIETY* (MAY 5, 2011)

"Because of the film *Forks Over Knives*, more people than ever are looking to try veganism. I'm happy to be a part of the *Forks Over Knives Cookbook* [whose dessert chapter she wrote], because the better people find vegan food, the more people will stay! Because of the low-fat guidelines, which I don't typically adhere to, I enjoyed rising to the challenge of using nut butters and avocado as fats, which helped to make the desserts really taste like desserts."
—ISA CHANDRA MOSKOWITZ, AUTHOR OF *ISA DOES IT* AND *VEGANOMICON*

The **Joe Cross** film *Fat, Sick & Nearly Dead* is released, contrasting two men's journeys to health via drinking vegetable and fruit juices. In its wake, sales of juice — and juice books — boom.

A November 7 *New York* magazine article by Robin Raisfeld and Rob Patronite announces "**Vegetables Are the New Meat**. . . . At serious restaurants all over town, carrots, peas, and the like are no longer just the supporting cast — they're the stars. Move over locavores, here come the vegivores."

Filmmaker **Marisa Miller Wolfson**'s documentary *Vegucated*, which tracks three meat-loving New Yorkers who agree to adopt a vegan diet for six weeks, premieres at the Toronto Film Festival and wins "Best Documentary." The audience of four hundred is double the size for that of any other film shown.

Chef **Rich Landau** and pastry chef **Kate Jacoby** open the vegan restaurant **Vedge** in Philadelphia, where it earns accolades as not just one of America's best new *vegan* restaurants, but as one of the best new restaurants of the year — period. Their 2013 *Vedge* cookbook is named one of *Entertainment Weekly*'s ten best cookbooks of the year.

2012   *Publishers Weekly* reports that **vegetarian cookbooks** are being read by others besides vegetarians.

By May, law school grad **Mark Devries** raises more than $15,000 on Kickstarter.com to finish his documentary film *Speciesism: The Movie*. Inspired in part by the argument by Princeton professor Peter Singer's book *Animal Liberation* that "no justifications exist for considering humans more important than members of other species" and the growing "speciesism" movement (which considers animal factories among the greatest evils in our history), the film will premiere in 2013.

In a May appearance on *The Rachael Ray Show*, TV talk show host **Ellen DeGeneres** and her wife, **Portia de Rossi**, extol the virtues of their vegan diet, including weight loss and the curing of a skin condition (rosacea) after just two meat-and-dairy-free weeks.

In press release issued May 23, **the International Food Information Council (IFIC) Foundation**'s *2012 Food & Health Survey* reports that **most Americans (52 percent) believe that figuring out their income taxes is easier than knowing what they should and shouldn't eat to be healthier.** Some 76 percent agree that ever-changing nutritional guidance makes it hard to know what to believe.

"I was amazed at the lengths people were going to in order to live a cruelty-free life. After seeing *Vegucated*, I understand for the first time ever why people would do this. . . . It helps me to be able to enjoy cooking for our vegetarian and vegan guests."
—CHEF MARK LEVY, THE POINT (SARANAC LAKE, NY)

"There may be no better example of the elevation of humble produce to sexy star of the culinary world than the food at **Vedge**."
—*COOKING LIGHT* MAGAZINE (2012)

"You don't have to eat fat to get flavor these days — or any animal products at all. Vegetarian, even vegan, cookbooks are striving to reach more general audiences. And they are succeeding."
—MARK ROTELLA, *PUBLISHERS WEEKLY* (FEBRUARY 10, 2012)

2012 In May, Microsoft founder **Bill Gates** sings the praises of companies pursuing plant-based alternatives to meat and dairy, saying, "Companies that are taking the animal products . . . and actually coming up with a way of using largely plant-based materials — soy, peas, a variety of things — to make these things that are both cheaper, probably more healthy, less cruelty involved, less greenhouse gas emissions." In 2013, his slideshow on "The Future of Food" extols the companies Beyond Meat and Beyond Eggs.

> "[Moving toward a vegetarian diet is] important, too, in light of the environmental impacts of large-scale meat and dairy production, with livestock estimated to produce nearly 51 percent of the world's greenhouse gases. . . . Flavor and texture have been the biggest hurdles for most people in adopting meat alternatives. But companies like Beyond Meat, Hampton Creek Foods and Lyrical are doing some amazing things. Their actual recipes are secret, but the science is straightforward. By using pressure and precisely heating and cooling oils and plant proteins (like powdered soybeans and vegetable fiber), you can achieve the perfect flavor and texture of meat or eggs. I tasted Beyond Meat's chicken alternative, for example, and honestly couldn't tell it from real chicken."
>
> —MICROSOFT FOUNDER AND CHAIRMAN BILL GATES, ON MASHABLE.COM (MARCH 21, 2013)

In July, a **Gallup Poll** reports than 5 percent of American adults polled consider themselves vegetarian, while 2 percent identify as vegan — marking the first time Gallup inquires about vegan status.

In August, *Shape* magazine names its **Top 10 Upscale Vegan Restaurants in America**, which include **Blossom** (NYC), **Candle 79** (NYC), **G-Zen** (Branford, CT), **Karyn's on Green** (Chicago), **Millennium** (San Francisco), **Plum Bistro** (Seattle), **Pure Food and Wine** (NYC), **Real Food Daily** (Los Angeles), **True Bistro** (Boston), and **Vedge** (Philadelphia).

2013 In January, *Cooking Light* magazine names the "**Best Vegetarian Restaurant Menus**" at chain restaurants. They include Chipotle Mexican Grill, Jason's Deli, Noodles & Company, Panera Bread, Papa Murphy's, Pei Wei Asian Diner, P. F. Chang's, Ruby Tuesday, and Subway, reflecting the widespread availability of vegetarian options even at national chains.

On March 4, *The Washington Post's* food editor **Joe Yonan** comes out — as a vegetarian. Yonan writes, "One interview subject, founder of an imitation-meat company, said something along the lines of, 'The food editor of a major daily newspaper is vegetarian? This is huge!' And several food journalists have confessed, under their breath, that if it weren't for their jobs, they'd do the same thing."

In March, LA's public radio station KCRW's *Good Food,* hosted by **Evan Kleiman**, airs its first-ever all-vegetarian show.

In March, *GQ* magazine's **Alan Richman** names the 12 Most Outstanding Restaurants of 2013, which includes vegan **Vedge** in Philadelphia.

LYFE (short for Love Your Food Everyday) **Kitchen**, a healthy fast-casual restaurant with a more than 50 percent vegan menu, run by former global president and COO of McDonald's **Mike Roberts**, opens its doors in Culver City, California, on March 13. Developing the restaurant's menu are executive chefs **Tal Ronnen** and Oprah Winfrey's former personal chef **Art Smith**. Roberts says he hopes to franchise 250 locations within five years.

On April 18, *The Wall Street Journal* publishes an article titled "La Nouvelle Veg," which states, "**Haute-vegetarian menus are conquering Europe.**"

In May, P.S. 244 — the Active Learning Elementary School — in Flushing, Queens, becomes the **first public school in America to serve only vegetarian meals** for breakfast and lunch.

From May through August, **Grant Achatz** (whose restaurant Alinea is on *Restaurant* magazine's list "The World's 50 Best Restaurants") and his executive chef, **Dave Beran**, serve a twenty-plus-course vegan menu at their Chicago restaurant **Next**, which since its opening in 2010 has showcased three set menus annually.

A six-year study of 73,000 members of the Seventh-day Adventist Church (which promotes a vegetarian diet) in the *Journal of the American Medical Association* reports that **vegetarians live longer than meat eaters.**

"Every dish [at **Vedge**] tasted better than I expected it would. Fingerling potatoes with a creamy — no cream, of course — Worcestershire sauce were intense, an attribute of most Vedge dishes. . . . All the dishes had extraordinary balance and savoriness. Nothing was absent from this meal, and let's not forget that meat and fish weren't present."
—ALAN RICHMAN, GQ (MARCH 2013)

"When President Clinton visited **LYFE Kitchen**, I had the privilege of sitting down to talk with him, and found him so present and so into what we're doing. He loved our sweet corn chowder, crispy Gardein chicken sandwich, and baked sweet potato fries."
—TAL RONNEN, CROSSROADS (LOS ANGELES)

"On many plates vegetables can be but an afterthought or quite literally a 'side dish' — the supporting actor. For our team vegetable driven dishes have always forced us to be more creative. Maybe, we thought, **it's time for vegetables to take the lead.**"
—FROM THE VEGAN MENU AT CHICAGO'S **NEXT**

2013

In June, the vegan restaurant **Kajitsu** — which specializes in shojin cuisine, an ancient Japanese culinary practice developed in Zen Buddhist monasteries — is awarded two stars from *The New York Times*. In his review, Pete Wells writes, "When I eat at Kajitsu . . . I am never shocked to find that I don't miss meat or fish. When the Japanese have been working on an idea for hundreds of years, they tend to figure out a few things."

In its August cover story, *Food & Wine* magazine declares "**Vegetables are the new pork, the new cupcake and the new craft beer all in one. They are the biggest mega-trend ever.**" The magazine names the twenty best vegetarian and vegan restaurants in America as **The Butcher's Daughter** (NYC), **Café Gratitude** (Venice, CA), **Canteen** (Portland, OR), **Clover** (Boston), **Crossroads** (Los Angeles), **Dirt Candy** (NYC), **Elizabeth's Gone Raw** (Washington, DC), **Gracias Madre** (San Francisco), **Green Seed Vegan** (Houston), **Green Zebra** (Chicago), **Greens Restaurant** (San Francisco), **Kajitsu** (NYC), **M.A.K.E.** (Santa Monica, CA), **Millennium** (San Francisco), **Natural Selection** (Portland, OR), **Plant** (Asheville, NC), **Plum Bistro** (Seattle), **Sutra** (Seattle), **Vedge** (Philadelphia), and **Watercourse Foods** (Denver).

In October, *Travel & Leisure* names the best vegetarian restaurants in the U.S.: **Café Flora** (Seattle), **Café Sunflower** (Atlanta); **Candle 79** (New York City); **Choices Vegan Café** (Miami); **Crossroads** (Los Angeles); **Dell'z Uptown** (Charleston, SC); **G-Zen** (Branford, CT); **Green Elephant** (Portland, ME); **Kajitsu** (New York City); **Leaf** (Boulder, CO); **Mana Food Bar** (Chicago); **Millennium** (San Francisco); **Mother's Café** (Austin); **Natural Selection** (Portland, OR); **Plant** (Asheville, NC); **Sage's Café** (Salt Lake City); **Samosa House** (Culver City, CA); **Vedge** (Philadelphia); **Vegeria** (San Antonio); and **Veggie Galaxy** (Cambridge, MA). Promoting the list, *Travel & Leisure* Tweeted, *"Best vegan and vegetarian restaurants in America? They're some of the most innovative in the country."*

The November 23 *Forbes* article "**Bill Gates' Food Fetish: Hampton Creek Foods Looks to Crack the Egg Industry**" mentioning "**newly turned vegan Al Gore**" starts to spread the news of the former vice president's new diet.

On December 4, the *Intelligence Squared* debate "**Don't Eat Anything with a Face**" airs live on National Public Radio (see sidebar), with the team arguing "for" — PCRM's **Dr. Neal Barnard** and Farm Sanctuary's **Gene Baur** — declared the winner.

"The country's most exciting chefs have become vegetable worshippers. . . . **Vegetables are the future of American cooking.**"
—*FOOD & WINE* (AUGUST 2013)

"While **[Josh] Tetrick**, Hampton Creek's CEO, hasn't been able to persuade everyone, it's the type of people he has convinced that has the San Francisco food startup turning heads. **Bill Gates** is a backer, handpicking the company as one that could change future food production. Tetrick has raised $6 million to date from the likes of **Peter Thiel**'s Founders Fund, **Vinod Khosla**'s Khosla Ventures and environment-friendly billionaire **Tom Steyer**. Newly turned vegan **Al Gore** is also circling."
—RYAN MAC, *FORBES* (NOVEMBER 23, 2013)

A CONVERSATION WITH DR. NEAL BARNARD

"According to a 2009 poll, around 1% of American adults reported eating no animal products [i.e., eating a vegan diet]. In 2011 that number rose to 2.5% — more than double, but still dwarfed by the 48% who [then] reported eating meat, fish, or poultry at all of their meals. In this country, most of us are blessed with an abundance of food and food choices. So taking into account our health, the environment, and ethical concerns, which diet is best? Are we or aren't we meant to be carnivores?"

—INTELLIGENCESQUAREDUS.ORG

NPR hosted a live debate titled "**Don't Eat Anything With a Face**" in front of an audience of more than 400 guests (including me) on December 4, 2013, airing nationally as part of its award-winning *Intelligence Squared (IQ2)* series and moderated by ABC News correspondent John Donovan.

Clinical researcher **Neal Barnard, MD**, the bestselling author of such books as *Power Foods for the Brain* and *Dr. Neal Barnard's Program for Reversing Diabetes* and founder and president of the Physicians Committee for Responsible Medicine (PCRM), joined Farm Sanctuary co-founder Gene Baur to argue for the proposition while researcher/blogger Chris Masterjohn and farmer/author Joel Salatin argued against it.

Audience members were polled electronically both before and after the debate, with each side's aim being to persuade more voters to shift their position. In the pre-debate poll, 24% of the audience were for, 51% against, and 25% undecided. In the post-debate poll, 45% were for, 43% against, and 12% undecided — with the "for" team declared the winner.

I spoke with Dr. Barnard during the week following his team's triumphant performance. Here are some of his thoughts:

"When the initial pre-vote was announced, it was very much against us. During the debate, there was a lot of applause for the other side — so I honestly couldn't tell which way things were going. It was good to see things went the way they did.

"The outcome fits with the times, in a way. Looking at ethical side of things, over the past year or two chimpanzees were basically retired from medical research. Over the past two or three months, people have been giving a lot of attention to orcas and the controversy over SeaWorld [in the wake of the October 2013 premiere of Gabriela Cowperthwaite's documentary *Blackfish* on CNN]. People are thinking about animals in a way they never did before. Over the past four or five years, climate change has started transitioning from being controversial to being accepted — and the animal part of that may not yet be at the forefront of people's minds, but it's there. And then it seems that every day a new celebrity announces that he or she is going vegan. So, the times do seem to be changing."

ENVIRONMENTAL CONSIDERATIONS

"While the environmental arguments are quite accurate, most people find them a little too abstract — and they can't quite use them as a motivator. There's a diffusion of responsibility, so people think, "This steak that I'm eating isn't going to affect things very much." But of course if you put all of the cows in the United States on one side of a balance, and you put all of the people on the other side of the balance, the cows' mass is much greater than ours. Every last cow is as big as a sofa, exhaling methane hour by hour. And for climate change, that's a big issue."

HEALTH CONCERNS

"Health arguments cast a much wider net. People want to lose weight, get their cholesterol down, improve their diabetes, improve their skin, or whatever. However, often people's commitment to it might be 'thinner' than it is if they come to it through an ethical standpoint. If a person feels they can't eat a chicken leg because they're eating a living being, that's not something they're going to cheat on during the holidays; it's grotesque no matter what day it is. If a person thinks they're only doing it for their blood pressure, they may not be so committed. But even that's not entirely true, because I see a lot of folks who felt that shifting to a vegan diet has absolutely saved their lives, so there's no way they're going to cheat on it.

"For older folks — say, over 50 — who get news from their doctor that their blood pressure and everything else is not so hot, health issues are bigger for them just in general. Almost invariably, when people go vegan for health reasons, after about a month or so, somebody will say, 'It just hit me what a weird diet most people eat — they're eating animals all day!' So the animal issues start kicking in to them, or they start to get the environmental part. No matter which door a person walks in, eventually the others start to make sense to them, too. [Bestselling author Dr.] John McDougall initially followed a vegan diet only for health — however, a year or so ago, I heard him say, 'After a while, the animal part starts to make sense.'"

ETHICAL ISSUES

"I recognize that if you're 16 years old, you're not worried about prostate cancer. Sometimes it's environmental issues, sometimes it's health issues, but very often it's animal issues that well up for young people.

"People are extremely physically perceptive in many ways. Humans have eyes that can detect color, whereas cats and dogs really don't do that very well. On the other hand, animals are more perceptive in different ways. They have better hearing, for example, and a much better sense of smell. There are dogs who can sniff out cancer. However, people are amazingly imperceptive in relation to the feelings of others. A human being can barely sniff out what another person is thinking when they look into their eyes. I think that we specifically and intentionally don't see things when they're pointed out, like the fact that this is actually slaughtering an animal, and not 'dressing' them [a euphemism used by the opposing team during the IQ2 debate].

"Dairy is the same way. For many years, I consumed dairy products. Of course there are many health reasons to get away from it — it's the biggest source of bad fat. But the ethical reasons against dairy are extremely profound. Cows stop producing milk very soon after giving birth, just as lactating women do. So to keep the cows lactating, farmers artificially inseminate them year after year. Half the offspring are male, and what do you do with a male dairy cow? You put him in a veal crate. No civilized person would eat veal — but veal will still be produced as long as there's a dairy industry."

THE PRACTICAL SIDE

"Eating vegan [which Barnard has done since 1984] is easier than it ever was. When I first went vegetarian in 1977, health food stores were tiny, dark little places playing folk music, where the cashiers were named Sunshine. The veggie burgers were kind of bready, and if you bought soy milk, it was a powder that you had to mix up like nonfat dried milk. But now when you go into health food stores, they are enormous — and they have every possible product you could ever want. It's easy, and it's everywhere.

"Everybody is different. There are some people who kind of drag themselves toward a vegetarian or vegan diet very slowly, while there are others who take to it instantly. There are some who need a lot of support, while others have no trouble at all. It's like quitting smoking: There are some folks for whom it's really rough, and there are others who say, 'I've made up my mind — this is it.' "

2
Chapter

MAXIMIZING FLAVOR:
CREATING A NEW, COMPASSIONATE CUISINE

"I had no idea so much flavor could be delivered without butter, cream, milk, eggs, and other kitchen staples. Chef Richard Landau's staff must include a benevolent gremlin or a fairy godmother who sprinkles magic dust over the pots and the pans. I had trouble understanding how vegan food had advanced this far and this fast without an accompanying outpouring of acclaim."

—ALAN RICHMAN, FIFTEEN-TIME JAMES BEARD AWARD–WINNING RESTAURANT CRITIC, IN *GQ*, NAMING VEDGE ONE OF 2013's MOST OUTSTANDING RESTAURANTS

"I wasn't trying to make vegan food. I was trying to make great food. . . . I still am a caveperson at heart who craves these carnal flame-roasted flavors, and that is what I have always cooked. My goal is to turn people on to what food can be once you take away all the labels."

—RICH LANDAU, VEDGE (PHILADELPHIA)

Throughout history, people have chosen vegetarianism for many reasons. The most common motivations fall into three primary categories: eating animals isn't good for you (health), isn't good for others (environment), and isn't good, period (ethics). The current generation, however, appears to have pioneered a new reason for the shift away from meat and dairy products: maximizing flavor.

Terrance Brennan, whose twenty-year-old Manhattan restaurant, Picholine, has earned many accolades, including two stars from the Michelin Guide and three stars from the *New York Times*, and offers one of America's best vegetarian tasting menus, described to me the process of perfecting his winter squash soup: "I switched from chicken stock to vegetable stock when I realized the flavor of the

chicken stock was overpowering the flavor of the squash. And then I switched from vegetable stock to squash stock in order to intensify the squash flavor further," he said. "And I didn't stop there — I also came to realize that by adding cream to my squash soup, I was only diluting the flavor of the squash and not adding flavor, so I eliminated it."

Wait — what? This classically French-trained chef, in the course of creating one of the best winter squash soups in America, had actually made it *vegan*?

This discovery reminded me of my surprise at learning, while researching *The Flavor Bible* in the mid-2000s, that French chef Michel Richard had eliminated the meat stock in his French onion soup and replaced it with miso broth, which he found brought as much if not more richness and umami to the soup without overpowering the flavor of the onions. In his 2006 book *Happy in the Kitchen*, Richard provides recipes for mushroom water and tomato water, which can be used as lighter, vegetarian alternatives to meat stock in sauces.

Just a few decades earlier, when the 1970s movement toward *nouvelle cuisine* saw a decrease in the use of butter and cream in French cooking, the continued use of meat stock appeared sacrosanct. However, with the publication of Jean-Georges Vongerichten's groundbreaking 1990 book *Simple Cuisine*, his use of vegetable stocks, juices, and vinaigrettes in lieu of traditional stocks and sauces gained traction. "I have always been fascinated with the Mushroom Broth [made from caramelized white button mushrooms, shallots, garlic, parsley, and water] and its reduction, which, after a mere 30 minutes, closely resembles a veal stock," Vongerichten writes in its pages, "and, if reduced further [another 10 minutes, when it becomes a syrup], a veal demi-glace that would take a day to prepare." The world-renowned chef has since opened Manhattan's vegetable-centric ABC Kitchen, which serves a deliciously crusty falafel-inspired veggie burger, and Vongerichten has announced plans to open a vegetarian restaurant in 2014.

Likewise, Daniel Boulud's restaurant menus have always emphasized vegetables. New York's Café Boulud has long highlighted dishes inspired by the farmer's market under the heading "Le Potager." After a 2013 redesign, Boulud's db Bistro Moderne reopened with a new "Cuisine du Marché" section of the menu that is mostly vegetarian, including a db market salad with kohlrabi and radish and a dish of salt-baked celery root with wild mushrooms, apple confit, and toasted barley jus. His eponymous restaurant DANIEL (one of *Restaurant* magazine's "World's 50 Best Restaurants") is also vegetarian-friendly and has offered a vegetarian tasting menu since the 1990s. Its November 2013 vegetarian menu included such flavor-rich dishes as lentil velouté with root vegetables, Orleans mustard cream, chive oil, and watercress; and glazed butternut squash with roasted black radish, pumpkin seed oil, and mustard salad.

Indeed, more restaurants from coast to coast and around the world (from Calgary to London to Sydney) have been offering vegetarian tasting menus, making this one of the fastest-growing trends in the industry. Today, it's virtually expected that every city's very best restaurants — such as DANIEL, Eleven Madison Park, and Per Se in New York City; CityZen, the Inn at Little Washington, and Komi in the Washington, DC, area; and Mélisse in the Los Angeles area — will accommodate vegetarian and vegan guests. Many kitchens of the elite Relais & Châteaux–affiliated restaurants throughout North America have gone to great lengths to please their vegetarian guests, including Camden Harbour Inn in Maine, Canoe Bay in Wisconsin, Fearrington House Restaurant in North Carolina, Hotel Fauchère in Pennsylvania, Lake Placid Lodge and The Point in New York, and Winvian in Connecticut.

Leading destination spas have also been on top of this trend for years. Rancho La Puerta in Mexico is well known for its mostly vegetarian cuisine, including a signature version of guacamole whose flavor is lightened and enhanced by the addition of pureed green peas (or alternatively asparagus, broccoli, or edamame). Its California sister property the Golden Door's longtime chef Michel Stroot, who was the first spa chef nominated for a James Beard Foundation Award, has long insisted, "I want my asparagus soup to taste like *asparagus* — not cream, not butter, not chicken broth. You don't need butter or cream when you have freshness and intensely flavored ingredients."

The Lodge at Woodloch in Pennsylvania, which has its own vegetable and herb gardens (plus master herbalist Nathaniel Whitmore, who waxes lyrical to guests on the health benefits of herbs), inevitably offers at least one veg option on its dinner menu, with many more available during breakfast and lunch. Nate Curtis, chef of Rowland's at the Westglow Resort & Spa in North Carolina, handcrafted two completely different vegetarian tasting menus for us during the first night of our visit, highlighted by two completely different tofu entrees: pesto-marinated tofu with root vegetable risotto, verjus-braised squash pudding, and pecan tuile; and black garlic–marinated grilled tofu with bamboo rice, orange kanzuri broth, radish slaw, and soy sauce. (Nate's Southern-inspired veg menu the next night kicked off with a whimsical spin on the regional specialty fried pickles.)

A number of high-end chefs are turning their talents to bringing a new level of vegetarian food to supermarket aisles. In 2013, Dan Barber came out with a line of Blue Hill savory yogurts from milk from grass-fed cows; flavors include beet, butternut squash, carrot, parsnip, sweet potato, and tomato and are sold at retailers such as Whole Foods. Diane Forley (who apprenticed with Michel Guérard, Gaston Lenôtre, and Alain Passard before opening her restaurant Verbena) teamed with her chef-husband, Michael Otsuka (who had apprenticed with Michel Bras and Jacques Maximin), in 2009 to create Flourish Baking Company, which offers top-of-the-line pot pies and other baked goods "with a savory twist" — not to mention fresh vegetables, vegetable infusions, and organic whole grains, ensuring equal attention to nutrition and flavor.

There has been a national explosion in vegan bakeries (e.g., BabyCakes, Dun-Well Doughnuts, and Vegan Divas in New York City; Pomegranate Café in Phoenix; Petunia's Pies & Pastries and Sweetpea Baking Co. in Portland, OR; Sticky Fingers in Washington, DC; Vegan Treats in Bethlehem, Pennsylvania),

VEGETARIAN FOOD FAST

It isn't just higher-end places that are finding new ways of extolling the flavor of veg cuisine: In 2013, Chipotle Mexican Grill started testing an organic, non-GMO vegan option called "Sofritas." Made from shredded tofu braised with chipotle chiles, roasted poblanos, and spices, it has a texture akin to ground meat and can be added to the chain's burritos, tacos, bowls, and salads. (Chipotle's previous test of Garden Blend, a grain-based protein, didn't lead to a national roll-out.) Shortly before, the company had eliminated the bacon from its pinto beans, with a Chipotle spokesperson telling Consumerist.com, "In testing some recipes, we simply didn't think the bacon added anything and, by removing it, we make the pinto beans vegetarian."

confectionaries (e.g., Chalk Hill Cookery in Healdburg, CA; Lagusta's Luscious in New Paltz, NY; Sweet & Sara in Long Island City, NY), food trucks (e.g., Cinnamon Snail in New York City; Homegrown Smoker Vegan BBQ in Portland, OR; and that of Plum Bistro in Seattle, funded via a Kickstarter campaign), and ice cream shops (e.g., FoMu in Boston; Blythe Anne's in New York City; Maddy's in Los Angeles). The food they're turning out is so decadently delicious that it's winning over non-vegan customers, too — contributing to owners' reticence to use the monikers "vegan" or "vegetarian" for fear they might turn off potential customers who could be easily won over on the basis of flavor alone.

FIVE TRENDS INTERSECTING TO FORGE A NEW, COMPASSIONATE CUISINE

"I have long thought of the food at the restaurant as vegetable-driven cuisine where, besides outright vegetarian dishes, the preparations derive much of their identity and character from a liberal use of vegetables, herbs, and grains. . . . It boils down to preserving clean, explosive flavors — flavors that maintain their integrity and elegance."
—CHARLIE TROTTER OF CHARLIE TROTTER'S, WHICH HAS BEEN CREDITED AS THE FIRST CHICAGO RESTAURANT AND ONE OF THE FIRST AMERICAN RESTAURANTS TO OFFER A VEGETARIAN TASTING MENU

A number of trends are coalescing to create a new, contemporary way of cooking and eating that sacrifices neither deliciousness nor wholesomeness. My prediction? The coming decade will see the evolution of a new, compassionate cuisine that represents the intersection of the following:

- vegetarianism
- health
- globalization
- gastronomy
- flavor

VEGETARIANISM: FROM THE MARGINS TO THE MAINSTREAM

"Probably 70 percent of our dishes are vegetarian. We're moving away from all the meat."
—DANIEL HUMM OF ELEVEN MADISON PARK, TO GRUBSTREET.COM

"Generally speaking, you're looking at 70 to 80 percent vegetables or grains [on Blue Hill's menu] now."
—DAN BARBER OF BLUE HILL AT STONE BARNS, TO BLOOMBERG.COM

While the percentage of committed vegetarians has remained steady since 1999, the past fifteen years have seen bursts of growth in both more stringent veganism and less stringent flexitarianism. Together, this has fueled a 22 percent rise in vegetarian dishes on American restaurant menus from 2012 to 2013, as reported by *Nation's Restaurant News*. Many of America's best high-end restaurants — such as Eleven Madison Park and Blue Hill — appear to be naturally downshifting the amount of meat they're serving as their cuisines evolve. And many are also making a pointed effort to promote "Meatless Mondays" at their restaurants (see page 60).

Centuries after Asian Buddhist monks began their development of some of the world's first meat analogs — based on soy or wheat gluten, and approximating the appearance, texture, and flavor of various meats (including beef, chicken, duck, pork, and shrimp) — these non-animal proteins went mainstream in the U.S. through the advent of vegetarian Asian restaurants such as New York's Zen Palate, as well as wholesale suppliers such as May Wah. Other meat, dairy, and egg alternatives that have hit the mainstream are not likely to leave supermarket shelves or the menus of vegetarian and vegan restaurants anytime soon.

The number of dedicated vegetarian and vegan restaurants has also grown at all points along the spectrum, from quick-service and fast-casual chains (e.g., Maoz Vegetarian, Native Foods, and **Veggie Grill**, the last of which characterizes 90 percent of its customers as omnivores looking to reduce their meat intake through its vegan "Chickin'" sandwiches and vegan "carne" asada) to casual-to-midscale spots (e.g., Blossom, Café Blossom, and the Candle Cafes in New York City; Café Gratitude, Gracias Madre, and Real Food Daily in Los Angeles; Root near Boston) to upscale restaurants (e.g., Candle 79 in New York City; Greens and Millennium in San Francisco). These represent a wide range of approaches to meatless cuisine, from naturally homey (e.g., Garden Café in Woodstock; Moosewood Restaurant in Ithaca, New York; and Follow Your Heart near Los Angeles) to diner delights (e.g., Champs in Brooklyn, Chicago Diner in Chicago) to sophisticated (e.g., Crossroads in Los Angeles, Dirt Candy in New York City, Green Zebra in Chicago, Vedge in Philadelphia), and from vegetarian to vegan to raw vegan (e.g., G-Zen in Branford, Connecticut, and M.A.K.E. in Santa Monica).

HEALTH: AN OLDER POPULATION GROWS WISER

"As of 2010, diet surpassed smoking as the No. 1 risk factor for disease and death in America."
—MICHAEL MOSS, WRITING IN A NOVEMBER 3, 2013, *NEW YORK TIMES MAGAZINE* COVER STORY ON BROCCOLI

As this book's Introduction suggests, Americans are finally waking up to the importance of diet and allowing health concerns to reshape what we eat — moving *away* from meat, eggs, and dairy

MEATLESS MONDAYS

"As I started to question what I ate, I realized I ate meat simply because I always had. That didn't seem like a good enough reason."
—JOHN FRASER OF DOVETAIL, A *NEW YORK TIMES* THREE-STAR RESTAURANT OFFERING VEGETARIAN AND VEGETABLE-FOCUSED "MEATLESS MONDAY" MENUS (NEW YORK CITY)

As of February 2014, more than two hundred restaurants were participating in the Meatless Monday program by agreeing to spotlight the meatless dishes on their menus, including

Almond (East Hampton and NYC)	Gurney's Inn (Montauk, NY)
Babbo (NYC)	Hard Rock Café (London)
Benson Brewery (Omaha)	Lupa (NYC)
Border Grill (Las Vegas and Los Angeles)	M Café (Los Angeles)
Canyon Ranch (Tucson)	Matsuhisa (Aspen)
Casa Mono (NYC)	Osteria Mozza (Los Angeles)
Cookshop (NYC)	Pizzeria Mozza (Los Angeles)
Del Posto (NYC)	SD26 (NYC)
Dell'Anima (NYC)	Smorgas Chef (NYC)
Dovetail (NYC)	Susan Feniger's Street (Los Angeles)

The foodservice industry's Sodexo serves more than 10 million meals daily and has established "Meatless Mondays" in more than 2,000 college, corporate, government, and hospital cafeterias.

For more information, visit meatlessmonday.com.

(not to mention refined and processed foods, and often added salt, sugar, and fat), and increasingly *toward* a nutrient-dense, whole-food, plant-strong diet. With the aging of the population, we're getting not only older but wiser — and increasingly seeking out food that's as healthful as it is delicious.

Matthew Kenney found that his classical French training, with its layering of "fat on fat," was "anti-flavor": "It masked the flavor of the ingredients, and eating it didn't make me feel good," he recalls of the period before his evolution toward an olive oil–based, Mediterranean style of cooking. Then, in his thirties, he found himself sensitive to the way food made him feel and started eating less animal protein. But it was his transition to eating only vegetarian and raw food that he found life-changing. "My aches and pains went away," he recalls. "I looked and felt younger. And as a chef, this new way of eating and preparing food reignited my passion."

Kenney went on to open a number of raw-food restaurants, including Manhattan's Pure Food & Wine (with then-partner Sarma Melngailis) in 2004 and Santa Monica's M.A.K.E. in 2012, not to mention raw-foods academies in Miami, New England, and Santa Monica. "Most of the food being served in the world is so outdated — it's more harmful than helpful to people's health," Kenney observes. "There's definitely a correlation between a Bacchanalian approach to food and ill health. But I believe health and wellness and the culinary arts should be friends, not foes. You should not have to compromise."

GLOBALIZATION: A SHRINKING WORLD'S EXPANDING CHOICES

"The pork-loving chef [David Chang], whose menu once read, 'We do not serve vegetarian-friendly items here,'. . . has become obsessed with vegetables. . . . Chang couldn't believe dishes prepared without meat, onions, or garlic could have such intense flavor."

—GISELA WILLIAMS, WRITING IN *FOOD & WINE* (MARCH 2011) OF CHANG'S EYE-OPENING VISIT TO SOUTH KOREA TO EXPERIENCE THE VEGETARIAN BUDDHIST TEMPLE CUISINE PREPARED BY MONKS AND NUNS, ON THE HEELS OF SERVING A MEATLESS SUMMER VEGETABLE DINNER AT THE JAMES BEARD HOUSE ON AUGUST 20, 2009

As people from all corners of the earth come together to address the problems facing the planet, they are also embracing the diversity of cuisines from around the globe. Food has long been a portable embodiment of culture and a key driver of globalization (think of the spice routes), which continues to expand the range of ingredients, cooking techniques, and flavor profiles of interest today. Long a global melting pot, the United States is the world's largest spice importer and consumer and has seen spice consumption grow nearly three times as fast as the population over the past decade. Ten years ago, an average American spice rack might have a mere ten spices; it now has forty.

Patty Penzey Erd, who owns The Spice House in the greater Chicago area with her husband, Tom, counts a long list of seasonings that her store couldn't sell ten years ago and that it can barely keep in stock today, such as asafoetida powder, curry leaves, epazote, mango powder, pomegranate molasses, and tamarind. "These are all things that pair better with vegetarian dishes than with meat dishes, for the most part," she observes. "Also, curries sell so much more than they ever did before, along with our garam masala mixture, and both work beautifully with vegetable dishes. Last night I attended a dinner for [Milwaukee chef] Sandy D'Amato at [Carrie Nahabedian's Chicago restaurant] NAHA, where my favorite dish was the garam masala–spiced kohlrabi soup with tamarind-glazed almonds."

Our evolving cuisine reflects our ongoing incorporation of these spices — in authentic, contemporized, and even melded (i.e., fusion) dishes. As *The Flavor Bible* points out, cuisine is undergoing a startling historic transformation: with the advent of the global availability of ingredients, dishes are no longer based on geography but on *flavor*. This radical shift calls for a new approach to cooking — as well as a new genre of vegetarian "cookbook" that serves not to document classic dishes via recipes but to inspire the creation of new ones based on imaginative and harmonious flavor combinations. Thus the book you hold in your hands.

THE VEGETARIAN KITCHEN: ONE WITHOUT BORDERS

"With optimum cooking and seasoning, vegetables have a capacity for flavor that meat simply doesn't have. If legumes and grains are the backbone of Indian cuisine, vegetables provide the flesh. What we do in India with a plant-based diet that is different from other places is we add flavors in the beginning of cooking, before the vegetables, taking a little oil and adding cumin, coriander, mustard, cinnamon. . . . With an arsenal of flavorings that are easy to keep all year long, we are able to take boring greens and gnarly root vegetables and make them shine at the table and dance on your tongue."

—SUVIR SARAN, CHEF AND AUTHOR OF *AMERICAN MASALA* (2007) AND *MASALA FARM* (2011)

There's an entire world of vegetarian cuisine far beyond the bland brown-rice-and-kale fare many omnivores still mistakenly believe defines it. Countries, their customs, and their cuisines are inextricably linked, with each country or region offering its own take on delicious dishes based on vegetables, fruits, legumes, grains, nuts, and seeds — which collectively suggest a world of endless possibilities. Mollie Katzen was a folk-dancing aficionado who traveled to folk festivals where she fell in love with a new world of foods — which is how she ended up tasting her first hummus, tabbouleh, and other Mediterranean and Middle Eastern dishes that would become staples of her vegetarian kitchen and bestselling cookbooks (including the original *Moosewood Cookbook,* which features more than seventy recipes for dishes like mushroom moussaka, spinach-ricotta pie, and "soy gevult"). Others have drawn their inspiration from different parts of the globe, and I count myself lucky to be able to relish them all on a regular basis from my home base in Manhattan.

Restaurants serving **Caribbean** cuisine often feature vegetarian options. Believing that human beings are natural vegetarians based on anatomy and physiology and that "you are what you eat," Jamaica's Rastafarians opt for only those foods they see as enhancing vitality (the root of the word "ital" used to describe their cuisine). They eat close to nature, often seasoning their food with peppers (and sometimes the herb marijuana, as Indonesians do). I was utterly charmed by the cafeteria-style vegan restaurant Fire & Spice in Hartford, which I lucked into visiting after a Yelp search from nearby Interstate 84; its coconut-milk-enhanced chayote was incredible.

You can almost always find vegetable dishes on **Chinese** restaurant menus. Those favoring Cantonese-style cuisine should seek out Buddha Bodai (and especially its watercress dumplings and its impressive vegan barbecued "pork") and the Vegetarian Dim Sum House in Manhattan's Chinatown. My favorite neighborhood Chinese restaurant was Hunan Manor, which I started frequenting weekly after being turned on to it by *qigong* master Robert Peng, who confided at a dinner party that — at that time — it was the restaurant whose food most reminded him of home. Two of my favorite dishes there were the Chinese long beans and eggplant over brown rice, as well as the bean curd with mixed vegetables in black bean sauce.

I've enjoyed **Ethiopian** cuisine since college, but I love it even more now as a fun way of eating vegetarian. Because of the culture's traditional periods of fasting and avoiding meat, eggs, and dairy, every Ethiopian restaurant I know has a vegetarian combination option that includes the spongy pancakes called *injera*, which are used to scoop up bites of various braised legumes, greens, and other vegetables.

Indian cuisine isn't an imitation or approximation of an earlier meat-based cuisine — it is an *original* vegetarian cuisine. Hindus, Jains, and Taoists all advocate vegetarianism, either loosely or strictly, and India is said to have the highest percentage of practicing vegetarians of any country in the world, making Indian restaurants one of the safest bets for vegetarian dining. I'm fortunate to live just a few blocks from Hemant Mathur's Tulsi, one of the best Indian restaurants in America, and I am confident its ranks will be joined by Suvir Saran's new San Francisco restaurant (as Saran and Mathur were partners in New York's Devi, the first Indian restaurant in the U.S. to earn a Michelin star).

Not only did **Indonesian** cuisine give us tempeh, but its restaurants also invariably offer vegetarian options. Bali Nusa Indah in Manhattan's Theater District offers several vegetarian combinations showcasing dishes such as coconut-milk-based vegetable stews, corn fritters, and gado gado (peanut sauce over assorted vegetables).

Kosher **Israeli** restaurants do not serve meat and dairy together, so you can be confident that dishes served in kosher dairy restaurants do not contain meat (although you should confirm that they do not contain fish, which is not considered meat under Jewish dietary laws). Roughly 8.5 percent of Israel's population opts for vegetarianism, and veganism has been on the rise there ever since Gary Yourofsky's 2010 "Best Speech You Will Ever Hear" talk at Atlanta's Georgia Tech was translated into twenty-seven languages and became the most-watched speech on YouTube in Israel.

Pastas and pizzas have long been vegetarian staples, but restaurants like Brooklyn's Paulie Gee's and Portland's Portobello Vegan Trattoria are doing their part to make pizza a *vegan* staple, too. Now that we Americans have assimilated northern **Italian** cuisine via restaurants and cooking shows, more and more of us are prepared to make the leap to the idea of farro or other grains prepared in the style of risotto. Boulud Sud in New York City sets the bar for farrotto, while the version of wheatberry risotto we tasted in 2013 at Canoe Bay in Wisconsin (which featured multiple local cheeses and a Parmesan foam) inspired Andrew to duplicate and then elaborate on it at home several times since, using Lucky Dog Farm's wonderful organic wheat berries.

Enthusiasts of **Japanese** cuisine welcomed Manhattan's vegan Michelin-starred restaurant Kajitsu, which specializes in dinnertime tasting menus showcasing seasonal ingredients such as matsutake mushrooms (which are as prized in Japanese cuisine as white truffles are in Italian). Lunchtime is a great value; a composed tray might feature a main dish of ramen noodles seasoned with three different kinds of miso, or rice topped with bamboo shoots, alongside seasonal vegetable accents and perhaps a spring roll or yuba (tofu skin) filled with seasoned rice. Manhattan's popular Beyond Sushi creates vegan sushi from ingredients such as "mighty mushrooms" served on a six-grain blend. The lovely organic vegan Japanese restaurant Shojin in Los Angeles is also worth a visit, for dishes like Apricot-Kale Salad with Soy Vinaigrette and Spicy "Tuna" and Avocado Dynamite Roll.

Several years ago, I silently balked when a friend, the psychic Fahrusha, suggested the informal **Korean**-inspired vegan restaurant Franchia for our lunch date — but after tasting its spicy mock duck salad and vegetable bibimbap, I became a regular customer years before I stopped eating meat in 2012. It's the sister restaurant of the acclaimed, more formal Hangawi, which strives to achieve the Korean ideal of *um* and *yang* (yin and yang in Korean) through a healthy balanced menu of green vegetables and fruits (*um*) and root vegetables such as radishes, carrots, and potatoes (*yang*).

I first tasted **Malaysian** cuisine in Los Angeles in the company of restaurant critic Jonathan Gold. There could have been no better introduction to the delights of coconut milk, galangal, lemongrass-infused curries, and fried noodle dishes. Malaysian cuisine is based on three different cuisines: Chinese, Indian, and Malay, with more meatless options among menus influenced by the first two than the last. Manhattan has its own Michelin-starred Malaysian-influenced restaurant, Laut, near Union Square, which delights with vegetarian takes on classics such as *masak kicap* (seasoned with cinnamon, garlic, ginger, onions, shallots, star anise, and turmeric), Malaysian vegetable curries, and a banana-and-homemade-peanut-butter roti dessert it calls "the Elvis."

I've been a fan of Manhattan's oldest **Mexican** restaurant, El Parador Café, for two decades of its fifty-five years in business. (How can you not love a restaurant whose motto is "The answer is yes. What's your question?") And I discovered a year or two ago that it offers vegetarian salsa upon request (its standard warm salsa is not), along with an excellent vegetarian menu — and owner Alex Alejandro will substitute mushrooms in the restaurant's *chilaquiles* to make the dish veg. After two decades of loving one of America's most renowned Mexican restaurants — Chicago's Frontera Grill — and later its sister restaurant, Topolobampo, I was surprised to discover that the latter, too, offers a vegetarian menu. It blew me away — especially chef Andres Padilla's extraordinary chayote dish, the best I've ever tasted. The organic vegan Mexican restaurant Gracias Madre on Mission Street in San Francisco is a charmer, with specialties like butternut squash tamales and enchiladas con mole.

Middle Eastern cuisines (e.g., Israeli, Lebanese, Syrian, and Turkish) offer an abundance of vegetarian options, from stuffed grape leaves to countless spreads and grains. The Lebanese-inspired *mujadara* (green lentils + bulgur + fried onions) sandwich at Kalustyan's in New York City has a cult following, and I'm definitely among the true believers. I had one of the best falafel sandwiches I've ever tasted at New York's hole-in-the-wall Taïm, which also serves the fried eggplant and hummus sandwich known as *sabich*. The fast-growing vegetarian chains serving Middle Eastern food, such as Boston's Clover and New York's Maoz, attest to its deliciousness.

Southern / Soul food–influenced vegetarian spots win raves from coast to coast. I'll never forget my disbelief that the macaroni and cheese at Everlasting Life Restaurant & Lounge in Washington, DC, was actually vegan — it's the best version I've ever tasted. Then again, I've not yet tried the wildly popular original version of Mac and Yease (which features nutritional yeast) created by Plum Bistro's Makini Howell's parents at their two-decades-old vegan restaurant Quickie Too in Tacoma, but I can hardly wait.

Thanks to Buddhist beliefs, which influence an estimated 10 to 15 percent of the country to practice vegetarianism, **Taiwanese** restaurants typically offer many vegetarian options, often without garlic, leeks, and onions (reflecting Buddhist teachings against eating overstimulating foods). These include a variety of mock meats (such as ham, ribs, sausages, and seafood) as well as tofu, rice, noodles, and vegetables. Taiwan-born culinary consultant Yuki Chen has brought some of these influences to the pan-Asian vegan cuisine at Manhattan's Gobo, whose website indicates that she originally developed them as "the mastermind behind the menu at Zen Palate."

Restaurants featuring the cuisine of countries where Buddhism has significant numbers of followers are often vegetarian-friendly, with **Thai** restaurants a prime example. While it's relatively easy to avoid most meat and dairy by sticking with vegetable curries or tofu pad thai, it's sometimes a challenge to avoid the ubiquitous fish sauce seasoning — although naturally fermented Golden Mountain Seasoning Sauce, Thai (aka white) soy sauce, or fermented black bean sauce can be substituted.

Vietnamese restaurants often have vegetarian options, although you just as often have to watch out for the seemingly ever-present *nuac cham* (fish sauce) that flavors them. Manhattan's Lan Cafe is 100 percent vegetarian, serving dishes such as the Vietnamese baguette sandwiches known as bánh mì, lemongrass seitan on rice vermicelli, and of course pho: Vietnamese noodle soup served here with mock beef and sprouts and seasoned with herbs and lime.

Other cuisines are certainly less veg-friendly by tradition. Given that **French** cuisine has long incorporated meat stocks and demi-glace as foundational ingredients, I was all the more impressed with the debut of Manhattan's first French-inspired vegetarian restaurant, Table Verte, where Chef Ken Larsen served dishes such as vegan onion tarts (made with Earth Balance), plus a meatless cassoulet based on black and pinto beans, garlic, and shallots and seasoned with bay leaf, cardamom, chili powder, cumin, and thyme.

GASTRONOMY: SETTING A HIGHER BAR FOR HAUTE CUISINE

"The natural progression of my thinking over thirty years as a chef."

—ALAIN PASSARD OF THE MICHELIN THREE-STAR RESTAURANT L'ARPÈGE, ON HIS 2001 DECISION TO FOCUS ON A TASTING OF VEGETABLES — "THE GRANDS CRUS DU POTAGER" — AS HIS SIGNATURE MENU

"When you take a custard into the savory realm, it's much more versatile, happily taking on any number of flavor profiles. . . . As oils can be infused with herbs, so, too, can custards: a basil custard in tomato soup, for instance; a tarragon custard with diced orange as a refreshing opening course. **Some of the cream in the custard can be replaced by a vegetable juice to lighten it and intensify the flavor.**"

—THOMAS KELLER, IN HIS BOOK *BOUCHON* (2004)

"I never, ever eat anything for health reasons. I eat for taste," says Rene Redzepi . . . [of] Noma, otherwise known as the best restaurant in the world. . . . [H]e offered to help with my remedial education. Beginning with this: The reason we should eat our vegetables isn't because they're better for us. We should be plucking and pan roasting our friends in the plant kingdom, first and foremost, because they are damned delicious."

—ADAM SACHS, *BON APPÉTIT* (DECEMBER 2012)

Gastronomy has been described by philosopher Jean-Anthelme Brillat-Savarin as "the rational study of all related to man as he is eating; its purpose is to keep humankind alive with the best possible food." It all comes down to two things: the **ingredients** themselves and the **techniques** with which they are prepared.

The variety and quality of ingredients available in the United States took a giant leap forward after Alice Waters opened the doors of Chez Panisse in 1971 and then decided that she wasn't going to settle for sub-par ingredients. In rejecting industrialized food, she launched a revolution — and a new food economy — by developing direct relationships with farmers and other suppliers. Recent decades have seen the rise of specialty producers such as the Chef's Garden in Ohio and Chino Farms in California and the explosive growth of farmers markets and community-supported agriculture (CSA). Vegetables are clearly eclipsing meat as the new stars of the plate and palate.

Diane Forley, whose 2002 book *The Anatomy of a Dish* chronicled her botanical approach to cooking and delineated the family trees of various vegetables (a theme later taken up in Deborah Madison's 2013 *Vegetable Literacy*), observes how many vegetables thought to be odd twenty years ago are considered commonplace today. "Lots of nutritious plants are starting to be popular, like purslane, nettles, miner's lettuce, and things previously thought of as 'weeds,'" she observes. "And root vegetables like parsley root and kohlrabi are just not considered unusual anymore."

Long-time chef of the vegetarian Greens Restaurant in San Francisco

AARON WOO OF PORTLAND'S NATURAL SELECTION ON CREATING DEPTH OF FLAVOR

"The challenge in vegetable-based cooking is finding depth of flavor. I don't ever want people to get bored eating one of our dishes. We attack things in regard to texture, because that is the single primary way to get bored: having everything the same texture, regardless of how flavorful it is. Then we use all of our techniques to give each vegetable a different profile.

"Today, we have a lot more going for us than we did ten years ago; we dehydrate, roast, sauté, or char. When charring vegetables, such as ramps or fennel, we roast them at 300 to 400 degrees in the oven for however long is appropriate, and it slowly changes the flavor profile. Then we puree them to create ash to use as a seasoning.

"By focusing on cooking vegetables, I think more about flavor than I ever have before in my cooking career, and I feel I am by far a better cook than I have ever been before in my life."

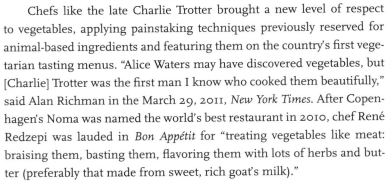

Annie Somerville has noted, "When most people don't like a vegetable, it's typically for one of three reasons: It's overcooked, it's undercooked, or it's under-seasoned." Over the years, chefs have learned how to cook and season vegetables for maximum flavor, drawing on the principles of flavor compatibility and leveraging classic flavor pairings while forging new ones.

Chefs like the late Charlie Trotter brought a new level of respect to vegetables, applying painstaking techniques previously reserved for animal-based ingredients and featuring them on the country's first vegetarian tasting menus. "Alice Waters may have discovered vegetables, but [Charlie] Trotter was the first man I know who cooked them beautifully," said Alan Richman in the March 29, 2011, *New York Times*. After Copenhagen's Noma was named the world's best restaurant in 2010, chef René Redzepi was lauded in *Bon Appétit* for "treating vegetables like meat: braising them, basting them, flavoring them with lots of herbs and butter (preferably that made from sweet, rich goat's milk)."

Vegetarian cooks have long used blenders (such as immersion blenders and Vitamixes), dehydrators, juicers, smokers, and spiralizers. And after a decade of intense culinary experimentation inspired by Chef Ferran Adrià of Spain's El Bulli restaurant (creating foams, gels, and caviar-like spheres), there is a new arsenal of culinary techniques being developed and employed to enhance flavor.

M.A.K.E.'s Matthew Kenney builds his dishes around vegetables but takes pains to explain, "It is not simply a pile of carrots. It will be carrots cooked sousvide until tender, while others are raw and still others pickled. A dish will feature a wide variety of variations on an ingredient, with the foundation being fresh ingredients and any sauces simply enhancements."

Tal Ronnen of Crossroads restaurant in Los Angeles conducts master vegetarian workshops at Le Cordon Bleu, which shared his vegan adaptations of the five classic mother sauces of French cuisine (béchamel, espagnole, hollandaise, tomato, and velouté). "It was an elective for students and required for the whole staff on all nineteen campuses," he recalls. "It was great because this is influencing literally hundreds of future chefs who would never have looked at vegan cuisine seriously. By the time the course was over, they saw vegan cuisine in a different light."

As one the country's most gifted vegan chefs, Ronnen is already elevating the vegan restaurant experience to a level never seen before. And as more of the world's best restaurant chefs turn their own attention, talent, and creativity to vegetarian and even vegan menus, he and they are starting to demonstrate the true potential of plant-based cuisine.

FLAVOR:
EXPLORING THE FLAVOR EQUATION

"Flavor profiles are really in the herbs or the vegetables, not the protein. That is what determines the character of the dish."
—TOM COLICCHIO, TO STEPHANIE MARCH OF *HAMPTONS* MAGAZINE (NOVEMBER 2012)

"[When creating new dishes], I will choose an ingredient to focus on, and that is where *The Flavor Bible* comes in — I look for [a pairing] that is out of the ordinary, then I'll come up with the other components that I want to use. Next, I'll sit down with my sous chef and work it out in a collaborative, organic, and democratic process. I might come up with two parts [of a dish], hit a roadblock, and then talk to someone and open *The Flavor Bible*. Usually it is a matter of hitting on a single ingredient that will spark the dish into a different direction and make it all come together."

—JON DUBOIS, GREEN ZEBRA (CHICAGO)

Flavor stands at the center of the intersection of these trends, uniting them all. No matter what other factors come into play, it is a love of flavor that is leading chefs to explore new, meatless avenues of flavor enhancement. There's an aspect of flavor that is intensely personal — and a reflection of one's experiences, preferences, and values.

FLAVOR = TASTE + MOUTHFEEL + AROMA + "THE X FACTOR"

Taste = What we perceive via the taste buds
Mouthfeel = What we perceive via the rest of the mouth
Aroma = What we perceive via the nose
"The X Factor" = What we perceive via the other senses — plus the heart, mind, and spirit

Understanding flavor is just as important to vegetarian and vegan cooking as it is to any other style of cooking. The first chapter of *The Flavor Bible* (2008) outlines the basic principles of flavor. I am happy to recap these basics here and to expand upon them for the purposes of contemporary vegetarian cuisine.

Our taste buds perceive five basic tastes: sweet, salty, sour, bitter, and umami. The essence of good cooking is to bring these five tastes into balanced harmony to create deliciousness. It's that simple — and that difficult. After all, flavor is a function of our other senses — that is, not only taste, but also smell, touch, sight, and hearing. And because we're human beings, other nonphysical factors come into play, including our emotions, thoughts, and spirits.

Learning to recognize as well as manipulate both the obvious and subtle components of flavor will make you a much better cook.

VEGETARIAN SHOW-STOPPER DISH AT BETONY

One of my favorite dishes of 2013 was Eleven Madison Park alum Bryce Shuman's grain salad at New York City's Betony, which won a three-star rave from Pete Wells of the *New York Times* shortly after opening. It's deceivingly simple-looking: a smear of thick Greek yogurt on a plate, topped with mixed grains, which are in turn topped with a variety of sprouts. Knowing by its extraordinary flavor that there was a lot more to it, I had to ask Bryce to tell me about the secrets behind it.

That yogurt? It's been pressed and strained until very thick, in order to anchor the grains on the plate. Those grains? They're a combination of barley, bulgur, farro, quinoa, spelt, and wheat berries. Each is cooked separately — the bulgur and quinoa steamed, and the barley, farro, spelt, and wheat berries simmered. The grains are mixed, and half are dehydrated. The dehydrated grains are submerged (via a strainer) in very hot (450 – 470 degree) oil for literally one second, so that they puff — creating a crunchy texture. Finely chopped shallots and chives are added to the unpuffed mixed grains, which are seasoned with kosher salt and drizzled with lemon vinaigrette. The grains are then tossed with the puffed grains and placed on the yogurt base. Then they are draped with a combination of mostly clover sprouts, some pea sprouts, and a few mung bean sprouts, and finished with another drizzle of lemon vinaigrette.

This book will be your companion in the kitchen whenever you wish to use plant-based ingredients to create deliciousness.

Everyone who cooks — or even merely seasons their food at the table before eating — can benefit from mastering the basic principles of making food taste great. This complex subject is simplified by one fact: while the universe may contain a vast number of ingredients and a virtually infinite number of ingredient combinations, the palate can register only the five basic tastes.

Great food balances these tastes beautifully. A great cook knows how to taste, to discern what is needed, and to make adjustments. Once you learn how to season and how to balance tastes, a whole new world opens up to you in cooking. Great cooking is never as simple as merely following a recipe. The best cooking requires a discerning palate to know when a dish needs a little something or other — and what to add or do to elevate the flavor.

WHAT WE PERCEIVE VIA THE MOUTH

TASTE

Sweet. Salty. Sour. Bitter. Umami. Every delicious bite you've ever tasted has been a result of these five tastes coming together on your taste buds. We taste them as individual notes and in concert. Each taste affects the other. For example, bitterness suppresses sweetness. In addition, different tastes affect us in different ways. Saltiness stimulates the appetite, while sweetness satiates it. Take the time to explore the five basic tastes, and you'll find that they're often influenced by factors such as freshness and ripeness, which are also helping to fuel the trend toward local cuisine.

Sweetness It takes the greatest quantity of a substance that is sweet (versus salty, sour, bitter, or umami) to register on our taste buds. However, we can appreciate the balance and "roundness" that even otherwise imperceptible sweetness adds to savory dishes. Sweetness can work with bitterness, sourness — even saltiness. Whether delivered via honey, maple syrup, molasses, sugar, or another ingredient, sweetness can also bring out the flavors of other foods, such as fruits and certain vegetables (e.g., tomatoes) and grains (e.g., oats).

Saltiness When (for our 1996 book, *Culinary Artistry*) Andrew and I banished more than thirty of America's leading chefs to their own desert islands with only ten ingredients to cook with for the rest of their lives, the number-one ingredient they chose was salt. Salt is nature's flavor enhancer. It is the single most important taste for making savory food delicious. (Sweetness, by the way, plays the same role in desserts). Salts flavored with smoke or truffles offer even more ways to enhance the flavor of soups or risottos, and New York City's venerable spice store Kalustyan's lists dozens of varieties on its website. Beyond salt, regionally appropriate salty ingredients also play an important role in enhancing veg meals, such as Parmesan cheese with dishes like pastas, pizzas, and risottos, and soy sauce and tamari with stir-fries and veg sushi.

Sourness Sourness is second only to salt in savory food and sweeteners in sweet food in its importance as a flavor enhancer. Sour notes — whether a squeeze of lemon or lime, or a drizzle of vinegar — add sparkle and brightness to a dish. Honing your choices for adding acidity, such as by selecting the right vinegar (whether apple cider vinegar for fruit salad, rice wine vinegar for nori rolls, or sherry vinegar for gazpacho) can enhance it even further. Balancing a dish's acidity with its other tastes is critical to the dish's ultimate success.

Bitterness Humans are most sensitive to bitterness, and our survival wiring allows us to recognize it in even relatively tiny amounts. Bitterness balances sweetness and can also play a vital role in cutting richness in a dish. For example, the bitterness of walnuts balances the sweetness of a beet salad while cutting the richness of the goat cheese that often accompanies it. Chocolate's bitterness is an innate counterbalance in rich desserts. While bitterness is more important to certain people than to others, some chefs see it as an indispensible "cleansing" taste — one that makes you want to take the next bite, and the next.

Umami (Savoriness) In addition to the four original tastes, there is now widespread acceptance of a fifth taste, umami, which Andrew and I first wrote about in 1996 in *Culinary Artistry*. It is often described as the savory or meaty "mouth-filling" taste that is noticeable in such ingredients as aged cheese (e.g., blue, Parmesan), fermented foods (e.g., miso, sauerkraut), mushrooms, and sea vegetables, and in such flavorings as monosodium glutamate (MSG), which is the primary component of branded seasonings such as Accént. Vegetarian dishes loaded with umami range from miso soup with shiitakes, tofu, and wakame to pastas with tomato sauce, mushrooms, and Parmesan cheese.

MOUTHFEEL

In addition to its sense of taste, the mouth has a sense of "touch" and can register other sensations, such as temperature and texture, that play a role in flavor. These aspects of food, generally characterized as mouthfeel, help to bring food into alignment with our bodies, and bring some of a dish's greatest interest and pleasure. The crunchiness and crispiness of a dish contribute sound as well as textural appeal.

Temperature Temperature is one of the foremost among the other sensations that can be perceived by the mouth. The temperature of our food even affects our perception of its taste; for example, coldness suppresses sweetness. A food's temperature can affect both the perception and enjoyment of a dish. A chilled carrot soup on a hot summer day — and hot roasted carrots on a cold winter day — could be said to be "healing" through their ability to bring our bodies into greater alignment with our environment.

Texture A food's texture is central to its ability to captivate and please. We value pureed and/or creamy foods (such as soup and mashed potatoes) as "comfort" foods, and crunchy and crispy foods (such as nachos and caramel corn) as "fun" foods. We enjoy texture as it activates our other senses, including touch, sight, and sound.

While babies by necessity eat soft or pureed foods, most adults enjoy a variety of textures, particularly crispiness and crunchiness, which break up the smoothness of texture — or even the simple monotony — of dishes. At New York City's Kajitsu restaurant, Chef Ryota Ueshima often incorporates a crispy tempura-fried element into his silky ramen or udon noodle dishes for a pleasing contrast in texture and flavor.

Much of the flavor of meat is conveyed by its texture, such as its chewiness (e.g., chicken) or its crispiness (e.g., crisp-fried bacon). It's possible to approximate a similar texture with meatless ingredients (e.g., fried Provolone slices can approximate crispy bacon in a "vegetarian BLT") or plant-based ingredients (e.g., lentils, whole grains, mushrooms, or frozen-then-cooked and crumbled tofu can approximate chewy ground beef, such as in tacos or chili, while thinly sliced crisp-fried tempeh can approximate bacon, e.g., in a club sandwich). In playful cuisine, caviar can be approximated via spherification, a chemical process introduced by Ferran Adrià at Spain's El Bulli restaurant in 2003, which involves the creation of spherical caviar-like substances from calcium lactate mixed with sodium alginate and one's choice of flavorings, from sea vegetables to watermelon.

Likewise, many people enjoy the creamy texture of milk and cream. These can be approximated by plant-based milks, such as those made from almonds, coconut, hazelnuts, hemp, oat, rice, and soy, or by plant-based creams such as cashew cream and coconut cream. If you haven't yet tried some of the better vegan "ice creams" available, you're in for a treat: you'll be amazed by the silky, creamy texture of FoMu's or Maddy's ice creams or the commercially available Coconut Bliss nondairy frozen dessert.

For other examples of non-veg foods that can be approximated by vegetarian or vegan substitutes, check out "Getting to the Root of Cravings" on pages 76 – 80.

Piquancy Our mouths can also sense what we often incorrectly refer to as "hotness," meaning piquancy's "sharpness" and/or "spiciness" — whether boldly as in chile peppers, or more subtly as in a sprinkle of cayenne pepper. Some people find the experience of these *picante* (as the Spanish say, or *piccante* as the Italians do) tastes more pleasurable than others, and have varying levels of toleration — hence the "mild," "medium," "hot," or "very hot" labels on many salsas. Mexican cuisine most famously celebrates chiles' piquancy, although other cuisines — from Thai to Italian (in which you'll commonly find garlicky broccoli rabe accented with a shake of chili pepper flakes) — do, too.

Astringency Our mouths pucker to register astringency. This is a drying sensation caused by the tannins in red wine or strong tea and occasionally in foods such as walnuts, cranberries, and unripe persimmons. The astringency of cranberries is often a welcome addition to sweeter apple and pear desserts such as pies or crisps, while a handful of astringent pomegranate seeds can add a refreshing counterbalance when sprinkled atop rich Mexican moles or Persian walnut sauces.

WHAT WE PERCEIVE VIA THE NOSE

AROMA

Aroma is thought to be responsible for 80 percent or more of flavor. This helps to explain the popularity of aromatic ingredients, from fresh herbs and spices to grated lemon zest. Incorporating aromatic ingredients can enhance the aroma of your dish and, in turn, its flavor.

While there are only five basic tastes, there is an almost infinite number of aromatic notes that contribute to the flavor of food. Most aromas can be characterized as either sweet or savory.

Sweet notes are largely associated with sweeteners, fruits, and certain vegetables (e.g., sweet potatoes), herbs (e.g., basil), and spices (e.g., cinnamon). **Savory** notes are typically associated with "meatiness" almost as much as with alliums such as garlic and onions, even across different cultures. Other savory notes can include *cheesiness, smokiness,* and *spiciness.* Cheesiness can even be found in vegan cuisine, such as in nutritional yeast, or in vegan cheeses. Smokiness can be imparted via cooking techniques (e.g., grilling, hot or cold smoking) and/or ingredients (e.g., smoked paprika, liquid smoke). And spiciness can reflect flavor chords that are regionally specific combinations of flavors (e.g., garlic + ginger + soy sauce = Asia; garlic + lemon + oregano = Mediterranean).

Some qualities are perceived through both taste and smell:

Pungency Pungency refers to the taste and aroma of ingredients, such as horseradish and mustard, that are as irritating — albeit often pleasantly — to the nose as they are to the palate. The simple sweetness of a beet soup can be punched up with a dollop of horseradish cream sauce, while bitter green salads often find mustard vinaigrettes a welcome enhancement.

Chemesthesis *Chemesthesis* refers to other sensations that tickle (e.g., the tingle of carbonated beverages) or play tricks on (e.g., the false perception of "heat" from chile peppers or "cold" from spearmint) our gustatory senses. Experimental chefs have had fun introducing sugar combined with carbon dioxide (commercially known as Pop Rocks) into high-end desserts, providing mini-explosions of flavor in the mouth.

WHAT WE PERCEIVE VIA THE OTHER SENSES, THE HEART, THE MIND, AND THE SPIRIT

"THE X FACTOR"

When we are conscious of and alert to what we are eating, food has the power to affect our entire selves. We experience food not only through our physical senses — including our sense of sight, which we address below — but also emotionally, mentally, and even spiritually.

The X Factor takes into consideration the fact that different people will perceive the same dish differently. For example, someone who grew up loving strawberries and someone who is allergic to strawberries will perceive the flavor of the same hypothetical "perfectly prepared" strawberry tart differently. Likewise, an omnivore and a vegetarian will perceive the aroma or flavor of the same hypothetical "perfectly prepared" meat stew differently.

When vegetarians or vegans say that they have "lost their taste for meat," they don't actually mean that their taste buds have changed, but that — physically, emotionally, mentally, and/or spiritually — they perceive its flavor as no longer palatable.

THE VISUAL

The visual presentation of a dish can greatly enhance the pleasure we derive from it. During the best vegan tasting menu of my life at Eleven Madison Park, I was as delighted by the visual presentation of the carrot tartare, which was ground before my eyes in a meat grinder temporarily attached to our table for this purpose, and accompanied with a palette of spices and herbs we could use to season it ourselves, as I was with its exquisite resulting flavor.

Just a few decades ago, it was still possible to taste a dish with the eyes, but only those who'd spent time in world-class kitchens knew the tricks of such artistic plate presentation or modern techniques. Since the widespread dissemination of photos of dishes from the world's best restaurants via the Web, it's become easier to reproduce a great dish's elaborate form than its exquisite flavor.

How a dish looks can also affect our perception of its flavor in more direct ways; for example, the deeper the color of a berry sorbet, the more berry flavor is perceived. The stronger the connection between a particular food and a particular color, the stronger the flavor impact — such as raspberries and strawberries with red, lemon with yellow, and lime with green.

THE EMOTIONAL

"I say all the time that [my mother's Spanish potato and egg tortilla] is my favorite because it conveys a point: that sentimental value comes above all else."
—FERRAN ADRIÀ, FOUNDING CHEF OF EL BULLI (SPAIN)

We taste with our hearts as much as with our tongues. What else could explain adult preferences for one's mother's dishes over those prepared by a great chef? This also helps to explain the lasting appeal of traditional dishes and cuisines of countries around the globe, which stem from our love for their people, their cultures, and the deeply rooted culinary traditions that have sustained them over centuries.

I am in awe of the pivotal moment in the animated film *Ratatouille*, which is the single best on-screen depiction of the transformative power of food I've ever seen. Knowing that chef Thomas Keller had consulted on the design of the movie's namesake dish, I found the flavor of the extraordinary ratatouille I was served during my veg tasting menu at Per Se in New York City all the more pleasurable.

THE MENTAL

If we ate only for sustenance, we might be able to survive on nutritive pills and water. But we also eat for pleasure. Because we typically eat three times a day, 365 days a year, we enjoy novelty, such as a twist on the traditional construct of a dish. Increasingly, since the 1980s and the advent of "tall" food, chefs have played with the presentation of their ingredients. Since the 1990s, the advent of avant-garde cuisine and so-called molecular gastronomy has seen chefs experiment more and more with both the chemical composition and presentation of dishes as well.

Conceptual dishes provide pleasurable "food for thought." Chef Amanda Cohen of New York City's Dirt Candy goes to great lengths, through a development process often lasting months, to reinvent fun vegetable-centric versions of meaty classics, smoking broccoli and nestling it into a hot dog bun to become a **"Broccoli Dog"** and subbing cornflake-crusted cauliflower for the namesake meat in a veg spin on chicken-and-waffles. And the Inn at Little Washington in Virginia, the site of some of the very best meals of my life, is well known for its signature dish "Portobello Mushrooms Pretending to Be a Filet Mignon."

THE SPIRITUAL

The preparation, cooking, and eating of food is a sacrament. Treating it as such has the potential to elevate the quality of our daily lives as nothing else can. Several of the world's leading chefs have worked to perfect each aspect of the dining encounter — from the food and drink to the ambiance to the service — to raise the overall experience to a new level imbued not only with pleasure, comfort, and interest, but also with meaning.

DR. NEAL BARNARD ON THE X FACTOR UNDERLYING CHEESE ADDICTION

"Part of some people's addiction to cheese is physical. Back in 2003, the NIH [National Institutes of Health] funded us to do a diabetes study using a vegan diet. As the [diabetic] participants began to go vegan, they started losing weight, their blood sugars came down, and everything got better. But I noticed that a lot of them had what I might call food addictions. Some would specifically say, 'I miss cheese.' Not necessarily milk, and maybe not even ice cream, but cheese in particular. So I thought, 'Why is that? It smells like old socks — why cheese?'

"There are a couple of things going on here. First, it turns out that there is a gene that causes some people to be born with too few dopamine receptors in their brains. If you have that DRD2 Taq1 allele, you have fewer dopamine receptors, and that means you don't feel dopamine's effects so much — so you need extra dopamine stimulation. So you might smoke, or drink, or get into compulsive gambling or compulsive eating. About half the people with type 2 diabetes have this gene that causes them to overeat — and it leads them to really want things that give them extra dopamine, particularly food.

"But cheese is a special case. Nutritionally, it is awful — with a very high content of saturated fat, cholesterol, and sodium. However, cheese is extremely high in casein, the dairy protein, which is not like other proteins. It breaks apart to release opiates into the bloodstream, and these mild casomorphins attach to the same opiate receptors in the brain that heroin attaches to, called the mu-receptor. So it's not just taste, it's not just mouthfeel — dairy products are unique in that they release casomorphins, and cheese has a much higher concentration of them than milk or ice cream.

"If I stuck a needle in your arm a half-hour after you ate cheese, there would be opiates in your bloodstream and attaching to your brain. While it's not enough to make you drive dangerously or rob a convenience store, it's enough to make you say the next day, 'I think I'd like a little more cheese.' Completely stinky, repugnant cheeses become attractive when a person associates what's going on in the brain with the smell and the flavor.

"If you are hooked on cheese — or anything else — you might consider trying to make a clean break. That's easier than teasing yourself with little bits here and there.'"

TOWARD A MORE COMPASSIONATE CUISINE

"Will three or four meals [at Matthew Kenney's Santa Monica raw foods restaurant, M.A.K.E.] be enough to sway a hardened raw-foods cynic? Of course not. . . . But it may be enough to make him take a second look."
—PULITZER PRIZE–WINNING RESTAURANT CRITIC JONATHAN GOLD, WRITING IN THE *LOS ANGELES TIMES* (APRIL 13, 2013)

"This is a chance for a personal revolution: to leave your mark on this planet by causing the least amount of harm possible. What's the argument for not causing the least amount of harm? Inconvenience? Indifference? Apathy? . . . Here's the coolest thing about being vegan in this day and age: It's never been easier. You can have the same smell, taste, and texture of meat, cheese, and milk without it. Nobody has to suffer and die for dinner any more, including you."
—GARY YOUROFSKY, THE VEGAN ACTIVIST WHOSE 2010 TALK AT GEORGIA TECH, TITLED "BEST SPEECH YOU WILL EVER HEAR," BECAME A YOUTUBE SENSATION

Here at the crossroads of our history and our future, we have choices to make every day with every meal we make and eat. I hope that those choices will be more conscious, informed, and compassionate — for ourselves, for others, and for our planet.

In a recent Technomic poll, two out of three Americans agree that a vegetarian meal can be just as satisfying as a non-vegetarian one. My aim with this book is to help make that fraction even larger. Given the extraordinary talent that is being brought to the realm of plant-based cuisine via vegetarian and vegan menus and restaurants, I have no doubt that fraction will continue to grow.

"José Andrés, Mario Batali, and Tom Colicchio are all preaching that vegetables are the next big thing. They are really helping," Rich Landau and Kate Jacoby of Vedge in Philadelphia observe. "They are not going vegan, or dressing up in cow suits with 'Meat is Murder' signs — they are just out there to say what is true: meat is getting boring, and vegetables are the most interesting food there is to cook. It is an amazing perspective and a great way to look at what is happening on our dining scene."

It is easier than ever to eat vegetarian and even vegan today — and more are doing so. The easiest places I've ever tried to do so are New York City and Los Angeles, where there is an embarrassment of riches. The hardest was a suburb two hours east of Minneapolis, where we had to point out to our waitress at one of the "better" restaurants in town that our guacamole was served brown, and were informed, "It always comes out of the can that color." But we found a little mom-and-pop southeast Asian restaurant in the same town, where we had wonderful veg dishes, so it just took a bit of perseverance.

I'd have imagined that Omaha (land of Omaha Steaks!) might be one of the very toughest. So I was shocked when I first heard that Brooklyn-based vegan cookbook queen Isa Chandra Moskowitz had moved there and was planning to open a vegan café, which underscored how widespread veg cuisine is becoming even outside major metropolitan areas. My eyes opened wider when *VegNews* named a dozen small towns notable for their vegan friendliness in 2013 and I saw that they included choices from north to south and from coast to coast, including Asheville, North Carolina; Ashland, Oregon; Athens, Georgia; Boulder, Colorado; Ithaca, New York; Portland, Maine; and Santa Cruz, California.

Tal Ronnen of Crossroads in Los Angeles takes it all in stride. "There is nothing that can surprise me anymore," he told me. "Because this is not a trend or fad: It is something we are going to have to turn to sustain the future of our world. And I am looking forward to every day as it comes."

FLAVOR COMPATIBILITY

An essential aspect of great cooking is harnessing compatible flavors — which involves knowing which herbs, spices, and other flavorings best accentuate particular ingredients.

A process of trial and error over centuries resulted in classic cuisines and dishes, some of which feature timeless combinations of beloved flavor pairings — for example, apples with cinnamon, bananas with rum, rice with soy sauce, tomatoes with basil, jícama with lime.

It's fascinating to find that certain combinations of ingredients can fool us into believing we're eating something other than what we're actually eating because of their context. As a child of four or five, I once believed that the slice of pie I was eating with soft, layered sugar-and-cinnamon-scented filling was apple pie — and utterly shocked when I learned it was something called "mock apple pie" made with Ritz crackers standing in for sliced apples! The experience was so profound that it started me thinking about food more deeply at a very young age, and deconstructing what makes a dish that dish.

Mock apple pie isn't such a far cry from the avant-garde creations of modernist kitchens that turn classic dishes on their heads. Homaro Cantu of Chicago's moto has made the point that classic flavor combinations are what help make experimental dishes work, because they bring a sense of familiarity and comfort to the unfamiliar and novel. So, too, do they further veg interpretations of classic meat-based dishes, such as veg Reuben sandwiches, a cult dish that appears on countless vegetarian restaurant menus. By the time you put together rye bread, Thousand Island dressing, Swiss cheese, and sauerkraut, the context has the eye so convinced that it is really a Reuben sandwich that the palate is more forgiving to the seasoned seitan, tempeh, or other stand-in for corned beef. Likewise, I was so enamored with the flavor and texture of Dave Anderson's delicious mock tuna salad sandwich at Maddy's in Los Angeles — with its chopped celery and Vegenaise served on fresh-baked ciabatta bread — that it was a cinch to get me to buy into the slight resemblance of mashed chickpeas to mashed canned tuna.

GETTING TO THE ROOT OF CRAVINGS

"People don't really crave bacon — they crave something smoky and crispy. And they don't really crave fish sauce — they crave that fermented umami flavor you can get from fermented black bean sauce."

—AMANDA COHEN, DIRT CANDY (NEW YORK CITY)

"People associate a lot of flavor properties with meat that are due to the other umami-rich ingredients in a dish. If you put a heavy braised stew made with caramelized onions and tomato paste and red wine next to the same stew made without meat, you'd find virtually the same umami and richness in both."

—ERIC TUCKER, MILLENNIUM (SAN FRANCISCO)

"Most people think they want milk, cream, and cheese, when what they're really craving is creaminess. If you sauté onions to caramelize them and puree them with vegetable stock and red wine, it mimics a creamy texture."

—JON DUBOIS, GREEN ZEBRA (CHICAGO)

"I am not against soy, but we don't cook tofu or seitan or reshape something into meat here. Nor do we serve fake cheese. Instead, we will try to give you the satisfaction your memory seeks whether it is texture, caramelization, or fat content. If I want to serve a creamy dish with the texture or voluptuousness that you might normally get from butter or cream, I will use root vegetables like carrots, parsnips, celery, or parsley and confit them. We'll shave them really thin on the mandoline, then add some fat in the form of olive oil with herbs or citrus, and cook them at 85 degrees for six to eight hours, which breaks down the cell wall structure. I will add that I am not a scientist — I am just a cook — but [this approach] achieves everything you're looking for."

—AARON WOO, NATURAL SELECTION (PORTLAND, OREGON)

IF YOU ARE CRAVING . . .

This	Try This Instead
anchovies (e.g., in Caesar salad dressing)	capers
anchovy paste	dark miso paste
	umeboshi plum paste
bacon	crisply fried provolone cheese
	liquid smoke
	pimenton
	portobello mushroom "bacon"
	sautéed dulse
	smoked paprika
	smoked salt
	smoked tofu
	tempeh "bacon"
	toasted sesame oil
	tofu, extra-firm — marinated in liquid smoke, maple syrup, nutritional yeast, and soy sauce

	Lightlife Smart Bacon (bacon-style meatless protein strips)
	Lightlife Fakin' Bacon Organic Smoky Tempeh Strips
beef	Gardein Beefless Tips
beef, ground	bulgur, seasoned (e.g., in vegetarian burritos, chili, enchiladas, tacos, etc.)
	lentils, seasoned
	tempeh, crumbled
	Field Roast's Classic Meatloaf
beef stock	dark miso broth
	Better Than Bouillon "No Beef" base
Bolognese sauce	tomato sauce with Italian-seasoned lentils
	tomato sauce with tempeh
burgers	veggie burgers
butter, e.g., on grilled or toasted sandwiches	olive oil, e.g., on bread
	vegan margarine, e.g., Earth Balance
caramel	pureed dates + salt + vanilla
caramel corn	popcorn drizzled with warm brown rice syrup
cheese	cashew or other nut-based "cheese"
	soy "cheese"
	Daiya and Follow Your Heart vegan "cheeses"
cheese, cream	soy "cream cheese"
cheese, e.g., smoked Gouda or mozzarella	smoked tofu
cheese, e.g., Parmesan (e.g., in onion soups, pesto-like sauces, even Caesar salads)	ground almonds + lemon zest + salt + sesame seeds
	miso
	Parma brand vegan "Parmesan"
cheese, ricotta	ground almond, cashew, or pine nut "ricotta"
	half nondairy cream cheese + half firm tofu, mashed together
	tofu "ricotta," made from crumbled tofu
chicken	chicken of the woods mushrooms
	jackfruit
	seitan
	Gardein Chik'n Filets or Scallopini, Lightlife Smart Strips: Chick'n Style, May Wah Vegetarian Market's "chicken," Trader Joe's Chicken-less Strips
chicken stock	light or sweet miso broth
	Better Than Bouillon "No Chicken" base
chili, meat-based	chili with quinoa
chocolate	cacao nibs
chopped liver	walnut-lentil paté
chorizo sausage	Melissa's Soyrizo
cottage cheese	soy "cottage cheese"
crabcakes	"Cape Cod cakes" made with hijiki seaweed and tofu + Old Bay seasoning, served with vegan tartar sauce
	"crabfree cakes" made with grated zucchini + Old Bay seasoning
	mock crabcakes made with hearts of palm + breadcrumbs + kelp + lemon + mustard + Old Bay seasoning
crab dip	white bean dip + dill + kelp + lemon + Old Bay seasoning

IF YOU ARE CRAVING . . .

This	Try This Instead
cream	cashew cream
	coconut milk
	soy milk
cream, heavy	coconut milk (esp. in baking)
cream, whipped	cashew cream
dairy, in general	coconut milk
	other nondairy milks
	nuts and seeds and their milks
	silken tofu
egg salad	mock version made with extra-firm tofu, vegan mayonnaise, and black salt
eggs, in baked goods	applesauce, egg replacer, flax seeds, mashed banana, silken tofu
eggs, in quiches	silken or firm tofu
eggs, scrambled	tofu "scrambles" (esp. with a pinch of turmeric to turn them yellow)
escargot	mushrooms (e.g., cremini, forest) braised in butter + garlic + parsley, and stuffed into pasta shells or plastic novelty "snail" shells and served with sliced French baguette
feta cheese	cashew "feta"
	soy "feta"
fish sauce	fermented black bean sauce
	Thai soy sauce (aka white soy sauce)
	umeboshi plum paste, thinned with water or dashi
fish stock	light or sweet miso broth
gyro	substitute fried eggplant slices or Taft Seitan Gyro for meat in a pita; top with lettuce, tomato, and tzatziki sauce
ham	smoked paprika (e.g., in soup)
	smoked tofu (esp. w/maple syrup + tamari)
hamburgers	See "burgers," above.
mayonnaise	vegan "mayonnaise," e.g., Vegenaise
meat	grains
	legumes
	nuts (e.g., walnuts)
	seitan
	tempeh
	tofu
	meat sauce (on pasta) sauce with crumbled tempeh
meat, smoked	chipotle chiles with adobo, liquid smoke, smoked cheese, smoked tofu
meatballs	"wheatballs" (made from seitan)
	Nate's Meatless Meatballs
"meatiness"	chiles (e.g., chipotle — use the adobo sauce from canned chiles), garlic (e.g., roasted), liquid smoke, miso, mushrooms, onions (e.g., roasted), paprika (e.g., smoked), shallots (e.g., roasted), soy sauce

milk	nondairy milk, e.g., almond (e.g., Almond Breeze), cashew, hazelnut, hemp, nut, oat, rice, soy
onion soup	onion soup with miso instead of beef stock
	onion soup with molasses + sherry vinegar instead of beef stock
oysters	oyster mushrooms
	salsify (which has notes of oysters)
pasta	spaghetti squash
	zucchini spirals
pepperoni	Lightlife Smart Deli Pepperoni
pie crusts	pie crusts made with Earth Balance natural shortening
pork	chicken of the woods mushrooms
	jackfruit
	seitan
	Field Roast's Celebration Roast
pork fat	toasted sesame oil
pork, pulled	jackfruit, seasoned with chili powder and other seasonings
salad dressing (creamy)	tahini and tahini-based dressings
salad dressing (nonoily)	balsamic vinegar, champagne vinegar, rice wine vinegar, verjus (which are all mild enough to be used without oil)
sausage (e.g., on pizza)	crumbled tempeh
	Field Roast Italian Grain Meat Sausage
sautéed dishes made with oil	sautéed dishes made with stock, vinegar, or wine
seafood	simmered dulse
sloppy Joes	seasoned lentils on whole-grain bun
soup, cream	soup, creamy — made so via adding pureed grains (such as oats or rice, e.g., brown or white); or pureed vegetables (e.g., cauliflower)
sour cream	cashew "sour cream" (raw cashews + lemon juice + miso + nutmeg + sea salt + water)
	nonfat yogurt, or tofu "sour cream" (e.g., firm silken tofu + lemon juice + salt + umeboshi vinegar, or tofu + cider vinegar + lemon juice + oil + salt, or light miso + lemon juice + tofu)
	soy milk + oil, emulsified together
	pureed silken tofu + hint of lemon juice
	Tofutti non-hydrogenated Better Than Sour Cream
stock, meat	stock, mushroom or vegetable; miso broth;
	see also "beef stock," "chicken stock," "fish stock"
tacos, ground beef	tacos filled with seasoned brown lentils
tuna	smoked tofu
tuna salad	ground cashews with chopped celery
	mashed chickpeas with chopped celery and nori
	mashed tofu with chopped celery, onion, kelp powder
turkey	Tofurky (made from tofu, and stuffed on the inside)
	Field Roast's Celebration Roast
tzatziki sauce, Greek	vegan "tzatziki" made with raw cashews + cucumber + garlic + lemon + olive oil + seasonings
yogurt	coconut or soy "yogurt"

"I typically don't like fake anything and believe in cooking from scratch. We didn't like any of the premade veggie burger patties we tried, and only make our own. But realizing that Buddhists have been making faux meats for ages, we've found some to be very good. For example, May Wah Vegetarian Market's 'chicken' has amazing flavor and texture. It's great broiled, because it gets crispy and has a nice stringy texture, but I probably wouldn't use it for a cold chicken salad. . . . And while Tofutti sour cream has a texture that's a bit stiff, I've enjoyed it in soups like borscht or on potato latkes."

—SELMA MIRIAM, BLOODROOT (BRIDGEPORT, CT)

Note: In the interest of helping omnivores in their shift toward flexitarianism / vegetarianism / veganism, several processed foods are included on the list above. While these can be very useful transitional "crutches," it seems important to underscore that a subsequent move toward a *whole-food* diet is even better for optimal health.

HOW *RESTAURANT* MAGAZINE'S WORLD'S 50 BEST RESTAURANTS (2013) LOCATED IN THE U.S. ACCOMMODATE VEGETARIANS

"Having trained in so many great kitchens [in the late 1980s and early 1990s, including Gotham Bar & Grill and the River Café in New York City, as well as those of Guerard and Passard in France], I can still remember the days when the 'veg plate' was whatever you could pull together when someone asked for one, and definitely an afterthought. It is nice to see how it has evolved."

—DIANE FORLEY, FLOURISH BAKING COMPANY (SCARSDALE, NY), WHOSE CELEBRATED MANHATTAN RESTAURANT, VERBENA, OFFERED AN ELABORATE VEGETARIAN TASTING MENU WITH WINE PAIRINGS IN THE 1990'S

#5) Eleven Madison Park (New York City) — Offers vegetarian tasting menu that can be served vegan upon request

#11) Per Se (New York City) — Offers vegetarian tasting menu that can be served vegan upon request

#14) Alinea (Chicago) — Alinea's menu states, "Alinea accommodates vegetarian diners without compromise to the quality and originality of the cuisine. Please indicate that you wish to have a vegetarian menu when we call to confirm your ticket purchase."

#19) Le Bernardin (New York City) — Le Bernardin's seafood-centric menu offers a single vegetarian option for an appetizer (salad) and entrée (vegetable risotto).

#29) DANIEL (New York City) — Offers vegetarian tasting menu that can be served vegan upon request

#47) The French Laundry (Yountville, California) — Offers vegetarian tasting menu that can be served vegan upon request

VEGETABLE-CENTRIC RESTAURANT MENUS

Vegetables are being elevated to new heights at the most rarified levels of the restaurant world. No longer mere "side dishes," they are the main event and the stars of their own celebrated tasting menus.

The following menus shine a spotlight on some of the vegetarian and vegan dishes that have been served in some of the world's best dining rooms.

Picholine

New York, New York

Winter 2014

Vegetarian Tasting Menu

Amuse Varie

Winter Vegetable Salad
Parsnip, Mushrooms à la Grecque, Truffle Vinaigrette

Blue Hubbard Squash Bisque
Chestnuts, Pear Butter, Quatre Épices Meringue

Celery Root-Apple Agnolotti
"Borscht," Celery Tempura

Potato Crusted Hen Egg
Confit Potato, Frisee, Sauce Gribiche

Grilled King Trumpet Mushroom
Wild Rice Fritter, Red Endive, Vanilla-Cranberry Vinaigrette

Potato "Mille-Feuille"
Carrots, Salsify, Parsley Vinaigrette

Fromage Affinés
Selections from our Cheese Cart

Guanaja Chocolate Marquise
Blood Orange, Nicoise Olives, Fennel-Yuzu Sorbet

Per Se

New York, New York

August 24, 2013

Vegetarian Tasting Menu

White Bean Flan
Black Winter Truffle, Nori "Tempura," Compressed Scallions
and Barrel Aged Tamari

Sweet Corn Sorbet
Poached Huckleberries, Red Radishes and Pea Tendrils

Charred Eggplant "Barbajuan"
Cocktail Artichokes, Armenian Cucumbers, Herb Salad and "Romesco"

Coddled Hen Egg
San Marzano Tomato "Soffritto," Summer Squash,
Toasted Pine Nuts and Rosemary Bialy

"Celeri Farci en Façon Subric"
Haricots Verts, Pearl Onions and "Crème de Morilles"

Caramelized Sunchoke "Agnolotti"
Roasted Scarlet Grapes, Romaine Lettuce Hearts and Smoked Ricotta "Glaçage"

"Burrata" Tart
Heirloom Tomatoes, Castelvetrano Olives, Petite Basil and
Armando Manni Extra Virgin Olive Oil

"Gin & Juice"
Vanilla Poached Blackberries, Hendricks Gin "Granite" and Tonic Gelée

"Peach Bellini"
Champagne Gelée and Peaches

Fig Leaf "Glace"
Mirin Gelée and Tiger Striped Figs

Chocolate Caramel
Maralumi Chocolate "Ganache," "Orange Genoise" and Candied Cocoa Nibs

DANIEL

New York, New York

February 12, 2014

Vegetarian Tasting Menu

Leek and Potato Velouté with Romaine Lettuce
Black Trumpet, Chervil Cream, Cremini Mushroom, Black Garlic

Fricassée of Wild Rice with Cilantro
Young Turnips, Swiss Chard, Pearl Onion

Glazed Celery Root with Caramelized Torpedo Shallot
Sautéed Chanterelle, Pomme Dauphine

Radicchio Tardivo Glazed with Blood Orange
Crosnes Tempura and Castelfranco Salad

Cauliflower Cromesquis with Cubeb Pepper
Potato "Saint-Florentin," Red Ribbon Sorrel

Sunchoke Ravioli with Sautéed Black Trumpet
Swiss Chard Fricassée, Black Garlic, Vadouvan Sauce

. . . .

Bitter Brew
Fleur de Sel Chocolate Foam, Puffed Wheat, Abbey Ale Ice Cream

Molasses Poached Pear
Lime-Pain de Gênes, Cranberry Confit, Pear-Gewürztraminer Sorbet

Bergamot Parfait
Citrus Gelée, Honey Sablé Breton, Ginger Emulsion

This was the best vegetarian tasting menu of my life:

The Inn at Little Washington

Washington, Virginia

July 22, 2012

Our Garden of Eatin' Harvest Menu

Tempura Squash with Asian Dipping Sauce

A Shot of our Heirloom Tomato Soup with Truffled Grilled Cheese Sandwich

Blistered Shishito Peppers with Sea Salt

Beet Fantasia: A Mélange of Our Garden Roasted Beets with
Virginia Goat Cheese, Beet Sorbet and Orange Essence

Pappardelle Pasta with a Medley of Virginia Mushrooms and Local Peaches

Sweet Corn Custard Wreathed with a Mélange of Garden Beans,
Cauliflower and Truffle Vinaigrette

Our Club Sandwich of Eggplant, Grilled Shiitake Mushrooms and
Fried Green Tomato on Charred Onions with Burgundy Butter Sauce

Buttermilk Panna Cotta with Sour Cherry Preserves from our Orchard

Grandmother's Warm Local Peach Tart with Peach Leaf Ice Cream

This was the best vegan tasting menu of my life:

Eleven Madison Park

New York, New York

August 22, 2013

Vegan Tasting Menu

Almonds: Nuts for Nuts with Smoked Paprika and Pimente d'Espelette

Watermelon: Compressed with Beets and Raspberries

Zucchini: Marinated with Teff Crisp and Lemon, Smoked with
Shallot Crumble, Pickles and Zucchini Caviar

Cucumber: Salad with Pickled Mustard Seeds

Wax Beans: Salad with Lettuce

Carrot: Tartare with Baguette and Condiments

Sunflower: Barigoule with Sunchokes and Black Truffle

Eggplant: Roasted with Bulgur Wheat, Licorice, and Greens

Fruit Plate: Seasonal Berries

Chocolate: Soy Milk Egg Cream

Mint: Sorbet with Fernet Branca and Chocolate Ganache

Red Pepper: Cheesecake with Strawberry and Cashew

Pretzel: Chocolate Covered with Sea Salt

Apricot: Sweet Black and White Cookie

VEGETARIAN FLAVOR MATCHMAKING: THE LISTS

"I am obsessed with the relationship between cooking and health. When one goes to the opera, one does not expect to return having gone deaf; one does not expect to go blind as a result of going to the theatre. Why then must one do oneself damage by going out to eat? For people who think this way, there is, on one hand, the cuisine for pleasure — but full of menace — and on the other, the diet — for the redemption of the body. This separation is odious, and we must find the means of reconciling pleasure and health. I dream of a cuisine that no longer does anyone harm."

—ALAIN SENDERENS, PARIS-BASED MICHELIN THREE-STAR CHEF, AS QUOTED IN MIRIAM KASIN HOSPODAR'S 2001 BOOK *HEAVEN'S BANQUET*

"Chefs hold the key to health in the twenty-first century. And they will be the ones to change the perception that a plant-based diet has anything to do with lack — because, in truth, it opens up a world of abundance. There's no need to sacrifice any of the mouthfeel, the richness, or the satisfaction that comes from eating the most delicious food."

—CHEF CHAD SARNO, CO-AUTHOR WITH KRIS CARR OF THE BESTSELLING BOOK *CRAZY SEXY KITCHEN*

Chef Chad Sarno healed himself of his childhood asthma within six months of giving up dairy products, and he went on to embrace a plant-based diet. Having co-authored the bestselling cookbook *Crazy Sexy Kitchen: 150 Plant-Empowered Recipes to Ignite a Mouthwatering Revolution* with Kris Carr and served as lead culinary educator of Whole Foods Market's healthy eating program, he now leads the Plant-Based Professional Certification Course at Rouxbe.com, which includes the unit "Flavor, Seasoning, and Texture."

"As an educator and chef, the greatest hurdle that I have witnessed when budding chefs and students dive into the kitchen is the awakening and development of the instinct for flavor balancing, combining, and building," says Sarno. "I have been telling people for years that *The Flavor Bible* is one of the greatest resources on the market to help guide this intuitive nature that comes with experience, and it is my own go-to book to get the ideas flowing. I think it should be a cornerstone resource for the modern chef and for every home and professional kitchen."

Sarno has introduced the book and its flavor-pairing approach to participants in bestselling author Dr. John McDougall's renowned weekend program when teaching seminars on the use of herbs and spices. "The starting point is typically thinking about seasonal products," says Sarno. "I then skim the book to refresh my memory about classic combinations or to discover unique combinations I almost didn't believe would work until I tried them for myself and found them awesome."

The starting point for your creativity in the kitchen can be anything. As Sarno suggests, it often begins with the seasonal availability of a particular ingredient — such as spring's first morel mushrooms or the arrival of pomegranates in autumn — or even the desire to cook in a particular way, such as firing up the grill in summer or warming the house with an oven-braised dish in winter. It can begin with a craving for the flavors of a particular country or region: the garlic and herbs of Provence, or the chiles and coconut milk of southeast Asia. Or it can begin with simple curiosity, such as the urge to experiment with a new ingredient or technique.

Recognizing this, I've provided a broad range of starting points in the A-to-Z (açai to zucchini blossoms) lists that follow: the seasons (with listings for autumn, spring, summer, and winter); an extensive variety of vegetables, fruits, legumes, grains, nuts, seeds, mushrooms, sea vegetables, and other ingredients; dozens of world cuisines; and a broad array of flavorings and seasonings (from asafoetida to elderflower to toasted pumpkin seed oil), including dozens of different salts, peppers, herbs, spices, oils, and vinegars.

Below each entry, you'll find a distillation of an ingredient's essence and summary of its key aspects: its season, flavor, volume, nutritional profile, and more. You'll also find its most highly recommended cooking techniques and some useful tips to keep in mind when working with it. After all, some ingredients lend themselves to being prepared in a particular manner: While potatoes are versatile enough to be cooked in a number of ways (from baked to fried to mashed), delicate salad greens beg to be served raw, and root vegetables to be roasted or stewed.

When perusing the listings of compatible flavors, readers of *The Flavor Bible* and *What to Drink with What You Eat* will recognize the same ranking system used in those books to let you know which pairings are truly stellar. Those ingredients that appear in **BOLD CAPS** (*) are out-of-this-world, time-honored classics: these "marriages made in heaven" make up the top 1 or 2 percent of pairings. Next you'll find very highly recommended pairings in **BOLD CAPS**. **Bold**, lowercase listings are frequently recommended pairings; and plain-text pairings are recommended pairings. And even when just a single top expert recommends a flavor combination, it's very high praise indeed.

"If you like a mixture such as broccoli rabe, toasted almonds, and manchego cheese with pasta, chances are it'll be great on pizza, too."

— ANNIE SOMERVILLE, CHEF OF SAN FRANCISCO'S GREENS RESTAURANT AND AUTHOR OF *EVERYDAY GREENS*

For many listings, you'll also find groups of three or more **"Flavor Affinities"** (as they are called in *The Flavor Bible*; they are called "flavor cliques" in *Culinary Artistry*). These affinities will get you started on complex flavor combinations. In other cases, you'll find some of America's most creative chefs' signature vegetarian dishes, so you can gain inspiration from some of the most celebrated vegetable-loving restaurant kitchens across the country.

Annie Somerville's quotation gets to the heart of the usefulness of these listings: Once you understand flavors that work well together, you can use them in countless different applications, from pasta or pizza toppings to mix-ins for quiches or salads, or as the basis of soups or stews.

As the starting point for creating a dish can be anything at all, you'll find a range of categories offering inspiration for any interest, such as specific ingredients (from açai to zucchini blossoms), particular cuisines (with alphabetical listings such as Ethiopian cuisine, French cuisine, Indian cuisine, etc.), the seasons (with alphabetical listings for autumn, spring, summer and winter), and more.

Throughout these pages, you'll also find sidebars on subjects ranging from harnessing the "meatiness" of mushrooms to making pasta sauces from vegetable purees other than tomato. They'll help you learn not only the "whats" of combining flavors, but also the "whys" and "hows."

Keep an eye out for the distinctions being made among ingredients. After all, not even all salty condiments (e.g., salt itself, not to mention Bragg Liquid Aminos, soy sauce, tamari, etc.) are created equal. As you hone your selections, you'll hone the quality of the flavors you're able to create.

For years, I have traveled throughout North America, spending thousands of hours interviewing creative chefs and other experts on their most highly recommended flavor combinations. I've scoured their memories — along with their restaurant menus, websites, cookbooks, and other favorite books — for insights into building flavors. Their wisdom has been synthesized into the comprehensive, easy-to-use listings that follow. These listings represent a treasure trove of ideas for you to put to work in your own kitchen.

Armed with the extensive information that follows, you'll learn how to better show off virtually any ingredient or to re-create the flavors of any world cuisine you can think of. From here on out, you'll have the expert advice of some of America's most imaginative vegetable-loving chefs at your disposal when you want to spark your own creativity. Whether you're exploring a new flavor or looking for additional ideas for working with an ingredient you've cooked a thousand times, you'll find helpful tips and a plethora of options here.

MATCHING FLAVORS: KEY INGREDIENT

● Much Higher ● Higher ● Moderate ● Lower ● Much Lower (nutrient concentration) [pro-nun-see-AY-shun]

Season: The ingredient's general seasonal peak(s) in North America, which may vary by location and climate

Flavor: The ingredient's primary taste (e.g., bitter, salty, sour, sweet, umami), plus primary flavor notes and a brief description of its texture

Volume: The ingredient's relative flavor "loudness," from quiet to loud

What it is: A brief description of less common ingredients (and/or the nutritional category, e.g., grain, legume, vegetable)

What's healthful about it: Key vitamins, minerals, other nutrients, and/or health benefits

Gluten-free: Whether grains are free of gluten, a protein composite found in wheat and related grains

Nutritional profile: The ingredient's macronutrient content, i.e., percentage of calories from carbohydrates, fat, or protein, in decreasing order

Calories: Number of calories per stated serving size

Protein: Number of grams of protein per stated serving size

Techniques: Methods commonly used to prepare the ingredient (and their general **Timing** and/or the recommended **Ratio** of ingredient to cooking liquid)

Tips: Suggestions for preparing, using, and/or serving the ingredient

Botanical relatives: Plant family of origin, which sometimes inspires ideas for pairing experiments

Possible substitutes: In a pinch, other ingredients that may be substituted for the named ingredient (and vice versa)

Flavors mentioned in regular type are pairings suggested by at least one expert.

Bold marks those recommended by a number of experts.

BOLD CAPITALS mark those very highly recommended by an even greater number of experts.

***BOLD CAPITALS** with an asterisk (*) mark "Holy Grail" pairings that are the most highly recommended by the greatest number of experts.

Italics mark either specific dishes or cuisines that make use of that particular ingredient.

"Quotation marks" mark meatless versions of typical meat dishes (e.g., tempeh "bacon") or dishes made in the style of another dish (e.g., farro "risotto").

NOTE: Those who prefer not to consume butter, cream, mayonnaise, milk, and yogurt (e.g., vegans) can easily substitute their preferred eggless and nondairy versions of these ingredients.

AÇAI

[ah-sah-EE]

Flavor: sour/bitter; with earthy notes of berries (e.g., blackberries, blueberries and/or raspberries) and/or chocolate

What it is: a berry-like fruit, more commonly available as concentrate, juice, powder, or pulp

Techniques: dry, juice, raw

agave nectar
bananas
berries
cassava
desserts, e.g., cheesecake, ice cream, sorbet
drinks, e.g., cocktails, lemonade
granola
ice cream
jellies
juices
pomegranates
raspberries
SMOOTHIES
sorbets
South American cuisine
yogurt

Dishes

Açai Sunset Smoothie: Açai Berry, Banana, Strawberry, Orange Juice, Mango, Pineapple, Lime
— Pomegranate Café (Phoenix)

Deep Purple Smoothie: Açai Berry, Raspberry, Blueberry, Strawberry, Banana, Goji Berry, Pomegranate Juice
— Pomegranate Café (Phoenix)

Açai Bowl: Sambazon Açai Berry, Granola, Bananas, Berries, Drizzled Agave Nectar
— Real Food Daily (Los Angeles)

ACHIOTE SEEDS (aka ANNATO SEEDS)

Flavor: sour, with earthy and/or musky notes of citrus, paprika, pepper, and/or turmeric

Volume: quiet – moderate

Tip: Used as much for its (yellow/orange) coloring as for its flavor

Possible substitutes: saffron (for color)

beans
Caribbean cuisine
cheese
chiles, e.g., habanero, jalapeño
cilantro
citrus, e.g., sour orange
cloves
coriander
cumin
garlic
gravies
Latin American cuisines
lime
marinades
MEXICAN CUISINE
oil, e.g., corn, olive, vegetable
onions
ORANGES and SOUR ORANGES, e.g., juice
oregano
pastes
pepper, black
polenta
potatoes
Puerto Rican cuisine
RICE
sauces
seitan
sofritos
soups
South American cuisines
squash, winter, e.g., butternut
stews

tacos
tofu
tomatoes
vinegar, e.g., wine
yuca

Flavor Affinities

achiote seeds + cumin + garlic + lime + oil + oregano

ADOBO SAUCE and/or SEASONING (see also CHILES, CHIPOTLE)

Flavor: salty/sour/hot

Volume: moderate – loud

What it is: seasoning or sauce made from some or all of the following:

(ground) chiles / cayenne + cumin + **garlic** + herbs (e.g., oregano) + onion + **(black) pepper** + salt + turmeric + vinegar

avocado
beans, e.g., black
burritos
Caribbean cuisines [+ cumin + garlic + orange juice + oregano]
cauliflower
cheese, e.g., cheddar
CHILES, e.g., CHIPOTLE, or chili powder
enchiladas
Filipino cuisine [+ annatto seeds + coconut milk + garlic]
guacamole
Latin American cuisines
lemon
lime
marinades
Mexican cuisine [+ chipotle chiles + cinnamon + garlic + orange juice + oregano]
orange, e.g., juice
polenta

potatoes, e.g., baked, fried
sauces
soups
stews
stock, e.g., vegetable
tortilla chips

Flavor Affinities
adobo + avocado + chili powder + **lime** + **salt**
adobo + **lime** + **salt** + seitan

AFRICAN CUISINES (see also ETHIOPIAN CUISINE and MOROCCAN CUISINE)

bananas
beans
bell peppers
black-eyed peas
braised dishes
cabbage
coconut
curries
fruit, tropical, e.g., pineapple
garlic
grains, e.g., millet, teff
greens, e.g., stewed
lentils
okra
peanuts and peanut butter
plantains
salad dressings, e.g., peanut
salads, e.g., bean, lentil
sauces, e.g., peanut
soups, e.g., bean, black-eyed pea, peanut, yam
stews, e.g., peanut, vegetable
sweet potatoes
tomatoes
yams, esp. west African

Flavor Affinities
beans + rice + sweet potatoes
chickpeas + coconut + curry powder
coriander + cumin + lemon + lentils + nutmeg

green beans + peanuts + sweet potatoes

● AGAR or AGAR-AGAR (see also KANTEN)
[AH-gahr or AG-er AG-er]
Flavor: virtually none
Volume: extremely quiet
What it is: a thickening agent made from seaweed; a vegetarian substitute for gelatin
Nutritional profile: 94% carbs / 5% protein / 1% fat
Calories: 0 per 1-tablespoon serving

> **Tips:** To gel, use about 2 – 3 teaspoons of agar powder (or 2 – 3 tablespoons of agar flakes) per 1 cup of boiling liquid. Unlike regular gelatin (which requires refrigeration), agar can gel at room temperature in about an hour (although it will gel twice as fast in the refrigerator). Substitute agar powder for the same amount of gelatin in recipes. Avoid raw mangoes, papayas, pineapple (whose enzymes won't let agar set); cook these fruits first if you'd like to gel them.

Possible substitute: gelatin

apple, e.g., cider, juice
apricots, dried or fresh
aspics
bananas
beans, adzuki
berries, e.g., blueberries
coconut and coconut milk
desserts, gelled
fruit juice
Japanese cuisine
jellies
kanten
kiwi fruit
lemon
macrobiotic cuisine

melon, e.g., cantaloupe
milk, coconut
"panna cotta," vegan
peaches
pears
pomegranates
puddings
soups
strawberries
sugar
vanilla
watermelon
yogurt, e.g., vegan

Flavor Affinities
agar + fruit juice + sugar

AGAVE NECTAR
[ah-GAH-vay NECK-ter]
Flavor: sweet, with notes of caramel, fruit, honey, and/or maple syrup
Volume: quiet (light) – moderate (amber or dark)
What it is: sweetener similar in color and texture to honey, made from the agave plant, a Mexican succulent
Nutritional profile: 100% carbs
Calories: 20 per teaspoon

> **Tips:** Agave is sweeter than sugar, so you can use less. Because baked goods made with agave may brown more quickly, lower oven temperature by 25°F and slightly extend baking time.

apples
baked goods, e.g., breads
cereals, hot breakfast
cheese, e.g., goat
cinnamon
cocktails, e.g., tequila-based
desserts, e.g., fruit
drinks
fruits
ice cream

pancakes, as a topping (esp. amber
    or dark)
pears
pumpkin (esp. amber or dark)
salad dressings
sauces, e.g., barbecue, caramel
smoothies
squash, winter (esp. amber
    or dark)
waffles, as a topping (esp. amber
    or dark)

"It's easier to make caramel sauce
from **agave nectar** than it is to
make it from sugar — because it's
already a liquid! Heat it on low,
slow heat until it caramelizes,
then stir in a little Earth Balance
and almond or soy milk."
— DAVE ANDERSON, MADDY'S AND
FORMERLY MADELEINE BISTRO (LOS
ANGELES)

ALLIUMS (see GARLIC, LEEKS, ONIONS, etc.)

● ALLSPICE
Season: autumn – winter
Flavor: sweet, with hot,
pungent, and/or spicy notes of
black pepper, cinnamon, cloves,
cumin, mace, and/or nutmeg
Volume: loud

Tip: Add early in cooking
process.

Botanical relatives: cloves

BAKED GOODS, e.g., cakes,
    cookies
beans, e.g., baked beans, black
beets
berbere, the Ethiopian spice
    blend
beverages, e.g., chai, cocoa
Caribbean cuisine, e.g., jerk seasoning
carrots
chiles, e.g., habanero

chocolate
cinnamon
cloves
coconut
compotes, fruit
cucumbers
cumin
curry powder, e.g., Indian,
    Jamaican; and curries, e.g.,
    Caribbean
desserts, e.g., crumbles
English cuisine
Ethiopian cuisine
fruits, e.g., apples, bananas,
    mangoes, peaches, pears,
    pineapple
ginger
grains, e.g., quinoa
gravies, e.g., mushroom
ice cream
Indian cuisine
JAMAICAN CUISINE, e.g., jerk
    dishes
ketchup
marinades
Mexican cuisine
Middle Eastern cuisines
Moroccan cuisine
nutmeg
nuts, e.g., pecans
oats
onions
pepper, black
pickled vegetables, e.g., broccoli,
    cauliflower, cucumber, green beans
pies, e.g., apple, fruit
pilafs
puddings
pumpkin
punch
ras el hanout
rum
salad dressings
sauces, e.g., barbecue, jerk, mole
soups, e.g., fruit, tomato
squash, **winter**, e.g., kabocha
stews

sugar
sweet potatoes
tamarind
teas
vegetables, esp. root
vinegar, e.g., apple cider, red wine
wine, mulled

Flavor Affinities
allspice + black pepper + rum

● ALMONDS (and UNSWEETENED ALMOND BUTTER; see also MILK, ALMOND)
Flavor: nutty, slightly sweet (and
sometimes salty), with a crunchy
texture
Volume: quiet
Nutritional profile: 72% fat /
15% carbs / 13% protein
Calories: 165 per 1-ounce
serving (about 20 – 25 whole
almonds)
Protein: 6 grams
Tips: Buy organic almonds.
Toast almonds to bring out
their flavor and crunchiness.
Almonds are arguably the most
versatile nut, and they pair
well with a great number of
ingredients.
Botanical relatives: apricots,
cherries, nectarines, **peaches**,
plums

amaretto
anise
apples
apricots
arugula
baked goods, e.g., cookies, pie crusts,
    quick breads
bananas
barley
beans, green, e.g., French

bell peppers, e.g., red or yellow,
  esp. roasted
BERRIES, e.g., blackberries,
  blueberries, strawberries
beverages, e.g., chocolate
biryanis
brandy
bread/toast, seven-grain
broccoli
Brussels sprouts
bulgur
butter
cabbage, napa
candies
caramel
caraway seeds
cardamom
carrots
cauliflower
cayenne
celery
celery root
cheese, e.g., blue, cream, goat,
  manchego, ricotta, Romano,
  Stilton
CHERRIES
chiles, e.g., ancho, and chili
  powder
CHOCOLATE / COCOA /
CACAO NIBS
chocolate, e.g., dark, milk, white
cinnamon
citrus
coconut
coffee
cornmeal
couscous
cranberries
cream
cumin
currants, e.g., black
curries
DATES
desserts, e.g., mousses, puddings
dips
figs
FRUITS, e.g., dried, fresh,
  roasted

Dishes

Almond Olive Oil Cake with Blackberries and Greek Yogurt
— True Food Kitchen (Santa Monica)

GARLIC
ginger
granola
grapes
greens, e.g., bitter, salad
hazelnuts
hiziki
HONEY
ice cream
icings, e.g., for cakes, cupcakes, etc.
Indian cuisine
kale
lavender
leeks
LEMON, e.g., juice, zest
lime, e.g., juice, zest
liqueurs, fruit (e.g., orange)
MAPLE SYRUP
mascarpone
Mediterranean cuisines
Middle Eastern cuisines
milk
molasses
Moroccan cuisine
muesli
mushrooms, e.g., chanterelle,
  portobello
mustard powder
nectarines
noodles, soba
nuts, other, e.g., walnuts
oats and oatmeal
oil, e.g., olive
olives
onions, e.g., red
ORANGE, e.g., juice, zest
paprika
passion fruit
PEACHES
pears
pecans
pepper, e.g., black
"pestos"

pilafs
pine nuts
pistachios
plums, e.g., dried, fresh
polenta
praline
quinces
raisins
raspberries
rhubarb
RICE, e.g., sweet
rose water
rosemary
rum
salads
salt, e.g., kosher, sea
SAUCES, e.g., mole, romesco
sesame, e.g., seeds
sherry
smoothies
soups, e.g., white gazpacho
soy sauce
Spanish cuisine
spiced almonds
spinach
spreads
strawberries
stuffings
sugar, e.g., brown
thyme
tofu
tomatoes
trail mix
Turkish cuisine
VANILLA
vinegar, e.g., champagne, sherry
watercress
yogurt
zucchini

Flavor Affinities

almond butter + bananas + seven-grain toast
almonds + apricots + lemon
almonds + basil + French green beans + peaches
almonds + bell peppers + chiles + garlic + sherry vinegar + tomatoes
almonds + bell peppers + garlic + tomatoes
almonds + blackberries + yogurt
almonds + blueberries + ricotta
almonds + blue cheese + watercress
almonds + bread crumbs + garlic + olive oil + parsley + tomatoes
almonds + cayenne + chili powder + lime
almonds + cayenne + cumin + mustard powder + paprika
almonds + chocolate + coconut
almonds + cream + orange + polenta
almonds + dates + garlic + ginger + soy sauce
almonds + dates + rice
almonds + honey + ricotta + vanilla
almonds + lemon + maple
almonds + oats + peaches

ALMONDS, MARCONA

Flavor: sweet/salty, with a rich, dense, crunchy texture
What they are: almonds from Spain
Calories: 180 per 1-ounce serving
Techniques: fry, raw

Tip: Marcona almonds are richer, softer, and sweeter than California almonds.

baked goods
beans, e.g., green
beets
cheeses, e.g., manchego
chickpeas
dates
desserts
figs
garlic
honey, e.g., orange blossom
lemon
maple syrup
oil, e.g., olive, sunflower
paprika, smoked
parsnips
quince paste
rosemary
salads, e.g., green, vegetable
salt
Spanish cuisine
squash, summer and winter
thyme
vegetables, root
vinegar, sherry

Flavor Affinities

Marcona almonds + green beans + lemon
Marcona almonds + manchego cheese + quince paste
Marcona almonds + olive oil + salt

● AMARANTH (THE GRAIN) (see also GREENS, AMARANTH)

Flavor: slightly sweet, with earthy notes of corn, grass, malt, molasses, nuts, pepper, sesame seeds, spinach, and/or woods, and a somewhat creamy/sticky, porridge-like texture
Volume: quiet – moderate
What it is: considered a whole grain, even though not in the grain family

Gluten-free: yes
Nutritional profile: 74% carbs / 13% protein / 13% fat
Calories: 250 per 1-cup serving (cooked)
Protein: 9 grams
Techniques: pop, simmer, sprout, steam
Timing: Cook about 15 – 30 minutes, covered, until tender. (Do not overcook, or it will become gummy.)
Ratio: 1:3 (1 cup amaranth to 3 cups cooking liquid)
Tips: Toast lightly before cooking. If toasted long enough, grains will pop like popcorn and can be enjoyed as a snack or as a garnish on salads or vegetables.
Brands: Bob's Red Mill, Hodgson Mill
Possible substitutes: cornmeal, polenta

almonds
apples and **apple juice**
baked goods, e.g., breads, cookies
beans, e.g., black, cannellini, pinto
blueberries
cabbage
cardamom
casseroles
CEREALS, e.g., hot breakfast
chia seeds
chickpeas
chili
chocolate, dark
cinnamon
corn
garlic
ginger
GRAINS, OTHER MILDER, e.g., buckwheat, bulgur, millet, quinoa, rice, wild rice
greens
honey
lemon
maple syrup

Mexican cuisine
milk
oil, e.g., olive
onions
orange, e.g., juice, zest
parsley
persimmons
pistachios
"*polenta*"
"*popcorn*"
porridges
puddings
raisins
salads, *when popped or sprouted*
scallions
SOUPS, *e.g., bean, clear*
  (used as a thickener or as a
  garnish when popped)
South American cuisines
soy sauce
spinach
stews
stock, vegetable
tamari
tomatoes, e.g., *stuffed*
veggie burgers
walnuts
yams
yogurt

Flavor Affinities
amaranth + almonds + bulgur +
  herbs
amaranth + apples + walnuts
amaranth + black beans + sweet
  potatoes
amaranth + cinnamon +
  maple syrup
amaranth + corn + pinto beans +
  scallions
amaranth + lemon + olive oil
amaranth + quinoa + wild rice
amaranth + raisins + soy milk

AMERICAN CUISINE
(see also CAJUN/
CREOLE CUISINE,
SOUTHERN CUISINE,
TEX-MEX CUISINE, etc.)
beans
blueberries
chives
corn
cranberries
grapes, Concord
maple syrup
peanuts
pecans
popcorn
pumpkin and pumpkin seeds
rice, wild
squash
sunflower seeds
vinegar, apple cider
walnuts

Flavor Affinities
dried cranberries + sunflower
  seeds + wild rice

● **ANISE SEEDS**
[AN-iss]
Flavor: slightly sweet, with
pungent notes of fruit and licorice
Volume: moderate – loud
  Tip: Add early in cooking.
Botanical relatives: carrots,
parsley

allspice
almonds
apples and applesauce
Asian cuisines
BAKED GOODS, *e.g., biscotti,*
  breads (esp. rye), *cakes, cookies,*
  pies, shortbread
beets
cabbage
cardamom
carrots
cauliflower

celery
cheese, e.g., goat, Munster, ricotta
chestnuts
Chinese cuisine
cinnamon
cloves
coffee
compotes
cranberries
cream
cumin
curry powder and *curries (e.g.,*
  Indian)
dates
desserts
drinks
fennel and fennel seeds
FIGS
French cuisine, esp. Provençal
fruits, e.g., cooked, dried
garlic
ginger
hazelnuts
Italian cuisine
lemon
lentils
maple syrup
marinades
mayonnaise
[Eastern] *Mediterranean cuisines*
melon
Middle Eastern cuisines
Moroccan cuisine
nutmeg
nuts, e.g., almonds
orange
parsnips
peaches
pears
pepper, e.g., black
pickles
pineapple
pine nuts
plums, fresh or dried
Portuguese cuisine
pumpkin
quince

raisins
rhubarb
rice
salad dressings
salads, fruit
sauces, e.g., cream, mole, tomato
sauerkraut
Scandinavian cuisine
soups, e.g., sweet potato
Southeast Asian cuisines
star anise
STEWS, e.g., vegetable
strawberries
sugar
sweet potatoes
teas
tomatoes and tomato sauce
vanilla
vegetables, e.g., **root**
Vietnamese cuisine
walnuts
wine

Flavor Affinities
anise + cranberries + walnuts
anise + maple syrup + pine nuts
   + vanilla
anise + orange + pine nuts

ANISE HYSSOP
(aka LICORICE MINT)
Season: summer
Flavor: sweet, with notes of
licorice and mint
Volume: quiet – moderate
Botanical relatives: mint
Possible substitutes: anise,
mint

apricots
baked goods, e.g., cookies, scones
basil
beans, e.g., green
beets
berries, e.g., blackberries,
   blueberries, raspberries
beverages

carrots
cherries
chervil
chocolate
cream
currants
desserts, e.g., crisps, custards, pies
fennel
fruit, esp. summer
grains, e.g., bulgur, couscous
honey
ices and ice creams
lavender
lemon
lychees
melons, e.g., cantaloupe,
   honeydew
mint
nectarines
oranges
parsley
parsnips
peaches
pears
raspberries
rhubarb
rice
salads, e.g., fruit, grain, green
sauces, e.g., crème anglaise, custard
soups, e.g., melon
spinach
squash, winter
sweet potatoes
"tabboulehs"
teas
tomatoes
vegetables, root
watermelon
wine, e.g., sparkling and/or sweet
zucchini

Flavor Affinities
anise hyssop + almonds +
   peaches
anise hyssop + beets + orange
anise hyssop + berries +
   cantaloupe + Moscato d'Asti

anise hyssop + blueberries +
   honey + lemon
anise hyssop + fennel + orange

ANISE, STAR
(see STAR ANISE)

ANNATTO
(see ACHIOTE)

APPLES (and APPLE
CIDER, APPLE JUICE
and/or APPLESAUCE)
Season: autumn
Flavor: sweet (and sometimes
sour), with astringent notes
of baking spices, honey, and/or
lemon, and a crispy texture
(when raw)
Volume: quiet – moderate
What they are: fruit
Nutritional profile: 95% carbs
/ 3% fat / 2% protein
Calories: 65 per 1-cup serving
(chopped, raw)
Techniques: bake, caramelize,
dry, fry (e.g., fritters), grill, juice,
poach, puree, raw, sauté, stew
Tips: Opt for organic apples.
Eat the peels, which are high
in antioxidants. Buy sugar-free
applesauce. Substitute applesauce for fat in baking recipes.
Botanical relatives:
apricots, blackberries, cherries,
peaches, pears, plums, quinces,
raspberries, strawberries

agave nectar
allspice
almonds
apple butter and ***applesauce***
apricots
BAKED APPLES
BAKED GOODS, e.g., cakes,
   muffins, pies
bananas

beets
blackberries
blueberries
brandy, e.g., apple
butter
buttermilk
butterscotch
cabbage, e.g., red
Calvados
caramel
cardamom
carrots
cashews
cayenne
celery
celery root
CHEESE, e.g., blue, Camembert,
    cheddar, cream, feta, goat,
    Gorgonzola, Gruyère,
    Roquefort, white
cherries
chestnuts
chiles, e.g., chipotle, jalapeños
chutneys
cider, e.g., apple
*****CINNAMON**
cloves
coconut
compotes, fruit, e.g., apple
coriander
CRANBERRIES, dried or fresh
cream
crepes
cucumbers
currants, e.g., black
custards and flans
dates
DESSERTS, e.g., cobblers, crisps,
    crumbles
eggs
endive
fennel and fennel seeds
figs
fruit, dried, e.g., raisins
GINGER
GRAINS, e.g., amaranth, farro,

kasha, millet, oats, quinoa,
wheat berries
granola (esp. dried apples)
grapes
greens, salad
HONEY
horseradish
jícama
juices
kale
lamb's lettuce
lavender
LEMON, e.g., juice, zest
lentils
lettuce, e.g., romaine
mace
MAPLE SYRUP
mascarpone
mint
molasses
muesli
mustard and mustard seeds
nutmeg
NUTS, e.g., almonds, hazelnuts,
peanuts, **pecans**, pistachios,
walnuts
OATS and OATMEAL
oil, nut, e.g., hazelnut, peanut,
walnut
onions
oranges, e.g., juice, zest
parsnips
pears
pepper, black
phyllo dough
pine nuts
plums, e.g., dried, fresh
puddings
pumpkin
quince
RAISINS
raspberries
rhubarb
rice, e.g., basmati, brown, wild
rosemary
sage

Dishes

Apple Cobbler: Walnut Crust and Layers of Apples, Cinnamon, and Agave, topped with Macadamia Vanilla Sauce
— 118 Degrees (California)

Cinnamon Apple Sticks with Brandy Caramel Sauce
— Blossom (New York City)

Apple and Celery Salad with Hazelnut Vinaigrette, Cider Gelée, Young Mesclun
— DANIEL (New York City)

Salad of Honeycrisp Apples: Peanut Brittle, Celery Branch "Ribbons" and Condensed Milk Tuile
— Per Se (New York City)

Caramel Apple Beignets with Bourbon Caramel Sauce and Candied Pecans
— Plum Bistro (Seattle)

Honeycrisp Apple Tarte Tatin with Smoked Grand Marnier Ice Cream
— The Point (Saranac Lake, NY)

Flavor Affinities

apples + allspice + cinnamon + cloves + ginger + maple syrup + orange
apples + almonds + cinnamon + rosemary
apples + apple cider vinegar + greens + maple syrup + walnut oil
apples + blue cheese + celery
apples + brown sugar + caramel + cinnamon
apples + buttermilk + horseradish + sorrel
apples + caramel + nuts (e.g., peanuts, pecans)
apples + cheese (e.g., blue) + greens (e.g., salad, spinach) + **nuts** (e.g., pecans, walnuts)
apples + cinnamon + cranberries + ginger + maple + raisins + walnuts
apples + cinnamon + dates + oatmeal
apples + cinnamon + honey + lemon
apples + cinnamon + honey + vanilla + yogurt
apples + cinnamon +maple syrup + mascarpone
apples + cinnamon + maple syrup + rice
apples + cinnamon + nuts + raisins
apples + cinnamon + raisins + walnuts
APPLES + CLOVES + CRANBERRIES + ORANGES
apples + cucumbers + mint + yogurt
apples + fennel + walnuts
apples + figs + honey
apples + ginger + lemon + scallions + sesame seeds
apples + grains (e.g., oats, quinoa, wild rice) + **nuts** (e.g., walnuts)
apples + maple syrup (+ vanilla) + **walnuts**

SALADS, e.g., fennel, fruit, grain, green, Waldorf
sauerkraut
seeds, e.g., caraway, sesame, sunflower
slaws
sorrel
soups, e.g., butternut squash, sweet potato
sour cream
spinach
spirits, e.g., apple brandy, applejack, Armagnac, Calvados, cognac, Cointreau, Kirsch, Madeira, rum, sherry, vermouth
SQUASH, WINTER, e.g., acorn, butternut, delicata
stuffings
SUGAR, e.g., brown
sumac
SWEET POTATOES
trail mix, esp. dried apples
vanilla
verjus
vinegar, e.g., cider
WALNUTS
watercress
wine, red
yogurt
zucchini

● APRICOTS (see also APRICOTS, DRIED)

Season: summer
Flavor: sour/sweet, with notes of almonds, honey, peaches, or plums, and a juicy, soft texture
Volume: moderate
Nutritional profile: 83% carbs / 10% protein / 7% fat
Calories: 20 per apricot
Techniques: bake, broil, dried, grill, poach, raw, stew
Botanical relatives: apples, blackberries, cherries, peaches, pears, plums, quinces, raspberries, strawberries

Dishes

Apricots: Almonds, Olive Oil and Lemon Basil Ice Cream
— Blue Hill (New York City)

Poached Apricots with Toasted Meringue and Apricot Sorbet with Jasmine, Rolled Oats, Ricotta, Lemon
— Fearrington House (Fearrington Village, NC)

ALMONDS
apples
arugula
basil
bay leaf
beets
berries, e.g., blueberries
brandy
buttermilk
caramel
cardamom
carrots
cereals, e.g., hot breakfast
cheese, e.g., cottage, cream, goat, ricotta, soft white
cherries
chocolate, e.g., dark
chutneys
cinnamon
cloves
coconut
compotes
coriander
couscous
cranberries
cream
cumin
curry powder and curry spices
desserts, e.g., crisps, crumbles, custards
fennel and fennel seeds
figs
fruit, dried
garlic
ginger
grains, e.g., barley, bulgur, quinoa, rice, wheat berries
granola

grapefruit
hazelnuts
HONEY, e.g., chestnut
ice cream
jícama
juices
juices, fruit
Kirsch
lemon, e.g., juice, zest
lemongrass
lemon thyme
lime
mangoes
maple syrup
mascarpone
Middle Eastern cuisines
mint
nectarines
nutmeg
nuts, e.g., walnuts
onions
orange, e.g., juice, liqueur, zest
peaches
pecans
pepper, e.g., black, white
pilafs, rice
pineapple
pine nuts
pistachios
plums, e.g., dried, fresh
preserves
puddings, e.g., rice
raisins
raspberries
rice, e.g., brown
saffron
salads, e.g., fruit, rice
salsas

sesame, e.g., seeds
smoothies
sorbets
soups, e.g., fruit
sour cream
strawberries
sugar, e.g., brown, powdered
tagines, i.e., Moroccan stews
tarragon
tarts, e.g., fruit
thyme
VANILLA
vinegar, e.g., balsamic, white wine
yogurt
wine, e.g., sweet, white, e.g.,
Moscato d'Asti

• APRICOTS, DRIED
(see also APRICOTS)
Flavor: similar to fresh apricots,
but more concentrated, and
chewy in texture
Volume: moderate
Calories: 315 per 1-cup serving
(uncooked)
Techniques: poach, raw, stew
Tip: Look for organic,
unsulphured dried apricots.

allspice
apples
baked goods, e.g., breads, cakes,
cookies, muffins, pies
bananas
brandy
cabbage, e.g., napa
cayenne
cereals, cold or hot breakfast
cheese, e.g., Brie, goat, ricotta
chestnuts
chiles, e.g., green, serrano
chocolate
cinnamon
coconut
Cognac
compotes
couscous
cranberries

curry powder
desserts, e.g., custards
dried fruit, other, e.g., cherries,
currants, plums, raisins
French toast
ginger
grains, e.g., bulgur
honey
jams and preserves
kale
lemon, e.g., juice, zest
lettuce, e.g., iceberg, romaine
lime
maple syrup
mascarpone
Middle Eastern cuisines
Moroccan cuisine
mint
NUTS, e.g., almonds, hazelnuts,
pecans, pine nuts, **pistachios**
oats and oatmeal
orange, e.g., juice, zest
pancakes and crepes
parsley
pears
porridges
puddings, e.g., rice
raspberries
rice and wild rice
salads, e.g., fruit, grain
sauces
seeds, e.g., pumpkin
stews
stuffings
sugar, e.g., brown
sweet potatoes
tamarind paste
vanilla
vinegar, e.g., champagne, rice
walnuts
wine, sweet, e.g., Madeira, Muscat
zucchini

Flavor Affinities
dried apricots + brown sugar +
sweet potatoes + vanilla
dried apricots + chiles + **ginger** +
honey + **lime** + vinegar

dried apricots + chocolate +
walnuts
dried apricots + citrus (lemon,
lime) + **ginger**
dried apricots + grains
(e.g., couscous, wild rice) +
nuts (e.g., pistachios)

ARAME (see also
SEA VEGETABLES)
[ah-rah-may or AIR-uh-may]
Flavor: slightly sweet, with a
firm texture
Volume: quiet
What it is: sea vegetable that has
been shredded, cooked, and sun-
dried, so it has the appearance of
very thin, black noodles
Nutritional profile: 80% carbs
/ 20% protein
Calories: 60 per 1-ounce
serving
Protein: 2 grams
Techniques: sauté, steam
Tip: Rinse well, then soak for
5 – 10 minutes before using.

almonds
apple juice
baked goods, e.g., breads, savory
pastries, strudels, tarts, turnovers
bell peppers, e.g., red
broccoli
buckwheat
cabbage, e.g., Chinese, red
CARROTS
casseroles
cilantro
citrus
coriander
corn
cucumbers
dill
edamame
eggs, e.g., *omelets, quiches*
garlic
ginger, fresh
gomashio

greens, salad, esp. Asian, e.g.,
  baby bok choy, mizuna, tatsoi
horseradish
Japanese cuisine
kale
lettuce
lotus root
mirin
miso
mushrooms, e.g., shiitake
mustard, e.g., spicy
noodles, Asian, e.g., soba, udon
oil, e.g., olive, sesame
onions, e.g., green, red
quiches
radishes
rice, brown
SALADS, e.g. cucumber, pasta
scallions
sea vegetables, other, e.g., hiziki,
  wakame
sesame, e.g., oil, paste, seeds
shoots, e.g., snow pea
snow peas
soups, e.g., split pea
soy sauce
squash, winter, e.g., buttercup,
  butternut
stews
stir-fries
strudels, e.g., phyllo dough
stuffed cabbage
stuffed peppers
sweeteners, e.g., agave nectar,
  maple syrup
tahini
tamari
tempeh
tofu
tofu scrambles
turmeric
turnips
vegetables
vinegar, e.g., brown rice, rice wine
wasabi

Flavor Affinities
arame + carrots + garlic +
  onions
arame + carrots + onions
arame + carrots + snow peas
arame + hiziki + mirin + miso
arame + mirin + sesame paste

"Among all sea vegetables, I love
arame for its versatility. It's great
in cucumber salads with toasted
sesame vinaigrette or tahini
dressing, or in a phyllo dough
strudel with spicy wasabi
mustard, or cooked with cabbage,
carrots, and onions and seasoned
with rice vinegar, tamari, and
scallions."
— PAM BROWN, GARDEN CAFÉ
(WOODSTOCK, NY)

ARROWROOT (aka ARROWROOT FLOUR, POWDER, or STARCH)
Flavor: virtually none
Volume: very quiet
What it is: a thickening agent,
less processed than cornstarch,
made from the arrowroot plant (a
tuber grown in the tropics)
Gluten-free: yes

Tips: Dissolve in a little cold
water before adding to sauces;
or dissolve about one tablespoon
of powder per cup of cold liquid
before bringing it to a simmer.
It becomes clear as it cooks. Stir
constantly, and do not overheat,
which makes arrowroot lose its
thickening power.

Brand: Authentic Foods, Bob's
Red Mill
Possible substitutes:
cornstarch, flour, kuzu, tapioca
starch

*baked goods, e.g., biscuits, breads,
  cakes, cookies, muffins, pies,*
scones
crepes
custards
desserts
flours, other
gravies
ice creams
milk, e.g., coconut
pie fillings
puddings
**SAUCES, e.g., fruit, sweet-and-
  sour*
soups
stews
stir-fries

ARTICHOKE HEARTS (see also ARTICHOKES)
Flavor: bitter/sweet, with earthy
notes, and a soft, tender, leafy
texture
Volume: quiet – moderate
What they are: vegetables (the
inner part of artichoke buds)
Techniques: deep-fry, marinate,
pickle, sauté (Note: never raw)
Tip: For ease, look for canned,
frozen, or jarred.

almonds
arugula
basil
beans, e.g., cannellini, **fava**, white
bell peppers, e.g., red
bread crumbs
bulgur
capers
casseroles, e.g., rice
cheese, e.g., goat, mozzarella,
  Parmesan, pecorino, ricotta
chickpeas
couscous
crostini

crudités
dill
DIPS
eggplant
eggs, e.g., *frittatas*, poached
focaccia
fritters
garlic
gratins
horseradish
Italian cuisine
leeks
LEMON, e.g., juice, zest
MUSHROOMS, e.g., porcini,
   shiitake, wild
oil, e.g., olive
olives, e.g., black
onions, e.g., red, white
oregano
palm, hearts of
parsley
PASTAS, e.g., fettuccine, penne

peas
pepper, black
pesto
pine nuts
PIZZAS
potatoes
relishes
rice
risotto
SALADS, e.g., green, pasta, potato
scallions
soups
sorrel
SPINACH
thyme
tomatoes
tomatoes, sun-dried
Turkish cuisine
walnuts
wheat berries
wine, e.g., dry white
zucchini

Flavor Affinities

artichoke hearts + arugula + **lemon juice + olive oil + Parmesan cheese**
artichoke hearts + bread crumbs + **garlic + lemon juice + olive oil +**
   Parmesan cheese
artichoke hearts + capers + lemon
artichoke hearts + carrots + potatoes
artichoke hearts + couscous + walnuts
artichoke hearts + eggs + Parmesan cheese + spinach
artichoke hearts + fava beans + lemon
artichoke hearts + garlic + leeks + pesto + potatoes
ARTICHOKE HEARTS + garlic + **LEMON + OLIVE OIL +**
   white beans
ARTICHOKE HEARTS + LEMON + OLIVE OIL
artichoke hearts + pasta + sun-dried tomatoes

Dishes

Artichoke Dip: Artichoke Hearts, Fennel, Roasted Garlic, Red Peppers,
and an assortment of Cheeses baked and served with House-Made
Whole-Wheat Pita
— Laughing Seed Café (Asheville, NC)

● ARTICHOKES (see also ARTICHOKE HEARTS)

Season: spring – summer
Flavor: bitter/sweet, with notes of nuts
Volume: moderate – loud
What they are: unopened flower buds from a member of the thistle family
Nutritional profile: 82% carbs / 13% protein / 5% fat
Calories: 64 per medium artichoke
Protein: 3 grams
Techniques: bake, boil, braise, broil, deep-fry, grill, pressure-cook (3 – 12 minutes, depending on size), roast, sauté, **steam** (about 15 – 45 minutes, depending on size), stew, stuff (Note: never raw)
Tip: The smaller the artichoke, the more tender it is.

Botanical relatives:
chamomile, chicory, dandelion greens, endive, lettuces (e.g., Bibb, iceberg, romaine), radicchio, salsify, tarragon

artichokes, Jerusalem
asparagus
basil
BAY LEAF
BEANS, e.g., **fava**, green, **white**
bell peppers, e.g., red, yellow
bouquet garni
BREAD CRUMBS, e.g., panko
butter and brown butter
capers
carrots
casseroles
celery
celery root
CHEESE, e.g., Fontina, **GOAT**, Gruyère, dry Jack, **PARMESAN**, Pecorino Romano, ricotta, ricotta salata

Flavor Affinities

artichokes + arugula + capers + lemon + olive oil + Parmesan cheese

artichokes + balsamic vinegar + olive oil

artichokes + bread crumbs + capers + **olives** + **Parmesan cheese** + tomatoes

artichokes + fennel + mushrooms

artichokes + fennel + potatoes

artichokes + garlic + herbs + onions

ARTICHOKES + GARLIC + LEMON + mayonnaise

ARTICHOKES + GARLIC + LEMON + olive oil + olives + Parmesan cheese

ARTICHOKES + GARLIC + LEMON + olive oil + parsley

ARTICHOKES + GARLIC + LEMON + pine nuts

artichokes + goat cheese + rosemary

artichokes + hazelnuts + lemon

ARTICHOKES + HERBS (e.g. mint, parsley, tarragon) **+ LEMON**

artichokes + lemon + mustard + tarragon

artichokes + olive oil + Parmesan cheese + tomatoes

artichokes + orange + white wine

artichokes + spinach + walnuts

Dishes

Buckwheat Ravioli filled with Ricotta and Fresh Artichokes
— Al Forno (Providence, RI)

Artichoke Barigoule with Tomato-Jalapeño Chutney, Glazed Pattypan Squash, and French Beans
— DANIEL (New York City)

Artichoke Salad: Oven Roasted Artichokes, Crumbled Feta Cheese, Shaved Radishes, Pickled Fennel, Lemon Artichoke Vinaigrette
— The Golden Door Spa Café at The Boulders (Scottsdale, AZ)

Artichoke and Sunchoke Gratin with Tomatoes, Peppers, Leeks, Green Garlic, Manchego and Fromage Blanc Custard
— Greens Restaurant (San Francisco)

Grilled Artichokes with Lemon Oil, Mint, and Romesco
— Greens Restaurant (San Francisco)

Baby Vegetable Salad: Braised Baby Artichokes, Grilled Baby Gold Zucchini, Truffle Vinaigrette, Mâche
— Plume (Washington, DC)

Crispy Artichoke, Harissa, Baby Spinach, Israeli Couscous, Preserved Lemon, Dukkah
— True Bistro (Somerville, MA)

chervil

chickpeas

chili pepper flakes

cilantro

cloves

coriander

curry

eggs, e.g., hard-boiled

endive

FENNEL and fennel seeds

fines herbes

French cuisine

GARLIC

ghee

gratins

greens

gremolata

herbs

Italian cuisine

leeks

LEMON, e.g., juice, oil, preserved, zest

lentils

lime

marjoram

mayonnaise

mint

MUSHROOMS, e.g., dried, porcini, trumpet

mustard, e.g., Dijon

nutmeg

nuts, e.g., **hazelnuts**, walnuts

oil, **nut**, e.g., hazelnut, walnut

OIL, OLIVE

OLIVES, e.g., black, green, kalamata

ONIONS, e.g., Spanish, sweet, yellow

oranges and **blood oranges**

paprika

PARSLEY

pasta

peas

pepper, e.g., black

pesto

pine nuts

pizza

potatoes, e.g., new

Provençal cuisine
ragouts
rice
risotto
rosemary
rutabagas
saffron
sage
salads, e.g., green, tomato
salsify
salt, e.g., sea
savory
scallions
shallots
sorrel
soups, e.g., artichoke
soy sauce
spinach
stews
stock, vegetable
stuffed artichokes
tahini
tarragon
THYME and lemon thyme
tomatoes
vinaigrette
vinegar, e.g., balsamic, cider, rice
   wine, sherry, white wine
walnuts
WINE, e.g., dry white
yogurt
za'atar

● ARTICHOKES, JERUSALEM (aka SUNCHOKES)

Season: autumn – spring
Flavor: slightly sweet, with earthy notes of artichoke hearts, nuts, potatoes, salsify, or smoke, and a crisp, crunchy, potato-like texture (when raw)
Volume: quiet – moderate
Nutritional profile: 92% carbs / 8% protein
Calories: 110 per 1-cup serving (raw, sliced)
Protein: 3 grams

Dishes

Organic Connecticut Farm Egg with Steamed Polenta, Artichoke, Sunchoke, Coconut Garlic Broth
— Bouley Restaurant (New York City)

Sesame-Crusted Jerusalem Artichoke with Chioggia Beets, Citrus-Braised Beet Greens, and Navel Orange
— CityZen (Washington, DC)

Globe Artichoke with Roasted Sunchokes and Eggplant Caviar and Pinenut Crosnes, Beluga Lentils, Tarragon, Baby Carrot
— Fearrington House (Fearrington Village, NC)

Creamy Sunchoke Soup, Granny Smith Apple, Preserved Lemon, Pine Nuts, German Thyme
— Green Zebra (Chicago)

Coddled Jidori Hen Egg, Sunchoke Mousse, Black Winter Truffle Coulis, Garlic Melba, and Brown Butter-Hazelnut Vinaigrette
— Per Se (New York City)

Techniques: bake (at 400°F, 20 – 25 minutes), blanch, boil (12 – 15 minutes), cream, deep-fry, fry, glaze, grate, mash, puree, raw (sliced thin, as for salads), roast (at 400°F, 30 minutes), sauté, shred, simmer, steam (about 15 – 20 minutes), stir-fry, tempura-fry

Tips: Scrub well, so there's no need to peel. Bake like a potato in the oven. Steam before sautéing.

Botanical relatives: sunflowers (Note: Jerusalem artichokes are not a type of artichoke, but both are in the daisy family.)
Possible substitutes: water chestnuts

almonds
(Native) American cuisine
apples
artichoke hearts
basil
bay leaf
broccoli

butter and brown butter
capers
cardamom
cardoons
carrots
celery
celery root
chard, Swiss
CHEESE, e.g., blue, cheddar, feta, Fontina, Gouda, **Gruyère**, PARMESAN, Saint-Nectaire, Swiss
chervil
chestnuts
chips, fried
chives
citrus, e.g., juice
coconut
CREAM
crème fraîche
croutons, e.g., whole grain
cumin
dill
eggs
fennel
French cuisine
GARLIC

ghee
ginger
grains, whole, e.g., quinoa
grapefruit
gratins, e.g., potato
greens, e.g., arugula, mâche
HAZELNUTS
herbs
Italian cuisine
kale
LEEKS
LEMON, e.g., juice
lentils
lime, e.g., juice
maple syrup
"mashed potatoes"
mint
mushrooms, e.g., chanterelle
mustard, e.g., Dijon
nutmeg
OIL, e.g., canola, grapeseed,
   hazelnut, nut, **OLIVE**, peanut,
   pecan, pumpkin seed, safflower,
   sunflower seed, truffle, walnut
olives, e.g., kalamata
ONIONS, e.g., spring, white
oranges
pancakes
PARSLEY
pastas, e.g., linguini, ravioli,
   spaghetti
pepper, e.g., black
pine nuts
polenta
POTATOES
purees, e.g., potato, root vegetable,
   turnip
radicchio
radishes
rice, wild
risotto
rosemary
sage
SALADS, e.g., green, spinach,
   wild rice
salt, e.g., sea
scallions
seeds, e.g., sesame, sunflower

shallots
SOUPS, e.g., Jerusalem artichoke,
   potato, vegetable
soy sauce
spelt
spinach
sprouts, e.g., sunflower
squash, winter, e.g., butternut
stews
stir-fries
STOCK, VEGETABLE
sugar, e.g., brown
sweet potatoes
tamari
tarragon
tarts

Flavor Affinities

Jerusalem artichoke + apple cider vinegar + hazelnuts
Jerusalem artichoke + carrots + fennel
Jerusalem artichoke + chard + feta cheese + garlic
Jerusalem artichoke + garlic + lemon + **rosemary**
Jerusalem artichoke + lemon + olive oil + parsley + **walnut oil/walnuts**
Jerusalem artichoke + lemon + *risotto* + thyme
Jerusalem artichoke + mushrooms + onions + spinach
Jerusalem artichoke + mustard + watercress
Jerusalem artichoke + nutmeg + parsley + potatoes
Jerusalem artichoke + olives + tomatoes

tempura
thyme
tomatoes, e.g., cherry, **and tomato**
   paste
turnips
vegetables, root
vermouth
vinaigrette
VINEGAR, e.g., apple cider,
   sherry, white wine
walnuts
WATERCRESS
wine, e.g., dry white
yogurt

● ARUGULA
(aka ROCKET)
[ah-ROO-guh-lah]
Season: spring – summer
Flavor: bitter/hot, with
earthy, pungent, and/or spicy
notes of horseradish, mustard,
nuts, and/or pepper, and a
chewy, lightly crunchy texture
(when raw)
Volume: moderate (younger
leaves) – loud (older)
Nutritional profile: 53% carbs /
25% protein / 22% fat
Calories: 10 per 1½-cup serving
(raw)
Protein: 1 gram
Techniques: braise, **raw**, sauté,
wilt

Tips: Rinse leaves thoroughly
before using. If older, stronger-
flavored arugula is used, combine with milder-flavored greens
and/or a more acidic dressing to
balance the flavor.

Botanical relatives: mustard,
radishes, watercress
Possible substitutes: Belgian
endive, dandelion greens,
escarole, spinach, watercress

apples
apricots
asparagus
avocado
basil
BEANS, e.g., black, cannellini,

fava, **green**, **white**
beets
bell peppers, e.g., roasted, green
  or red
carrots
cashews
CHEESE, e.g., blue, cheddar,
  FETA, **GOAT**, Grana Padano,
  manchego, Monterey Jack,
  mozzarella, **PARMESAN**,
  PECORINO, ricotta, ricotta
  salata, Roquefort, sheep's milk,
  vegan
chervil
chickpeas
chiles, e.g., chipotle, piquillo, and
  chili pepper flakes
cilantro
corn
croutons, e.g., whole grain
cucumbers
daikon
dates
eggplant
EGGS, e.g., hard-boiled, *omelets*
endive, e.g., Belgian
FENNEL and fennel seeds
FIGS
GARLIC
ginger
grains, whole, e.g., bulgur, millet
grapefruit
gratins
GREENS, milder and softer salad,
  e.g., Bibb
hazelnuts
honey
horseradish
Italian cuisine
jícama
leeks
LEMON, e.g., juice, zest
lentils
lettuce, e.g., romaine
lime
maple syrup
Mediterranean cuisine
melon, e.g., honeydew

mint
mushrooms, e.g., porcini,
  portobello, shiitake
mustard, e.g., Dijon
NUTS, e.g., macadamia
OIL, e.g., canola, hazelnut,
  lemon, **nut**, **OLIVE**, walnut
OLIVES, e.g., black, kalamata
onions, green
ONIONS, e.g., red

ORANGES
PASTA, e.g., linguini, penne, spaghetti
peaches
PEARS
peas
pecans
pesto
"PESTOS" (arugula + garlic +
  Parmesan + pine nuts)
pine nuts

Flavor Affinities
arugula + apples + cheddar cheese + mustard + **walnuts**
arugula + apples + lemon juice + **maple syrup** + olive oil
arugula + balsamic vinegar + endive + Parmesan cheese + radicchio
ARUGULA + BALSAMIC VINEGAR + PARMESAN CHEESE
arugula + balsamic vinegar + Parmesan cheese + red onions + *risotto* +
  tomatoes
ARUGULA + BEETS + FETA CHEESE (+ garlic)
ARUGULA + CHEESE (e.g., blue, goat, Parmesan, ricotta) + **FRUIT**
  (e.g., apricots, figs, grapefruit, peaches, pears — or sweet vegetables,
  e.g., beets, tomatoes) + **NUTS** (e.g., hazelnuts, walnuts)
arugula + cheese (e.g., Parmesan, pecorino) **+ garlic + olive oil** + pasta
  + pine nuts
arugula + chickpeas + red onions + spinach
arugula + chipotle chiles + orange + tomatoes
arugula + corn + tomatoes
arugula + cucumbers + feta cheese + quinoa + red onions + tahini +
  tomatoes
arugula + fennel + figs
arugula + fennel + grapefruit + *salad*
arugula + fennel + hazelnuts + orange + radicchio
arugula + fennel + lemon + pasta
arugula + feta cheese + figs
arugula + feta cheese + watermelon + white balsamic
arugula + garlic + lemon juice + olive oil + Parmesan cheese + pine nuts
arugula + garlic + pesto + portobello mushrooms + white beans
arugula + goat cheese + honey + lemon
arugula + goat cheese + onions
arugula + goat cheese + potatoes
arugula + horseradish + jícama + mustard + red onions
arugula + lemon + olives + red onions
arugula + lemon + pecorino cheese + summer squash
arugula + mint + pecorino cheese + pine nuts
arugula + mozzarella cheese + tomatoes
arugula + olives + oranges + Parmesan cheese
arugula + olives + tomatoes
arugula + pears + rosemary

pizza
pomegranate seeds
POTATOES, e.g., fingerling, new
pumpkin seeds
quinoa
radicchio
raisins
rice, e.g., brown
risotto
SALADS, e.g., arugula, endive,
  green, mesclun, radicchio,
  tricolore salad (arugula + endive
  + radicchio)
salt, sea
sandwiches, e.g., grilled cheese
scallions
shallots

SOUPS, *e.g., arugula, leek, potato*
sprouts, e.g., sunflower
spinach
SQUASH, e.g., summer, winter
  (e.g., butternut, delicata)
stir-fries
strawberries
sweet potatoes
TOMATOES and **sun-dried**
  tomatoes
VINEGAR, e.g., apple cider,
  balsamic, fig balsamic,
  raspberry, red wine, sherry,
  white balsamic, white wine
WALNUTS
watermelon

Dishes

Arugula Salad, served with Red Onion, Garbanzo Beans, Hearts of Palm, and Avocado, tossed in a Roasted Garlic Vinaigrette
— Café Blossom (New York City)

Market Arugula and Mushroom Salad with Celery, Parmigiano Reggiano, Sherry Vinaigrette
— Boulud Sud (New York City)

Arugula Ravioli with Tomato Confit and Braised Fennel, Piquillo Peppers, Tomato Emulsion
— DANIEL (New York City)

Arugula, Spinach, and Radicchio with Mountain Gorgonzola, Spiced Almonds, Honey-Fig Vinaigrette
— Nora (Washington, DC)

Sylvetta Arugula, Beet and Citrus Salad with Roast Beets, Blood Oranges, Toasted Hazelnuts, and Shaved Fennel with Muscatel Vinaigrette
— Portobello (Portland, OR)

Corn, Cilantro, and Arugula Salad with Yogurt Dressing
— Rancho La Puerta (Mexico)

ASAFOETIDA POWDER (aka HING)

Flavor: bitter, with pungent notes of garlic, onion, and/or shallots
Volume: moderate (cooked) – loud (uncooked)
Tips: Temper asafoetida powder by sautéing it in oil or ghee before adding to other ingredients. Use sparingly.
Possible substitutes: garlic powder, onion powder

beans, e.g., dried
butter or ghee
cabbage
cauliflower
chaat masala
chutneys
cumin
curries
Indian vegetarian cuisines
legumes
lentils, e.g., red, yellow
mushrooms
potatoes
rice, e.g., basmati
spinach
vegetables, assorted

"**Asafoetida powder** is a critical seasoning in Jain cuisine, as they are vegetarians who do not consume root vegetables (e.g., garlic, onions, potatoes). It gives dishes garlicky or oniony notes."
— HEMANT MATHUR, TULSI
(NEW YORK CITY)

ASIAN CUISINES (see CHINESE CUISINE, JAPANESE CUISINE, THAI CUISINE, VIETNAMESE CUISINE, etc.)

● ASPARAGUS

Season: spring
Flavor: bitter/sweet, with pungent notes of grass and/or nuts, and a crisp, tender texture
Volume: quiet – **moderate**
What it is: vegetable – green
Nutritional profile: 68% carbs / 27% protein / 5% fat
Calories: 30 per 1-cup serving (raw)
Protein: 3 grams
Techniques: blanch, boil, broil, deep-fry (e.g., tempura), grill, pan-roast, pickle, raw, roast (oiled, at 350 – 400°F for 5 – 20 minutes), sauté, simmer, steam (1 – 5 minutes, depending on thickness), stir-fry (1 – 3 minutes)

artichokes and artichoke hearts
arugula
avocado
basil
bay leaf
BEANS, e.g., **fava**, green, haricots verts, white
bell peppers, red, esp. roasted
bread crumbs
butter, e.g., brown, fresh
capers
CHEESE, e.g., Asiago, blue, Brie, Camembert, chèvre, **feta**, Fontina, goat, Gruyère, mild, Muenster, **PARMESAN**, pecorino, ricotta, Romano, Taleggio, soft, triple cream
chervil
chili paste and chili pepper flakes
chives
cilantro
corn
cream and crème fraîche
custards
dill
EGGS, e.g., fried, *frittatas*,

Dishes

Roasted Asparagus, Crispy Egg, and Mustard Vinaigrette
— ABC Kitchen (New York City)

Country Flatbread, Grilled Asparagus, Melted Leeks, Lightly Smoked Brie, Basil
— Green Zebra (Chicago)

Asparagus Pizza with Spring Onions, Knoll Farm Green Garlic, Feta, Asiago, Meyer Lemon, Pepper Flakes, and Italian Parsley
— Greens Restaurant (San Francisco)

Grilled Zuckerman's Farm Asparagus with Lemon Pistachio Gremolata, Regina Olive Oil, and Andante Dairy Fresh Goat Cheese
— Greens Restaurant (San Francisco)

Green Asparagus and Avocado Salad, Sorrel Dressing, and Sesame
— Jean-Georges (New York City)

Asparagi alla Milanese: Grilled Asparagus with Fried Egg, Charred Scallion, Piquillo Pepper, and Parmigiano-Reggiano
— Le Verdure (New York City)

Shaved Asparagus Salad with Fennel, Orange, Pickled Shallots, Lemon Vinaigrette
— Natural Selection (Portland, OR)

hard-boiled, *omelets*, POACHED, *quiches*, scrambled, soft-boiled
fennel and fennel seeds
French cuisine
GARLIC and green garlic
ginger
grains, whole, e.g., barley, couscous, farro, quinoa
greens, salad
hoisin sauce
honey
horseradish
LEEKS
*LEMON, e.g., juice, zest
lemon, Meyer, e.g., juice, zest
mayonnaise
mint
miso
MUSHROOMS, e.g., chanterelle, cremini, morel, oyster, porcini, shiitake, wild
mustard, e.g., Dijon
noodles, e.g., Japanese
NUTS, e.g., almonds, hazelnuts, pecans, pistachios, walnuts
OIL, e.g., canola, OLIVE, peanut

(esp. roasted), pumpkin seed, sesame, vegetable
olives, e.g., black
ONIONS, e.g., green, red, spring, yellow
orange, e.g., juice, zest
PARSLEY
PASTA, e.g., farfalle, fettuccine, pappardelle
peanuts and peanut sauce
peas, e.g., spring
pepper, e.g., black, white
pine nuts
pizza
polenta
potatoes, e.g., new
rice, e.g., basmati, wild
RISOTTO
rosemary
sage
salad dressing, e.g., vinaigrette
SALADS, e.g., asparagus, green, potato, vegetable
salt, e.g., kosher, sea
sauces, e.g., romesco, tahini
scallions

SESAME, e.g., oil, paste, seeds (black, white)
SHALLOTS
sorrel
soufflés
SOUPS
soy sauce
spinach
stir-fries
stock, e.g., vegetable
sushi, vegetarian
TARRAGON
tarts, e.g., asparagus, vegetable
thyme
tofu
tomatoes
vinaigrette
VINEGAR, e.g., balsamic, champagne, red wine, sherry, tarragon, white wine
watercress
wine, dry white
yogurt

Flavor Affinities

asparagus + avocado + lime + mint + olive oil
asparagus + basil + olives
asparagus + bell peppers + eggs + garlic + lemon juice + thyme
asparagus + chives + hard-boiled eggs + mustard + olive oil + vinegar
ASPARAGUS + CITRUS (e.g., lemon, orange) + garlic + HERBS (e.g., parsley, tarragon) + olive oil
asparagus + couscous + orange
asparagus + fava beans + mint
asparagus + garlic + ginger + scallions + sesame + sesame oil + soy sauce + vinegar
asparagus + ginger + hoisin sauce + sesame oil + soy sauce
asparagus + goat cheese + lemon + olive oil + pistachios
asparagus + hazelnuts + Parmesan cheese + parsley
ASPARAGUS + LEMON + PARMESAN (or pecorino) + *risotto*
asparagus + lemon + pecans + rice
asparagus + onions + orange
asparagus + pasta + pistachios
asparagus + peas + *risotto* + saffron
asparagus + sesame + tofu

"I love to grill asparagus simply and dress it with a Meyer lemon vinaigrette and serve it with some nice beets, goat cheese, and greens. We also make an asparagus pizza that people love. The asparagus is seasoned with olive oil, lemon zest, salt, and pepper and we let it sit to drain off some of its liquid so it won't make the dough too soggy. Then we add some raw spring onions and raw green garlic, a little Fontina, feta, or Asiago cheese, and chili flakes, and put it on the dough. People are happy. I love to make asparagus with spring peas and fava beans in pasta or in a farro risotto."
— ANNIE SOMERVILLE, GREENS RESTAURANT (SAN FRANCISCO)

• ASPARAGUS, WHITE

Season: spring

Flavor: slightly sweet, with notes of artichokes and/or hearts of palm

Volume: quiet – moderate (and quieter in flavor and texture than green asparagus)

What it is: asparagus that has been grown in the dark so that it doesn't turn green

Techniques: bake, blanch, boil, broil, pickle, sauté, simmer, stir-fry

Tips: The lower, woody stalks of white asparagus should be peeled. Note that white asparagus has fewer antioxidants than green.

asparagus, green
Austrian cuisine
basil
butter
cheese, e.g., Comte, manchego, Parmesan
chervil
chili pepper sauce
corn
cream
dill
eggs
French cuisine, esp. Alsatian
garlic
German cuisine
hazelnuts
herbs
Italian cuisine
LEMON, e.g., **juice**, zest

Dishes

Jumbo French White Asparagus and Roasted Green Asparagus with Pencil Asparagus, Basil Dressing, in a Comté Cloud
— Bouley (New York City)

White Asparagus and Garlic Velouté: Garlic and Tofu Mousse, Black Garlic Powder, Asparagus Ribbons
— Plume (Washington, DC)

mayonnaise
mushrooms, e.g., morel, porcini, portobello
mustard
oil, e.g., olive, truffle
onions, yellow
parsley
peas
pepper, e.g., black, white
pesto
potatoes, e.g., new
risottos
salads, e.g., bean, green
salt, e.g., sea
SAUCES, e.g., **HOLLANDAISE, mayonnaise, romesco**
shallots
SOUPS, e.g., white asparagus
Spanish cuisine
sugar
Swiss cuisine
tarragon
terrines
tofu
vinaigrette
vinegar, e.g., champagne, white wine
wine, e.g., Riesling

Flavor Affinities

white asparagus + butter + eggs

white asparagus + hazelnuts + Parmesan cheese + truffle oil

white asparagus + herbs + mayonnaise

white asparagus + lemon + mushrooms + parsley

AUSTRIAN CUISINE

asparagus, esp. white
cabbage
cauliflower
cinnamon
coffee
cream
cucumbers
dill
dumplings
goulash
marjoram
oil, pumpkin seed
paprika
parsley
pastries
pickles
potatoes
pumpkin
schnitzel
soups, e.g., dumpling, noodle
spinach
stews
strudels
wine, e.g., Grüner Veltliner

AUTUMN

Weather: typically cool

Techniques: bake, braise, glaze, roast

allspice (peak: autumn/winter)
almonds (peak: October)
apples (peak: September – November)
artichokes (peak: September – October)
basil (peak: September)
beans, e.g., green (peak: summer/ autumn)
beets
bell peppers (peak: September)
bok choy (peak: summer/ autumn)
broccoli
broccoli rabe (peak: July – December)

Brussels sprouts (peak: November – February)

cabbage, e.g., red, savoy (peak: autumn/winter)

cakes, esp. served warm

caramel

cardoons (peak: October)

cauliflower

celery

celery root (peak: October – November)

chard (peak: June – December)

chestnuts (peak: October – November)

chiles

cinnamon

coconut (peak: October – November)

corn (peak: September)

cranberries (peak: September – December)

crosnes

cucumbers (peak: September)

daikon (peak: autumn/winter)

dates (peak: autumn/winter)

eggplant (peak: August – November)

eggplant, Japanese

endive, Belgian

escarole (peak: summer/autumn)

fennel (peak: autumn/winter)

figs (peak: September – October)

frisée

garlic (peak: September)

goji berries (peak: summer/ autumn)

grains

grapes (peak: September)

greens, e.g., beet, bitter, turnip

guava (peak: summer/autumn)

heavier dishes

horseradish (peak: summer/ autumn)

huckleberries (peak: August – September)

kale (peak: November – January)

kohlrabi (peak: September – November)

lentils

lettuce, e.g., green leaf, red leaf (peak: summer/autumn)

lovage (peak: September – October)

lychees (peak: September – November)

miso, dark

mushrooms, e.g., chanterelle, chicken of the woods, hedgehog, hen of the woods, lobster, matsutake, **porcini**, shiitake, wild

nutmeg

nuts

okra

onions

oranges, blood (peak: November – February)

papaya (peak: summer/autumn)

parsnips

passion fruit (peak: November – February)

pears (peak: July – October)

pecans

persimmons (peak: October – January)

pistachios (peak: September)

plums (peak: July – October)

polenta

pomegranates (peak: October – December)

potatoes

pumpkin (peak: September – December)

quince (peak: October – December)

radicchio

rice, wild

rutabagas

sage

salsify (peak: November – January)

seeds, e.g., pumpkin, sunflower

slow-cooked dishes

snow peas (peak: spring; autumn)

spices, warming, e.g., black pepper, cayenne, cinnamon, chili powder, cloves, cumin, mustard powder

spinach

squash — e.g., acorn, buttercup, butternut, delicata, Hubbard, kabocha (peak: October – December)

stuffings

sweet potatoes (peak: November – January)

todok (peak: autumn/winter)

tomatoes (peak: September)

truffles, e.g., black, **white**

turnips (peak: **autumn**/winter)

vegetables, root

vinegar, red wine

walnuts

watercress (peaks: spring, autumn)

yams (peak: November)

● AVOCADO

Season: spring – summer

Flavor: buttery in flavor and texture, with fruity and nutty notes

Volume: quiet

What it is: technically a fruit

Nutritional profile: 77% fat / 19% carbs / 4% protein

Calories: 325 per avocado (raw)

Protein: 4 grams

Techniques: Always serve raw, as cooking makes avocados taste bitter. Mash into guacamole, hummus, or sandwich spreads, or slice for salads.

Tips: Haas avocados are the smaller, dark green, firm variety (more flavorful, and better for guacamole), while Florida avocados are larger and brighter green (and they can sometimes be watery). Use avocados to add richness to a dish, whether a dip or spread or even a dessert.

Botanical relatives: bay leaf, cinnamon

artichoke, Jerusalem

arugula

asparagus

basil

beans, e.g., **black**, fava

beets

bell peppers, red

breads, e.g., sprouted grain, whole wheat

bulgur

burritos

buttermilk

cabbage

California cuisine

carrots

cashews

cayenne

celery

Central American cuisine

cheese, e.g., feta, Monterey Jack, queso añejo

chickpeas

CHILES, e.g., chipotle, jalapeño, poblano, serrano; chili pepper flakes, and **chili powder**

chili, vegetarian

chives

CILANTRO

citrus

coffee

coriander

corn

couscous

CUCUMBERS

cumin

desserts, e.g., chocolate mousses

dips

eggs, e.g., *huevos rancheros, omelets*

endive

fajitas

fennel

galangal

garlic

ginger

GRAPEFRUIT

GREENS, e.g., bitter, collard, dandelion, mesclun, salad

*GUACAMOLE
ice cream
jícama
kumquats
leeks
LEMON, e.g., juice, zest
lemongrass
lemon verbena
lettuces, e.g., romaine
LIME, e.g., juice, zest
mangoes
mayonnaise
melon
milk
mint
miso
mushrooms, e.g., shiitake
mustard, Dijon
nachos
nori
OIL, e.g., avocado, canola, **olive**, sunflower
olives and olive paste
onions, e.g., green, **red**, spring, white
oranges, esp. blood oranges, e.g., juice
oregano
papaya
paprika
parsley
pears
pecans
pepper, black
persimmons
pineapple
pistachios
pomegranates
pomelo
pumpkin seeds
quesadillas
quinoa
radishes
relishes
rice, e.g., brown, red
rum

SALAD DRESSINGS, *e.g., Green Goddess*

SALADS

SALSAS

salt, *e.g., kosher, sea*

sandwiches, e.g., cheese

sauces

scallions

sesame, *e.g., seeds*

shallots

shiso

smoothies

sorbets

sorrel

SOUPS, e.g., avocado, cold, tortilla

sour cream

spinach

spreads

sprouts, *e.g., alfalfa, mung bean*

stock, vegetable

stuffed avocados

sushi, vegetarian, e.g., hand rolls, nori rolls

tacos

tempeh

tofu

tomatillos

TOMATOES

veggie burgers, e.g., as a topping

vinegar, esp. balsamic, fruit, rice, wine

walnuts

wasabi

YOGURT

zucchini

"**Avocados** are key vegetables for raw foodists. They're meaty and creamy at the same time, and versatile enough to be used in salad dressings, soups, and wraps."
— AMI BEACH, G-ZEN (BRANFORD, CT)

Flavor Affinities

avocado + almond butter + banana + cocoa powder + *mousse*

avocado + asparagus + lime + mint + olive oil

avocado + basil + lime

avocado + basil + onions + tomatoes

avocado + black beans + tomatoes

avocado + celery + **chiles** + **CILANTRO** + cumin + garlic + **LIME** + spinach

AVOCADO + **chiles** + **CILANTRO** + **LIME** + onions

avocado + chiles + citrus + ginger + shiso

avocado + chili powder + cilantro + jícama + onions + orange juice

AVOCADO + **CILANTRO** + **CUCUMBER** + jalapeño + **LIME** + mint + yogurt

AVOCADO + **CILANTRO** + garlic + **LIME** + red onions + tomatoes

avocado + citrus (e.g., lime, orange) + jícama

AVOCADO + **CUCUMBER** + green onions + **LIME** + yogurt

avocado + **cucumber** + mint + yogurt

avocado + cucumber + nori + rice

avocado + endive + grapefruit

avocado + **fennel** + **citrus** (e.g., grapefruit, orange)

avocado + grapefruit + papaya

avocado + grapefruit + pistachios + pomegranates

avocado + honey + yogurt

avocado + lemon + shallots

avocado + lime + wasabi

avocado + olives + tomatoes

avocado + oranges + red onions

Dishes

Grilled Brokaw Avocado and Quinoa Salad with Pumpkin Seeds, Chilies, Watermelon Radish, Cilantro, and Grilled Serrano Salsa Verde
— Greens Restaurant (San Fancisco)

Hass Avocado Sorbet: "Ajo Blanco," Lemon Confit, Sicilian Pistachios, and Nasturtium Capers
— Per Se (New York City)

Avocado Sorbet in Papaya with Aged Balsamic Vinegar
— Rancho La Puerta (Mexico)

Tarte au Chocolat Vegetalienne et Sans Gluten: Vegan Chocolate Tart, Dark Callebaut Chocolate Avocado "Ganache" with Rice, Almond, and Raisin Crust
— Table Verte (New York City)

"I love **avocados** and eat one every day. In one of my favorite salads, the richness of avocado is balanced by the acidity of tomato and the sweetness of watermelon. And avocados are versatile; as a pastry chef, I even use them in my chocolate mousse."

— FERNANDA CAPOBIANCO, VEGAN DIVAS (NEW YORK CITY)

"Mashed **avocado** on bread is like the PB&J of Jamaica. After my friends and I played soccer, we'd raid the cupboard for bread and climb the tree in my backyard for 'pears,' as we call them there, to eat on the bread, maybe with just a little salt. Their flavor is so fresh and bright."

— SHAWAIN WHYTE, CAFÉ BLOSSOM (NEW YORK CITY)

● BAMBOO SHOOTS

Season: spring – summer
Flavor: bitter (raw) / sweet (cooked); with woody notes of artichokes, corn, nuts, and/or water chestnuts, and a crisp yet tender, juicy, pineapple-like texture
Volume: quiet
Nutritional profile: 54% carbs / 31% protein / 15% fat
Calories: 15 per 1-cup serving (boiled, sliced)
Protein: 2 grams
Techniques: boil (about 60 minutes), braise, pickle, sauté, steam, stew, stir-fry

Dishes

Bamboo Shoot Chazuke: Bamboo Shoots, Shiitake, Enoki Mushrooms, Sansho Peppercorn

— Kajitsu (New York City)

Tips: Rinse well in cold water before using. Look for pre-cooked, vaccum-sealed bamboo shoots, or whole (not sliced) canned shoots.

Asian cuisines
basil
beans, e.g., long
bell peppers
bok choy
cabbage, e.g., Chinese, napa
carrots
chiles, e.g., red
Chinese cuisine
cilantro
curries, e.g., green, red, Thai
daikon
dashi
dill
eggs
garlic
ginger
jícama
kombu
lime
lotus root
mirin
miso
mushrooms, e.g., enoki, oyster, portobello, shiitake, white noodles, Asian, e.g., shirataki
oil, e.g., peanut, sesame, vegetable
onions
pineapple
pumpkin seeds
rice
sake
salads, e.g., Asian, green

---

scallions
sea vegetables, e.g., hiziki, **wakame**
seitan
shallots
slaws
snow peas
soups, e.g., hot-and-sour, mushroom, noodle, vegetable
soy sauce
spinach
stews
stir-fries
sugar snap peas
tamari
tempeh
Thai cuisine
tofu
Vietnamese cuisine
vinegar, rice
wasabi
water chestnuts
wine, rice
zucchini

Flavor Affinities
bamboo shoots + basil + bell peppers + coconut milk + red chili paste
bamboo shoots + chiles + cilantro + lime
bamboo shoots + dashi + mirin + rice + soy sauce
bamboo shoots + rice + sake + scallions + shirataki noodles + **soy sauce** + tofu
bamboo shoots + soy sauce + wasabi

● BANANAS

Flavor: sweet, with astringent notes, and a firm, creamy texture
Volume: quiet
What it is: fruit
Nutritional profile: 93% carbs / 4% protein / 3% fat
Calories: 105 per medium banana (raw)

Protein: I gram

Techniques: bake, broil, caramelize, deep-fry, freeze (e.g., for smoothies), grill, poach, puree, raw, sauté

Tips: Freeze before adding to smoothies to eliminate or reduce the need for ice. Puree frozen bananas — or put through a Champion juicer (using the "Blank" instead of the "Screen"), and they will come out the texture of soft-serve ice cream to enjoy as-is or with toppings such as maple syrup and nuts.

agave nectar
apples and apple juice
apricots, e.g., dried, fresh
Armagnac
baked goods, e.g., breads, cakes, cookies, muffins, pies, quickbreads
berries, e.g., blackberries, **blueberries**, raspberries, **strawberries**
bourbon
bread and toast, whole grain
butter
Calvados
caramel
cardamom
cereals, breakfast
cherries
cheese, e.g., cream, ricotta
chiles
chocolate, e.g., dark, white
cilantro
cinnamon

COCONUT and COCONUT MILK
cognac
CREAM and ICE CREAM
cumin
curry powder
dates
figs
flax seeds
French toast
fruit, other tropical
ginger
granola
honey
Kirsch
lassis
lemon
lime
malt
mangoes, e.g., green, ripe
MAPLE SYRUP
nectarines
nutmeg
NUTS and NUT BUTTERS, e.g., **ALMONDS**, cashews, macadamia, **peanut**, pecans
oats and oatmeal
oil, e.g., olive
onions
oranges
pancakes
papaya
passion fruit
peaches
pears
PINEAPPLE
raisins
RUM
salads, fruit

sesame seeds, e.g., black, white
SMOOTHIES
sugar, e.g., brown
sunflower seeds
sweet potatoes
tamarind
vanilla
walnuts
yogurt
yuzu

Flavor Affinities
bananas + almond milk + nutmeg + vanilla
bananas + almonds + oatmeal
bananas + apple juice + cinnamon
bananas + apricots + yogurt
bananas + blueberries + yogurt
bananas + cashews + pineapple
bananas + chocolate + peanuts
bananas + cinnamon + orange
bananas + citrus (e.g., lime, orange) **+ coconut**
bananas + coconut + pineapple + sesame
bananas + dates + flax seeds
bananas + honey + peanut butter
bananas + maple syrup + oatmeal
bananas + oranges + papaya
bananas + peaches + raspberries
bananas + pineapple + sesame seeds

Dishes

Banana Walnut Bread with Maple Cinnamon Butter
— Greens Restaurant (San Francisco)

Banana Caramel Cake with Toasted Almonds and Milk Chocolate Ice Cream
— Greens Restaurant (San Francisco)

• BARLEY (e.g., HULLED)

Flavor: sweet, with astringent notes of nuts, and chewy in texture
Volume: quiet – **moderate**
What it is: whole grain
Nutritional profile: 82% carbs / 13% protein / 5% fat
Gluten-free: no
Calories: 100 per 1-ounce serving (yields about ½ cup)
Protein: 3 grams
Techniques: boil, pressure-cook, simmer, steam, toast

Timing: Soak overnight before cooking. Cook presoaked whole barley about 35 – 40 minutes or longer, covered. If not presoaked, cook about 75 minutes, until tender. (Note: Quick-cooking barley takes only 10 – 15 minutes.)

Ratio: 1:3 (1 part barley to 3 parts cooking liquid)

Tips: For a deeper flavor, toast barley before soaking and cooking. For maximum nutrition, opt for hulled barley (which has an extra layer of fiber-rich bran), versus pearl barley (which has its outer husk removed). Try barley flakes instead of rolled oats in breakfast cereals.

Botanical relatives: corn, kamut, rye, spelt, triticale

Dishes

Warm Barley Cereal with Natural Honey, Flaxseed, Orange Segments, Fresh Figs, Almond Milk, and Organic Almonds
— Mayflower Inn & Spa (Washington, CT)

Flavor Affinities

barley + almonds + cauliflower
barley + arugula + orange
barley + basil + corn + garlic + *risotto*
barley + beets + fennel
barley + beets + lemon
barley + butternut squash + portobello mushrooms
barley + carrots + herbs + mushrooms
barley + cashews + cilantro + mint
barley + cashews + parsley + *salads*
barley + cinnamon + milk + raisins
barley + dill + lentils + mushrooms
barley + feta cheese + *risotto*
barley + feta cheese + shiitake mushrooms + *salads*
barley + garlic + marjoram + white wine + wild mushrooms
barley + honey + milk
barley + kale + tomato + *soups*
barley + mint + peas
barley + parsley + white beans

agave nectar
almonds
apples
arugula
avocados
basil
bay leaf
beans, e.g., kidney, lima, white
beer
beets
bell peppers, e.g., red, yellow
black-eyed peas
breads
broccoli de Cicco and broccoli rabe
burdock
buttermilk
cabbage
capers
cardamom

CARROTS
cashews
casseroles
cauliflower
celery
cereals, hot breakfast
cheese, e.g., feta, goat, pecorino
chiles, e.g., jalapeños
chives
cilantro
cinnamon
coconut
corn
currants
curry powder
dill
eggplant
fennel
figs
fruits, dried
GARLIC
gratins
greens
herbs, fresh
honey
kale
leeks
LEMON, e.g., juice, zest
lentils
loaves
maple syrup
marjoram
milk, dairy or non-dairy, e.g., rice or soy
mint
miso
*MUSHROOMS, esp. cremini, porcini, portobello, shiitake, trumpet, wild
nutmeg
OIL, e.g., grapeseed, **OLIVE**, **sesame**, sunflower
olives, e.g., black, green, kalamata
ONIONS, e.g., spring, white
oranges
oregano
"paellas"
PARSLEY

peas
pepper, black
pilafs
pomegranates and pomegranate
   molasses
puddings
quinoa
raisins
rice, e.g., brown
"RISOTTOS"
sage
SALADS, e.g., barley, grain, green
salt, sea
scallions
seeds, e.g., sesame, sunflower
sesame, e.g., oil, seeds
shallots
SOUPS, e.g., mushroom
sour cream
soy sauce
spelt
spinach
squash, e.g., butternut
stews
stir-fries
stock, e.g., mushroom or
   vegetable
stuffed peppers
stuffings
sweet potatoes
tamari
tarragon
thyme
tomatoes and sun-dried tomatoes
vegetables, root
veggie burgers
vinegar, e.g., umeboshi
yogurt
zucchini

BARLEY MALT

Flavor: sweet to very sweet, with
notes of caramel, honey, malt,
and/or molasses, and the thick,
sticky, syrupy texture of molasses
(syrup)
Volume: quiet (powder) –
moderate/loud (syrup)

What it is: sweetener

Tips: Barley malt powder can
be substituted for sugar. Barley
malt syrup can be substituted
for brown rice syrup, honey,
or molasses. Select organic
100-percent barley malt syrup.

baked goods, e.g., breads, cakes,
   cookies, gingerbread, muffins
beans, e.g., baked
cereals, hot breakfast
desserts, e.g., custards
macrobiotic cuisine
maple syrup
nuts
pancakes
popcorn and caramel corn
pumpkin
squash, e.g., winter
sweet potatoes

"**Barley malt syrup** is a great
liquid sweetener I'll use to
sweeten desserts like custards,
or when making candied nuts.
Its flavor is distinctive — it's
already caramelized, almost like
a great Madeira or sherry. I use
it in a dessert based on beer and
pretzels, where it plays against
the maltiness of the beer."
— KATE JACOBY, VEDGE (PHILADELPHIA)

● BARLEY, PEARL (or PEARLED)

Flavor: slightly sweet, with notes
of nuts, and a soft, chewy texture
Volume: quiet – moderate
What it is: grain (*not* whole)
Nutritional profile: 90% carbs
/ 7% protein / 3% fat
Calories: 195 per 1-cup serving
(cooked)
Protein: 4 grams
Techniques: boil, simmer
Timing: Cook about 30 – 75
minutes, until tender.

Ratio: 1: 2 ½ – 3 ½ (1 cup barley
to 2 ½ – 3 ½ cups cooking liquid)

Tip: Opt for whole-grain barley
(which is higher in fiber;
see BARLEY) when you have the
extra time to cook it; otherwise,
faster-cooking pearl barley
(which doesn't require presoaking) will do.

allspice
asparagus
basil
beans, e.g., black, kidney, white
beets
bell peppers, e.g., green
black-eyed peas
butter
cabbage
carrots
casseroles
celery
cereal, hot breakfast
chard, Swiss
cheese, e.g., blue, cheddar,
   dry Jack, **feta**, goat, Gruyère,
   Parmesan, pecorino, provolone
chili pepper flakes
chili, vegetarian
cinnamon
corn
cream
crème fraîche
cucumbers
cumin
currants
dill
fennel
garlic
grains, other
gratins
hazelnuts
herbs, fresh
honey
kale
leeks
lemon, e.g., juice, zest
lentils, e.g., red

lime, e.g., juice, zest
loaves, e.g., mock "meatloaf"
milk
mint
MUSHROOMS, e.g., button,
    oyster, porchini, white, wild
nutmeg
nuts, e.g., pecans
OIL, e.g., hazelnut, olive,
    sunflower, walnut
ONIONS, e.g., red, white, yellow
orange
parsley, flat-leaf
peas, e.g., split
pepper, black
pilafs
pistachios
porridges
potatoes
raisins
"RISOTTOS"
rosemary
saffron
sage
salads
salsify
salt
shallots
*SOUPS, e.g., barley, lentil, Scotch
    broth, vegetable*
squash, butternut
stews, e.g., vegetable
stock, e.g., mushroom, vegetable
stuffed vegetables, e.g., peppers,
tomatoes
stuffings
tarragon
thyme
tomatoes and tomato paste
turnips
vanilla
vinegar, e.g., balsamic

Dishes

Pearl Barley and Chanterelle Mushroom "Potage": Crème Fraîche "Royale," Brioche
Croûtons, and Celery Branch "Ribbons"
— Per Se (New York City)

walnuts
watercress
wine, dry red or white
zucchini

Flavor Affinities

pearl barley + basil + tomatoes +
    zucchini
pearl barley + beets + fennel +
    lemon
pearl barley + blue cheese +
    mushrooms
pearl barley + chard + fennel +
    soup
pearl barley + cucumbers +
    feta cheese + red onions
pearl barley + garlic +
    mushrooms + onions
pearl barley + nuts + raisins
pearl barley + Swiss chard +
    white beans

● BASIL

Season: summer
Flavor: slightly sweet, fragrant,
with pungent notes of anise,
cinnamon, citrus, cloves, licorice,
mint, and/or pepper
Volume: moderate – loud

Tips: Add this herb just before
serving. Use to add a note of
freshness to a dish.

Botanical relatives: lavender,
marjoram, mint, oregano,
rosemary, sage, summer savory,
thyme

aioli
almonds
artichoke hearts
artichokes
asparagus

avocados
beans, e.g., fava, green
beans, summer
beans, white, e.g., cannellini
bell peppers, e.g., red, roasted,
    yellow
beverages, e.g., cocktails, lemonade
breads
broccoli rabe
bulgur
capers
cauliflower
CHEESE, e.g., feta, fresh white,
    goat, **mozzarella**, Parmesan,
    pecorino, ricotta
chickpeas
cilantro
corn
couscous
Cuban cuisine
cucumbers
curries
EGGPLANT
eggs, e.g., *frittatas, omelets*
French cuisine
galangal
***GARLIC**
gazpacho
ginger
Greek cuisine
greens, e.g., salad
hazelnuts
Indian cuisine
ITALIAN CUISINE
jícama
kale
leeks
lemon
lemongrass
marjoram
Mediterranean cuisines
Mexican cuisine
millet
mint
mushrooms, e.g., portobello
nectarines
noodles, Asian rice, e.g., *pad thai*
nuts

OIL, OLIVE

olives
onions, e.g., yellow
oregano
parsley
PASTAS, e.g., cannelloni,
   *fettuccine, lasagna, penne,
spaghetti*
peaches
peanuts
peas
pepper, e.g., black, white
*PESTOS
PINE NUTS
pistachios
pistou
PIZZAS
polenta
potatoes, esp. new
quinoa
ratatouille
rice
risotto
rosemary
sage
salad dressings
salads, e.g., *pasta*
salt, e.g., kosher, sea
sandwiches, e.g., panini
sauces, e.g., *pasta, tomato*
soups, e.g., *Asian, bean, chowder, corn,
   minestrone, tomato, vegetable*
Southeast Asian cuisines
spinach
squash, e.g., *spaghetti, summer*
stews
sweet potatoes
Thai cuisine, e.g., green curries
tofu
**TOMATOES and TOMATO
   SAUCE*
tomatoes, sun-dried
vegetables, summer, e.g., corn,
   tomatoes, zucchini
vinegar, e.g., balsamic, sherry
walnuts
watermelon
ZUCCHINI

Flavor Affinities

basil + asparagus + peas + risotto
   + saffron
basil + capers + tomatoes
basil + chiles + cilantro + garlic +
   lime + mint
basil + chiles + olive oil + pine
   nuts + sun-dried tomatoes
basil + corn + tomatoes
basil + cucumbers + mint + peas
**BASIL + GARLIC + OLIVE OIL +
   Parmesan cheese + pine nuts**
**BASIL + GARLIC + OLIVE OIL +
   TOMATOES**
basil + lemon + olive oil
basil + mint + pistachios
**basil + mozzarella cheese +
   olive oil**
basil + mushrooms + tomatoes
basil + tomatoes + white beans

BASIL, THAI

Flavor: bitter/**sweet**; aromatic,
with pungent/spicy notes of
anise, basil, cinnamon, flowers,
licorice, and/or mint
Volume: moderate – loud
Tips: Add this herb to dishes
just before serving. Do *not*
substitute for Italian basil.

Asian cuisines
bamboo shoots
cashews
chiles and chili pepper paste
   (e.g., Thai)
cilantro
coconut milk
corn
*curries, e.g., green, Indian red, **Thai***
eggplant
garlic
ginger
Kaffir lime leaves
lemongrass
lime
mango
marinades

mint
mushrooms, e.g., shiitake
noodles, e.g., Asian
oil, e.g., grape seed, pumpkin
   seed
papaya, green
peanuts
salads
scallions
shallots
soups, e.g., *Asian, coconut milk–
   based, vegetarian pho*
Southeast Asian cuisines
soy sauce
stir-fries
stock, vegetable
sugar, e.g., maple, palm
Thai cuisine
tofu
Vietnamese cuisine
zucchini

Flavor Affinities

Thai basil + chiles + Kaffir lime
   leaves
Thai basil + cilantro + mint
Thai basil + coconut milk +
   peanuts

● BAY LEAF

Flavor: bitter/sweet; aromatic,
with pungent/spicy notes of
cloves, flowers, grass, mint,
nutmeg, pepper, pine and/or
wood
Volume: quiet (if used in
moderation) – loud
Techniques: braise, simmer,
stew
Tips: Use at the start of the
cooking process, and remove
before serving. Use judiciously,
to avoid too-strong bitterness.
Botanical relatives: avocado,
cinnamon

(North) African cuisines
apples, baked

beans — in general, e.g., broad, dried, white
bell peppers
black-eyed peas
bouquets garnis
chili, vegetarian
custards
French cuisine
garlic
grains, whole
Greek cuisine
Indian cuisine
lentils
marinades
***Mediterranean cuisine*s**
milk and cream
Moroccan cuisine
onions
parsley
pâtés
peas, split
pickles
plums, dried
potatoes
puddings, e.g., rice
pumpkin
rice, e.g., basmati
risottos
salad dressings
sauces, *e.g., white*
SOUPS, e.g., bean
squash, winter, e.g., acorn
STEWS
stocks, *vegetable*
thyme
tomatoes and tomato sauce
vegetables

• BEANS — IN GENERAL (or MIXED)

What they are: legumes
Techniques: Always cook *thoroughly.*
Timing: Most beans require anywhere from a half-hour to two hours to cook, depending on the type of bean and length of presoaking.

Tips: Soak dried beans overnight (or for 8 – 10 hours) before cooking. Drain and rinse the beans before cooking in fresh water for about 1 – 3 hours, depending on the type of bean. While you can add alliums (e.g., garlic, onions) or herbs (e.g., parsley, thyme) during the cooking process, do *not* add acid (e.g., lemon, tomato, vinegar) during cooking; acids may interfere with the cooking process. If you don't buy salt-free canned beans, rinse before using. Dried beans will typically yield three times their quantity in cooked beans (i.e., $1/3$ cup dried beans = 1 cup cooked beans). Certain compatible seasonings also aid in the digestion of beans, e.g., asafoetida, cumin, fennel, ginger, kombu, savory.

Botanical relatives: lentils, peanuts, peas
Brands: Eden

avocado
basil
bay leaf
bell peppers
butter
carrots
cassoulet, vegetarian
cayenne
celery

cheese, e.g., Jack
chervil
chiles
chili powder
cilantro
cloves
coriander
cumin
dips
epazote
fennel
GARLIC
ginger
grains, whole
greens
KOMBU
lemon, e.g., juice
lime, e.g., juice
marjoram
mayonnaise
mint
oil, olive
onions
oregano
paprika and smoked paprika
PARSLEY
pastas
pesto
quesadillas
*****RICE**, e.g., brown
rosemary
saffron
sage
salads, e.g., bean, green
salsa, tomato
salt, e.g., sea

Dishes

Three-Bean Chili: Piquant Chili made with Homemade Seitan, Kidney, and Pinto Beans and Lentils; slowly simmered with Sun-Dried Tomatoes and a blend of Chiles; topped with Lime-Jalapeño Tofu Sour Cream
— Angelica Kitchen (New York City)

Vegetarian Cassoulet made with White Beans, Cauliflower, Brussels Sprouts, Pearl Onions, Swiss Chard, and Cremini Mushrooms, finished with Arethusa Farm Cream and an Herbed Bread Crumb Crust
— Arethusa Al Tavolo (Bantam, Connecticut)

• BEANS, ADZUKI (aka ADUKI or AZUKI BEANS)

[ah-ZOO-kee]

Flavor: sweet/sour, with earthy notes of chestnuts and/or nuts

Volume: moderate – **loud**

What they are: small red Japanese legumes

Nutritional profile: 79% carbs / 20% protein / 1% fat

Calories: 295 per 1-cup serving (boiled)

Protein: 17 grams

Techniques: bake, boil, mash, simmer, stew, stir-fry

Timing: Presoak beans for at least an hour or two (or ideally overnight); bring to a boil, and then simmer 30 – **90 minutes**, until soft.

almonds
apples
arame
Asian cuisines
barley
basil
bay leaf
bean cakes
beans, other, e.g., mung, red
bell peppers, e.g., green
carrots
casseroles
celery
chiles, e.g., Anaheim, fresno, jalapeño, poblano; chili pepper flakes, and chili powder
chili, vegetarian

Chinese cuisine
cilantro
cinnamon
cloves
cocoa
coconut and coconut milk
corn, e.g., summer sweet
cumin
DESSERTS, esp. Japanese, e.g., yōkan
dips, e.g., bean
garlic
GINGER
grains, e.g., barley, millet, quinoa
honey
ice cream
JAPANESE CUISINE
kale
kombu
lemon, e.g., juice
lime
macrobiotic cuisine
maple syrup
mirin
miso
mochi
mushrooms, e.g., oyster, shiitake
mustard
noodles, e.g., Asian
nori
oil, e.g., canola, **olive, sesame**
onions, e.g., green, red
orange, e.g., zest
oregano
pancakes
parsley
pepper, e.g., black, white
pilafs

*SAVORY
soups*
thyme
tomatoes
tortillas, whole wheat
turmeric
vinegar, e.g., rice

"We only cook our **beans** in clay pots, called olla de barro, because they taste so much better cooked that way. When we first experimented, we soaked the beans overnight, then cooked half in a traditional metal pot and the other half in a clay pot [which transmits heat more gently, allowing flavors to develop more slowly but with greater depth]. You could absolutely taste the difference."

— SELMA MIRIAM, BLOODROOT (BRIDGEPORT, CT)

Dishes

Heirloom BLT: Heirloom Tomatoes, Adzuki Bacon, Bibb Lettuce, Basil Mayo, Toasted Sourdough
— The Butcher's Daughter (New York City)

Adzuki Bean Vegetable Burger made with Cabbage, Carrots, Celery, Oats, Onions, and Rice (Brown, Red, Wild)
— Flourish Baking Company (Scarsdale, NY)

porridges
posole
pumpkin
raisins
red bean paste
RICE, e.g., basmati, **brown**, sticky, sushi, white short-grain, wild
SALADS, e.g., bean, grain, green
salt, sea
sauces
scallions
SESAME, e.g., oil, seeds
shallots
SOUPS, e.g., vegetable
soy sauce
spinach
spreads
squash, summer, e.g., zucchini
SQUASH, WINTER, e.g., acorn, buttercup, butternut, kabocha
stews, e.g., bean, vegetable
stir-fries
stock, vegetable
sugar
sweets, Japanese
tamari
teas
tempeh, e.g., smoked
Thai cuisine
thyme
tomatillos
tomatoes and tomato puree
turmeric
veggie burgers
vinegar, e.g., apple cider, rice, umeboshi
wakame

Flavor Affinities
adzuki beans + brown rice + garlic + **ginger** + **scallions** + **sesame oil** + tamari
adzuki beans + carrots + ginger + sea salt
adzuki beans + cilantro + coconut milk + lime
adzuki beans + coriander + cumin + ginger

adzuki beans + ginger + sesame oil and seeds + rice
adzuki beans + miso + scallions + shiitake mushrooms
adzuki beans + sesame seeds + sushi rice
adzuki beans + soy sauce or tamari + winter squash

● BEANS, ANASAZI

Flavor: slightly sweet, with a firm, somewhat mealy texture
Volume: quiet
What they are: legumes
Calories: 150 per ¼-cup serving (dry)
Protein: 7 grams
Techniques: boil, braise, pressure-cook (20+ minutes), simmer (for 60 – 90 minutes, until tender)
Ratio: 1:3 (1 cup beans to 3 cups cooking liquid)

Tip: Presoak beans for several hours, or overnight, before cooking.

Botanical relatives (and possible substitutes):
pinto beans

avocado
baked beans
beans, other, e.g., black
bell peppers
bread crumbs
carrots
casseroles
cayenne
celery
cheese
chiles, e.g., Anaheim, ancho, chipotle, jalapeno
chili powder
chili, vegetarian
cilantro
cinnamon
cloves
coriander

corn
cumin
dips, e.g., bean
epazote
garlic
kombu
Latin American cuisines
Mexican cuisine
molasses
Native American cuisine
oil, e.g., olive
onions, e.g., green, yellow
oregano
parsley
potatoes
pumpkin
quinoa
refried beans
salsas
soups, e.g. bean, vegetable
sour cream
Southwestern (U.S.) cuisine
stews
stock, vegetable
tomatoes, e.g., fresh, sun-dried
veggie burgers
vinegar, e.g., red wine

Flavor Affinities
anasazi beans + carrots + celery + onions + pumpkin + *stews*
anasazi beans + garlic + tomatoes

● BEANS, BLACK (aka TURTLE BEANS)

Flavor: slightly sweet, with earthy and meaty notes, and a rich, creamy yet dense, firm texture
Volume: moderate
Nutritional profile: 74% carbs / 23% protein / 2% fat
Calories: 225 per 1-cup serving (cooked)
Protein: 15 grams
Techniques: simmer
Timing: Presoak beans overnight (or 6 – 8 hours); boil about 1 – 2 hours, until tender.

Dishes

Modern Black Beans with Baja Olive Oil, Roasted Garlic, Crispy Onions, Queso Añejo, Cilantro
— Frontera Grill (Chicago)

Traditional Black Beans: Epazote, Manteca, Sweet Plantains, Queso Fresco
— Frontera Grill (Chicago)

Black Bean Pozole with Heirloom Yellow Hominy, Shaved Radish, Cilantro, Cotija Cheese
— Green Zebra (Chicago)

Black Bean Chili with Cheddar, Crème Fraîche and Cilantro
— Greens Restaurant (San Francisco)

Pan-Seared Spicy Organic Black Bean Dumplings with Miso-Mango Sauce
— Josie's (New York City)

Black Bean Torte: Whole Wheat Tortilla, Caramelized Plantains, Smoky Black Bean Puree, Pumpkin-Habanero Salsa Verde, Cashew Sour Cream, Pomegranate Salsa
— Millennium (San Francisco)

avocado
basil
bay leaf
BELL PEPPERS, e.g., green, red, yellow, esp. roasted
black bean cakes
Brazilian cuisine
BURRITOS
CARIBBEAN CUISINE
carrots
casseroles
cayenne
celery
Central American cuisines
cheese, e.g., cheddar (esp. white), cotija, goat, Monterey Jack
chickpeas
chilaquiles
CHILES, e.g., Anaheim, ancho, CHIPOTLE, jalapeño, poblano, serrano
chili pepper flakes, **chili powder,** chili pepper sauce
CHILI, VEGETARIAN
chives
chocolate
CILANTRO
citrus

coffee
coriander
CORN
cucumbers
Cuban cuisine
CUMIN
dips
eggs, e.g., *huevos rancheros*
empanadas
enchiladas
epazote
GARLIC
ginger
grains
Jamaican cuisine
jícama
kombu
Latin American cuisines
lemon, e.g., juice
LIME, e.g., juice, zest
liquid smoke
MANGOES
Mexican cuisine
mint
miso
mushrooms
mustard
nachos

oil, e.g., **olive**, peanut, sesame, vegetable
olives, e.g., green
ONIONS, e.g., green, **red**, white, yellow
ORANGE
OREGANO, e.g., Mexican
paprika
parsley
pâtés
pepper, e.g., black, white
plantains
potatoes
Puerto Rican cuisine
purees
quesadillas
quinoa
refried beans
RICE, e.g., brown
rosemary
SALADS, e.g., bean, corn, taco
salsa
SALT, e.g., kosher, sea
savory
scallions
sherry, dry
SOUPS, e.g., black bean
sour cream
South American cuisines
Southwestern (U.S.) cuisine
soy sauce
spinach
spreads
squash, e.g., acorn, spaghetti, winter
stews
stock, vegetable
sweet potatoes
tacos
tempeh
Tex-Mex cuisine
thyme
TOMATOES and tomato paste
tortillas, e.g., whole wheat
tostadas
VEGGIE BURGERS
vinegar, e.g., apple cider, red wine, sherry

Flavor Affinities

BLACK BEANS + AVOCADO + CILANTRO + corn + LIME JUICE

black beans + avocado + cilantro + onions + rice

black beans + avocado + salsa + spinach + *burritos*

black beans + bell peppers + corn + lettuce + scallions

BLACK BEANS + BELL PEPPERS + GARLIC + ONIONS

black beans + brown rice + salsa + tomatoes

black beans + cheddar + chickpeas + corn + green onions

BLACK BEANS + chiles + CILANTRO + coriander + **cumin** + lime + scallions

black beans + chiles + garlic + sesame oil + sugar

black beans + chili powder or chili pepper flakes + cumin + garlic + onions + tomatoes

black beans + chipotle chiles + coffee + cumin + orange

BLACK BEANS + CILANTRO + LIME + oregano + red onions

black beans + cilantro + orange

black beans + coriander + cumin + ginger

black beans + garlic + thyme

black beans + ginger + kombu + soy sauce

black beans + kale + sweet potatoes

black beans + oregano + sage + thyme

black beans + mango + quinoa

black beans + salsa + sweet potatoes + tortillas

**BEANS, BORLOTTI
(see BEANS,
CRANBERRY)**

**BEANS, BROAD
(see BEANS, FAVA)**

**● BEANS, CANNELLINI
(see also BEANS, WHITE)**

Flavor: notes of nuts, with a creamy, smooth texture

Volume: quiet – moderate

What they are: white Italian kidney beans

Techniques: braise, puree, simmer

Tips: Presoak dried beans overnight (or 6 – 8 hours); boil and simmer until tender, about 1 to 2 hours.

Possible substitutes: other white beans, navy beans

artichokes and artichoke hearts

arugula

BASIL

bay leaf

bell peppers, e.g., red, roasted

broccoli rabe

bruschetta

carrots

"cassoulets," vegetarian

celery

chard, e.g., Swiss

chiles, e.g., jalapeño

chili, vegetarian

chives

cilantro

cloves

couscous

cumin

dips, e.g., bean

escarole

fennel

GARLIC

greens, bitter, e.g., beet

ITALIAN CUISINE

KALE

kombu

leeks

lemon, e.g., juice, zest

lime

mushrooms

OIL, e.g., grapeseed, **OLIVE**

olives, e.g., kalamata

onions, e.g., red, Spanish, spring

oregano

paprika

parsley

PASTAS, e.g., fettuccine, linguini, pasta e fagioli

pepper, e.g., black

pesto

pistou

potatoes

purees

rice, e.g., brown

rosemary

SAGE

SALADS, e.g., bean, green, tomato

salt, e.g., kosher, sea

savory

shallots

SOUPS, e.g., minestrone, pasta e fagioli, tomato

spelt

spinach

spreads

stews

stock, vegetable

sweet potatoes

thyme

TOMATOES

tomatoes, sun-dried

vinegar, e.g., balsamic, sherry

walnuts

Flavor Affinities

cannellini beans + balsamic vinegar + herbs (basil, rosemary, sage) + olive oil

cannellini beans + basil + tomatoes

cannellini beans + bay leaf + savory

cannellini beans + beet greens + walnuts

cannellini beans + bell peppers + garlic

cannellini beans + chard + garlic + olive oil + rice + vinegar

CANNELLINI BEANS + cilantro + GARLIC + lemon juice + OLIVE OIL

CANNELLINI BEANS + GARLIC + OLIVE OIL + *pasta*

CANNELLINI BEANS + GARLIC + OLIVE OIL + rosemary or sage

CANNELLINI BEANS + GARLIC + herbs (e.g., sage, thyme) + TOMATOES

cannellini beans + lemon + spinach

• BEANS, CRANBERRY (and BORLOTTI BEANS, a popular type of cranberry bean)

Season: summer (fresh); year-round (dried)

Flavor: slightly sweet, with earthy notes of chestnuts, meat, nuts, and/or peas, with a creamy, yet firm texture

Volume: quiet

Nutritional profile: 73% carbs / 24% protein / 3% fat

Calories: 240 per 1-cup serving (boiled)

Protein: 17 grams

Techniques: boil, braise, pressure-cook, simmer

Timing: Boil and simmer presoaked dried cranberry beans until tender, about 1 – 2 hours. Boil fresh beans about 10 minutes.

Possible substitutes: kidney beans, pinto beans

bay leaf
beans, baked
bell peppers, e.g., red *"brandade"*
broccoli rabe
butter
carrots
casseroles
celery
chard, Swiss
cheese, e.g., feta, Gorgonzola, Parmesan
chili, vegetarian
cinnamon
dips
farro
garlic
gratins
herbs
hummus
ITALIAN CUISINE
lemon juice
oil, olive
olives
onions, e.g., yellow
oregano
parsley
PASTAS
Portuguese cuisine
quinoa
rosemary
sage
salads
scallions
SOUPS, e.g., bean, minestrone, pasta e fagioli
Spanish cuisine
spinach
stews
stock, vegetable
succotash
thyme
tomatoes
walnuts
zucchini

Flavor Affinities

cranberry beans + cinnamon + tomatoes

cranberry beans + feta + walnuts

cranberry beans + garlic + green onions + lemon + olive oil

cranberry beans + garlic + sage

• BEANS, FAVA (aka BROAD BEANS)

Season: spring – summer

Flavor: bitter/sweet, with earthy notes of butter, nuts (e.g., chestnuts) and/or split peas, and a dense, grainy, rich texture

Volume: moderate (fresh) – louder (dried)

Nutritional profile: 73% carbs / 24% protein / 3% fat

Calories: 190 per 1-cup serving (boiled)

Protein: 13 grams

Techniques: blanch (then peel), boil, braise, puree, raw (young beans), sauté, simmer (8 – 10 minutes fresh, 1½ – 2 hours dried), steam, stir-fry

Timing: Boil and simmer presoaked fava beans until tender, about 1½ – 2 hours. Note: If skins are removed, fava beans will cook in less than an hour.

Tip: Never overcook.

artichokes and artichoke hearts
arugula
ASPARAGUS
avocado
basil
beans, other, e.g., green
beets
bell peppers
bread crumbs
broccoli rabe
bruschetta
butter
buttermilk

carrots
cayenne
celery
CHEESE, e.g., blue, feta, goat,
    mozzarella, Parmesan, **pecorino**,
    ricotta, ricotta salata, white
chervil
chicory
CHILES, e.g., dried, jalapeño
chili pepper flakes, chili powder,
    and chili sauce
chives
cilantro
couscous
cream
crostini
cumin
dill
dips
eggs, *e.g., frittatas, omelets*
epazote
"falafel"
fennel
GARLIC and spring garlic
ginger
Greek cuisine
greens, e.g., **bitter**, salad
"hummus"
Italian cuisine

kale
leeks
LEMON, e.g., juice, zest
lemon, Meyer
lettuce
lime
lovage
marjoram
MEDITERRANEAN CUISINES
Middle Eastern cuisines
MINT
Moroccan cuisine
MUSHROOMS, e.g., lobster,
    morel
nettles
nutmeg
OIL, **e.g., OLIVE**, sesame, **walnut**
olives
ONIONS, e.g., red, spring
parsley
PASTAS, e.g., orecchiette, spaghetti
peas
pesto
pistachios
Portuguese cuisine
potatoes
purees
quinoa
radishes

ramps
rice
risottos
rosemary
sage
SALADS, e.g., beet
salt, e.g., kosher, sea
savory, *e.g., summer*
scallions
snap peas
SOUPS
Spanish cuisine
spinach
spreads
stews
tahini
thyme
tomatoes, esp. sun-dried
vinaigrette
walnuts
yogurt
zucchini

Flavor Affinities

fava beans + asparagus + peas + *pastas*
fava beans + avocado + quinoa
fava beans + black pepper + herbs (e.g., basil, chives, parsley) + olive oil
    + salt
fava beans + beets + mint + ricotta salata cheese
fava beans + chiles + cilantro + garlic + lime
fava beans + cilantro + feta cheese + radishes
fava beans + cumin + garlic + lemon + olive oil + parsley + tomatoes
fava beans + dill + lemon + yogurt
fava beans + dill + mint
fava beans + garlic + lemon + mint + olive oil + ricotta cheese
fava beans + garlic + olive oil + onions
fava beans + garlic + thyme
fava beans + goat cheese + lemon + olive oil + yogurt
fava beans + lemon + pasta + ricotta
fava beans + marjoram + pasta
fava beans + mint + pecorino cheese + pistachios

BEANS, FERMENTED BLACK (and SAUCE)

Flavor: SALTY/sweet/**umami**, with pungent notes
Volume: loud – very loud
What it is: condiment made of fermented and salted black soybeans, sometimes combined with ginger and orange zest

Tips: Rinse fermented black beans before cooking for a "quieter" flavor. Chop well to season more evenly.

arame
asparagus
basil
beans, e.g., green, long, mung
bell peppers
bok choy
broccoli
cabbage, e.g., Chinese
cauliflower
CHILES, e.g., serrano

chili oil, chili paste, and chili
   pepper flakes
Chinese cuisine
cilantro
eggplant, e.g., Asian
GARLIC
GINGER
greens, Asian, e.g., bok choy
hoisin
honey
kale, e.g., black, green
ketchup
leeks
lemon, e.g., juice
lime
mushrooms, e.g., shiitake
noodles, e.g., Asian, rice, soba,
   udon
oil, e.g., peanut, scallion, sesame
onions
orange, e.g., zest
pepper, e.g., black
rice, e.g., brown
rice syrup
salads, e.g., onion, spinach
sauces
scallions
seitan
sesame, e.g., oil, seeds
sherry
soups
soy sauce
spinach
star anise
STIR-FRIES
stock, e.g., vegetable
sugar, e.g., brown
tamari
tofu
vinegar, e.g., balsamic, rice,
   sherry
wine, e.g., dry white, rice
yogurt
zucchini

Flavor Affinities
fermented black beans + balsamic
   vinegar + sesame + soy sauce

fermented black beans + chiles +
   garlic + vinegar
fermented black beans + eggplant
   + yogurt
**FERMENTED BLACK BEANS +
   GARLIC + GINGER**
fermented black beans + garlic +
   star anise
**fermented black beans + ginger +
   orange zest**
**fermented black beans + ginger +
   scallions + tofu** + *soups*
fermented black beans + onions +
   sesame oil + scallions

"I love the umami flavor that
fermented black beans add to
dishes, from Asian eggplant
to onion salads."
— AMANDA COHEN, DIRT CANDY
(NEW YORK CITY)

● BEANS, FLAGEOLET

[flah-zhoh-LAY]
Flavor: creamy and delicate in
texture
Volume: quiet
What they are: immature
kidney/navy beans removed from
their pods
Techniques: Boil and simmer
until tender, about 30 – 90
minutes.

arugula
asparagus
basil
bay leaf
beans, other, e.g., Anasazi, fava,
   green
carrots
cassoulets
celery
cheese, e.g., goat
chervil
citrus, e.g., lemon, lime, orange
couscous
cream

cucumbers
fines herbes
FRENCH CUISINE
garlic
gratins
herbs
Italian cuisine
leeks
lemon
mint
oil, e.g., olive
olives
onions, e.g., red, sweet, yellow
parsley
pastas
pesto
pistachios
rice, e.g., wild
rosemary
salads, e.g., tomato
salt
sauces, e.g., butter, tomato
savory
shallots
soups
stews
tarragon
thyme
tomatoes and tomato sauce
wine, e.g., dry white

Flavor Affinities

flageolet beans + basil + tomatoes
flageolet beans + garlic + thyme
flageolet beans + garlic +
   tomatoes
flageolet beans + goat cheese +
   olives
flageolet beans + green beans +
   onions + parsley + tomatoes
flageolet beans + pistachios +
   wild rice

● BEANS, FRENCH GREEN (aka HARICOTS VERTS)

Tip: Haricots verts are smaller
and more delicate than regular
green beans, with a crisp texture.

almonds
arugula
avocados
basil
bell peppers, red, e.g., roasted
butter
carrots
chervil
chives
crème fraîche
dill
French cuisine
garlic
greens, e.g., mesclun
hazelnuts
lemon
mint
oil, e.g., hazelnut, **olive**, walnut
olives, e.g., black, kalamata,
   niçoise
onions
orange
parsley
pepper, e.g., black
pesto
potatoes, e.g., new
salads, e.g., Niçoise
savory, summer
scallions
shallots
soups
stir-fries
tarragon
thyme
tomatoes
vinegar, e.g., apple cider,
   balsamic, herb, red wine,
   sherry, tarragon
walnuts

Flavor Affinities

French green beans + almonds + garlic + olive oil

French green beans + hazelnuts + orange

French green beans + onions + tomatoes

BEANS, GARBANZO (see CHICKPEAS)

• BEANS, GIGANTE (aka GIGANDE BEANS or GIANT BEANS)

[zhee-GAHN-teh]

Flavor: slightly sweet, with savory notes, and a firm yet creamy texture

Volume: moderate

Techniques: bake, stew

anise seeds
bay leaf
bread crumbs
carrots
casseroles
cassoulet, vegetarian
celery
cheese, e.g., feta
chili pepper flakes
coriander
dill
fennel
GARLIC
grains
GREEK CUISINE
honey
lemon, e.g., juice, zest
oil, olive
olives
onions, e.g., cippolini
oregano, e.g., Greek
parsley
pepper, e.g., black
rice
rosemary
salads, e.g., bean
salt
soups

spinach
stock, e.g., vegetable
thyme
TOMATOES
vinegar, e.g., red wine

Flavor Affinities

gigante beans + bell peppers + carrots + tomatoes

gigante beans + dill + garlic + tomatoes

gigante beans + dill + honey + olive oil + red wine vinegar + tomatoes

gigante beans + feta cheese + olive oil + olives

• BEANS, GREAT NORTHERN (see BEANS, WHITE)

• BEANS, GREEN (aka SNAP BEANS, STRING BEANS or WAX BEANS; see also BEANS, FRENCH GREEN)

Season: **summer** – autumn

Flavor: slightly sweet, with a firm texture

Volume: quiet – **moderate**

What they are: legumes that can be eaten pod and all; considered a vegetable nutritionally

Nutritional profile: 80% carbs / 13% protein / 7% fat

Calories: 45 per 1-cup serving (cooked)

Protein: 2 grams

Techniques: blanch, boil (2 – 5 minutes, depending on the thickness of the beans), pressure-cook, roast, **sauté**, simmer, **steam** (5 minutes), stew, stir-fry

ALMONDS
arugula
barley

BASIL
beans, other, e.g., cannellini, shell, white
bell peppers, e.g., red
butter
capers
carrots
cashews
casseroles
cauliflower
cayenne
celery
CHEESE, e.g., cheddar, Gorgonzola, mozzarella, **PARMESAN**, **pecorino**, Swiss
chervil
chickpeas
chiles and chili pepper flakes
chives
cilantro
coconut
corn
cream
crème fraîche
cucumbers
cumin
curry and *curries*
dill
eggs, e.g., hard-boiled
fennel
French cuisine
frisée
GARLIC
ghee
ginger
greens, e.g., mesclun, salad
hazelnuts
hiziki
honey
Indian cuisine
kale
kasha
leeks
LEMON, e.g., juice, preserved, zest
lentils
lettuce, e.g., Boston
lime

maple syrup
marjoram
millet
mint
miso, esp. white
MUSHROOMS, e.g., chanterelle, cremini, shiitake
MUSTARD, e.g., Dijon or seeds
nutmeg
nuts
OIL, e.g., canola, nut, **OLIVE**, peanut, sesame, **walnut**
okra
olives, e.g., black, niçoise
onions, e.g., green, pearl, red
orange
oregano
PARSLEY
pastas, e.g., farfalle
peanuts
pecans
pepper, e.g., black
pesto
pilafs
pine nuts
pistachios
POTATOES
pumpkin seeds
quinoa
rice, e.g., brown, wild
risotto
rosemary
SALADS, e.g., bean, chickpea, Niçoise, tomato
salt, e.g., kosher, sea
savory
scallions
sesame, e.g., sauce, seeds
SHALLOTS
soups, e.g., bean, vegetable
soy sauce
spinach
stews
stir-fries
stock, vegetable
succotash
sunflower seeds
TARRAGON

tempeh
thyme
tofu
TOMATOES, e.g., cherry, plum
turmeric
VINEGAR, e.g., balsamic, cider, red wine, sherry, tarragon
WALNUTS
watercress
zucchini

Flavor Affinities
green beans + almonds + lemon
green beans + garlic + lemon
green beans + garlic + nuts (e.g., pine nuts, walnuts) + olive oil
green beans + herbs (e.g., parsley, rosemary) + **nuts** (e.g., pistachios, walnuts) + shallots
green beans + honey + lemon + mustard
green beans + lemon + pine nuts
green beans + mustard + potatoes + tarragon
green beans + onions + tomatoes
green beans + pesto + *risotto*

"I snack on **green beans** — their chlorophyll is like caffeine, in that it gives you an energy boost!"
— KEN LARSEN, TABLE VERTE (NEW YORK CITY)

● BEANS, KIDNEY (see also BEANS, RED)

Flavor: sweet, with astringent and/or earthy notes, and a dense, "meaty" texture
Volume: moderate
Nutritional profile: 73% carbs / 24% protein / 3% fat
Calories: 225 per 1-cup serving (boiled)
Protein: 15 grams
Techniques: boil, simmer, stew
Timing: Soak dried beans overnight (or for 6 – 8 hours) before cooking; boil for at least

15 minutes and then simmer about 45 minutes to 2 hours, until soft and very thoroughly cooked.

anise seeds
avocados
barley
basil
bay leaf
bell peppers, e.g., green, red
black-eyed peas
Cajun cuisine
Caribbean cuisine
carrots
casseroles
cayenne
celery
Central American cuisines
chiles, e.g., chipotle, jalapeño
CHILI, VEGETARIAN
chili pepper sauce and chili powder
chives
cilantro
corn
Creole cuisine
cumin
dips, e.g., bean
epazote
fennel
GARLIC
ginger
greens
gumbo, e.g., vegetarian
Jamaican cuisine
kamut
lemon, e.g., zest
lime
"meatballs," e.g., with pasta
Mexican cuisine
oil, e.g., **olive**, sunflower
ONIONS, e.g., red, sweet, white
orange
oregano
paprika
PARSLEY
parsnips

pasta
peanuts
peas
potatoes
pumpkin seeds
quinoa
red beans and rice
refried beans
RICE, e.g., brown
rice and beans
sage
SALADS, *e.g., bean, green*
sauces, e.g., pasta
SAVORY
scallions
SOUPS, *e.g., minestrone, pasta,*
vegetable
South American cuisines
soy sauce
spreads
stews, e.g., vegetable
stock, vegetable
tarragon
thyme
tofu
tomatoes, e.g., juice, paste
veggie burgers
vinegar, e.g., red wine, sherry,
white wine
walnuts
wheat berries
zucchini

Flavor Affinities
kidney beans + chipotle peppers
+ garlic + rice + tomatoes
kidney beans + oregano + sage
+ thyme

"Every Jamaican family eats 'rice
and peas' every Sunday —
which is rice made with coconut
milk and Scotch bonnet
[chili] peppers served with red
kidney beans."
— SHAWAIN WHYTE, CAFÉ BLOSSOM
(NEW YORK CITY)

● BEANS, LIMA (aka BUTTER BEANS)

Season: summer
Flavor: faintly bitter/sweet, with
notes of butter, cream, and/or
nuts, and a rich, meaty, smooth
texture
Volume: quiet – **moderate**
What they are: legumes;
nutritionally, considered a starchy
vegetable
Nutritional profile: 79% carbs
/ 19% protein / 2% fat
Calories: 210 per 1-cup serving
(boiled, baby)
Protein: 12 grams
Techniques: mash, puree,
simmer (15 minutes), steam
(Note: never raw)
Timing: Presoak dried lima
beans overnight (or 6 – 8 hours)
before cooking in salted water;
cook until tender, about 45 – 90
minutes (if beans are smaller)
to 60 – 90 minutes (if beans are
larger).

basil
bay leaf
beans, green
bell peppers, e.g., green, red
butter
buttermilk
carrots
casseroles
cheese, e.g., cheddar, **feta**,
Parmesan
chervil
chili pepper flakes
chives
cilantro
CORN
cream
cucumber
dill
dips
eggplant
fennel and fennel seeds

garlic
HERBS, e.g., basil, cilantro,
rosemary, sage, thyme
horseradish
kale
leeks
LEMON, e.g., juice
lettuce
marjoram
mint
molasses
mushrooms
nutmeg
OIL, OLIVE
olives
onions, e.g., red, yellow
oregano
PARSLEY
pepper, e.g., black
purees
quinoa
rosemary
sage
salads, e.g., three-bean
salt, sea
scallions
sorrel
soups
Southern (U.S.) cuisine
spinach
spreads
squash, e.g., Hubbard, summer
stews
SUCCOTASH
sumac
tamari
thyme
TOMATOES and tomato paste
vinegar, e.g., cider, red wine
wine, dry white
yogurt

Flavor Affinities
lima beans + chili pepper flakes +
garlic + lemon juice + olive oil
lima beans + corn + tomatoes
(succotash)

lima beans + **corn** + garlic + rosemary + **tomatoes** (succotash)

lima beans + fennel + garlic

lima beans + feta cheese + olives + tomatoes

lima beans + feta cheese + spinach

lima beans + **garlic** + **lemon** + **olive oil** + oregano

lima beans + garlic + onions

lima beans + lemon + parsley + *soup*

lima beans + scallions + yogurt

● BEANS, LONG (aka YARD-LONG BEANS)

Flavor: bitter/sweet, with notes of legumes (e.g., beans, peas) and/or nuts, and a crunchy texture

Volume: quiet – moderate

What they are: legumes, resembling green beans, that often reach 12 inches long — or much longer!

Nutritional profile: 79% carbs / 19% protein / 2% fat

Calories: 50 per 1-cup serving (boiled)

Protein: 3 grams

Techniques: boil, braise, deep-fry, sauté, steam, stew, stir-fry

Tip: Cut into three-inch pieces for easier cooking and serving.

Botanical relative: black-eyed peas

Asian cuisines

beans, e.g., fermented black

bell peppers, e.g., red

chiles, e.g., jalapeño, Thai

chili paste and chili sauce

cilantro

coconut and coconut milk

coriander

cumin

curry powder

eggs, e.g., *omelets*

fennel

fennel seeds

fenugreek

garlic

ginger

lemon, e.g., juice, zest

liqueur, anise-flavored, e.g., Pernod

mint

mushrooms

nuts

oil, e.g., canola, peanut, vegetable

onions

paprika

pasta

pepper, e.g., black, Szechuan

pesto

salads

salt, e.g., sea

sesame, e.g., oil, paste, seeds

shallots

soy sauce

stir-fries

sugar

tahini

tamarind

tomatoes

vinegar, e.g., rice wine, sherry, white wine

walnuts

water chestnuts

Flavor Affinities

long beans + chiles + ginger + rice wine vinegar

long beans + chiles + lemon

long beans + cilantro + sesame oil/seeds + soy sauce

long beans + coconut milk + ginger + shallots

"I loved a dish I had at Mission Chinese of stir-fried **long beans** with lots of cumin."

— AMANDA COHEN, DIRT CANDY (NEW YORK CITY)

Dishes

Chilled Vietnamese Long Beans with Radish, Cucumber, and Shaved Carrot
— FnB Restaurant (Scottsdale, AZ)

● BEANS, MUNG

Flavor: slightly sweet, with notes of butter, grass, and/or split pea soup, and a soft texture

Volume: quiet – moderate

Nutritional profile: 74% carbs / 23% protein / 3% fat

Calories: 215 per 1-cup serving (boiled)

Protein: 14 grams

Techniques: pressure-cook, sauté, simmer (30 – 60 minutes), sprout, stir-fry

Tip: Presoaking mung beans is optional.

Ratio: 1:3 (1 cup mung beans to 3 cups cooking liquid)

asafoetida powder
Asian cuisines
bay leaf
bell peppers
bok choy
cabbage, napa
carrots
casseroles
cayenne
chiles, e.g., jalapeño, red
Chinese cuisine
chives
cilantro
cinnamon
coconut and coconut milk
coriander
CUMIN
CURRIES
dals
dill
garam masala
GARLIC
ghee
GINGER
grains, e.g., bulgur
gravies
greens
hummus
Indian cuisine
leeks

lemon, e.g., juice
lentils
lime
millet
moong dal
mujadura
mushrooms
mustard seeds
noodles, Asian
oil, e.g., coconut, mustard, olive
ONIONS, e.g., red
pancakes
parsley
peas, e.g., split
pho, vegetarian
pilafs
purees
RICE, e.g., basmati, brown, long-grain
salads
salt, e.g., sea
sauces
SOUPS, e.g., miso, mung bean
Southeast Asian cuisines
spinach
sprouts, mung bean
stews
sugar snap peas
tempeh
tofu
tomatoes
turmeric
vegetables
yogurt

Flavor Affinities

mung beans + bulgur + olive oil + onions
mung beans + coconut milk+ **cumin** + **garlic** + **ginger** + onions
mung beans + coriander + **cumin** + **garlic** + **ginger**

Dishes

Zucchini-Mung Bean Pancake and Skeena Cherry, Basil, and Purslane Salad served with a Sorrel-Truffle Sauce and Blue Majestic Potato Crisps
— Sutra (Seattle)

● BEANS, NAVY (aka YANKEE BEANS)

Flavor: slightly sweet, with notes of cream, and a soft, mealy texture

Volume: quiet – moderate

Nutritional profile: 76% carbs / 20% protein / 4% fat

Calories: 255 per 1-cup serving (boiled)

Protein: 15 grams

Techniques: simmer

Timing: Presoak dried beans overnight (or 6 – 8 hours) before cooking. Boil and simmer until tender, about 1 – 2 hours.

Factoid: They are the second-most popular bean in America (after pinto beans).

Possible substitute: cannellini beans

arugula
asparagus
BAKED BEANS
barley
basil
beets
Boston cuisine
broccoli rabe
cabbage, e.g., red
carrots
casseroles
cauliflower
celery
celery root
cheese, e.g., ricotta
chiles
chili, vegetarian
cloves
corn

dips
fennel
garlic
ketchup
leeks
maple syrup
molasses
mushrooms
mustard, e.g., Dijon, yellow
onions, e.g., white, yellow
orange
parsley
pastas, e.g., pasta e fagioli
pepper, e.g., black
pilafs
potatoes
purees
quinoa
rice
rosemary
SALADS, e.g., tomato, vegetable
salt, e.g., kosher, sea
savory
shallots
SOUPS, e.g., bean, tomato
spreads
squash, summer
stews
sugar, e.g., brown
sweet potatoes
thyme
tomatoes and tomato paste
vinegar, e.g., cider

Flavor Affinities
navy beans + black pepper +
    maple syrup + mustard + sugar
navy beans + brown sugar +
    molasses + vinegar

● BEANS, PINTO
Season: winter
Flavor: earthy and savory notes,
with a mealy, soft texture (when
cooked)
Volume: quiet – moderate

Nutritional profile: 74% carbs
/ 22% protein / 4% fat
Calories: 245 per 1-cup serving
(boiled)
Protein: 15 grams
Techniques: mash, puree, refry,
simmer, stew
Timing: Soak dried beans
overnight (or 6 – 8 hours) before
cooking. Boil about 1 – 2 hours,
until tender.
Botanical relative: kidney
beans
Factoid: They are the most
popular beans in America.

anise seeds
avocado
barbecue sauce
bay leaf
beans, other, e.g., black, kidney
burritos
casseroles
cheese, e.g., cheddar or Jack
CHILES, e.g., ancho, chipotle,
    jalapeño, poblano, serrano, and
    chili powder
CHILI, VEGETARIAN
chips, tortilla
cilantro
corn
CUMIN
dips
eggs, e.g., *huevos rancheros*
epazote

fennel
frijoles, e.g., refritos
GARLIC
kale
kombu
lemon
lime
liquid smoke
maple syrup
MEXICAN CUISINE
mushrooms, e.g., portobello
mustard
nachos
oil, olive
ONIONS
oregano
parsley
pâtés
pepper, black
purees
quinoa
REFRIED BEANS
RICE, e.g., brown
sage
salads, e.g., taco
salsas
salt, e.g., sea
savory
scallions
soups
Southwestern (U.S.) cuisine
spelt
spreads
STEWS, vegetarian
stock, e.g., vegetable

Dishes

Canyon Rancheros — Our take on Huevos Rancheros: Grilled Corn Tortilla topped with
Mashed Pinto Beans and broiled with Cheddar Cheese, served with a Poached Egg and
Pico de Gallo Salsa
— Canyon Ranch (Tucson)

Organic Pinto Bean Tostada Stack, Avocado Salsa, Red Rice, and Ancho Chile Sauce
— Golden Door (Escondido, California)

tacos
Tex-Mex cuisine
thyme
tomatoes and tomato puree
tortillas
tostadas
veggie burgers

Flavor Affinities
pinto beans + chiles + sage
pinto beans + chili powder + cumin
pinto beans + cilantro + liquid smoke + onions
pinto beans + cumin + garlic + onions + quinoa
pinto beans + oregano + sage + thyme

● **BEANS, RED (see also similar BEANS, KIDNEY)**
Flavor: slightly sweet, similar to kidney beans, with a firm texture
Volume: quieter than kidney beans
Timing: Cook presoaked red beans about 1½ – 2 hours, until tender.
Possible substitute: kidney beans

casseroles
chilaquiles
chiles, e.g., ancho
chili, vegetarian
coffee
Creole cuisine
jambalaya
Mexican cuisine
parsley
red beans and rice
RICE
salads, e.g., bean, green
savory
soups
Southwestern (U.S.) cuisine

BEANS, SHELL (see BEANS, CRANBERRY; BEANS, FAVA; BEANS, LIMA)

BEANS, SOY (see EDAMAME and SOY BEANS)

BEANS, STRING (see BEANS, GREEN)

● **BEANS, WHITE (see also BEANS, CANNELLINI; BEANS, NAVY)**
Season: winter
Flavor: neutral, with notes of nuts, and a creamy texture
Volume: quiet – moderate
Nutritional profile: 74% carbs / 24% protein / 2% fat
Calories: 250 per 1-cup serving (boiled)
Protein: 17 grams
Techniques: bake, simmer

artichokes
arugula
asparagus
baked beans
barley
BASIL
bay leaf
bell peppers, red, esp. roasted
bread crumbs
bruschetta
cabbage, e.g., savoy
capers
carrots
casseroles
cassoulets
cauliflower
celery
celery root
chard, e.g., Swiss
cheese, e.g., cheddar, Parmesan

chervil
chickpeas
chiles, e.g., green chili pepper flakes, chili pepper sauce, and chili powder
chili, vegetarian
chives
couscous
croutons, whole grain
cumin
dates
dill
dips
eggs, e.g., hard-boiled
escarole
fennel, fennel pollen, and fennel seeds
French cuisine
frisée
GARLIC
greens, bitter, e.g., beet, mustard
honey
"hummus," i.e., white bean
Italian cuisine
kale, esp. black
kombu
leeks
LEMON, e.g., juice, zest
lettuce, e.g., butter
maple syrup
molasses
mushrooms, e.g., cremini, oyster, portobello, shiitake
mustard, e.g., Dijon, dry
OIL, e.g., **OLIVE**, peanut
olives, e.g., green
ONIONS, e.g., red, sweet, white
orange
oregano
parsley
PASTAS
peas
pepper, e.g., black, white
pesto
potatoes
pumpkin

purees
ROSEMARY
SAGE
SALADS, e.g., bean, fennel, green
salt, e.g., kosher, sea
sauces, e.g., tomato
sauerkraut
sausages, vegan
savory
scallions
shallots
SOUPS, e.g., white bean
spelt
spinach
spreads
squash, e.g., butternut
stews

stock, vegetable
sugar, e.g., brown
sweet potatoes
tahini
tarragon
thyme
TOMATOES
tomatoes, sun-dried
Tuscan cuisine
vegetables, root
VINEGAR, e.g., balsamic, cider, red wine, rice, umeboshi, white wine
wheat berries
wine, dry red

Flavor Affinities
white beans + asparagus + garlic
white beans + basil + celery
white beans + basil + escarole + Parmesan cheese
white beans + basil + garlic
white beans + basil + scallions + *dips*
white beans + basil + tomatoes
white beans + cabbage + Parmesan cheese
white beans + cumin + garlic + lemon + sage
white beans + dill + garlic + lemon
white beans + garlic + olive oil + rosemary
white beans + garlic + rosemary
WHITE BEANS + GARLIC + HERBS (e.g., oregano, parsley, **sage**, thyme) + lemon + olive oil + pasta + tomatoes
white beans + garlic + sun-dried tomatoes
white beans + lemon + olives + rosemary + thyme
white beans + mushrooms + tarragon + thyme
white beans + orange + thyme

Dishes

Bangers and Mash: White Bean and Fennel Sausage, Rustic Mashed Potatoes, Sautéed Spinach, Caramelized Onions, Mushroom Jus
— The Butcher's Daughter (New York City)

Tuscan White Bean Pâté Sandwiches with Arugula and Tomato
— Candle Cafe (New York City)

Pasta with White Beans, Arugula, Mushrooms, and Peas
— Telepan (New York City)

● **BEETS**
Season: year-round, esp. late summer – autumn
Flavor: sweet, with very earthy, pungent notes, and a crisp, dense texture
Volume: moderate – loud
Nutritional profile: 86% carbs / 11% protein / 3% fat
Calories: 60 per 1-cup serving (raw)
Protein: 2 grams
Techniques: bake (350°F, about 60 minutes), boil (about 20 – 45 minutes, depending on size), grate (e.g., for grains, salads), julienne, pickle, pressure-cook (10 – 25 minutes), raw, roast, sauté, shred, steam (about 25 – 40 minutes)
Botanical relatives: chard, quinoa, spinach, Swiss chard

agave nectar
allspice
anise hyssop
anise seeds
APPLES and **apple juice**
arame
ARUGULA
asparagus
avocado
baked goods, e.g., cakes
basil
bay leaf
beans, e.g., fava, green
bell peppers, e.g., green, red, yellow
blackberries
black-eyed peas
breads, e.g., dark, rye
butter
buttermilk
cabbage, e.g., green, red, savoy
capers
CARAWAY SEEDS
cardamom
"carpaccio"
CARROTS

cauliflower
celery and celery leaves
celery root
chard, Swiss
CHEESE, e.g., **blue**, Cambozola,
 cashew, cream, **FETA**, **GOAT**,
 Gorgonzola, Gouda, Havarti,
 Monterey Jack, Parmesan,
 queso blanco, **ricotta**, **ricotta
 salata**, Roquefort, salty
chervil
chickpeas
chicory
chiles and chili pepper flakes
chips, e.g., fried
CHIVES
chocolate and cocoa
chutneys
cilantro
cinnamon
citrus, e.g., juice
cloves
coriander
couscous
cranberries
cream
crème fraîche
crudités
cucumbers
cumin
curry powder
desserts, e.g., "red velvet"
DILL
edamame
eggs, esp. hard-boiled
endive
escarole hearts
falafel
**FENNEL, fennel fronds, and
 fennel seeds**
frisée
fruit, dried
GARLIC
GINGER
grains
grapefruit, e.g., juice
GREENS, e.g., baby, **BEET**, **bitter**,
 collard, dandelion, mesclun,
 mixed, mustard

harissa
hash, e.g., red flannel
herbs
hiziki
honey
HORSERADISH
juices, e.g., *beets + carrots + celery*
kale
kumquats
lavender

leeks
LEMON, e.g., juice, zest
lemon, preserved
lemongrass
lentils, e.g., green, red
lettuce, e.g., butter
lime
mace
mâche
mangoes

Flavor Affinities

BEETS + arugula + feta cheese + balsamic vinegar + walnuts
beets + arugula + horseradish + pecans
beets + avocado + orange
beets + balsamic vinegar + blackberries
beets + balsamic vinegar + carrots + **chives** + greens
beets + balsamic vinegar + chives + parsley + **red onions**
beets + balsamic vinegar + fennel + oranges
beets + beet greens + dill + lemon + yogurt
beets + beet greens + marjoram + pine nuts
beets + black olives + oranges
BEETS + CHEESE (e.g., blue, feta, queso blanca) **+ FRUIT**
 (e.g., apples, currants, oranges) **+ GREENS** (e.g., arugula, dandelion,
 endive) **+ NUTS** (e.g., hazelnuts, pine nuts, walnuts)
BEETS + CHEESE (e.g., feta, goat, mascarpone, ricotta) **+ NUTS** (e.g.,
 hazelnuts, pecans, pine nuts, pistachios, walnuts)
beets + chives + cucumbers + horseradish + onions + **yogurt**
beets + chives + radishes + **yogurt**
beets + coriander + cumin + goat cheese + yogurt
beets + crème fraîche + dill + orange
beets + Dijon mustard + goat cheese + spinach + walnuts
beets + dill + fennel + *risotto*
beets + fennel + ginger + yogurt
BEETS + FENNEL + ORANGE + watercress + yogurt
beets + garlic + olive oil + parsley
beets + garlic + olive oil + tarragon
beets + garlic + yogurt
beets + ginger + mint + **orange**
beets + goat cheese + lentils
beets + horseradish + **pistachios + ricotta**
beets + horseradish + shallots + tarragon
beets + mint + yogurt
beets + mustard + orange
beets + orange juice/zest + (sherry/wine) **vinegar + walnut oil +**
 walnuts
beets + pistachios + watercress + yogurt
beets + tahini + yogurt
beets + yogurt + za'atar

Dishes

Chocolate Beet Cake, Roasted Pear Sorbet, Beet, and Pear Leather
— Dirt Candy (New York City)

Ricotta Gnudi, Horseradish, Beets, Pistachios
— Dovetail (New York City)

Beet-Chocolate Cupcakes with Vegan Cream Cheese Frosting
— Fire & Spice (Hartford, CT)

Roasted Baby Beets, Pearled Barley, Horseradish Whipped Goat Cheese, Walnut Vinaigrette
— Green Zebra (Chicago)

Roasted Baby Beets and Raspberry Salad, Savory Chocolate, Spiced Pecans, Tarragon
— Green Zebra (Chicago)

Three-Beet Salad with Devoto Fuji Apples, Walnuts, Arugula, Andante Dairy-Fresh Goat Cheese, and Cider Vinaigrette
— Greens Restaurant (San Francisco)

Roasted Beets with Hazelnut Oil, Balsamic Vinegar, and Thyme
— Millennium (San Francisco)

Vegan Red Flannel Hash Scrambled Tofu with Smoked Tofu, Red Beets, Sweet Potato, Potato, Shallot, Fresh Thyme, Choice of Toast
— Mohawk Bend (Los Angeles)

Beet-Lime Ganache, Chèvre Frozen Yogurt, Pistachio Crunch
— Momofuku (New York City)

Rotisserie-Crisped Beets with Bulgur Salad, Apples, and Creamed Horseradish
— Narcissa (New York City)

Assortment of Roasted Baby Beets with Fresh Catapano Goat Cheese, Pistachios and Sherry-Shallot Dressing
— North Fork Table & Inn (Southold, NY)

Tartare of Beets, Dill Flat Bread, Soft Quail Egg, Crispy Capers, and Blood Orange Pepper
— The Point (Saranac Lake, NY)

Beet Tartare: Roasted Beets, Carrot Aioli, Cashew Cheese, Served with Baguette
— Portobello (Portland, OR)

Flannel Hash with Tempeh: Roasted Beets, Sweet Potatoes and Tempeh with Caramelized Onions and Worcestershire Sauce
— Portobello (Portland, OR)

Salad of Summer Greens and Sweet Beets with Warm Local Goat's Milk Cheese Fritters, Caramelized Oranges, and Shallot Vinaigrette
— The White Barn Inn (Kennebunk, ME)

maple syrup
marjoram
mascarpone
mayonnaise
milk
MINT
mizuna
mushrooms
MUSTARD, e.g., Dijon
nutmeg
NUTS, e.g., **hazelnuts,**
macadamia, **pecans, pine nuts,**
pistachios, WALNUTS
OIL, e.g., canola, hazelnut,
macadamia nut, mustard,
nut, **OLIVE**, peanut, safflower,
vegetable, **WALNUT**
olives, e.g., black, kalamata
ONIONS, **e.g.**, **green**, **red**, white,
yellow
ORANGE, e.g., juice, zest
oregano
paprika
PARSLEY
parsnips
pasta
pears
pepper, e.g., black, white
pomegranate, e.g., molasses,
seeds
poppy seeds
potatoes
pumpkin seeds
purslane
quinoa
radishes
raisins
relishes
rhubarb
risottos, e.g., beet
Russian cuisine
rye, e.g., bread
sage
*SALADS, e.g., beet, carrot, green
salsa verde
salt, e.g., kosher, sea
savory
scallions

sea vegetables, e.g., arame, wakame
seeds, e.g., poppy, sunflower
SHALLOTS
sorrel
SOUPS, e.g., BORSCHT
SOUR CREAM
soy sauce
spinach
star anise
stews
stock, vegetable
sugar, e.g., brown
sunflower seeds
TARRAGON
*"tartares," e.g., **beet** (resembling
   steak tartare)*
thyme
tofu
tomatoes
turnips
vegetables, root
veggie burgers, e.g., beet-lentil
verjus
vinaigrette, e.g., citrus
*****VINEGAR**, e.g., **BALSAMIC**,
   champagne, **cider**, fruit,
   raspberry, **RED WINE**, rice,
   sherry, tarragon, **white
   balsamic**, **white wine**
wakame
wasabi
WATERCRESS
watermelon
wine, dry red
YOGURT
za'atar

"Our **beet** tartare is a play on beef
tartare, so I thought about my
associations with both tartare
and with beets. The tartare
inspired the capers, shallots, and
[vegan] Worcestershire sauce, while
the beets inspired the dill and
orange. Quail eggs are a lighter,
more delicate take on traditional
egg yolks."
— MARK LEVY, THE POINT (SARANAC
LAKE, NY)

• BELL PEPPERS — IN GENERAL, or MIXED

Season: summer – autumn
Flavor: bitter (raw)/sweet (roasted), with peppery notes, and a crunchy, juicy texture
Sweetness: green (more bitter) < yellow < orange < red (sweeter)
Volume: moderate (red/roasted) – loud (green/raw)
What they are: Green peppers are immature red bell peppers (the latter are allowed to ripen on the vine).
Nutritional profile: 86% carbs / 8% protein / 6% fat
Calories: 40 per 1-cup serving (boiled red)
Protein: 1 gram
Techniques: bake, blanch, braise, broil, grill, marinate, puree, raw, **roast** (over open flame, before placing in a covered bowl to steam), sauté, steam, stew, stir-fry (3 – 5 minutes), stuff

Tips: Opt for organic bell peppers. Red and yellow bell peppers are also known as sweet peppers and are more nutritious than green bell peppers.

Botanical relatives: chiles, eggplant, gooseberries, potatoes, tomatillos, tomatoes

anise
arame
artichokes
arugula
barley
BASIL
bay leaf
BEANS, e.g., **BLACK**, **fava**, red
bok choy
bread
broccoli
broccoli rabe
bruschetta
bulgur

cabbage
capers
carrots
casseroles
cauliflower
cayenne
celery
celery seeds
chard
CHEESE, e.g., cheddar, feta, Fontina, **goat**, **mozzarella**, **Parmesan**, provolone, soft
chervil
chickpeas
chiles, chili flakes, and chili powder
chili, vegetarian
chives
cilantro
coconut milk
coriander
corn
corn bread
coulis
couscous
cucumbers
cumin
curries
dips
eggplant
EGGS, e.g., *frittatas, omelets, quiches, scrambled, tortillas*
fennel
GARLIC
gazpacho
ginger
grains, whole
gratins
greens, salad
harissa
hash
honey
jícama
leeks
lemon, e.g., juice, zest
lemons, preserved
lentils
lime

mango
marjoram
"meatloaf," vegetarian
Mediterranean cuisines
Mexican cuisine
millet
mint
miso
mushrooms, e.g., button, portobello, shiitake
noodles, Asian, e.g., pad thai
OIL, e.g., canola, corn, **OLIVE**, peanut, sesame
olives, e.g., black, green, kalamata
ONIONS, e.g., red, sweet, yellow
oregano
paprika, e.g., smoked, sweet
PARSLEY
PASTAS, e.g., lasagna, linguini, orzo, spaghetti
peaches
pears
pepper, black
pilafs
pineapple
pine nuts
pizzas, e.g., mushroom
polenta
pomegranate molasses
potatoes
purees
quesadillas
quinoa
raisins
ratatouille
relishes
RICE, e.g., **brown**, wild
risottos
romesco sauce
saffron
sage
SALADS, e.g., bean, green, pasta, potato, tomato, vegetable
salt
sandwiches, e.g., grilled cheese, Italian
sauces
sesame seeds

shallots
slaws
snow peas
sofritos
SOUPS, e.g., bean, gazpacho, gumbo, red pepper, tomato, vegetable
South American cuisines
spreads
squash, summer
stews
stir-fries
stock, vegetable
STUFFED PEPPERS
stuffings, e.g., Israeli couscous, quinoa, rice
sweet potatoes

tahini
tempeh
Tex-Mex cuisine
Thai cuisine
thyme
tofu
tomatoes, e.g., green, sun-dried
*****TOMATOES, tomato paste, and tomato sauce**
Turkish cuisine
vegetables, summer
VINEGAR, e.g., balsamic, red
wine, sherry
walnuts
wine, dry red or white
yogurt
zucchini

Flavor Affinities

bell peppers + almonds + bread crumbs + garlic + paprika + sherry vinegar + tomatoes

bell peppers + balsamic vinegar + basil + garlic + olive oil

bell peppers + balsamic vinegar + chili pepper flakes + garlic + **olive oil**

bell peppers + balsamic vinegar + olive oil + red onions

bell peppers + basil + chiles + **garlic**

bell peppers + basil + eggplant + **garlic**

bell peppers + basil + fennel + goat cheese

BELL PEPPERS + basil + garlic + OLIVE OIL + onions + oregano + tomatoes

bell peppers + cheese + eggs + tomatoes

bell peppers + chiles + cilantro + lime + mint + scallions

bell peppers + cucumbers + garlic + tomatoes

bell peppers + dried cranberries + mushrooms + sage + wild rice

bell peppers + eggs + **mushrooms + onions**

bell peppers + fava beans + garlic + lemon

bell peppers + garlic + ginger + sesame oil + soy sauce

bell peppers + garlic + miso + vegetable stock

BELL PEPPERS + GARLIC + OLIVE OIL + tomatoes + zucchini

BELL PEPPERS + cider vinegar + garlic + honey + olive oil + red onions

bell peppers + lemon juice + mint + pine nuts + rice

bell peppers + olive oil + onions + red wine vinegar + thyme

bell peppers + pomegranate molasses + walnuts

bell peppers + red beans + rice

"Many people say they don't like the flavor of **bell peppers**, but I think they actually don't like *raw* bell peppers. Their season in California is short [September – October], but red and yellow peppers are wonderful grilled, roasted, or sautéed in curries and soups — and yes, even raw when served with hummus. They're easy to peel if you oven-roast them, then put them in a covered bowl to steam — the peel will come right off."

— ANNIE SOMERVILLE, GREENS RESTAURANT (SAN FRANCISCO)

Dishes

Yellow Pepper Soup with 62-Degree Egg and Confit Red Pepper, Brown Butter, Brioche, Radish, Parmesan

— Fearrington House (Fearrington Village, NC)

● BERRIES — IN GENERAL, or MIXED BERRIES (see also SPECIFIC BERRIES, e.g., BLACKBERRIES, BLUEBERRIES, RASPBERRIES, STRAWBERRIES)

Season: spring – summer
Flavor: sweet/sour
Volume: quiet – moderate
Techniques: poach, raw

almonds
apricots
basil
cereals, breakfast
chamomile
cheese, e.g., cream, ricotta
chocolate, e.g., dark, milk, white
cinnamon
cream and crème fraîche
desserts, e.g., tarts, trifles
elderflower syrup

Dishes

Warm Three Berry-Ginger Pie with Walnut Oat Crumb Topping, Multi-Grain Crust (Organic Spelt, Oat, Barley, and Brown Rice Flours), and Non-Dairy, Low-Fat Vanilla Soy Ice Cream
— Josie's (New York City)

ginger
granola
honey
lemon
lime
liqueurs, e.g., crème de cassis, crème de menthe, Grand Marnier, Kirsch
maple syrup
mascarpone
meringue
mint
nectarines
orange
peaches
pepper, black
pie fillings
puddings, e.g., summer
salads, fruit
seeds, e.g., poppy
smoothies
sour cream
sugar, e.g., brown
vanilla
vinegar, e.g., balsamic
wine, e.g., sparkling, sweet, e.g., **Moscato d'Asti**
yogurt

Flavor Affinities

berries + honey + yogurt

BITTERNESS

Taste: bitter
Function: cooling; stimulates appetite; promotes other tastes
Tips: Bitterness relieves thirst. When a bitter component is added to a dish, it creates a sense of lightness. The hotter the food or drink, the lesser the perception of bitterness.

Examples of bitter foods:
arugula
baking powder and baking soda
beans, lima
beer, esp. hoppy (e.g., bitter ales)
bell peppers, green
bitters
broccoli rabe
Brussels sprouts
cabbage, green
caffeine (e.g., coffee, tea)
chard
chicory
chocolate, dark
cocoa
cranberries
eggplant
endive
escarole
fenugreek
frisée
grapefruit
greens, bitter, dark leafy, e.g., beet, dandelion, mustard, turnip
herbs, bitter
horseradish
kale
lettuce, e.g., romaine
melon, bitter
olives
radicchio
rhubarb
tonic water
turmeric
walnuts, e.g., black
watercress
wine, red, esp. tannic
zest, e.g., lemon, orange, etc.
zucchini

● BLACKBERRIES
(see also BERRIES)

Season: summer
Flavor: sour/sweet, with a juicy texture and lots of crunchy seeds
Volume: moderate
Nutritional profile: 79% carbs / 11% protein / 10% fat
Calories: 65 per 1-cup serving (raw)
Protein: 2 grams
Techniques: cooked, fresh, frozen (e.g., blended into a smoothie)
Botanical relatives: apples, apricots, cherries, peaches, pears, plums, quinces, raspberries, strawberries

almonds
apples
bananas
blueberries
caramel
cinnamon
coulis
CREAM AND ICE CREAM
*DESSERTS, e.g., cobblers, **crisps**, crumbles*
endive
figs
ginger
hazelnuts
honey
LEMON
lemon herbs, e.g., lemon balm, lemon verbena
lime
mangoes
maple syrup
mascarpone
melon, e.g., honeydew
milk, e.g., almond
mint
muesli
nectarines
nutmeg
oats

oranges, e.g., juice, zest
papaya
pecans
peaches
pepper, e.g., black
pies
pumpkin seeds
raspberries
rhubarb
rose geranium
salads, e.g., fruit
sauces
smoothies
sorbets
soups*, e.g., fruit*
strawberries
sugar, e.g., brown
vanilla
watermelon
wine, e.g., fruity, red
yogurt

Flavor Affinities

blackberries + apples + brown
   sugar + cinnamon
blackberries + apples + cinnamon
   + hazelnuts
blackberries + cinnamon +
   orange
blackberries + lime + mint
blackberries + lime + yogurt
blackberries + papaya + yogurt

● BLACK-EYED PEAS [aka COWPEAS]

Flavor: slightly sweet, with
earthy and/or savory notes of
beans, butter, dirt, nuts, and/or
peas, and a firm texture
Volume: quiet – moderate/loud
What they are: legumes
Nutritional profile: 71% carbs /
24% protein / 5% fat
Calories: 200 per 1-cup serving
(boiled)
Protein: 14 grams (vs. 9 grams
per cup for other peas)

Dishes

Black-Eyed Pea Cake with Red Pepper Coulis, Chipotle Aioli
— Café Blossom (New York City)

Timing: For maximum
digestibility, presoak before
cooking. Boil and simmer about
30 – 45 minutes (if presoaked) to
90 minutes (if dry), until tender.
Tip: Black-eyed peas are more
easily digested than other
legumes.
Brand: Eden Organic (canned)

AFRICAN CUISINE
agave nectar
allspice
arugula
barbecue sauce
barley
basil
BAY LEAF
beans, e.g., green, kidney
BELL PEPPERS, e.g., green, red,
   roasted
burritos
cabbage
Cajun cuisine
capers
Caribbean cuisine
carrots
casseroles
celery
chard, Swiss
cheese, e.g., feta
chiles, e.g., chipotle, habenero,
   jalapeño; chili pepper flakes,
   chili pepper sauce, chili powder
chili, vegetarian
cilantro
coconut, e.g., butter, **milk**
coriander
corn
corn bread
Creole cuisine
cumin

dill
dips
GARLIC
ginger
GREENS, BITTER, e.g.,
   COLLARD, mustard, or turnip
gumbo
herbs, e.g., fresh
HOPPIN' JOHN
"hummus"
Indian cuisine
kombu
lemon, e.g., juice
marjoram
mushrooms, e.g., cremini,
   shiitake
oil, e.g., **olive**, safflower,
   sunflower
olives
ONIONS, e.g., **red**, yellow
oregano
parsley
pepper, black
potatoes
RICE, e.g., brown, long-grain,
   sticky
sage
salads, e.g., bean, green, Hoppin'
   John, tomato
salt
scallions
shallots
soul food
soups*, e.g., collard green*
SOUTHERN (U.S.) CUISINE
spinach
stews
stock, vegetable
succotash
tahini
tamari
tamarind

"Texas caviar"
thyme
TOMATOES
vinegar, e.g., apple cider, balsamic
yogurt

Flavor Affinities
black-eyed peas + bell peppers +
  celery + onions
black-eyed peas + brown rice +
  onions
black-eyed peas + coconut milk
  + sticky rice
black-eyed peas + corn + dill
black-eyed peas + feta cheese +
  tomatoes
black-eyed peas + garlic + greens
black-eyed peas + herbs + lemon
  + olive oil
black-eyed peas + onions +
  tomatoes
black-eyed peas + pumpkin + rice

● BLUEBERRIES

Season: spring – summer
Flavor: sour/**sweet**, with a soft,
juicy texture
Volume: quiet – moderate
Nutritional profile: 91% carbs
(high in sugar) / 5% fat / 4%
protein
Calories: 85 per 1-cup serving
(raw)
Protein: 1 gram
Techniques: dry, freeze, fresh,
simmer (10 minutes)

Tips: Frozen blueberries work
as well as fresh in smoothies.
Use dried blueberries when
you're worried about bursting
berries, e.g., in thicker batters
or smaller-sized tins (e.g., for
mini-muffins).

Possible substitutes:
huckleberries

agave nectar
almonds

(North) American cuisine
apples and apple juice
apricots
BAKED GOODS, e.g., breads,
  MUFFINS, pies, quick breads,
  scones, tarts
bananas
blackberries
buttermilk
cereals, breakfast
cheese, e.g., blue, **cream**, ricotta
CINNAMON
corn
corn cakes
cream and ice cream
crème fraîche
crepes
cucumbers
currants
DESSERTS, e.g., clafoutis, cobblers,
  ***crisps**, crumbles*
drinks, e.g., cocktails
fennel
fruit, tropical
ginger
grains, whole, e.g., spelt
granola
hazelnuts
honey
lavender
LEMON, e.g., juice, zest
lime, e.g., juice, zest
mango
MAPLE SYRUP
MASCARPONE
melon, e.g., cantaloupe
mint
nectarines
nutmeg
nuts
oats and oatmeal
orange, e.g., juice, zest
PANCAKES
PEACHES
pecans
pies
pineapple
raspberries

rhubarb
rice, brown
SALADS, e.g., FRUIT, green
salsas
sauces, fruit
SMOOTHIES
soups, fruit
sour cream
strawberries
SUGAR, e.g., brown
thyme
vanilla
watermelon
yogurt

Flavor Affinities
blueberries + cinnamon + lemon
  + rice
blueberries + cinnamon +
  nutmeg + peaches
blueberries + corn + nectarines
blueberries + cream cheese +
  lemon + nutmeg
blueberries + ginger + orange
blueberries + hazelnuts + rhubarb
  + ricotta
blueberries + honey + lime +
  mango
blueberries + lemon + ricotta
blueberries + maple syrup +
  pecans

● BOK CHOY (aka CHINESE CABBAGE or PAK CHOI)

[bahk CHOY]
Season: year-round, esp.
summer – autumn
Flavor: bitter/**sweet**, with spicy
notes of cabbage, chard, milk,
and/or spinach, and a soft, yet
crispy/crunchy and juicy texture
Volume: quiet
What it is: vegetable
Nutritional profile: 57% carbs
/ 32% protein / 11% fat
Calories: 20 per 1-cup serving
(shredded, boiled)

Protein: 3 grams
Techniques: blanch, boil, braise, raw, roast (at 400°F for 5 minutes), sauté (over high heat), simmer, steam, **STIR-FRY**

Tips: Bok choy is a quick-cooking green. Buy small (and tender) heads.

Botanical relatives: cabbage

agave nectar
almonds, e.g., roasted or
   smoked
Asian cuisines
beans, black, and **fermented black
   bean sauce**
bell peppers, red
broccoli
broccoli rabe
cabbage, e.g., napa, purple
cardamom
carrots
cashews
casseroles
cauliflower
celery
chiles, e.g., jalapeños
**chili pepper flakes, chili paste,
   and chili sauce**
Chinese cuisine
cilantro
cinnamon
coconut milk
curry powder and *curries*
five-spice powder
GARLIC
GINGER
greens, e.g., Asian, dandelion
hoisin
leeks
lemon
lemongrass
lime
lotus root
mirin
miso
MUSHROOMS, e.g., Chinese,
   shiitake

NOODLES, e.g., Asian, soba,
   udon
OIL, e.g., canola, chili, grapeseed,
   olive, peanut, SESAME,
   sunflower
onions, e.g., yellow
peanuts and peanut sauce
ponzu
potatoes
quinoa
rice, e.g., brown, short-grain

salads, when leaves are young
salt, sea
scallions
sesame seeds
shallots
slaws
SOUPS
soybeans, black
SOY SAUCE
sprouts, bean
squash, butternut

Flavor Affinities

bok choy + Asian noodles + peanut sauce
bok choy + Asian noodles + tofu + *stir-fries*
bok choy + bell peppers + olive oil + shiitake mushrooms
bok choy + black bean sauce + water chestnuts
bok choy + brown rice vinegar + sesame oil + tamari
bok choy + chiles + garlic + ginger + sesame oil
bok choy + chili flakes + coconut milk + red bell peppers
bok choy + fermented black bean sauce + **garlic + ginger**
BOK CHOY + GARLIC + GINGER + soy sauce
bok choy + garlic + olive oil
bok choy + garlic + sesame + tofu
bok choy + ginger + peanuts + ponzu
bok choy + ginger + tofu
bok choy + hoisin + shiitake mushrooms
bok choy + lemon + tahini
bok choy + lemongrass + lime
bok choy + mushrooms + tofu
bok choy + scallions + shiitake mushrooms

Dishes

Stir-Fried Bok Choy with Garlic and Ginger, served with Brown Rice and Plum Sauce
— Bloodroot (Bridgeport, CT)

Giant Asian Dumplings: Steamed Dumplings filled with Wok-Seared Vegetables, Edamame, Ginger, and Garlic, served with Sweet Chili Dipping Sauce and Grilled Bok Choy
— Canyon Ranch (Lenox, MA)

Bok Choy with Broccoli, Vinton Soybeans, and Hakurei Turnips
— Gramercy Tavern (New York City)

Sautéed Baby Bok Choy, Ginger Ponzu, Toasted Peanuts
— Green Zebra (Chicago)

Baby Bok Choy, Kimchi-Tokyo Turnips, Cashew, Chili Vinaigrette
— Picholine (New York City)

stews
STIR-FRIES
stock, e.g., mushroom or
vegetable
sugar, brown
tahini
tamari
tempeh
Thai cuisine
TOFU
turmeric
turnips
vinaigrette
vinegar, e.g., brown rice, rice, or
umeboshi
water chestnuts
wine, e.g., dry sherry
zucchini

● BORAGE

[BOHR-ij]
Season: spring
Flavor: sweet, with notes of
celery, **cucumber**, herbs, and/or
honey; and fuzzy-textured leaves
Volume: quiet – moderate
What it is: herb / leafy green
Nutritional profile: 51% carbs /
28% fat / 21% protein
Calories: 20 per 1-cup serving
(raw)
Protein: 2 grams
Techniques: raw, sauté, steam
Tips: Chop finely before adding
to dishes. Use bluish-purple bor-
age flowers as an edible garnish
for cocktails, salads, or other
dishes.
Possible substitutes: celery
(for stems), spinach (for leaves)

Dishes

Garden Borage Risotto with Smoked Local
Hen Egg, Borage, Housemade Ricotta
— Hotel Fauchère (Milford, PA)

basil
cheese, e.g., cream, ricotta, ricotta
salata
chervil
chickpeas
chives
cocktails, e.g., gin-based, e.g.,
Pimm's cup
cream
cucumbers
dill
drinks, e.g., fruit, iced
eggs, e.g., boiled, poached,
smoked
European cuisines
fennel
garlic
German cuisine
gin
lemon, e.g., juice
mint
mustard
oil, e.g., olive, vegetable, walnut
parsley
pasta, e.g., ravioli
pepper, e.g., white
potatoes
rice, e.g., Arborio
risottos
salad dressings
salads, e.g., bread, chickpea, fruit,
green
sauces, e.g., green, herb
scallions
sorrel
soups, e.g., cold, cucumber,
vegetable
sour cream
stocks, vegetable
teas
thyme
tomatoes
vegetables
vinegar, e.g., fruit, rice wine
watercress
wine, white
yogurt

Flavor Affinities
borage + chervil + chives + cream
cheese + parsley + sorrel +
yogurt + *sauces*
borage + eggs + potatoes

"I love **borage**, burnet, and
comfrey, three herbs that all taste
like cucumber and are wonderful
to add to salads when you don't
have cucumbers on hand.
Comfrey is also good for broken
bones, and [Bloodroot partner]
Noel [Furie] once healed herself
with comfrey."
— SELMA MIRIAM, FOUNDER OF
BLOODROOT (BRIDGEPORT, CT)

● BOYSENBERRIES (see also BLACKBERRIES)
Tip: Use like blackberries, one
of the three berries (along with
raspberries and loganberries)
of which boysenberries are a
hybrid.

BRAGG LIQUID AMINOS
Flavor: complex notes of beef
stock, soy sauce, and/or red wine
Volume: moderate – loud
What it is: an unfermented,
soy-based condiment that offers
a gluten-free (though not low-
sodium) alternative to soy sauce
Tip: Add to toasted sesame
oil for an instant sauce for
vegetables.
Possible substitutes: soy
sauce, tamari

beans
carrots
casseroles
cauliflower
celery
cilantro
daikon

eggplant
garlic
ginger
grains, whole
gravies
greens, e.g., collard
honey
juices, e.g., carrot
kale
lemon, e.g., juice
lentils
mushrooms, e.g., shiitake
oil, e.g., olive, **sesame**
onions
parsley
popcorn
potatoes
raw cuisine
rice, e.g., brown
salad dressings, e.g., Caesar
salads
sauces
scallions
seitan
soups, e.g., gazpacho
spreads
stews
stir-fries
stock, vegetable
tofu
tomatoes
vegetables, e.g., steamed
veggie burgers

Flavor Affinities
Bragg Liquid Aminos + brown
  rice + carrots + celery + onions
  + tofu
Bragg Liquid Aminos + garlic +
  lemon juice + olive oil

BRAZIL NUTS (see NUTS, BRAZIL)

BRAZILIAN CUISINE
beans, black
cardamom
chiles

cilantro
cloves
coconut milk
feijoada
garlic
ginger
greens, e.g., collard
kale
nutmeg
onions
orange
parsley
pepper, black
peppers, Brazilian
pumpkin
rice
saffron
salsa
thyme

Flavor Affinities
black beans + onions + orange

● BREAD CRUMBS, WHOLE-GRAIN
Flavor: typically neutral, with a
crunchy texture
Volume: quiet

Tips: Make your own healthful
bread crumbs by drying
or lightly toasting whole-grain
or sprouted grain bread (e.g.,
Ezekiel brand), then puls-
ing in a food processor until
lightly crumbed — or, for larger
crumbs and more texture, grate
the dried bread on a cheese
grater right over the dish. Use to
add a crunchy texture to gratins,
pastas, salads, soups, etc.

arugula
asparagus
beans, e.g., green
breadings, e.g., for seitan
casseroles
cassoulets
cauliflower

cheese, e.g., goat, Parmesan,
  pecorino
endive
fennel
garlic
gratins
Italian cuisine
legumes, e.g., lentils
macaroni and cheese
marjoram
mushrooms
nuts, e.g., pistachios
oil, olive
onions
parsley
*pastas, e.g., linguini, macaroni,
  spaghetti*
pesto
radicchio
rosemary
*salads, e.g., bean, Caesar, green,
  mushroom*
soups, e.g., gazpacho, white bean
stuffings
thyme
tomatoes, e.g., *broiled*
veggie burgers
watercress
zucchini

Flavor Affinities
bread crumbs + garlic + olive oil +
  Parmesan cheese
bread crumbs + kale + lemon
  juice + Parmesan cheese

BREAD CRUMBS, PANKO

Flavor: neutral, with a very
crunchy texture
Volume: quiet
What it is: Japanese bread
crumbs
Calories: 110 per ½-cup serving
Tip: Makes a crunchy crust for
seitan and tofu or a coating for
deep-fried foods, e.g., vegetables

artichokes
asparagus
baked dishes
breadings
cheese, e.g., goat, mozzarella,
    Parmesan, pecorino
crusts
deep-fried dishes
eggplant
herbs, e.g., basil, parsley
Japanese cuisine
lemon
"*meatballs*"
mushrooms, e.g., oyster
nuts, e.g., pecans
seitan
squash, e.g., kabocha
stuffings, e.g., for artichokes
tofu

BREAKFAST and BRUNCH

Tips: Eating breakfast jump-
starts your metabolism and
can prevent overeating later
in the day.

When you can't decide what
you're in the mood for at
breakfast, consider these:

almond butter, e.g., on whole-
    grain bread
apples and apple juice
bagels, whole grain, e.g., with nut
    butter
bananas
biscuits with "sausage" and gravy
breads, whole-grain, e.g., sliced
    or toasted, with or without
    nut butter
burritos, breakfast
cereal, e.g., cold
cereal, e.g., hot, whole grain:
    amaranth, millet, oats, quinoa,
    wheat berries; e.g., with berries,
    cinnamon, cocoa powder,
    coconut flakes, flax seeds, maple

syrup, and/or milk — such as
    almond, rice or soy)
*chilaquiles (i.e., beans + cheese +
    salsa + tortillas or tortilla chips +
    optional egg)*
crepes, e.g., fruit or savory
egg dishes: frittatas, omelets,
    scrambled
*French toast, e.g., cinnamon-date,
    vegan (e.g., substitute almond milk,
    or ground flaxseed and water, for
    egg), whole-grain bread*
frittatas, e.g., broccoli-cheese
fruit, fresh, e.g., apples, bananas,
    blueberries, strawberries
fruit and cheese
granola, e.g., cranberry-maple
*hash, e.g., bell peppers, cheese, eggs,
    onions, potatoes, scallions,
    spinach, sweet potatoes, tomatoes,
    vegetables*
*huevos (or tofu) rancheros: eggs on
    tortillas with dairy or vegan
    cheese, pico de gallo, guacamole,
    and (cashew) sour cream*
melon, e.g., cantaloupe or
    honeydew
muesli
muffins, fruit and/or whole grain
nut butters, e.g., almond, peanut,
    on whole-grain bread, or sliced
    fruits or vegetables
*oatmeal, e.g., with dried or fresh
    fruit, flaxseeds, nuts*
*pancakes, e.g., apple/walnut,
    banana/walnut, blueberry,
    pumpkin, vegan*
pies or tarts, e.g., ricotta
porridge, e.g., nut
rice, brown, e.g., with cinnamon
scrambles, egg or tofu
smoothies, e.g., fruit
soufflés
soups, e.g., fruit
tacos, breakfast
toast, whole wheat with nut butter
    and banana
tofu, scrambled

*tostada, breakfast: avocado + beans
    + corn tortilla + egg + salsa*
waffles, whole-grain, e.g., with fruit
wheat germ, e.g., mixed into yogurt
wraps, breakfast
yogurt, e.g., with fruit (e.g.,
    bananas, berries, peaches),
    granola

● BROCCOLI

Season: autumn – winter
Flavor: slightly bitter, with notes
of cabbage, cauliflower, and/
or grass, and a crunchy texture
(when raw)
Volume: moderate
What it is: vegetable – green
Who says it's healthful:
The Center for Science in the
Public Interest's *Nutrition Action*
includes broccoli on its "10 Best
Foods" list.
Nutritional profile: 73% carbs
/ 17% protein / 10% fat

Calories: 55 per 1-cup serving (boiled)

Protein: 4 grams

Techniques: Better served cooked than raw — but cook only until tender, and do *not* overcook: boil (3 – 5 minutes), deep-fry (e.g., tempura), pressure-cook (2 – 3 minutes, puree, roast, sauté, simmer (5 – 6 minutes), **steam**, stir-fry (2 – 3 minutes)

Tip: Make a salad from leftover stems of broccoli florets.

Botanical relatives: Brussels sprouts, cabbage, cauliflower, collard greens, horseradish, kale, kohlrabi, land cress, radishes, rutabagas, turnips, watercress

almonds
avocado
basil, e.g., Italian or Thai
beans, e.g., black, **cannellini**, green, **white**
BELL PEPPERS, e.g., red, esp. roasted
bread crumbs
bulgur
butter and brown butter
capers
cashews
casseroles
cauliflower
cayenne
CHEESE, e.g., blue, **feta**, **cheddar**, goat, Gorgonzola, Gouda, mozzarella, **PARMESAN**, pecorino, Romano
chickpeas
CHILES, e.g., green, red; and **chili pepper flakes**
chives
cilantro
coconut and coconut milk
coriander
cream
crepes
crudités

Dishes

Iacopi Farm Broccoli Soup with Cheddar and Chives
— Greens Restaurant (San Francisco)

curries and **curry**, e.g., paste, powder, spices
dill
eggs, e.g., *custards, omelets, quiches*
flax seeds
GARLIC
ginger
gomashio
gratins
greens, mesclun
"*guacamole*"
hazelnuts
"*hummus*"
leeks
LEMON, e.g., juice, zest
lime
marjoram
mayonnaise
miso, e.g., barley
mushrooms, e.g., oyster, shiitake
mustard, e.g., Dijon, and mustard seeds
noodles, e.g., Asian, rice, soba, udon
nuts, e.g., peanuts, pecans
OIL, e.g., OLIVE, peanut, sesame, walnut
olives, e.g., black
ONIONS, e.g., red, yellow
orange
oregano
parsley, e.g., Italian
PASTA, e.g., fettuccine, linguini, penne, spaghetti
pepper, e.g., black
pestos
pine nuts
pizzas
potatoes, *e.g., baked potatoes*, red
pumpkin seeds
rice, e.g., brown
rosemary

sage
SALADS, e.g., green, pasta, tomato, vegetable
salsify
salt, esp. sea
sauces, e.g., hollandaise
savory
scallions
seitan
sesame, e.g., oil, seeds
shallots
slaws
soufflés
SOUPS, e.g., broccoli, creamy
soybeans
soy sauce
spinach
sprouts, mung bean
squash, e.g., spaghetti
stews
stir-fries
stock, vegetable
tahini
tamari
tarragon
tempura
thyme
tofu
tomatoes
tomatoes, sun-dried
turmeric
vinaigrette
vinegar, e.g., balsamic, rice, tarragon
walnuts
watercress
wheat berries
wine, dry white
yogurt

Flavor Affinities

broccoli + almonds + citrus (e.g., lemon, orange) (+ garlic)

broccoli + almonds + mushrooms

broccoli + almonds + Romano cheese

broccoli + basil + **garlic + olive oil** + Parmesan cheese + walnuts

broccoli + bell peppers + capers + olives

broccoli + bell peppers + mozzarella cheese

broccoli + chiles + garlic + ginger + lime + olive oil

BROCCOLI + CHILES (fresh or chili pepper flakes) + GARLIC + olive oil

broccoli + chiles + garlic + orange (juice, zest)

broccoli + feta cheese + mint + red onions

broccoli + flax seeds + lemon

broccoli + garlic + ginger + **sesame oil/seeds** + tamari

broccoli + garlic + lemon + olive oil + chili pepper flakes

broccoli + garlic + lemon + tahini

broccoli + ginger + orange

broccoli + lemon + parsley

broccoli + lime + noodles + peanuts

broccoli + miso + sesame

broccoli + onions + orange

broccoli + orange + Parmesan cheese + tomatoes

broccoli + pasta + pecorino cheese + white beans

broccoli + red onions + yogurt

broccoli + rice vinegar + sesame oil + **sesame seeds + soy sauce/tamari**

• BROCCOLI, CHINESE (aka CHINESE KALE or GAI LAN)

Flavor: slightly bitter, with a crisp, crunchy texture

Volume: quiet – moderate

Nutritional profile: 60% carbs / 27% fat / 13% protein

Calories: 20 per 1-cup serving (cooked)

Protein: 1 gram

Techniques: blanch, sauté, steam, stir-fry

Tip: Opt for Chinese broccoli when you need a quick-cooking green.

beets

carrots

chives

citrus

five-spice powder

GARLIC

GINGER

grains

leeks

lemon, e.g., juice, zest

mirin

miso

mushrooms, e.g., shiitake

mustard

oil, e.g., chili, grapeseed, olive, **peanut**, or **sesame**

olives

pasta

peanuts

raisins

sauces, e.g., black bean, hoisin

scallions

soy sauce

squash, winter

stir-fries

sugar

tofu

tomatoes

vinegar, e.g., balsamic or rice

wine, e.g., rice

Flavor Affinities

Chinese broccoli + black bean
   sauce + chives + garlic
CHINESE BROCCOLI + GARLIC
   + GINGER + peanuts +
   scallions + soy sauce
CHINESE BROCCOLI + GARLIC
   + GINGER + shiitake
   mushrooms + tofu
CHINESE BROCCOLI + GARLIC
   + GINGER + soy sauce
Chinese broccoli + mustard +
   soy sauce

• BROCCOLI RABE (aka BROCCOLI RAAB or RAPINI)

Flavor: bitter, with pungent
notes of mustard, pepper, spices,
and/or turnips
Volume: moderate – **loud**
Nutritional profile: 46%
protein / 40% carbs / 14% fat
Calories: 30 per 1-cup serving
(cooked)
Protein: 3 grams
Techniques: boil, braise, fry,
parboil, roast, **sauté**, simmer,
steam, stir-fry
(Note: not raw)
Botanical relatives: broccoli,
cabbage, **turnips** and turnip
greens

almonds
barley
basil
beans, e.g., fava, shell, white
bell peppers, e.g., red or yellow,
   esp. roasted
bread crumbs
bruschetta
capers
carrots
CHEESE, e.g., feta, Fontina,
   fresh, mozzarella, **Parmesan**,
   pecorino, **ricotta**, ricotta salata,

Romano, sheep's milk, smoked
   mozzarella, white
chestnuts
chickpeas
chiles, e.g., jalapeño, and **CHILI**
   PEPPER FLAKES
Chinese cuisine
chives
cilantro
citrus
cream
currants
eggplant
eggs
*****GARLIC**
ginger
grains, e.g., barley
hazelnuts
Italian cuisine
lemon

lemon, Meyer
mushrooms
mustard seeds
noodles, rice
OIL, e.g., **OLIVE**, peanut
olives
onions, e.g., yellow
oregano
paprika, e.g., smoked
PASTA, esp. whole grain, e.g.,
   fettuccine, orecchiette,
   penne, spaghettini
peanuts
pepper, black
pesto
pine nuts
pizza
polenta
potatoes
raisins

Flavor Affinities

broccoli rabe + beans + pasta
BROCCOLI RABE + BREAD CRUMBS + CHILI FLAKES + GARLIC
broccoli rabe + brown rice + chickpeas + garlic
broccoli rabe + brown rice + cilantro + peanuts + soy sauce
broccoli rabe + cheese (e.g., pecorino, ricotta) + pasta
broccoli rabe + chiles + citrus + feta cheese + pasta
broccoli rabe + chiles + garlic
BROCCOLI RABE + CHILI PEPPER FLAKES + GARLIC + lemon +
   OLIVE OIL
broccoli rabe + chili pepper flakes + olives + smoked mozzarella +
   pizza
broccoli rabe + chili flakes + lemon + pasta
broccoli rabe + garlic + lemon + pine nuts + raisins
BROCCOLI RABE + GARLIC + OLIVE OIL + PASTA
broccoli rabe + garlic + pine nuts

Dishes

Grilled Broccoli Rabe with Spicy Tomato Sauce and Sour Cream
— ABC Kitchen (New York City)

Charred Broccoli Rabe with Peperoncini, Crispy Shallots
— Boulud Sud (New York City)

Spaghetti and Wheatballs, Broccoli Rabe, Black Olives, Basil Marinara
— Café Blossom (New York City)

rice, e.g., brown
risotto
salad dressing, e.g., lemon
 vinaigrette
salads
salt, sea
scallions
shallots
soups, e.g., bean, broccoli rabe
soy sauce
squash, summer
stews
stir-fries
stock, vegetable
tempeh
tofu
tomatoes
turmeric
vinegar, e.g., balsamic, red wine,
 sherry, white wine
walnuts
wine, dry white

● BROCCOLINI

Flavor: slightly sweet, with
peppery notes of grass, and a
tender yet crisp texture
Volume: quiet – moderate
What it is: a hybrid of broccoli
and gai-lan (a type of Chinese
broccoli)
Calories: 35 per 1-cup serving
Techniques: Cooks quickly:
blanch, boil, raw, sauté, steam,
stir-fry

almonds
basil
bell peppers, e.g., red
bread crumbs

Dishes

Grilled Olive Pesto Tofu with Broccolini and Smashed Purple Potatoes
— Plum Bistro (Seattle)

Mushroom Home Fries with Pan-Roasted Broccolini, Mushrooms, and Parsley-Walnut Pesto
— Portobello (Portland, OR)

broccoli and broccoli rabe
cheese, e.g., feta, Parmesan
chiles, e.g., dried, and chili paste,
 chili pepper flakes, and
 chili sauce
cilantro
eggs, e.g., *frittatas*
garlic
ginger
lemon, e.g., juice, zest
mushrooms, e.g., porcini
mustard, e.g., Dijon
oil, e.g., **olive**, porcini, sesame,
 vegetable
olives
onions, e.g., red
orange, e.g., juice, zest
parsley
pastas, e.g., fettuccine
peanuts and peanut sauce
pepper, e.g., black
potatoes
salads
salt, sea
sesame, e.g., oil, seeds
shallots
soups
soy sauce
stock, e.g., vegetable
tofu
tomatoes
vinegar, e.g., balsamic, cider

Flavor Affinities

broccolini + balsamic vinegar +
 Dijon mustard + olive oil
broccolini + chiles + cilantro +
 garlic + ginger
broccolini + egg + mushrooms +
 Parmesan cheese + pasta
**broccolini + garlic + olive oil +
 Parmesan cheese + pasta**
broccolini + ginger + orange
**broccolini + orange + sesame oil
 + soy sauce**

BROWN RICE (see RICE, BROWN)

BROWN RICE SYRUP (aka RICE MALT SYRUP)

Flavor: sweet, with notes of
butterscotch, caramel, malt, and/
or rice, and a thick, liquid texture
Volume: quiet
Nutritional profile: 97% carbs
/ 3% protein
Calories: 75 per tablespoon
serving

Tip: Half as sweet as regular
sugar, it can substitute for honey
(e.g., on toast) or maple syrup
(e.g., on waffles).

Possible substitute: barley
malt syrup

*baked goods, e.g., cakes, cookies,
 muffins*
coffee
cookies, esp. crisp
ice cream
marinades
pancakes
popcorn, e.g., *"caramel corn"*
salad dressings
waffles

BRUNCH (see BREAKFAST and BRUNCH)

● BRUSSELS SPROUTS

Season: autumn – winter
Flavor: bitter/sweet, with
pungent notes of broccoli,
cabbage, and/or nuts, and a
crisp texture

Volume: quiet (younger) – moderate/loud (older)
What they are: green vegetable
Nutritional profile: 71% carbs / 17% protein / 12% fat
Calories: 30 per ½-cup serving (boiled)
Protein: 2 grams
Tips: Look for smaller Brussels sprouts. Better served lightly cooked than raw. Cook only until tender. Do *not* boil them, as they will lose nutritional value — and overcooking heightens their sulphur notes, ruining the flavor.
Techniques: blanch, boil, **braise**, fry, grill, mandoline, pressure-cook (2 – 3 minutes), puree, roast (20 – 30 minutes at 350°F), **sauté**, shred, simmer, **steam** (7 – 10 minutes), stir-fry, tempura-fry
Botanical relatives: broccoli, **cabbage**, **cauliflower**, collard greens, horseradish, **kale**, **kohlrabi**, land cress, radishes, rutabagas, turnips, watercress

almonds
apples (dried and fresh), **apple cider**, and **apple juice**
artichokes, Jerusalem
basil
bay leaf
bell peppers, e.g., red
bread crumbs
butter and brown butter
capers
caraway seeds
carrots
cashews
cauliflower
celery
celery root
CHEESE, e.g., **blue**, **cheddar**, feta, goat, Gorgonzola, Gouda, Gruyère, **Parmesan**, pecorino, provolone, ricotta, Roquefort, Swiss
CHESTNUTS (traditional)
chili pepper flakes
chives
coconut milk
coriander
cranberries, dried
cream and crème fraîche
crudités
cumin
curry powder
dill
eggs, e.g., fried, hard-boiled, *omelets,* poached
endive, e.g., Belgian
fennel
fennel seeds
GARLIC

ghee
ginger
grains, whole, e.g., buckwheat
grapefruit
grapes
hazelnuts
juniper berries
kale
kasha
LEMON, e.g., juice, zest
lentils, e.g., French
lime
maple syrup
marjoram
mint
mirin
miso
mushrooms, e.g., shiitake
MUSTARD, e.g., **Dijon**, mustard powder, and mustard seeds
nutmeg

Flavor Affinities
Brussels sprouts + almonds + orange juice
Brussels sprouts + apples + goat cheese + hazelnuts
Brussels sprouts + black pepper + pecorino
Brussels sprouts + blue cheese + walnuts
Brussels sprouts + bread crumbs + hard-boiled eggs + lemon + parsley
Brussels sprouts + buckwheat + mushrooms
Brussels sprouts + caraway seeds + mustard
Brussels sprouts + caraway seeds + orange
Brussels sprouts + caraway + sour cream
Brussels sprouts + cauliflower + garlic + olive oil + rosemary
Brussels sprouts + chestnuts + maple syrup
Brussls sprouts + chili pepper flakes + garlic + shallots
Brussels sprouts + cream + nutmeg + Parmesan cheese
Brussels sprouts + dried cranberries + walnuts
Brussels sprouts + garlic + lemon + olive oil
Brussels sprouts + garlic + pine nuts + shallots
Brussels sprouts + garlic + vinegar + walnuts
Brussels sprouts + ginger + thyme
Brussels sprouts + hazelnuts + maple syrup
Brussels sprouts + juniper berries + orange juice
BRUSSELS SPROUTS + LEMON + MUSTARD + parsley + walnut oil
Brussels sprouts + miso + mustard
Brussels sprouts + mushrooms + pine nuts
Brussels sprouts + orange + sesame oil

Dishes

Seared Brussels Sprouts with Garlic, Italian Chilies, Preserved Lemon, and Toasted Pistachios
— Millennium (San Francisco)

OIL, e.g., canola, hazelnut, mustard, nut, **OLIVE**, peanut, pumpkin seed, sesame, **walnut**
onions, e.g., green, red
orange, e.g., juice
oregano
paprika, e.g., smoked
parsley
parnips
pasta, e.g., whole grain
pears
pecans
pepper, e.g., black, white
pine nuts
pistachios
potatoes
raisins
rice, e.g., basmati
rosemary
rutabagas
salads
salt, e.g., **kosher, sea**, smoked
scallions
sesame seeds
shallots
slaws
soups, e.g., chestnut, vegetable
sour cream
soy sauce
sprouts, e.g., bean, mung bean
squash, e.g., winter
stir-fries
stock, vegetable
sugar
sunflower seeds
tamari
thyme
tofu, e.g., smoked
turnips
vegetables, root
vermouth

vinaigrette
VINEGAR, e.g., apple, balsamic, rice wine, sherry, tarragon, white wine
WALNUTS
water chestnuts
wine, e.g., dry white, rice
yogurt

"The way Jean-Georges Vongerichten thinks about flavors is exceptional. I made his recipe for **Brussels sprouts** [with toasted pecans and avocado] that appeared in *Food and Wine*, and it was amazingly good."
— SELMA MIRIAM, BLOODROOT (BRIDGEPORT, CT)

"In mainstream restaurants, you'll inevitably see **Brussels sprouts** served with bacon. We serve them with smoked tofu, whose smokiness serves as the 'bacon,' accented by the sweetness of orange juice and a hint of agave plus the umami of miso."
— ERIC TUCKER, MILLENNIUM (SAN FRANCISCO)

● **BUCKWHEAT (aka BUCKWHEAT GROATS; see also KASHA and NOODLES, SOBA)**
Flavor: slightly sweet, with earthy notes of nuts
Volume: quiet – **moderate**
What it is: considered a whole grain, though it's not a grain but the seed of a non-grass crop

Gluten-free: yes
Nutritional profile: 82% carbs / 12% protein / 6% fat
Calories: 155 per 1-cup serving (cooked)
Protein: 6 grams
Techniques: bake, boil, pan-roast, roast, simmer (about 10 – 20 minutes, until tender), stir-fry, toast
Ratio: 1:2 – 3 (1 part buckwheat to 2 – 3 parts cooking liquid)
Tips: Toast until crunchy (to bring out flavor). Sprinkle on salads or vegetable dishes. Roasted buckwheat groats are sold as kasha (see also KASHA).
Botanical relatives: rhubarb, sorrel (*not* wheat)

almonds and almond butter
apples, e.g., cider, fruit, juice
arame
asparagus
bananas
basil
bay leaf
beans, e.g., black
bell peppers, e.g., red
berries, e.g., blueberries
Brazil nuts
butter
cabbage
cardamom
carrots
cashews
casseroles
celery
cereals, hot breakfast
chard, Swiss
cheese, e.g., feta, Fontina, goat, Gruyère, Parmesan
chickpeas
chives
cinnamon
corn
crepes

dates

Eastern European cuisine

eggs or egg whites, e.g., fried, poached, roasted

flax seeds

(Northern) French cuisine

fruit, dried

garlic

ginger

grains, other milder, e.g., cracked wheat, millet, rice

herbs

honey

ice cream

KASHA

kohlrabi

leeks

lemon, e.g., juice, zest

maple syrup

"meat loaf," made with grains, nuts, and/or vegetables

MUSHROOMS, e.g., wild

noodles, e.g., soba

oil, olive

ONIONS, e.g., caramelized

PANCAKES

parsley

PASTAS, e.g., FARFALLE

pears

pepper, black

pilafs

pine nuts

"polentas"

porridges

potatoes

quinces

Russian cuisine

sage

salads

salt, sea

scallions

sesame, e.g., oil, sauce, seeds

soups, e.g., black bean, potato

sour cream

soy sauce

spinach

squash

stock, e.g., mushroom, vegetable

stuffed vegetables, e.g., cabbage, mushrooms, winter squash

stuffings

thyme

tofu

tomatoes

vanilla

vegetables, e.g., root

veggie burgers

walnuts

yogurt

Flavor Affinities

buckwheat + apples + maple syrup

buckwheat + bananas + walnuts

buckwheat + basil + mushrooms + tomatoes

buckwheat + blueberries + cinnamon + ginger + vanilla

buckwheat + carrots + mushrooms

buckwheat + eggs (e.g., fried, poached) + garlic + thyme

buckwheat + feta cheese + parsley

buckwheat + garlic + mushrooms + onions

buckwheat + garlic + parsley + soy sauce

buckwheat + lemon + olive oil + parsley + scallions

buckwheat + mushrooms + scallions + sesame oil

buckwheat + potatoes + thyme

● BULGUR, WHOLE WHEAT (see also WHEAT, CRACKED and WHEAT BERRIES)

[BUHL-guhr]

Flavor: notes of nuts, with a fluffy (i.e., fine) or chewy (i.e., medium to coarse) texture

Volume: quiet – moderate

What it is: pre-cooked (e.g., steamed), dried, cracked/ground, whole-grain wheat berries

Gluten-free: no

Nutritional profile: 85% carbs / 13% protein / 2% fat

Calories: 150 per 1-cup serving (cooked)

Protein: 6 grams

Techniques: boil (10 – 20 minutes), simmer (15 – 20 minutes), steam

Timing: Cook about 15 – 20 minutes, covered.

Ratio: 1 : 1½ (finer) – 2½ (coarser) (1 cup bulgur to 1½ – 2½ cups cooking liquid)

Tips: Different grinds are better for different uses — fine grinds make better tabboulehs, while coarse grinds make better pilafs. Enhance its nutty flavor by sautéing before steaming. Seasoned, it can substitute for ground meat in vegetarian chili, tacos, etc.

almonds

apples and apple juice

apricots, e.g., dried

arugula

beans, e.g., cannellini, fava

bell peppers, e.g., green

broccoli

butter

buttermilk

cabbage, e.g., red

carrots

casseroles

cauliflower

cereals, hot breakfast

celery

chard

cheese, e.g., feta, goat

CHICKPEAS

chiles, e.g., ancho, and chili powder

chili, vegetarian

cilantro

cinnamon

citrus, e.g., zest

coriander

corn
cranberries, dried
cucumbers
cumin
currants
dill
eggplant
falafel
figs
fruit, dried
garlic
grape leaves
grapes
greens, e.g., collard
herbs, fresh
honey
kibbeh, vegetarian (use fine grain)
leeks

Dishes

Vegan Taco Salad: Bulgur Wheat seasoned with Chili Powder and Cumin, served with Tortilla Chips and (Soy Milk-based Vegan) Sour Cream
— Soul Gourmet Vegan (Chicago)

LEMON, e.g., juice, zest
lentils, e.g., green, red
lettuce, e.g., Bibb, romaine
lime
"meatballs" and "meat sauce"
Mediterrean cuisines
Middle Eastern cuisines
MINT
mushrooms, e.g., cremini
mustard
nuts
oil, e.g., olive, sesame, walnut

olives
ONIONS, e.g., green, red, sweet, white
orange
PARSLEY
peas
pepper, black or white
PILAFS (use large grain)
pine nuts
pistachios
plums
pomegranates
puddings
pumpkin
radishes
raisins
rice
"risottos"
SALADS, e.g., grain, tomato, vegetable
salsa, e.g., tomato
salt, e.g., sea
sauces
scallions
seeds, e.g., sesame, sunflower
sesame, e.g., oil, seeds
shallots
soups
spinach
squash, e.g., spaghetti, **summer,** winter, **yellow**
stews
stock, vegetable
stuffed vegetables, e.g., bell peppers, cabbage, grape leaves, tomatoes
stuffings
TABBOULEH (use fine grain)
tamari
tangerines
tarragon
thyme
tofu

Flavor Affinities

bulgur + almonds + amaranth
bulgur + almonds + apples + cinnamon (+ honey) (+ raisins)
bulgur + arugula + white beans
bulgur + basil + tomatoes + *pilaf*
bulgur + basil + tomatoes + walnuts + *tabbouleh*
bulgur + bell peppers + chickpeas + **cumin**
bulgur + bell peppers + chili powder + **cumin** + lemon juice + mustard + olive oil + onions + tomatoes
bulgur + chickpeas + **lemon** + mint + **olive oil** + parsley + **tomatoes**
bulgur + cilantro + lime
bulgur + cinnamon + lemon + pine nuts
bulgur + coriander + onions + **parsley**
BULGUR + cucumbers + ONIONS + PARSLEY + TOMATOES
bulgur + cucumbers + tomatoes
bulgur + dill + feta cheese + garlic + spinach
bulgur + dried currants + lemon juice + mint + onions + parsley
bulgur + dried fruit (e.g. apricots, currants, raisins) + **nuts** (e.g., pistachios, walnuts)
bulgur + eggplant + yogurt
bulgur + garlic + leeks + mushrooms + Swiss chard
bulgur + garlic + **lemon** + **mint** + **parsley**
bulgur + goat cheese + parsley + tomatoes
bulgur + lentils + walnuts
bulgur + mint + parsley + tomatoes
bulgur + mint + shallots + **tomatoes**
bulgur + mushrooms + spinach + *pilafs*
bulgur + orange + pistachios

TOMATOES and tomato paste
tomatoes, sun-dried
vinegar, e.g., balsamic
walnuts
yogurt
za'atar
zucchini

● BURDOCK (aka BURDOCK ROOT or GOBO ROOT)

Flavor: sweet; with rich, earthy notes of artichokes, nuts, and/or potatoes, and a tender yet crunchy (when raw) or chewy (when cooked) texture
Volume: moderate
What it is: Japanese root vegetable
Nutritional profile: 92% carbs / 7% protein / 1% fat
Calories: 110 per 1-cup serving (boiled)
Protein: 3 grams
Techniques: sauté, shred, simmer, stir-fry

Tips: Do not use raw. Doesn't need to be peeled, but scrub well.

Botanical relatives: artichokes

apples, e.g., cider, juice
arame
artichokes, Jerusalem
barley
brown rice syrup
cabbage, e.g., savoy
CARROTS
celery
celery leaves
chiles, e.g., jalapeño, Thai; and chili pepper flakes
dashi
dates
fennel seeds
garlic
GINGER

grains, e.g., millet
greens, e.g., dandelion
hiziki
JAPANESE CUISINE
kale
kinpira
leeks
lemon, e.g., juice, zest
lime
lotus root
macrobiotic cuisine
marinades
mirin
miso
mushrooms, e.g., shiitake
mustard
noodles, Asian, e.g., shirataki
nuts
oil, e.g., canola, corn, safflower, **sesame,** sunflower, vegetable
ONIONS, e.g., yellow
parsnips
potatoes
rice, e.g., basmati, brown, wild
sake
salads
salsify
scallions
SESAME, e.g., OIL, SEEDS
soups
SOY SAUCE
spinach
squash, winter
stews
stir-fries
stock, e.g., mushroom, vegetable
sugar
tahini
tamari
tarragon
tempura and kinpira

teriyaki sauce
tofu
tomatoes
vinegar, e.g., umeboshi
walnuts
watercress

Flavor Affinities
burdock + apple juice + **carrots** + **ginger** + sesame + soy sauce
burdock + **carrots** + lotus root + **sesame**
BURDOCK + CARROTS + SESAME+ SESAME OIL/ SEEDS + SOY SAUCE
burdock + chili pepper + mirin + sake + soy sauce
burdock + garlic + ginger
burdock + ginger + sesame
burdock + **ginger** + **soy sauce**
burdock + onions + shiitake mushrooms
burdock + potatoes + tarragon
burdock + rice + scallions + sesame oil + **sesame seeds** + **soy sauce**

"A mix of **burdock root** and carrots, cut into matchsticks, and seasoned with toasted sesame oil and tamari, is incredibly simple and incredibly delicious."
— MARK SHADLE, G-ZEN (BRANFORD, CT)

BURMESE CUISINE

beans, e.g., long
chiles, e.g., dried, red; and chili paste
cilantro
coconut
curries

eggplant
flour, chickpea
garlic
ginger
greens, e.g., Asian
lemongrass
lime
noodles, Asian, e.g., rice noodles
oil, e.g., peanut
peanuts
rice
scallions
shallots
soy sauce
sprouts, bean
sweet potatoes
tofu
turmeric

Flavor Affinities
greens + garlic + lime + peanuts
+ shallots

BUTTER, CLARIFIED
(see also GHEE)

Tip: Can be used for higher-
temperature cooking, as solids
have been removed.

BUTTER
Vegan substitute: Earth
Balance natural buttery spread
(0 g trans fat, non-GMO)

BUTTER, PEANUT
(see PEANUTS and
PEANUT BUTTER)

● BUTTERMILK,
LOW-FAT
Flavor: sour, with a thick,
creamy texture
Volume: moderate – loud
Nutritional profile: 46% carbs
/ 35% protein / 19% fat
Calories: 100 per 1-cup serving
Protein: 8 grams

Dishes

Southern Style Hushpuppies, Mesclun, Honey Butter, and Buttermilk Dressing
— Verjus (Paris)

avocados
bananas
baked goods, e.g., *biscuits, corn
breads, muffins, scones, shortcakes*
barley, e.g., pearl
basil
beets
berries, e.g., blackberries,
blueberries, raspberries,
strawberries
biscuits
broccoli
bulgur
cayenne
cherries
chickpeas
chives
chocolate
cilantro
cinnamon
citrus
corn
corn bread
cucumbers
cumin
dates
dill
garlic, e.g., roasted
ginger
HERBS, fresh, e.g., basil, chives,
cilantro, dill, parsley
honey
horseradish
lemon, e.g., juice
lime, e.g., juice
maple syrup
mayonnaise
mint
molasses
mustard, e.g., Dijon, powder,
seeds
nectarines

nutmeg
oatmeal and oats
onions
orange
pancakes and waffles
parsley
peaches
pepper, black
plums
potatoes
raisins
raitas
rhubarb
SALAD DRESSINGS, esp. creamy,
herb, ranch
sauces, e.g., pasta
scallions
slaws
smoothies
sorbets
soups, e.g., buttermilk, butternut
squash, cucumber, grain
squash, butternut
sugar, e.g., brown
vanilla
vegetables, green

Ranch dressing = **BUTTERMILK**-
based salad dressing often blended
with some of the following:
basil + bell peppers + black pepper + cayenne + chili pepper
sauce + **chives** + cilantro + **dill** +
GARLIC + **HERBS** + lemon juice +
mayonnaise + mustard + olive oil
+ **onions** + oregano + paprika +
parsley + salt + scallions + shallots
+ sour cream + sugar + tarragon +
thyme + vinegar + Worcestershire
sauce + yogurt

vinegar, e.g., cider, sherry, white wine
walnuts
wheat berries
Worcestershire sauce, vegetarian
yogurt

● CABBAGE, IN GENERAL, or MIXED CABBAGES

Season: autumn – winter
Flavor: bitter/sweet, with pungent and/or peppery notes, and a crunchy texture
Volume: quiet – moderate
Nutritional profile: 85% carbs / 12% protein / 3% fat
Calories: 25 per 1-cup serving (raw, chopped)
Protein: 1 gram
Techniques: bake, boil, braise, grate, pickle, pressure-cook (3 – 4 minutes), raw, sauté, shred, simmer, steam (6 – 8 minutes), stir-fry (2 – 4 minutes), stuff, tempura-fry (Better cooked than raw, but overcooking brings out its pungent, sulphuric notes.)

Tip: Red cabbage's firmer texture makes it a bit slower to cook than green cabbage.

Botanical relatives: broccoli, Brussels sprouts, cauliflower, collard greens, horseradish, kale, kohlrabi, land cress, radishes, rutabagas, turnips, watercress

APPLES, APPLE JUICE, and APPLE CIDER
bell peppers
butter and brown butter
CARAWAY SEEDS
CARROTS
celery
cheese, e.g., blue, cheddar, feta, Parmesan
cilantro
cole slaw

cream
dill
garlic
ginger
horseradish
juniper berries
leeks
lemon, e.g., juice, zest
lime, e.g., juice
mushrooms
mustard, e.g., Dijon, dry, prepared; mustard seeds
nutmeg
OIL, e.g., flax seed, hemp, mustard, nut, **OLIVE,** safflower, **sesame,** vegetable, walnut
onions, e.g., green, red, white
parsley
pepper, e.g., black, white
POTATOES
rice
salads
salt, e.g., kosher, sea, smoked
seeds, e.g., hemp, poppy, sesame, sunflower
sesame, e.g., oil, seeds
SLAWS
soups
soy sauce
stuffed cabbage
turnips
VINEGAR, e.g., apple cider, champagne, rice wine, sherry, wine

Flavor Affinities

cabbage + arame + sesame seeds + sesame oil
cabbage + brown rice + pine nuts + tomatoes
cabbage + caraway seeds + garlic + sea salt
cabbage + caraway seeds + lemon + safflower oil
cabbage + carrots + cider vinegar + mayonnaise + mustard
cabbage + carrots + ginger + mint + rice **wine vinegar** + sesame oil
cabbage + cream + nutmeg
cabbage + ginger + lime
cabbage + ginger + soy sauce
cabbage + mirin + sesame oil + umeboshi paste
cabbage + potatoes + turnips

● CABBAGE, CHINESE (aka NAPA CABBAGE; see also BOK CHOY)

Flavor: sweet, with notes of cabbage and celery, and a crisp/crunchy yet tender and juicy texture
Volume: quiet (combines well with louder greens)
Nutritional profile: 57% carbs / 32% protein / 11% fat
Calories: 20 per 1-cup serving (shredded, cooked)
Protein: 3 grams
Techniques: bake, blanch, boil, braise, grill, marinate, pickle, raw, sauté, shred, simmer, steam, stir-fry (4 – 5 minutes), stuff

Tips: Napa cabbage is one of the most popular types of Chinese cabbage. Do not over-cook, or its flavor will be lost.

almonds
arame
arugula
Asian cuisines
bamboo shoots
basil and Thai basil
beans, black, and black bean sauce
beans, green
beets
bell peppers
brown rice syrup

butter
cabbage, other, e.g., green, savoy
CARROTS
cayenne
chicory
chiles, e.g., dried red, jalapeño;
chili pepper flakes, chili pepper
paste, and chili powder
Chinese cuisine
cilantro
cloves
cornstarch
cucumbers
cumin
dill
fennel seeds
garlic
GINGER
greens, louder
hiziki
honey
kimchi
lemon
lettuce, e.g., mizuna
lime
lotus root
mint
mirin
miso
MUSHROOMS, e.g., black,
shiitake, wild
mustard seeds
noodles, Asian, e.g., mung bean,
udon
oil, e.g., chili, coconut, olive,
peanut, safflower, **sesame**,
vegetable
onions, e.g., green
parsley
peanuts and peanut butter
pears
peas
pepper, black
pickles
pine nuts
radicchio
radishes

raisins
rice, e.g., brown
SALADS, e.g., Asian, cabbage
salt, e.g., sea
scallions
seeds, e.g., sesame, sunflower
seitan
sesame, e.g., oil, sauce, seeds
slaws, e.g., Asian
snow peas
soups, e.g., Asian, cabbage, vegetable
soy sauce
spring rolls
stews
stir-fries
stock, e.g., vegetable
stuffed cabbage
sugar
sugar snap peas
tamari
tofu
turmeric
vegetables, Asian
vinegar, e.g., apple cider,
balsamic, black, brown rice,
rice wine
walnuts
watercress
wine, rice

Flavor Affinities
Chinese cabbage + Asian noodles + **cilantro + sesame oil + sesame
sauce** + soy sauce
Chinese cabbage + bell peppers + carrots + peanut dressing
Chinese cabbage + chili oil + sesame seeds
Chinese cabbage + chili pepper flakes + **garlic + ginger**
Chinese cabbage + cilantro + lemon + mint
Chinese cabbage + cilantro + peanuts
Chinese cabbage + garlic + ginger + sesame oil
Chinese cabbage + ginger + lemon
Chinese cabbage + ginger + peanuts
Chinese cabbage + ginger + sesame + soy sauce
Chinese cabbage + ginger + tofu
Chinese cabbage + lemon juice + sesame oil + soy sauce
Chinese cabbage + peanut butter + rice wine vinegar + soy sauce
Chinese cabbage + rice + shiitake mushrooms + tofu

• CABBAGE, GREEN

Flavor: slightly sweet (and more
so when cooked), with notes of
pepper, and a soft, rubbery texture
(when raw)
Volume: quiet
Techniques: blanch (to quiet
flavor), boil, braise, raw (e.g.,
slaw), roast, shred, simmer,
steam, stir-fry

apples and apple cider/juice
bay leaf
beans, e.g., green
bell peppers, e.g., red
bread, e.g., rye
bread crumbs, whole grain
butter
cabbage rolls
caraway seeds
cardamom
carrots
celery
celery root
celery salt / seeds
cheese, e.g., Gruyère, Swiss
cilantro
coriander
cream

croutons, e.g., pumpernickel, rye
cumin
curries, curry powder, and curry
    spices
dill
fennel
garlic
ginger
Hungarian cuisine
juniper berries
leeks
lentils, brown
lime
milk
mustard, e.g., Dijon
oil, olive
onions, e.g., yellow
parsley
pepper, e.g., black
potatoes
relishes

rice, e.g., brown or white
risottos
rosemary
salads, e.g., cabbage
salt, e.g., sea
slaws
soups, e.g., borscht, cabbage
sour cream
stock, e.g., vegetable
stuffed cabbage
tamari
thyme
tomatoes and tomato paste
vinegar, e.g., apple cider, red
    wine, white wine
walnuts

Flavor Affinities
green cabbage + apples + caraway
    seeds

● **CABBAGE, NAPA (see
CABBAGE, CHINESE)**
What it is: a popular type of
Chinese cabbage

● **CABBAGE, RED**
Season: autumn – winter
Flavor: more pungent notes
and a firmer texture than green
cabbage
Volume: quiet – moderate
Techniques: braise, mandoline,
marinate, raw (e.g., slaw), sauté,
stew, wilt

> **Tip:** Cook in water with a dash
> or more of apple juice or vinegar
> to maintain its redness.

allspice
APPLES AND APPLE JUICE

bay leaf
broccoli
caraway seeds
carrots
celery seeds
CHEESE, e.g., blue, feta, goat,
  Roquefort
chestnuts
cider, apple or pear
cinnamon
cloves
cranberries, e.g., dried, fresh,
  juice
cumin
dill
dulse
fennel and fennel seeds
fruit, e.g., sour
garlic
ginger
greens, salad
honey
juniper berries
kale
lemon, e.g., juice
lime, e.g., juice
lovage
marjoram
mint
MUSTARD, e.g., Dijon, dried,
  seeds
nutmeg
OIL, e.g., canola, **grapeseed**, nut,
  OLIVE, peanut, walnut
ONIONS, e.g., **red**, white
pears and Asian pears
pecans
pepper, e.g., black
pomegranates
raisins
salads, e.g., cabbage (cold or warm),
  green
salt
scallions
sesame, e.g., seeds
shallots
SLAWS
soups, e.g., borscht, sweet-and-sour

stews
sugar, e.g., organic brown
tarragon
thyme
VINEGAR, e.g., **apple cider**,
  balsamic, **RED WINE**, sherry
walnuts
wine, esp. dry red
yogurt

Flavor Affinities
RED CABBAGE + APPLES +
  BROWN SUGAR + caraway
  seeds + vinegar
RED CABBAGE + APPLES +
  BROWN SUGAR + onions +
  vinegar
red cabbage + apples + garlic +
  olive oil + tarragon + vinegar
red cabbage + apples + yogurt
red cabbage + balsamic vinegar +
  feta cheese + sunflower seeds
red cabbage + cheese (e.g., blue,
  goat) **+ walnuts**
red cabbage + ginger + sesame
red cabbage + pears + red onions
  + walnuts

● CABBAGE, SAVOY
Season: autumn – winter
Flavor: slightly bitter/sweet,
with a tender texture
Volume: very quiet
Techniques: boil, braise, raw,
roast, steam

apples
beans, e.g., white

bell peppers
bread, rye
butter
cabbage rolls
caraway seeds
carrots
celery
chard, Swiss
cheese, e.g., Gouda, Gruyère,
  Parmesan, Swiss
chiles, e.g., serrano
corn
cream and crème fraîche
cumin
dill
fennel
fruits, dried, e.g., dried apricots,
  raisins
garlic
ginger
grains, e.g., pearl barley
grapefruit
juniper berries
kale
leeks
lemon, e.g., juice
mint
miso
mushrooms
mustard
nutmeg
nuts, e.g., cashews, hazelnuts,
  peanuts, pecans
oil, e.g., canola, grapeseed, **olive**,
  peanut, sesame, vegetable
onions, e.g., red, white, yellow
parsley
pastas

Dishes

Pan-Seared Tenderloin of Savoy Cabbage with Pearl Barley Gratin, Tarragon, and
Hazelnut Gremolata
— CityZen (Washington, DC)

Savoy Cabbage Spring Rolls filled with Marinated Tempeh, Baby Corn, Chinese Leaves,
Mange Tout, and Carrots, with a Ginger-Spiked Lemon Miso Dressing
— Manna (London)

pepper, e.g., black
pistachios
potatoes
rice, e.g., Arborio, long-grain
rosemary
sage
salads
salt, e.g., kosher
sauerkraut
sesame, e.g., oil, seeds
slaws, Asian
snow peas
soups, e.g., *cabbage*, **minestrone**, rice
spinach
stews
stock, vegetable
stuffed cabbage
tamari
tarragon
tempeh
thyme
vinegar, e.g., cider, red wine, rice wine, white wine
yogurt

Flavor Affinities
savoy cabbage + dried fruits + rice
savoy cabbage + garlic + olive oil + parsley + rice + tomatoes

CACAO or CACAO NIBS (see also CHOCOLATE, DARK)

Flavor: bitter, with notes of **chocolate** (and smoke, if roasted), and a crunchy texture
Volume: moderate – loud
What nibs are: dried, roasted, crushed cacao beans (that when crushed to a powder become unsweetened cocoa powder)

baked goods, e.g., brownies, cakes, cookies, muffins
beverages, e.g., hot chocolate
candies and confections, e.g., fudge
caramel

cereals, breakfast
chocolate, e.g., dark, milk
desserts, esp. raw
granola
ice creams and gelatos
nuts, e.g., almonds, pecans
oatmeal
popcorn
puddings
salads, fruit
smoothies
spreads
sugar
trail mix and energy bars
vanilla

"**Cacao**, which is essentially unprocessed chocolate, is one of nature's most powerful superfoods. In addition to its nutritional benefits, it is a stimulant without negative side effects. I use cacao nibs or powder or pods for our chocolate frostings and truffles. I'll substitute raw carob powder if I want a similar flavor with no stimulants."

— AMI BEACH, G-ZEN (BRANFORD, CT)

CAJUN CUISINE
bay leaf
beans, e.g., green, kidney
bell peppers, e.g., green
black-eyed peas
Cajun seasoning
carrots
cayenne
celery
chiles
cumin
garlic
gumbos
jambalaya
okra
onions
oregano
paprika

peas
rice, e.g., *dirty rice*
sweet potatoes
tomatoes

Flavor Affinities
bell peppers + celery + onions

CALLALOO (see GREENS, AMARANTH)

CANNELLINI BEANS (see BEANS, CANNELLINI)

CANTALOUPE (see MELON, CANTALOUPE)

• CAPERS
Flavor: salty and/or sour (depending on curing solution, e.g., brine, vinegar), with sharp, pungent notes of lemon
Volume: loud
What they are: pickled, green, immature flower buds

Tips: Rinse, or soak for up to 24 hours before using to quiet their flavor. Consider crisping for a minute or two in very hot oil before using them to garnish salads.

Possible substitutes: green olives, esp. chopped

artichokes
arugula
asparagus
basil
beans, e.g., green, kidney
beets
bell peppers, e.g., roasted
Brussels sprouts
butter
caponata
carrots
cauliflower
celery
chervil
chickpeas

couscous
dill
dips
eggplant
escarole
French cuisine
garlic
Greek cuisine
greens, e.g., collard
gremolata
Italian cuisine
kale
LEMON, e.g., juice, zest
marjoram
mayonnaise
Mediterranean cuisines
mustard, e.g., Dijon
oil, e.g., canola, olive
OLIVES, e.g., black, Greek, green,
    Italian, kalamata
onions
oregano
parsley
pasta, e.g., farfalle, linguini
pepper, black
pickles
pine nuts
pizza
polenta
potatoes, e.g., new, red
Provençal cuisine
raisins
salad dressings, e.g., vinaigrettes
salads, e.g., bean, Caesar, grain
SAUCES, e.g., butter, piccata,

puttanesca, tartar, tomato
seitan
shallots
Spanish cuisine
spreads
tapenades
tarragon
tofu
TOMATOES
tomatoes, sun-dried
vegetables
vinegar, e.g., balsamic,
    champagne or white wine
wine, dry white
zucchini

Flavor Affinities

capers + basil + garlic + **pasta +**
    (fresh or sun-dried) **tomatoes**
capers + basil + olives
capers + beets + celery + dill
capers + black olives + black
    pepper + garlic + mustard
capers + cauliflower + lemon zest
    + pasta
capers + eggplant + tomatoes
capers + garlic + greens + olive oil
    + vinegar
capers + garlic + lemon +
    mustard + olive oil
capers + garlic + lemon + parsley
    + shallots + white wine
CAPERS (+ garlic) + OLIVES +
    TOMATOES
capers + lemon + olive oil + olives
    + parsley

Dishes

Chanterelle Mushroom and Potato Flatbread with Smoked Leek Confit, Fried Capers,
Roasted Garlic, and Cashew Cream
— Millennium (San Francisco)

Tartare of Beets with Dill Flatbread, Soft Quail Egg, Crispy Capers, and Blood Orange Pepper
— The Point (Saranac Lake, NY)

Seitan Piccata: Seitan Cutlets in White Wine-Lemon-Caper Sauce with Mashed Potatoes
and Grilled Escarole
— V-Note (New York City)

"Theo Schoenegger [of Sinatra
Restaurant in Las Vegas] is
awesome and is one of the best
Italian chefs working in America.
He is also one of the most open-
minded people I have worked
with. He likes to eat healthy and
acknowledges that Americans eat
far too much meat and animal
protein three times a day / seven
days a week, so he was digging
the vegan stuff I was showing
him. Together, we created a vegan
agnolotti and a vegan Caesar salad.
For Caesar salad, to add the briny
flavor you need, I use **capers** instead
of anchovies — and people love it."
— TAL RONNEN, CROSSROADS
(LOS ANGELES)

CARAMEL

"We make a vegan dessert based
on a Snickers bar, and the **caramel**
is made from pureed dates flavored
with a little salt and vanilla."
— MARLENE AND CASSIE TOLMAN,
POMEGRANATE CAFÉ (PHOENIX)

• CARAWAY SEEDS
Flavor: bitter/sour/sweet;
aromatic, with notes of anise,
cumin, dill, licorice, and/or nuts
Volume: moderate – **loud**
Tip: Add later in the cooking
process.
Botanical relatives: anise,
carrots, celery, celery root, chervil,
coriander, cumin, dill, fennel,
parsley, parsley root, parsnips
Possible substitutes: dill seeds

almonds
apples, and apple cider, *applesauce*
aquavit
Austrian cuisine
baked goods, e.g., breads, cakes,
    crackers

barley
beans, green
beets
BREADS, e.g., Irish soda,
    pumpernickel, rye
Brussels sprouts
CABBAGE, e.g., red
carrots
cauliflower
cheese, e.g., cheddar, feta,
    Parmesan
chiles, e.g., dried
cole slaw
cream, sour
cucumbers
drinks, e.g., liqueurs
dukkah
Eastern European cuisines
eggs, e.g., *omelets*
fruits
garlic
German cuisine
harissa
hazelnuts
Hungarian cuisine
juniper berries
lemon
mushrooms
noodles
nutmeg
onions
orange
parsley
potatoes
pumpkin
rye breads
salt, sea
sauces
sauerkraut
soups/bisques, e.g., potato,
    pumpkin, sweet potato
spreads, e.g., vegan "cheese"
squash, e.g., winter
stews
sweet potatoes
tempeh
tofu, e.g., extra firm
vanilla

vegetables, esp. root
vinegar

Flavor Affinities
caraway seeds + apples + nutmeg
    + orange
caraway seeds + cabbage +
    potatoes
caraway seeds + lemon + salt +
    tofu

• CARDAMOM
[CAR-duh-mum]
Flavor: slightly sweet; aromatic,
with pungent/spicy notes of
cinnamon, eucalyptus, flowers,
fruit (e.g., **lemon**), mint, and/or
pepper
Volume: loud

Tips: Add early in the cooking
process. Use whole for a more
delicate flavor, and ground for a
more pronounced flavor. Also,
look for black cardamom, which
can add a delicate bacon-y flavor
to dishes.

Botanical relatives: ginger,
turmeric
Factoid: The world's third-most
expensive spice, after saffron and
vanilla.

almonds
apples
BAKED GOODS, e.g., breads,
    cakes, coffee cakes, cookies,
    pastries, pies
beans, e.g., black
butter
cabbage
caramel
carrots
cereals, hot breakfast
chiles
chocolate
cilantro
cinnamon
cloves

coconut and coconut milk
coffee, e.g., *Turkish coffee*
coriander
cumin
CURRIES, curry leaves, curry
    powder, and curry spices
custards
dates
desserts
drinks, e.g., chai
Ethiopian cuisine
fenugreek
fruits
garam masala
garlic
ginger
grains
honey
ice cream
INDIAN CUISINE
lemon
lentils, e.g., red
mangoes
maple syrup
marinades
Middle Eastern cuisines
milk
mint
orange, e.g., juice, zest
parsley
pears
pepper, e.g., black
pilafs
pistachios
puddings, e.g., rice
quince
raisins
ras el hanout
rice
rose water
saffron
salads, fruit
Scandinavian cuisine
soups
Southeast Asian cuisines
stews
sweet potatoes
tea, e.g., chai

tofu
Turkish cuisine
turmeric
vanilla
vegetables
yogurt

Flavor Affinities
cardamom + chocolate + coffee
cardamom + curry leaves + garlic
  + ginger + turmeric
cardamom + honey + orange +
  pistachios + yogurt
cardamom + pears + sugar +
  vanilla + wine
cardamom + raisins + rice
**cardamom + rice + rose water
  + saffron**
**cardamom + rose water + saffron
  + yogurt**

CARIBBEAN CUISINES
(see also JAMAICAN
CUISINE)
allspice
basil
bay leaf
chayote
chiles, e.g., habanero, Scotch
  bonnet; and chili pepper sauce
cilantro
cinnamon
citrus
cloves
coconut milk
culantro (aka chadon beni)
curry
dill
fruit, tropical
garlic
ginger
Jamaican cuisine
jerk dishes
lemon
lime
mangoes
marjoram
molasses

nutmeg
onions, e.g., green
orange
oregano
parsley
pineapple
plantains
rum, e.g., dark
salsas
sugar, e.g., brown
tamarind
thyme
yuca

● CARROTS
Season: summer – autumn
Flavor: sweet; aromatic, with a
crisp, juicy texture
Volume: quiet – moderate
What they are: root vegetables
Nutritional profile: 89% carbs
/ 6% protein / 5% fat
Calories: 55 per 1-cup serving
(raw, chopped)
Protein: 1 gram
Techniques: bake, blanch, boil,
braise, grate, grill, pressure-cook
(2 – 5 minutes), puree, raw, roast,
sauté, simmer, steam (5 – 10
minutes), stir-fry (5 – 10 minutes)
Tips: Scrub carrots well, but
resist peeling them and deny-
ing yourself the pleasure of the
peels' flavor and nutrition. Better
served lightly cooked than raw.
Botanical relatives: anise,
caraway, celery, celery root,
chervil, coriander, dill, fennel,
parsley, parsley root, parsnips
Possible substitutes:
pumpkin, winter squash

allspice
almonds
apples, e.g., cider, fruit, juice
apricots
arame
artichokes, e.g., baby, Jerusalem

asparagus
avocados
***BAKED GOODS**, e.g., **cakes,**
  muffins
basil and Thai basil
bay leaf
beans, e.g., black, broad, **green**
beets
bell peppers, e.g., red
broccoli and broccoli rabe
burdock
butter
cabbage, e.g., green, napa, red
caraway seeds
cardamom
cashews
celery and celery root
CHEESE, e.g., cheddar, cream,
  feta, **goat**, Parmesan, ricotta,
  Swiss
chervil
chickpeas
chiles, chili pepper flakes, and/or
  chili powder
chili, vegetarian
chives
cilantro
CINNAMON
citrus
cloves
coconut, coconut butter, coconut
  milk
coriander
cream and crème fraîche
crudités
cucumbers
CUMIN
curries, **curry powder, and curry**
  spices
daikon
dates
desserts, e.g., cakes, mousses
DILL
fennel and fennel seeds
fruit, dried
GARLIC
***GINGER**

grains, e.g., barley, bulgur,
    couscous, farro, millet, quinoa
greens, e.g., carrot, collard, salad
HONEY
leeks
LEMON, e.g., juice, zest
lentils
lime, e.g., juice, zest
maple syrup
marjoram
mascarpone
mint
miso
Moroccan cuisine
mushrooms, e.g., enoki, lobster
MUSTARD, e.g., Dijon, and
    mustard seeds
noodle dishes, Asian, e.g., pad thai
nutmeg
nuts, e.g., hazelnuts, macadamia,
    pecans, pine nuts
oil, e.g., coconut, olive, peanut,
    sesame
olives
ONIONS, e.g., green, pearl, red
ORANGE, e.g., juice, zest
paprika
PARSLEY
parsnips
peanuts and peanut butter
peas
pepper, e.g., black, white
pesto
pineapple
POTATOES
purees, e.g., carrot, root vegetable
RAISINS
rice
risotto
rosemary
SALADS
salt, esp. kosher, sea, savory
    scallions
seeds, e.g., anise, **caraway**, **poppy**,
    sesame, sunflower
sesame, e.g., oil, paste, seeds
shallots
slaws, e.g., cole

Flavor Affinities

carrots + almonds + pineapple + vanilla
carrots + apples + cinnamon + pecans + vanilla
carrots + apples + **raisins + walnuts**
carrots + balsamic vinegar + beets + chives + greens
carrots + brown sugar + orange + pineapple + raisins
carrots + capers + dill
carrots + caraway seeds + cumin
carrots + caraway seeds + garlic + lemon + olive oil + parsley
carrots + cardamom + maple + orange + yogurt + *soups*
CARROTS + CELERY + ONIONS
carrots + chiles + **cilantro + lime juice**
carrots + cilantro + ginger + scallions + **sesame oil**
carrots + cinnamon + coconut + nuts + pineapple
carrots + cinnamon + nutmeg + pineapple + walnuts
carrots + cinnamon + orange + vanilla
carrots + citrus + cumin
carrots + coconut + garlic + ginger + **lime juice**
carrots + cranberries + orange + walnuts
carrots + cumin + garlic + lemon + parsley
carrots + curry + ginger + Kaffir lime
carrots + dates + sunflower seeds + yogurt
carrots + dill + lemon + lentils
carrots + fennel + garlic
carrots + fennel + yogurt
CARROTS + FRUIT (e.g., apples, oranges, pineapple, raisins) + **NUTS**
    (e.g., almonds, cashews, pecans, walnuts)
carrots + garlic + ginger + walnut oil
carrots + garlic + potatoes + thyme
carrots + ginger + honey + rosemary
carrots + ginger + miso + sesame **seeds** + snap peas
CARROTS + GINGER + ORANGE (or other citrus, e.g., lime)
carrots + ginger + sea vegetables + **sesame oil/seeds** + soy sauce
carrots + harissa + raisins
carrots + honey + lemon juice + olive oil + **raisins** + vinegar + **walnuts**
carrots + honey + orange
carrots + honey + pineapple + yogurt
carrots + lemon juice + mustard + parsley
carrots + maple syrup + mustard
carrots + miso + spinach + tofu
CARROTS + NUTS (e.g., pine nuts, walnuts) + **RAISINS**
carrots + parsnips + thyme
carrots + sesame + sugar snap peas

Dishes

Roasted Carrot Soup, Beluga Lentils, Carrot Top Pesto, Paprika Croutons
— The Acorn (Vancouver)

Chilled Carrot Velouté: Carrot Fritter, Cilantro Cream, Lime
— Café Boulud (New York City)

Carrot Cake with Pineapple Compote, Vanilla Cream, Candied Almonds
— Candle 79 (New York City)

Carrot Parsnip Soup with Orange Crème Fraîche and Chives
— Greens Restaurant (San Francisco)

Carrot Cake: Moist and Decadent with Organic Sugar, Raisins, Pineapple, Coconut, and a Vegan Cream Cheese Frosting
— Laughing Seed Café (Asheville, NC)

Roasted Carrots with Yogurt, Date, and Sunflower Seeds
— Menton (Boston)

Carrots Wellington with Bluefoot Mushrooms, Sunchokes, Gremolata
— Narcissa (New York City)

Carrot Butter Crostini: Slices of Toasted 7-Grain Bread with Our Macadamia Creamed Carrot Butter Pâté
— Sage's Cafe (Salt Lake City)

"Use the whole **carrot**. Put the greens in salad, or cook them with some risotto — they are very good for you."
— FERNANDA CAPOBIANCO, VEGAN DIVAS (NEW YORK CITY)

"**Carrots** and cumin are great together."
— AMANDA COHEN, DIRT CANDY (NEW YORK CITY)

"We juice **carrots** to use for stocks or other dishes, and then dehydrate the pulp. We confit carrots in oil, herbs, and spices to get that nice, fatty, succulent confit texture out of a carrot. We will fry some carrots into chips and pulse them into crumbs. We might pickle some carrots or ferment them, then dehydrate them and grind them into a powder to use as a seasoning. So we have now taken a carrot eight ways and give you those components back on one dish or throughout the four courses that you have during the course of a meal here. You have now gotten this whole depth of flavor from this carrot. If we do that with anywhere from two to eight components on a menu, all of a sudden you and your palate have been elevated to a whole different level. I equate it to an Old World wine compared to a New World wine: it is still red wine, but it is completely different."
— AARON WOO, NATURAL SELECTION (PORTLAND, OR)

snap peas
SOUPS, e.g., carrot, onion, vegetable
soy sauce
spinach
stews, e.g., Moroccan tagines
stock, vegetable
sugar, e.g., brown
tahini
tarragon
thyme
tofu
tomatoes
turmeric
turnips
vanilla
vegetables, e.g., other root
vinegar, e.g., balsamic, cider, red wine, rice wine, white wine
walnuts and walnut oil
watercress
yogurt
zucchini

CASHEW CREAM (see CREAM, CASHEW)

• CASHEWS and CASHEW NUT BUTTER

Flavor: sweet, with buttery and vegetal notes (esp. when raw), and a rich texture
Volume: quiet/moderate (raw) – moderate/loud (toasted)
Nutritional profile: 66% fat / 23% carbs / 11% protein
Calories: 155 per 1-ounce serving (raw nuts)
Protein: 5 grams
Techniques: raw, roast, toast
Tips: Roast cashews to bring out their flavor and crunchiness. Add at the end of the cooking process or just before serving.
Botanical relatives: mangoes, pistachios

almonds
apricots
baked goods, e.g., cookies
bananas
beans, e.g., green
bell peppers, e.g., roasted
blueberries
bok choy
butter / ghee
cabbage
cardamom
carrots
cauliflower
cayenne
celery
celery root
Central American cuisines
cheese, e.g., goat, nut
chickpeas
chiles, e.g., serrano
chili, vegetarian
Chinese cuisine
chocolate / cacao nibs
cilantro
cinnamon
cloves
**COCONUT AND COCONUT
   MILK**
corn
cream, e.g., raw
cumin
CURRIES
curry powder
desserts
dips and dipping sauces
garam masala
garlic
ginger
GRANOLA and granola bars
hazelnuts
hoisin sauce
honey
hummus

Indian cuisine
lemon, e.g., juice
lime
mangoes
milk, coconut
miso
mushrooms, e.g., portobello,
   shiitake
mustard
nutmeg
oil, olive
onions
orange
papaya, green
pâtés
peanut butter
peas
pepper, e.g., black
pineapple
pine nuts
potatoes
pumpkin
RICE, e.g., basmati, jasmine,
   sushi
risottos
salad dressings
salads
salt, sea
satays
sauces, e.g., nut
sesame, e.g., seeds
smoothies
snow peas
soups, *e.g., carrot, cauliflower*
sour cream
South American cuisines
soy sauce
spinach
squash, winter, e.g., butternut
stews
stir-fries
stuffings
sugar, e.g., brown, maple

sugar snap peas
tahini
tempeh
thyme
tofu
tomatoes and sun-dried tomatoes
vanilla
veggie burgers
wasabi
wheat berries
yogurt

Flavor Affinities

cashews + carrots + ginger
cashews + carrots + orange
cashews + chickpeas + curry +
   potatoes
cashews + chiles + cilantro +
   coconut milk + garlic + ginger +
   lime + tofu
cashews + cilantro + spinach
cashews + honey + orange
cashews + mustard + snow peas
   + soy sauce
cashews + orange + rice

"The texture of **cashews** is so
incredibly creamy, and works well
in everything from appetizers to
cashew cheese to entrees to
desserts, which I'll even top with
a whipped cashew cream. Most
live raw cheesecakes — which
can range from German chocolate
to key lime in flavor — are cashew-
based, and they're delicious."
— AMI BEACH, G-ZEN (BRANFORD, CT)

• CAULIFLOWER

Season: autumn – winter
Flavor: sweet, with pungent
notes of butter, mustard, nuts,
and/or pepper, and a soft yet
crunchy (when raw) / creamy
(when cooked) texture
Volume: moderate
Nutritional profile: 64% carbs
/ 20% protein / 16% fat

Dishes

Sunflower-Chocolate-Fig Crusted Lavender-Cashew Cheesecake with Fresh Blueberry
— Sutra (Seattle)

Calories: 15 per ½-cup serving (boiled)

Protein: 1 gram

Techniques: Better served cooked than raw. Bake, blanch, boil, braise, deep-fry, dry, fry, juice, mash, pressure-cook (2 – 3 minutes), puree, roast (20 – 25 minutes at 400°F), sauté, simmer, smoke, steam (5 – 10 minutes), stir-fry (2 – 5 minutes); however, overcooking highlights sulphur notes.

Tips: Do not overcook. Add pureed cauliflower to vegetable soups to give a creamy texture. Or slice thickly (¾ inch) into "steaks" and sauté to brown.

Botanical relatives: broccoli, Brussels sprouts, cabbage, collard greens, horseradish, kale, kohlrabi, land cress, radishes, rutabagas, turnips, watercress

almonds
aloo gobi
apples
asparagus
barley
basil
bay leaf
beans, e.g., black, fermented black, green, white
bell pepper, e.g., green, red
black-eyed peas
bok choy
BREAD CRUMBS, e.g., whole wheat
broccoli
Brussels sprouts
bulgur
BUTTER and BROWN BUTTER
buttermilk
CAPERS
cardamom
carrots
cashews
cayenne

celery
CHEESE, e.g., blue, cheddar, Emmental, **feta,** goat, Gorgonzola, Gouda, **Gruyère,** Havarti, manchego, mozzarella, Pantaleo, **Parmesan,** pecorino, Roncal, Stilton, Swiss
chervil
chickpeas
CHILES, e.g., green, red; **chili pepper flakes, chili pepper sauce,** and **chili powder**
chili, vegetarian
chives
chowders
cilantro
cinnamon
citrus
coconut and coconut milk
coriander
corn
couscous
cream and milk
cress, e.g., land
crudités
CUMIN

CURRIES and **CURRY,** e.g., oil, powder, spices
dill
eggs, e.g., *quiches*
fenugreek
frito misto
garam masala
GARLIC
ghee
ginger
gratins
greens, e.g., bitter
hazelnuts
herbs
honey
horseradish
Indian cuisine
kale
kasha
leeks
LEMON, e.g., juice, zest
lentils
lime
mango
marjoram

Dishes

Cauliflower and Date Ragoût with Roasted Sunchokes, Cauliflower and Parmesan Velouté, Lemon Poached Salsify, Rye Berries, and Chestnuts
— Beckta Dining and Wine (Ottawa, Canada)

Garlic Parsley Linguine with Roasted Mariquita Farm Cauliflower, Spring Onions, Green Garlic, Pine Nuts, Lemon, Mustard Caper Butter, Pecorino Fiore Sardo
— Greens Restaurant (San Francisco)

Seared Cauliflower with Garlic, Almond, Sweet and Spicy Peperonata, Capers
— Millennium (San Francisco)

Cavolfiore: Cauliflower Steak, Riso Venere, Almonds, and Pecorino Toscano
— Salumeria Rosi (New York City)

Frito Misto: Crispy Cauliflower, Sweet Chili Sauce, Sesame Seed
— Sublime (Fort Lauderdale)

Cauli-Mashed Potatoes and Gravy: Fresh Cauliflower Blended with Mashed Potatoes, Porcini Mushroom Gravy with Fresh Rosemary
— Veggie Grill (Los Angeles)

mashed cauliflower, à la mashed
   potatoes
mayonnaise
Mediterranean cuisines
Middle Eastern cuisines
milk, dairy or nondairy, e.g.,
   cashew
millet
mint
mushrooms, e.g., portobello
MUSTARD, e.g., Dijon or seeds
noodles, Asian, e.g., rice noodles
nutmeg
nutritional yeast
nuts
OIL, e.g., mustard, **OLIVE**,
   walnut

OLIVES, e.g., black, green,
   kalamata
ONIONS, e.g., **red**, yellow
orange
oregano
paprika
PARSLEY
PASTA, e.g., farfalle, lasagna,
   linguini, penne, rigatoni
peas
pepper, e.g., black, white
pesto
pine nuts
pistachios
polenta
potatoes, e.g., red
pumpkin

purees
raisins
rice, e.g., Arborio, basmati, brown
risottos
rosemary
saffron
sage
salads, e.g., cauliflower, green, pasta
salt, e.g., kosher, sea
savory
scallions
seeds, e.g., caraway, poppy,
   pumpkin, sesame
sesame, e.g., oil, paste, seeds
shallots
snow peas
soufflés
SOUPS, e.g., cauliflower, curry,
   vegetable
sour cream
soy sauce
spelt
spinach
squash
sriracha sauce
"steaks"
stews
stir-fries
stock, e.g., mushroom, vegetable
sweet potatoes
"tabbouleh"
tacos
tahini
tamarind
tarragon
thyme
tofu
TOMATOES and TOMATO
   SAUCE
tomatoes, sun-dried
truffles
turmeric
VINEGAR, e.g., balsamic, rice,
   white wine
wakame
walnuts
watercress
wine, e.g., dry white
yogurt

Flavor Affinities
cauliflower + almonds + barley
cauliflower + almonds + brown butter + lemon
cauliflower + almonds + raisins
cauliflower + balsamic vinegar + garlic + olive oil + raisins
cauliflower + basmati rice + chickpeas + coconut
CAULIFLOWER + bread crumbs + **CAPERS + LEMON + PARSLEY**
cauliflower + bread crumbs (+ cheese) + chives + pasta + parsley
cauliflower + Brussels sprouts + capers + lemon
cauliflower + Brussels sprouts + garlic + olive oil + rosemary
cauliflower + capers + dill + garlic + tomatoes
CAULIFLOWER + CAPERS + green olives + **LEMON** + olive oil
cauliflower + cashews + cilantro + coconut + nut milk + onions + turmeric
cauliflower + cheddar cheese + mustard
cauliflower + cheddar cheese + Parmesan cheese + **parsley** + pasta
cauliflower + chickpeas + eggplant + raisins
cauliflower + chiles + lime juice
cauliflower + chili pepper flakes + parsley + pasta
cauliflower + cilantro + ginger
CAULIFLOWER + COCONUT + CURRY
cauliflower + cumin + ginger + tamarind + turmeric
cauliflower + garlic + tomatoes
cauliflower + ginger + orange
cauliflower + Gorgonzola cheese + pasta + thyme
cauliflower + lemon + parsley
cauliflower + lemon zest + mustard + shallots
cauliflower + mint + Parmesan cheese + pine nuts
cauliflower + olives + orange
cauliflower + sage + walnuts
cauliflower + scallions + sesame oil + soy sauce

"I learned through testing that I don't like maple-smoked cauliflower — I prefer it hickory-smoked. I'll smoke, bread, and deep-fry **cauliflower**, which looks like chicken, and serve it with waffles for a play on chicken-and-waffles."

— AMANDA COHEN, DIRT CANDY (NEW YORK CITY)

"I make a soup out of **cauliflower** that's been crushed with a potato masher so that it's the texture of rice, and cook it with saffron, tomato, white wine, and garlic. It's something that's unusual while tasting interesting and familiar."

— RICH LANDAU, VEDGE (PHILADELPHIA)

CAVIAR, VEGAN

Flavor: salty, with notes of the sea, and a delicately crisp, caviar-like texture
What it is: seaweed-based product resembling caviar
Brands: Cavi-Art, Kelp Caviar
Tip: Can be used in both cold and hot dishes.

avocado
canapes
eggs, e.g., hard-boiled, *omelets*
pastas
potatoes
salads, e.g., mock seafood
sour cream
sushi, vegetarian

"Cavi-Art is a **vegan caviar** made from seaweed that is rich in salt, which complements the freshness of avocado. It is absolutely amazing!"

— SHAWAIN WHYTE, CAFÉ BLOSSOM (NEW YORK CITY)

CAVOLO NERO (see KALE, BLACK)

● CAYENNE (aka RED PEPPER)

Flavor: hot/picante
Volume: loud
What it is: powder made from ground red peppers
Tips: Long used as a flavor enhancer. Cayenne tastes hotter the longer it cooks.

allspice
almonds
beans, e.g., black, green, mung, red
bell peppers
Cajun cuisine
cashews
cauliflower
cheese — in general
chickpeas
chili, vegetarian
chocolate and cocoa
cilantro
corn
cumin
curries
dill
dips, e.g., bean, chickpea
dulse
eggplant
eggs, e.g., hard-boiled, esp. deviled
enchiladas
garlic
lemon
lentils
lime
low-fat dishes
low-salt dishes
marinades
onions, e.g., white
paprika
peas
pecans

pine nuts
plantains
potatoes
refried beans
salads, e.g., "egg," potato, tofu
sauces, e.g., barbecue, nut
seeds, e.g., pumpkin, sunflower
soups, e.g., beet, carrot, legume, mushroom
sour cream
stews
sugar
tofu
tomatoes
veggie burgers
walnuts, e.g., *spiced walnuts*
yogurt

Flavor Affinities
cayenne + almond + dulse (or salt)
cayenne + corn + lime
cayenne + dill + garlic + yogurt

● CELERY

Season: year-round, esp. summer – autumn
Flavor: slightly sweet, with earthy notes of herbs, minerals, and/or nuts, and a crisp/crunchy (when raw) and stringy texture
Volume: quiet/moderate (e.g., heart or inner stalks) – moderate/loud (e.g., outer stalks)
What it is: vegetable
Nutritional profile: 73% carbs / 17% protein / 10% fat
Calories: 15 per 1-cup serving (raw, chopped)
Protein: 1 gram
Techniques: boil, braise, cream, mandoline, pressure-cook (2 – 5 minutes), raw, sauté, steam, stir-fry (2 – 5 minutes)
Tips: Opt for organic celery. Don't overlook celery leaves, which contain the most nutrients.

Botanical relatives: anise, caraway, carrots, celery root, coriander, dill, fennel, parsley, parsley root, parsnips

almonds and almond butter
anise seeds
APPLES
artichokes
barley
basil
bay leaf
beans, e.g., black, kidney
beets
bell peppers, red
bread crumbs, e.g., whole grain
bulgur
butter and brown butter
cabbage
capers
caraway
CARROTS
casseroles
cauliflower
celery root, celery salt, and celery seeds
CHEESE, e.g., BLUE, Brie, cheddar, cream, goat, Gorgonzola, Gouda, Gruyère, **Parmesan, Stilton**, Swiss
chervil
chestnuts
chickpeas
chives
cloves
cocktails, e.g., Bloody Marys
cream
crudités
cucumbers
cumin
curries
dill
eggs, e.g., hard-boiled, esp. deviled
endive
fennel
garlic
grapes

gratins
greens, mesclun
hazelnuts
kohlrabi
leeks
lemon, e.g., juice
lentils
lime
lovage
mâche
maple syrup
marjoram
mayonnaise
mirepoix (celery + carrots + onions)
mushrooms, e.g., oyster, wild
mustard, e.g., Dijon
nuts, e.g., almonds, hazelnuts, walnuts
OIL, e.g., nut, **olive**, walnut
olives, e.g., green
ONIONS, e.g., red
oranges, e.g., fruit, juice
PARSLEY
peanuts and peanut butter
pears
peas
pecans
pepper, e.g., black
pineapple
pistachios
potatoes
purslane
radishes
raisins
rice
risotto
rosemary
SALADS, e.g., egg, fruit, pasta, potato, vegetable
salt, e.g., sea
sauces
scallions
seeds, celery
shallots
slaws
snow peas
SOUPS, e.g., celery, celery root, potato, vegetable

soy sauce
squash
stews
stir-fries
STOCKS, e.g., vegetable
stuffed celery
stuffings
tarragon
thyme
tomatoes
turmeric
turnips
umeboshi paste
vinegar
walnut oil
WALNUTS
water chestnuts
watercress
yogurt

Flavor Affinities
celery + almond butter + raisins
CELERY + APPLES + WALNUTS
CELERY + CARROTS + ONIONS
CELERY + CHEESE (e.g., blue) **+ FRUIT** (e.g., apples, oranges, pears) **+ NUTS** (e.g., hazelnuts, pecans, walnuts)
celery + cucumbers + mustard
celery + garlic + tomatoes
celery + oranges + pecans
celery + parsley + tomatoes
celery + pistachios + yogurt

● CELERY ROOT (aka CELERIAC)
Season: autumn – spring
Flavor: bitter/sour/sweet, with earthy notes of anise, celery, hazelnuts, minerals, parsley, potatoes, truffles, and/or walnuts, and a crunchy (when raw) or fluffy (when cooked) texture
Volume: quiet – moderate (quieter than celery)
Nutritional profile: 84% carbs / 10% protein / 6% fat
Calories: 45 per 1-cup serving (boiled)

Protein: 1 gram

Techniques: bake (at 350°F, about 30 – 40 minutes), blanch, boil, braise, deep-fry, fry, grate, marinate, mash, pressure-cook (3 – 5 minutes), puree, raw (as a slaw), roast, **sauté**, steam (5 – 20 minutes), stir-fry

Tips: Must peel before using. Use pureed celery root instead of butter to add richness to sauces.

Botanical relatives: anise, caraway, carrot, celery, coriander, dill, fennel, parsley, parsley root, parsnips

*APPLES, apple cider, apple juice
artichokes
beans, e.g., cannellini, green
beets
bell peppers, e.g., green, roasted
bread crumbs, e.g., whole grain
butter, e.g., brown, goat's milk
buttermilk
cabbage, e.g., savoy
capers
caraway seeds
carrots
cayenne
celery
celery leaves
celery seeds
chard, Swiss
CHEESE, e.g., **blue**, Comté, Emmental, goat, **GRUYÈRE**, mozzarella, **Parmesan**, pecorino, Swiss
chervil
chestnuts
chickpeas
chips, celery root (i.e., deep-fried)
chives
chowders
CREAM and crème fraîche
dill
eggs
endive, Belgian

fennel
GARLIC
gratins
hazelnuts
honey
kale
kohlrabi
leeks
LEMON, e.g., juice
lentils, e.g., French
lime, e.g., juice
mascarpone

mayonnaise
millet
mint
miso
mushrooms, e.g., chanterelle, cremini, oyster, porcini
MUSTARD, e.g., Dijon, Pommery, and/or whole-grain
nutmeg
nuts, e.g., cashews
OIL, e.g., hazelnut, nut, **olive**, pecan, **sunflower**, truffle, walnut

Flavor Affinities

celery root + apples + celery
celery root + apples + crème fraîche + **mustard**
celery root + apples + fennel + hazelnuts + lemon
celery root + apples + parsley + raisins
celery root + apples + walnuts
celery root + arugula + Parmesan cheese + porcini mushrooms
celery root + black truffles + potatoes
celery root + blue cheese + chives
celery root + buttermilk + herbs + olive oil + olives
celery root + chanterelles + wild rice
celery root + cheese + **garlic** + mustard + **potatoes**
celery root + chestnuts + cider + cream + mushrooms
celery root + chestnuts + tarragon
celery root + chives + leeks + thyme
celery root + fennel + potato + *soups*
CELERY ROOT + GARLIC + parsnips + POTATOES
celery root + garlic + parsnips + rutabagas
celery root + lemon juice + mayonnaise
celery root + lemon juice + mustard + walnut oil
celery root + maple syrup + mustard
celery root + Parmesan cheese + parsley
celery root + parsnips + potatoes
celery root + parsnips + thyme
celery root + rosemary + rutabagas

Dishes

Celeriac Soufflé with Celery Salad and Black Truffle
— Chez Panisse (Berkeley, CA)

Roasted Celery Root with Mushrooms and Polenta
— Gramercy Tavern (New York City)

Braised Kale with Celery Root, Compressed Apple, Cipollini Aigre-Doux
— Picholine (New York City)

olives, e.g., black
onions
oranges, juice, zest
oranges, blood
paprika, e.g., smoked
PARSLEY
parsnips
pears
peas
peas, split
pecans
pepper, black
pine nuts
POTATOES, e.g., mashed
purees, e.g., potato
ramps
remoulades
rice, e.g., Arborio, wild
risottos
root vegetables, other, e.g.,
    carrots, turnips, etc.
rosemary
rutabaga
saffron
sage
salad dressings, e.g., creamy,
    vinaigrette
SALADS, e.g., winter
salsify
salt, e.g., kosher, smoked, truffle
sauces
shallots
slaws
sorrel
SOUPS, e.g., celery, celery root, leek,
    tomato
soy sauce
stews
stock, vegetable
sugar, e.g., brown
tarragon
THYME
tomatoes and tomato paste
truffles, e.g., black, oil, salt
vegetables, root, e.g., turnips
vinegar, e.g., cider, red wine,
    sherry, white wine
walnuts

watercress
wild rice
wine, dry red or white
yogurt

CELERY SALT
Flavor: salty, with notes of celery

beets
Bloody Marys
cabbage
celery
chili pepper sauce
dill
dips
eggs, e.g., hard-boiled
garlic
juices, e.g., tomato, vegetable
onions
salad dressings
salads, e.g., potato
slaws, cole
soups, esp. bean, gazpacho, lentil,
    tomato
sour cream
stock, vegetable
tomatoes

● CELERY SEEDS
Flavor: **bitter** and/or slightly
sweet, with pungent notes of
celery, celery leaves, herbs (e.g.,
parsley), lemon, and/or spices
Volume: moderate – **loud**

baked goods, e.g., breads
cabbage
carrots
celery
cheese, e.g., Parmesan
cocktails, e.g., Bloody Marys
cucumbers
dill
dips
eggs
garlic
lemon
marinades

mayonnaise
mustard, e.g., Dijon
nuts
oil, e.g., almond, olive
onions
pepper, black
pickles
potatoes
SALAD DRESSINGS
SALADS, e.g., egg, fruit, macaroni,
    potato, and vegetable
sauces
sauerkraut
slaws, e.g., cole
soups, e.g., celery, noodle, onion,
    zucchini
sour cream
spinach
stews, e.g., vegetable
tomatoes and tomato juice
vegetables and vegetable juices
vinegar, e.g., apple cider, white
    wine
Worcestershire sauce, vegetarian

● CHARD, e.g., RAINBOW, RED/RUBY, SWISS, or MIXED
Season: year-round, esp.
summer – autumn
Flavor: bitter/slightly salty;
the leaves have earthier spinach
notes, and the stalks quieter
celery-like notes
Volume: moderate (cooked) –
loud (raw)
What it is: vegetable – green
Nutritional profile: 74% carbs
/ 23% protein / 3% fat
Calories: 35 per 1-cup serving
(chopped, boiled)
Protein: 3 grams
Techniques: This quick-cooking
green is better served cooked
than raw. Cook the stalks like
asparagus and the leaves like
spinach, e.g., bake, blanch, boil
(3 – 4 minutes), **braise**, parboil,

pickle, **sauté**, steam (3 – 4 minutes), stir-fry

Tip: Opt for younger chard, which is tender, for salads.

Botanical relatives: beets, quinoa, spinach

Possible substitutes: spinach

almonds
apples
basil
BEANS, e.g., dried, white
bell peppers
bread crumbs
bulgur
butter
capers
carrots
CHEESE, e.g., blue, cheddar, cottage, feta, goat, Gruyère, mozzarella, **Parmesan**, pecorino, **RICOTTA**, Taleggio
CHICKPEAS
chiles, e.g., chipotle, dried, red; and **chili pepper flakes**
cilantro
cinnamon
coconut
coriander
cream
crepes, e.g., buckwheat
cumin
currants
curries
dolmas
eggplant
EGGS, e.g., fried, *frittatas, omelets,* poached, *quiches*
fennel and fennel seeds
French cuisine, e.g., Niçoise
***GARLIC**
ginger
gratins
greens, other
kale
lamb's quarters
leeks

LEMONS, e.g., juice, zest
LENTILS
lime, e.g., juice, zest
lovage
mascarpone
millet
mint
mirin
mushrooms, e.g., porcini, portobello, shiitake
mustard and mustard seeds
nettles
noodles, e.g., Asian, rice
nutmeg
OIL, e.g., canola, chili, **OLIVE,** peanut, sesame
olives, e.g., kalamata
ONIONS, e.g., red
orange, e.g., juice, zest
paprika, e.g., smoked, sweet
parsley

Flavor Affinities
chard + acorn squash + garlic + Gruyère cheese
chard + balsamic vinegar + garlic + **olive oil** + red onions
chard + basil + eggs + onions
chard + cheese (e.g., Parmesan, ricotta) + **onions**
chard + chickpeas + eggs + lemon + *soups*
chard + chickpeas + fennel
chard + chickpeas + pasta
chard + chiles + garlic + olive oil + vinegar
chard + chiles + tomatoes
CHARD + CURRANTS + PINE NUTS + rice
chard + dill + leeks
chard + garlic + ginger + soy sauce
CHARD + GARLIC + LEMON + OLIVE OIL
chard + lemon + mustard
chard + lemon + olive oil + Parmesan cheese
chard + lemon + tahini
chard + mirin + shiitake mushrooms + soy sauce
chard + orange + smoked paprika
chard + Parmesan cheese + polenta + portobello mushrooms
chard + pasta + ricotta + tomato sauce
chard + pasta + white beans
chard + peanuts + pineapple
chard + pine nuts + raisins
chard + pine nuts + tahini + yogurt

PASTAS, e.g., cannelloni, farfalle, fusilli, gnocchi, lasagna, orecchiette, penne, ravioli, tortellini
pepper, black
PINE NUTS
polenta
POTATOES, e.g., red
quinoa
raisins
rice, e.g., basmati, brown
risottos

saffron
salads, e.g., *green, watercress*
salt, e.g., kosher, sea
scallions
seeds, e.g., pumpkin, sesame
shallots
sorrel
SOUPS, e.g., chard, lentil,
minestrone, potato
sour cream
soy sauce
stews
stir-fries
stock, vegetable
stuffed chard, e.g., with currants +
pine nuts + rice
tahini
tamari
thyme
tofu
TOMATOES and TOMATO
SAUCE
tomatoes, sun-dried
VINEGAR, e.g., apple cider,
balsamic, red wine
walnuts
wheat berries
Worcestershire sauce, vegetarian
yogurt
zucchini

"I love **chard**! I love cooking the stems of rainbow chard, which have so much flavor. Just slice them and toss them in hot olive oil for one or two minutes, then add the greens, some garlic, some water or stock, and salt and pepper, and let them cook another two or three minutes. You can finish them with almonds, pine nuts, or pumpkin seeds for a little texture — and a shake of chili pepper flakes if you want a little kick."

— ANNIE SOMERVILLE, GREENS RESTAURANT (SAN FRANCISCO)

"What we do here is build flavors: For example, we will stew **chard** with onions, garlic, and other traditional stewing ingredients that are really tasty, and then dehydrate some of it and turn it into a powder that will get worked into a gnocchi or pasta dough. It is a seasoning component that you would use about 5 percent in the dough. Next, you take the chard you didn't dehydrate and put that in the dish with the gnocchi on top. We will also fry some chard as a garnish. All of the sudden, the chard takes on a whole level of flavor because we have incorporated it into different forms within the dish. So when people eat it, they say, 'Wow — I have never tasted chard like this!' This happens because we did not simply sauté some chard; we manipulated it, thought it through, and gave it back to you on a dish in a whole multitude of ways."

— AARON WOO, NATURAL SELECTION (PORTLAND, OR)

CHARD, RED / RUBY (see CHARD)

CHARD, SWISS (see CHARD)

● CHAYOTE (aka CHAYOTE SQUASH and MIRLITON; see also SQUASH, SUMMER)

Season: winter
Flavor: neutral, with notes of cucumbers and zucchini, and a crisp, fibrous texture; its soft, edible seed has been described as a cross between an almond and a lima bean

Volume: very quiet – quiet
What it is: technically a fruit
Nutritional profile: 77% carbs / 17% fat / 6% protein
Calories: 40 per 1-cup serving (boiled)
Protein: 1 gram
Techniques: bake, boil (8 – 10 minutes), broil, grate, grill, parboil, puree, raw, sauté, sous-vide, steam, stew, stuff
Tip: It can be prepared as you would zucchini.
Botanical relatives: gourds, squash
Possible substitutes: summer squash, zucchini

almonds
apples
bell peppers, e.g., red
bread crumbs
butter
Caribbean cuisines
Central American cuisine
cheese, e.g., Monterey Jack
chiles, e.g., chipotle, jalapeño
cilantro
cinnamon
coconut milk
corn
cream
Creole / Cajun cuisine, in which the
chayote is known as mirliton
curries
enchiladas
fennel and fennel seeds
garlic
ginger
gratins
honey
Jamaican cuisine
Latin American cuisines
lemon
lime
Louisiana cuisine, in which the
chayote is known as mirliton

Dishes

Chayote en Mole Verde: Braised Chayote in Aroma of Acorn Squash, Herby Green Pumpkin Seed Mole, Creamy Pumpkin Seed Tamal, Yogurt-Infused Chayote Pearls

— Topolobampo (Chicago)

mango
Mexican cuisine
oil, olive
onions, e.g., spring, white, yellow
orange
oregano
parsley
pumpkin seeds
salads, e.g., fruit, green, potato
salsas
scallions
slaws
soups
sour cream
Southern (U.S.) cuisine
squash, acorn
stews
stir-fries
stock, vegetable
stuffed chayotes
sushi, e.g., nori rolls
sweet potatoes
tarragon
thyme
tofu, e.g., firm
tomatoes
tortillas, corn
tostadas
turmeric
vanilla
watercress

Flavor Affinities

chayote + almonds + cinnamon + honey
chayote + garlic + onions + tomatoes

● CHEESE, ASIAGO

Volume: quiet – moderate
Possible substitutes:
Parmesan, Romano

almonds
arugula
breads, e.g., focaccia
eggs, e.g., *frittatas*
enchiladas
figs
garlic
grapes
Italian cuisine
pastas
pizzas
potatoes
salads, e.g., green, pasta
spinach
squash, summer
tomatoes
zucchini

Flavor Affinities

blue cheese + almonds + watercress
blue cheese + apples + celery
blue cheese + apples + fennel
blue cheese + apricots + balsamic vinegar + celery + hazelnuts
blue cheese + celery + dates
blue cheese + cucumbers + tomatoes
BLUE CHEESE + FRUIT (e.g., figs, peaches, pears) **+ greens** (e.g., spinach) **+ NUTS** (e.g., hazelnuts, pecans, walnuts)
blue cheese + fruit (e.g., pears) + **greens** (e.g., spinach)
blue cheese + **greens** (e.g., romaine, spinach) + **nuts** (e.g., walnuts)
blue cheese + leeks + thyme
blue cheese + onions + pears + pecans + spinach
blue cheese + onions + walnuts

● CHEESE, BLUE (e.g., GORGONZOLA, ROQUEFORT, STILTON)

Volume: loud

almonds
apples
apricots
beets
bread, e.g., nut, pumpernickel, raisin, **walnut**
buttermilk
cayenne
celery
cheese, cream
chestnuts, roasted
chives
cucumbers
dates
dill
dips
endive
fennel

Dishes

Hearth-Fired Fig and Maytag Blue Cheese Flatbread with Caramelized Onion, Arugula, Balsamic Glaze

— Canyon Ranch (Miami Beach, FL)

"Bleu d'Auvergne": Swiss Chard "Subric," Michigan Sour Cherries, and Brown Butter Toasted Walnuts

— Per Se (New York City)

figs
fruit
garlic
grapes
greens, e.g., baby, bitter, salad
hazelnuts
HONEY
leeks
lettuce, e.g., iceberg
mascarpone
mayonnaise
milk
mushrooms
NUTS, e.g., hazelnuts, walnuts,
   esp. toasted
oil, olive
onions
parsley
pastas
peaches
PEARS
pecans
pepper, black
pine nuts
plums
potatoes, e.g., baked
radishes
SALAD DRESSINGS
salads
salt
sandwiches
sauces
sour cream
spinach
sunflower seeds
thyme
tomatoes
vegetables, e.g., raw, steamed
vinegar, e.g., balsamic, red wine,
   sherry, white wine
WALNUTS
watercress
watermelon
yogurt

CHEESE, BRIE
Volume: moderate
Techniques: bake

Possible substitutes:
Camembert

almonds
apples
argula
bread, esp. baguettes
cherries
dates
fennel
figs
melon
mesclun
mushrooms, morel
nuts, e.g., pistachios
onions
pears
salads
sandwiches
strawberries
vegetables, e.g., raw
vinegar, fruit, e.g., raspberry

Flavor Affinities
brie cheese + arugula + pears

CHEESE, BURRATA
Volume: quiet

basil
beans, e.g., fava
bread
carrots
cucumbers

garlic
Italian cuisine
melon, e.g., cantaloupe
nuts, e.g., cashews
oil, olive
onions, red
pastas
peaches
pesto
plums
salt
tomatoes
vinegar, balsamic

Flavor Affinities
burrata + balsamic vinegar + basil
   + red onions + tomatoes

"I love **burrata cheese**. We have
served it warm with pasta and
pesto, or with pickled vegetables
and crispy quinoa, or with carrot
top pesto along with carrots and
fava beans, and even with
cantaloupe with melon granite
and toasted cashews. I want to
take a cheese that people are
familiar with and show that you
can use it during all four seasons.
There is a cheese maker here in
the U.S. from Puglia who makes
incredible cheese [sold by
Zingerman's]."
— JON DUBOIS, GREEN ZEBRA (CHICAGO)

Dishes

"Caprese Salad": Marinated French Laundry Garden Tomatoes, Jellied Burrata, Aged
Balsamic Vinegar, Toasted Pine Nuts, and Petite Basil
— The French Laundry (Yountville, CA)

Zingerman's Burrata, Salted Cucumber, Pomelo, Shallot Aigre-Doux, Pumpernickel–Pine
Nut Streusel
— Green Zebra (Chicago)

Zingerman's Burrata, Nichols Farm Tomato Jam, Basil Granita, Preserved Lemon
— Green Zebra (Chicago)

Burrata Mozzarella, White Peaches, Chili Powder, Fresh Almonds, Mint
— Verjus (Paris)

● CHEESE, CHEDDAR

Volume: moderate

APPLES, apple cider, apple juice
arugula
asparagus
avocado
beans, white
biscuits
bread crumbs
breads, e.g., French,
    pumpernickel, whole rye,
    whole wheat
broccoli
caraway seeds
cauliflower
cayenne
chiles, e.g., chipotle, jalapeño,
    poblano
chiles rellenos
chili powder
corn
custard
dates
dill
eggs
enchiladas
fennel
garlic
grapes
gratins
grits
honey
horseradish
kale
leeks
loaves, vegetarian
MACARONI AND CHEESE
mushrooms
mustard
nuts

Dishes

Mac and Cheese with Horseradish, Sharp
Cheddar, and Cracked Black Pepper
— Mana Food Bar, Chicago

oats
onions, e.g., caramelized
paprika
pasta, e.g., macaroni
pears
pecans
pepper, black
pie crusts
popcorn
potatoes
quesadillas
quince paste
rice
salads
sandwiches, e.g., grilled cheese
sauces
scallions
soufflés
spinach
thyme
tomatillos
tomatoes
vinegar, apple cider
walnuts

● CHEESE, CHÈVRE (aka FRESH GOAT CHEESE; SEE CHEESE, GOAT)

● CHEESE, COTIJA (see CHEESE, QUESO AÑEJO)

● CHEESE, COTTAGE

Volume: quiet – moderate
Nutritional profile: 73%
protein / 15% carbs / 12% fat
Calories: 165 per 1-cup serving
(lowfat)
Protein: 28 grams

> **Tip:** Puree cottage cheese with
> lemon juice and herbs into a
> sauce to pour over spaghetti or
> other pasta.

Brand: Check out Nancy's sour
and complex low-fat organic
cottage cheese, which is in a
league of its own.

apples
arugula
bananas
basil
bell peppers, e.g., green
berries
breads, whole grain
carrots
celery
cheese, other, e.g., blue,
    Parmesan
cheesecake
chives
cilantro
cinnamon
coriander
cucumbers
dill
dips
eggs
flaxseed and flaxseed oil
fruit, esp. fresh, e.g., cantaloupe,
    pineapple
garlic
ginger
gratins
greens, e.g., beet
herbs
honey
lemon, e.g., juice, zest
oil, olive
olives
onions
onions, green, e.g., scallions
oranges
pancakes
paprika
parsley
pastas, e.g., lasagna
pears
pepper, e.g., black, white
pesto
raisins
raspberries
salad dressings, e.g., creamy
salads
salt, e.g., sea
seeds, e.g., sunflower

sour cream
spinach
tomatoes
walnuts
watercress
yogurt
zucchini

Flavor Affinities
cottage cheese + black pepper + olive oil

● CHEESE, CREAM (see also FROMAGE BLANC)

Flavor: sour, with a rich yet spreadable texture
Volume: moderate – **loud**
What it is: a fresh, unripened cheese
Nutritional profile: 88% fat / 7% protein / 5% carbs
Calories: 50 per 1-tablespoon serving
Protein: 1 gram
Tip: Opt for ● fat-free cream cheese.
Possible Substitute: Neufchâtel

apples
apricots
avocado
beets
bell peppers, e.g., red
BERRIES
blueberries
breads, fruit and/or nut, e.g., date-nut
capers
carrots
celery
cheese, e.g., blue, chèvre, fresh, goat, ricotta
cheesecake
cherries,
chives
chocolate
cinnamon
coconut

coffee
cranberries
dates
desserts
dips
frostings, e.g., for carrot cake
fruit, dried
garlic
ginger
graham crackers
guava
honey
kiwi
LEMON, e.g., juice, zest
maple syrup
mascarpone
mint
mustard
nutmeg
nuts
olives
orange, e.g., juice, zest
oregano
parsley
pineapple
pistachios
plums, dried
quince paste
raisins
raspberries
rhubarb
salt
sandwiches, e.g., grilled cheese
sauces
scallions
seeds, e.g., sesame
sour cream
spinach
spreads
strawberries
sugar, e.g., powdered
thyme
tomatoes, e.g., sun-dried
vanilla
yogurt

Flavor Affinities
cream cheese + avocado + chili pepper sauce + garlic + lemon juice
cream cheese + maple syrup + mascarpone
cream cheese + spinach + sun-dried tomatoes

"CHEESE, CREAM" — CASHEW NUT (VEGAN)

Tip: Use as you would regular cream cheese.
Brand: Dr. Cow Tree Nut Cheeses (made with cashews or macadamia nuts)

"We make our own 'cream cheese' served on our raw 'everything bagel' by soaking cashews and macadamia nuts and pureeing them with garlic, lemon juice, red onions, salt and pepper, and water."
— CASSIE AND MARLENE TOLMAN, POMEGRANATE CAFÉ (PHOENIX)

"CHEESE, CREAM" — SOY

Brands: Check out tofu cream cheese from Follow Your Heart, Galaxy, or Tofutti, but make sure it has no added trans-fats.

bagels
desserts
icing, e.g., cakes, cupcakes (e.g., carrot, zucchini)

Flavor Affinities
tofu cream cheese + maple syrup + orange juice/zest + vanilla

---

● CHEESE, EMMENTAL (FRENCH) or EMMENTALER (SWISS)

Techniques: shred
Possible substitute: Swiss cheese

bread, e.g., rye
cabbage, e.g., napa
fondues
fruit
mushrooms
onions, e.g., red
pasta, e.g., lasagna
pears
sandwiches
spinach

Dishes

Napa Cabbage, Pears, Winter Truffles,
Emmentaler Cheese Fondue
— Dovetail (New York City)

• CHEESE, FETA

Flavor: salty and sour; semi-firm/crumbly
Techniques: bake, fresh, smoke
Vegan Tip: Substitute fluffy macadamia nut "feta."

apples
arugula
asparagus
barley
basil
beans, e.g., borlotti, lima, red
beets
bell peppers, e.g., red, roasted
breads, e.g., olive, whole wheat
   pita
capers
chard, e.g., Swiss
chickpeas
cilantro
cucumbers
dates
dill
eggplant
EGGS, e.g., *frittatas, omelets,*
   quiches
farro
fennel
figs

garlic
grapes
gratins
Greek cuisine
honey
kale
lemon, e.g., juice, zest
lentils, e.g., red
lettuce, e.g., romaine
marjoram
Mediterranean cuisines
mint
mushrooms
oil, olive
OLIVES, e.g., black, Greek,
   kalamata
onions, e.g., pickled, red
orange
oregano
parsley
pasta, e.g., farfalle, **orzo**
pepper, black
pistachios
pizza
potatoes

Dishes

Hearth-Fired Mediterranean Flatbread
with Babaganoush, Feta Cheese,
Roasted Fennel, Kalamata Olives,
Roasted Peppers
— Canyon Ranch (Miami Beach, FL)

Flavor Affinities
feta cheese + artichoke hearts + garlic + spinach + *pizza*
feta cheese + arugula + figs
feta cheese + asparagus + eggs + tomatoes
feta cheese + balsamic vinegar + sun-dried tomatoes
feta cheese + bell peppers + mushrooms
feta cheese + black olives + orzo + sun-dried tomatoes
feta cheese + dill + eggs + spinach
feta cheese + fennel + watermelon
feta cheese + garlic + oregano
feta cheese + lemon + scallions
feta cheese + marjoram + mint + tomatoes
feta cheese + olive oil + olives + parsley + red onions + tomatoes
feta cheese + rosemary + spinach

quinoa
risotto
rosemary
sage
salad dressings
SALADS, *e.g., Greek, vegetable*
sandwiches
sauces
savory
scallions
sesame
sorrel
soups, e.g., tomato
spanakopita, i.e., spinach pie
SPINACH
spreads, e.g., whipped feta
sumac
thyme
TOMATOES
tomatoes, sun-dried
vinegar, e.g., balsamic, red wine
walnuts
watermelon
yogurt
zucchini

"We smoke **feta cheese** in cherry wood. Feta really absorbs flavor, so you need a mild wood."
— AMANDA COHEN, DIRT CANDY
(NEW YORK CITY)

• CHEESE, FONTINA

artichokes
arugula
basil
bell peppers, e.g., roasted
eggs, e.g., *omelets*
endive
fondues / fondutas
fruit, esp. fresh
grapes
Italian cuisine
mushrooms, e.g., chanterelle
mustard, Dijon
onions, e.g., grilled and/or red
pastas, e.g., cannelloni, macaroni
pears
pizzas
plums
potatoes
quesadillas
sage
salads
sandwiches, e.g., grilled cheese,
   panini
sauces
squash, butternut
tomatoes
tomatoes, sun-dried
truffles, white
walnuts
zucchini

Flavor Affinities

Fontina cheese + arugula + red
   onions + sun-dried tomatoes +
   sandwiches
Fontina cheese + tomatoes +
   zucchini + *pizza*

Dishes

**Macaroni with Fontina Cheese and
Chanterelle Mushrooms**
— White Barn Inn (Kennebunk, ME)

• CHEESE, GOAT
Techniques: bake, fresh

almonds
apples
apricots, dried or fresh
artichokes
arugula
asparagus
basil
beans, e.g., fava, wax
BEETS
bell peppers, **red**, esp. roasted
berries, e.g., blackberries,
   raspberries, **strawberries**
breads, e.g., fruit and/or nut;
   whole grain
broccoli
capers
carrots
cayenne
celery
chard
cheese, other, e.g., cream,
   Neufchâtel, ricotta
cheesecake

cherries, e.g., dried, fresh, sour,
   sweet
chervil
chiles, e.g., pequillo; and chili
   pepper flakes, chili pepper sauce
chives
cinnamon
corn
cranberries, dried
cream
dates
dill
dips
eggplant
EGGS, *e.g., frittatas, omelets, quiches*
endive
fennel and fennel seeds
FIGS
GARLIC grains, e.g., millet
grapes
greens, e.g., salad
hazelnuts
herbs
honey
kohlrabi

Flavor Affinities

goat cheese + apples + beets
goat cheese + apples + celery + *salads*
goat cheese + arugula + eggs
goat cheese + arugula + pears
goat cheese + balsamic vinegar + beets + dill + sage
goat cheese + balsamic vinegar + figs
goat cheese + basil + garlic
goat cheese + beets + cider vinegar
goat cheese + capers + garlic + oregano + sun-dried tomatoes
goat cheese + caramelized onions + sage
goat cheese + figs + pomegranate seeds
goat cheese + garlic + greens + **thyme**
goat cheese + garlic + olive oil + **thyme**
goat cheese + grapes + pistachios
goat cheese + mushrooms + pine nuts + spinach
goat cheese + pears + walnuts
goat cheese + pesto + sun-dried tomatoes
goat cheese + red onions + tomatoes
goat cheese + scallions + sun-dried tomatoes

Dishes

Bohemian Creamery Goat's Milk Cheeses with Heirloom Apple-Quince Pâte de Fruit and Candied Walnuts
— Chez Panisse (Berkeley, CA)

Goat Cheese Gnocchi, Caramelized Baby Artichokes, Lemon, and Olive Oil
— Jean-Georges (New York City)

LEEKS
lemon, e.g., juice, zest
lentils
lettuce
lime
marjoram
mint
mushrooms, e.g., shiitake
nuts, e.g., pecans
oil, e.g., hazelnut, **olive**, pine nut, walnut
olives, e.g., black
ONIONS, e.g., caramelized, green, red
orange, e.g., juice, zest
oregano
parsley
pasta, e.g., lasagna, ravioli, tortellini
peaches
pears
pepper, e.g., black, white
pesto
pine nuts
pistachios
pizzas
plantains
plums, dried or fresh
polenta
pomegranates
potatoes
quesadillas
quince
quinoa
raisins
ramps
risotto
rosemary
sage

SALADS, e.g., fruit, green
salt, sea
sandwiches, e.g., grilled cheese
sauces
savory
scallions
seeds, e.g., poppy
soufflés
SPINACH
squash, e.g., summer
sweet potatoes
tapenade
tarts
thyme
TOMATOES
TOMATOES, SUN-DRIED
vanilla
vegetables, roasted
vinaigrette
vinegar, e.g., balsamic, cider, red wine, sherry
walnuts
wheat berries
yogurt
za'atar
zucchini
zucchini blossoms

● CHEESE, GORGONZOLA (see CHEESE, BLUE)

● CHEESE, GOUDA

apples
apricots
arugula
bread, e.g., sourdough
cherries
honey

mushrooms
onions
pears
pizzas
salads
soups, e.g., onion
spinach
walnuts

● CHEESE, GRUYÈRE

apples
arugula
asparagus
breads, e.g., nut
cayenne
celery
cherries
chives
EGGS, e.g., *frittatas, omelets,* **quiches**
endive
fondues
garlic
gratins
hazelnuts
leeks
mayonnaise
mushrooms
mustard
nutmeg
oil, e.g., olive, walnut
onions, e.g., caramelized
parsnips
pears
potatoes
quince
rosemary
salads

Dishes

Onion Soup "2013," with Smoked Gouda, Sourdough "Sponge," Onion Bouillon
— Picholine (New York City)

Heirloom Apple and Smoked Gouda Salad with Honey Walnut Dressing
— Rancho La Puerta (Mexico)

Dishes

Vermont Egg Omelette with Wilted Spinach, Gruyère Cheese, and Chives
— Café Boulud (New York City)

sandwiches, e.g., *grilled cheese*
sauces
soufflés
soups, *e.g., onion*
spinach
thyme
tomatoes
vegetables, roasted
walnuts

Flavor Affinities

Gruyère cheese + asparagus + chives + eggs
Gruyère cheese + cayenne + nutmeg
Gruyère cheese + leeks + mushrooms + thyme

● CHEESE, HALLOUMI

Flavor: salty/sour, with notes of feta cheese and sometimes mint, and a firm, chewy, almost meaty texture that can even stand up to grilling without melting
Volume: quiet
What it is: Greek cheese made from sheep's or, sometimes, goat's milk
Techniques: bake, GRILL, sauté, sear — or serve fresh

arugula
bell peppers, e.g., red, roasted
bread, e.g., pita, whole grain

Dishes

Grilled Halloumi Cheese and Peaches with Chard Rib Salad, Sun-Dried Olive, and Sweet Pepper Broth
— Oleana (Cambridge, MA)

capers
carrots
chard
Cyprian cuisine
dates
dill
eggplant
figs
garlic
ginger
Greek cuisine
greens, salad
harissa
honey
kebabs
Lebanese cuisine
leeks
lemons
lentils
limes
melon
mint
oil, olive
olives, e.g., kalamata
parsley
peaches
pears
pepper, black
pesto
pine nuts
salads, e.g., green
salt, sea
sandwiches
Syrian cuisine
tomatoes
walnuts
za'atar

Flavor Affinities

Halloumi cheese + capers + lemon

● CHEESE, HAVARTI

Flavor: notes of butter
Volume: quiet

bell peppers, e.g., roasted
breads, e.g., whole rye
cucumbers
dill
fruits, esp. autumn
horseradish
mustard
nuts, e.g., almonds
pears
pesto
sandwiches
sour cream
zucchini

● CHEESE, JACK (aka MONTEREY JACK)

almonds
American cuisine
beans, e.g., pinto
bell peppers
chilaquiles
chiles, e.g., serrano
chiles rellenos
cilantro
corn
eggs, *e.g., omelets, scrambled*
enchiladas
figs
lime
Mexican cuisine
olives
pastas
pears
pecans
peppers, e.g., piquillo
plums, dried
polenta
pumpkin seeds
quesadillas
quince paste
salsa
sauces
tacos
vegetables, roasted

walnuts
yams

Flavor Affinities
Jack cheese + bell peppers + corn
Jack cheese + chiles + corn

● CHEESE, MANCHEGO
ALMONDS
artichokes
bell peppers, e.g., roasted
breads, e.g., crusty, fruit (e.g., fig)
broccoli rabe
dates
eggs, e.g., *omelets, tortillas*
figs
membrillo (quince paste)
oil, olive
olives, e.g., black, green, Spanish
onions, e.g., caramelized
parsley
peppers, e.g., piquillo, red,
  roasted
plum paste
*QUINCE PASTE
salads
Spanish cuisine
tomatoes
walnuts

Flavor Affinities
manchego cheese + almonds +
  broccoli rabe
manchego cheese + almonds +
  quince paste
manchego cheese + artichokes +
  olives
manchego cheese + dates +
  walnuts
manchego cheese + figs + walnuts

Dishes

Manchego Chopped Salad of Garbanzo
Beans, Vegetables, Olives, Capers, and
Manchego Cheese, tossed with Roasted
Lemon Vinaigrette
— Canyon Ranch (Miami Beach, FL)

● CHEESE, MOZZARELLA

Vegan Tip/Brand: Check
out Follow Your Heart soy
mozzarella.

almonds
artichoke hearts and artichokes
arugula
asparagus
*BASIL
BELL PEPPERS, esp. roasted
bread crumbs
broccoli and broccoli rabe
calzones
capers
celery
cheese, other, e.g., Parmesan
EGGPLANT
eggs, e.g., *quiches*
figs
garlic
gratins
greens, bitter or salad
Italian cuisine
leeks
lemon, e.g., juice, zest
melon
mint
mushrooms, e.g., cremini,
  portobello
oil, olive
olives, e.g., black, green; and
  olive paste
oregano

Dishes

Hearth-Fired Whole-Wheat Margherita Flatbread: Flatbread Crust with Hearth-Roasted
Tomatoes, Fresh Buffalo Mozzarella and Basil
— Canyon Ranch (Miami Beach, FL)

Hand-Pulled Mozzarella, with Grapes, Capers, and Olives
— FnB Restaurant (Scottsdale, AZ)

Heirloom Tomato and Mozzarella Cheese: Buffalo Milk Mozzarella, Panzanella, Cannellini
Crema, Pesto, and 25-Year-Old Balsamic Vinegar
— Mayflower Inn & Spa (Washington, CT)

---

pasta, e.g., *lasagna, rigatoni*
peaches
pepper, e.g., black, white
peppers, esp. roasted
pesto
PIZZA
pumpkin
radicchio
rice, e.g., Arborio
rollatini
rosemary
sage
salads
salt, e.g., kosher, sea
sandwiches, e.g., *panini*
spiedini
spinach
*TOMATOES, green and
  sundried
truffles
vanilla
vegetables, roasted
vinaigrette
vinegar, e.g., balsamic, red wine
zucchini
zucchini blossoms

Flavor Affinities
mozzarella cheese + basil
  + figs
MOZZARELLA CHEESE
  + BASIL + OLIVE OIL +
  TOMATOES
mozzarella cheese + bell peppers
  + portobello mushrooms

mozzarella cheese + black olives
+ tomatoes + zucchini
mozzarella cheese + capers +
lemon
mozzarella cheese + pesto +
sundried tomatoes

• CHEESE, PARMESAN

Vegan Tip: To add saltiness
and texture to pastas, substitute
bread crumbs and capers for
Parmesan cheese on top of
the dish.

artichoke hearts and artichokes
arugula
asparagus
basil
beans, e.g., borlotti, fava, green,
white
bread crumbs
broccoli
casseroles
celery root
chard, Swiss
chestnuts
chickpeas
dates
eggplant
eggs, e.g., *frittatas*
endive
escarole
fennel
figs
frittatas
fruits, e.g., grapes
garlic
gratins
grits
honey
Italian cuisine
kale, e.g., black, green

Dishes

**Parmesan Cheese Ice Cream with Crisp
Fig Fritter**
— The White Barn Inn (Kennebunk, ME)

kohlrabi
leeks
lemon
melon
mushrooms, e.g., portobello
oil, olive
onions
*PASTA, e.g., farfalle, gnocchi,
lasagna, macaroni, manicotti*
pears
pesto
pine nuts
pizza
polenta
popcorn
potatoes
pumpkin
quiches
risottos
rosemary
sage
salad dressings, e.g., Caesar
SALADS, e.g., Caesar
sauces
soups
squash, summer
stuffings
sugar snap peas
thyme
TOMATOES
tomatoes, green
vinegar, e.g., balsamic
walnuts
zucchini

Flavor Affinities

Parmesan cheese + basil + tomato
Parmesan cheese + dates + walnuts
Parmesan cheese + honey +
thyme + walnuts
Parmesan cheese + portobello
mushrooms + rosemary

• CHEESE, PECORINO
almonds
arugula
beets

Dishes

**Heirloom Tomato Tasting with
Arugula Pesto, Pecorino, and
Smoked Olive Oil**
— Plume (Washington, DC)

bell peppers, esp., roasted,
sweet
broccoli
cauliflower
cheese, other, e.g., Parmesan,
ricotta
eggs, e.g., *frittata*
endive
grapes
greens, salad
honey, e.g., chestnut
Italian cuisine
lemon
mushrooms, portobello
oil, e.g., olive
parlsey
pasta, e.g., spaghetti
pears
pepper, e.g., black
pesto
polenta
risottos
salads
squash, summer
truffles
vinegar, e.g., balsamic
walnuts
watercress

Flavor Affinities

pecorino cheese + arugula +
walnuts

• CHEESE, PROVOLONE

Tip: Fry thinly sliced provolone
(optionally topped with a
sprinkle of smoked paprika) to
a crisp for a quick bacon
substitute on baked potatoes,
salads, or sandwiches.

artichokes
bell peppers, red, esp. roasted
fennel
figs
grapes
greens, salad
Italian cuisine
lettuce
lime
oil, olive
olives
***pasta**, e.g., lasagna, ziti*
pears
pesto
pizzas
polenta
potatoes, e.g. *baked*
radicchio
salads
sandwiches, e.g., vegetarian BLT
sauces
tomatoes
vegetables, roasted
zucchini

• CHEESE, QUESO AÑEJO

What it is: Mexican aged cheese
Techniques: crumble or grate on top of dishes
Possible substitutes: Parmesan, pecorino, Romano

basil
beans, e.g., refried
cayenne
chilaquiles
chiles and chili powder
cilantro
corn, e.g., grilled (e.g., with mayonnaise)
eggs and *egg dishes, e.g., frittatas, huevos rancheros*
enchiladas
garlic
greens, salad
lime

Mexican cuisine
oil, olive
onions
pastas
"pesto"
pumpkin seeds
salad dressings
salads, e.g., Caesar
soups
tacos
tortillas
vegetables
vinegar

Flavor Affinities
queso añejo cheese + cayenne + corn + mayonnaise
queso añejo cheese + cilantro + pumpkin seeds

• CHEESE, QUESO FRESCO

Techniques: crumble on top of dishes
Possible substitutes: mild feta or other mild fresh goat cheese

avocados
beans, black
corn
eggplant
enchiladas
Mexican cuisine
plantains
quesadillas
refried beans
salads, e.g., green, vegetable
squash, summer
tacos
tomatoes

• CHEESE, RICOTTA

Flavor: neutral, with a creamy texture
Volume: quiet
Nutritional profile: 66% fat / 28% protein / 6% carbs

Calories: 215 per ½-cup serving (whole-milk ricotta)
Protein: 14 grams
Techniques: bake, raw

Vegan Tip: Substitute pine nut (which has a similar fluffy texture), macadamia nut / pumpkin seed, or tofu "ricotta."

almonds
apples
apricots
artichokes
arugula
BASIL
beans, fava
bee pollen
beets
bell peppers, e.g., red, esp. roasted
BERRIES, e.g., blueberries, raspberries, strawberrries
blintzes
bread and bread crumbs, whole grain
broccoli
chard
CHEESE, other, e.g., cream, goat, Gruyère, mozzarella, **PARMESAN**, pecorino, Romano
cheesecake
chestnuts
chives
chocolate
cinnamon
cloves
coffee
crostini
dates
EGGPLANT
eggs, e.g., *frittatas, omelets*
fennel
figs
fruit, e.g., dried, fresh
GARLIC
gnocchi
greens, bitter
herbs

HONEY, e.g., chestnut,
   eucalyptus, lavender
Italian cuisine
kale, e.g., black
leeks
LEMON, e.g., juice, zest
marjoram
mascarpone
melon
mint
mushrooms, e.g., porcini,
   portobello
mushrooms, stuffed
nettles
nutmeg
nuts, e.g., hazelnuts
oil, olive
olives, e.g., black
oranges, e.g., blood
oregano
pancakes
paprika
parsley
PASTAS, *e.g., cannelloni, gnocchi,*
   lasagna, manicotti, ravioli, ziti
peaches
peanuts and peanut butter
peas
pepper, e.g., black
pesto
phyllo dough
pies
pine nuts
pizza
plums
polenta
potatoes
rollatini
saffron
sage
salt
shallots
soups
sour cream
SPINACH
squash, buttercup
sugar, e.g., brown
tarragon

Dishes

House-Made Ricotta Ravioli: Fennel, Tomato, Lemon Breadcrumb
— Boulud Sud (New York City)

"Vacherin": Ricotta Pound Cake, Bing Cherries, Lemon Verbena, and Tahitian Vanilla-Lime Ice Cream
— The French Laundry (Yountville, CA)

Genovese Basil "Tortellini" with Ricotta, Brentwood Corn, Shishito Peppers, and French Laundry Garden Squash
— The French Laundry (Yountville, CA)

Ricotta Pie: Baked Ricotta with Fresh Herbs and One Egg
— North Fork Table & Inn (Southold, New York)

Grilled Figs with Creamy Honeyed Ricotta and Almonds
— Rancho La Puerta (Mexico)

ricotta + almonds + cinnamon + honey + peanut butter + vanilla
ricotta + almonds + honey
ricotta + apricots + arugula
ricotta + artichokes + leeks + *pizza*
ricotta + balsamic vinegar + strawberries
ricotta + basil + Parmesan cheese + pasta + pine nuts
ricotta + blueberries + lemon
ricotta + chestnuts + honey
ricotta + chocolate + strawberries
ricotta + dried fruit + honey
ricotta + egg + herbs + Parmesan cheese + *pies*
ricotta + fava beans + lemon + pasta
ricotta + figs + honey + pistachios
ricotta + figs + walnuts
ricotta + greens + pasta
ricotta + honey + lemon + sour cream
ricotta + peas + thyme
ricotta + sage + zucchini blossoms

tarts
thyme
TOMATOES and TOMATO
   SAUCE
vanilla
vinegar, e.g., balsamic, cider, red
   wine, sherry
walnuts, e.g., candied, toasted
watercress
zucchini and *stuffed zucchini*
zucchini blossoms

● CHEESE, RICOTTA SALATA

What it is: moist, fresh salted, and pressed ricotta (similar to feta)
Techniques: grate, shave

apples
artichokes
arugula
avocados
basil

beans, e.g., fava
beets
cheesecake
citrus fruits
cucumbers
eggplant
endive
fennel
fruit
garlic
greens, salad
honey
Italian cuisine
kale
lemon
lettuces, e.g., butter
mushrooms, e.g., wild
oil, olive
olives
orange
parsley
parsnips
PASTAS, *e.g., lasagna, manicotti,*
  pappardelle, spaghetti
pears
peas
pistachios
pizzas
radicchio
raisins
salads, *e.g., green, pasta, spinach*
shallots
spinach
squash, e.g., butternut, summer
thyme
tomatoes and tomato sauce
vegetables, grilled
vinegar, balsamic
walnuts
watermelon

Flavor Affinities

ricotta salata + eggplant + garlic
  + olive oil + parsley + tomato
ricotta salata + greens + lemon +
  mustard + pears
ricotta salata + kale + lemon +
  olive oil + shallots

● CHEESE, ROQUEFORT (see CHEESE, BLUE)

● CHEESE, ROMANO

almonds
broccoli
Italian cuisine
mushrooms, e.g., portobello
pastas, e.g., fettuccine
pesto
pizzas
salads
soups

● CHEESE, SMOKED MOZZARELLA

artichokes
arugula
asparagus
basil
bell peppers, roasted
broccoli
bruschetta
escarole
figs
gratins
honey
mushrooms
olive paste
onions, e.g., caramelized
pastas, e.g., baked, penne
pesto
pizza
potatoes
radicchio
risotto
sandwiches, e.g., panini
scallions
spinach
tomatoes

Flavor Affinities

smoked mozzarella + basil +
  tomatoes
smoked mozzarella + potatoes +
  scallions

CHEESE, STILTON (see CHEESE, BLUE)

● CHEESE, SWISS

apples
asparagus
bread, e.g., pumpernickel
eggs, e.g., *frittatas, quiches*
fennel
grapes
gratins
kale
leeks
mushrooms, portobello
onions
parsnips
pears
potatoes
sandwiches, e.g., "Reuben"
sauces
Swiss cuisine

● CHEESE, TALEGGIO

arugula
asparagus
hazelnuts
Italian cuisine
lemon
mostarda (mustard fruits)
nuts
pears
pesto
pizzas
polentas
radicchio

Dishes

Tomato Artichoke Romano Salad: Tomatoes, Cannellini Beans, Artichokes, Green Olives, and Romano Cheese, tossed in a Lemon Dressing
— Canyon Ranch (Tucson, AZ)

raisins
risottos
salads, e.g., green
sandwiches, e.g., grilled
tomatoes

"CHEESE," VEGAN

calzones
cheese plates, e.g., with fruits, nuts
dips, e.g., cheese
eggplant, e.g., baked eggplant
enchiladas
fondues
pastas, e.g., macaroni
pizzas

Say (Vegan) Cheese!

Many vegans enjoy Daiya or Follow Your Heart brand vegan cheeses, which come in various flavors (e.g., cheddar, mozzarella) and often melt and stretch much as dairy cheese does.

I have been more impressed with the flavor of the artisanal vegan cheeses I've tasted, such as those at Pure Food and Wine in Manhattan. Portobello in Portland, Oregon, serves an artisanal vegan cheese plate that showcases cheeses from cheese-makers across the country, including **Field Roast**, Seattle-based producer of Chao Cheese (herb-crusted, tofu-based cheeses), **Door 86** (Nashville), **Heidi Ho** (Portland, OR), **Kite Hill** (Hayward, CA), **Punk Rawk Labs** (Minneapolis), and **Treeline Treenut Cheese** (Kingston, NY).

Interested in making your own? Check out Miyoko Schinner's 2012 book **Artisan Vegan Cheese**, which is developing a cult following among vegan chefs and foodies.

quesadillas
sandwiches, e.g., grilled cheese, "Reuben"
veggie burgers

• CHERRIES, SOUR and SWEET

Season: summer
Flavor: sweet and/or sour, with a juicy texture
Volume: moderate
What they are: fruit
Nutritional profile: 88% carbs / 7% protein / 5% fat (sour)
Calories: 80 per 1-cup serving (e.g., sour, raw)
Protein: 2 grams
Techniques: bake, dry, flambé, poach, raw, stew
Tips: Off-season, consider frozen cherries. Sour cherries are more nutritionally dense than sweet.
Botanical relatives:
apples, apricots, blackberries, peaches, pears, plums, quinces, raspberries, strawberries

allspice
ALMONDS
apples and **apple juice**
apricots
baked goods, e.g., cakes, cookies, crisps
basil
blackberries
brandy
butter
caramel
cardamom
CHEESE, e.g., cream, GOAT, ricotta
cherries jubilee
chiles, e.g., jalapeño
CHOCOLATE
chutneys
CINNAMON
citrus, e.g., juice
clafoutis, cherry

cloves
coconut
compotes
corn / cornmeal
cream and crème fraîche
crisp, fruit
currants, red
ginger
granola
hazelnuts
honey
ice cream
*KIRSCH
lemon, e.g., juice, zest
lemon verbena
mint
nectarines
nutmeg
nuts
oatmeal and oats
orange, e.g., juice, zest
peaches
pears
pecans
pepper, black
pies
pistachios
plums
rhubarb
salads, e.g., fruit, green
sauces, dessert
smoothies
sorbets
soups, e.g., fruit
sour cream
star anise
sugar
tarts
VANILLA
vinegar, e.g., balsamic, regular or white
wine, esp. dry, red or port
yogurt

Flavor Affinities
cherries + almonds + apricots
cherries + almonds + balsamic vinegar

cherries + almonds + chocolate
cherries + apricots + oats
cherries + basil + vanilla
cherries + cinnamon + ginger +
    orange juice + vanilla
cherries + cinnamon + wine
cherries + ginger + pears
cherries + lemon + mascarpone
    + vanilla
cherries + peaches + pecans
cherries + pistachios + yogurt

"When **cherries** come in, I love to
use them in savory dishes. I like
to pair them with a creamy
burrata, which is a nice textural
contrast. I might use them in a
gastrique to create a sweet
and sour flavor to play off the
creaminess of the cheese.
Cherries are also great with
grains like farro or freekeh with
lots of lemon. I like cherries
with sweeter herbs like chervil
or parsley, and they are great
with basil. Cherries pair well with
nuts, but since they're used
with almonds so much, I will pair
them with black walnuts."
— JON DUBOIS, GREEN ZEBRA (CHICAGO)

CHERRIES, DRIED, esp. SOUR

Flavor: sour, with a chewy
texture
Volume: moderate – loud

apples and apple juice
*baked goods, e.g., biscotti, breads,
    pastries*
cereals, hot breakfast
cheese, e.g., goat
cherries and cherry juice
chocolate, e.g., dark
compotes
dates
desserts

fruit, other dried, e.g., apricots
ginger
grains, e.g., quinoa, wild rice
granola
greens, e.g., mesclun, salad
lemon, e.g., juice, zest
muesli
oats
oranges
pears
pilafs
popcorn
quince
salads
sauces
stuffings
trail mix
vanilla
vinegar, e.g., balsamic
walnuts

Flavor Affinities
dried cherries + apple juice +
ginger + quince + sugar

● CHERVIL

Season: spring – autumn
Flavor: slightly sweet; aromatic;
with notes of anise, licorice,
parsley, pepper, and/or tarragon
Volume: very quiet

> **Tips:** Chervil is best when
> used fresh (not dried). Add at
> the end of cooking, just before
> serving.

Botanical relatives: caraway,
carrots, coriander, cumin,
parsley

almonds
artichokes
asparagus
basil
beans, e.g., fava, green, white,
yellow
bouquets garnis

Dishes

Glenmere Salad: Baby Mixed Greens, Beets, Radishes, Candied Walnuts, Dried Cherries,
Goat Cheese, and Cherry Vinaigrette
— Glenmere Mansion (Chester, New York)

bulgur
butter
carrots
cheeses, e.g., chèvre, goat,
pecorino, Romano, soft white
chives
cilantro
cold dishes
couscous
cream
crème fraîche
cucumbers
dill
EGGS, e.g., hard-boiled, and *egg
dishes*
FINES HERBES
FRENCH CUISINE
grains, whole
greens, e.g., dandelion, salad
leeks
lemon
lettuces
marjoram
mint
mushrooms, e.g., morel
mustard
nuts
oil, olive
parsley
pastas
peas
pestos
potatoes, e.g., new
rice
salad dressings
SALADS, e.g., egg, green, potato
sauces, e.g., creamy
shallots
sorrel
*SOUPS, e.g., creamy, potato,
vegetable*

spinach
stuffings
tarragon
tomatoes, **tomato sauces**, and
sun-dried tomatoes
vinegar, e.g., champagne, white
wine
zucchini

Flavor Affinities
chervil + chives + parsley +
tarragon (*fines herbes*)

● CHESTNUTS

Season: autumn – winter
Flavor: sweet, with earthy notes
of nuts, smoke (esp. roasted),
and/or vanilla, and a creamy, rich,
starchy texture
Volume: quiet – moderate
What they are: nuts
What's healthful about them:
low in fat versus other nuts
Nutritional profile: 92% carbs
/ 5% fat / 3% protein
Calories: 55 per 1-ounce serving
(peeled, raw)
Techniques: bake, boil (15 –
40 minutes), braise, candy,
dry, grill, mash, pressure-cook
(5 – 20 minutes, depending on
whether fresh or dried), puree,
roast (400°F for 15 – 20 minutes),
sauté (about 20 minutes), steam
(about 10 minutes)

> **Tips:** Must be cooked and
> peeled. If dried, they can keep
> for years. If you're a fan of
> cream of chestnut soup, also try
> Jerusalem artichoke soup.

apples, apple cider, and apple juice
baked goods, e.g., cakes, pies
bay leaf
beans, e.g., white
brandy
bread crumbs
broccoli and broccoli rabe
BRUSSELS SPROUTS
butter
cabbage, e.g., red
carrots
casseroles
cayenne
celery
celery root
cheese, e.g., blue, Fontina
chickpeas
chiles, e.g., chipotle
chocolate
cinnamon
cloves
coffee
Cognac
cranberries
cream
currants
DESSERTS
dips
eggs
farro
fennel and fennel seeds
garlic
ginger
grains, whole
grapes
greens, bitter
honey, e.g., chestnut
Italian cuisine
kale

leeks
lemon, e.g., juice
lentils, e.g., French, red
madeira
maple syrup
milk
mirin
mushrooms, e.g., button, porcini, white
nutmeg
oil, e.g., canola, grapeseed, olive, sesame
onions
orange, e.g., zest
parsley
parsnips
pastas, e.g., gnocchi, pappardelle, tortellini
pâtés, e.g., chestnut-lentil
pears
pecans
pepper, e.g., black
"pestos"
pine nuts
plums, dried
puddings
pumpkin
purees
raisins
raspberries
rice, e.g., glutinous, medium- or short-grain, wild
risottos
rosemary
rum
sage
sake
salads
salt, e.g., sea

sesame seeds, black
shallots
sherry
soufflés
SOUPS, e.g., chestnut, butternut squash
Spanish cuisine
SQUASH, WINTER, e.g., butternut, kabocha
stir-fries
stock, vegetable
STUFFINGS, e.g., corn bread
sugar, e.g., brown
tarragon
vanilla
vegetables, root, e.g., beets, celery root, turnips
vinegar, e.g., balsamic, sherry
wine, red, e.g., dry or sweet, e.g., port

Flavor Affinities
chestnuts + black sesame seeds + rice
chestnuts + broccoli rabe + garlic + olive oil
chestnuts + Brussels sprouts + squash
chestnuts + butternut squash + garlic + sage
chestnuts + celery root + tarragon
chestnuts + cinnamon + garlic + pumpkin
chestnuts + Fontina cheese + pasta + white truffles
chestnuts + lemon + parsley
chestnuts + pasta + rosemary

● **CHIA SEEDS**
Flavor: notes of nuts and/or poppy seeds, with the texture of tapioca pearls (when soaked)
Volume: quiet
Who says they're healthful: Joel Fuhrman lists it as a top-10 "Super Food for Super Immunity."
Nutritional profile: 53% fat / 36% carbs / 11% protein

Dishes

Mascarpone Enriched Chestnut "Agnolotti": "Beurre Noisette," Bartlett Pears, Brussels Sprouts, and Black Winter Truffle
— Per Se (New York City)

Chestnut Agnolotti with Chocolate Granola, Huckleberries, Brown Butter Sage
— Picholine (New York City)

Calories: 140 per 1-ounce serving

Protein: 4 grams

Tips: Sprinkle ground chia seeds over breakfast cereals. Use to thicken soups, as the seeds become gelatinous in liquids. Stir ¼ cup chia seeds into ⅔ cup water, and then refrigerate for 10 minutes to achieve a pudding-like consistency.

Factoid: Chia seeds can hold 12 times their weight in water.

Botanical relatives: mint, sage

apples
baked goods, *e.g., biscuits, breads, cakes, cookies, muffins*
bananas
beans, black
berries, e.g., blueberries
carob
cereals, breakfast
chili, vegetarian
chocolate and cocoa / cacao
cinnamon
coconut, coconut butter, and coconut milk
dates
drinks, e.g., limeade
flax seeds
ginger
goji berries, e.g., dried
granola
honey
kale
lemon
lime, e.g., juice
maca
mango
maple syrup
milk, e.g., cashew, coconut, hemp seed
mint
nutmeg
nuts and nut butters, e.g., Brazil
oatmeal, oats, and oat bran
pears

C

pecans
porridge
PUDDINGS
raisins
sage
salads
smoothies
soups
squash, spaghetti
sugar, e.g., coconut
tofu, silken
vanilla
veggie burgers
walnuts
yogurt and frozen yogurt

Flavor Affinities
chia seeds + almond milk + apples
    + buckwheat + cinnamon
chia seeds + cashews + coconut
    + dates
chia seeds + cocoa + honey +
    silken tofu + vanilla
chia seeds + ginger + pear + pears

Dishes

I Am Free: Chia-Seed Porridge with
Hempseed Milk, Lucuma, Maca,
Cinnamon, Maple Syrup, Goji Berries, and
Seasonal Fruit
— Café Gratitude (Los Angeles)

Apple Cinnamon Buckwheat and Chia
Cereal, Almond Milk
— In the Raw (Highland Park, IL)

**● CHICKPEAS (aka
GARBANZO BEANS)**
Season: year-round, esp.
summer (for fresh)
Flavor: slightly sweet, with
earthy/starchy notes of nuts (e.g.,
chestnuts, walnuts), and a rich,
creamy yet firm texture
Volume: quiet
Who says they're healthful:
The Center for Science in the
Public Interest's *Nutrition Action*
lists garbanzo beans on its "10
Best Foods" list.
Nutritional profile: 68% carbs
/ 19% protein / 13% fat
Calories: 270 per 1-cup serving
(boiled)
Protein: 15 grams
Techniques: boil, fry, pressure-
cook, roast, simmer, smoke,
sprout, stew

Tips: Presoak dried chickpeas
overnight (or 6 – 8 hours) before
cooking. Boil until tender and
cooked thoroughly, about 1½ –
3 hours. Note that chickpeas
require longer cooking than
most legumes.

(North) African cuisine
almonds
apples, apple cider, or apple
    juice
apricots, dried
artichokes
avocados
basil and Thai basil
bay leaf
beans, green
bell peppers, e.g., roasted
Bragg Liquid Aminos
bread, e.g., pita, whole grain
bulgur
buttermilk
cabbage, e.g., napa
capers
cardamom
carrots
cashews
cauliflower
cayenne
celery
chana masala
chard, Swiss
cheese, e.g., cheddar, **feta**, goat,
    Parmesan
chiles, e.g., chipotle, jalapeño;
    and chili pepper flakes

chili, vegetarian
cilantro
cinnamon
citrus, e.g., lemon, lime, orange
cloves
coconut and coconut milk
coriander
couscous
cucumbers
CUMIN, e.g., toasted
currants
CURRIES, e.g., Indian, curry
    powder, curry spices
dill
dips, e.g., hummus
EGGPLANT
FALAFEL
fennel
GARLIC
ginger
grains, e.g., farro, millet, quinoa,
    rice, wheat berries
Greek cuisine
greens, bitter, e.g., amaranth, beet
greens, salad
herbs
*HUMMUS
INDIAN CUISINE
Italian cuisine
kale
LEMON, e.g., juice
lemons, preserved
lentils, e.g., green
lime
mangoes
mayonnaise
Mediterranean cuisines
Mexican cuisine
MIDDLE EASTERN CUISINES
mint
Moroccan cuisine
mushrooms, e.g., porcini,
    portobello
mustard seeds
OIL, e.g., **OLIVE**, sesame,
    sunflower, vegetable
olives, e.g., kalamata, niçoise
ONIONS, e.g., red, yellow

oregano
paprika, e.g., smoked, sweet
PARSLEY
pasta, e.g., whole grain
pepper, e.g., black, white
peppers, roasted red
pine nuts
pistachios
polenta
potatoes
pumpkin
quinoa
RICE, e.g., basmati, brown, wild
rosemary
saffron
sage
salad dressings
*SALADS, e.g., bean, chopped,
    green, vegetable*
salt, e.g., kosher, sea
scallions
seeds, e.g., pumpkin, **sesame**
*SOUPS, e.g., minestrone, tomato,
    vegetable*
SPINACH
spreads
squash, e.g., summer, yellow
STEWS, e.g., vegetable
stock, vegetable
sumac
sweet potatoes
tabbouleh
tagines
TAHINI
tamari, low-sodium
tamarind
tarragon
thyme
**TOMATOES, TOMATO PASTE,
    and sun-dried tomatoes**
tortillas, whole wheat
turmeric
veggie burgers
vinegar, e.g., balsamic, red wine,
    sherry
walnuts
yogurt
zucchini

Dishes

Chickpea and Eggplant: Herb Falafel, Spicy Fava Bean Hummus, Babaganoush, Lavash
— Boulud Sud (New York City)

Spiced Chickpeas with Oven-Dried Tomatoes and Parsley Garlic Whip
— Crossroads (Los Angeles)

Stewed Chickpeas, Tamarind, Curry Roasted Cauliflower, Eggplant, Cilantro, Yoghurt
— Green Zebra (Chicago)

Chickpea Terrine with Apricot, Pistachio, and Tahini Sauce
— Oleana (Cambridge, MA)

Coriander, Chickpea, and Kale Soup
— Real Food Daily (Los Angeles)

Sun-Dried Tomato Hummus: Homemade Chickpea Dip, Cucumbers, Toasted Pita Tips
— Real Food Daily (Los Angeles)

Flavor Affinities

chickpeas + apricots + pistachios + tahini
chickpeas + basil + brown rice + curry
chickpeas + basil + cucumber + feta cheese + garlic + red onions
chickpeas + bay leaf + cinnamon + ginger
chickpeas + brown rice + mushrooms + *veggie burgers*
chickpeas + bulgur + eggplant + mint + quinoa
chickpeas + cayenne + feta cheese + garlic + spinach + tomatoes
chickpeas + cayenne + garlic + lemon + olive oil + tahini
chickpeas + chiles + cilantro + lime
chickpeas + cilantro + coriander + cumin + garlic + lemon + olive oil
chickpeas + coconut milk + cumin
chickpeas + coriander + cumin + mint + sesame seeds
chickpeas + cucumbers + tomatoes
chickpeas + cumin + eggplant
chickpeas + cumin + garlic + lemon + tahini
chickpeas + cumin + red onions + tomatoes + turmeric
chickpeas + currants + pine nuts + rice
chickpeas + curry powder + garlic + lime juice + onions
chickpeas + feta cheese + onions + tomatoes
CHICKPEAS + GARLIC + LEMON + TAHINI
chickpeas + garlic + mint
chickpeas + goat cheese + olives + tomatoes
chickpeas + kale + Parmesan cheese + *soups*
chickpeas + mint + onions + yogurt
chickpeas + potatoes + saffron + Thai basil
chickpeas + spinach + sweet potatoes

"Some of the dishes I come up with don't sound as good on paper as they taste in your mouth. Some had doubts hearing about my smoked **chickpea** salad made with carrots, celery, and [vegan] mayonnaise, and served with veggies in a wrap — but everyone loved the taste of it!"
— JORGE PINEDA, CANDLE 79 (NEW YORK CITY)

CHICORIES (see ENDIVE, ESCAROLE, and RADICCHIO)

• CHICORY (see also RADICCHIO, aka RED CHICORY)

Season: autumn – spring
Flavor: bitter, with notes of broccoli rabe, and a hearty, crunchy texture
Volume: moderate – loud
Nutritional profile: 71% carbs / 18% protein / 11% fat
Calories: 10 per 1-cup serving (chopped, raw)
Techniques: braise, grill, raw, sauté (about 15 – 20 minutes.)
Botanical relatives:
artichokes, chamomile, dandelion greens, endive, lettuces (e.g., Bibb, iceberg, romaine), radicchio, salsify, tarragon

almonds
apples, e.g., Fuji
artichokes, Jerusalem
arugula
beans, e.g., kidney
beets
bread crumbs
butter
capers
carrots
CHEESE, e.g., **blue**, cheddar, feta, Fontina, fresh, Gorgonzola, Gruyère, **PARMESAN**, Roquefort, Stilton, Swiss
chili pepper flakes
chives
cranberries, dried
cream
eggs, e.g., hard-boiled
fennel
figs
garlic
grapefruit
grapes
gratins
greens, other
hazelnuts
honey
lemon
lettuces, e.g., mesclun, mixed
mint
mustard, e.g., Dijon
nutmeg
nuts, e.g., hazelnuts, walnuts
oil, nut, e.g., hazelnut, walnut
oil, olive
olives, e.g., black, green
onions
oranges, e.g., blood
parsley
parsnips
pastas
pears

Flavor Affinities

chicory + almonds + pears
chicory + apples + blue cheese + pecans
chicory + apples + figs + goat cheese
chicory + blue cheese + dried cranberries + pecans
chicory + blue cheese + hazelnuts + **pears**
chicory + blue cheese + walnut oil + walnuts
chicory + bread crumbs + garlic + onions + Parmesan cheese + rice
CHICORY + CHEESE (e.g., blue, goat, Parmesan) + **FRUIT**
   (e.g., apples, pears) + **NUTS** (e.g., hazelnuts, pecans, walnuts)
chicory + garlic + rice
chicory + grapefruit + sunchokes
chicory + lemon + olive oil + Parmesan cheese
chicory + Parmesan cheese + walnuts

pecans
persimmons, e.g., fuyu
pine nuts
potatoes
raisins
rice
salads, e.g., bitter green, mixed green
scallions
shallots
sorrel
soufflés
soy sauce
sugar, e.g., brown
tomatoes
vegetables, root
vinegar, e.g., balsamic, red wine, sherry
walnuts
watercress
Worcestershire sauce, vegan
zucchini

• CHILES — IN GENERAL, or MIXED

Season: summer – autumn
Flavor: hot (and sometimes sweet)
Volume: moderate – extremely loud
What they are: vegetables
Nutritional profile: 84% carbs / 12% protein / 4% fat

Calories: 30 per ½-cup serving (e.g., raw, green, chopped)
Protein: 1 gram
Techniques: raw, roast, sauté, toast

Tips: Opt for organic chiles. Toast dry chiles to bring out their flavor. Add at the end of the cooking process.

Botanical relatives: bell peppers, eggplant, gooseberries, potatoes, tomatillos, tomatoes

Asian cuisines
avocados
basil, e.g., Thai
BEANS, e.g., black, pinto
bell peppers
Cajun cuisine
caraway seeds
Caribbean cuisines
cheese, e.g., cheddar, Fontina, goat, Monterey Jack, mozzarella, Parmesan, queso fresco
Chinese cuisine
chocolate, e.g., bitter, dark
CILANTRO
cinnamon
coconut and coconut milk
coriander
corn
corn bread
cucumbers
cumin
curries
eggplant
eggs, e.g., omelets
galangal
GARLIC
GINGER
greens
guacamole
Indian cuisine, e.g., South
Latin American cuisines
lemon, e.g., juice
lemongrass
lentils

LIME, e.g., juice
mangoes
marjoram
*MEXICAN CUISINE
moles
mushrooms
noodles
nuts
oil, e.g., olive, sesame, sunflower
olives
onions, e.g., red
oregano, e.g., Mexican
parsley
pasta
peanuts, esp. in Asian dishes
peas
pineapple
potatoes
relishes
rice
salads, e.g., bean, Thai
SALSAS
sauces, e.g., fruit, moles, salsas
seeds, e.g., pumpkin
sesame, e.g., oil, seeds, esp. in Asian cuisines
shallots
soups
sour cream
South American cuisines
Southeast Asian cuisines
Southwestern (U.S.) cuisine
soy sauce
stews
stuffed chiles
sugar, e.g., palm
tamarind
Tex-Mex cuisine
*THAI CUISINE
thyme
tomatillos
TOMATOES and TOMATO SAUCE
tortillas and tortilla chips
turmeric
vegetables, sweet, e.g., beets, carrots, corn

vinegar, e.g., balsamic, red wine, rice wine, sherry
yogurt

Flavor Affinities
chiles + chocolate + garlic + nuts + onions + seeds
chiles + cilantro + garlic + red onions + tomatoes + vinegar + salsas

"I use Fresno **chiles** a lot. They look like red jalapeños but are sweeter. If a red bell pepper and a jalapeño got together and produced offspring, this is what it would taste like."
— CHARLEEN BADMAN, FnB (SCOTTSDALE, AZ)

CHILES, ANAHEIM
[AN-uh-hyme]
Flavor: hot; bitter (esp. green) or sweet (esp. red)
Volume: quiet (for a chile!) – moderate
Techniques: roast, stuff

beans, e.g., black
cheese, e.g., cheddar
chiles rellenos
chiles, other, e.g., chipotle
chili, vegetarian
chowders, e.g., corn
cilantro
coriander
corn
corn bread
cumin
dips
eggs, e.g., omelets
salads
salsas
salt
sauces
stews
stir-fries
stuffed peppers

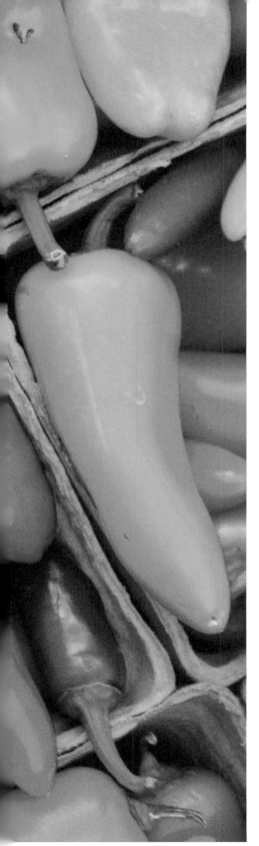

tacos
tomatillos
tomatoes
veggie burgers
vinegar, rice

● CHILES, ANCHO

Flavor: hot/sweet, with notes of coffee and/or fruit (e.g., dried plums or raisins)
Volume: quiet – moderate-plus
What they are: dried poblano chiles

> **Tip:** Grind to make chili powder.

achiote seeds
bay leaf
BEANS, e.g., black, kidney, pinto, red
bulgur
cashews
chiles, other, e.g., guajillo
chili, vegetarian
chocolate
cloves
coriander
corn
cumin
eggplant
epazote
garlic
lentils, e.g., brown
lime, e.g., juice
Mexican cuisine
oil, e.g., grapeseed, vegetable
onions
oregano, e.g., dried, Mexican
pepper, e.g., black
rice
salsas
salt, e.g., sea
sauces, e.g., adobo, mole
soups, e.g., vegetable
stews
stock, e.g., vegetable
stuffed ancho chiles
tacos

tamales
tofu
tomatoes

Flavor Affinities
ancho chiles + garlic + oregano + tomatoes + *sauces*
ancho chiles + lime + tofu

CHILES, CASCABEL
[KAH-skah-bel]
Flavor: hot, with rich notes of earth, fruit, nuts, smoke, tobacco, and/or wood
Volume: **moderate** (for a chile!) – loud
Techniques: roast

> **Tip:** Remove chiles before serving, as their skins do not dissolve readily.

almonds
beans
casseroles
chiles, other, e.g., chipotle
chili
cilantro
enchiladas
fajitas
grapefruit
honey
lemon
lime
Mexican cuisine
mushrooms
orange
peaches
pumpkin
salsas, esp. raw
sauces, e.g., mole
soups
squash, e.g., winter
stews
tacos
tamales
tomatillos
tomatoes

CHILES, CHIPOTLE

[chih-POHT-lay]

Flavor: hot/bitter/sweet, with notes of chocolate, nuts, and/or smoke

Volume: moderate – **loud**

What they are: dried smoked jalapeños

> **Tip:** Buy canned peppers packed in adobo sauce (a tomato-based sauce that adds acidity and saltiness).

agave nectar
arugula
avocados
basil
BEANS, e.g., **BLACK**, pinto
bell peppers, e.g., red
carrots
casseroles
Central American cuisines
cheese
chilaquiles
chiles, other; and chili sauce, e.g., Thai sweet
CHILI, VEGETARIAN
chocolate
cilantro
corn
cumin
empanadas
GARLIC
honey
lemon, e.g., juice, zest
lime, e.g., juice, zest
maple syrup
marinades
mayonnaise
Mexican cuisine
miso
molasses
mushrooms, e.g., portobello
mustard
oil, e.g., canola, **olive**, vegetable
ONIONS, e.g., red, white
orange, e.g., juice, zest
oregano

paprika
pepper, e.g., black
pizzas
pomegranates
posole
potatoes
quesadillas
quinoa
rice
salad dressings
salads
salsas
salt, e.g., kosher, sea
sandwiches, e.g., grilled cheese
SAUCES, e.g., dipping
sherry, dry
SOUPS, e.g., black bean
Southwestern (U.S.) cuisine
soy sauce
spinach
spreads
squash, butternut
STEWS
stock, vegetable
sugar, e.g., brown
sweet potatoes
tacos
tamales
tamari
tempeh
Tex-Mex cuisine
tofu
tomatillos
TOMATOES (canned or fresh) and tomato paste, puree, sauce, etc.
tortillas and tortilla chips
vinegar, e.g., apple cider, balsamic, champagne, rice wine, white
yams

Flavor Affinities

chipotle peppers + balsamic vinegar + cumin + **onions** + **tomatoes**

chipotle peppers + cilantro + **garlic + lime**

chipotle peppers + citrus (e.g., lime, orange) + **garlic**

chipotle peppers + garlic + **onions + tomatoes**

chipotle peppers + lime juice + **onions + tomatoes**

CHILES, GREEN (see CHILES, JALAPEÑO and CHILES, SERRANO)

CHILES, GUAJILLO

Flavor: hot, with notes of berries, smoke, and/or tea

Volume: moderate – loud

What it is: dried chiles

achiote seeds
bay leaf
chiles, other, e.g., ancho chiles
chili, vegetarian
cloves
coriander
cumin
eggs
epazote
garlic
jícama
lime
Mexican cuisine
oil, e.g., grapeseed
oregano, Mexican
pepper, black
salt, sea
sauces, e.g., pasta
soups
stews
tomatoes

CHILES, HABANERO

Flavor: hot, with notes of fruit (not to mention fire and brimstone)

Volume: extremely loud

> **Tip:** Also known as Scotch bonnet peppers, these are one of the world's hottest chiles.

allspice
apples
avocados
bell peppers, red
Caribbean cuisines
carrots
cilantro
cloves
fruit, tropical
guacamole
ketchup
lemon, e.g., juice
lime
mangoes
mint
oil, vegetable, e.g., olive
onions, e.g., red, white
oregano
papaya
pineapple
pumpkin
radishes
salsas
salt, sea
SAUCES, e.g., hot, jerk
sugar
tomatillos
tomatoes
vinegar, rice wine

"Because their flavor is so strong once they're cut, I'll throw whole **Scotch bonnet peppers** into a dish for a much milder flavor, and remove them before serving."
— SHAWAIN WHYTE, CAFÉ BLOSSOM (NEW YORK CITY)

• CHILES, JALAPEÑO

Flavor: hot, with notes of pepper
Volume: moderate – very loud
Techniques: stuff (e.g., with cheese)
Tip: Add jalapeños at the end of the cooking process.

apples
avocados

beans, e.g., black, pinto
carrots
cayenne
cheese, e.g., anejo, cheddar
chiles rellenos
chutneys
cilantro
cinnamon
coconut milk
corn
corn bread and corn muffins
cucumbers
cumin
curries
dips
figs
guacamole
honey
jícama
lemon, e.g., juice
LIME
mangoes
Mexican cuisine
mint
oil, e.g., olive
onions, e.g., white
palm, hearts of
peanut butter
"pesto"
pumpkin seeds
sage
salad dressings, e.g., citrus
salads
salsas, e.g., salsa verde
salt, e.g., sea
sauces, e.g., ranchero
soups
squash, e.g., butternut, summer
stews
tacos
tomatillos
tomatoes
vermouth
vinegar, champagne

Flavor Affinities
jalapeños + champagne vinegar + lime + olive oil

• CHILES, PASILLA

Flavor: hot/sweet, with notes of chocolate, dried fruit, and/or nuts
Volume: moderate – loud
What they are: dried chilaca chiles

avocado
bell peppers
cabbage
cheese, e.g., cotija
chiles, other, e.g., ancho
chili, vegetarian
chocolate, Mexican
corn
crema
enchiladas
epazote
garlic
guacamole
lime
mushrooms, e.g., button, shiitake
oil, olive
onions
potatoes
salsas
SAUCES, e.g., MOLES
scallions
slaws
soups, e.g., garlic, pumpkin, tomato, tortilla
stuffed peppers
tacos
tomatoes

Flavor Affinities
pasilla peppers + epazote + garlic + mushrooms

• CHILES, POBLANO

Season: summer
Flavor: hot, with notes of smoke, and a rich, velvety texture
Volume: moderate – loud
Factoid: Dried poblanos are ancho chiles.
Techniques: bake, fire-roast, fry, grill, roast, stuff

avocado
beans, e.g., black, pinto, white
bell peppers, sweet, e.g., red,
  yellow
carrots
casseroles
cayenne
chard, Swiss
cheese, e.g., cheddar, goat,
  Monterey Jack, queso fresco
chiles, other, e.g., ancho, **chipotle**
CHILES RELLENOS
chili pepper flakes and chili
  powder
chili, vegetarian
cilantro
CORN
cumin
eggs, e.g., *frittatas, scrambled*
enchiladas
fajitas
garlic
grains
hominy
leeks
lime
Mexican cuisine
mushrooms, e.g., oyster,
  portobello, shiitake
oil, olive
onions, e.g., red
orange
oregano
posole
potatoes
pumpkin
quesadillas
quinoa
rice, e.g., brown
salad dressings
salads
salsas
scallions
soups, e.g., black bean, corn,
  mushroom, potato
sour cream
stews
stock, vegetable
stuffed peppers

tacos
tempeh
tofu
tomatillos
tomatoes
tortillas, corn
vegetables, e.g., roasted
veggie burgers
zucchini

Flavor Affinities
poblano chiles + cheese + cilantro
  + *enchiladas* + garlic + spinach +
  tortillas
poblano chiles + cilantro + lime +
  onions + tomatoes
poblano chiles + cumin + orange
  + rice
poblano chiles + garlic + onions

"I didn't grow up with chiles [in
Michigan], but they've grown on
me over the years. **Poblano chiles**
are my favorite. I love their great
aroma and smoky flavor, and
will fire roast them on an Asador
grill [aka a chile pepper grill or
dry roaster] on the stovetop. I'll
stuff them with quinoa and goat
cheese, and serve with ancho
and chipotle chiles, corn, cilantro,
marjoram, and a little lime to
perk it all up!"
— ANNIE SOMERVILLE, GREENS
RESTAURANT (SAN FRANCISCO)

● CHILES, SERRANO
Flavor: hot/spicy, with savory
notes
Volume: loud – very loud

> **Tip:** Serranos are even hotter
> than jalapeños (but not as hot as
> habaneros).

beans, e.g., pinto
Bloody Marys
chili powder
chili, vegetarian
cilantro

coriander
corn
cucumbers
cumin
eggs, e.g., *huevos rancheros*
enchiladas
garlic
guacamole
jícama
lime
Mexican cuisine
molasses
oil, e.g., olive, vegetable
onions, e.g., yellow
orange, e.g., juice
pineapple
pumpkin and pumpkin seeds
salads
salsas
sauces, e.g., ranchero
tomatillos
tomatoes
vinegar, e.g., white wine

Flavor Affinities
serrano chiles + cilantro +
  coconut milk + **ginger** + Indian
  spices + **lemongrass** + tomatoes
serrano chiles + ginger + lentils
  + rice
serrano chiles + onions + tomatoes

"I really like **serrano chiles** —
they bring food to life! With some
tomatoes, cilantro, and salt, I am
in heaven."
— ANNIE SOMERVILLE, GREENS
RESTAURANT (SAN FRANCISCO)

CHILES, THAI
Flavor: hot
Volume: very loud

basil, Thai
beans, e.g., green
bell peppers
bok choy
broccoli
cashews

cilantro
curries, Thai
garlic
ginger
Kaffir lime
lemongrass
lime, e.g., juice, zest
mushrooms
noodles, Asian, e.g., rice
oil, e.g., peanut
onions, e.g., red
oyster sauce, vegetarian
pad thai
rice, e.g., jasmine
scallions
soy sauce
spinach
sprouts, bean
Thai cuisine
tofu

● CHILI PEPPER FLAKES
Flavor: hot
Volume: loud (but quieter than chili powder)
Possible substitute: Aleppo pepper flakes (made from sun-dried Syrian peppers)

baked goods, e.g., breads
bamboo shoots
bell peppers
broccoli and broccoli rabe
chickpeas
chili, vegetarian
garlic
Italian cuisine
lentils
marinades
mushrooms
oil, e.g., olive
pastas, *e.g., spaghetti*
pizzas
refried beans
salad dressings
salads
sauces, *e.g., dipping, pasta, tomato*
soups

stews
stir-fries
tomatoes and tomato sauce

● CHILI POWDER
Flavor: hot
Volume: very loud
What it is: ground, dried chiles; sometimes also contains allspice, cayenne, cloves, coriander, **cumin**, **garlic powder**, onion powder, **oregano**, paprika, and/or salt
Tip: Store chili powder in the freezer.

avocado
beans, e.g., black, pinto
cheese, e.g., cheddar
chickpeas
chili pepper sauce
CHILI, VEGETARIAN
corn
corn bread
cumin
dips
enchiladas
garlic
guacamole
Italian cuisine
lime
marinades
mayonnaise
Mexican cuisine
nachos
pecans, e.g., spiced
popcorn
refried beans
rice
salad dressings
sauces, e.g., tomato
seeds
soups, *e.g., black bean*
stews
stir-fries
tequila
Tex-Mex cuisine
tomatoes and tomato sauce
trail mix, spicy
vegetables, e.g., sautéed

CHINESE CUISINE
Techniques: bake, fry, steam, stir-fry

asparagus
bamboo shoots
cabbage, e.g., Chinese
chiles
cinnamon
five-spice powder
garlic
ginger
hoisin sauce
noodles, Asian, e.g., wheat
peanuts
RICE, e.g., brown
scallions
sesame, e.g., oil, seeds
snow peas
SOY SAUCE
spring rolls
star anise
steamed dishes
stir-fries
sugar
tofu
vegetables
vinegar, rice wine
wheat, e.g., noodles (esp. in northern China)
wine, rice

"I spent two years in **Hong Kong** and found what they were doing with vegetarian food was very inspiring. At the time there was nowhere [in North America] to eat vegetarian food unless you wanted 'hippy and crunchy.' But in Hong Kong, it was natural because people ate vegetarian once or more a week and it was not considered weird. The flavors they were able to coax from meatless ingredients were amazing."
— AMANDA COHEN, DIRT CANDY (NEW YORK CITY)

CHINESE FIVE-SPICE POWDER (see FIVE-SPICE POWDER)

• CHIVES
Season: spring – autumn
Flavor: pungent, with notes of onions or scallions
Volume: quiet – moderate
Tips: Use fresh. Add chives toward the end of cooking, or just before serving.
Botanical relatives: asparagus, garlic, leeks, onions, shallots

asparagus
avocados
beans, e.g., black, green, navy, pinto
beets
bell peppers, red
butter
buttermilk
carrots
celery
cheese, e.g., cheddar, cottage, goat, Parmesan, ricotta
chervil
chiles, jalapeño
Chinese cuisine
cole slaws
corn
couscous
cucumbers
dips
EGGS, e.g., *deviled, frittatas,* hard-boiled, *omelets,* scrambled
FINES HERBES
French cuisine, e.g., Provençal
garlic
grains, whole
gratins
gravies
herbs, other, e.g., basil, mint, parsley, tarragon
Italian cuisine, e.g., Tuscan
leeks
lemon

lentils
lettuce, e.g., romaine
lime
mushrooms, e.g., morel
mustard, Dijon
noodles, egg
oil, olive
olives
onions
parsley
pasta, e.g., *fettuccine, spaghetti*
peas
peas, split
pecans
POTATOES, e.g., *baked, mashed*
salad dressings
SALADS, e.g., bean, egg, grain, pasta, potato
sandwiches
sauces, e.g., cheese, cream
shallots
SOUPS and **CHOWDERS**, *e.g., cold, cream-based, cucumber, vichyssoise*
sour cream
squash, winter, e.g., butternut
stews
stir-fries
stock, e.g., vegetable
stuffings
tarragon
tomatoes
vegetables, e.g., root
vinegar, e.g., white wine
yogurt
zucchini

Flavor Affinities
chives + garlic + lemon + olive oil + Parmesan cheese + *pasta*

CHIVES, GARLIC (aka CHINESE CHIVES)
Season: spring
Flavor: pungent, with notes of garlic and onion
Volume: moderate – loud

butter
cheese
chiles
Chinese cuisine
dumplings, e.g., Asian
eggplant, Japanese
eggs, e.g., scrambled
garlic
ginger
lemon
miso
mushrooms, e.g., shiitake
Japanese cuisine
noodles, e.g., Asian
oil, sesame
parsley
potatoes
rice and *fried rice*
salad dressings
shallots
soups, e.g., miso
soy sauce
sprouts, bean
stir-fries
tofu
tomatoes
vegetables, e.g., root, stir-fried
vinegar

Flavor Affinities
garlic chives + Asian noodles + sesame oil + shiitake mushrooms + soy sauce

CHOCOLATE, DARK (see also CACAO and COCOA POWDER)
Flavor: bitter (and sometimes sweet), with nutty notes
Volume: moderate – loud
What's healthful about it: antioxidants (which are more plentiful in dark chocolate than in milk chocolate; the more bitter the chocolate, the more antioxidants)

achiote
allspice
apples and applesauce
apricots
baked goods, e.g., brownies, cakes,
  cookies, muffins
BANANAS
berries
beverages, e.g., hot chocolate
brandy
Brazil nuts
brown rice syrup
butter
candies
CARAMEL
cashews
cheese, cream
cherries, e.g., fresh, dried
chestnuts
chiles
chili, vegetarian
CINNAMON
cloves
coconut
*COFFEE and ESPRESSO
cookies
cream
dates
DESSERTS
figs, e.g., dried
fruit, dried and fresh
ginger
goji berries
graham crackers
granola
HAZELNUTS
honey
hot chocolate / hot cocoa
ice cream
lemon
lemongrass

Dishes

Chocolate Bread Pudding: Salted Caramel, Pine Nuts, and Cocoa Nib Ice Cream
— Blue Hill (New York City)

Mexican Chocolate Brownie with Caramelized Bananas, French Vanilla Ice Cream, Candied Pecans, and Chocolate Ancho Sauce (pictured on page 211)
— Candle Cafe West (New York City)

Chocolate Layer Cake: Coffee Bean Cream, Chocolate Ganache, Lucky Hand Black Lager Caramel, Peanut Brittle, Malt Chip Ice Cream
— Millennium (San Francisco)

Banana Chocolate Tart with Mesquite Flour Crust and Brazil Nut
— True Food Kitchen (Santa Monica)

Chocolate Uber Chunk Pretzel-Peanut Crust, Malt Custard, Stout Ice Cream
— Vedge (Philadelphia)

macadamia nuts
malt
maple syrup
marshmallows
Mexican cuisine
MILK
MINT
mocha
mole sauces
mousses
nutmeg
*NUTS, e.g., **ALMONDS,
HAZELNUTS**, peanuts, **pecans,
pistachios, WALNUTS,** and
NUT BUTTERS**
oats
oil, nut, e.g., almond or walnut
orange
passion fruit
pears
plums, dried
popcorn
puddings
raisins
raspberries
rum
sauces, e.g., dessert, mole
sorbets

sour cream
strawberries
SUGAR or Sucanat
tofu
VANILLA
wine, sweet, e.g., Banyuls, port,
    Pedro Ximénez sherry
yogurt

Flavor Affinities

chocolate + almond oil + cocoa +
    nuts
chocolate + almonds + coconut
**chocolate + almonds + maple
    syrup** + tofu
chocolate + caramel + coffee
chocolate + caramel + vanilla
chocolate + cherries + dates +
    nuts
chocolate + cinnamon + dried/
    fresh fruit + milk
chocolate + coconut + ginger
chocolate + coconut + pecans
chocolate + coffee + orange
chocolate + hazelnuts + dried
    plums
chocolate + pecans + vanilla
chocolate + pistachios + walnuts

● **CHOCOLATE, WHITE**
Nutritional profile: 52% fat /
43% carbs (high in sugar) / 5%
protein

apricots
baked goods, e.g., cookies
BERRIES, e.g., blackberries,
    raspberries, strawberries
cheese, e.g., cream
cherries
chocolate, other, e.g., dark
cinnamon
citrus
coconut
cream
desserts, e.g., cheesecake, mousses
ginger
hazelnuts
lemon, e.g., juice, zest
lime, e.g., juice, zest
mint
nuts, e.g., hazelnuts, macadamia
oatmeal
orange, e.g., juice, zest
pears
rhubarb
rum
vanilla

Flavor Affinities
white chocolate + rhubarb +
    strawberries

● **CILANTRO (aka
CHINESE PARSLEY or
FRESH CORIANDER
LEAF)**
[sill-AHN-troh]
Season: year-round, esp.
spring – summer
Flavor: bitter/sour/sweet, with
pungent notes of lemon, lime,
and/or parsley (and, to non-
lovers, soap)
Volume: loud
What it is: an herb

Tips: Cilantro is best used fresh (not dried or cooked). Add at the very last minute, or ideally just before serving. Use cilantro to add a cooling note to chile-spiced dishes.

Botanical relatives: coriander, parsley

Possible substitute: parsley

(North) African cuisines
almonds
ASIAN CUISINES (except Japanese)
avocado
basil
BEANS, e.g., **black**, fava, pinto, white
beets
bell peppers
cardamom
Caribbean cuisines
carrots
cauliflower
cayenne
celery
chard
chickpeas
CHILES, e.g., ancho, chipotle, jalapeño, serrano
chili, vegetarian
chimichurri sauce
Chinese cuisine
chutneys
cinnamon
citrus
coconut and **coconut milk**
coriander
CORN
corn bread
couscous
cucumbers
cumin
curries, e.g., Indian
dips
edamame
eggplant

eggs, e.g., hard-boiled
enchiladas
epazote
fajitas
GARLIC
ginger
greens, e.g., mustard
guacamole
INDIAN CUISINE
jícama
Latin American cuisines
lemon, e.g., juice
lemongrass
lentils
LIME, e.g., juice
mangoes
marinades
melon, e.g., cantaloupe
MEXICAN CUISINE
mint
miso
moles

mushrooms, e.g., shiitake
mustard
noodles, esp. Asian, e.g., soba
nuts
oil, e.g., **olive**, vegetable
okra
onions, e.g., red
oranges and blood oranges, e.g., juice
pad thai
papaya, e.g., red
parsley
pasta, e.g., orzo
peanuts
pears
peas
pepper, black
"PESTOS"
posole
potatoes
pumpkin seeds
quinoa

Flavor Affinities

cilantro + almonds + garlic **+ olive oil**
cilantro + avocado + chiles + garlic + red onions + tomatoes
cilantro + basil + chiles + garlic + lime + mint
cilantro + basil + garlic + Parmesan cheese
cilantro + black pepper + garlic
cilantro + carrots + **lime + rice**
cilantro + cayenne + cumin + garlic + lemon + olive oil + parsley
cilantro + chiles + coconut milk + lime
cilantro + chiles + coriander + cumin + garlic + lime + mint + olive oil
cilantro + chiles + corn
cilantro + chiles + garlic + lime
cilantro + chiles + lime
cilantro + chiles + lime + onions + tomatillos/tomatoes
cilantro + coconut milk + lemon
cilantro + corn + lime
cilantro + corn + tomatoes
cilantro + cumin + lime
cilantro + garlic + ginger + rice vinegar + sesame (oil/seeds) + soy sauce
cilantro + garlic + walnuts
cilantro + jícama + lime + onions + orange + papaya
cilantro + onions + pinto beans
cilantro + tomatoes + winter squash

RICE, e.g., basmati, brown
salad dressings
SALADS, e.g., Asian, Thai
SALSAS, e.g., green, Mexican,
  tomato
sandwiches
sauces
scallions
sorrel
SOUPS, e.g., chickpea, gazpacho,
  tortilla
South American cuisines
Southeast Asian cuisines
soy sauce
squash, e.g., summer, winter
stews
sweet potatoes
tacos
tahini
tamarind
Tex-Mex cuisine
THAI CUISINE
tofu
tomatillos
TOMATOES
tortillas
vegetables
Vietnamese cuisine
vinegar, e.g., white wine
wakame
walnuts
wheat berries
yogurt
zucchini

● CINNAMON

Season: year-round, esp.
autumn – winter
Flavor: bitter/sweet; very
aromatic
Volume: loud
Factoid: One teaspoon
of cinnamon has as many
antioxidants as a ½-cup of
blueberries.

> **Tips:** Add early in the cooking
> process. Overcooking cinnamon,
> however, brings out its bitterness.

Botanical relatives: avocado,
bay leaf

almonds
APPLES, apple cider and
  apple juice
BAKED GOODS, e.g., breads,
  cakes, cookies, muffins, pastries,
  pies
bananas
beans
beets
beverages, e.g., cocoa, eggnog, hot
  chocolate
blueberries
breakfast / brunch, e.g., coffee cake,
  French toast, pancakes
butter
carrots
cauliflower
cereals, breakfast, e.g., hot
chiles
chili, vegetarian
CHOCOLATE and **COCOA**
cloves
coconut
coffee and **espresso**
compotes, fruit
corn
couscous
curries, e.g., Indian
curry powder
custards
dates
DESSERTS, e.g., crisps, custards
French toast
FRUITS and fruit desserts
garam masala
ginger
grapefruit
grapes
honey
ice cream
Indian cuisine
lemon, e.g., juice
maple syrup
Mediterranean cuisines
Mexican cuisines

Middle Eastern cuisines
milk
Moroccan cuisine
nutmeg
nuts
oatmeal
onions
orange flower water
oranges and **blood oranges**, e.g.,
  juice
pancakes
peaches
pears
pecans
popcorn
puddings
raisins
rhubarb
rice
rose water
sauces, e.g., chocolate
stews
stuffings, e.g., rice
sugar, e.g., brown
sweet potatoes
teas
tomatoes
vanilla
wine, e.g., mulled, red
yogurt

Flavor Affinities
cinnamon + almonds + grains
  (e.g., couscous, oats) + **raisins**
cinnamon + almonds + rice
cinnamon + chocolate + milk
cinnamon + maple syrup + pecans

CITRUS — IN GENERAL (see GRAPEFRUIT, LEMON, LIME, ORANGE, and TANGERINE)

> **Tips:** Using citrus is one of the
> best ways to add flavor without
> adding extra fat or sodium to a
> dish. Both the juice and the zest
> of citrus fruits are full of flavor.

CLEMENTINES (see MANDARINS, ORANGES, and TANGERINES)

• CLOVES

Flavor: bitter/**sweet**, with pungent/spicy notes

Volume: loud

Tip: Add early in cooking process.

Botanical relative: allspice

allspice
apples, apple cider, and apple juice
baked goods, e.g., breads, biscuits, cakes, cookies, fruitcakes, gingerbread, muffins, pastries, pies
beets, e.g., pickled
cardamom
chiles
chocolate
cinnamon
coriander
cranberries
cumin
desserts, e.g., custards
drinks
fenugreek
fruits, esp. cooked/stewed
garam masala
ginger
honey
lemon, e.g., zest
lentils
maple syrup
marinades
nutmeg
nuts
onions
ORANGE, e.g., juice, zest
pears, e.g., *poached*
pepper, e.g., black
pilafs
puddings
pumpkin
quatres épices

ras el hanout
relishes, e.g., cranberry
rice
salad dressings
sauces, e.g., barbecue, dessert, mole
sloppy Joes, vegetarian
soups
soy sauce
squash, winter
stews
stock, vegetable
sugar, e.g., brown
sweet potatoes
tamarind
teas
turmeric
vanilla
wine, e.g., *mulled*

Flavor Affinities

cloves + allspice + apple cider + cinnamon + maple syrup + vanilla
cloves + apples + cranberries
cloves + cinnamon+ cumin + green lentils + onions + oranges
cloves + cinnamon + oranges + pears + vanilla + wine

• COCOA POWDER (see also CACAO and CHOCOLATE, DARK)

Factoid: More antioxidants than in green tea or red wine!

avocado
BAKED GOODS, e.g., brownies, cakes, cookies
beverages, e.g., hot chocolate, hot cocoa
chili, *vegetarian*
coconut and coconut milk
milk, e.g., almond, dairy, hemp, rice, soy
nuts and **nut butters**, e.g., almonds

Flavor Affinities

cocoa powder + agave nectar + avocado

• COCONUT, COCONUT CREAM, and COCONUT MILK (see also COCONUT BUTTER, COCONUT NECTAR, COCONUT WATER, and MILK, COCONUT)

Flavor: sweet, with notes of nuts, and a chewy (meat) or creamy (milk) texture

Volume: moderate – loud

Nutritional profile: 82% fat / 14% carbs / 4% protein

Calories: 185 per 1-ounce serving (e.g., coconut meat, dried, unsweetened)

Protein: 2 grams

Techniques: dried (flakes, shredded), raw, roast, shave

Tip: For convenience, try frozen grated coconut.

Brand: Thai Kitchen premium organic coconut milk

almonds
apricots
"bacon"
BAKED GOODS, e.g., breads, cakes, cobblers, cookies (e.g., oatmeal), macaroons, muffins, pie crusts
bananas
basil
beans, e.g., green
bell peppers, e.g., red
beverages
butterscotch
cabbage, e.g., julienned, napa
caramel
Caribbean cuisines
carrots
cauliflower
*cereals, **breakfast**, e.g., **granola**, muesli*
cherries
chiles, e.g., dried, serrano
CHOCOLATE, e.g., dark, white
cilantro
cinnamon

coconut water
coriander
cranberries, dried
cream and crème fraîche
cucumbers
cumin
CURRIES, e.g., Indian, Thai,
  vegetable; curry paste and curry
  powder
dates
DESSERTS, e.g., cakes, custards,
  ICE CREAMS, *pies, puddings,*
  sorbets
eggplant
FRUITS, esp. fresh, tropical, e.g.,
  guavas, lychees, **MANGOES,**
  papayas, **passion fruit, pineapple**
galangal
garlic
ginger
graham crackers
grapefruit
honey
icings
Indian cuisine
Kaffir lime leaves
kale
kiwi
LEMON
lemongrass
lentils, e.g., red
lettuce, e.g., romaine
LIME
macaroons
maple syrup
marinades
melon, e.g., honeydew
milk, e.g., almond, rice
mint

miso
NUTS, e.g., Brazil, **cashew,**
  hazelnuts, macadamia, peanuts,
  pecans, pistachios, walnuts
oats / oatmeal
oil, e.g., sesame
orange
paprika
parsnips
peas
pepper, e.g., black
plantains
pomegranates
potatoes
raspberries
RICE, e.g., jasmine, sticky
rum
salads, e.g., fruit, green
sauces
scallions
sesame seeds
SMOOTHIES

SOUPS
Southeast Asian cuisines
soy sauce
spinach
squash, e.g., butternut
strawberries
sugar, e.g., brown, coconut
sweet potatoes
tapioca
tempeh
THAI CUISINE
tofu
tomatoes
trail mix
turmeric
VANILLA
vinegar, wine
watercress
yogurt
zucchini

Flavor Affinities

coconut + banana + goji berries + maca powder + *smoothies*
coconut + banana + yogurt
coconut + brown sugar + ginger + vanilla
coconut + cashews + maple syrup + vanilla
coconut + chiles + sweet potatoes + tomatoes
coconut + citrus (e.g., lemon, lime) **+ mango**
coconut + cranberries + *granola* + hazelnuts
coconut + curry + peanuts + tofu
coconut + curry powder + sweet potatoes
coconut + dates + nuts + orange
coconut + lemongrass + passion fruit
coconut + lime + pomegranate seeds + watercress
coconut + lime + tropical fruits + yogurt
coconut + pineapple + rum
coconut + rice milk + vanilla

Dishes

Coconut Meringue with Mango, Papaya, and Passion Fruit
— Eleven Madison Park (New York City)

Coconut Lime Pot de Crème with Mango Compote and Sesame Seed Cookies
— Greens Restaurant (San Francisco)

"I love fresh young **coconut** meat, even plain. But if you add avocado and lime, you can make a pudding to die for! And you can also take it savory by making a 'beef jerky' from dehydrated coconut blended with cayenne, liquid smoke, and raw agave or maple syrup — it's incredible."
— AMI BEACH, G-ZEN (BRANFORD, CT)

"I'll whip very cold **coconut cream** with a little agave nectar and vanilla in the KitchenAid with the whisk attachment for about 5 – 10 minutes to make a really luscious topping. The colder the coconut cream, the less time it takes to whip."

— DEENA JALAL, FOMU AND ROOT (ALLSTON, MA)

COCONUT BUTTER

Flavor: notes of cream, with a creamy consistency
Volume: quiet
What it is: ground coconut meat + coconut oil (like nut butter, made from coconut)
Brands: Artisana (organic, raw), Nutiva Coconut Manna (organic)

apples
avocado
baked goods, e.g., cakes, pie crusts
bananas
breads and quick breads
cheeses, vegan
chia seeds
chocolate
cinnamon
coconut
dates
*desserts, e.g., cheesecake, flan, **ice cream**, pudding*
dressings
frostings
goji berries
honey
lentils, e.g., red
milk, e.g., almond, hemp
muffins
pistachios
pumpkin
raw cuisine
sauces
sautéed dishes
smoothies

soups, e.g., lentil
spreads
vanilla

Flavor Affinities
coconut butter + avocado + banana + chocolate
coconut butter + cinnamon + honey + vanilla
coconut butter + cumin + fennel seeds + onions + red lentils + spinach

"I use extra-virgin raw **coconut butter** or oil in all my raw cheeses and desserts like cheesecakes."

— AMI BEACH, G-ZEN (BRANFORD, CT)

COCONUT MILK (see COCONUT and MILK, COCONUT)

COCONUT NECTAR

Flavor: sweet, with notes of caramel, cream, maple syrup, molasses, and/or vanilla, and the rich texture of honey or molasses
Volume: quiet
What it is: sweetener
Tip: Substitute for agave nectar, honey, or molasses.
Brand: Coconut Secret, Sweet Tree (both organic, raw)

cereals, breakfast
cheesecake
desserts
nuts, e.g., almond, macadamia
oatmeal
pancakes
peanut butter
raw cuisine
sauces, fruit, e.g., raspberry
smoothies
waffles

"The flavor of **coconut nectar** is to die for. And it's a neutral-flavored sweetener, in contrast to much stronger-flavored sweeteners like corn syrup."

— CASSIE TOLMAN, POMEGRANATE CAFÉ (PHOENIX)

● COCONUT WATER

Nutritional profile: 78% carbs / 13% protein / 9% fat
Calories: 45 per 1-cup serving
Protein: 2 grams
Tip: Substitute for water in recipes (e.g., for smoothies) for added nutrients.

almonds
avocados
beverages, e.g., cocktails
coconut
lemon
lime
mangoes
pineapple
puddings
rum
sauces
smoothies
sorbets
soups

COFFEE / ESPRESSO

Flavor: bitter, with notes of chocolate, fruit (e.g., berries), nuts, spices, and/or vanilla
Volume: quiet/moderate (lighter roast) – moderate/loud (darker roast)

allspice
baked goods
beverages, e.g., lattes
caramel
cardamom
chicory
chocolate, e.g., dark, white
cinnamon

cocoa
coconut and coconut milk
cream
desserts, e.g., custards
fruits
ice cream
Kaffir lime leaf
lemon
lime
liqueurs, e.g., brandy, cognac,
Irish whiskey
mango
milk, e.g., dairy, nondairy (e.g.,
almond, hemp, soy)
nuts, e.g., almonds, **hazelnuts,**
macadamia
salsas, e.g., cooked
sauces
smoothies
sorbets
spices
sugar, e.g., brown
tamarind
vanilla
walnuts

Flavor Affinities
coffee + chocolate + cinnamon
coffee + cinnamon + lemon
coffee + coconut milk + vanilla

"In our **coffee,** Rich and I will use
[vegan] Silk brand creamer
instead of heavy cream or milk.
It's got a nice texture and color."
— KATE JACOBY, VEDGE (PHILADELPHIA)

"I use Wildwood Soy Creamer, or
Trader Joe's creamer, in my
coffee, which gives it such a
wonderful richness."
— ISA CHANDRA MOSKOWITZ, AUTHOR
OF *ISA DOES IT* AND *VEGANOMICON*

● CORIANDER
Flavor: bitter/sour/**sweet**;
aromatic, with astringent,
pungent, and/or spicy notes of

caraway, cedar, flowers, **lemon,**
mustard, orange, and/or **sage**
Volume: quiet – moderate/loud
Tips: Add near the end of
cooking. Toast coriander seeds
to release their flavor.
Botanical relatives: anise,
caraway, carrots, celery, celery
root, chervil, **cilantro,** cumin,
dill, fennel, **parsley,** parsley root,
parsnips

apples
Asian cuisines
baked goods, e.g., biscuits, breads,
cookies, pastries, pies
beans, e.g., red
beets
bok choy
cakes
carrots
chiles, e.g., green
chili, vegetarian
cinnamon
citrus and citrus zest
cloves
coconut milk
coffee
couscous
cumin
curries, e.g., Indian
curry powder
desserts
fennel
fenugreek
garam masala
ginger
grains
Indian cuisine
lemon
lentils, e.g., red
marinades
Mediterranean cuisines
Middle Eastern cuisines
mushrooms
onions
orange
peas

pepper, e.g., black
polenta
potatoes
pumpkin
salad dressings
salads
sesame seeds
soups, e.g., lentil
squash, winter
stews
tofu
turmeric
vegetables

● CORN
Season: summer – early autumn
Flavor: sweet
Volume: quiet – moderate
What it is: whole grain (not a
vegetable)
Gluten-free: yes
Nutritional profile: 80% carbs
/ 11% fat / 9% protein
Calories: 135 per 1-cup serving
(sweet, yellow, raw)
Protein: 5 grams
Techniques: bake (husks on, at
375°F for 20 minutes), boil (1 –
3 minutes), cream, grill (husks
on), pressure-cook, roast, sauté,
steam
Tips: Serve corn very fresh. Use
the flavored water from boiling
corn as stock for soups.
Botanical relatives: barley,
kamut, rye, spelt, triticale

American cuisine
arugula
avocados
baked goods, e.g., corn bread,
corn muffins
barley and pearl barley
BASIL, e.g., lemon, sweet, Thai
BEANS, e.g., BLACK, fava, **green,**
kidney, **lima,** pinto
BELL PEPPERS, e.g., green, red
black-eyed peas

blueberries
bulgur
butter
buttermilk
caraway seeds
carrots
casseroles
cauliflower
cayenne
celery
celery seeds
Central American cuisines
chayote
CHEESE, e.g., **CHEDDAR**, cotija, **feta**, goat, manchego, Monterey Jack, Parmesan, Swiss
CHILES, e.g., Anaheim, chipotle, jalapeño, poblano, red, roasted
chili, vegetarian
chili pepper sauce and chili powder
chives
CILANTRO
coconut, coconut milk, and coconut oil
coriander
corn on the cob
cream
cumin
curries, curry powder, and curry spices
dill
edamame
eggs, e.g., *custards, quiches,* scrambled
epazote
fennel
fritters
GARLIC
ghee
ginger
grits
herbs, e.g., basil, parsley
honey
jícama
leeks
lemon
LIME, e.g., juice

lovage
maple syrup
marjoram
mayonnaise
Mexican cuisine
milk
millet
mint
miso, e.g., light, white
mushrooms, e.g., chanterelle, morels, oyster, **porcini**, shiitake, wild
mustard and mustard seeds
nectarines
nutmeg
oil, e.g., coconut, **olive**, sesame
ONIONS, e.g., green, red, yellow
oregano
pancakes
parsley
pastas
pepper, e.g., black, white
pepper, e.g., Szechuan
pesto
pine nuts
polenta
POTATOES
puddings
pumpkin and pumpkin seeds
quinoa
relishes
rice, esp. wild
saffron
sage

SALADS, *e.g., bean, corn, egg, pasta, potato, vegetable*
salsas
SALT, e.g., kosher, sea, smoked
savory
scallions
sesame seeds
shallots
soufflés
SOUPS and CHOWDERS, *e.g., corn, potato, vegetable*
Southwestern (U.S.) cuisine
soy sauce
squash, e.g., butternut, summer, yellow
stews
stock, vegetable
succotash
sugar
sweet potatoes
tarragon
thyme
tomatillos
TOMATOES, e.g., cherry, red, yellow
tortillas, e.g., corn
turmeric
vinegar, e.g., apple cider, champagne, rice wine, white wine
wheat berries
yogurt
zucchini

Dishes

Chilled Corn Soup with Pickled Eggplant and Chervil
— Blue Hill (New York City)

Fricassee of Jersey Corn: Braised Lacinato Kale, Creeping Jenny Flower, Corn Shoot Salad
— DANIEL (New York City)

Grilled Corn on the Cob: Chili Mayo, Coconut Flakes, Chili Powder
— Num Pang (New York City)

Corn Custard: Corn Bread Crumbs, Jalapeño-Pomegranate Gastrique
— Vedge (Philadelphia)

Flavor Affinities

corn + avocado + black beans + **cilantro + lime juice**

corn + balsamic vinegar + bell peppers + olive oil + onions + sun-dried tomatoes

corn + basil + fennel + tomatoes

corn + basil + garlic

corn + basil + onions + tomatoes

corn + beans + rice

corn + bell peppers + scallions

corn + black beans + tomatoes

corn + blueberries + maple syrup

corn + cayenne + chili powder + cumin + garlic + lime

corn + chiles + cotija cheese + lime

corn + chiles + garlic + lime + olive oil + onions + tomatoes

corn + chives + onions

corn + coconut + ginger

CORN + COCONUT MILK + CURRY SPICES

corn + garlic + miso

corn + garlic + mushrooms + **sage**

corn + garlic + potatoes + thyme

corn + honey + soy sauce

corn + jalapeños + maple syrup

corn + quinoa + scallions

"**Corn** is a religion where I grew up [in the New York Finger Lakes region]. We treat corn like the French treat their baguettes. You don't eat the baguettes you bought in the morning for dinner! Likewise, you buy and serve corn as fresh as possible. Corn is all about timing because it loses fifty percent of its sweetness after harvest. Farmers pick corn three times a day: at seven in the morning, at noon, and at three. Seven a.m. is the best, but you have to eat it for lunch. You buy your three o'clock corn for dinner. I like it simple: corn, butter, and salt. My wife Isabel [Bogadtke] likes her corn with lime and cumin seeds."

— CHRISTOPHER BATES, HOTEL FAUCHERE (MILFORD, PA)

"**Corn** is the one ingredient I work with best, and I get a non-GMO corn so it tastes great. I will focus in on it, and it will end up being the favorite of both our guests and our servers. I made a chilled corn soup that people loved: I cut the corn off the cob, made corn milk, made a stock out of corn cobs, sautéed the corn in a bunch of onion, thyme, and garlic, then added the corn milk and stock. I reduced it, pureed it all together, and added some half and half. I served the soup with shaved radishes and parsley. It's great because it is a cold soup when it is hot out, with the peppery radishes cutting the richness of the soup and an accent of vegetal green parsley rounding out the flavor and bringing it all together."

— JON DUBOIS, GREEN ZEBRA (CHICAGO)

• CORNMEAL and POLENTA (see also GRITS)

Flavor: sweet, with notes of butter and/or corn, and a creamy texture (when cooked)

Volume: quiet – moderate

What it is: grain, made of dried corn kernels, ground to fine (e.g., corn flour, cornstarch), medium, or coarse (e.g., grits, polenta) texture

Gluten-free: yes

Nutritional profile: 86% carbs / 8% fat / 6% protein

Calories: 220 per ½-cup serving (whole grain, yellow, uncooked)

Protein: 5 grams

Techniques: boil, broil, fry, grill, sauté, simmer

Timing: Cook until tender according to instructions on the back of the package, as this can vary from 1 minute (instant or fine) to 20 – 45 minutes (coarse).

Ratio: 1:3 (firm cornmeal, e.g., to grill or sauté) to 1:5 – 6 (soft, creamy cornmeal or polenta)

Tips: Opt for organic cornmeal. Use blue cornmeal, which is higher in protein than regular cornmeal, when you wish to add a light blueish, purplish hue to foods. Serve creamy polenta as an alternative to mashed potatoes. Alternatively, let polenta cool in a sheet pan; then cut into slices and broil, grill, or sauté lightly, before serving with tomato sauce and/or marinated vegetables.

Brand: Finely ground de la Estancia Organic Polenta is not an instant product but cooks to tender in less than 1 minute!

almonds and almond milk
amaranth
apples and apple butter
artichokes
asparagus
*BAKED GOODS, e.g., cakes, corn
    bread, corn muffins*
BASIL
beans, e.g., black, kidney
berries, e.g., blueberries
*breading, e.g., for mushrooms
    or tofu*
broccoli and broccoli rabe
butter
buttermilk
carrots
casseroles
cereals, hot breakfast
CHEESE, e.g., Asiago,
    **blue, cheddar, fontina, goat,
    GORGONZOLA**, Gruyère,
    Monterey Jack, mozzarella,
    PARMESAN, pecorino, ricotta,
    smoked, Taleggio
cherries
chiles, e.g., chipotle, jalapeño,
    and chili powder
chives
cinnamon
coconut cream
coriander
corn
cranberries, e.g., dried
cream and milk
croquettes
crusts, e.g., breads, pizzas
dumplings
eggplant
eggs, e.g., fried, poached
escarole
fennel
flours, e.g., spelt, whole wheat
"fries," e.g., baked
GARLIC
gratins
greens, e.g., dandelion
honey

Flavor Affinities

cornmeal + almonds + lemon
cornmeal + chipotle chiles + maple syrup
cornmeal + cinnamon + coconut + nutmeg + vanilla
cornmeal + eggs + Parmesan cheese
cornmeal + goat cheese + herbs
cornmeal + honey + mascarpone + orange
polenta + almond milk + cinnamon
POLENTA + ALMONDS + cream + lemon + **ORANGE**
polenta + almonds + raisins
polenta + artichokes + olives + tomatoes
polenta + artichokes + rosemary
POLENTA + BASIL + CORN + TOMATOES
polenta + carrots + garlic + rosemary
polenta + cheese + rosemary + tomatoes
polenta + garlic + mushrooms + parsley + **rosemary**
polenta + garlic + sage
polenta + goat cheese + kalamata olives
polenta + Gorgonzola cheese + portobello mushrooms + sage
polenta + Gorgonzola cheese + walnuts
polenta + honey + mascarpone + orange
polenta + maple syrup + sesame seeds
polenta + mascarpone + molasses
polenta + mascarpone + rosemary + walnuts
polenta + mozzarella cheese + mushrooms
polenta + mushrooms + Parmesan cheese + ricotta + **spinach**
polenta + mushrooms + tomatoes
polenta + mushrooms + zucchini
polenta + oregano + rosemary
polenta + Parmesan cheese + rosemary
polenta + porcini mushrooms + spinach + tomatoes

hush puppies
(Northern) ITALIAN CUISINE
johnnycakes
kale
lemon, e.g., juice, zest
maple syrup
mascarpone
milk, dairy or nondairy, e.g., soy
molasses
muffins
MUSHROOMS, e.g., chanterelle,
    porcini, portobello, shiitake,
    trumpet, wild

nutmeg
nutritional yeast
OILS, e.g., **corn**, nut, **OLIVE**,
    sesame, truffle, walnut
olives, e.g., kalamata
ONIONS, e.g., green, **white**
orange
oregano
pancakes and waffles
parsley
pepper, black
pesto
POLENTA

Dishes

Nut Crusted Polenta with Cranberry Bean, Pumpkin Seed Chili, and Garlic Sautéed Lacinato Kale and Collards with Cilantro Lime Cream
— Encuentro Cafe (Oakland, CA)

Grilled Ridgecut Gristmills Polenta with Grilled Wild Mushrooms, Crisp Shallots, Herb Cream, Shaved Grana Padano, and Arugula
— Greens Restaurant (San Francisco)

Polenta Gratin with Braised Fall Greens, Goat Cheese, and Roasted Bell Peppers
— Rancho La Puerta (Mexico)

porridges
rhubarb
ROSEMARY
SAGE
salt, e.g., sea
"sausage," vegan, e.g., Field Roast
  Italian
seeds, e.g., poppy, sesame,
  sunflower
sesame, e.g., oil, seeds
sour cream
spinach
spoonbread
squash, winter
stock, vegetable
sugar, brown
thyme
TOMATOES, TOMATO SAUCE,
  and **sun-dried tomatoes**
tortillas
truffles
vanilla
vegetables, root
vinegar, e.g., balsamic
walnuts
yogurt
zucchini

• CORNSTARCH
What it is: finely ground cornmeal, used as a binder or thickener
Techniques: To prevent lumps, dissolve in cold water before adding to very hot/boiling liquids or stir-fries to thicken.
Ratio: 1 teaspoon cornstarch to ¼ – ⅓ cup cold water
Tips: Opt for cornstarch when seeking a thickener that remains translucent (rather than turns opaque). Opt for organic (non-GMO) brands.
Possible substitutes:
arrowroot, corn flour, tapioca starch

baked goods, e.g., cookies
curries
custards
fondues
gravies
milk
pie fillings
puddings, e.g., chocolate, coconut
sauces
soups, e.g., fruit
stir-fries
sugar
vanilla

COTTAGE CHEESE
(see CHEESE, COTTAGE)

• COUSCOUS, ISRAELI
Flavor: notes of nuts, with a chewy texture
Volume: quiet
What it is: pasta (counts as a serving of grains)
Calories: 325 per ½-cup serving (boiled)
Protein: 18 grams
Brand: Bob's Red Mill

agave nectar
allspice
almonds
apples
apricots, dried
artichokes
asparagus
basil
beans, e.g., black, white
bell peppers, e.g., roasted
cardamom
carrots
cashews
cauliflower
celery
cheese, e.g., feta
chickpeas
chiles, e.g., poblano
chives
cinnamon
coconut and coconut milk
cranberries, dried
cucumbers
cumin
currants
curry
dill
eggplant
fennel
figs
fruit, dried
garlic
herbs
lemon, e.g., juice, preserved,
  zest
lentils, e.g., French, red
lettuce, e.g., butter
lime, e.g., juice, zest
milk, e.g., coconut
mint
miso

Flavor Affinities

Israeli couscous + almonds + apricots + coconut milk
Israeli couscous + almonds + parsley
Israeli couscous + asparagus + mushrooms
Israeli couscous + basil + eggplant
Israeli couscous + carrots + orange + raisins
Israeli couscous + chickpeas + eggplant
Israeli couscous + chickpeas + feta cheese + lemon
Israeli couscous + chickpeas + mint + parsley
Israeli couscous + chickpeas + tahini
Israeli couscous + cucumbers + feta cheese + mint
Israeli couscous + dried apricots + pistachios
Israeli couscous + dried fruit + pine nuts
Israeli couscous + feta cheese + spinach
Israeli couscous + lime + mint
Israeli couscous + mushrooms + tofu
Israeli couscous + parsley + pine nuts

mushrooms, e.g., shiitake
oil, e.g., olive
olives, e.g., kalamata
onions, e.g., red
oranges
paprika, e.g., smoked
parsley
peas
pepper, e.g., black, white
pesto
pine nuts
pistachios
purslane
raisins
"risottos"
saffron
salads, e.g., grain, green
salt, sea
scallions
shallots
soups, e.g., tomato, zucchini
spinach
squash, e.g., butternut
stews, vegetable
stock, vegetable
stuffed tomatoes
sugar, brown
tahini
tarragon
thyme

tofu
tomatoes and **tomato sauce**
turmeric
vinegar, e.g., balsamic or sherry
watercress
wine, e.g., dry white
yams
yogurt

● COUSCOUS, WHOLE-WHEAT

Flavor: neutral, with notes of nuts, and a fluffy texture
Volume: quiet – moderate
What it is: whole-grain pasta
Nutritional profile: 85% carbs / 14% protein / 1% fat
Calories: 175 per 1-cup serving (boiled)
Protein: 6 grams
Techniques: steam, steep (in boiling water)
Timing: Cover and steep about 5 – 10 minutes, until tender.
Ratio: 1:1 – 2 (1 cup couscous to 1 – 2 cups cooking liquid)
Possible substitute: millet

allspice
apples and apple juice

APRICOTS, e.g., DRIED, fresh
arugula
asparagus
beans, e.g., broad, white
bell peppers, e.g., green, red
cabbage
cardamom
carrots
cauliflower
cayenne
celery
cheese, e.g., feta
chervil
chickpeas
chiles, e.g., poblano
chives
cilantro
CINNAMON
citrus
coriander
corn
cucumbers
cumin
currants
curry, e.g., powder, spices
dates
eggplant
fennel
fruit, e.g., dried, juice
garlic
ginger
grapefruit, e.g., fruit, juice, zest
harissa
herbs
honey
kale
LEMON, e.g., juice, zest
lime
melon
milk, e.g., almond, rice
MINT
MOROCCAN CUISINE
mushrooms
NORTH AFRICAN CUISINES
NUTS, e.g., **almonds,** hazelnuts, **pine nuts, PISTACHIOS,** walnuts
oil, olive
olives, e.g., black

Flavor Affinities

whole-wheat couscous + almonds + apple juice + dates

whole-wheat couscous + almonds + cinnamon + saffron + turmeric

whole-wheat couscous + apricots + almond milk + orange + pistachios

whole-wheat couscous + apricots + almonds + cardamom + cinnamon

whole-wheat couscous + apricots + butternut squash

whole-wheat couscous + apricots + ginger + pine nuts

WHOLE-WHEAT COUSCOUS + (DRIED) APRICOTS + PISTACHIOS

whole-wheat couscous + asparagus + mushrooms

whole-wheat couscous + asparagus + orange

whole-wheat couscous + bell peppers + garlic

whole-wheat couscous + bell peppers + mint

whole-wheat couscous + carrots + chickpeas + cinnamon + onions + raisins + zucchini

whole-wheat couscous + cauliflower + cumin

whole-wheat couscous + chickpeas + curry powder

whole-wheat couscous + chickpeas + eggplant + feta cheese + orange

whole-wheat couscous + chickpeas + garlic + lemon + tahini

whole-wheat couscous + chickpeas + kale + tomatoes

whole-wheat couscous + chickpeas + pumpkin + raisins

whole-wheat couscous + cinnamon + honey + milk + raisins

whole-wheat couscous + cinnamon + orange + saffron

whole-wheat couscous + citrus + honey

whole-wheat couscous + coriander + cumin + ginger + saffron

whole-wheat couscous + dates + honey

whole-wheat couscous + feta cheese + pistachios

whole-wheat couscous + lemon + mint + parsley + pine nuts

whole-wheat couscous + mint + pomegranates

whole-wheat couscous + onions + parsley + pine nuts

whole-wheat couscous + raisins + saffron

onions, esp. red

ORANGES, e.g., fruit, juice, zest

oregano

papaya

paprika

parsley

peas

pepper, black

peppers

pilafs

pomegranates

potatoes

pumpkin

radicchio

raisins

"risottos"

saffron

salads, e.g., grain

salt, sea

sauces

scallions

shallots

spinach

squash, summer, e.g., yellow, zucchini; and **winter**, e.g., acorn, butternut

stews, e.g., vegetable tagines

stock, vegetable

sugar

sweet potatoes

"tabbouleh"

tahini

tarragon

TOMATOES (including cherry tomatoes), tomato juice, and tomato paste

turmeric

turnips

vegetables

zucchini

● CRANBERRIES

Season: autumn – winter

Flavor: sour, bitter

Volume: moderate – loud

Nutritional profile: 95% carbs / 3% protein / 2% fat

Calories: 50 per 1-cup serving (raw, chopped)

Techniques: boil, simmer (about 5 minutes)

Tips: Try dried as well as fresh. Look for cranberry juice low in added sugar.

agar-agar

agave nectar

allspice

American cuisine

APPLES, apple cider, and apple juice

apricots, e.g., dried

baked goods, e.g., breads, cakes, cookies, muffins, pies, quick breads, scones

beets

caramel

cheese, soft

chestnuts

chiles, e.g., jalapeño or serrano

CINNAMON

cloves

cobblers

compotes

cornmeal

currants

dates

desserts, e.g., fruit cobblers or crisps

drinks, e.g., cocktails, juices, punches

figs
ginger
granola
hazelnuts
honey
juices
kale
lemon, e.g., juice, zest
lime, e.g., juice, zest
maple syrup
miso
muffins
nutmeg
NUTS, e.g., almonds, macadamias, **PECANS**, pistachios, **WALNUTS**
oats and **oatmeal**
onions, e.g., pearl
*ORANGE, e.g., juice, zest
oranges, mandarin
pancakes
pears
PECANS
pepper, e.g., black
persimmons
pomegranates
puddings, e.g., bread
pumpkin
pumpkin seeds
raisins
raspberries
RELISHES, e.g., cranberry
rice, e.g. brown, **wild**
salad dressings
salads, *e.g., green*
salsas
salt, sea
sauces, *e.g., cranberry*
sorbets
soups, e.g., fruit
squash, winter, e.g., acorn, **butternut**
stuffings
SUGAR, e.g., brown
sweet potatoes
tangerines
trail mix
vanilla

Flavor Affinities

cranberries + apples + oranges
cranberries + apples + raisins
CRANBERRIES + balsamic vinegar + **GINGER** + honey + miso + **ORANGE**
CRANBERRIES + brown sugar + lime + **ORANGES + WALNUTS**
cranberries + chiles + lime
CRANBERRIES + cinnamon + **GINGER + ORANGES** + vanilla + walnuts
CRANBERRIES + cloves + **GINGER + ORANGES**
cranberries + dates + oranges
cranberries + maple syrup + vanilla
cranberries + nuts + wild rice
cranberries + oatmeal + walnuts
cranberries + oranges + pears + pecans

vinegar, e.g., balsamic
vodka
watermelon
wine, e.g., port
yogurt

● CRANBERRIES, DRIED
Flavor: sweet/sour, with a chewy texture
Volume: moderate – loud
> **Tip:** Look for dried cranberries sweetened with fruit juice.

Possible substitutes: dried cherries (esp. sour), raisins

allspice
almonds and almond butter
American cuisine
apples and **apple juice**
arugula
baked goods, e.g., breads, cookies, pastries
beets
bread crumbs
Brussels sprouts
cereals, hot breakfast
cinnamon
desserts
grains, e.g., farro, quinoa
granola
hazelnuts
maple syrup
milk
mint
muesli
nutmeg
oatmeal and oats
onions, e.g., caramelized
oranges, e.g., juice, zest
pears
pecans
persimmons
pilafs
pomegranates
popcorn
puddings, e.g., rice
pumpkin seeds

rice, e.g., long-grain, wild
salads, e.g., grain, green
sauces, e.g., cranberry
spinach
stuffings, e.g., corn bread
sugar
trail mixes
vanilla
walnuts

Flavor Affinities

dried cranberries + almonds + *pilafs* + quinoa
dried cranberries + couscous + pistachios
DRIED CRANBERRIES + GRAINS (e.g., couscous, oats, quinoa, wild rice) + **NUTS** (e.g., almonds, pecans, pistachios, walnuts)
dried cranberries + oats + walnuts
dried cranberries + orange zest + wild rice
dried cranberries + pears + pecans
dried cranberries + pecans + wild rice
dried cranberries + walnuts + wild rice

● CREAM, HEAVY
Nutritional profile: 94% fat / 3% carbs / 3% protein
> **Tips:** Use silken tofu instead of actual cream to create creamy vegan sauces. Or heed the insight of the Cooking Lab's director of applied research, Scott Heimendinger: "Dairy **cream** is an emulsion of fat and water. Once you realize that, with the right approach you can make 'cream' out of anything."

"CREAM," CASHEW
Flavor: neutral, with notes of nuts, and a rich, creamy texture

Volume: quiet – moderate
What it is: raw cashew nuts that have been soaked overnight in water and finely pureed with water to achieve the consistency of cream
> **Tip:** Substitute cashew cream for regular cream.

Brand: MimicCreme nondairy cream substitute, made from almonds and cashews

baked goods, e.g., cakes, muffins
crepes
desserts, e.g., mousses, puddings, semifreddos
fruit
gratins
gravies
ice cream
pancakes
pastas, e.g., ravioli
potatoes, e.g., *mashed*
sauces, e.g., alfredo, cream, pasta
smoothies
*soups, e.g., broccoli, butternut squash, **creamy**, tomato*

CREAM, WHIPPED — VEGAN
Brand: Soy Whip

CREAM CHEESE (see CHEESE, CREAM)

● CRÈME FRAÎCHE (see also FROMAGE BLANC)
Flavor: sour, with a smooth texture
Volume: moderate
What it is: fresh, cultured cream
> **Tip:** Can be used to thicken sauces, because, unlike sour cream, it will not curdle when cooked.

Possible substitutes: fromage blanc (which is made from milk), sour cream

apples, apple cider, and apple juice

berries, e.g. raspberries, strawberries

caramel

citrus, e.g., juice, zest

dates

figs

French cuisine

fruits, e.g., fresh, stone, tree

oranges, e.g., juice, zest

pastas

potatoes

risottos

sauces

soups, e.g., beet, butternut squash, carrot, mushroom, pea, pumpkin

squash, winter

stews

sugar, e.g., brown

tarts

CRESS (see LAND CRESS and WATERCRESS)

● CRUCIFEROUS VEGETABLES (see ARUGULA; BOK CHOY; BROCCOLI; BROCCOLINI; BROCCOLI RABE; BRUSSELS SPROUTS; CABBAGE; CAULIFLOWER; GREENS —e.g., COLLARD, MUSTARD, TURNIP; KALE; KOHLRABI; RADISHES; TURNIPS; WATERCRESS)

"**Cruciferous vegetables** are twice as powerful as other plant foods. [They are] not only the most powerful anticancer foods in existence; they are also the most nutrient-dense of all the vegetables."

— DR. JOEL FUHRMAN, AUTHOR OF *SUPER IMMUNITY*

CUBAN CUISINE

bay leaf

BEANS, e.g., BLACK, pinto

bell peppers

cabbage

cilantro

corn

cucumbers

garlic

lettuce

lime

oranges

peanuts

plantains

pumpkin

RICE

scallions

squash, e.g., calabaza

sweet potatoes

tomatoes

● CUCUMBERS

Season: spring – **summer**

Flavor: slightly sweet, with notes of melon, and a moist yet crisp texture

Volume: **quiet** – moderate

What it is: vegetable

Nutritional profile: 68% carbs / 20% protein / 12% fat

Calories: 15 per 1-cup serving (raw, chopped)

Protein: 1 grams

Techniques: best served raw; otherwise, blanch, braise, pickle, sauté, or steam

Tip: Opt for organic cucumbers.

Botanical relatives: melons, pumpkins, squashes

Possible substitutes: cucumber-flavored herbs, e.g., borage, burnet, comfrey

almonds

anise and anise hyssop

apples

apricots

arugula

avocado

basil

beans, e.g., black

beets

bell peppers, e.g., green

beverages, e.g., sparkling water

borage

butter

buttermilk

cabbage, e.g., Chinese

capers

caraway seeds

carrots

cayenne

celery and celery seeds

CHEESE, e.g., cream, FETA, goat, ricotta, soft white

chervil

chickpeas

CHILES, e.g., Anaheim, jalapeño, red, serrano; and chili pepper sauce

CHIVES and garlic chives

CILANTRO

citrus

coconut and coconut milk

couscous, e.g., Israeli

cream

cress, e.g., land

crudités

CUMIN

curries, curry powder, and curry spices

*DILL

dips

drinks, e.g., cocktails, sparkling waters

eggplant

eggs, e.g., hard-boiled

endive

escarole

fennel

galangal

GARLIC

ginger

grains, e.g., bulgur, farro, spelt

FARM FRESH
Vegetables

grapes, e.g., white
Greek cuisine
greens, salad
hibiscus
honey
horseradish
Indian cuisine
jícama
kale
kefir
lamb's lettuce
LEMON, e.g., juice, zest
lemongrass
lentils, e.g., red
lettuce, e.g., butter, romaine

lime, e.g., juice, zest
lovage
mangoes
marjoram
mayonnaise
melon, e.g., cantaloupe,
   honeydew
Middle Eastern cuisines
milk, soy
*MINT, esp. spearmint
mushrooms, e.g., shiitake
mustard, e.g., Dijon, powder
noodles, Asian, e.g., soba, udon
OIL, e.g., avocado, flaxseed,

grapeseed, **OLIVE**, sesame,
   sunflower, vegetable
olives, e.g., kalamata
ONIONS, e.g., green, red, spring,
   white
orange, e.g., juice
oregano
palm, hearts of
papaya
paprika
PARSLEY
peaches
PEANUTS
pears
peas, green
pepper, e.g., black, white
pesto
pickles
pineapple
pine nuts
plums
pomegranates
potatoes
pumpernickel
quinoa
radishes
RAITAS
rice
saffron
salad dressings
SALADS, e.g., chopped, cucumber,
   Greek, green, pasta
salsify
salt, e.g., kosher, sea
sandwiches
sauces, e.g., raita, tzatziki
savory
scallions
sea vegetables
seeds, e.g., poppy, pumpkin,
   sesame
sesame, e.g., oil, sauce, seeds
shallots
shiso
SOUPS, e.g., cold, **cucumber**,
   GAZPACHO, *summer,*
   vichyssoise, **white gazpacho**
SOUR CREAM

Flavor Affinities

cucumbers + almonds + avocados + cumin + mint
cucumbers + Asian noodles + sesame sauce
cucumbers + avocados + chiles + chives + lime **+ yogurt**
cucumbers + avocados + green onions + lime **+ yogurt**
cucumbers + avocados + nori + (sushi) rice
cucumbers + basil + garlic + tomatoes
cucumbers + beets + yogurt
cucumbers + buttermilk + dill + scallions
cucumbers + chiles + cilantro + lime + scallions
cucumbers + chiles + cilantro + peanuts
cucumbers + chiles + cilantro + rice vinegar + sugar
cucumbers + chiles + jícama + lime
cucumbers + cilantro + citrus (e.g., lime)
CUCUMBERS + CILANTRO + MINT
cucumbers + coconut milk + mint
cucumbers + cumin + lime + mint + **yogurt**
cucumbers + cumin + paprika + **yogurt**
cucumbers + curry + peanuts + yogurt
cucumbers + dill + garlic + **vinegar**
cucumbers + dill + mint + **yogurt**
cucumbers + dill + scallions + **vinegar** + wakame
cucumbers + feta cheese + lemon + **mint**
cucumbers + feta cheese + walnuts
CUCUMBERS + GARLIC + HERBS (e.g., DILL, MINT, PARSLEY) +
   YOGURT
cucumbers + garlic + lemon + olive oil + oregano
cucumbers + lemon + lime + mint + scallions + tofu
cucumbers + lime + mango + parsley + red onions
CUCUMBERS + MINT + YOGURT
cucumbers + miso + sesame
CUCUMBERS + RICE VINEGAR + sesame seeds + soy sauce

soy sauce
spinach
sprouts, e.g., radish
stews
strawberries
stuffed cucumbers
sugar
summer rolls
sushi, e.g., nori rolls
tabbouleh
tahini
tarragon
Thai cuisine
thyme
tofu, esp. silken
TOMATOES
turmeric
tzatziki sauce
VINEGAR, e.g., champagne,
  cider, red wine, rice wine,
  tarragon, white balsamic,
  white wine
wakame
walnuts
wasabi
watercress
watermelon
***YOGURT**
za'atar

"I like making hot **cucumber** soup at home: I'll cook the cucumbers with onion and a little extra-virgin olive oil and then add

Dishes

Cucumber Gazpacho: Greek Yogurt, Mint, Celery Stalk
— Café Boulud (New York City)

Chilled Cucumber Velouté: Ginger-Sake "Granité," Garden Blossoms, and Andante Dairy Yogurt
— The French Laundry (Yountville, CA)

Gazpacho: Onion, Cucumber, Kanzuri, Westglow Herbs
— Rowland's Restaurant at Westglow Resort and Spa (Blowing Rock, NC)

Chilled Cucumber Avocado Soup, Almond Picada, Cumin, Mint
— Vedge (Philadelphia)

cumin, coriander, and masala curry. If I want the soup bright green, I'll not add any white wine, but if I want a dull green, I'll add white wine. To finish the soup, I might add either yogurt or crème fraîche — or if I want to take it even farther, I'll add some kefir."
— CHRISTOPHER BATES, HOTEL FAUCHÈRE (MILFORD, PA)

● CUMIN

Flavor: bitter/sweet; aromatic, with earthy/musky/pungent/spicy notes of lemon, nuts, and/or smoke
Volume: quiet/moderate – loud
Tips: Bring out cumin's flavor by toasting in a dry pan. Add early in the cooking process.
Factoid: Cumin is the world's second most popular spice, behind black pepper.
Botanical relatives: caraway, chervil, coriander, **parsley**

(North) African cuisines
avocados
baba ghanoush
baked goods, *e.g., breads*
beans, e.g., black, kidney, long
bell peppers
bulgur

burritos
cabbage
carrots
cayenne
cheese, e.g., cheddar, Swiss
chickpeas
chiles
chili powder
CHILI, VEGETARIAN
chives
cilantro
cinnamon
cloves
cocoa
coriander
couscous
Cuban cuisine
CURRIES, e.g., *Indian*
curry leaves and curry powder
dals
eggplant
eggs
enchiladas
fenugreek
garlic
ginger
grains
Greek cuisine
hummus
INDIAN CUISINE
kebabs
Latin American cuisines
lemon
LENTILS, e.g., red
lime
marinades
Mediterranean cuisines
MEXICAN CUISINE
MIDDLE EASTERN CUISINES
mint
Moroccan cuisine
mushrooms, e.g., oyster
onions
oregano
paprika, e.g., sweet
peas
pepper, e.g., black
potatoes
purees

rice, e.g., basmati
salad dressings
salads, *e.g., bean, rice*
salsas
sauces, *e.g., tomato*
sauerkraut
sesame seeds
soups, *e.g., bean, lentil*
Southeast Asian cuisines
Spanish cuisine
squash, e.g., kabocha
stews
tacos
tamarind
Tex-Mex cuisine
tomatoes and tomato sauce
Turkish cuisine
turmeric
vegetables, e.g., root
walnuts
yogurt

Flavor Affinities

cumin + avocado + black beans + lime + tomatoes
cumin + black beans + cilantro + garlic
cumin + cilantro + curry spices
cumin + garlic + potatoes
cumin + paprika + tomatoes

"**Cumin** is one of my favorite spices, and a great supporting flavor. Its earthy/nutty/smoky flavor is very strong and can easily kill a dish — so you never want to use enough so that it can be tasted. Instead, just sprinkle a little on so that people will ask, 'What *is* that flavor?!'"
— RICH LANDAU, VEDGE (PHILADELPHIA)

"I love the smell of **cumin**, which reminds me of walking through the woods in Jamaica. . . . It's very good with grains, as it brings out their earthy, woody flavor."
— SHAWAIN WHYTE, CAFÉ BLOSSOM (NEW YORK CITY)

Dishes

Red Curry Vegetables: Pineapple, Vegetables, and Edamame simmered in Red Curry Coconut Milk Sauce, served over Brown Rice, and topped with Pistachio Nuts
— Canyon Ranch (Tucson)

Panang Curry: Brown Rice, Potato, Broccoli, Ginger, Carrot, Mushroom, and Coconut Broth
— True Food Kitchen (Santa Monica)

CURRY LEAVES (aka CURRY LEAF)

Flavor: bitter/sour, with earthy/pungent/spicy notes of curry powder, lemon, orange zest, and/or pine
Volume: quiet – moderately loud
Techniques: sauté, simmer, stew

Tip: Add later in cooking or to finish a dish.

Asian cuisines
beans
breads, e.g., naan
cabbage
cardamom
carrots
cauliflower
chiles
chutneys
cinnamon
citrus, e.g., lemon, lime
cloves
coconut and **coconut milk**
coriander
cumin
*CURRIES, e.g., **Indian**, Southeast Asian*
dals
eggplant
fennel seeds
fenugreek
garlic
ghee
ginger
Indian cuisine
lentils
mustard seeds
okra

onions
peas
pepper, e.g., black
potatoes
rice
salad dressings, e.g., yogurt-based
soups
stews
sweet potatoes
tamarind
tomatoes
TURMERIC
vegetables
yogurt

CURRY PASTE, THAI (e.g., GREEN or RED)

What it is: often made from **chiles** + **galangal** + garlic + ginger + Kaffir lime leaves + **lemongrass**
Brands: Maesri, Thai Kitchen

avocado
bamboo shoots
BASIL, THAI
beans, e.g., green
BELL PEPPERS
carrots
cauliflower
chickpeas
chili pepper paste
cilantro
***COCONUT MILK**
CURRIES, THAI
edamame
eggplant
galangal
grains
Kaffir lime leaf
lemongrass

lime
"mock duck"
noodles, e.g., Asian
onions
peanuts
pineapple
pistachios
potatoes, e.g., red
rice, e.g., brown, jasmine
scallions
soups
soy sauce
stir-fries
sugar, e.g., brown, palm
sugar snap peas
sweet potatoes
THAI CUISINE
tofu
vegetables, e.g., mixed
zucchini

Flavor Affinities
curry paste + coconut milk + rice
  + vegetables

• DAIKON
Season: autumn – winter
Flavor: bitter/**sweet** (and more
so when cooked)/hot, with notes
of pepper and/or radishes; and
crisp, tender, and juicy in texture
Volume: quieter/moderate
(cooked) – louder (raw)
What it is: Japanese radish, with
a carrot-like shape
Nutritional profile: 86% carbs
/ 9% protein / 5% fat
Calories: 60 per 7-inch daikon
Protein: 2 grams
Techniques: bake, braise, glaze,
grate, marinate, pickle, raw (e.g.,

julienne, spiralize), roast, sauté,
sear, shave (e.g., into noodles),
shred, simmer, steam, stew, stir-
fry (2 – 3 minutes)

Tips: Scrub before using. Use
raw daikon slices with dips
and spreads. Spiralize to make
veggie "noodles."

Botanical relatives: cabbage

agave nectar
apples
Asian cuisines
bamboo shoots
bell peppers
bok choy
cabbage, e.g., Chinese, napa
CARROTS
chiles, e.g., jalapeño; chili pepper
  flakes or chili powder
Chinese cuisine
cilantro
crudités
cucumbers
dashi
dulse
fatty foods
fried foods
garlic
ginger
grains
greens, daikon
honey
JAPANESE CUISINE
kohlrabi
kombu
lemon, e.g., juice, zest
lettuce
lime
macrobiotic cuisine
maple syrup

mirin
miso, e.g., sweet white
mushrooms, e.g., porcini,
  shiitake
mustard
noodles, Asian, e.g., buckwheat,
  soba, udon
oil, e.g., olive, peanut, sesame
onions, e.g., green, red
orange, e.g., juice, zest
papaya
parsley
pears, e.g., Asian
persimmons
pickles
potatoes
quinoa
radishes
raitas
rice, e.g., brown
sake
SALADS, e.g., fruit, vegetable
salsas
salt
sandwiches, e.g., bánh mì
scallions
sea vegetables
sesame, e.g., oil, seeds
sesame seeds, e.g., black
slaws, e.g., Asian
snow peas
SOUPS, e.g., miso, mushroom
SOY SAUCE
spring rolls
stews
stir-fries
stock, vegetable
sugar
tamari
tofu
umeboshi paste
VINEGAR, e.g., balsamic, cider,
  rice, sherry, umeboshi, wine
wasabi
yogurt
yuzu, e.g., juice, zest

Dishes

Caramelized Daikon with Sour Plum Coulis: Glazed Radish, Young Turnips, New Zealand
Spinach
— DANIEL (New York City)

Flavor Affinities

daikon + apples + *slaws*

daikon + carrots + cucumbers + lettuce + scallions

daikon + carrots + kohlrabi

daikon + carrots + rice vinegar

daikon + cilantro + yogurt

daikon + mirin + rice vinegar + soy sauce + yuzu

daikon + oranges + radishes

daikon + oranges + sesame

daikon + persimmons + rice vinegar + yuzu

daikon + scallions + sesame seeds

"Shredded raw **daikon** is good for your digestion, which is why it's traditionally served with tempura. Raw daikon helps to break down the fat in your stomach."

— MARK SHADLE, G-ZEN (BRANFORD, CT)

"I love **daikon**, as well as green meat radishes, which are smaller than daikon with green veins. They're sweet, bitter, and juicy, and when they're roasted then sautéed, they have a wonderful creamy texture."

— RICH LANDAU, VEDGE (PHILADELPHIA)

DANDELION GREENS (see GREENS, DANDE-LION)

DASHI (aka KOMBU DASHI) (see also STOCK, VEGETABLE)

Flavor: notes of the sea, and a watery texture

Volume: quiet – moderate

What it is: Japanese stock made of kombu + water

cilantro

ginger

hiziki

kombu

mirin

miso

mushrooms, e.g., shiitake

noodles, soba

nori

scallions

soups, miso

soy sauce

tofu

vinegar, brown rice

Flavor Affinities

dashi + rice vinegar + soy sauce

"**Dashi** is a staple for us to have on hand to serve our vegetarian and vegan guests. Its body and flavor are wonderful to use as a base for soups, sauces, or even faux consommés."

— MARK LEVY, THE POINT (SARANAC LAKE, NY)

● DATES

Season: autumn – winter

Flavor: sweet – very sweet, with a chewy texture

Volume: moderate

Nutritional profile: 98% carbs / 2% protein

Calories: 65 per pitted medjool date

Tips: Slip an almond inside a pitted date and eat like candy (in moderation). Use dehydrated, ground dates as date sugar.

(North) African cuisine

amaranth

APPLES, dried or fresh; and apple juice

apricots

BAKED GOODS, e.g., breads, cakes, muffins, pie crusts, scones

bananas

bourbon

bran

cabbage, red

caramel

cardamom

carrots

CHEESE, e.g., blue, cream, feta, halloumi, **Parmesan**

cherries

chocolate, e.g., dark, white

cinnamon

cloves

coffee

coconut

confections, e.g., truffles

cranberries

cream

desserts

flax seeds

ginger

granola

honey

LEMON

maple syrup

mascarpone

Middle Eastern cuisine

milk, almond or other nondairy

miso, e.g., light, sweet

nutmeg

NUTS, e.g., **ALMONDS**, pecans, pine nuts, **pistachios**, **WALNUTS**

oat flour

OATS and **OATMEAL**

oil, olive

onions, e.g., caramelized

ORANGE, e.g., juice, zest

parsley

parsnips

peanuts and **peanut butter**

pears and **pear juice**

puddings

pumpkin

quinoa

rice

Dishes

Pistachio Stuffed Dates with Orange, Cinnamon, and Aleppo Chile

— Millennium (San Francisco)

Flavor Affinities

dates + almond milk/almonds + bananas + cinnamon + nutmeg + vanilla

dates + almonds + Parmesan cheese

dates + apples + cinnamon + coconut + nutmeg + orange zest + pecans

dates + apples + cinnamon + oatmeal

dates + apricots + ginger

dates + balsamic vinegar + blue cheese

dates + bananas + coconut + *muesli*

dates + bananas + oats

dates + chocolate + walnuts

dates + coconut + nuts

dates + coconut + orange

dates + lemon + oatmeal

dates + nuts (e.g., walnuts) + **oats** + **sweetener** (e.g., brown sugar, maple syrup)

dates + orange + sesame seeds

dates + Parmesan cheese + walnuts

dates + peanuts + vanilla

---

rum

salad dressings

salt, sea

sauces

sesame, e.g., seeds

smoothies, *e.g., fruit*

soups

spreads

squash, winter, e.g., butternut

sugar, e.g., brown

tahini

tamarind

toffee

tofu, silken

vanilla

vinegar, e.g., balsamic

yogurt

"In addition to using soaked and liquefied **dates** as a sweetener, we serve dates on all our vegan cheese plates, and also serve an appetizer of dates and figs stuffed with vegan 'goat cheese.' We combine dates and walnuts and sea salt in a Cuisinart and press it into a pie pan to make a delicious raw dessert crust."

— AMI BEACH, G-ZEN (BRANFORD, CT)

DEHYDRATING

"We use our **dehydrator** for a variety of things, including our powders, which we use a lot of. For example, we will dehydrate celery and then turn it into a powder for celery cake. We also dehydrate yellow tomatoes for tomato powder. We'll also use the dehydrator for creating leathers with tomatoes, beets, and pears, or for turning cauliflower into crunchy little bits. Anything you can do in a dehydrator, you can do in an oven — it is simply faster using the dehydrator. The reason I use one is that if you are dehydrating something in the oven, you can't use your oven for anything else."

— AMANDA COHEN, DIRT CANDY (NEW YORK CITY)

DESSERTS

Minimizing sugar consumption is a tenet of healthful eating. When you crave something sweet, consider one of these desserts, which may contain less sugar than many others:

apples, *e.g., baked*

bananas, *e.g., baked, frozen-and-blended*

cakes, *e.g., carrot, fruit, spice, zucchini*

cheesecake, *e.g., vegan made with tofu*

chocolate, dark

cobblers, *fruit*

confections, *e.g., raw truffles*

cookies, *e.g., date/nut, oatmeal/raisin, raw*

crisps, *fruit*

crumbles, *fruit*

dates

fruit, dried (and unsweetened) or fresh

honey

ice cream, *e.g., coconut milk–based*

maple syrup

muffins

peaches, *e.g., grilled*

pears, *e.g., poached*

pies, *e.g., fruit, pumpkin*

puddings, *e.g., chia seed, chocolate, coconut, fruit, pumpkin, rice, tapioca*

smoothies, *e.g., banana, cacao, coconut*

sorbets, *fruit*

sweet potatoes

yogurt, *semi-frozen and drizzled with maple syrup*

Flavor Affinities

agave nectar + almonds + cacao nibs + *truffles* + vanilla

almonds + cocoa powder + dates

bananas + honey + sesame seeds

carrots + coconut + cream cheese + ginger + macadamia nuts

"Our number-one **dessert** is crumbles. They're seasonal, but often apple- or pear-based with berries. We'll sweeten them with agave or brown sugar and season with some citrus zest and a splash of gin. Our topping is simple: brown sugar, a gluten-free flour blend (such as chickpea, rice, tapioca, and sorghum flours), and margarine or palm shortening."

— AARON WOO, NATURAL SELECTION (PORTLAND, OR)

● DILL (see also DILL SEEDS and DILL WEED)

Season: spring – **summer**
Flavor: sour (seeds) / sweet (weed), with notes of anise and/or caraway
Volume: quiet/moderate (weed) – moderate/loud (seeds)
Note: Use dill weed for a quieter, sweeter flavor than dill seeds. Dill is quieter than caraway seeds, but louder than anise.

Tip: Use fresh, or at the very end of the cooking process.

Botanical relatives: anise, caraway, **carrots**, **celery**, **celery root**, chervil, coriander, **fennel**, **parsley**, **parsley root**, parsnips, wild fennel

artichokes
asparagus
baked goods, e.g., breads
basil
BEANS, e.g., dried, **green**, lima, white
beets
bell peppers, e.g., red
black-eyed peas
cabbage
capers
caraway seeds
CARROTS

cauliflower
celery
CHEESE, e.g., cottage, feta, **fresh white**, goat
chickpeas
chives
cilantro
corn
***CUCUMBERS**
dips
Eastern European cuisines
eggplant
eggs, e.g., hard-boiled or *omelets*
(Northern) European cuisines
fennel
garlic
German cuisine
ginger
grains, e.g., barley
honey
horseradish
kale
kasha
kohlrabi
lemon, e.g., juice
mayonnaise
millet
miso
mushrooms
noodles
Northern European cuisines
oil, olive
onions
paprika
parsley
pasta, e.g., farfalle, fettuccine, pappardelle, penne
peas
pepper, e.g., black, green
PICKLES, esp. dill seeds + cucumbers
Polish cuisine
poppy seeds
POTATOES
pumpkin
rice
Russian cuisine
salad dressings

SALADS, e.g., egg, potato
SAUCES, e.g., cheese, tomato, yogurt
sauerkraut
Scandinavian cuisines
slaws
soups and **chowders**, e.g., cold, *spinach, yogurt*
SOUR CREAM
spinach
squash, e.g., summer
stews
tahini
tofu, e.g., soft
tomatoes and tomato sauces
Turkish cuisine
vegetables
vinegar, e.g., balsamic
wheat berries
YOGURT
zucchini

Flavor Affinities

dill + beets + capers + celery
dill + cucumber + yogurt
dill + fennel + feta cheese
dill + feta cheese + kohlrabi
dill + feta cheese + spinach
dill + garlic + ginger + green pepper + lemon
dill + garlic + sour cream + yogurt
dill + horseradish + sour cream
dill + mushrooms + yogurt

● DILL SEEDS (see also DILL and DILL WEED)

Flavor: sour, with pungent notes of anise and/or caraway
Volume: moderate – **loud**
Tip: Add early in the cooking process.

Possible substitute: caraway seeds

bay leaf
beets
breads, e.g., rye
cabbage

carrots
cheese
chili powder
cucumbers
cumin
gravies
lemon
lentils
onions
paprika
parsley
PICKLES
potatoes
rice
salad dressings
sauces
soups, *e.g., beet, cucumber, potato*
spinach
thyme
turmeric
vegetables, e.g., roasted
vinegar

Flavor Affinities
dill seeds + bay leaf + beets
dill seeds + cabbage + carrots

● DILL WEED (see also DILL and DILL SEEDS)

Flavor: sweet, with earthy, spicy notes of anise, caraway, and/or licorice
Volume: quiet – moderate

asparagus
beans, e.g., green
beets
butter
cabbage
carrots
cheese, e.g., mild
cucumbers
eggs
Greek cuisine
Indian cuisine
lemon
mayonnaise

Middle Eastern cuisines
mustard
potatoes, esp. new
rice
Russian cuisine
salads, e.g., egg, potato
sauces, e.g., creamy, mustard
sour cream
yogurt

Flavor Affinities
dill weed + asparagus + butter + mushrooms
dill weed + cabbage + feta cheese + mint
dill weed + chard + cheddar cheese + cream + garlic

● DULSE (FLAKES)

Flavor: salty and sour, with rich notes of bacon, nuts, and/or seafood, and a chewy texture
Volume: moderate – loud
What it is: reddish-brown seaweed / sea lettuce / sea vegetable
Techniques: pan-fry, roast, sauté, simmer, stir-fry

Tips: Rinse, then soak (20 – 30 minutes) before use, to tame its saltiness. When sautéed, its bacon-like notes are louder (it can be used like bacon bits); when simmered, its seafood-like notes are louder.

Possible substitute: sea salt

apples
avocado
beans, e.g., black
butter
cabbage, e.g., Chinese, napa, red
capers
cashews
celery
chili, vegetarian
coconut

curry
dill
dips
eggs, e.g., scrambled
ginger
gomashio
grains, e.g., oats
greens, e.g., collard
Irish cuisine
lemon, e.g., juice, zest
miso
mushrooms, e.g., shiitake
noodles, e.g., soba
oil, e.g., olive, sesame
onions, e.g., red
parsley
pastas
pâtés, e.g., "fish"
peanuts and peanut butter
pizza
popcorn
potatoes, e.g., baked
rice, e.g., brown
salads
salt, e.g., sea
sandwiches, e.g., "BLTs"
scallions
Scottish cuisine
sesame, e.g., oil, paste, seeds
SOUPS, e.g., bean
spinach
sprouts, bean
stews
stir-fries
tahini
tofu
umeboshi paste
vegetables
wakame
walnuts
watercress
wraps

Flavor Affinities
dulse + basil + sun-dried tomatoes + walnuts
dulse + dill + lemon zest + parsley

dulse + ginger + sesame oil

dulse + lemon + tahini

dulse + lemon juice/zest + walnuts

dulse + sea salt + sesame seeds

● EDAMAME

[ed-ah-MAH-mee]

Season: summer

Flavor: slightly sweet, with notes of butter, green vegetables, and/or nuts, and a rich, tender yet crisp texture

Volume: quiet

What it is: fresh green soybeans in their pods

Nutritional profile: 36% fat / 32% carbs / 32% protein

Calories: 130 per 1-cup serving (frozen, unprepared)

Protein: 12 grams

Techniques: boil (about 5 minutes), raw, roast, steam

arugula
avocado
beans, green
beets
bell peppers, e.g., red, yellow
carrots
cashews
cheese, e.g., feta, pecorino
chiles, e.g., jalapeño; and chili pepper flakes
cilantro
coconut
corn
cucumber
daikon
dips
dumplings
escarole
garlic
ginger
grains, e.g., bulgur, couscous, quinoa, rice
greens, e.g., mesclun

herbs
hummus
Japanese cuisine
kombu
leeks
LEMON, e.g., juice
lime
mint
miso
mushrooms, e.g., cremini
noodles, Asian, e.g., rice, soba, udon
OIL, e.g., canola, **OLIVE**, **SESAME**, white truffle
onions, e.g., green, **red**, yellow
parsley
pastas, e.g., linguini
"*pâtés*"
peanuts
pepper, black
potatoes, e.g., new
quinoa
radishes
rice, e.g., Arborio, black, brown
risottos

salads, e.g., Asian, corn, green, potato
SALT, esp. **SEA**
sauces
scallions
sea vegetables
seeds, e.g. pumpkin, **sesame**
shallots
soups, e.g., miso
soy sauce
spinach
spreads
squash, butternut
stir-fries
stock, vegetable
sugar snap peas
tamari
tofu
tomatoes, e.g., cherry
veggie burgers
vinegar, rice wine
wasabi
watercress
zucchini

Flavor Affinities

edamame + Asian noodles + carrots + chile pepper flakes + rice vinegar + scallions + sesame oil + soy sauce

edamame + avocado + lemon + pumpkin seeds + tomatoes

edamame + bell peppers + quinoa

edamame + black pepper + sea vegetables + sesame seeds

edamame + carrots + corn + red onions

edamame + carrots + ginger + peanuts + *salads*

edamame + chile pepper + lemon + salt

edamame + chiles + garlic

edamame + corn + quinoa

edamame + ginger + soy sauce

edamame + lemon + lime + olive oil + rice wine vinegar

edamame + mint + scallions

edamame + sea salt + sesame oil + sesame seeds

edamame + soba noodles + soy sauce

Dishes

Edamame Dumplings with Daikon Radish and White Truffle Oil
— True Food Kitchen (Santa Monica)

• EGGPLANT
(aka AUBERGINE)

Season: summer – autumn
Flavor: bitter/sweet, with earthy notes, and a spongy texture
Volume: quiet – **moderate**
What it is: vegetable
Nutritional profile: 83% carbs / 10% protein / 7% fat
Calories: 20 per 1-cup serving (raw, cubed)
Protein: 1 gram
Techniques: Cook thoroughly: bake, blanch, boil, braise, broil, char, deep-fry, fry, grill, puree, roast, sauté, steam, stir-fry, stuff (e.g., rice, tomatoes)
Botanical relatives: bell peppers, chiles, gooseberries, potatoes, tomatillos, tomatoes

African cuisines
artichoke hearts
arugula
Asian cuisines
BABA GHANOUSH
BASIL, esp. Thai
bay leaf
beans, e.g., black, butter, cannellini, white
BELL PEPPERS, e.g., roasted green, red, or yellow
bok choy
bread crumbs, e.g., panko, whole-grain
bulgur
capers
caponata
cardamom
carrots
cashews
casseroles
celery
chard
*CHEESE, e.g., Asiago, **feta**, **goat**, Gruyère, **MOZZARELLA**, **PARMESAN**, **RICOTTA**, ricotta salata, sheep's milk, Swiss

chervil
chickpeas
CHILES, e.g., green, jalapeño, red, serrano; chili pepper flakes, chili pepper sauce, and chili powder
Chinese cuisine
cilantro
cinnamon
coconut and coconut milk
coriander
couscous and Israeli couscous
cream
cumin

curries, **curry powder**, and **curry spices**
custards
dashi
dill
dips
eggplant Parmesan
eggplant rollatini
eggplant, stuffed
eggs, e.g., *omelets, quiches,* scrambled
fennel seeds
fenugreek
French cuisine

Flavor Affinities

eggplant + Asian noodles + peanut sauce
eggplant + balsamic vinegar + basil + oregano
eggplant + balsamic vinegar + tomatoes + zucchini
eggplant + basil + bell peppers + **garlic** + tomatoes + zucchini
eggplant + basil + garlic + olive oil + parsley
eggplant + basil + ricotta + tomatoes
eggplant + bean sprouts + bok choy + edamame + sesame oil
EGGPLANT + BELL PEPPERS + GARLIC
eggplant + bell peppers + miso
eggplant + bell peppers + onions + tomatoes + zucchini
eggplant + bok choy + garlic
eggplant + bread crumbs + Parmesan cheese + rosemary + walnuts
eggplant + capers + celery + onions + pine nuts + tomatoes + vinegar
eggplant + cheese (e.g., mozzarella, Parmesan, ricotta) + **tomatoes**
eggplant + chickpeas + tomatoes + pomegranate molasses
eggplant + cucumbers + garlic + mint + yogurt
eggplant + cumin + yogurt
eggplant + dill + walnuts + yogurt
eggplant + feta cheese + mint
eggplant + garlic + ginger + scallions + sesame+ sesame oil + soy sauce
EGGPLANT + GARLIC + LEMON + OLIVE OIL (+ TAHINI)
eggplant + garlic + olive oil + parsley
eggplant + garlic + Parmesan cheese + parsley + ricotta + tomatoes
eggplant + garlic + tomatoes + zucchini
eggplant + ginger + miso + sesame seeds
eggplant + ginger + soy sauce
eggplant + herbs + lemon juice + olive oil
eggplant + mint + paprika + pine nuts + rice + **yogurt**
eggplant + mint + tomatoes + **yogurt**
eggplant + miso + sesame seeds + shiso
eggplant + *pasta + pesto* + ricotta + walnuts
eggplant + sesame seeds + soy sauce

*GARLIC
ginger
gratins
Greek cuisine
hoisin
honey
INDIAN CUISINE
Italian cuisine
Japanese cuisine
kohlrabi
LEMON, e.g., juice
lemongrass
lentils
lime
mace
marjoram
Mediterranean cuisines
Middle Eastern cuisines
millet
mint
mirin
miso, e.g., white, yellow
Moroccan cuisine
moussaka
mushrooms, e.g., portobello
noodles, Asian, e.g., soba
nutmeg
nuts
OIL, e.g., OLIVE, peanut, sesame,
  sunflower
okra
OLIVES, e.g., black, green,
  niçoise
ONIONS, e.g., green, red, white,
  yellow
orange, e.g., juice, zest
oregano
paprika and smoked paprika
PARSLEY
*PASTA, e.g., lasagna, linguini,
  orzo, penne, rigatoni*
peanuts and peanut sauce
pepper, e.g., black, white
pesto
pine nuts
pizza
polenta
pomegranates and pomegranate

Dishes

Braised Prosperosa Eggplant with Tomatoes, Capers, and Basil
— Blue Hill (New York City)

Summer Vegetable Tart, with Tomato Confit, Eggplant, Zucchini, and Arugula-Basil Pesto
— Café Boulud (New York City)

Charred Eggplant "Barbajuan," Bulgur Wheat "Tabbouleh," Parsley Shoots, and "Raita"
— Per Se (New York City)

Eggplant: Babaganoush, Fried/Grilled Heirloom Tomatoes, Mozzarella, Aged Balsamic
— Rowland's Restaurant at Westglow (Blowing Rock, NC)

molasses
potatoes
quinoa
radicchio
raisins
RATATOUILLE (+ bell peppers
  + garlic + onions + tomatoes +
  zucchini)
rice, e.g., brown, jasmine, wild
risotto
rosemary
saffron
sage
sake
salads, e.g., Asian, Mediterranean
salt, e.g., sea
sandwiches, e.g., grilled mozzarella
savory
scallions
seitan
sesame seeds, e.g., white
shallots
shiso leaves
soups
Southeast Asian cuisines
soy sauce
spinach
spreads
sprouts, e.g., bean
"steaks"
stews
stir-fries
stock, vegetable
tagines
TAHINI

tamari
tarragon
tempeh
Thai cuisine
thyme
tofu
*TOMATOES, TOMATO PASTE,
  and TOMATO SAUCE
turmeric
VINEGAR, e.g., balsamic, cider,
  red wine, sherry
walnuts
yogurt
za'atar
zucchini

"We use five or six different varieties of **eggplant** — including Japanese eggplant, which have thinner skin and more meat to them. We have eggplant from May to November, which is seven months of eggplant. To keep it new, we choose different countries for inspiration. For example, I did a pop-up dinner and made Chinese sweet-and-sour eggplant, cooking it with chiles, Chinese vinegar, garlic, dark soy sauce, and cilantro. Sautéing the eggplant with all these ingredients makes it soak up all the flavors."
— CHARLEEN BADMAN, FnB (SCOTTSDALE, AZ)

"I love vegetables in dessert because it is fun — that is number one! This is where we have our most creative dishes. The vegetable will be the catalyst, but I don't want you leaving with a vegetable flavor — I want your last bite to be a sweet, happy moment at the end of the meal that brings together everything you just ate. **Eggplant** is more fruit than vegetable because it has seeds. It's also like tofu in that it doesn't have much flavor but will soak up the flavors you put it with. Eggplant has a luscious texture. I don't know why I got obsessed with making eggplant tiramisu, but for some reason I did. We mix eggplant with mascarpone and then put it between layers of rosemary ladyfingers and it is just perfect!"

— AMANDA COHEN, DIRT CANDY (NEW YORK CITY)

"You can't *not* get the **Eggplant** Braciole when you come to Vedge The dish is thin layers of eggplant that have been poached in olive oil and that are then wrapped around a filling of eggplant and roasted crushed cauliflower, finished with a green salsa verde. It has a lot of fresh herbs, a good punch of salt, and cured black olive on top. It has so many strong flavors, but you still taste eggplant and cauliflower. These dishes transcend the season, which we thought was important to do."

— RICH LANDAU AND KATE JACOBY, VEDGE (PHILADELPHIA)

"I'm working on a new roasted and stuffed **eggplant** dish right now, and the secret is avoiding the monotony of texture. I'm sure the dish will have some pine nuts for crunch, and most likely also some bulgur for chewiness, accented by feta cheese, onions, and lemon zest."

— ANNIE SOMERVILLE, GREENS RESTAURANT (SAN FRANCISCO)

● EGGPLANT, JAPANESE

Season: year-round, esp. autumn
Volume: quieter than other eggplant
Techniques: bake, broil, deep-fry, **grill**, pickle, **roast**, simmer, steam, **stir-fry**

Tip: Japanese eggplant retains its texture after roasting and absorbs less oil.

Botanical relatives: peppers, potatoes, tomatoes
Possible substitute: eggplant

basil and **Thai basil**
bell peppers, red or yellow, esp. roasted
cabbage
capers
cheese, e.g., mozzarella
chiles, e.g., red
Chinese cuisine
dips
five-spice powder
GARLIC
ginger
gomashio
Indian cuisine

Japanese cuisine
lemon
lime
mint
mirin
miso
mushrooms, e.g., shiitake
oil, olive
olives
onions, red
pastas, e.g., lasagna
peanuts and peanut sauce
pine nuts
pizzas
relishes
rice
sake
salads
salt
sauces, e.g., oyster (vegetarian), peanut
scallions
sesame, e.g., oil, seeds
shiso
soy sauce
spinach
sugar, e.g., brown
tamari
tofu
vinegar, e.g., apple cider, balsamic, red wine, rice, sherry
yogurt

Flavor Affinities
Japanese eggplant + garlic + lime + miso
Japanese eggplant + ginger + soy sauce

EGGS (e.g., FRESH)
Flavor: slightly sweet, with astringent notes
Volume: quiet
Nutritional profile: 63% fat / 35% protein / 2% carbs
Calories: 70 per large egg (whole, raw)
Protein: 6 grams

Techniques: bake, fry, hard-boil, poach, scramble, soft-boil

Tips: Consider organic, omega-3-enriched eggs. If you eat eggs, make sure they are organic and humanely raised.

arugula
asparagus
avocado
basil
bell peppers, esp. roasted
bread, esp. whole-wheat
burritos
butter
capers
casseroles
CHEESE, e.g., cheddar, Comté, cream, Emmental, feta, **goat**, Gruyère, Havarti, Monterey Jack, mozzarella, **Parmesan**, ricotta, Roquefort
chervil
chili pepper sauce and **chili powder**
chives
cream
cumin
curry powder
custards
desserts
dill
egg foo yung
eggplant
eggs, deviled
fennel
French toast
frisée
frittatas
garlic
greens, e.g., braised, salad
herbs
huevos rancheros
kale
leeks
marjoram
mayonnaise
milk

Dishes

This Morning's Farm Egg: First of the Season Corn, and Stone Barns Celtuse
— Blue Hill (New York City)

Organic Connecticut Farm Egg, Steamed Polenta, Artichoke, Sunchoke, Coconut Garlic Broth
— Bouley (New York City)

"Shirred" Hen Egg: Brentwood Corn "Ragoût," Caramelized Okra, and Garden Dill Mousseline
— Per Se (New York City)

MUSHROOMS, e.g., morel, portobello
oil, olive
omelets
onions
oregano
paprika
parsley
pepper, e.g., black, white
pesto
pizzas
polenta
potatoes
quiches
salad dressings
salads, e.g., egg, green
salsas
salt, e.g., kosher, sea
savory
scallions
scrambles
shallots
sorrel
soufflés
soups, e.g., avgolemono
soy sauce
SPINACH
sweet potatoes
tacos
tarragon
thyme
tomatoes
tortilla, Spanish
vinegar
watercress
yogurt
zucchini

Flavor Affinities

eggs + asparagus + chives + Gruyère cheese
eggs + asparagus + *frittata* + goat cheese
eggs + basil + tomatoes
eggs + goat cheese + leeks
eggs + Gruyère cheese + spinach
eggs + kale + ricotta
eggs + lemon + rice + *soups*
eggs + mushrooms + scallions
eggs + nutmeg + spinach
eggs + peas + shiitake mushrooms
eggs + shallots + spinach

EGGS, HARD-BOILED

Techniques: chop, devil, half, pickle, sieve, slice
Vegan substitutes: firm or extra-firm tofu for hard-boiled egg whites, e.g., in egg salads

almonds
artichokes
arugula
asparagus
avocado
basil
beans, e.g., cannellini, green, white
bell peppers, e.g., green, red, yellow
capers
carrots
cayenne
celery

Vegan Egg Substitutes

For breakfast, instead of scrambling eggs, "scramble" tofu (e.g., extra-firm) with herbs and/or vegetables. Firm tofu also replaces hard-boiled egg whites in vegan dishes (e.g., "egg salads").

When baking, you can use Ener-G Egg Replacer, a potato starch–based product that can often replace eggs in the ratio of 1½ teaspoons Ener-G to 2 tablespoons water for each egg, or other commercial egg replacers. However, there are probably already egg replacers in your cupboard or refrigerator, as you'll see below.

How to know which other substitute to use? First, determine whether its need is for **binding** (i.e., holding the mixture together, without the need to rise, e.g., casseroles, veggie burgers), **leavening** (i.e., by adding air bubbles to a batter or dough, as well-beaten eggs do, e.g., in baked goods such as breads, cakes, cupcakes, or muffins), or simply **adding moisture**.

Egg Substitutes, each equivalent to 1 egg (best use)
- ¼ cup applesauce (adding moisture, e.g., in brownies, cakes, cupcakes, quickbreads)
- ¼ cup avocado, mashed (binding)
- 1 teaspoon baking soda + 1 tablespoon apple cider vinegar (leavening and adding moisture)
- ½ mashed banana (adding moisture and/or binding, e.g., in cakes, muffins, pancakes, quick breads)
- ¼ cup carbonated water (leavening)
- 1 tablespoon chia seed meal + 3 tablespoons water, mixed (adding moisture; for leavening, add ¼ teaspoon baking powder)
- ¼ cup full-fat coconut milk + 1 teaspoon baking powder (leavening, esp. in compatibly flavored dishes)
- ¼ cup dried fruit (e.g., apricot, prune) puree (adding moisture)
- 1 tablespoon ground flax seeds + 3 tablespoons water, mixed (binding; for leavening: add ¼ teaspoon baking powder, esp. in nut/seed-compatible dishes, e.g., whole-grain cookies, muffins, pancakes)
- 3 tablespoons nut butter, e.g., peanut (binding, e.g., grain-based veggie burgers)
- ¼ cup silken tofu, blended (adding moisture, esp. in heavier baked goods, e.g., brownies, carrot cakes)
- ¼ cup vegetable puree, e.g., beets, carrots, pumpkin (adding moisture)
- ¼ cup yogurt, dairy or nondairy (adding moisture, e.g., in cakes, muffins, pancakes, quick breads)

"We don't cook with eggs, so I use lemon juice or apple cider vinegar with baking powder to make my cakes rise. I've used **Ener-G Egg Replacer** when baking cookies. It has also worked surprisingly well in 'meringues' and looks beautiful."
— KATE JACOBY, VEDGE (PHILADELPHIA)

celery salt
chervil
chiles, e.g., green, jalapeño; and
  chili pepper sauce
chives
cilantro
cream
cucumbers

curries
curry powder
deviled eggs
dill
egg salad
endive
garlic
grains, e.g., brown rice, farro

Dishes

Deviled Eggs with Curry Powder and
Smoked Paprika
— The Library Bar at The Peacock
(New York City)

gratins
greens, winter, e.g., escarole, radicchio
leeks
lemon, **e.g.**, juice
lettuce, e.g., romaine
lovage
marjoram
mayonnaise, e.g., vegan
mint
mustard, e.g., Dijon, dry
oil, olive
olives, niçoise
onions, e.g., red, spring
paprika
parsley
pepper, e.g., black
potatoes
radicchio
radishes
SALADS, *e.g., egg, grain, green, lentil, niçoise, potato, spinach, tomato, vegetable*
salt, e.g., kosher
sandwiches, e.g., egg salad
scallions
shallots
soups, e.g., beet, borscht
sour cream
spinach
sprouts, e.g., mustard, radish
tarragon
tomatoes
vinegar, e.g., white wine
watercress
yogurt

Flavor Affinities
hard-boiled eggs + asparagus + chives + Dijon mustard + lemon juice + olive oil
hard-boiled eggs + celery + mayonnaise + mustard
hard-boiled eggs + celery + yogurt
hard-boiled eggs + lemon + mayonnaise + mustard

EGYPTIAN CUISINE
baba ghanoush
beans, e.g., fava
cheese, white
chickpeas
coriander
cucumbers
cumin
dill
dukkah
fennel seeds
garlic
grape leaves
hummus
lentils, e.g., red
marjoram
mint
nuts, e.g., almonds, hazelnuts, pistachios
oil, e.g., olive
pasta, e.g., macaroni
pepper, black
pine nuts
rice
salt, sea
seeds, e.g., sesame
soups, e.g., red lentil
spinach
stuffed cabbage
tabbouleh
tahini
thyme
tomatoes and tomato sauce
yogurt

Flavor Affinities
cucumber + mint + yogurt
cumin + fava beans + lemon juice + olive oil

● ENDIVE (aka BELGIAN ENDIVE)
Season: year-round, esp. autumn – spring
Flavor: slightly bitter/sweet, with a crisp, crunchy texture
Volume: quiet – moderate
What it is: vegetable

Nutritional profile: 72% carbs / 18% protein / 10% fat
Calories: 5 per ½-cup serving (chopped, raw)
Techniques: bake, boil, braise (5 – 10 minutes), broil, fry, glaze, grill, raw, roast, sauté, steam, stir-fry, stuff

Tips: Dip whole, raw endive leaves into dips instead of chips or serve leaves filled with purees or spreads.

Botanical relatives: artichokes, chamomile, chicory, dandelion greens, lettuces (e.g., Bibb, iceberg, romaine), radicchio, salsify, tarragon

almonds
APPLES
artichokes, Jerusalem
arugula
avocado
basil
beans, e.g., broad, white
BEETS
bell peppers, e.g., red
berries, e.g., blackberries
bread crumbs, e.g., whole-grain
butter
capers
caraway seeds
celery
CHEESE, e.g., **BLUE**, Cantal, cheddar, feta, fontina, goat, gorgonzola, **Gruyère**, **PARMESAN**, pecorino, ricotta, **Roquefort**, soft, Swiss
chervil
chiles and chili pepper flakes
chives
cilantro
citrus
clementines
cream
crudités
cucumbers
dill

Flavor Affinities

endive + arugula + pears + walnuts
endive + avocado + grapefruit
endive + avocado + red onion + watercress
endive + baby greens + fennel + garlic + Parmesan cheese + vinaigrette
endive + balsamic vinegar + garlic + olive oil
endive + blue cheese + farro + pears
endive + blue cheese + mushrooms + pecans
ENDIVE + CHEESE (e.g., blue, Gruyère, pecorino) **+ FRUIT** (e.g., apples, oranges, pears) **+ NUTS** (e.g., hazelnuts, walnuts)
endive + dill + hazelnuts + lemon + olive oil + potatoes
endive + lemon + olive oil + parsley
endive + Parmesan cheese + portobello mushrooms
endive + Parmesan cheese + white beans

eggs, e.g., hard-boiled, *quiches*
escarole
farro
fennel
figs
frisée
garlic
grapefruit
grapes
gratins
greens
hazelnuts
kumquats
leeks
LEMON, e.g., juice, zest

lettuce, e.g., romaine
mayonnaise
mint
mushrooms, e.g., portobello
mustard, e.g., Dijon, dry
nutmeg
nuts
OIL, e.g., grapeseed, hazelnut, **nut, OLIVE**, walnut
olives, e.g., black
onions, red
ORANGE and **blood orange**, e.g., juice, zest
oregano
palm, hearts of

papaya
parsley
PEARS
pecans
pepper, e.g., black
pizzas
polenta
pomegranate
potatoes
RADICCHIO
radishes
rice
SALADS, e.g., spinach, tricolore salad (i.e., endive + arugula + radicchio)
scallions
shallots
soups
stock, e.g., vegetable
stuffed endive leaves
sugar
sugar snap peas
tangerines
tarragon
thyme
tomatoes, e.g., cherry
truffles, black
vinaigrette
VINEGAR, e.g., **BALSAMIC**, fruit, sherry, **WHITE BALSAMIC**, wine
WALNUTS
watercress
yogurt

Dishes

Salad of Belgian Endive: Lychee, Navel Orange, Piedmont Hazelnuts, Mizuna, and Australian Black Truffle
— The French Laundry (Yountville, CA)

Endive: Grilled Endive and Radicchio, Toasted Hazelnuts, Amish Blue Cheese, and White Balsamic
— Mana Food Bar (Chicago)

Endive Salad with Pickled Asian Pears, Kale, Pomegranate, Red Quinoa, Pecans, and Persimmon Vinaigrette
— Mohawk Bend (Los Angeles)

Endive "Mikado" with Rutabaga Sauerkraut, Tarragon, and Mustard Sauce
— Picholine (New York City)

"I've been making savory vegetarian muffins based on combinations of vegetables, cheese, and nuts or seeds, and one of my favorites is based on caramelized **endive**, blue cheese, and walnuts."
— DIANE FORLEY, FLOURISH BAKING COMPANY (SCARSDALE, NY)

ENDIVE, CURLY
(see FRISÉE)

EPAZOTE
[eh-pah-ZOH-teh]
Flavor: bitter/sweet, with pungent notes of cilantro, coriander, fennel, herbs, lemon, mint, oregano, parsley, and/or sage
Volume: moderate – **loud**
What's healthful about it: enhances flavor and aids in the digestibility of beans
Possible substitute: Mexican oregano

avocados
BEANS, e.g., BLACK, pinto
beans, refried
Central American cuisines
chayote
cheese, e.g., manchego, Mexican, Monterey Jack, mozzarella
chilaquiles
chiles, e.g., chipotle; chili pepper flakes, chili pepper sauce, and chili powder
chili, vegetarian
cilantro
corn
crema
cumin
garlic
huitlacoche
lime
MEXICAN CUISINE
mushrooms
onions
potatoes
quesadillas, e.g., cheese
queso fundido
refried beans
rice
salads
salsas
sauces, e.g., mole

soups, e.g., bean, black bean, garlic, mushroom, tortilla
South American cuisines
Southwestern (U.S.) cuisine
squash, summer
stews
teas, Mexican
tomatillos
tomatoes
tortillas, e.g., corn
zucchini
zucchini blossoms

Flavor Affinities
epazote + chili pepper flakes + lime + zucchini

● ESCAROLE
Season: year-round, esp. summer – autumn
Flavor: bitter, with notes of nuts, and a crisp texture
Volume: moderate – loud
Nutritional profile: 75% carbs / 25% protein
Calories: 10 per 1-cup serving
Techniques: braise, grill, raw, roast, sauté, simmer, steam
Botanical relatives: chicory, endive, frisée, radicchio

almonds
apples
artichokes

Flavor Affinities
escarole + bread crumbs + cheese + *pasta*
escarole + capers + garlic + pine nuts + raisins
escarole + chickpeas + onions
escarole + chickpeas + porcini mushrooms
escarole + chili flakes + garlic + lemon
escarole + garlic + lemon zest + olive oil
escarole + garlic + Parmesan cheese
escarole + garlic + *pasta* **+ white beans**
escarole + garlic + *soups* + tomatoes
escarole + goat cheese + sun-dried tomatoes + watercress
escarole + lemon + orange + radishes
escarole + lemon juice + olive oil + Parmesan cheese

BEANS, e.g., borlotti, cannellini, white
beets
bell peppers, e.g., roasted
bread crumbs and **croutons**
bruschetta
butter
cabbage, e.g., red
capers
carrots
cauliflower
CHEESE, e.g., **blue**, Fontina, goat, mozzarella, **Parmesan**, Roquefort
chickpeas
chiles and **chile pepper flakes**
citrus
crème fraîche
cucumbers
currants
dill
eggs, e.g., *frittatas*
endive
fennel and fennel seeds
GARLIC
hazelnuts
ITALIAN CUISINE
kamut
leeks
LEMON, e.g., **juice**
lentils
lettuce, e.g., butter
mint
mushrooms, e.g., porcini

mustard, e.g., Dijon
nutritional yeast
OIL, e.g., nut, OLIVE
olives, e.g., black, green
ONIONS, e.g., white, yellow
oranges and blood oranges
parsley
parsnips
pasta, e.g., fettuccine, orzo, penne, spaghetti
pears
pepper, e.g., black, white
persimmons
pine nuts
pizzas
polenta
pomegranates
potatoes
radicchio
raisins
rice, e.g., Arborio, brown
salads
salt, e.g., kosher, sea
sauces, e.g., pasta
shallots
SOUPS, e.g., escarole, minestrone, potato, white bean
squash, e.g., yellow
stews, e.g., white bean
stock, vegetable
sumac
thyme
tofu
tomatoes and sun-dried tomatoes
vinegar, e.g., apple cider, balsamic, red, sherry, white wine
walnuts
watercress

Dishes

Betteraves et Escarole (Beets and Escarole): Roasted Red Beets, Goat Cheese Custard, Rhubarb, and Meyer Lemon Confit
— Bar Boulud (New York City)

Romaine Hearts and Escarole with Kalamata Olives, Toasted Pine Nuts, and Creamy Asiago Dressing
— Rancho La Puerta (Mexico)

ETHIOPIAN CUISINE

beans, green
beets
bell pepper, red
berbere
butter, spiced
cabbage
carrots
cloves
eggs, hard-boiled
garlic
ginger
greens, e.g., collard
INJERA
legumes, e.g., chickpeas, lentils, split peas
onions
paprika
peas
potatoes
spices
tibs (i.e., sautés)
turmeric
vegetables, stewed
wats (i.e., stews)

Flavor Affinities

berbere + garlic + onions

FALL (see AUTUMN)

FARRO (aka EMMER WHEAT)
[FAHR-oh]
Flavor: slightly sweet, with earthy notes of barley and/or nuts, and a chewy texture
Volume: quiet

What it is: whole grain; Note: farro is *not* the same as spelt, which is typically a *very* slow-cooking grain.
Gluten-free: no
Nutritional profile: 81% carbs / 12% protein / 7% fat
Calories: 170 per ¼ cup (uncooked)
Protein: 7 grams
Timing: Presoak farro for fastest cooking. Although whole farro is available, most of the farro available in the U.S. is semipearled (semi-*perlato* or pearled (*perlato*), i.e., with some or all of the outside husk removed. Whole farro takes longest to cook (45 – 60 minutes or longer), while pearled farro can cook in as little as half that time. Simmer farro, covered, until tender.
Ratio: 1: 2 – 3 (1 cup farro to 2 – 3 cups cooking liquid)
Tip: Add the cooking water from white cannellini beans to give a creamier, starchier texture to "farrotto."

apples and apple juice
apricots, dried
artichokes
arugula
asparagus
basil
bay leaf
beans, e.g., cannellini, fava, white
beets
bell peppers, esp. roasted
breads
butter
buttermilk
cabbage, e.g., green, savoy
carrots
casseroles
celery
CHEESE, e.g., feta, Grana

Padano, **PARMESAN**, pecorino, ricotta
chicory
chickpeas
chiles, e.g., guajillo

chives
citrus
coconut and coconut milk
corn
cucumbers

dates
dill
dukkah
eggplant
eggs
fennel
garlic
ginger
grapes
gratins
honey
ITALIAN CUISINE
kale
kefir
leeks
lemon, e.g., juice, zest
lemon, preserved
lentils
lovage
mangoes
marjoram
Mediterranean cuisines
mint
MUSHROOMS, e.g., chanterelle, cremini, porcini, shiitake, white, wild
nutmeg
nuts, e.g., almonds, cashews, pistachios
OIL, nut, **OLIVE**
olives, black
onions, e.g., caramelized, yellow
orange, e.g., juice, zest
oregano
PARSLEY
parsnips
pastas
pears
pilaf
pine nuts
pomegranates
quinoa
radicchio
radishes
rice, brown
"risottos," i.e., made with farro, aka *FARROTTOS*
rosemary

Dishes

Farro Salad: Roasted Artichokes, Asparagus, Sweet Peppers, Tomatoes, and White Balsamic Vinegar
— al di la Trattoria (Brooklyn)

Klaas Martens' Emmer Wheat and Quinoa: Wild Spinach, English Peas, and Zucchini
— Blue Hill (New York City)

Organic Farrotto with Pesto Genovese and Parmigiano Reggiano
— Boulud Sud (New York City)

Farrotto con Piselli e Asparagi: Farro cooked in the style of Risotto, with Fresh Peas, Shaved Asparagus, Parmigiano Reggiano, Pecorino Romano, Butter, and Mint
— Le Verdure (New York City)

Date Farro: Dukkah Spice, Squash, Mint, Pomegranate
— Picholine (New York City)

Zucchini and Farro Risotto: Toasted Grains of Farro simmered in Vegetable Stock and finished with a Coconut-Tofu Herb Cream and Fresh Roasted Diced Zucchini
— Sacred Chow (New York City)

Flavor Affinities

farro + apple cider vinegar + butternut squash + dried cranberries + olive oil
farro + basil + olive oil + Parmesan cheese + parsley + walnuts
farro + brown sugar + coconut milk + mangoes
farro + chicory + olive oil + pears + sherry vinegar
farro + citrus + ginger
farro + coconut + zucchini
farro + eggplant + tomatoes
farro + feta cheese + mushrooms
farro + garlic + kale
farro + leeks + parsnips
farro + lemon + orange + rosemary
farro + mint + pecorino cheese + vegetable stock
farro + onions + Parmesan cheese + *risottos* **+ wild mushrooms**
farro + parsley + shallots
farro + peas + quinoa + spinach + zucchini
farro + preserved lemons + radicchio

salads, e.g., grain, green
shallots
SOUPS, e.g., hearty, minestrone,
   mushroom, winter
spinach
squash, winter, e.g., acorn,
   butternut, kabocha
stews
stock, e.g., mushroom or
   vegetable
sugar, e.g., brown
thyme
tofu
tomatoes
vinegar, e.g., apple cider, red
   wine, sherry
walnuts
wine, dry white
zucchini

"**Farro** is my favorite grain
because of its nuttiness. I like
mixing it into green salads with
dried apricots and radishes."
— CHARLEEN BADMAN, FnB
(SCOTTSDALE, AZ)

"I love **farro**'s nutty flavor and
toothy texture, and the sensation
of eating farrotto. Farro doesn't
give off starch the same way
Arborio rice does, but it still has
some of its own sauce like
risotto. . . . You can make a
different version each season:
Spring calls for lots of peas,
spring onions, spinach, and
vegetable stock. **Summer** could
be corn with tomatoes. **Autumn**
farroto with butternut squash,
kale, and roasted garlic could
have Parmesan shaved on top.
Winter farrotto could feature wild
mushrooms and either vegetable
stock or the soaking water from
dried porcini."
— ANNIE SOMERVILLE, GREENS
RESTAURANT (SAN FRANCISCO)

● FENNEL

Season: year-round, esp.
autumn – winter
Flavor: sweet, with notes of
anise and/or licorice, and a crisp,
crunchy texture
Volume: quiet – moderate
Nutritional profile: 85% carbs
/ 10% protein / 5% fat
Calories: 30 per 1-cup serving
(sliced, raw)
Protein: 1 gram
Techniques: bake, blanch,
boil, braise, fry, grill, mandoline,
raw, roast, sauté, shave, simmer,
steam, stir-fry
Botanical relatives: anise,
caraway, celery, celery root,
coriander, dill, parsley, parsley
root, parsnips

almonds
anise
apples, e.g., green
artichokes and artichoke hearts
artichokes, Jerusalem
ARUGULA

asparagus
avocado
basil
bay leaf
BEANS, e.g., **CANNELLINI**, fava,
   green, **WHITE**
beets and beet juice
bell peppers, e.g., red, yellow
bread crumbs
butter
capers
carrots
cashews
casseroles
cauliflower
celery
celery root
chard
CHEESE, e.g., blue, feta, **GOAT**,
   Gorgonzola, Gouda, **Gruyère**,
   manchego, **PARMESAN**,
   pecorino, Piave, **ricotta**, ricotta
   salata, Swiss
cherries, e.g., dried
chervil
chestnuts
chickpeas

Dishes

Mushroom, Sausage, and Fennel Scramble: Tofu Scramble, sautéed with Seitan Sausage, Portobello Mushrooms, Leeks, Fennel, and Fresh Herbs, topped with Roasted Red Pepper Sour Cream
— Blossoming Lotus (Portland, OR)

Arugula Fennel Salad: Arugula, Heart of Palm, Fennel, Grapefruit, Sea Salt
— The Butcher's Daughter (New York City)

Homemade Fettuccine: Caramelized Fennel, Roasted Beets, Goat Cheese, Hazelnut,
Bread Crumbs
— Café Boulud (New York City)

Creamy Fennel Soup with Poached d'Anjou Pear, Shaved Almonds, Fines Herbes
— Green Zebra (Chicago)

Salad of K. K. Haspel's Bio-Dynamic Greens with Fennel and Radishes, tossed in
Shallot-Dijon Mustard Vinaigrette
— North Fork Table & Inn (Southold, NY)

Fennel Confit: Romesco Mousse, Baby Leeks, Pimenton de la Vera
— Picholine (New York City)

Flavor Affinities

FENNEL + ACID (e.g., orange juice, vinegar) + BEETS

fennel + almonds + avocados + mesclun greens

fennel + arugula + grapefruit + hazelnuts

fennel + avocados + citrus + mâche + olives

fennel + beets + Belgian endive

fennel + blood oranges + romaine

fennel + cashews + oranges + vanilla

FENNEL + CHEESE (e.g., Gouda, Parmesan, ricotta) + NUTS (e.g., almonds, walnuts) + TREE FRUITS (e.g., apples, pears)

fennel + cranberries + nuts + *salads* + wild rice

fennel + cucumbers + mustard + thyme

fennel + endive + pears

fennel + escarole + olives + ricotta salata cheese

fennel + escarole + oranges

fennel + fennel seeds + garlic + **olive oil** + thyme

fennel + fennel seeds + lemon juice + **olive oil**

fennel + feta cheese + lemon + parsley

fennel + garlic + olives + Parmesan cheese + **tomatoes**

fennel + garlic + potatoes

fennel + greens + Gruyère cheese + mushrooms

fennel + lemon + olive oil + Parmesan cheese + parsley + *salads*

fennel + mushrooms + Parmesan cheese

fennel + olives + oranges

FENNEL + ORANGES + NUTS (e.g., pecans, walnuts)

fennel + oranges + red onions + white beans

fennel + Parmesan cheese + risotto + tomatoes

chicory

chiles, e.g., jalapeño; and chili pepper flakes

Chinese cuisine

chives

citrus

clementines

coriander

couscous

cranberries, e.g., dried

cream

cucumbers

curries, curry powder, and curry spices

dill

edamame

eggplant

eggs, e.g., *custards*, hard-boiled, *omelets, quiches*

endive

escarole

fennel fronds, fennel pollen, and FENNEL SEEDS

figs

French cuisine

frisée

GARLIC

ginger

grains, e.g., millet, quinoa, spelt

grapefruit

gratins

greens, e.g., mesclun, winter

hazelnuts

honey

Italian cuisine

leeks

LEMON, e.g., juice, zest

lentils

lettuce, e.g., romaine

lime

liqueurs with anise/licorice flavor, such as Pernod, Ricard, sambuca

mâche

mango

Mediterranean cuisines

mint

MUSHROOMS, e.g., porcini, portobello, white, wild

mustard, e.g., Dijon, and mustard seeds

nuts

OIL, e.g., canola, hazelnut, nut, OLIVE, vegetable, walnut

olives, e.g., black, green, Italian

ONIONS, e.g., cippolini, red, spring

ORANGE, e.g., juice, zest

orange, blood

oregano

palm, hearts of

parsley

pasta, e.g., *linguini, orecchiette, orzo*

peaches

pears

pecans

pepper, e.g., black, white

Pernod

pistachios

pizza

pomegranates

potatoes

pumpkin seeds

radicchio

radishes

relishes

rice and wild rice

risottos

saffron

sage

SALADS, e.g., fennel, grain, green, tomato

salt, e.g., kosher, sea

sauces, e.g., tomato

scallions

sesame seeds, white

shallots

slaws
snap peas
soufflés
SOUPS, e.g., fennel, potato,
tomato, vegetable
soy sauce
squash, e.g., spaghetti, summer,
winter
star anise
stews, e.g., vegetable
stir-fries
stock, e.g., fennel, vegetable
stuffings
tamari
tarragon
thyme
TOMATOES and **tomato sauce**
turnips
vanilla
verjus
vermouth
VINEGAR, e.g., **balsamic**,
champagne, cider, raspberry,
sherry, **white wine**
WALNUTS
watercress
wine, dry white
zucchini

FENNEL FRONDS (or LEAVES)

Flavor: notes of anise/licorice
Volume: quiet
Techniques: garnish (esp.
fennel dishes), raw

beans
cabbage
cheese, e.g., Parmesan
citrus
cocktails, e.g., vodka-based
eggs and *egg dishes*
fennel
Italian cuisine
lemon
Mediterranean cuisines
oil
onions, e.g., red

pastas
"*pestos*" *(+ garlic + olive oil +*
Parmesan cheese + pine nuts)
rice
risottos
salad dressings, e.g., citrus
vinaigrettes
salads, *e.g., carrot, citrus, fennel,*
green
salsas
sausages, vegetarian
soups, *e.g., barley, cucumber*

Flavor Affinities

fennel fronds + avocado + fennel
+ grapefruit + *salads*

FENNEL POLLEN

Season: spring – summer
Flavor: bitter/**sweet**/umami;
aromatic, with pungent notes of
anise, citrus, fennel, herbs, honey,
and/or licorice
Volume: quiet – moderate/loud
Tip: Use to finish a dish.

apricots
asparagus
baked goods, e.g., cakes, cookies
carrots
cheese, e.g., Monterey Jack,
ricotta
chocolate
cinnamon
citrus
cream and crème fraîche
eggplant
fennel and fennel seeds
garlic
(Central and Northern) Italian
cuisine
leeks
lemon, e.g., juice, zest
mushrooms
nuts, e.g., almonds, pistachios
oatmeal
orange
pastas, e.g., ravioli

pepper, black
polentas
potatoes
rice
risottos
salads
salt, e.g., sea
tomatoes and tomato sauce
vegetables, e.g., roasted, spring
yogurt

• FENNEL SEEDS

Flavor: bitter/**sweet**, with notes
of anise, caraway, cumin, dill,
and/or licorice
Volume: quiet – moderate
Tips: Add at the end of the
cooking process. Nibble on a few
seeds to freshen the breath.
Possible substitute: anise
seeds

apples
artichokes, Jerusalem
baked goods, e.g., breads, cakes,
cookies, flatbreads
basil
beans, e.g., green
beets
broccoli
Brussels sprouts
cabbage
carrots
cauliflower
celery root
cheese
chickpeas
Chinese cuisine
cinnamon
cloves
coriander
cucumbers
curries
cumin
desserts, e.g., Indian
eggplant
English cuisine
European cuisines

fennel
fenugreek
figs
five-spice powder
garam masala
garlic
ginger
grapefruit, e.g., juice, zest
greens, e.g., beet
herbes de Provence
Italian cuisine
kohlrabi
leeks
lemon, e.g., juice
lentils
liqueurs
mangoes
marinades
marjoram
Mediterranean cuisines
mushrooms
mustard, e.g., Dijon
oil, olive
olives
orange
paprika
parsley
parsnips
pastas
peas, split
pepper, black
pickles
pizza
potatoes
pumpkin
ras el hanout
rice
saffron
salad dressings
salads**, e.g., pasta, **potato
SAUCES, e.g., pasta
sauerkraut
Scandinavian cuisine
shallots
***soups**, e.g., carrot, celery root, split pea, tomato*
star anise
stuffings

sweet potatoes
tarragon
teas
thyme
tomatoes and **tomato sauce**
vegetables, e.g., green, roasted
walnuts

Flavor Affinities
fennel seeds + grapefruit + lemon + mustard + shallots
fennel seeds + leeks + tomatoes
fennel seeds + marjoram + thyme

● FENUGREEK

Flavor: bitter/sweet; aromatic, with pungent and/or savory notes of burnt sugar, caramel, celery, chocolate, coffee, and/or maple syrup
Volume: quiet/moderate (leaves) – moderate/**loud** (seeds)
What it is: used as an herb (dried or fresh leaves), a spice (seeds), and as a vegetable (fresh)

Tips: Toast fenugreek seeds to bring out their flavor, which resembles maple syrup. (Indeed, fenugreek is used in making artificial maple syrup.) Long cooking (e.g., simmering) will quiet their flavor. Sprouted fenugreek seeds can be used in salads.

Botanical relatives: clover, peas

(Northern) African cuisine
baked goods
beans, e.g., dried, green, kidney, mung
breads
broccoli
cabbage
caraway seeds
cardamom
carrots
CAULIFLOWER

cheese, e.g., creamy, paneer, white
chickpeas
chiles and **chili paste**
chutneys
cilantro
cinnamon
cloves
coriander
cumin
CURRIES, curry leaves, and **curry powder**
dals
dosai, i.e., Indian crêpes
eggplant
eggs, e.g., *omelets*
fennel seeds
flours, e.g., lentil, rice
garlic
ginger
greens, e.g., collard, turnip
honey
INDIAN CUISINE
lemon
LENTILS
mayonnaise
Mediterranean cuisines
Middle Eastern cuisines
mustard seeds
onions
parsnips
peas
peas, split
pepper, e.g., black
pickles
POTATOES, e.g., curried, mashed
rice, e.g., basmati, long-grain
salad dressings
***salads**, e.g., potato*
sauces, e.g., raita, white
***soups**, e.g., lentil*
spinach
squash, winter, e.g., butternut
stews, vegetable
teas, e.g., mint
tomatoes
Turkish cuisine
turmeric

turnips
walnuts
yogurt
zucchini

Flavor Affinities
fenugreek seeds + chiles +
cilantro + garlic + tomatoes
fenugreek seeds + cumin + garlic
+ ginger + lentils + turmeric

● FIDDLEHEAD FERNS
Season: spring
Flavor: bitter, with notes of
artichokes, asparagus, green
beans, and/or mushrooms, and a
crunchy texture
Volume: moderate – loud
Nutritional profile: 57% carbs
/ 33% protein / 10% fat
Calories: 10 per 1-ounce serving
(raw)
Protein: 1 gram
Techniques: blanch, boil
(5+ minutes), braise, pickle,
poach, puree, sauté, steam (Note:
never raw)

almonds
arugula
asparagus
butter and brown butter
cheese, e.g., Comté, goat,
Gruyère, Parmesan
chiles, e.g., green
chives
coriander
cream
cumin
custards
eggs, e.g., hard-boiled, *quiches*
fenugreek seeds
garlic
ginger
leeks
lemon
marjoram
milk

miso
MUSHROOMS, e.g., chanterelle,
maitake, morel, wild
mustard
nettles
noodles, soba
nutmeg
oil, e.g., hazelnut, nut, **olive**
onions, e.g., green, red
oregano
paprika
parsley
pastas
peas
pepper, black
"pestos" (e.g., fiddleheads + almonds
+ olive oil + Parmesan)
ponzu sauce
potatoes, e.g., new
rice, wild
risottos
salads, e.g., warm
salt
sauces, e.g., cheese, cream,
hollandaise
savory
sesame, e.g., oil, seeds
shallots
soufflés
soups
soy sauce
squash, summer
stock, vegetable
turmeric
vinaigrette
vinegar, e.g., apple cider,
balsamic, sherry
zucchini

Flavor Affinities
fiddlehead ferns + butter + herbs
+ morel mushrooms + ramps
fiddlehead ferns + butter + lemon
fiddlehead ferns + chanterelle
mushrooms + risotto
fiddlehead ferns + garlic +
marjoram

fiddlehead ferns + garlic + olive
oil + parsley
fiddlehead ferns + mustard +
olive oil
fiddlehead ferns + sesame oil +
sesame seeds + soy sauce

● FIGS (see also FIGS, DRIED)
Season: summer – autumn
Flavor: sweet, with astringent
notes, and a soft texture when
ripe (studded with tiny, crunchy
seeds)
Volume: quiet – moderate
Nutritional profile: 94% carbs
(high in sugar) / 3% fat / 3%
protein
Calories: 50 per large fig (raw)
Techniques: bake, broil,
caramelize, deep-fry, grill, raw,
roast, sauté, simmer

anise seeds
apples
Armagnac
ARUGULA
baked goods, e.g., cakes, corn bread,
muffins, quick breads
basil
bay leaf
berries, e.g., blackberries,
blueberries
butter
caramel
cardamom
cereals, e.g., breakfast
CHEESE, e.g., blue, burrata,
Cabrales, chèvre, **cream, feta,**
fresh white, **GOAT, Gorgonzola,**
manchego, Monterey Jack,
mozzarella, Parmesan,
pecorino, **ricotta, Stilton**
chiles, e.g., jalapeño
chocolate
chutneys
cinnamon
cloves

coconut and coconut milk
Cointreau
compotes
cranberries
cream
desserts
endive, e.g., red

fennel and fennel seeds
frisée
ginger
grapes
HONEY
lavender
lemon, e.g., juice, zest

lettuce, butter
lime, e.g., juice, zest
mascarpone
Mediterranean cuisines
melon, e.g., cantaloupe
Middle Eastern cuisines
milk, coconut
mint
molasses
NUTS, e.g., ALMONDS,
   hazelnuts, pecans, pistachios,
   WALNUTS
oatmeal and oats
oil, e.g., coconut, grapeseed, **olive**
onions, caramelized
ORANGE, e.g., juice, liqueur, zest
pancakes
peaches
pears
pepper, black
persimmons
phyllo dough
pizza
pomegranates
quince
raspberries
relishes
rice
rosemary
salad dressings, e.g., blue cheese
salads, e.g., green, spinach
salt, sea
sesame seeds
sour cream
spinach
star anise
strawberries
stuffed figs
SUGAR, e.g., brown
tarts
thyme
vanilla
VINEGAR, e.g., **balsamic**, red
   wine, sherry, **white balsamic**
watercress
wine, e.g., Madeira, Marsala, red,
   sweet (e.g., port)
yogurt

Flavor Affinities

figs + almonds + anise
figs + almonds + pears + red wine
figs + anise + cardamom + pistachios + yogurt
figs + apples + honey
figs + apples + pecans
figs + arugula + basil + cheese + honey
figs + arugula + chèvre cheese
figs + arugula + feta cheese
figs + arugula + walnuts
figs + balsamic vinegar + cheese
figs + balsamic vinegar + olive oil
figs + balsamic vinegar + pistachios
figs + basil + goat cheese + pomegranate seeds
figs + basil + mozzarella cheese
figs + black pepper + cheese + honey
FIGS + CHEESE (e.g., blue, burrata, feta, goat, Gorgonzola, mascarpone,
   ricotta) **+ NUTS** (e.g., almonds, pecans, pistachios, walnuts)
figs + cinnamon + honey + vanilla
figs + cream cheese + honey + mint + ricotta
figs + goat cheese + thyme
figs + Gorgonzola cheese + (caramelized) onions
figs + honey + nuts + ricotta
figs + honey + pecans
figs + honey + port + rosemary
figs + honey + raspberries
figs + honey + vanilla + wine
figs + honey + walnuts + yogurt
figs + melon + mint
figs + melon + orange

Dishes

Roasted Hamada Farm Figs and Buratta on Grilled Walnut Levain with Arugula and Red Endive Salad
— Greens Restaurant (San Francisco)

Honey-Grilled Figs with Sweetened Ricotta
— Telepan (New York City)

"I believe Japanese **figs**, which are very popular in Japan, are the best — but I've found that candy-striped figs [also called raspberry figs, for their bright red color, sweet-tart flavor, and crunchy seeds] have even more flavor, and are better eaten as a fruit."

— RYOTA UESHIMA, KAJITSU (NEW YORK CITY)

• FIGS, DRIED

Flavor: sweet, with notes of honey, nuts, and/or raisins, and a soft, chewy texture studded by tiny crunchy seeds
Volume: moderate
Techniques: as is, stew

almonds
anise seeds
apples
baked goods, e.g., cakes, muffins, quick breads
bananas
brandy
cardamom
cheese, e.g., blue, cream, feta, goat, Gorgonzola, manchego, Parmesan, ricotta
chestnuts
cinnamon
coconut
cranberries
dates
desserts
granola
honey
jams
lemon, e.g., juice, zest
NUTS, e.g., almonds, macadamia, pecans, walnuts
oats and oatmeal
olives
orange, e.g., juice, zest
pears
pecans
pistachios

pumpkin seeds
raisins
snacks
stews
tagines
vinegar, e.g., balsamic
WALNUTS
wine, e.g., red, sweet
yogurt

Flavor Affinities
dried figs + almonds + cream cheese
dried figs + bananas + coconut
dried figs + chestnuts + orange
dried figs + goat cheese + salad greens + walnuts
dried figs + honey + nuts
dried figs + honey + orange + yogurt

FIVE-SPICE POWDER

Flavor: sweet
Volume: quiet – moderate
What it is: A spice blend made of cinnamon + cloves + fennel seeds + star anise + Szechuan peppercorns

braised dishes
Chinese cuisine
garlic
ginger
marinades
nuts, e.g. almonds, pistachios, walnuts
rice
roasted dishes
sauces
seeds, e.g., pumpkin
stews
stir-fries
tofu

FLAXSEED OIL (see OIL, FLAXSEED)

• FLAXSEEDS

Flavor: slightly sweet, with notes of nuts, and a crunchy texture
Volume: quiet
What they are: seeds
Who says they're healthful: Joel Fuhrman, in his "Top Super Foods for Super Immunity"
What's healthful about them: 1 tablespoon of ground flaxseeds every day — such as on cereal or in a smoothie — fulfills daily omega-3 fatty acids needs.

Tips: Buy whole seeds and grind immediately before using. Seeds must be ground to release their full nutritional value. Do not cook on high heat if you want to maintain nutritional benefits. To use as an egg substitute when baking, use 1 heaping tablespoon to substitute for 1 large egg: soak flaxseeds in hot water in a 1:3 ratio before blending into a thick paste (1 tablespoon flaxseeds to 3 tablespoons water).

apples and applesauce
avocados
*BAKED GOODS, e.g., **breads**, crackers, muffins, pie crusts, pizza crusts, quick breads*
bananas
carrots and carrot juice
CEREALS, e.g., breakfast
citrus
coriander
cottage cheese
desserts
fennel
flour, e.g., whole wheat
French toast
grains
granola
herbs
honey

F

Dishes

Pizza: Buckwheat, Sweet Potato, and
Flaxseed Crust topped with Red Bell
Peppers, Olives, Onions, Basil,
Choice of Marinara Sauce or Pesto
— Peacefood Café (New York City)

juices
kale
"meatloaf," vegetarian
nuts, e.g., peanuts and peanut
    butter, walnuts
oats, oat bran, oatmeal
oil, olive
*pancakes and waffles, e.g., add to
    batter*
pizza doughs
rice
salads, e.g., as a topping
sesame seeds
SMOOTHIES
soups
squash, winter
vegetables
veggie burgers
yogurt
zucchini

FLOUR, RICE

"I like to use **rice flour** —
grinding in some Arborio
rice for texture, and some
sesame or coriander seeds
for texture and flavor —
as a crust for fried mushrooms.
Just dip the mushrooms
into soy milk, or rice milk
with a little Dijon mustard
added for viscosity, and
then into the rice flour
mixture before frying."
— ERIC TUCKER, MILLENNIUM
(SAN FRANCISCO)

Diane Forley of Flourish Baking Company

As a chef, my interest is in whole-plant cooking — from root to
fruit — as integral to a more healthful and enjoyable way of living.
But food has to first satisfy taste, so the challenge is always to find the
right combination of ingredients and balance of flavors and textures.
I have been experimenting with grains and beans in nontraditional
ways: folded into muffins, added to savory custards, and pulverized
into tart crusts. This also allows me to bring energy-rich plant foods
into our products replacing white flours and sugars, which are devoid
of nutrition. Sprouted-grain flours are especially interesting to me
because they offer not only great flavor, but also an energy-rich ingredient for baked goods.

Because my kitchen is focused on developing savory baked items,
I try to create the flavors first and then select how they are best
presented.

Here are some combos:

Savory:
- sprouted spelt flour muffin with asparagus, sorrel, pumpkin seed,
  and parmesan
- sprouted corn flour muffin with pickled beet, macadamia nut, and
  goat cheese
- millet flour biscuit with roasted chickpeas, sumac, and sesame seed
- savory rice pudding with confit of fennel, carrot, and tarragon
- quinoa pudding with broccoli and cheddar

Fruit:
- coconut flour scone with wild blueberries, ginger root, and hempseed
- wild rice and quinoa muffin with bananas, dried cranberries, and
  walnuts
- chocolate cherry scone with vanilla bean kefir and almonds
- strawberry jam muffin with pomegranate molasses, Meyer lemon,
  and chia seed

FLOUR, SPELT

"Because **spelt flour** doesn't have
as much gluten as wheat flour,
muffins made with it don't rise as
high, so instead of filling muffin
tins two-thirds full, we fill them
three-quarters full."
— MARLENE TOLMAN, POMEGRANATE
CAFÉ (PHOENIX, AZ)

"We make apple cider
doughnuts with **spelt flour,**
which is very good for you, with
lots of vitamins and easy to
digest. We tried making the
doughnut with whole-grain wheat
flour, but it was very heavy. To
sweeten the doughnut as well as
other cakes, I use maple syrup,
which is not overpowering. In

2010, *Time Out* awarded us 'best doughnut,' and the funny thing is my partner owns a Dunkin' Donuts."

— FERNANDA CAPOBIANCO, VEGAN DIVAS (NEW YORK CITY)

"I think **spelt flour** pizza has more flavor than white flour pizza. It's really good served with pears and ricotta."

— MAKINI HOWELL, PLUM BISTRO (SEATTLE)

FLOUR, SPROUTED

Brands: Essential Eating, To Your Health

FLOWERS, EDIBLE

While several varieties of flowers are edible — such as (sweet licorice) anise hyssop, (cucumber-like, sweet honey-like) borage, carnations, chicory, (garlicy, oniony) chives, chrysanthemums, daisies, day lilies, (herbal, pungent, sweet) lavender, (bitter, floral, sour) marigolds, (honey, peppery) nasturtiums, (minty) pansies, and (sweet) violets — most do not add much flavor of their own. Rather, they're mostly decorative.

"We grow **edible flowers** on our roof at Mélisse. . . . Pollen is what gives most edible flowers their sweet, individual flavors. . . . Nasturtiums are stronger flavored than most edible flowers — they have a very strong, floral, peppery, spicy flavor. Yellow wood sorrel is also strongly sour."

— JOSIAH CITRIN, MÉLISSE (SANTA MONICA)

FREEKEH (aka FRIKEH)

[FREE-kah]

Flavor: earthy notes of grass, meat, nuts, and/or smoke, with a chewy texture
Volume: moderate
What it is: young green wheat that has been set on fire before harvesting; i.e., grain
Techniques: simmer (20 – 30 minutes)
Ratio: 1: 1½ – 2 (1 cup freekeh to 1½ – 2 cups cooking liquid)
Tip: To bring out its nuttiness, toast in a pan before cooking.
Possible substitute: bulgur + drops of liquid smoke

(North) African cuisines
allspice
apples
apricots, dried
asparagus
baked goods, e.g., breads
beans, e.g., adzuki, black, soy
beets
bell peppers, e.g., red
bread crumbs, e.g., panko
butter
carrots
cayenne
celery
cereals, hot breakfast
cheese, e.g., burrata, feta, Parmesan
chickpeas
chiles, e.g., green
cilantro
cinnamon
cloves
coriander
cucumbers
cumin
eggplant
eggs
fruit, dried, e.g., apricots, cranberries, plums, raisins
GARLIC
grains, other, e.g., oats
honey

lemon, e.g., juice, zest
lentils
"meatballs"
Mediterranean cuisines
Middle Eastern cuisines
mint
mushrooms, e.g., button, enoki, oyster, shiitake
North African cuisines
nutmeg
nuts, e.g., cashews, hazelnuts, walnuts
oil, e.g., nut, **olive**
olives, e.g., kalamata
ONIONS, e.g., red
oregano
paprika, e.g., hot, sweet
parsley
pepper, black
PILAFS
pine nuts
pistachios
pomegranate seeds
"risottos"
saffron
salads, e.g., grain
salt, sea
seeds, e.g., pumpkin, sesame, sunflower
shallots
soups
squash, butternut
stews
stock, e.g., mushroom, vegetable
stuffings
sweet potatoes
tabbouleh
thyme
tomatoes and **tomato paste**
tomatoes, sun-dried
veggie burgers
walnuts
yogurt
zucchini

Flavor Affinities
freekeh + apples + *breakfast cereal* + cinnamon + raisins

freekeh + bread crumbs + eggs + *meatballs* + Parmesan cheese + parsley

freekeh + cinnamon + coriander + cumin

"I've cooked **freekeh**, then dehydrated and fried it, so that it turns crispy like Rice Krispies, and paired it with a creamy burrata cheese."

— JON DUBOIS, GREEN ZEBRA (CHICAGO)

FRENCH CUISINE

apples

apricots

butter

cassoulets, vegetarian

cheese

cream

eggs, e.g., *omelets*

garlic

gratins

herbs, e.g., fines herbes

mirepoix (carrots + celery + onions)

mustard, e.g., Dijon

onions

parsley

pastries

pears

potatoes

rémoulades, e.g., celery root

salads, e.g., lentil

SAUCES

sautéed dishes

shallots

spirits

stocks

tarragon

tarts, e.g., savory (e.g., onion, zucchini), sweet (e.g., fruit)

thyme

tomatoes

truffles, e.g., black

vegetables, root

vinaigrettes

vinegars, wine, e.g., red, white

wheat, esp. as flour

WINE

zucchini

"When I was twenty-six, I went to **France** for the first time. My takeaway was that the French love vegetables! It was simple food with a tremendous impact. I also learned that they love to use pressure cookers to cook their vegetables. It makes the vegetables turn into a soft state, sort of a melting texture. The aromas from this technique are like nothing else. . . . During my time in France, it felt like every meal had a tart! Or if Americans are thought to always be eating hot dogs and hamburgers, I felt the same could be said about the French and their tarts. In France, lunch is the big meal of the day, so dinner is often lighter — such as a zucchini tart with custard and curry spices, served with a salad. I learned from a French woman to make my tart dough with half-butter, half-margarine, which made a crisper tart shell, but now I use 100 percent Earth Balance for our vegan tart."

— KEN LARSEN, TABLE VERTE, NEW YORK CITY'S FIRST FRENCH VEGETARIAN BISTRO

FRESHNESS

Season: spring – summer

Tips: Listed herbs are always used fresh (with little or no cooking), and add a note of freshness to a dish. Other listed flavors add a bright note to a dish. For the opposite, see the entry **SLOW-COOKED**.

basil

chives

cilantro

citrus

dill

fennel pollen

mint

tarragon

● FRISÉE (aka CURLY ENDIVE)

Flavor: bitter/slightly sweet, with a "fluffy" texture

Volume: quieter (younger) – louder (older)

What it is: a fine-leaved variety of curly endive

Techniques: braise, raw, sear, wilt

apples

arugula

asparagus

beans, green

beets

bread crumbs

cashews

celery

CHEESE, e.g., **blue**, chèvre, feta, *fromage blanc*, goat, Gorgonzola, manchego, **Parmesan**, Roquefort

chives

eggs, e.g., fried, poached

endive

escarole

fennel

garlic

ginger

grapefruit

greens, other salad

hazelnuts

lemon, e.g., juice

mâche

maple syrup

mint

mushrooms, e.g., chanterelle, king oyster, porcini, portobello, shiitake

mustard, Dijon

nuts, e.g., cashews, hazelnuts, walnuts

oil, e.g., canola, grapeseed, hazelnut, nut, **olive**, sunflower seed, walnut
oranges and blood oranges, and their juices
palm, hearts of
parsley
pears
pepper, e.g., black, white
pomegranates
potatoes
radicchio
radishes
salads, e.g., green, potato
salt, e.g., kosher, sea
savory
seeds, e.g., sunflower
shallots
soups
spinach
sprouts, e.g., sunflower
tarragon
thyme
tomatoes
VINEGAR, e.g., apple cider, balsamic, red wine, sherry, white wine
wakame
walnuts
watercress

Flavor Affinities

frisée + arugula + beets + goat cheese + hearts of palm + vinegar
frisée + balsamic vinegar + Dijon mustard + olive oil + potatoes
frisée + balsamic vinegar + goat cheese

Dishes

Roasted Beet and Frisée Salad with Fennel, Grapefruit, Sunflower Seed Brittle, Goat's Cheese, White Balsamic
— Mayflower Inn & Spa (Washington, CT)

Fricassee Vegetables with Fromage Blanc, Jumbo Asparagus, Frisée Salad
— Mayflower Inn & Spa (Washington, CT)

frisée + croutons + egg + garlic + lemon + mushrooms
frisée + Gorgonzola cheese + walnuts
frisée + Roquefort cheese + sherry vinegar + walnut oil

FROMAGE BLANC

Flavor: sour, with creamy notes, and a smooth and firm yet spreadable texture (somewhat similar to ricotta)
Volume: quiet – moderate
What it is: made from milk, "France's answer to yogurt"
What's healthful about it: low in fat or fat-free
Techniques: whip
Possible substitutes: cream cheese, crème fraîche (which is made from cream), pureed fresh ricotta, sour cream, yogurt

apricots
asparagus
bananas
basil
berries, e.g., blueberries, strawberries
blintzes
blueberries
breads
cheese, cream
cheesecakes
chives
citrus, e.g., juice, zest
crêpes
eggs, e.g., *frittatas*

desserts
dips
figs
fines herbes
French cuisine
fruit and fruit jams and preserves
garlic
granola
herbs
honey
ice cream
lavender
leeks
maple syrup
mustard, e.g., Dijon
nectarines
nuts
onions, e.g., spring
parsley
peaches
pistachios
pizzas
potatoes
salads, e.g., fruit
sandwiches
sorbets
soups, e.g., carrot
spreads
strawberries
sugar
tarragon
tomatoes
vanilla

Flavor Affinities

fromage blanc + eggs + fines herbes + *omelets*
fromage blanc + garlic + herbs
fromage blanc + granola + honey

FRUITS AND VEGETABLES, FROZEN

Tip: Frozen fruits and vegetables are frequently more nutritious than those purchased fresh that are a few days old.

FRUITS, DRIED (see APRICOTS, DRIED; CHERRIES, DRIED; CRANBERRIES, DRIED; CURRANTS, DRIED; PLUMS, DRIED; RAISINS, etc.)

Tips: Select *only* organic dried fruits. If the fruit is hard, steam before using.

GALANGAL (see also GINGER)

[guh-LANG-uhl]
Flavor: sour/hot, aromatic, with earthy, pungent notes of camphor, citrus, flowers, ginger, lemon, mustard seed, **pepper**, and/or tropical fruit, and a woody texture
Volume: very loud
What it is: "Thai ginger"
Botanical relative and Possible substitute: ginger

baked goods, e.g., cakes (e.g., carrot), cookies, quick breads (e.g., banana)
cauliflower
chiles, e.g., Thai
chocolate
cilantro
citrus, e.g., lemon, lime
COCONUT and **COCONUT MILK**
coriander
curries, e.g., green, red
GARLIC
ginger
honey
Indonesian cuisine
Kaffir lime leaves
LEMONGRASS
Malaysian cuisine
miso, e.g., white
mushrooms
onions
parsley
pears, e.g., Asian
potatoes
rice

sauces
scallions
shallots
shiso
SOUPS, e.g., coconut
Southeast Asian cuisines
squash, e.g., butternut, kabocha
stews
stir-fries
stock, e.g., vegetable
sugar, e.g., brown
tamarind
THAI CUISINE
turmeric
Vietnamese cuisine

Flavor Affinities

galangal + butternut squash + coconut milk + lemongrass + mushrooms + stock + tofu
galangal + chiles + cilantro + coconut milk + coriander + Kaffir lime leaf
galangal + ginger + kabocha squash + white miso

GARBANZO BEANS
(see CHICKPEAS)

GARDEN CRESS
(see LAND CRESS)

● GARLIC

Season: year-round, esp. spring (i.e., green) – autumn
Flavor: ranges from sweet to pungent, with notes of nuts and/ or onions
Volume: ranges from quiet/ moderate (esp. roasted) – loud (esp. raw)
Nutritional profile: 85% carbs / 12% protein / 3% fat
Calories: 5 per clove (raw)
Techniques: bake, grill, puree, raw (e.g., on salads), roast (400°F until soft, about a half hour), sauté, stew, stir-fry

Tips: Braise garlic in olive oil to use as a spread (e.g., for bread or crackers) or to use in cooking.

Botanical relatives: asparagus, chives, leeks, onions, shallots

Flavor Affinities
garlic + almonds + bread crumbs + **lemon + olive oil** + parsley
garlic + basil + olive oil + tomatoes
garlic + bread crumbs + mushrooms + parsley
garlic + broccoli + lemon
garlic + chard + potatoes + rosemary
garlic + feta cheese + oregano
garlic + ginger + mirin + sesame oil + soy sauce
garlic + ginger + parsley
garlic + kale + tamari
garlic + leeks + potatoes + saffron + *soups* + vegetable stock
GARLIC + LEMON + PARSLEY
garlic + olive oil + parsley
garlic + olive oil + rosemary
garlic + parsley + sage
garlic + potatoes + rosemary

aioli (i.e., garlic mayonnaise)
almonds
American cuisine
artichokes
artichokes, Jerusalem
asparagus
BASIL
bay leaf
BEANS, e.g., black, broad, cannellini, fava, green, lima, **pinto**, shell, **white**
beets
bread and **bread crumbs**
broccoli and broccoli rabe
butter
capers
carrots
casseroles
cauliflower

chard
cheese, e.g., feta, **goat**, Gruyère, **Parmesan**, ricotta, Swiss
chickpeas
chiles, e.g., chili pepper flakes, chili pepper paste, and chili pepper sauce
Chinese cuisine
chives
cloves
corn
couscous
curries
dips
eggplant
eggs and **egg yolks**
escarole
fennel
fiddlehead ferns
French cuisine
GINGER
Greek cuisine
greens, e.g., bitter, dandelion
herbs
Indian cuisine
Italian cuisine
kale
Latin American cuisines
leeks

legumes
LEMON, e.g., juice, zest
lentils
lettuce, e.g., romaine
Mexican cuisine
Middle Eastern cuisines
mint
mirin
MUSHROOMS, e.g., porcini
mustard, e.g., Dijon
noodles, Asian, e.g., pad thai
OIL, OLIVE
olives, e.g., kalamata
onions
orange
oregano
paprika
PARSLEY
PASTA, e.g., linguini, penne, spaghetti
peanuts
peas
pepper, e.g., black
pesto
pine nuts
pistou
pizza
POTATOES, e.g., mashed
purees

rosemary
saffron
sage
SALAD DRESSINGS, e.g.,
    vinaigrettes
salads
salt, e.g., sea
sauces, e.g., mole, skordalia, tzatziki
sesame oil
shallots
sorrel
SOUPS, e.g., garlic
sour cream
soy sauce
Spanish cuisine
spinach
spreads
squash, e.g., spaghetti, summer
stews
stir-fries
stock, vegetable
tahini
tamari
thyme
tofu
tomatillos
TOMATOES and **TOMATO
    SAUCE**
Turkish cuisine
turmeric
Vietnamese cuisine
vinegar, e.g., balsamic, red wine,
    rice wine
yams
yogurt
zucchini

GARLIC, BLACK

Flavor: salty/sweet/umami, with
earthy notes of balsamic vinegar,
chocolate, licorice, molasses,
syrup, tamarind, and/or truffles,
and a custardlike texture
Volume: quiet – moderate
What it is: aged, fermented
garlic
Brand: The Spice House
(thespicehouse.com)

Asian cuisines
basil
bell peppers, roasted
butter and brown butter
celery root
cheese, e.g., cream, Parmesan
chiles, e.g., milder
chives
dips
garlic
honey
kale
Korean cuisine
lemon
mushrooms
noodles, e.g., Asian
oil, olive
olives
parsley
pastas
pizza
potatoes
risottos
salad dressings
salads, e.g., potato
shallots
tapenades
tomatoes
vinegar, e.g., balsamic, white
    balsamic
wine

Flavor Affinities
black garlic + basil + olive oil
    + tomatoes + white balsamic
    vinegar

GARLIC, GREEN
(aka BABY GARLIC or
SPRING GARLIC)

Season: spring
Flavor: slightly sweet, with notes
of garlic and herbs
Volume: quiet – moderate
Possible substitute: scallions

aioli
artichokes

asparagus
baked goods, e.g., breads
basil
cheese, e.g., Parmesan
eggs, *e.g., frittatas, omelets*
garlic
gratins
leeks
lemon, e.g., juice, zest
oil, e.g., vegetable
parsley
pasta
pestos
pine nuts
pizza
potatoes, e.g., mashed
risottos
salad dressings
salads
sauces
soups
stir-fries

Flavor Affinities
green garlic + artichokes +
    balsamic vinegar + olive oil +
    parsley
green garlic + asparagus +
    Parmesan cheese + *pasta*
green garlic + basil + olive oil +
    Parmesan cheese + pine nuts
green garlic + leeks + potatoes

GARLIC SCAPES

Flavor: notes of garlic
Volume: quiet – moderate
What they are: flowering
shoots/stems of the garlic plant
Techniques: deep-fry, grill,
pickle, raw, sauté, steam
Botanical relatives: chives,
leeks, onions

almonds
basil
beans, green
bread
bruschetta

G

butter
celery
cheese, e.g., cream, **Parmesan,**
  ricotta
chickpeas
dill
EGGS, e.g., *frittatas, omelets*
garlic
greens, e.g., beet
hummus
lemon, e.g., juice, zest
lovage
mushrooms
nuts, e.g., almonds
oil, nut, e.g., walnut
OIL, OLIVE
parsley
pasta, e.g., *penne, spaghetti*
peanuts
pepper, black
PESTOS
pine nuts
potatoes
rice
sage
salad dressings
salads
salt, e.g., sea
soups, e.g., *garlic, leek, potato*
sour cream
spinach
stir-fries
stock, vegetable
sunflower seeds
teriyaki sauce
thyme
tomatoes
walnuts
wine, dry white

Flavor Affinities
garlic scapes + butter + thyme
garlic scapes + cream cheese +
  dill
garlic scapes + eggs +
  mushrooms
garlic scapes + nuts (e.g.,
  almonds, walnuts) + olive oil

● GHEE
Flavor: notes of caramel and/
or nuts, and a rich, smooth (and
often grainy) texture
Volume: quiet – moderate
What it is: Indian version of
clarified butter
What's healthful about it: less
fat and cholesterol than butter
because milk solids are removed
Tips: Can be used in higher-
temperature cooking (e.g., frying)
than butter can. Ghee lasts up to
six months when refrigerated.
Brand: Ancient Organics

breads
cardamom
chiles
cilantro
cloves
cumin
curry leaves
desserts
garlic
ginger
Indian cuisine
lemon
lentils
mint
potatoes
rice

● GINGER — IN GENERAL
Flavor: sour/sweet/hot;
aromatic, with pungent/spicy
notes of lemon and/or pepper,
and a juicy texture
Volume: moderate – **loud**
Nutritional profile: 86% carbs
/ 8% fat / 6% protein
Calories: 20 per ¼ cup (raw,
sliced)
Techniques: bake, candy, dry,
fresh, grate, pickle, raw, stir-fry

Tips: Fresh ginger is used more
often in savory Asian cuisines.
Dried ginger is used more often
in sweet baked goods, spice
blends, and slow-cooked dishes
(e.g., stews).
Botanical relatives:
cardamom, galangal, **turmeric**

African cuisines
agave nectar
almonds
apples and apple cider
apricots
ASIAN CUISINES
asparagus
baked goods, e.g., *breads, cakes,
  cookies, muffins, pies*
bananas
basil
beans, green
bell peppers, e.g., green, red
berries
beverages, e.g., *ales, beers, teas*
blueberries
bok choy
broccoli and broccolini
burdock
cabbage, e.g., red, savoy
cardamom
Caribbean cuisine
CARROTS
cashews
cauliflower
celery
cherries, e.g., tart
chickpeas
chiles, e.g., jalapeño; chili pepper
  flakes, chili powder
CHINESE CUISINE
chocolate, e.g., dark, white
cilantro
cinnamon
coconut and **coconut milk**
coriander
corn
cranberries
cream and *ice cream*

cumin
CURRIES, *esp. Asian or Indian*
deep-fried dishes, e.g., tofu,
    vegetables
desserts
dips
edamame
eggplant
fennel and fennel seeds
figs
fruit
garam masala
***GARLIC**
ginger ale
gingerbread
grains, whole, e.g., buckwheat
grapefruit
greens, e.g., Asian, collard
hiziki
hoisin sauce
honey

Flavor Affinities

ginger + agave nectar + *beverages* **+ soda water**
ginger + brown sugar + carrots + cinnamon
ginger + brown sugar + grapefruit
ginger + carrots + lemongrass
ginger + carrots + orange
ginger + chili powder + peanuts
ginger + cilantro + garlic + rice wine vinegar + sesame + soy sauce
ginger + citrus (e.g., **lemon**, lime) **+ honey**
ginger + garlic + mirin + sesame oil + soy sauce
ginger + garlic + olive oil + soy sauce
ginger + garlic + parsley
ginger + grapeseed oil + scallions + sherry vinegar + soy sauce
ginger + kombu + miso + tamari + tofu + wakame
ginger + lemongrass + peanuts
ginger + lime + mint
ginger + lime + pineapple + rum
ginger + maple syrup + yams
ginger + peanuts + yams
ginger + scallions + soy sauce
ginger + sesame (oil, seeds) + soy sauce

Dishes

Chilled Fruit Consommé with Lemon Ginger Sorbet and Compressed Melon
— The Golden Door Spa Café at The Boulders (Scottsdale, AZ)

ice cream
INDIAN CUISINE
Jamaican cuisine
Japanese cuisine
kiwi
kombu
leeks
LEMON
lemongrass
lentils
lime
lotus root
low-salt dishes
lychees
mango
maple syrup
marinades
melons, e.g., cantaloupe
mint
mirin
miso

molasses
Moroccan cuisine
mushrooms, e.g., shiitake
NOODLES, Asian, e.g., rice, soba,
    udon
oats and oatmeal
oil, e.g., grapeseed, sesame
okra
onions, e.g., green, spring
ORANGE, e.g., juice, zest
papaya
parsley
parsnips
passion fruit
pasta, e.g., orzo
peaches
peanuts
PEARS
peas
pickled ginger
pilafs
pineapple
plums
potatoes
pumpkin
raisins
rhubarb
RICE, e.g., basmati, brown
rum
sake
salad dressings
salt, e.g., kosher, sea
sauces, e.g., dipping, Kung Pao
scallions
seitan
sesame, e.g., oil, seeds
slaws, e.g., Asian
snow peas
SOUPS, e.g., Asian, hot-and-sour,
    sweet potato
Southeast Asian cuisines
SOY SAUCE
spinach
sprouts, e.g., bean, mung bean
squash, winter, e.g., butternut
stews, e.g., Moroccan
stir-fries
sugar, e.g., brown

sugar snap peas
sweet potatoes
tahini
tamari
tamarind
teas
TOFU, e.g., silken
tomatoes
turmeric
vegetables, e.g., Chinese, root
VINEGAR, e.g., apple cider,
  brown rice, champagne, red
  wine, **rice**, sherry, white wine
wasabi
water, soda
watercress
wheat berries
yams
yogurt
zucchini

"**Ginger** might not have been
a part of traditional Shojin
[Buddhist monk] cuisine, but I
can't imagine not using it — I
can't be restrained by the old
rules, which also prohibited tea
and alcohol. Ginger is a magical
ingredient with extraordinary
flavor and textures that goes well
with almost everything, and it
has healing properties that can
quickly and inexpensively heal my
wife's winter colds. . . . One of
my secrets when making pickled
ginger is instead of cooling the
ginger in the boiling pickling
liquid in the fridge, I'll drain it
and cool it with a fan, which
concentrates its flavor."
— RYOTA UESHIMA, KAJITSU
(NEW YORK CITY)

● **GINGER, POWDERED
(i.e., dried, ground)**
Flavor: sweet, with pungent
peppery notes
Volume: moderate – loud
Botanical relatives:
cardamom, turmeric

almonds
American cuisine
anise
apples
apricots
baked goods, *e.g., breads, cakes,
  cookies,* **gingerbread,** *gingersnaps*
braised dishes
carrots
chutneys
cinnamon
cloves
coconut
compotes, fruit
cumin
curries
dates
desserts
European cuisines
fruits
honey
lemon
mangoes
maple syrup
molasses
Moroccan cuisine
nutmeg
oranges
peaches
pumpkin
puddings
raisins
saffron
salad dressings
soups
squash, winter, e.g., butternut
stews

sugar, e.g., brown
sweet potatoes
tagines
turmeric
vanilla
vegetables, e.g., braised, root

GLUTEN
What it is: a protein composite
found in wheat and other grains

GLUTEN-FREE
Tip: Not all grains have gluten
(as wheat does). Gluten-free
grains include amaranth,
buckwheat, millet, quinoa, rice,
sorghum, teff, and wild rice.

GOJI BERRIES
[GOH-jee]
Season: summer (late) – autumn
Flavor: bitter/sour/sweet,
with notes of dried cherries,
cranberries, raisins, and/or wood,
and a chewy, grainy texture
Calories: 180 per half-cup
(dried)
Techniques: dry, raw
Tips: Look for berries that are
sweetened naturally. Soak dried
berries in water before adding to
smoothies.
Possible substitutes: dried
cranberries, raisins

almonds
apricots, e.g., dried
Asian cuisines
*baked goods, e.g., cookies, muffins,
  scones*
bananas
berries
cereals, hot breakfast
chocolate and **cacao nibs**
coconut

dates
energy bars
ginger
granola
lemon
lime
maple syrup
muesli
nuts, e.g., macadamia
oatmeal and oats
orange, e.g., juice, zest
pears
pomegranates and pomegranate
   juice
raspberries
salt, sea
sauces, e.g., fruit
seeds, e.g., flax, sesame,
   sunflower
smoothies
soups
stews
sweet potatoes
trail mix
walnuts
yogurt

Dishes

Raw Chocolate Ganache Tart:
Walnut Crust, Lemon Goji
Berry Preserve, Raspberry Coulis,
Pomegranate
— The Acorn (Vancouver)

Super Power Smoothie: Raspberry,
Strawberry, Banana, Mango,
Bee Pollen, Goji Berry, Sunwarrior
Protein, Orange Juice
— Pomegranate Café (Phoenix)

GRAINS, FAST-COOKING (see COUSCOUS and QUINOA)

[WHOLE] GRAINS AND CEREALS (see also COUSCOUS, WHOLE-WHEAT; POLENTA; QUINOA; RICE, BROWN; WHEAT BERRIES, etc.)

Tips: It's best to follow the specific directions on the package of grains you are using and to understand that timing can still vary depending on a number of factors, including heat level and heat conductivity of the pot you use. However, there are some general rules of thumb that may be helpful: Rinse grains before cooking. Combine grain with the cooking liquid (e.g., water, stock) in a heavy pot with a tight-fitting lid in the ratio indicated for the specific grain. Bring to a boil, add the grain, and bring to a boil again. Then reduce heat to low, cover the pot, and simmer for the cooking time indicated. Check to ensure that the desired tenderness has been achieved; then remove from heat and leave covered for 5 – 15 minutes before fluffing with a fork and serving.

Flavor Affinities

amaranth + brown rice + millet + rolled oats

"You can't overcook **grains** like **barley** or **farro**. Cooking farro risotto style as farrotto is common in Italy, and I'll cook barley the same way, so that it's chewy and toothy. But **bulgur** can overcook and turn mushy, so you really have to keep an eye on it. Grains are also great to dehydrate and powder for crusts . . . or to dry [dehydrate] and fry, to turn into 'Rice Krispies.' "
— JON DUBOIS, GREEN ZEBRA (CHICAGO)

"The secret is not to serve too large a portion of **grains** on a plate or people will get bored with them. I like to season grains with dried fruits, such as apricots, currants, figs, or apples and pears in the winter. Or I'll season them with powders and ashes [made from dehydrated vegetables]. Or I'll fill things like cabbage, chard, or kale with grains, and roll them up dolma-style — such as quinoa and dehydrated kimchi powder wrapped up in a cabbage leaf with dried figs or currants and pickled peppers or cucumbers. The overall impact it makes takes your brain on a ride."
— AARON WOO, NATURAL SELECTION (PORTLAND, OR)

GRAINS OF PARADISE

Flavor: bitter, with astringent, hot, and/or pungent notes of **black pepper**, butter, cardamom, chile, coriander, **flowers**, ginger, grapefruit zest, **lemon**, and/or nuts; and a crunchy texture
Volume: moderate – loud
Tip: Grind to a fine powder and add at the end of the cooking process.
Botanical relatives: cardamom
Possible substitute: black pepper
Brand: The Spice House (thespicehouse.com)

(North and West) African cuisines
allspice
apples
baked goods, e.g., cakes, pies
beer
cinnamon
cloves
coriander
couscous
cumin

eggplant
gin
ginger
lemon
lentils
Moroccan cuisine
nutmeg
okra
pepper, black
potatoes
pumpkin
ras el hanout
rice
rosemary
salad dressings
soups, e.g., butternut squash, lentil, potato
squash, e.g., butternut
stews
tomatoes
vegetables, root
vinegar
zucchini blossoms

● GRAPEFRUIT

Season: year-round, esp. **winter**
Flavor: sour, and ranges from bitter (e.g., white) to sweet (e.g., pink, red), with a very juicy texture
Volume: loud
What it is: a cross between an orange and a pomelo

Dishes

Avocado and Grapefruit Salad: Baby Spinach and Mixed Greens topped with Roasted and Marinated Shiitake Mushrooms, Daikon Radish, Fresh Grapefruit Segments, and Avocado tossed in a Ginger Miso Dressing
— Café Flora (Seattle)

Red Grapefruit Salad: Ruby Red Grapefruit, Avocado, Fennel, Arugula, Citrus Olive Oil, Marcona Almonds, and Farro
— Crossroads (Los Angeles)

Grapefruit with Frozen Yogurt and Mint
— Oxheart (Houston)

What's healthful about it:
antioxidants (with pink and red grapefruit delivering higher levels than white)
Nutritional profile: 90% carbs / 7% protein / 3% fat
Calories: 40 per ½ grapefruit (raw, white)
Protein: 1 gram
Techniques: bake (at 350°F for 10 minutes), broil, grill, raw
Botanical relatives: kumquat, lemon, lime, orange

agave nectar
artichokes, Jerusalem
arugula
AVOCADOS
bananas
beets
cabbage, e.g., napa
Campari
cashews
celery
celery root
cheese, e.g., feta, Parmesan
chicory
chiles and chili pepper flakes
cilantro
cinnamon
citrus fruits, other
coconut
compotes

coriander
drinks, e.g., sparkling wine cocktails
endive, Belgian
fennel
fromage blanc
ginger
granita
greens
hazelnuts
HONEY
ices
jícama
kale
kiwi
lemon
lime
maple sugar and **maple syrup**
mascarpone
melon
mint
mirin
mustard
oil, olive
oranges
parsley
passion fruit
pears
pineapple
pistachios
pomegranates
raspberries
rosemary
salad dressings
SALADS, e.g., fruit, green
salt, sea
sauces
scallions
smoothies
sorbets
soy sauce
strawberries
SUGAR, e.g., brown
tarragon
vanilla
vinegar, e.g., champagne, rice wine, sherry, white wine
vodka

walnuts
watercress
wine, e.g., sparkling
yogurt

Flavor Affinities
grapefruit + arugula + olive oil
grapefruit + arugula + hazelnuts
  + pomegranates
**grapefruit + avocado + Belgian
  endive/fennel / salad greens /
  watercress**
grapefruit + ginger + tarragon
grapefruit + *granita* + strawberries
grapefruit + honey + mint
grapefruit + maple syrup +
  strawberries
grapefruit juice + mirin + rice
  wine vinegar + soy sauce

• GRAPE LEAVES

Flavor: lemony, and a thick leafy
texture
Volume: quiet – moderate
Techniques: bake, blanch, boil,
grill, parboil, steam, stuff
Nutritional profile: 66% carbs
/ 19% fat / 15% protein
Calories: 15 per 1-cup serving
Protein: 1 gram

allspice
apricots, dried
beans
bulgur
CHEESE, e.g., Asiago, blue, **feta**,
  Fontina, **goat**, Gruyère, kasseri
cinnamon
currants
DILL
fennel
figs
garlic
GRAINS, e.g., quinoa, **RICE**
Greek cuisine
hazelnuts
Iraqi cuisine
Lebanese cuisine

LEMON, e.g., juice
lentils, e.g., red
MINT
mushrooms
nuts
oil, olive
onions, e.g., red, yellow
parsley
pepper, black
PINE NUTS
raisins
RICE, e.g., basmati, brown, long-
  grain
rosemary
scallions
soups, e.g., cabbage
stock, vegetable
*STUFFED GRAPE LEAVES, aka
  dolmades or dolmas (this region's
  answer to sushi!)*
thyme
tomatoes
Turkish cuisine
vinegar, e.g., balsamic
yogurt

Flavor Affinities
grape leaves + bulgur + dried
  apricots + lemon + mint
grape leaves + dill + garlic + **mint**
  + parsley + **rice** + yogurt
grape leaves + dill + lemon +
  mint + pine nuts + rice
grape leaves + feta cheese + *grill* +
  olive oil

• GRAPES (and
• GRAPE JUICE)

Season: summer – autumn
Flavor: sweet, with a very juicy
texture
Volume: quiet – moderate
Nutritional profile: 94% carbs
(high in sugar) / 4% protein /
2% fat
Calories: 65 per 1-cup serving
(raw, red or green)
Protein: 1 gram

Techniques: freeze, raw, roast
Tip: Opt for organic grapes.

almonds
apples and **apple juice**
arugula
bananas
basil
blueberries
Brussels sprouts
bulgur
cabbage, red
caramel
cardamom
carrots
celery
celery root
CHEESE, e.g., blue, Brie, cream,
  cow's milk, feta, fresh, goat,
  ricotta, soft, Taleggio
chocolate
cinnamon
cloves
cucumbers
desserts, e.g., tarts
endive, Belgian
farro
fennel and fennel seeds
figs
garlic
gazpacho, white
ginger
grains, e.g., brown rice, quinoa
grapefruit
greens, e.g., mesclun, salad
hazelnuts
honey
jícama
lemon, e.g., zest
lime
mango
mascarpone
melon
milk, almond
mint
nutmeg
nuts, e.g., almonds, walnuts
oil, e.g., grapeseed, **olive**, walnut

onions, e.g., red, sweet
orange
parsley
peanuts and peanut butter
pears
pecans
pizzas
raspberries
rice, e.g., brown
rosemary
rum
*salads, e.g., fruit, grain, green,
    vegetable*
salsas
salt
scallions
soups, e.g., fruit, white gazpacho
sour cream
sprouts, e.g., radish, sunflower
star anise
strawberries
sugar, e.g., brown

sumac
tomatoes
vanilla
verjus
vinegar, e.g., balsamic, sherry,
    white wine
WALNUTS
watercress
watermelon
wine
yogurt

Flavor Affinities
grapes + apples + bulgur + lemon
grapes + balsamic vinegar +
    ricotta cheese
grapes + cream cheese + ginger
grapes + endive + walnuts
grapes + feta cheese + hazelnuts
    + salad greens
grapes + feta cheese + lentils + mint
grapes + lemon + sugar

**GREEK CUISINE (see
also MEDITERRANEAN
CUISINES)**
allspice
anise seeds
baklava
basil
bay leaf
beans, e.g., gigante
bell peppers
cheese, e.g., feta, goat, halloumi,
    sheep's milk
cinnamon
cloves
dill
dolmades (stuffed grape leaves)
eggplant
eggs
fennel
figs
GARLIC
grape leaves

gyros, vegetarian, e.g., eggplant +
pita bread + tzatziki sauce
honey
kebabs
LEMON
mint
nutmeg
nuts
OIL, OLIVE
olives, e.g., kalamata
onions
OREGANO
parsley
phyllo dough
pine nuts
pita breads
potatoes
raisins
rice
salads, esp. mint-garnished
soups, e.g., bean
spanakopita, or spinach + cheese pie
spinach
stuffed grape leaves
thyme
tomatoes and tomato sauce
yogurt
zucchini

Flavor Affinities

artichokes + mint + potatoes +
   tomatoes
capers + cucumbers + feta cheese
   + kalamata olives + red onions
   + tomatoes
cheese + phyllo dough + spinach
cucumber + dill + garlic + yogurt
dill + lemon + olive oil
eggplant + garlic + olive oil
garlic + lemon + olive oil +
   oregano
gigante beans + garlic + onions +
   parsley + tomatoes

● **GREENS — IN GEN-
ERAL OR MIXED
(see also ARUGULA;
BOK CHOY; CAB-
BAGE; CHARD, SWISS;
GREENS, BEET; GREENS,
BITTER; GREENS,
COLLARD; GREENS,
DANDELION; GREENS,
SALAD; GREENS,
TURNIP; KALE; LETTUCE;
and SPINACH)**
What they are: green, leafy
vegetable
Techniques: blanch, boil,
braise, raw, sauté, steam, stir-fry
Tip: Cook quickly to retain
nutrients.

arugula
basil
beans, e.g., white
butter
cheese, e.g., Asiago, feta, goat,
   Monterey Jack, mozzarella,
   Parmesan, Swiss
chiles, chili pepper flakes, and
   chili pepper sauce
eggs, e.g., *frittatas, omelets, quiches*
GARLIC
ginger
grains, e.g., quinoa, rice, spelt
lemon
mushrooms
mustard
nuts, e.g., walnuts
OIL, OLIVE
onions, e.g., green, red
pastas
pepper, black
potatoes, e.g., new, red
salads
salt, e.g., kosher, sea
sandwiches
seeds, e.g., caraway, celery,
sesame
smoothies
soups, e.g., bean, lentil

soy sauce
stews
stock, vegetable
veggie burgers
VINEGAR, e.g., balsamic, red wine

"There are two ends of the
cooking spectrum you want to
concentrate on — one is high
heat and the other is low heat.
On high heat you want to cook
your vegetable higher and faster
than you normally would to get
that sear and caramelization and
let it stay crunchy on the inside
so you have a textural contrast.
Or go low and slow; that way
you get a crispy outside and a
dehydrated chew on the inside.
Home cooks know how to do
this with meat; they just need to
do it with vegetables. A good
example of a high-heat, fast-
cooking dish we do now is the
Chinese green choy sum.
It gets a nice crispiness, it is
barely cooked, and it gets tossed
in a bowl and wilts on itself.
If we cook the choy sum really
low, it turns into a flat,
dehydrated, crispy green."
— AMANDA COHEN, DIRT CANDY
(NEW YORK CITY)

● **GREENS, AMARANTH
(LEAVES/STEMS, aka
CALLALOO; see also
LAMB'S-QUARTER and
SPINACH)**
Season: summer
Flavor: slightly sweet, with
earthy notes of artichoke,
asparagus, beet greens, cabbage,
chard, kale, and/or **spinach**
Volume: quiet – moderate
Nutritional profile: 62% carbs
/ 26% protein / 12% fat
Calories: 5 per 1-cup serving (raw)

Protein: 1 gram
Techniques: braise, raw, sauté, steam, stir-fry

Tips: Choose young greens for most tender leaves. Prepare like spinach.

Possible substitutes: lamb's-quarter, **spinach**

basil
bell peppers, e.g., green, red
butter
Caribbean cuisines
celery root
cheese, e.g., cheddar, goat, ricotta, sharp, sheep's milk, Swiss
chiles, e.g., dried, Scotch bonnet
coconut milk
coriander
corn
cumin
curry powder and curry spices
eggs, e.g., *frittatas*, **quiches**
GARLIC
ginger
grains, e.g., bulgur, rice
Jamaican cuisine
kale
leeks
lemon, e.g., juice
lentils, e.g., red
lime
oil, e.g., corn, **olive**, peanut, sesame
okra
onions
parsley
plantains
rice
salads
salt
sandwiches
scallions
sesame seeds
shallots
soups
soy sauce
stews, e.g., *callaloo*
stir-fries

stock, vegetable
sweet potatoes
thyme
tomatoes
vinegar, e.g., apple cider
wine, dry white

Flavor Affinities
amaranth greens + coconut milk + okra
amaranth greens + sesame oil + sesame seeds + soy sauce

"One of the Jamaican women who work here introduced us to **callaloo** [amaranth greens] a few years ago. She brought us some seeds, and we discovered that it grows very easily. While it's traditionally served in soups and stews, we've also served it in quiches, and our customers are always intrigued by it."
— SELMA MIRIAM, FOUNDER OF BLOODROOT (BRIDGEPORT, CT)

GREENS, ASIAN (see BOK CHOY; BROCCOLI, CHINESE; CABBAGE, NAPA; MIZUNA, and TATSOI)

● GREENS, BEET
Season: summer – autumn
Flavor: bitter/slightly sweet, with earthy notes of cabbage and/ or spinach, and a tender texture
Volume: quieter (when young) – moderate (when older)
Nutritional profile: 71% carbs / 24% protein / 5% fat
Calories: 10 per 1-cup serving (raw)
Protein: 1 gram
Techniques: better cooked than raw; sauté, steam, wilt
Possible substitutes: chard, spinach

apples
beans, e.g., fava, fermented black, white
BEETS
cabbage
chard, e.g., rainbow
cheese, e.g., blue, chèvre, feta, goat, ricotta, ricotta salata
chickpeas
chili pepper flakes
chili, vegetarian
cinnamon
coconut milk *curries*
dill
eggs, e.g., *quiches*
figs
GARLIC
ginger
grains, e.g., buckwheat, bulgur
greens, other, e.g., chard or kale
hazelnuts
horseradish
kale, e.g., Tuscan
leeks
lemon
lentils
nutmeg
oil, olive
oranges
oregano
pastas
pecans
pine nuts
pizzas
potatoes
raisins
risottos
salad dressings, e.g., vinaigrettes
smoothies
SOUPS, e.g., beet, borscht, chickpea
stews
stock, vegetable
vinegar, e.g., balsamic, red wine, sherry
walnuts
yogurt

Flavor Affinities

beet greens + apples + cinnamon

beet greens + balsamic vinegar + beets

beet greens + garlic + olive oil

beet greens + walnuts + white beans

Dishes

Roasted Beetroot Steak and Pickled Beets: Baby Beet Greens, Red Watercress, Housemade Ricotta, and Beetroot Dressing
—The Peacock at the William Hotel (New York City)

● GREENS, BITTER (see GREENS, BEET; GREENS, COLLARD; GREENS, DANDELION; GREENS, MUSTARD; KALE, etc.)

● GREENS, COLLARD

Season: autumn – spring

Flavor: bitter/sweet, and sometimes hot, with earthy, pungent notes of cabbage, kale, and/or mustard, and a smooth texture

Volume: **moderate** (younger) – loud (older)

Nutritional profile: 68% carbs / 20% protein / 12% fat

Calories: 10 per 1-cup serving (raw, chopped)

Protein: 1 gram

Techniques: blanch, boil, braise, julienne, marinate, raw, **sauté** (3 – 5 minutes), shred, simmer (60 minutes, or until tender), **steam** (3 – 5 minutes), stew, stir-fry

Tips: Opt for organic collard greens. Remove stems; cut leaves into two-inch pieces. Best long-braised or simmered, to soften.

Botanical relatives: broccoli, Brussels sprouts, cabbage, cauliflower, horseradish, kale, kohlrabi, land cress, radishes, rutabagas, turnips, watercress

African cuisines

agave nectar

allspice

almonds and almond butter

apples, e.g., cider, juice

barley, e.g., pearl

bay leaf

BEANS, e.g., black, cannellini, navy, pinto, white

beer

bell peppers, red

BLACK-EYED PEAS

buckwheat

bulgur

butter

cabbage, e.g., green, red

cardamom

carrots

celery

chickpeas

chiles, e.g., chipotle, jalapeño; **chili pepper flakes**, **chili pepper sauce**, and chili powder

Dishes

Flourish Vegetable Pot Pie: Slow-Cooked Greens with Yogurt and Lemon
— Flourish Baking Company (Scarsdale, NY)

Maki: Raw Vegetables wrapped in Collard Greens, with Ponzu Sauce
— Mana Food Bar (Chicago)

Flavor Affinities

collard greens + apple cider vinegar + black-eyed peas

collard greens + apple cider vinegar + chili flakes + garlic

collard greens + chiles + garlic + lemon + olive oil

collard greens + chipotle peppers + liquid smoke

collard greens + citrus + raisins

collard greens + garlic + lemon

collard greens + garlic + olive oil + tamari

collard greens + garlic + tomatoes

collard greens + lemon juice + olive oil + rice

collard greens + rice vinegar + sesame oil + sesame seeds + soy sauce

collard greens + tomatoes + zucchini

cinnamon

citrus

cloves

coconut, e.g., butter, milk, water

collard wraps, i.e., stuffed with tofu, vegetables, etc.

corn bread

coriander

cream

cumin

curry powder and curry spices

dill

"dolmas"

dulse

Egyptian cuisine

Ethiopean cuisine

farro

GARLIC

ghee

ginger

grains

hazelnuts

Indian cuisine

Jamaican cuisine

kale

kamut

leeks

lemon, e.g., juice
lentils
liquid smoke
milk, coconut
mushrooms
mustard, Dijon
noodles, e.g., udon
nutmeg
OIL, e.g., canola, mustard, nut, olive, peanut (e.g., toasted), sesame (e.g., roasted)
olives
ONIONS, e.g., yellow
orange, e.g., juice
paprika, smoked
pasta, e.g., lasagna, whole-grain
peanuts and peanut butter
pepper, black
pine nuts
potatoes
quinoa
raisins
RICE, e.g., brown
salt, e.g., sea, smoked
scallions
seeds, e.g., hemp, sesame
sesame, e.g., oil, seeds
shallots
smoky-flavored foods, e.g., smoked paprika or tofu
soups, e.g., bean, lentil, sweet potato
sour cream
South American cuisines
SOUTHERN (U.S.) CUISINE
soy sauce
Spanish cuisine
squash, e.g., buttercup, kabocha
stews
stock, vegetable
stuffed collard greens
sushi rolls, vegetarian
sweet potatoes
tamari
tempeh
tofu
tomatoes
turmeric
vegetables, root

VINEGAR, e.g., apple cider, rice wheat berries
zucchini

"After cutting the spiny part out of the collard greens, soak them in lemon juice to soften them, and wrap them around ingredients for a breadless 'sandwich,' or use them instead of nori to make vegetarian maki rolls. Use a mandoline to slice vegetables to tuck inside."
— AMI BEACH, G-ZEN (BRANFORD, CT)

"When collard greens are cooked right, they have a buttery, melt-in-your-mouth texture. I like to cook them with a little olive oil, sliced garlic, a splash of water, and a pinch of salt, and to serve them as a side dish to Creole-style tempeh with mashed potatoes."
— MARK SHADLE, G-ZEN (BRANFORD, CT)

● GREENS, DANDELION

Season: spring – early autumn
Flavor: bitter/sour, with pungent, spicy notes of pepper, and a soft texture
Volume: moderate – **loud**
Nutritional profile: 72% carbs / 15% protein / 13% fat
Calories: 25 per 1-cup serving (raw, chopped)
Protein: 1 gram
Techniques: boil, blanch, braise, raw (when young), sauté, steam, stew (when older), wilt

Tips: Salt before cooking. Put in boiling water (never cold water, which "sets" the bitterness). Combine with other, milder vegetables or miso to neutralize bitterness. Use young greens (which are milder and more tender) in salads.

Botanical relatives: artichokes, chamomile, chicory, endive, lettuces (e.g., Bibb, iceberg, romaine), radicchio, salsify, tarragon
Possible substitutes: chard, kale, mustard greens, spinach

almonds
apples
avocado
basil
beans, e.g., cannellini
beets
butter
carrots
casseroles
cayenne
celery
CHEESE, e.g., cheddar, goat, Gorgonzola, Gruyère, mozzarella, Parmesan, sheep's milk
chickpeas
chiles, e.g., jalapeño; and chili pepper flakes
chives
croutons, e.g., whole-grain
curry powder
dill
eggs, e.g., frittatas, hard-boiled, quiches
endive
fennel
French cuisine
GARLIC
ginger
gratins
greens, other, e.g., milder, mustard
hazelnuts
hemp seeds
kale
LEMON, e.g., juice
lentils, e.g., red
lettuce, e.g., butter, romaine
maple syrup

Mediterranean cuisines
miso
mulberry
mushrooms, e.g., shiitake
mustard, e.g., Dijon
noodles, e.g., udon
oranges, e.g., blood
OIL, e.g., flaxseed, **OLIVE,**
  peanut, walnut
onions, e.g., raw, sliced
orange, e.g., juice
parsley
pasta, e.g., penne
peanuts
pepper, e.g., black
pine nuts
potatoes
raisins
risottos
sage
SALADS, e.g., dandelion, green,
  pasta
salt, e.g., sea
scallions
shallots
soups, e.g., vegetable
soy sauce
spinach

Dishes

Organic Dandelion and Avocado Salad, with Wasabi Dressing
— Hangawi (New York City)

Flavor Affinities
dandelion greens + almonds + blood oranges
dandelion greens + avocado + peanuts + wasabi
dandelion greens + balsamic vinegar + garlic + olive oil
dandelion greens + beets + goat cheese + sunflower seeds
dandelion greens + chickpeas + orange juice
dandelion greens + chili pepper flakes + garlic + olive oil
dandelion greens + cider vinegar + garlic + olive oil + soy sauce
dandelion greens + Dijon mustard + garlic + hard-boiled eggs + olive
  oil + Parmesan cheese
dandelion greens + garlic + lemon + mustard + **olive oil**
dandelion greens + garlic + lemon + olive oil + vinegar
dandelion greens + garlic + pine nuts
dandelion greens + olive oil + onions + vinegar

stews
stir-fries
strawberries
sunflower seeds
tarragon
tempeh
tomatoes, e.g., cherry
tomatoes, sun-dried
vegetables, milder
VINEGAR, e.g., **balsamic**, **cider,**
  raspberry, **red wine**, sherry
walnuts
wasabi

• GREENS, LEAFY (see GREENS, BITTER; and GREENS, SALAD)

What they are: bitter greens
and salad greens
Who says they're healthful:
The Center for Science in the
Public Interest's *Nutrition Action*
includes leafy greens on its "10
Best Foods" list, mentioning
"powerhouse greens" like collard
greens, kale, mustard greens,
spinach, Swiss chard, and turnip
greens.

• GREENS, MIZUNA

Season: spring – summer
Flavor: bitter, with pungent
notes of grass, mustard, and/or
pepper, and a crisp, tender texture
Volume: quiet (smaller leaves) –
loud (larger leaves)
Techniques: boil, braise, pickle,
raw, sauté, simmer, steam, stir-fry
Botanical relatives: coriander,
mustard, parsley

almonds
apples
arugula
asparagus
avocado
beans, e.g., fava
beets
carrots
celery
cheese, e.g., goat, pecorino
chestnuts
Chinese cuisine
chives
coriander
cranberries, dried
cucumbers
edamame
frisée
ginger
grains, e.g., quinoa
greens, milder salad
honey
Japanese cuisine
lemon
miso, e.g., dark, light
noodles, Asian, e.g., soba, somen
oil, e.g., olive, peanut, sesame
onions, green
orange, blood
pears, e.g., Asian
peas
plums
potatoes, e.g., new
radicchio
rice, e.g., brown

SALADS (esp. young leaves), e.g.,
    Asian, green, noodle
seeds, e.g., pumpkin, sesame
SESAME, e.g., oil, seeds
soups, e.g., Asian
soy sauce
STIR-FRIES (esp. older leaves)
tahini
tamari
tatsoi
tempeh
tofu
tomatoes
vinegar, e.g., balsamic, rice wine,
    sherry

Flavor Affinities
mizuna + almonds + plums
mizuna + avocado + tomato
mizuna + lemon + olive oil
**mizuna + rice wine vinegar +
    sesame oil + sesame paste +
    soy sauce**

• GREENS, MUSTARD

Season: winter – spring
Flavor: bitter/hot, with sharp
pungent/spicy notes of mustard
Volume: moderate/loud (when
young) – **loud/very loud** (when
older)
Nutritional profile: 69% carbs
/ 25% protein / 6% fat
Calories: 15 per 1-cup serving
(raw, chopped)
Protein: 2 grams
Techniques: boil, braise, grill,
puree, raw, sauté, simmer, steam,
stew, stir-fry, wilt

Tips: Put in boiling water
(never cold water, which "sets"
the bitterness). Combine with
miso or with other, milder-
tasting vegetables to neutralize
mustard greens' loudness.

Botanical relatives: cabbage
Possible substitutes: chard,
escarole, kale, spinach

African cuisines
Asian cuisines
beans, e.g., kidney
black-eyed peas
bread crumbs
capers
carrots
cashews
cayenne
celery
cheese, e.g., goat, Gouda
    (smoked), Parmesan, ricotta
chickpeas
chiles, e.g., jalapeño; chili pepper
    paste, chili pepper flakes and
    chili powder
Chinese cuisine
cumin
currants
curry powder
dill
eggs
farro
frisée
GARLIC
ginger
grains
gratins
greens, other, e.g., dandelion,
    milder (e.g., spinach)
Indian cuisine
Japanese cuisine
kale
lemon, e.g., juice
mango
millet
miso
mizuna
molasses
mushrooms
noodles, e.g., Asian, soba
OIL, e.g., chili, mustard, **OLIVE**,
    peanut, **sesame**, sunflower seed
olives
ONIONS, e.g., green, red, yellow
oranges
peanuts and **peanut butter**
pears

pepper, black
pine nuts
potatoes
raisins
rice
salads, e.g., pasta, potato
salt, e.g., sea
sandwiches
sauces
scallions
sesame seeds
shallots
SOUPS, e.g., bean
Southeast Asian cuisines
Southern (U.S.) cuisine
soy sauce
stews
stir-fries
stock, e.g., vegetable
sweet potatoes
tamari
thyme
tofu
tofu scramble
tomatoes
vegetables, milder and/or sweeter
VINEGAR, e.g., apple cider,
    balsamic, red wine, white wine
walnuts
wine, e.g., rice
Worcestershire sauce, vegetarian
yams

Flavor Affinities
mustard greens + capers + lemon
mustard greens + chiles + cumin
    + garlic + olive oil + vinegar
mustard greens + cider vinegar +
    molasses + peanuts
mustard greens + garlic + ginger
    + soy sauce
mustard greens + garlic + peanuts
mustard greens + lemon juice +
    olive oil + walnuts
mustard greens + onions +
    tomatoes
mustard greens + scallions +
    sesame oil + tamari

• GREENS, SALAD — IN GENERAL AND MIXED (e.g., MESCLUN) (see also ARUGULA, ENDIVE, ESCAROLE, FRISÉE, LETTUCE, MÂCHE, MIZUNA, RADICCHIO, SALAD DRESSINGS, SPINACH, WATERCRESS, etc.)

What they are: encompasses all greens that may be served raw in salads, including lettuces (which are almost always best served raw)
Note: The mix of salad greens known as "mesclun" may include several of the following: arugula + chervil + dandelion + endive + frisée + mizuna + mustard greens + oak leaf lettuce + mâche + radicchio + sorrel
Tip: Rinse well, and serve raw.

almonds
anise seeds
apples
avocados
basil
beets
blackberries
capers
celery
cheese, e.g., blue, Brie, goat, Gorgonzola
chervil
chives
cilantro
cranberries, dried
croutons

dill
fennel
garlic
hazelnuts
honey
lemon, e.g., juice
lentils
mâche
mangoes
marjoram
mint
mustard, e.g., Dijon, dry
nuts
oil, e.g., flaxseed, grapeseed, **olive**
onions, red
oranges, e.g., blood
parsley
pears
pepper, e.g., black
pine nuts
pistachios
potatoes, e.g., new
radishes
rice
SALADS, e.g., grain, green, potato
salt, e.g., sea
savory
sesame seeds
shallots
tamari
tarragon
thyme
tofu
veggie burgers
vinegar, e.g., balsamic, red wine, sherry, white wine
walnuts

Dishes

Orchard Salad: Mesclun Lettuces, Seasonal Fruit, Toasted Pecans, Dried Bing Cherries, and Sourdough Croutons, tossed in a Rosemary Vinaigrette
— Angelica Kitchen (New York City)

Mesclun Greens, Green Olives, Toasted Almonds, Lemon-Caper Vinaigrette
— True Bistro (Somerville, MA)

Flavor Affinities

mesclun greens + apples + celery + hazelnuts
mesclun greens + avocado + cilantro
mesclun greens + balsamic vinegar + garlic + mustard + olive oil
mesclun greens + blue cheese + pears
mesclun greens + goat cheese + pecans
mesclun greens + goat cheese + strawberries
mesclun greens + lentils + rice

• GREENS, TURNIP

Season: autumn – winter
Flavor: bitter, with hot notes of mustard greens
Volume: loud
Nutritional profile: 81% carbs / 11% protein / 8% fat
Calories: 20 per 1-cup serving (raw, chopped)
Protein: 1 gram
Techniques: blanch first, then **sauté** or steam; boil or braise older, tougher greens; otherwise, bake, sauté, wilt

apples
beans, e.g., pinto, white
black-eyed peas
bread crumbs
butter
cayenne
cheese, e.g., Parmesan, pecorino
chickpeas
chiles and **chili pepper flakes**
coconut and coconut milk
cream
cumin
curry powder
dashi
eggs
GARLIC
ginger

Dishes

Turnip Greens, Garlic, Chiles, Mint, and Pecorino
— Heirloom at the Study (New Haven, CT)

grains
lemon, e.g., juice, zest
lime
mint
miso
mushrooms, e.g., oyster
mustard, e.g., Dijon
noodles, Asian, e.g., somen
oil, olive
olives, e.g., black
onions
orange
parsley
pastas
pecans
potatoes
rice
saffron
salads
salt, e.g., kosher
"sausage"

sesame, e.g., oil, seeds
soups, e.g., bean, potato, root
    vegetable
Southern (U.S.) cuisine
soy sauce
stock, vegetable
sweet potatoes
tofu
tomatoes
turmeric
turnips
vinegar, e.g., apple cider
walnuts
wine, dry white

Flavor Affinities

turnip greens + garlic + lemon +
    olive oil + onions
turnip greens + *pasta* + white
    beans

GRILLING

Many vegetables and other plant-based foods are delicious when grilled, including these:

artichokes
asparagus
bell peppers
bok choy
breads
carrots
corn, e.g., on the cob (in husks)
eggplant
endive
fennel
garlic
kebabs, e.g., fruit, mushrooms, tofu,
    vegetables, etc.
leeks
mushrooms, e.g., portobello
onions
peaches
pineapple
pizzas
potatoes
quesadillas

rosemary
squash, e.g., summer
sweet potatoes
tofu
tomatoes
vegetables, root
zucchini

"I **grill** almost every vegetable —
radishes, kohlrabi, cabbage. Even
spinach, kale, and chard — I'll
put some olive oil and salt on
them, pile them up, and grill
them on high heat, flipping them
twice. Grilled beets are great,
although I'll parcook them for
about five minutes first, so they're
a little soft — and you can cook
parsnips and radishes the same
way."
— AMANDA COHEN, DIRT CANDY
(NEW YORK CITY)

● GRITS
What it is: grain — the coarsest
grind of dried corn
Nutritional profile: 89% carbs
/ 8% protein / 3% fat
Calories: 145 per 1-cup serving
(cooked with water)
Protein: 3 grams
Techniques: bake, boil (about
15 – 40 minutes), simmer

Tip: Look for coarse stone-
ground grits, which contain
bran and germ.

butter
cayenne
cereals, hot breakfast
chard

Dishes

Tortellini of Carolina Gold Rice Grits, Fall Vegetables, and Butternut Butter Sauce
— The Point (Saranac Lake, NY)

cheese, e.g., cheddar, Parmesan,
pecorino, ricotta salata
chiles, e.g., green; chili pepper
flakes and chili pepper sauce
cilantro
corn
cream
eggs
fruit
garlic
greens, e.g., collard
kale
maple syrup
mascarpone
milk
molasses
nutmeg
oil, olive
onions, e.g., sweet, yellow
paprika
pepper, e.g., black
polenta
porridges
puddings
salt, e.g., kosher, sea
scallions
seeds, sunflower
Southern (U.S.) cuisine
stock, e.g., corn, vegetable
vinegar, e.g., apple cider
watercress
wine, e.g., dry white

"Gary Jones of Le Manoir
aux Quat'Saisons served a
risotto ravioli that was
surprisingly delicious —
and inspired me to fill my
tortellini with **grits**."
— MARK LEVY, THE POINT
(SARANAC LAKE, NY)

● GUAVA, GUAVA JUICE
(or ● NECTAR),
and GUAVA PASTE
Season: summer – autumn
Flavor: **sweet**/sour, with floral
and fruity notes (apple, pear,
pineapple, and/or strawberry)
Volume: quiet (e.g., fresh) –
moderate (e.g., sweet guava paste)
Nutritional profile: 75% carbs
/ 13% protein / 12% fat
Calories: 115 per 1-cup serving
(raw)
Protein: 4 grams
Techniques: bake, juice, poach,
raw

apples
*baked goods, e.g., cakes, muffins,
tarts*
BANANAS
beverages, e.g., cocktails, juices
cashews
CHEESE, e.g., cream, farmer's,
goat, manchego, queso blanco
chili pepper sauce
chocolate, e.g., white
chutneys
cinnamon
citrus, e.g., lemon, lime, orange
cloves
coconut, coconut cream, and
coconut milk
compotes
cream
***desserts**, e.g., cakes, cheesecakes*
fruits, other tropical, e.g., kiwi,
mango, papaya, pineapple,
star fruit
ginger
greens, e.g., salad
hazelnuts
honey
Indian cuisine
jams and preserves
lemon
lime, e.g., zest

mangoes
mascarpone
mustard
nutmeg
nuts, e.g., cashews, macadamia
oil, olive
onions
orange
papayas
pears, e.g., Asian
phyllo dough
pineapple
plums
quince
raisins
rum
salads, e.g., fruit
sauces
smoothies
sorbets
South American cuisine
soy sauce
stock, vegetable
strawberries
sugar, e.g., brown
tamales
vanilla
vinegar, e.g., balsamic
wine, e.g., sparkling
yogurt, e.g., low-fat

Flavor Affinities
guava + cream cheese + sugar +
    tamales

● HAZELNUTS (aka FILBERTS)

Flavor: slightly salty/sweet,
with notes of butter (esp. when
roasted), coconut, cream, grass
(e.g., when raw), and/or smoke
(e.g., when roasted), and a crisp,
rich texture
Volume: quieter (e.g., raw) –
louder (e.g., roasted)
Nutritional profile: 81% fat /
11% carbs / 8% protein
Calories: 360 per ½ cup
(chopped)

Protein: 8 grams
Techniques: roast (275°F for
20 – 30 minutes), toast (350°F for
5 minutes)

almonds
apples
apricots, e.g., dried
artichokes
arugula
asparagus
*BAKED GOODS, e.g., biscotti,
    cakes, cookies, pies*
bananas
beans, e.g., green
beets
berries, e.g., blackberries,
    blueberries
Brussels sprouts
caramel
cauliflower
celery root
cereals, hot breakfast
CHEESE, e.g., blue, feta, **goat,**
    Gorgonzola, Gruyère,
    manchego, ricotta, Taleggio

Dishes

Hazelnut Caramel Bombe: Dark Chocolate Mousse, Hazelnut Praline, Chocolate Cake,
and Chocolate Glaze
— Portobello (Portland, OR)

Flavor Affinities

hazelnuts + apples + Brussels sprouts
hazelnuts + arugula + blue cheese + endive + radicchio
hazelnuts + asparagus + beets
hazelnuts + bananas + chocolate
hazelnuts + blue cheese + peaches
hazelnuts + brown sugar + cinnamon + pears
hazelnuts + caramel + dried apricots + chocolate
hazelnuts + feta cheese + grapes + salad greens
hazelnuts + figs + goat or ricotta cheese
hazelnuts + garlic + kale + sun-dried tomatoes
hazelnuts + goat cheese + pears
hazelnuts + goat cheese + raisins + spinach
hazelnuts + hazelnut oil + mandarin oranges + salad greens + vinegar
hazelnuts + mushrooms + parsley

cherries
CHOCOLATE, e.g., dark, white
chutneys
cinnamon
coffee and espresso
couscous
cranberries
cream and *ice cream*
***desserts**, e.g., crisps*
dukkah
eggplant
endive
fennel
figs
frisée
fruits, e.g., dried, fresh
granola
grapes
greens, bitter, e.g., beet
greens, salad, e.g., mesclun
honey, e.g., chestnut
ice cream
kale
leeks
lentils
lettuce

liqueurs, e.g., almond

loaves

maple syrup

meringue

mint

mushrooms, e.g., morel, wild

oil, e.g., hazelnut, orange

oranges, e.g., mandarin, e.g.,
   juice, zest

parsley

passion fruit

pastas

pâtés

peaches

PEARS

persimmons

pesto

pineapple

plums, dried

puddings

pumpkin

quinoa

radicchio

raisins

raspberries

rhubarb

risottos

rosemary

SALADS, e.g., fruit, green, spinach,
   tricolore

sauces, e.g., romesco

soups

Spanish cuisine

spinach

squash, winter, e.g., acorn,
   butternut

strawberries

stuffings

sugar, e.g., brown

sweet potatoes

toffee

tomatoes, sun-dried

trail bars

vanilla

veggie burgers

vinegar, e.g., balsamic,
   champagne, sherry, white wine

zucchini

HERBS, DRIED

Volume: typically louder than
their fresh versions, so adjust
accordingly

> **Tip:** Use dried herbs early in
> the cooking process, as they
> need time to reconstitute and
> release their flavor.

HIZIKI (aka HIJIKI)

[hee-ZEE-kee; hee-JEE-kee]

Flavor: salty, with notes of the
earth and/or sea, and a delicate
yet firm texture

Volume: moderate – **loud**

What it is: sea vegetable, with
the appearance of dried black
threads

Calories: 5 per ½-cup serving

Protein: 1 gram

Techniques: sauté, simmer
(about 30 – 40 minutes)

> **Tips:** Its grittiness requires it to
> be soaked (twice) in cold water
> for 10 minutes each time before
> use (discarding the gritty soak-
> ing water). Soaking will also
> tame its saltiness. Also, hiziki
> will expand fourfold, taking on
> the appearance of black angel
> hair pasta.

Asian cuisines

beans, e.g., green

bell peppers, e.g., red, yellow

bok choy

Bragg Liquid Aminos

brown rice syrup

burdock

cabbage, napa

CARROTS

casseroles

cayenne

Dishes

Cape Cod Cakes: Blend of Hiziki Seaweed, Tofu, and Herbs, served with Tartar Sauce
— V-Note (New York City)

celery

cheese, Parmesan

chiles, e.g., jalapeño

cilantro

citrus

corn

"crabcakes," vegetarian

edamame

eggplant

GARLIC

GINGER

grains

herbs

Japanese cuisine

leeks

lotus root

macrobiotic cuisine

mirin

miso, e.g., red

mushrooms, e.g., shiitake

NOODLES, ASIAN, e.g., brown
   rice or soba

oil, e.g., olive, sesame

onions, e.g., green, white, yellow

parsley

pâtés

peanuts

peas, green

rice, e.g., brown

salad dressings, e.g., miso

SALADS, e.g., green, noodle, sea
   vegetable

salt, sea

scallions

SESAME OIL

sesame seeds

shallots

SOUPS, e.g., miso

soybeans

SOY SAUCE

squash

stews

stir-fries

sugar, e.g., brown
sunflower seeds
tahini
tamari
tartar sauce
tempeh
TOFU
tomatoes, e.g., cherry
turnips
vegetables, esp. root, sweet
vinegar, e.g., **brown rice**, rice,
  umeboshi
water chestnuts
watercress
yams

Flavor Affinities
hiziki + brown rice + carrots +
  shiitake mushrooms
**hiziki + carrots + garlic + ginger +
  miso + sesame (oil, seeds)**
**hiziki + dashi + sesame oil +
  sesame seeds + soy sauce + tofu**
hiziki + garlic + ginger
hiziki + ginger + soy sauce
**hiziki + herbs + tartar sauce +
  tofu**
hiziki + rice vinegar + sesame
  (oil, seeds) + soy sauce
hiziki + sesame oil + tamari

● HOMINY

Flavor: notes of butter and corn,
with a chewy texture
Volume: quiet
What it is: dried corn kernels
that have had the germ and hull
removed

avocado
beans, e.g., Anasazi, pinto, red
bell peppers
carrots
casseroles
celery
cheese, e.g., goat, Monterey Jack,
  queso fresco

CHILES, e.g., dried red, fresh
  green, jalapeño; chili pepper
  sauce and chili powder
cilantro
corn
cumin
garlic
lime
Mexican cuisine
mushrooms, e.g., portobello
Native American cuisine
oil, e.g., olive, sesame, sunflower,
  vegetable
ONIONS, e.g., white
OREGANO, MEXICAN
pepper, black
POSOLE, vegetarian
pumpkin seeds
radishes
sage
SOUPS
Southwest (U.S.) cuisine
squash, butternut
STEWS
stock, vegetable
thyme
tomatillos
tomatoes

Flavor Affinities
hominy + chiles + cilantro +
  tomatillos
hominy + chiles + garlic + lime
hominy + chiles + onions +
  oregano

● HONEY —
IN GENERAL

Flavor: sweet to very sweet, with
astringent notes, and a thick,
syrupy texture
Volume: quieter (e.g., acacia
< clover) – louder (e.g., wildflower
< buckwheat)
Nutritional profile: 100%
carbs
Calories: 65 per tablespoon

Techniques: raw

Tip: As a general rule, the
darker the color of the honey,
the greater its nutritional value
(e.g., antioxidants, minerals,
vitamins).

Possible substitutes: agave
nectar, brown rice syrup, maple
syrup, molasses

apples
apricots
arugula
*baked goods, e.g., biscuits, breads,
  cakes, cookies, muffins*
bananas
beans, e.g., dried
beets
beverages, hot or iced, e.g., coffee, tea
*breakfast dishes, e.g., cereals, French
  toast, pancakes, toast, waffles*
butter
cardamom
carrots
CHEESE, e.g., blue, cream, goat,
  pecorino, **ricotta**
chestnuts
chiles, e.g., jalapeños
chocolate
cinnamon
citrus
cloves
coconut
couscous
cream
desserts, e.g., fruit
dips
fennel
FIGS
fruit, e.g., dried, fresh
ginger
grains, e.g., quinoa
granola
grapefruit
hazelnuts
lavender
LEMON, e.g., juice, zest

lentils
lime
marinades
mascarpone
melon, e.g., honeydew
mint
miso
MUSTARD, e.g., Dijon
nutmeg
NUTS, e.g., **almonds**, pecans,
   pistachios, **walnuts**
oats and oatmeal
orange, e.g., juice, zest
pears
pepper, black
plantains
plums
quince
quinoa
raisins
raspberries
rhubarb
rice
rosemary
salad dressings
salads, e.g., fruit, green
sandwiches, e.g., peanut butter
sauces, e.g., barbecue, peanut
seeds, e.g., pumpkin, sesame,
   sunflower
smoothies
soy sauce
spreads, e.g., for biscuits, breads
squash, winter, e.g., delicata
sugar, e.g., brown
tarragon
tofu
turnips
vanilla
vinegar, e.g., balsamic
yams
yogurt

Flavor Affinities
honey + almond + ricotta
honey + figs + ricotta
honey + ginger + lemon/lime

HONEY, VEGAN
(see also HONEY)
Flavor: sweet, with notes of
apples or apple blossoms, and the
texture of honey
What it is: vegan honey
substitute made from apples
Tip: Use 50/50 with agave
nectar.
Possible substitutes: agave
nectar, maple syrup
Brand: Bee Free Honee

"Bee-free **vegan honey** made from
a reduction of apples is one of the
most amazing products I've ever
come across. It looks and tastes
just like regular honey!"
— SHAWAIN WHYTE, CAFÉ BLOSSOM
(NEW YORK CITY)

HORSERADISH —
● PREPARED or ● FRESH
Season: summer – autumn
Flavor: bitter/very hot, with
pungent notes of mustard and/
or pepper
Volume: very loud
Techniques: grate, shred
Tips: Add just before serving.
Opt for white (not pink) horse-
radish.
Botanical relatives: broccoli,
Brussels sprouts, cabbage,
cauliflower, collard greens, kale,
kohlrabi, land cress, **mustard**,
radishes, rutabagas, turnips,
watercress

apples and applesauce
arugula
avocado
beans, e.g., adzuki, *baked beans*,
   green, *purees*
BEETS and beet juice
Bloody Marys
butter

---

cabbage
carrots
cauliflower
celery
cheese
chilled dishes
chives
cream
crème fraîche
cucumbers
dill
dips
eggs, e.g., hard-boiled
(Central and Northern) European
   cuisines
garlic
greens, bitter, e.g., beet
ketchup
lemon, e.g., juice, zest
lime, e.g., juice, zest
mascarpone
mayonnaise
miso, e.g., light
mushrooms, e.g., porcini
mustard, e.g., Dijon
oil, olive
onions
parsley
parsnips
pasta, e.g., gnocchi
peas, e.g., green
pepper, black
potatoes
ramps
relishes
rosemary
sage
salad dressings
salads, e.g., grain, macaroni, potato
salt
sandwiches
SAUCES, *e.g., creamy*
scallions
sorrel
SOUR CREAM
soy sauce
sugar, brown

tempeh
thyme
tofu, e.g., silken
tomatoes, tomato juice, and
 sun-dried tomatoes
vegetables, root
veggie burgers
VINEGAR, e.g., apple cider,
 balsamic, red wine, white wine
watercress
YOGURT
zucchini

Flavor Affinities

horseradish + apples + carrots
horseradish + beets + lemon
horseradish + beets + rosemary +
 yogurt
horseradish + bitter greens
 (e.g., arugula, sorrel) + potatoes
horseradish + carrots + parsnips
 + potatoes
horseradish + celery + tomato juice
horseradish + chives + yogurt
horseradish + vinegar + yogurt

HUCKLEBERRIES

Season: summer
Flavor: sour/sweet, with notes of
blueberries
Volume: moderate – loud
Nutritional profile: 94% carbs
/ 4% protein / 2% fat
Calories: 10 per 1-ounce serving
(raw)
Possible substitute:
blueberries

agave nectar
apples
bananas
buttermilk
cheese, cream, e.g., low-fat
cheesecake
cinnamon
coulis
crème fraîche
desserts, *e.g., cobblers, crisps, custards,*

*galettes, ice creams, panna
 cottas, pastries, pies,
 soufflés, tarts*
graham crackers
jams
lemons, e.g., Meyer
lime, e.g., juice
orange
pancakes, e.g., buckwheat
pears
pine nuts
puddings, e.g., bread
sugar
walnuts

HUITLACOCHE

[weet-lah-COH-chay]
Flavor: umami, with complex
earthy, pungent notes of corn,
meat, mushrooms, and/or smoke
Volume: quiet – moderate
What it is: a fungus that grows
on corn; known as corn smut or
"Mexican truffles"

avocado
Central American cuisines
cheese, e.g., cotija, goat, queso
 bianco
chiles
chiles rellenos
chocolate
cilantro
corn
crêpes
empanadas
epazote
garlic
ice cream
lettuce
lime
Mexican cuisine
mushrooms, e.g., wild
onions
quesadillas
soups
stews
sweet potatoes
tacos

Dishes

**Huitlacoche y Hongos: Just-Made Tortillas with Organic Otter Creek Cheddar,
Nichols Farm Huitlacoche, Local Woodland Mushrooms, and Herby Roasted
Tomatillo Salsa**
— Topolobampo (Chicago)

tamales
tortillas, e.g., corn
vanilla
zucchini blossoms

Flavor Affinities
huitlacoche + avocado + cheese +
  cilantro + mushrooms + onions
  + tortillas
huitlacoche + cheese + zucchini
  blossoms
huitlacoche + cilantro + corn +
  lime + lettuce + onions + tortillas

INDIAN CUISINE

Tip: India is considered the
world's leading country for
vegetarianism, which is
espoused by an estimated 20 –
42 percent of its population.

allspice
almonds
anise seeds
beans
breads, esp. in northern India
cardamom
cashews
cassia (or cinnamon)
cauliflower
cayenne
cheese, e.g., paneer
chickpeas
chiles
cilantro, esp. in southern India
cinnamon
cloves
coconut, esp. in desserts and
  southern India
coriander
cumin, esp. in northern India
CURRIES
**curry leaves, curry powder, and
  curry spices**
dosas
eggplant
fennel seeds
fenugreek

garam masala (Indian spice blend
  that often includes bay leaf, black
  pepper, cardamom, cassia/
  cinnamon, cloves, coriander,
  cumin, fennel, and/or nutmeg)
garlic, esp. in northern India
ghee (clarified butter)
ginger, esp. in northern India
herbs
lentils
mint
mustard seeds, esp. in southern
  India
nutmeg
oil, e.g., canola, grapeseed
onions
paprika
peas
pepper, e.g., black
pistachios, esp. in desserts
poppy seeds
potatoes
rice, basmati, esp. in southern
  India
saffron
sage
sauces, e.g., raita
SPICES
spinach
star anise
sugar, palm
tamarind, esp. in southern India
tomatoes
turmeric
vegetables, esp. in southern India
wheat, esp. in northern India
yogurt

INDONESIAN CUISINE
chiles
coconut
coriander
garlic
grilled dishes
lemongrass
molasses
noodles
peanuts and *peanut sauces*

pepper
rice
satays, i.e., skewers
seitan
soy sauce
spices, e.g., cloves, nutmeg,
  pepper
stir-fries
sugar, e.g., brown
tamarind
tempeh
vegetables

Flavor Affinities
chiles + garlic + lime + peanuts +
  soy sauce + sugar

● IRISH MOSS
Flavor: neutral, with a
gelatinous texture
Volume: quiet
What it is: sea vegetable, used
as a thickener (e.g., for desserts,
vegan cheeses)
Nutritional profile: 89% carbs
/ 8% protein / 3% fat
Calories: 15 per 1-ounce serving

Tips: Rinse *very* well (as it can
be sandy in its raw form), and
soak in cold water overnight or
longer before using.

almond milk
bananas
breads
cacao and chocolate
cheeses, vegan (e.g., nut-based)
cinnamon
coconut and **coconut milk**
*creams, dessert (e.g., vegan
  whipped)*
desserts, e.g., creamy, custards, flans,
  mousses, pies
ice creams
jams and jellies
salad dressings, creamy, e.g., ranch
smoothies
soups

stocks

tiramisu

vanilla

yogurt, vegan, e.g., nut-based

Flavor Affinities

Irish moss + almond milk + banana + cinnamon + vanilla

Irish moss + cacao nibs + coconut + coconut milk

Irish moss + garlic + hemp seeds + herbs + lemon juice

"We use **Irish moss** as a thickener more than agar-agar. It provides a better, creamier consistency, it sets beautifully, plus it's higher in nutritional value."
— CASSIE AND MARLENE TOLMAN, POMEGRANATE CAFÉ (PHOENIX, AZ)

ISRAELI CUISINE (see also MEDITERRANEAN CUISINES)

beans, e.g., fava

beets

bell peppers, red

bread, e.g. pita

cheese, e.g., feta

chickpeas, e.g. *hummus*

couscous, Israeli

dips

eggplant, e.g. *baba ghanoush*

falafel

harissa

honey

salads, e.g., cucumber, tabbouleh, tomato

sandwiches, e.g., sabich (eggplant + hard-boiled egg + hummus), seitan shawarma

tahini

tomatoes

yogurt, e.g., strained (aka *labneh*)

za'atar

ITALIAN CUISINE, NORTHERN

asparagus

basil

beans

butter

cheeses, e.g., Asiago, Fontina, Gorgonzola, Parmesan, Taleggio

cream and **cream-based sauces**

hazelnuts

lemon, e.g., juice

mascarpone

nuts

pasta, esp. fresh, richer egg-based or ribbon-shaped (e.g., *fettuccine, linguini, ravioli*), often combined with other starches, such as beans

pesto

pine nuts

polenta

potatoes

rice, e.g., Arborio, carnaroli; and *risottos*

rosemary

sage

sauces, e.g., cream-based

truffles, white

vinegar, esp. balsamic, wine

wine, e.g., Marsala, red, white

ITALIAN CUISINE, SOUTHERN

artichokes

basil

bell peppers

cheese, e.g., mozzarella, ricotta

chiles and chili pepper flakes

cinnamon

eggplant

fennel

garlic

herbs

marjoram

nutmeg

oil, olive

olives

oregano

pasta, esp. dried, tube-shaped, and served with tomato sauce

pizza, e.g., Neopolitan

raisins

sauces, e.g., red tomato-based

tomatoes and **tomato sauce**

wine

zucchini

● JACKFRUIT, UNRIPE GREEN

Season: summer

Flavor: neutral, with faint notes of apple, banana, lychee, mango, melon (e.g., cantaloupe), and/or pineapple; and the chewy, flaky, juicy, or meaty texture of dry pineapple, shredded chicken, or pulled pork

Volume: quiet

What it is: tropical fruit

Nutritional profile: 92% carbs / 5% protein / 3% fat

Calories: 155 per 1-cup serving (sliced, raw)

Protein: 2 grams

Technique: marinate

Tips: Look in Asian or Indian markets for *unripe* (aka green or young) jackfruit in cans (packed in brine, *not* sweet syrup!) or frozen (packed in brine). Chef Susan Feniger prefers using shredded and cooked jackfruit to processed faux meats in Street's vegan dishes such as baos and tacos. She has found that jackfruit takes on whatever flavors it's cooked with and even fools meat eaters. You'll typically want to rinse, drain, and shred before using; alternatively, cut into bite-sized triangles, as you would pineapple. Jackfruit is the world's largest tree fruit and can grow up to three feet long. Keep an eye out for products from Annie Ryu's Global Village Fruits.

Asian cuisines
bananas
barbecue dishes
barbecue sauce
bay leaf
bell peppers
biryani
butter or Earth Balance "butter"
carnitas
carrots
cashews
cauliflower
chiles, e.g., chipotle, green; and chili powder
chili, vegetarian
Chinese cuisine
cilantro
coconut milk
coriander
"crabcakes"
cumin
curries, e.g., *Indian, Thai*
desserts, i.e., made with ripe jackfruit
enchiladas
garam masala
garlic
ginger
gyros
Indian cuisine
Kaffir lime leaf
leeks
lemon, e.g., juice
lemongrass
lime, e.g., juice
Malaysian cuisine

molasses
mushrooms
nachos
oil, e.g., canola
onions, e.g., red, white
oregano
pasta
peas, green
potatoes
rice, e.g., basmati
sandwiches, e.g., baos, "pulled pork," "Reuben"
smoke, liquid
Southeast Asian cuisines
soy sauce
stews
stock, vegetable
tacos
tomatoes, tomato paste, and tomato sauce
tortillas, e.g., corn
turmeric
wine, e.g., dry

Flavor Affinities

jackfruit + barbecue sauce + liquid smoke + *"pulled pork"*
jackfruit + bell peppers + coconut milk + *curries* + curry paste + garlic + lemongrass
jackfruit + cilantro + onions + salsa + *tacos* + tortillas
jackfruit + coriander + cumin + *curries* + tomatoes + turmeric
jackfruit + coriander + *gyros* + lemon + oregano + *pita bread* + soy sauce + tzatziki

Dishes

Dum Biryani: A time-honored Mughal Rice Dish, slowly baked in a Handi Pot sealed with Naan Dough: Jackfruit, Potatoes, and whole Spices
— Tulsi (New York City)

"In eastern India, **jackfruit** is eaten ripe as a fruit, but in northern India it's more often eaten green [i.e., unripe] as a vegetable, where it's added to biryani."
— HEMANT MATHUR, TULSI (NEW YORK CITY)

JAGGERY
Flavor: sweet; aromatic, with notes of butter, caramel, maple syrup, and/or molasses
Volume: quiet – moderate
What it is: unrefined sugar made from cane or palm
Possible substitute: dark brown sugar

almonds
bananas
beverages, e.g., coffee, tea
breads
candies
cardamom
cashews
chickpeas
coconut milk
desserts, e.g., puddings
Indian cuisine
milk
peanuts
raisins
rice
syrups
yogurt

Flavor Affinities

jaggery + cardamom + cashews + coconut milk + raisins

JAMAICAN CUISINE (see also CARIBBEAN CUISINES)
avocados
beans, e.g., black, **red**
bell peppers
black-eyed peas

cabbage
carrots
cilantro
coconut and coconut milk
curries
garlic
ginger
greens, mustard
jerk dishes, e.g., tempeh, tofu,
   vegetables
onions
oranges
plantains
raisins
rice
spinach
stews
sweet potatoes
tomatoes

JAPANESE CUISINE
broccoli
broiled dishes
burdock root
carrots
chiles
daikon
DASHI
edamame
eggplant, Japanese
garlic
ginger
grilled dishes
gyoza
kelp
kinpira
kombu
mirin, i.e., rice wine
miso
MUSHROOMS, e.g., maitake,
   oyster, shiitake
noodles, Asian, e.g., ramen, soba
   udon
nori rolls, e.g., avocado, cucumber
pickled dishes
pineapple
poached dishes
RICE, e.g., black, brown, sushi

sauces, e.g., ponzu, teriyaki
scallions
sea vegetables, e.g., kelp, nori
sesame, e.g., oil, seeds
soups, e.g., miso
*****SOY SAUCE**
squash
steamed dishes
sweet potatoes
tea, e.g., green
tempura
vinegar, rice wine
wasabi
wine, rice, e.g., sake
yuzu
zucchini

Flavor Affinities
garlic + ginger + soy sauce
ginger + sake + soy sauce
ginger + scallions + soy sauce

• JÍCAMA
[HEE-kah-mah]
Season: winter – spring
Flavor: slightly sweet, with notes of water chestnuts, and crispy/crunchy and juicy texture
Volume: quiet
What it is: root vegetable
Nutritional profile: 93% carbs / 5% protein / 2% fat
Calories: 50 per 1-cup serving (raw, sliced)
Protein: 1 gram
Techniques: bake, boil, braise, fry, **raw**, sauté, shred, steam, stir-fry

Tips: Peel before using. Slice thinly and serve instead of chips with guacamole, hummus, or other dips.

Botanical relative: sweet potato

apples
arugula
AVOCADO
basil, e.g., Thai
beans, black
beans, green, e.g., haricots verts
beets
bell peppers, e.g., green, red
blackberries
broccoli
Brussels sprouts
cabbage, e.g., green, red
carrots
cayenne
Central American cuisines
chayote
chickpeas
*****CHILES**, e.g., jalapeño, serrano;
  chili pepper flakes and **chili
  powder**
CILANTRO
citrus
corn
crudités
CUCUMBERS
fruit
garlic
ginger
grapefruit

guacamole
horseradish
kumquats
lemon, e.g., juice
lemon, preserved
lettuce, mild, e.g., Bibb, butter,
  romaine
*****LIME**, e.g., juice
Malaysian cuisine
mangoes
melon
Mexican cuisine
millet
mint
mushrooms, e.g., button
mustard
noodles, e.g., rice
oil, e.g., chili, grapeseed, olive,
  peanut, sesame
olives
onions, e.g., green, red
ORANGES, e.g., fruit, juice
papaya
paprika
peanuts
pears
pecans
pepper, e.g., black, white
pineapple

pumpkin seeds
quinoa
radishes
relishes
rice
SALADS, e.g., fruit, green
salsas
salt
scallions
sesame, e.g., oil, seeds
SLAWS
South American cuisine
soy sauce
spinach
sprouts, e.g., sunflower
sugar
tacos
tangerines
tomatoes
vinaigrette
vinegar, e.g., balsamic, rice, white
  wine
watercress
watermelon
wheat berries
zucchini

Flavor Affinities

jícama + apples + zucchini
jícama + arugula + horseradish + mustard + red onions
jícama + avocado + cilantro + **citrus** (e.g., grapefruit, orange)
jícama + avocado + citrus (e.g., orange, grapefruit) + radishes
jícama + black beans + cucumbers + mint + rice wine vinegar
jícama + cayenne + cilantro + **lime** + onions + orange + **papaya**
jícama + cayenne + greens + lemon + **lime + papaya**
jícama + chili pepper flakes + lime + peanuts
JÍCAMA + CHILI POWDER + LIME JUICE + SALT
JÍCAMA + CILANTRO + ORANGE
jícama + cucumbers + lime
jícama + grapefruit + pecans + red cabbage + *salads*

Dishes

Jícama Street Snack: Jícama, Cucumber, Pineapple, Fresh Lime, Crushed Guajillo Chile
— Frontera Grill (Chicago)

J

JUICES (see also SMOOTHIES)

Technique Tips: We love our Champion juicer (as do many of the other experts interviewed for this book) and know others who are happy with their Omega juicers. Diane Forley of Flourish makes juice in her Vitamix, adding a little water and then straining the juice through a nut milk bag — and finds the cleanup even easier than with a juicer.

Flavor Tips: Avoid mixing kale with romaine, which ends up "tasting like mud," according to NYC's Blossom owner Pamela Elizabeth. To add a sweet note, mix green juices with agave nectar, beets, coconut water, dates, fruit, honey, or maple syrup.

"My favorite green **juice** is made from apples, celery, collard greens, kale, and lemon."
— DIANE FORLEY, FLOURISH (SCARSDALE, NEW YORK)

"My default morning **juice** is one made from cilantro, fennel, ginger, kale, lemon, pears, and pineapple."
— MATTHEW KENNEY, M.A.K.E. (SANTA MONICA)

"A dash of lemon juice is the best way to cut the 'fresh-mown grass' flavor of some of the stronger **green juices**. Even better is adding lemon juice, apple juice, and ginger."
— MARLENE TOLMAN, POMEGRANATE CAFÉ (PHOENIX)

JUNIPER BERRIES

Flavor: **bitter**/sour/sweet; aromatic, with astringent notes of gin, lemon, and/or pine resin
Volume: moderate – loud
Possible substitute: gin

apples
artichokes, Jerusalem
bay leaf
bread
butter
cabbage, e.g., red
caraway seeds
cheese
choucroute
eggs
fennel
garlic
gin
marinades
oil, olive
pastas
pepper, black
pickles
potatoes
rice

rosemary
sage
sauerkraut
squash, winter
stuffings
sweet potatoes
vegetables, root
vinegar

Flavor Affinities
juniper berries + apples + fennel
juniper berries + garlic + potatoes

KAFFIR LIME and KAFFIR LIME LEAVES

Flavor: bitter/**sour**, and aromatic, with astringent or pungent notes of citrus, flowers, and/or lemon; and a chewy texture
Volume: moderate – **loud**
What it is: Southeast Asian citrus fruit
Technique: stir-fry
Tips: While also used for its juice and zest, this fruit is especially valued for its aromatic leaves.
Possible substitute: lime zest

apples, e.g., juice
Asian cuisines
Balinese cuisine
basil, e.g., Thai
Cambodian cuisine
carrots
chiles (esp. Thai) and **chili pepper paste**
chili, vegetarian
cilantro
coconut and **coconut milk**
corn
cucumbers
CURRIES
custards
drinks
fruits, tropical
galangal
garlic

ginger
Indian cuisine
Indonesian cuisine
lemongrass
lime, e.g., juice
Malaysian cuisine
mangoes
marinades
mint
mushrooms
noodles, e.g., Asian
okra
pears, e.g., Asian or prickly
"pestos"
rice
salad dressings
salads, e.g., Thai, tomato
sauces
sesame, e.g., seeds
SOUPS, e.g., coconut, hot-and-sour, Thai
SOUTHEAST ASIAN CUISINES
star anise
stews
stir-fries
stocks, e.g., vegetable
sugar
tamarind
THAI CUISINE
turmeric
vegetables, e.g., green

Flavor Affinities
Kaffir lime leaf + carrots + lemongrass + *soups*
Kaffir lime leaf + coconut milk + galangal + lemongrass
Kaffir lime leaf + coconut milk + peanuts + tofu
Kaffir lime leaf + ginger + lemongrass + lime
Kaffir lime leaf + rice + turmeric

● KALE

Season: autumn – spring
Flavor: bitter/sweet (esp. in winter), with pungent notes of cabbage, and a rather tough texture

Volume: quiet – **moderate**
What it is: leafy, green vegetable
Nutritional profile: 72% carbs / 16% protein / 12% fat
Calories: 35 per 1-cup serving (raw, chopped)
Protein: 2 grams
Techniques: blanch, boil (4 – 5 minutes), braise, grill, long cooking, marinate, parboil, puree, raw, sauté (about 8 minutes over medium heat), steam (4 – 5 minutes), stew, stir-fry

Tips: Opt for organic kale. Many kale aficionados prefer the variety known as black kale (aka dinosaur kale or Tuscan kale), for its greater flavor complexity and silky texture. Macerate (and marinate) raw kale in Dijon mustard to flavor it and soften its texture.

Botanical relatives: broccoli, Brussels sprouts, cabbage, cauliflower, collard greens, horseradish, kohlrabi, land cress, radishes, rutabagas, turnips, watercress

almonds
anise
apples
arame
arugula
avocados
barley
basil
BEANS, e.g., adzuki, cranberry, green, kidney, mung, red, **white**
beets
bell peppers, e.g., red, esp. grilled
black-eyed peas
bok choy
bread crumbs, e.g., whole-grain
Brussels sprouts
bulgur
butter, brown
cabbage, e.g., red
capers
caraway seeds
carrots
cashews
casseroles
cauliflower
cayenne
celery
celery root
chard
CHEESE, e.g., **cheddar**, cottage, **feta**, goat, Gruyère, mozzarella, **PARMESAN, pecorino,** provolone, ricotta, ricotta salata, Romano, Swiss, vegan
cherries, dried
chestnuts
chickpeas
CHILES, e.g., chipotle, dried red, poblano, serrano; **chili paste, chili pepper flakes,** and chili pepper sauce
chips, e.g., dehydrated (not fried)
chives
cilantro
coconut milk
corn
cranberries, dried
cream

K

Flavor Affinities

kale + apples + vinegar (e.g, balsamic, cider) + walnuts

kale + avocado + dried apricots + lemon + orange + pistachios + raisins + soy sauce

kale + avocado + mushrooms + red onions

kale + balsamic vinegar + beets + feta cheese + walnuts

kale + balsamic vinegar + oranges + pistachios + tomatoes

kale + basil + noodles + sesame sauce

kale + beets + walnuts

kale + brown rice + garlic + ginger + soy sauce

kale + butternut squash + *risotto* + tomatoes

kale + capers + Parmesan cheese + *pasta*

kale + cheese (e.g., cheddar) + **fruit** (e.g., apples) + **nuts** (e.g., almonds)

kale + chickpeas + feta cheese + lemon

kale + chickpeas + mushrooms

kale + chickpeas + Parmesan cheese + *soups*

kale + chiles + garlic + ginger

kale + chili flakes + garlic + olive oil + Parmesan cheese + pine nuts

kale + chili paste + egg + garlic + potatoes

kale + flaxseed oil + lemon juice + tamari

kale + garlic + hard-boiled egg + lemon + Parmesan cheese

KALE + GARLIC + LEMON

KALE + GARLIC + LEMON + OLIVE OIL

kale + garlic + lemon + olive oil + pine nuts

kale + garlic + olive oil + Parmesan cheese + red wine vinegar

kale + garlic + sesame oil/seeds + soy sauce + vinegar

kale + garlic + shiitake mushrooms

kale + garlic + soy sauce

kale + ginger + tahini

kale + grapefruit + red onions

kale + miso + sesame seeds + tofu + walnuts

kale + olive oil + olives + *pasta* + pine nuts

kale + olive oil + onions + orange + raisins

kale + rosemary + white beans

cumin
curries
dates
dill
dulse
eggs, e.g., *frittatas*, hard-boiled, *omelets*, poached, *quiches*
escarole
farro
fennel seeds
GARLIC
garlic scapes
ginger

grapefruit
gratins
greens, other, e.g., collard, dandelion, mustard
juices
kombu
leeks
LEMON, e.g., juice, zest
lentils
maple syrup
mint
miso
mizuna

MUSHROOMS, e.g., brown, porcini, portobello, shiitake
mustard, e.g., Dijon
noodles, Asian, e.g., soba, udon
nori
nuts
OIL, e.g., canola, **flaxseed**, grapeseed, nut, **OLIVE, sesame**, vegetable
olives, e.g., black
ONIONS, e.g., caramelized, **RED**, Spanish, spring, white, yellow
oranges, e.g., juice
oregano
papaya, e.g., green
paprika, e.g., smoked
parsley
pastas, e.g., lasagna
peanuts
pecans
pepper, black
pestos
pine nuts
pistachios
pizza
polenta
Portuguese cuisine
POTATOES
purees
quinoa
radicchio
radishes
raisins, e.g., brown, yellow
RICE, e.g., Arborio, **brown**, wild
risottos
rosemary
SALADS
SALT, e.g., kosher, pink, sea, smoked
savory
scallions
sea vegetables
seeds, e.g., **hemp**, pumpkin, **sesame**
sesame, e.g., sauce, seeds
shallots
slaws
smoothies

Dishes

Marinated Kale Salad: Chopped Marinated Kale, Olives, Avocado, Walnuts, and Creamy Garlic Dulse Dressing
— 118 Degrees (California)

Kale Salad with Lemon, Serrano Chiles, and Mint
— ABC Kitchen (New York City)

Chiffonade of Kale with Miso-Marinated Tofu Feta, Diced Sun-Dried Tomatoes, and Toasted Walnuts, dressed with Olive Oil, Lemon, and Garlic
— Angelica Kitchen (New York City)

Thai Me Up: An All-Raw Entree: Delicate strands of Daikon Radish, Butternut Squash, and Carrot, on a bed of Garlic-Lemon Marinated Kale, dressed with Thai Tahini Sauce
— Angelica Kitchen (New York City)

Tuscan Kale Salad: Dried Cranberry, Pine Nut, Pecorino Romano
— Boulud Sud (New York City)

The Best Kale Salad: Baby Kale, Sunflower Seed Tahini, Avocado, Green Apples, Toasted Sunflower Seeds, Smoked Sea Salt
— The Butcher's Daughter (New York City)

Spicy Kale Caesar Salad: Baby Kale, Avocado, Almond Parmesan, Toasted Almonds, Crispy Shallots, and 7-Grain Croutons
— The Butcher's Daughter (New York City)

Kale and Radicchio Salad: Candied Walnut, Grapes, Shaved Pecorino, Sherry Vinaigrette
— Café Boulud (New York City)

Kale Spanakopita: Harissa Spiced Smoked Tomato Fondu / Mint Oil
— Crossroads (Los Angeles)

Red Chile Kale: Local Black Kale, Guajillo Chile Sauce, Local Potatoes, Wood-Grilled Onions, Anejo Cheese
— Frontera Grill (Chicago)

Raw Kale and Apples Salad: Marinated Kale, Apples, Red Cabbage, and Shaved Fennel tossed in a Cucumber Mint Dressing, topped with Beet Curls
— Great Sage (Clarksville, MD)

Grilled Spicy Kale: Chili, Garlic, Local Sunny Egg
— Hotel Fauchère (Milford, PA)

Warm Kale Salad, Avocado, Corn Chips, Spicy Carrots, Chipotle Dressing
— M.A.K.E. (Santa Monica)

Kale Salad with Basil, Almonds, Mango Pickle with Tahini Dressing and Sesame Wafer
— Oleana (Cambridge, MA)

Smoky Kale with Spanish Almonds, Smoked Tofu, and Roasted Garlic
— Plum Bistro (Seattle)

Raw Kale Salad with Ginger Oil, Tamari, Raw Tofu, Seaweed, and Lime Juice
— Plum Bistro (Seattle)

Rennie's Peanut-Kale Salad: Hearty Kale, Carrots, Butternut Squash, and Red Peppers, in a Peanut-Cider Marinade
— Seva (Ann Arbor, MI)

Tuscan Black Kale, tossed with Lemon Juice, Olive Oil, Garlic, Chili Pepper Flakes, Grated Pecorino Tuscano Cheese, and Bread Crumbs
— True Food Kitchen (Phoenix)

snow peas

SOUPS, e.g., bean, kale, minestrone, potato, vegetable, white bean

soy sauce

spelt

spinach

squash, summer and esp. winter, e.g., butternut, delicata, kabocha

stews, e.g., barley, winter

stir-fries

stock, vegetable

stuffings

sunflower seeds

sweet potatoes

tahini

tamari

thyme

tofu

tomatoes

turnips

VINEGAR, e.g., apple cider, **BALSAMIC, brown rice,** red wine, sherry, umeboshi

walnuts

yogurt

yuca

"**Kale** isn't a summer crop, but there's so much demand for it that it's served year-round. In the summer, the hot sun can make it more bitter and tougher, so it's less of a salad green and more of a braising green, requiring longer cooking to soften it."
— PAM BROWN, GARDEN CAFÉ (WOODSTOCK, NY)

"If I'm making a **kale** salad, I'll massage the kale with oil and maybe Dijon mustard. I want a combination of acid, oil, and salt."
— AMANDA COHEN, DIRT CANDY (NEW YORK CITY)

"I love serving charred **kale** with smoked tofu, which I'll mince like bacon bits and let provide the same kind of smoky accent."
— MAKINI HOWELL, PLUM BISTRO (SEATTLE)

"I love **kale** — and was an early adapter. I've only eaten it raw over the past couple of years. Before that, I preferred it braised, or sautéed with garlic and olive oil, or added to pasta along with feta cheese and pine nuts."
— MOLLIE KATZEN, AUTHOR OF *THE MOOSEWOOD COOKBOOK* AND *THE HEART OF THE PLATE*

"We go through crates and crates of **kale** every week, and always prefer the less bitter, more refined blue-green Tuscan kale over regular kale, which is much tougher. With either kale, we'll marinate it in garlic, lemon juice, and olive oil to soften it."
— CASSIE AND MARLENE TOLMAN, POMEGRANATE CAFÉ (PHOENIX)

"I'll use my hands to massage avocado into **kale** leaves, and season them with salt and pepper and lemon juice."
— SHAWAIN WHYTE, CAFÉ BLOSSOM (NEW YORK CITY)

● KALE, BLACK (aka CAVOLO NERO, DINOSAUR KALE, LACINATO KALE, or TUSCAN KALE)

Flavor: slightly sweet (and less bitter), with more flavor complexity and a silkier texture than green kale

Volume: quieter than regular kale

almonds

beans, e.g., borlotti, white

bread crumbs, e.g., whole-wheat

cheese, e.g., Parmesan, pecorino

chestnuts

chili pepper flakes

croutons, whole-grain

garlic

Italian cuisine, esp. Tuscan

lemon juice

millet

mushrooms, e.g., porcini, portobello

oil, olive

pastas, e.g., lasagna

potatoes

risottos

sage

salt

soups

tomatoes

vinegar, red wine

Flavor Affinities

black kale + almonds + **garlic** + **olive oil**

black kale + chili pepper flakes + **garlic** + lemon + **olive oil** + pecorino

black kale + **garlic** + new potatoes + **olive oil**

black kale + potatoes + sage

● KAMUT
[kah-MOOT]

Flavor: slightly sweet, with rich notes of butter and/or nuts, and a rich, chewy texture

Volume: quiet – moderate

What it is: a whole-grain wheat, aka Khorasan wheat

Gluten-free: no

Nutritional profile: 79% carbs / 16% protein / 5% fats

Calories: 250 per 1-cup serving (cooked)

Protein: 11 grams

Techniques: pressure-cook, slow cook, steam

Timing: Cook presoaked kamut about 15 – 20 minutes, covered; unsoaked, it can take up to 2 hours to become tender.

Ratio: 1:4 (1 cup kamut to 4 cups cooking liquid)

Botanical relatives: barley, corn, rye, spelt, triticale, wheat

almonds
apples and apple juice
asparagus
avocado
baked goods, e.g., breads
basil
bay leaf
beans, e.g., kidney, lima
beets
bell peppers, e.g., red, yellow
broccoli and broccoli rabe
butter
buttermilk
cabbage, e.g., savoy
carrots
cashews
celery
celery root
cereals, hot breakfast
cheese, e.g., feta, goat, Parmesan
chervil
chickpeas
chili pepper flakes
chili, vegetarian
chives
cilantro
cinnamon
coriander
cumin

dill
escarole
fennel
fruit, dried, e.g., apricots, cranberries
GARLIC
ginger
grains, other, e.g., barley, quinoa, rice
honey
kefir
lemon, e.g., juice, zest
lentils, e.g., green
lime
lovage
marjoram
mushrooms, e.g., maitake, oyster
mustard, e.g., Dijon
nuts
oil, e.g., avocado, nut, **olive**
olives, e.g., kalamata
ONIONS, e.g., green, red
oranges
PARSLEY
parsnips
pecans
pepper, black
PILAFS
pizzas
pomegranates
raisins
rice, e.g., wild
risottos
sage
SALADS, e.g., grain, green, tomato, vegetable
salt, sea
scallions
SOUPS, e.g., minestrone

soy sauce
spinach
squash, e.g., winter, e.g., acorn
stews
stock, e.g., vegetable
stuffings
sugar snap peas
tabbouleh
thyme
tomatoes, tomato paste, and tomato puree
tomatoes, sun-dried
vanilla
vegetables, root
veggie burgers
vinegar, e.g., balsamic, brown rice, cider, wine
watercress
yogurt

Flavor Affinities

kamut + apples + pecans + vanilla

kamut + dried cranberries + winter squash

kamut + kidney beans + mushrooms

KANTEN

What it is: a firm, opaque, gelatin-like dessert made with fruit juice (and often served with fruit), agar-agar, and kuzu

Ratio: 1 quart fruit juice (e.g., apple) + 4 tablespoons agar flakes + 2 tablespoons kuzu

Tips: Try substituting ginger or green tea for fruit juice. Serve with cashew cream or whipped cream and/or fruit. Vary kanten by the season:
autumn: cranberries + pears
winter: adzuki beans + chestnuts
spring: berries + lemon
summer: apples + peaches

Try making kanten with the following fruits:

Dishes

Winter Squash Kamut Risotto: Grilled Maitake Mushrooms, Cashew Cream, Fresh Shelling Beans, Roasted Blue Banana Squash, Braised Fennel and Leek, Fall Greens, Fried Capers, Lemon Zest, Porcini Oil, and Squash Tempura
— Millennium (San Francisco)

apples and **APPLE JUICE**
berries, e.g., blueberries,
  raspberries, strawberries
cherries and cherry juice
citrus, e.g., grapefruit, lemon
cranberries and cranberry juice
mangoes and mango juice
melons and melon juice
oranges, e.g., mandarins, and
  orange juice
peaches and peach juice
pears and **pear juice**
pomegranates and pomegranate
  juice
yuzu and yuzu juice

● **KASHA (aka TOASTED BUCKWHEAT GROATS; see also BUCKWHEAT)**

Flavor: slightly bitter, with earthy notes of nuts and toast, and a crunchy texture
Volume: loud
What it is: whole grain (toasted buckwheat groats)
Nutritional profile: 82% carbs / 12% protein / 6% fat
Calories: 155 per 1-cup serving (cooked)
Protein: 6 grams
Timing: Cook about 15 minutes, covered; let stand 10 minutes before serving.
Ratio: 1:2 (1 cup kasha to 2 cups cooking liquid)
Botanical relative: rhubarb

apples
beans, green

Dishes

The Butcher's Burger: Kasha Portobello Burger, Cashew Cheddar Cheese, Bibb Lettuce, Heirloom Tomatoes, Pickles and Special Sauce, served with Roasted Potato Wedges and Housemade Ketchup
— The Butcher's Daughter (New York City)

beets
bell peppers
cabbage
carrots
casseroles
cauliflower
celery
chickpeas
chili pepper paste
corn
croquettes
cucumbers
dates
DILL
Eastern European cuisines
eggs, e.g., hard-boiled and grated
garlic
gravies, e.g., mushroom
jícama
kale
leeks
lemon, e.g., juice
lentils, e.g., red
mint
MUSHROOMS, e.g., portobello,
  shiitake
oil, e.g., olive, vegetable
onions
oranges
peas, split
parsley
PASTA, whole-grain, e.g.,
  FARFALLE
pepper, black
pilafs
pistachios
rice, brown
Russian cuisine
salads, e.g., corn, grain

salt, sea
scallions
SOUPS, e.g., beet, cabbage, lentil,
  mushroom, split pea, vegetable
soy sauce
spinach
squash, acorn
stews
stock, vegetable
stuffed vegetables, e.g., cabbage,
  squash, tomatoes
stuffings
sunflower seeds
tofu
tomatoes
varnishkes, i.e., kasha + farfalle
vegetables, root
veggie burgers
vinegar, e.g., balsamic
walnuts
watercress
yogurt and frozen yogurt (e.g., as
  a topping)
zucchini

Flavor Affinities

kasha + dates + pistachios
kasha + dill + mushrooms
kasha + gravy + mushrooms +
  onions
kasha + onions + *pasta* +
  watercress

"I love **kasha** in salads, where its earthy flavor is balanced nicely by the sweetness of corn. Not only is it great in stuffed cabbage and pilafs, but I like it as croquettes: I'll make them from kasha and mashed potatoes, browning them in a skillet, and serving them with a sauce or just some caramelized onions."
— PAM BROWN, GARDEN CAFÉ (WOODSTOCK, NY)

• KELP, KELP GRANULES, and KELP POWDER (see also ARAME, KOMBU, SEA VEGETABLES, and WAKAME)

Flavor: salty, with notes of the sea
Volume: quiet/moderate (e.g., powder) – moderate/loud (e.g., granules)
What it is: a family of sea vegetables
Nutritional profile: 79% carbs / 11% fat / 10% protein
Calories: 5 per 2-tablespoon serving (raw)

Tip: Season mashed chickpeas or tofu with kelp powder to give mock tuna salad a seafood-like flavor.

almonds, e.g., raw
barley
beans
bonito flakes, dried
carrots
chickpeas
chips, e.g., deep-fried
citrus, e.g., lemon, lime
"crabcakes," meatless
daikon
DASHI
"fish filets" (i.e., with tofu)
garlic
ginger
grains
Japanese cuisine
kimchi
lemon
lettuces, e.g., romaine
lime
mirin
miso
mushrooms, e.g., oyster
nutritional yeast
oil, e.g., canola
onions
pepper, black

popcorn
potatoes
rice, e.g., sushi
salad dressings
salads, e.g., mock tuna
sauces, e.g., ponzu
sesame, e.g., oil, seeds
soups and chowders, e.g., oyster mushroom
soy sauce
spinach
stews
stir-fries
STOCKS, *e.g., dashi*
sugar
tamari
tempeh
tofu
vinegar, rice
zucchini

Flavor Affinities

kelp + rice vinegar + soy sauce + sushi rice
kelp powder + celery + lemon juice + mayonnaise + *salads* + scallions + soy sauce + tofu

• KIWI (aka KIWIFRUIT)

Season: late autumn – spring
Flavor: sweet/sour, with notes of melon and/or strawberries, and a soft texture punctuated by tiny, crunchy seeds
Volume: quiet – moderate
Nutritional profile: 87% carbs / 7% fats / 6% protein
Calories: 110 per 1-cup serving (raw)
Protein: 2 grams
Technique: raw

Tip: When stored at room temperature, kiwi will continue to sweeten.

almonds
apples
avocado

bananas
berries
brown rice syrup
cashews
cereals, breakfast
cheese, cream
cherries
chocolate, e.g., dark, white
cinnamon
citrus
coconut
Cointreau
cream and **ice cream**
cucumbers
desserts
drinks
ginger
grapefruit
grapes
greens, e.g., baby
hazelnuts
honey
jícama
kebabs
Kirsch
lemon, e.g., juice, zest
LIME, e.g., juice, zest
lychees
macadamia nuts
mangoes
marinades
melon, e.g., honeydew
mint
nuts
orange, e.g., juice, zest
oranges, blood
papaya
passion fruit
pineapple
pistachios
pomegranates
poppy seeds
puddings
raspberries
rum
salad dressings
salads, fruit
sorbets

star fruit
strawberries
sugar, brown
tarts, fruit
vanilla
watermelon
wine, sparkling, e.g., Champagne;
   sweet, e.g., ice wine
yogurt

Flavor Affinities
kiwi + bananas + orange juice
kiwi + bananas + strawberries
kiwi + honey + lime
kiwi + mint + yogurt

• KOHLRABI
Season: summer – autumn
Flavor: slightly sweet, with notes
of broccoli, cabbage, cauliflower,
cucumber, mustard, radish,
turnip, and/or water chestnut;
and a crisp, crunchy, juicy texture

Flavor Affinities
kohlrabi + apples + lemon + mustard + *slaws*
kohlrabi + basil + mushrooms
kohlrabi + celery root + nutmeg + onions + potatoes
kohlrabi + chili pepper flakes + mustard
kohlrabi + chives + lemon
kohlrabi + cream + *German cuisine* + nutmeg
kohlrabi + dill + feta cheese + *Greek cuisine*
kohlrabi + dill + horseradish + lemon juice + **sour cream**
kohlrabi + garlic + Parmesan cheese + parsley + risotto
kohlrabi + garlic + soy sauce
kohlrabi + paprika + sour cream
kohlrabi + sesame seeds + soy sauce

Dishes

Kohlrabi Salad with Fennel, Evalon [semi-firm goat cheese], Toasted Almonds, Roasted
Shiitakes, Pears and Ginger Dressing
— Girl & the Goat (Chicago)

"Purple" Kohlrabi braised with a broth of its roasted leaves, Wild Rice, Ricotta, Dill
— Oxheart (Houston)

Volume: quieter (esp. when younger) – louder (esp. when older)

Nutritional profile: 82% carbs / 15% protein / 3% fats

Calories: 40 per 1-cup serving (raw)

Protein: 2 grams

Techniques: boil (20 – 30 minutes), braise, glaze, grate, grill, parboil, puree, raw, roast, sauté, steam (about 30 – 45 minutes), stew, stir-fry, stuff

Botanical relatives: other cruciferous vegetables, e.g., broccoli, Brussels sprouts, **cabbage**, cauliflower, collard greens, kale

Factoid: Chicago chef Stephanie Izard is kohlrabi's self-described number-one fan.

almonds
anise
apples
basil
beans
blueberries
broccoli
butter
cabbage, e.g., napa
caraway seeds
carrots
casseroles
cayenne
celery
celery root
CHEESE, e.g., blue, feta, goat, Gouda, **Parmesan**, ricotta, Swiss
chervil
chiles
(Southern) Chinese cuisine
chives
corn
couscous
cream
crudités
cucumbers

cumin
curry powder and curry spices
daikon
DILL
(Northern) European cuisines
fennel
garlic
German cuisine
ginger
gratins
greens, e.g., mustard
horseradish
Hungarian cuisine
Indian cuisine
leeks
lemon, e.g., juice, zest
lentils, e.g., red
lettuces, e.g., romaine
maple syrup
marjoram
mayonnaise
melon, esp. muskmelon
mint
mushrooms
mustard, e.g., Dijon, and mustard seeds
nutmeg
oil, e.g., grapeseed, mustard, **olive**, peanut, sesame
onions, e.g., green, spring, Vidalia
paprika
parsley
peas
pies
potatoes
purees
radishes
rémoulades
risottos
rosemary
salad dressings
SALADS, e.g., grain, green, vegetable
salt, e.g., sea
sauces
sesame, e.g., oil, seeds
shallots

slaws
soups
sour cream
soy sauce
spring rolls
stews
stir-fries
stock, vegetable
sugar, e.g., brown
tarragon
thyme and lemon thyme
tomatoes
turmeric
turnips
vegetables, root
VINEGAR, e.g., balsamic, fruit, red wine, rice wine, white wine
za'atar

"**Kohlrabi** can be cubed and smoked, then baked in a hotel pan with stock and oil so that it confits but is still toothsome. It's great in a root vegetable Bolognese, served with polenta and portobello mushrooms."
— ERIC TUCKER, MILLENNIUM (SAN FRANCISCO)

KOMBU

Flavor: slightly sweet/umami, with notes of the sea

Volume: moderate – loud

What it is: sea vegetable (a type of edible kelp), used as a flavor enhancer

Techniques: deep-fry, pickle, roast, simmer, stew

Tips: Kombu breaks down indigestible sugars in beans. Soak and chop kombu before adding to salads and vegetable dishes. Use kombu and water to make vegetarian dashi (shojin dashi). Kombu adds richness to soup stocks.

Botanical relative: kelp

BEANS, e.g., adzuki, cannellini, dried, lima
carrots
cilantro
cream
daikon
DASHI
dips
eggplant
garlic
ginger
grains
JAPANESE CUISINE
kale
legumes
lemon
macrobiotic cuisine
millet
mirin
miso
MUSHROOMS, e.g., dried, oyster (e.g., smoked), shiitake
noodles, e.g., soba, udon
nori
oil, e.g., chili, sesame
onions
pumpkin seeds
radishes
rice, e.g., brown
sage
salads
sauces, esp. dipping sauces
scallions
sea vegetables, e.g., dulse, wakame
SOUPS, e.g., bean, onion
soy sauce
squash, e.g., kambocha
stews, e.g., root vegetable
STOCKS, e.g., Japanese, soup
tamari
thyme
tofu
vegetables, esp. root
vinegar, brown rice
wakame

Flavor Affinities
kombu + carrots + kale + miso + shiitake mushrooms
kombu + ginger + shiitake mushrooms
kombu + miso + onions + shiitake mushrooms
kombu + miso + shiitake mushrooms + tofu + wakame

"I had no clue how to create a vegan seafood dish. Creating vegan clam chowder was a by-product of having extra **kombu** broth around. We ended up adding some potatoes, smoked oyster mushrooms, and cashew cream to replace traditional cream, and it worked out great."
— TAL RONNEN, CROSSROADS (LOS ANGELES)

KOREAN CUISINE
bean paste
CHILES and **chili pepper flakes, chili paste,** and **chili powder**
garlic
ginger
grilled dishes
kimchi
mustard
noodles, Asian, e.g., buckwheat
RICE, e.g., short- to medium-grain
scallions
sesame, e.g., oil, seeds
soups (served very hot)
soy bean paste
SOY SAUCE
sprouts, mung bean
stews (served very hot)
sugar
tofu
vegetables, e.g., cold/raw, pickled (e.g., kimchi), warm/steamed
vinegar
wine

Flavor Affinities
CHILI PEPPER PASTE + SOY SAUCE + SOYBEAN PASTE

● KUMQUAT
Season: autumn – winter
Flavor: bitter/sweet/sour, with sweet edible skin and a juicy texture
Volume: moderate – loud
Nutritional profile: 81% carbs / 10% fats / 9% protein
Calories: 15 per kumquat (raw)
Techniques: candy, pickle, raw, stew
Botanical relatives: grapefruit, lemon, lime, orange

anise
apples, esp. green
apricots
arugula
avocado
baked goods, e.g., cakes, muffins
bananas
beets
blueberries
brandy
bulgur
butter
buttermilk
chili powder
Chinese cuisine
chocolate, e.g., dark, white
chutneys
cilantro
citrus
cloves
compotes
couscous
cranberries
currants
dates
figs
ginger
graham cracker, e.g., crust
grapefruit
honey

ice cream
Japanese cuisine
jícama
lemon, e.g., juice
lemon curd
lime, e.g., juice
mangoes
marmalades
mint
mushrooms, e.g., shiitake
onions, red
ORANGE, e.g., juice
papaya
parsley
pepper, e.g., pink
pineapples
pistachios
preserves
puddings, e.g., bread
raisins
rhubarb
rum
salad dressings
salads, *e.g., fruit, grain, green*
sauces
smoothies
star fruit
strawberries
stuffings
sugar, e.g., brown
syrups
tangerine
vanilla
vinegar, wine
walnuts

Flavor Affinities
kumquat + avocado + beet +
    citrus

Dishes

White Chocolate Panna Cotta,
Candied Kumquats, Dates,
Toasted Walnuts
— Print (New York City)

KUZU (aka KUDZU ROOT)
Flavor: neutral
Volume: very quiet
What it is: a root-based starch
that serves as a **thickening agent**
Ratio: 1½ tablespoons kuzu per
1 cup cooking liquid for gravies,
sauces; 2 tablespoons kuzu per
1 cup liquid for gelling liquids
Tip: Dissolve kuzu in a little
cold water before adding to
other ingredients.
Possible substitute: arrowroot

bay leaf
breadings
Chinese cuisine
dashi
desserts, e.g., kanten, puddings
gelled dishes
ginger
grains
gravies
Japanese cuisine
lemon
macrobiotic cuisine
maple
mirin
noodles, e.g., Asian
oil, sesame
onions
parsley
peaches
pears
pie fillings, e.g., fruit
plums
puddings
radishes
rice
SAUCES
scallions
sesame, e.g., seeds
shiso
soups
soy sauce
stews
stock, mushroom, e.g., shiitake

tamari
umeboshi plum

Flavor Affinities
kuzu + bay leaf + mushroom
    stock + onion + sesame oil + soy
    sauce
kuzu + *gravies* + sesame seeds +
    tamari

● LAMB'S-QUARTER (aka QUELITE or WILD SPINACH; see also tips for GREENS, AMARANTH; and SPINACH)
Season: summer
Flavor: notes of asparagus,
nuts (peanuts, walnuts), and/or
spinach, with a soft texture
Volume: moderate – loud
Nutritional profile: 58% carbs
/ 24% protein / 18% fats
Calories: 60 per 1-cup serving
(chopped, boiled)
Protein: 6 grams
Techniques: bake, sauté, steam
(better cooked than raw)
Tips: Put in boiling water
(never cold water, which sets
the bitterness). Cooking brings
out its nuttiness. Combine
with miso or other, milder
vegetables to quiet its flavor.
Botanical relatives: chard,
epazote, spinach
Possible substitutes:
amaranth greens, spinach

almonds
asparagus
avocado
beans, e.g., Anasazi, pinto
casseroles
cayenne
celery root
cheese, e.g., goat, Monterey Jack,
    Muenster, Parmesan

chiles, e.g., jalapeño
chili paste
chives
cilantro
cream
crema, Mexican
eggs, e.g., *omelets, quiches,*
    scrambled
freekeh
GARLIC
herbs
leeks
lemon
miso, esp. light
mushrooms, e.g., morel
mustard, e.g., Dijon
nutmeg
nuts
oil, e.g., nut, olive, sesame
olives, e.g., kalamata
onions
orange
pastas
pea shoots
peas
pestos
potatoes
pumpkin
purees
SALADS
sauces
scallions
soups
sour cream
squash, e.g., butternut
stews
stir-fries
tomatoes
tortillas, e.g., corn
vegetables, milder
vinaigrette
walnuts

Flavor Affinities
lamb's-quarter + chipotle chiles
    + cilantro + garlic + tomatoes +
    tortillas

lamb's-quarter + eggs +
    mushrooms + potatoes
lamb's-quarter + garlic + olive oil

LAMB'S LETTUCE (see LETTUCE, LAMB'S)

● LAND CRESS (aka GARDEN CRESS; see also WATERCRESS)

Flavor: mild (esp. in winter) to
hot (esp. in summer), with notes
of arugula, horseradish, mustard,
pepper, and/or watercress, and a
crunchy texture
Volume: quiet – loud
Nutritional profile: 62% carbs
/ 20% protein / 18% fats
Calories: 20 per 1-cup serving
(raw)
Protein: 1 gram
Techniques: cooked, raw
Botanical relative: mustard
Possible substitute: watercress

beets
butter
carrots
cauliflower
celery
dashi
eggs, e.g., hard-boiled
endive
lemon, e.g., juice
Mediterranean cuisines
noodles, Asian, e.g., somen
peas
pizzas
potatoes
sake
SALADS, e.g., green, vegetable
sandwiches
soups, e.g., creamy, potato
soy sauce
spinach
vinegar

LAVENDER
Flavor: bitter/sour/sweet; very
aromatic, with pungent notes of
flowers, herbs, lemon, and/or
woods
Volume: loud
Techniques: fresh, cook, infuse
Botanical relatives: basil,
marjoram, mint, oregano,
rosemary, sage, summer savory,
thyme
Possible substitute: caraway
seeds

apricots
arugula
BAKED GOODS, e.g., biscotti,
    cakes, cookies, scones, shortbread
basil
BERRIES, e.g., blackberries,
    blueberries, raspberries,
    strawberries
butter
candies
caraway seeds
carrots
cheese, e.g., blue, fromage blanc,
    goat, Gorgonzola
cherries
cinnamon
citrus, e.g., juice
coconut
corn
cream, crème fraîche, and *ice*
    cream
custards
desserts
drinks, e.g., lemonade
figs
French cuisine, esp. Provençal
fruit and fruit preserves
guava
herbes de Provence
HONEY
ICE CREAMS
LEMON, e.g., zest

lemonades
mangoes
mayonnaise
Mediterranean cuisines
mint
nectarines
oil, e.g., nut, olive, walnut
oranges
peaches
plums
potatoes
pumpkin seeds
rhubarb
rice
rosemary
saffron
salad dressings
salads, e.g., fruit
sauces
savory
soups
stews
sugar, e.g., powdered
syrups
teas, herbal
thyme
tofu
vanilla
vinegar, e.g., white wine
walnuts
watercress
yogurt

Flavor Affinities
lavender + butter + rosemary
lavender + blue cheese + figs +
  honey

"I like to dry my herbs from fresh
while still green and run them
through a coffee grinder to make
a seasoning salt — for example,
dried rosemary with salt, or dried
lavender with sugar."

— DIANE FORLEY, FLOURISH BAKING
COMPANY (SCARSDALE, NY)

● LEEKS

Season: autumn – spring
Flavor: slightly sweet, with notes
of onions
Volume: quiet
Nutritional profile: 89% carbs
/ 7% protein / 4% fats
Calories: 55 per 1-cup serving
(raw)
Protein: 1 gram
Techniques: boil, braise,
fry, grill, pressure-cook (2 –
4 minutes), roast, sauté, steam
(5 – 6 minutes), stew, stir-fry
(2 – 3 minutes)

Tips: Very, very carefully rinse
away all dirt or sand between
leek layers with cold water. Add
early in the cooking process.
Do not overcook (or brown), or
leeks become bitter.

Botanical relatives: asparagus,
chives, garlic, **onions**, shallots

artichokes
artichokes, Jerusalem
asparagus
barley
basil
bay leaf

Dishes

Braised Leeks with Mozzarella, Mustard Bread Crumbs, and a Fried Egg
— FnB Restaurant (Scottsdale, AZ)

Leek Tart, Thyme, and Cashew Cheese, Herbed Olive Oil Crust, Arugula
— True Bistro (Somerville, MA)

Leeks with Pumpkin Seed Romesco Sauce
— Vedge (Philadelphia)

BEANS, e.g., cannellini, fava, flageolet, green, **white**
beets
bell peppers, e.g., red, esp. roasted
bread crumbs/croutons, e.g., whole-grain
butter
cabbage
capers
carrots
casseroles
celery
CHEESE, e.g., **blue, cheddar,** feta, **GOAT,** Gorgonzola, **GRUYÈRE,** halloumi, mozzarella, **PARMESAN,** ricotta, sheep's milk
chervil
chestnuts
chives
coconut milk
cream and crème fraîche
custards and flans
dill
EGGS, e.g., fried, *frittatas,* hard-boiled, *omelets, quiches,* scrambled, *soufflés*
FENNEL
garlic, e.g., green, scapes, spring
ginger
gratins
kale

LEMON, e.g., juice, zest
lentils, e.g., green
lovage
mint
mushrooms, e.g., oyster, shiitake, wild
mustard, e.g., Dijon
OIL, e.g., hazelnut, nut, **olive,** peanut, walnut
olives, e.g., black, kalamata
onions, e.g., green, white
oranges
oregano
PARSLEY
pasta, e.g., fettuccine, gnocchi
peas
pepper, e.g., black, white
pesto
pizzas
POTATOES
pumpkin and pumpkin seeds
quinoa
rice, e.g., Arborio, brown
risotto
romesco sauce
rosemary
saffron
salad dressings, e.g., mustard vinaigrette
salads
salt, e.g., kosher, sea
sauces, e.g., cheese
scallions

shallots
sorrel
SOUPS, e.g., barley, Jerusalem artichoke, lentil, potato, vichyssoise
soy sauce
spinach
squash, e.g., butternut
stews
stir-fries
STOCKS, VEGETABLE
tarragon
tarts, e.g., cheese, potato
thyme
tofu, *e.g., scrambles*
tomatoes and **tomato sauce**
turnips
vinegar, e.g., white wine
walnuts
watercress
wheat berries
WINE, e.g., **dry red, white**
yogurt
zucchini

Flavor Affinities

leeks + blue cheese + thyme
leeks + butternut squash + thyme
leeks + carrots + celery + onions
leeks + celery + onions + potatoes + stock
leeks (+ cream) + Dijon mustard + garlic + thyme + white wine
leeks + eggs + Gruyère cheese + *quiche*
leeks + fennel + Gorgonzola cheese
leeks + fennel + lemon + thyme
leeks + feta cheese + garlic + nutmeg + ricotta + spinach
leeks + garlic + lemon
leeks + lemon + mustard
leeks + onions + tomatoes
leeks + potatoes + watercress

LEGUMES (see also specific BEANS, CHICKPEAS, LENTILS, PEANUTS, PEAS, and SOYBEANS)

Tip: Many chefs are experimenting with smoking legumes to enhance their "meatiness."

● LEMONGRASS

Flavor: sour/sweet, with notes of citrus (e.g., lemon or lemon zest) and/or flowers
Volume: quiet – moderate/loud
What it is: Southeast Asian grass used as a flavoring
Techniques: puree, simmer
Tips: Use fresh. Remove whole stalks after cooking and before serving. Otherwise, puree or slice these fibrous stalks very, very thinly.
Possible substitute: lemon zest

Cooking Legumes

There are three major categories of legumes:

- pulses, including chickpeas, lentils, dried beans, dried peas
- fresh beans and fresh peas
- peanuts and soybeans

It's best to follow the specific directions on the package of legumes you are using and to understand that timing can still vary depending on a number of factors, including heat level and heat conductivity of the pot you use. However, here are some helpful rules of thumb:

- Rinse legumes to remove any dirt or foreign objects (e.g., tiny pebbles).
- Soak most legumes overnight in water before cooking. This shortens their cooking time and increases their digestibility. Discard the soaking water. (If time is of the essence, legumes can still benefit from a quick soak achieved by bringing them to a boil in water, then removing from heat, and letting them stand for at least an hour. Drain and rinse before proceeding.)
- Combine legumes with cooking liquid (e.g., water, stock) in a pot. Bring to a boil, then reduce heat to low, partially covering the pot, and simmer. Check to ensure that the desired tenderness has been achieved, and then remove from heat.

Asian cuisines
bamboo shoots
basil, Thai
Cambodian cuisine
carrots
chiles, e.g., fresh, green, red
chili paste
cilantro
coconut and **COCONUT MILK**
coriander
corn
CURRIES, esp. Thai
desserts
eggplant
galangal
garlic
ginger
grains
Indonesian cuisine
Kaffir lime leaf
lemon, e.g., juice, zest
lime, e.g., juice, zest
lotus root
Malaysian cuisine
mushrooms, e.g., shiitake
noodle dishes
oil, sesame
onions, e.g., yellow
pho, vegetarian
pineapple
rice, e.g., brown
salad dressings
salads, e.g., tomato
sauces
scallions
shallots
SOUPS, e.g., Asian or fruit
SOUTHEAST ASIAN CUISINES
soy sauce
stews
stir-fries
stocks, vegetable
sugar, e.g., palm
tamari
tamarind
teas
THAI CUISINE

tofu
tomatoes
turmeric
VIETNAMESE CUISINE
vinegar, rice
yogurt

Flavor Affinities
lemongrass + chiles + garlic + ginger + shallots
lemongrass + coconut + lime + pineapple + yogurt
lemongrass + coconut + lychee + mango + mint + papaya + pineapple + *salads*
lemongrass + coconut milk + palm sugar
lemongrass + garlic + ginger

• LEMONS

Flavor: sour, with floral notes
Volume: moderate – **loud**
What they are: citrus fruit
Nutritional profile: 63% carbs / 24% protein / 13% fat
Calories: 20 per medium lemon (raw, with peel)
Protein: 1 gram
Tip: Use both the juice (for vitamin C) and the zest (for limonin and limonene).
Botanical relatives: grapefruit, kumquat, lime, orange

aioli
almonds
amaranth
artichokes
arugula
asparagus
avocados
baked goods, e.g., biscuits, cakes, cookies, quick breads, scones
basil
beans, e.g., fava, green
beets
bell peppers, red

BERRIES, e.g., **blackberries,**
  BLUEBERRIES, gooseberries,
  raspberries, strawberries
broccoli
butter
capers
cardamom
carrots
cauliflower
cheese, e.g., cream, goat,
  pecorino, **ricotta**
cheesecake
chickpeas
chives
chocolate
COCONUT
coriander
corn
couscous
cream

cucumbers
cumin
currants
desserts, e.g., cheesecake, puddings
dill
drinks, e.g., cocktails, lemonade
edamame
eggplant
eggs
fennel
flax, e.g., oil, seeds
GARLIC
GINGER
grains, whole, e.g., barley, bulgur
Greek cuisine
gremolatas
guavas
hazelnuts
herbs
HONEY

kale
lavender
leeks
lemon curd
lentils, e.g., red
lime
mango
maple syrup
marinades
mascarpone
milk, almond
mint
miso
mushrooms, e.g., portobello
mustard, e.g., Dijon
noodles
nuts, e.g., hazelnuts
OIL, OLIVE
olives, e.g., green
onions
orange, e.g., juice, zest
*OREGANO
pancakes
papaya
paprika
parsley
parsnips
pastas, e.g., linguini, orzo, spaghetti
peaches
pears
peas
pecans
pepper, black
pistachios
plantains
poppy seeds
potatoes
radicchio
radishes
rice
rice, wild
risottos
rosemary
saffron
SALAD DRESSINGS, e.g., lemon
  "vinaigrette"
sauces
shallots

Dishes

White Chocolate Lemon Mousse, Roasted Pineapple, Lemon Almond Tuile
— Green Zebra (Chicago)

Lemon Bar: Almond Coconut Crust, Tart Lemon Custard
— Pure Food and Wine (New York City)

Flavor Affinities

lemon + almond + coconut
lemon + apples + honey + romaine + *salads*
lemon + arugula + Parmesan cheese
lemon + asparagus + black pepper + *pasta*
lemon + asparagus + lemon + pecans + rice
lemon + basil + mint
lemon + blueberries + honey + ricotta
lemon + blueberries + yogurt
lemon + capers + *sauces* + white wine
lemon + cauliflower + tahini
lemon + coconut + strawberries
lemon + cream + *sauces* + tarragon
lemon + garlic + mustard + olive oil + oregano + vinegar
lemon + garlic + oregano
LEMON + GARLIC + PARSLEY
lemon + green beans + parsley
lemon + mint + zucchini
lemon + risotto + thyme + zucchini

soups, e.g., *avgolemono, lentil*
squash, e.g., summer
sugar, e.g., brown sugar
snap peas
tabbouleh
tahini
tarragon
teas
thyme
tofu
tomatoes
vanilla
vinegar, e.g., champagne, rice,
  sherry, wine

wasabi
wine, e.g., dry white
yogurt
za'atar
zucchini

"**Lemon juice** is one of the most important ingredients I use as a raw chef. In addition to being a seasoning, it is a tenderizer that gives vegetables pliability."
— AMI BEACH, G-ZEN (BRANFORD, CT)

LEMONS, MEYER

Season: autumn – spring
Flavor: sour/sweet, with notes of lemon and orange
Volume: moderate – loud (but quieter than regular lemons)

almonds
arugula
asparagus
baked goods, e.g., cakes, cookies, muffins, scones, tarts
bananas
berries, e.g., blackberries, blueberries, raspberries
beverages, e.g., cocktails
celery
cheese, e.g., blue, ricotta
cheesecake
citrus, e.g., grapefruit, lemon, lime
coconut
compotes
cream
custards
dates
desserts, e.g., puddings
fennel
fruit, e.g., dried, other
ginger
grains, e.g., bulgur
grapefruit
honey
ice creams
lemon
lime
maple syrup
mint
mousses
onions, e.g., Maui, sweet
orange, e.g., juice

Dishes

Mesclun Greens with Meyer Lemon Vinaigrette and Crumbled Oregon Blue Cheese
— Marché (Eugene, OR)

parsley

pastas

pine nuts

pineapple

pistachios

poppy seeds

risottos

salad dressings

salads, e.g., grain, green, vegetable

sauces, e.g., butter

shallots

sugar, e.g., brown

tarragon

thyme

tomatoes, cherry

vanilla

vegetables, e.g., root, steamed

zucchini

Flavor Affinities

Meyer lemon + almond + vanilla

Meyer lemon + ginger + vanilla

Meyer lemon + parsley + shallots
  + thyme

Meyer lemon + pine nuts + sugar

"I love **Meyer lemon**, which adds such nice acidity to dishes. It's especially great with asparagus, sweet Maui onions, or zucchini. I even grill them."

— JOSIAH CITRIN, MÉLISSE (SANTA MONICA)

LEMONS, PRESERVED

Flavor: salty/**sour**/umami, with citrus notes

Volume: moderate – **loud**

Tip: Either blanch in boiling water for a few seconds or rinse to quiet the flavor.

apricots, e.g., dried, fresh

arugula

barley, e.g., pearl

beans, e.g., green, white

bell peppers, e.g., green, red

cardamom

carrots

chickpeas

chiles, e.g., red

cinnamon

cloves

couscous, e.g., Israeli

cucumbers

eggplant

fennel

garlic

ginger

grains

legumes, e.g., chickpeas, lentils

lemon, fresh, e.g., juice

lentils

mint

MOROCCAN CUISINE

nigella seeds

olives, e.g., black, green

onions

parsley

pastas

pine nuts

potatoes

relishes

rice

risottos

saffron

salad dressings

salads, e.g., green, pasta, potato

soups, *e.g., lentil*

spinach

squash, e.g., butternut

stews

stock, vegetable

tagines, e.g., root vegetable

tofu, e.g., extra-firm

tomatoes

turnips

Flavor Affinities

preserved lemons + black olives +
  garlic + parsley

preserved lemons + butternut
  squash + chickpeas

preserved lemons + carrots +
  cumin + *salads*

preserved lemons + fennel +
  green olives

LEMON THYME

Flavor: sour, with notes of flowers, lemon, and thyme

Volume: quieter – louder

Tip: Lemon thyme is quieter than regular thyme.

asparagus

basil

bay leaf

beets

beverages

carrots

chives

eggs

fennel

figs

fruits

ginger

mint

mushrooms

orange

parsley

potatoes

rice

salad dressings

salads, *e.g., fruit, green*

sauces

spinach

stuffings

tofu

turnips

vegetables, esp. spring

LEMON VERBENA

Flavor: sour, with notes of flowers, fruit (e.g., lemon, lime), and/or herbs

Volume: loud

almonds

apricots

baked goods, e.g., cakes, shortbread

berries, e.g., blueberries,
  raspberries, strawberries

beverages, e.g., fruity, iced teas, lassis

cherries

compotes

custards, flans, and panna cottas

desserts
European cuisines
fruits
honey
ice creams
lemon, e.g., juice
lime, e.g., juice
marinades
mayonnaise
mint
mushrooms
nectarines
peaches
puddings
raspberries
salads, e.g., fruit, green
sauces, e.g., crème anglaise
sorbets
strawberries
sugar
tamarind
teas, e.g., green, herbal
vanilla
waters, mineral
zucchini

● LENTILS — IN GENERAL (see also specific LENTILS)

Season: autumn – winter
Flavor: sweet, with astringent/earthy notes, and textures ranging from firm to mushy when cooked
Volume: moderate
What they are: legumes
Nutritional profile: 70% carbs / 27% protein / 3% fats
Calories: 230 per 1-cup serving (boiled)
Protein: 18 grams
Techniques: boil, simmer (always cook thoroughly)
Timing: Cook until tender, typically less than 30 minutes.
Ratio: 1:2½ (1 cup lentils to 2½ cups cooking liquid, e.g., water)

Tips: Rinse well, and remove any pebbles or small stones before cooking. Unlike other legumes, lentils require no presoaking. Don't salt the cooking water, which can slow the cooking process. As a general rule, the darker the lentil, the louder the flavor and the firmer the texture.

Botanical relatives: beans, lentils, peanuts, peas

apples and apple juice
artichokes
arugula
asparagus
barley
basil

Flavor Affinities

lentils + beets + goat cheese
lentils + bell peppers + mushrooms
lentils + brown rice + onions + spinach
lentils + carrots + celery + Dijon mustard + leeks
lentils + cayenne + cinnamon + coriander + cumin
lentils + celery + tomatoes + zucchini
lentils + chiles + mint
lentils + cilantro + garlic + lemon
lentils + cilantro + sweet potatoes + yogurt
lentils + cinnamon + orange + spinach
lentils + coconut + lime
lentils + coriander + cumin + ginger
lentils + cumin + garlic
lentils + cumin + turmeric
lentils + curry powder + garlic + ginger + lemon
lentils + curry powder + yogurt
lentils + Dijon mustard + lemon juice
lentils + frisée + goat cheese + onions
lentils + garlic + lemon + parsley + sun-dried tomatoes
lentils + garlic + mint
lentils + garlic + olive oil + salt
lentils + grains (e.g., quinoa) **+ herbs** (e.g., basil, dill, mint, parsley) **+ lemon**
lentils + leeks + *pasta* + spinach
lentils + olive oil + onions + rice
lentils + *dals* + onions + tomatoes
lentils + spinach + yogurt

bay leaf
beans, green
beer
beets
BELL PEPPERS, e.g., red, roasted
buckwheat
bulgur
butter
cabbage
capers
cardamom
CARROTS
cashews
casseroles
cauliflower
cayenne
celery
celery root
CHARD, e.g., Swiss

Dishes

Lentil Soup, Celery Root, Parmesan, and Herbs
— ABC Kitchen (New York City)

Cassoulet with Lentils, Wild Mushrooms, Grilled Treviso, and Buttered Leeks
— Crossroads (Los Angeles)

Crimson Lentil Croquettes with Mango Chutney, Scallion, Mint, and Cilantro
— Green Zebra (Chicago)

Lentil Walnut Pâté with Tofu Sour Cream, Wheat-Free Rice Crackers, and Crudités
— Real Food Daily (Los Angeles)

CHEESE, e.g., **feta, GOAT** (esp. fresh), Gorgonzola, Parmesan
chickpeas
chiles, e.g., ancho or green, or serrano, and chili powder
chili, vegetarian
chives
cilantro
cinnamon
cloves
coconut
coriander
cream
cucumbers
CUMIN
curry powder, **curry spices**, and *CURRIES*
DALS, i.e., Indian stewed lentils
dill
dips
eggplant
eggs, e.g., hard-boiled
escarole
European cuisines
fennel
French cuisine, esp. French lentils
frisée
garam masala
GARLIC
ghee
GINGER
gratins
greens
hazelnuts
herbs

"hummus"
Indian cuisine
Italian cuisine
kale
leeks
LEMON, e.g., juice, zest
lemon, preserved
lime
loaves, e.g., mock meatloaf
marjoram
Mediterranean cuisines
Middle Eastern cuisines
mint
mujadara
mushrooms
MUSTARD (e.g., Dijon) and mustard seeds (e.g., black)
nutmeg
OIL, e.g., canola, coconut, **OLIVE**, peanut, sunflower, walnut
ONIONS, e.g., green, red, white, yellow
orange, e.g., juice, zest
oregano
palm, hearts of
paprika
PARSLEY
pasta, e.g., macaroni, spaghetti
pâtés
pepper, e.g., black, white
pilafs
pine nuts
potatoes
purees
quinoa

RICE, e.g., basmati, brown, wild
rosemary
SALADS, e.g., lentil, vegetable
salt, e.g., kosher, sea
sauces
scallions
shallots
sorrel
soups
soy sauce or tamari
SPINACH
squash, e.g., butternut
STEWS
STOCK, VEGETABLE
sunflower seeds
sweet potatoes
tabbouleh
tacos (season lentils with taco spices)
tagines
tamarind
tarragon
THYME
TOMATOES and sun-dried tomatoes
turmeric
vegetables, esp. root or winter
veggie burgers, e.g., with rice
VINEGAR, e.g., **red wine**, rice wine, **sherry**, wine
wakame
walnuts
watercress
yogurt, e.g., low-fat or sheep's milk
zucchini

"I love cooking **lentils** until they're soft, then combining them with vegetables — especially onions and mushrooms, but also things like broccoli — and pressing the mixture into a loaf pan and baking it for 40 minutes. After it's cool, I'll slice it and serve it with mashed potatoes and gravy."
— PAM BROWN, GARDEN CAFÉ (WOODSTOCK, NY)

"Yellow and red **lentils** are the lightest in texture and flavor, while black lentils are the heaviest and strongest in flavor. Green lentils fall in-between."

— HEMANT MATHUR, TULSI (NEW YORK CITY)

● LENTILS, BLACK (aka BELUGA)

Flavor: earthy notes of nuts, with a chewy yet soft texture
Volume: quiet – moderate
Tip: Black lentils hold their shape when cooked.
Techniques: boil, braise
Timing: Boil until tender, about 20 – 30 minutes.
Ratio: 1:2¼ (1 cup lentils to 2¼ cups water)

bay leaf
bell peppers
bread crumbs
butter
carrots
celery
cilantro
coriander
cream
cumin
dill
eggplant
Indian cuisine, esp. northern
Middle Eastern cuisines
oil, olive
onions
pasta
purslane
rice
SALADS, e.g., lentil, vegetable

Dishes

Carrots Cooked Shawarma Style, Black Lentils, Green Garbanzos, Tomato Olive Stew, Green Harissa

— Vedge (Philadelphia)

soups, e.g., lentil, winter
South Asian cuisines
stock, e.g., vegetable
stuffed bell peppers or stuffed
   eggplant
sweet potatoes
thyme
vegetables
walnuts
wine, e.g., red
yogurt

"I learned how to make **black lentils** when I cooked for two years at Bucara in Delhi, which is one of the best Indian restaurants in the world. After soaking them overnight and draining them, we would slow-boil them over low heat for two hours before seasoning them with ginger, garlic paste, tomato puree, salt, chili powder, unsalted butter, and heavy cream. They were so rich and delicious that we'd make 50 or 60 pounds of them every day to serve 300 guests! I still make them the same way today."

— HEMANT MATHUR, TULSI (NEW YORK CITY)

● LENTILS, BROWN

Flavor: earthy notes of nuts and/or pepper, with a soft texture (when cooked)
Volume: moderate – loud
Techniques: boil, mash, puree, simmer
Timing: Boil until tender, about 20 – 60 minutes.

Ratio: 1:3 (1 cup lentils to 3 cups water)
Tip: Use when a soft (or even mushy) texture is desired.

avocados
bell peppers
celery seeds
couscous
dals
eggplant
loaves
oil, olive
onions
pâtés
patties
purees
rice
salads
scallions
SOUPS, e.g., winter
South Asian cuisines
soy sauce
stews
stuffed vegetables, e.g., bell peppers,
   eggplant
tamari
veggie burgers
walnuts

Flavor Affinities

brown lentils + olive oil + onions + scallions + tamari + walnuts

● LENTILS, CHICKPEA

"I'll use **chickpea lentils** to make chickpea flour, which I use instead of cornstarch to bind ingredients. I use chickpea flour in my Indian vegetable fritters."

— HEMANT MATHUR, TULSI (NEW YORK CITY)

● LENTILS, FRENCH

Flavor: slightly sweet, with earthy notes of nuts and/or pepper, and a firm, chewy texture

Volume: quiet – **moderate**
Techniques: braise, marinate
Timing: Boil until tender, about 20 – 45 minutes.
Ratio: 1:2½ (1 cup lentils to 2½ cups water or stock)

> **Tip:** Use French green lentils when you want lentils that will hold their shape.

bay leaf
beer
bell peppers, e.g., red, yellow
carrots
cayenne
celery
celery root
chard
cheese, e.g., feta, goat, ricotta salata
chili pepper flakes
cilantro
couscous
croutons, whole-grain
cumin
dals
French cuisine
garlic
gravies
kale
leeks
lemon, e.g., juice
mint
mustard, e.g., Dijon
oil, olive
ONIONS, e.g., red, Spanish, yellow
paprika
parsley
pastas
pepper, black
radishes
rice, long-grain white
rosemary
sage
SALADS, e.g., lentil
sauces

SOUPS, e.g., lentil, minestrone, winter
South Asian cuisines
stuffed vegetables, e.g., bell peppers, eggplant
tarragon
thyme
tomatoes and tomato paste
vinegar, e.g., balsamic, red wine, sherry
wine, e.g., dry red
yogurt

Flavor Affinities
French lentils + carrots + celery + onions
French lentils + cumin + lemon
French lentils + garlic + greens
French lentils + garlic + lemon + mint + olive oil + spinach
French lentils + mustard + vinegar
French lentils + tarragon + thyme

● LENTILS, GREEN

Flavor: earthy notes of meat and/or nuts, with a firm texture
Volume: moderate – loud (for lentils)
Techniques: simmer
Timing: Cook green lentils about 20 – 45 minutes.
Ratio: 1:2½ (1 cup lentils to 2½ cups water)

> **Tip:** These are good in salads, as they keep their firm texture.

baked dishes
bay leaf

beets
bell peppers, red, e.g., roasted
carrots
celery
chard, Swiss
cheese, e.g., feta, **goat,** ricotta salata
chili pepper flakes
cilantro
coriander
cucumbers
cumin
curries
curry powder
dals
dill
eggs, hard-boiled
garlic
grains
greens
Indian cuisine
leeks
lemon, e.g., juice
Middle Eastern cuisines
mint
mushrooms, shiitake
mustard
nettles
North American cuisines
oil, e.g., **olive,** sunflower
olives, e.g., kalamata
onions
parsley
pasta
pâtés
pepper, e.g., black
rice, e.g., brown
SALADS, e.g., green, lentil
salt, sea

Dishes

Green Lentil Velouté, Piquillo Pepper Harissa, Caramelized Pearl Onion, Root Vegetables, Tatsoi Salad
— DANIEL (New York City)

Flourish Vegetable Pot Pie: Lentil Simmer with Spinach and Broccoli
— Flourish Baking Company (Scarsdale, NY)

scallions
sorrel
SOUPS, *e.g., lentil*
South American cuisines
spinach
stews
stock, vegetable
tarragon
thyme
tomatoes
turmeric
yogurt
zucchini

Flavor Affinities

green lentils + goat cheese + mint
 + *salads*

"I love **green lentils**, because they have the same flavor as the gungo peas I grew up with in Jamaica. They're great with [coconut] rice, or in lentil-thyme soup."

— SHAWAIN WHYTE, CAFÉ BLOSSOM (NEW YORK CITY)

● LENTILS, RED

Flavor: slightly sweet, with earthy notes of split peas, and a soft, mushy texture when cooked
Volume: quiet – moderate
Techniques: boil, puree, simmer, stew
Timing: Cook red lentils until tender, about 10 – 30 minutes.
Ratio: 1:2 (1 cup red lentils to 2 cups water)
Tip: Red lentils cook quickly, even without presoaking.

Dishes

Crimson Lentil Croquettes, Mango Chutney, Scallion, Mint, Cilantro
— Green Zebra (Chicago)

Red Lentil Ravioli with Apple-Fennel Tempeh, Golden Beets, and Apple White Wine Sauce
— Plum Bistro (Seattle)

asafoetida powder
arugula
avocado
basil
bay leaf
beets
bell peppers, e.g., green or red
bread, e.g., pita
broccoli
bulgur
burdock
cardamom
CARROTS
cashews, e.g., raw
cauliflower
cayenne
celery
chard, e.g., feta, Swiss
chickpeas
CHILES, e.g., Indian, jalapeño, serrano, Thai; and **chili pepper flakes / chili powder**
CILANTRO
cinnamon
coconut milk
coriander
corn
croquettes
cucumbers
CUMIN
CURRY LEAVES, PASTE, or **POWDER,** and *CURRIES*
dals
dill
eggplant
fennel seeds
fenugreek seeds
GARLIC
ghee

ginger
greens, e.g., amaranth, mustard
hummus
INDIAN CUISINE
Italian cuisine
kibbe
kombu
Lebanese cuisine
leeks
LEMON, e.g., juice, zest
lettuce, e.g., romaine
lime, e.g., juice
loaves
mango
marjoram
milk, coconut
mint
miso
mushrooms
MUSTARD, e.g., Dijon, mustard powder, and mustard seeds
OIL, canola, **OLIVE**, sesame
olives, e.g., black
ONIONS, e.g., red, white, yellow
orange
oregano
paprika, e.g., sweet
PARSLEY
pasta, e.g., fettuccine, orecchiette
pâtés, vegetarian, e.g., lentil, nut
patties
pepper, black
pilafs
pistachios
pomegranates and pomegranate molasses
potatoes, e.g., red, sweet, white
purees
RICE, e.g., basmati, black, brown
rosemary
salads
salt, sea
sauces, e.g., "Bolognese"
scallions
seeds, sunflower
shallots

L

SOUPS, e.g., harira, lentil, Mulligatawny, pureed, winter

spinach

spreads

squash, winter, e.g., butternut

stews

STOCK, vegetable

sweet potatoes

tamarind

thyme

TOMATOES and TOMATO PASTE

turmeric

veggie burgers

vinegar, e.g., cider, umeboshi, wine

wheat berries

wine, e.g., white

yogurt

"**Red lentils** are my favorite lentils. I love their flavor, which is both lentil-y and unique at the same time. And I love how they break down to reach such a creamy texture. I like to cook them Egyptian-style with potatoes, then puree them, seasoning them with cumin, salt, and pepper before finishing them with a squeeze of lemon."
— PAM BROWN, GARDEN CAFÉ (WOODSTOCK, NY)

Flavor Affinities

red lentils + avocado + cilantro + lemon

red lentils + brown rice + scallions

red lentils + carrots + celery + garlic + parsley + *pasta* + tomatoes

red lentils + carrots + leeks

red lentils + cilantro + curry powder + yogurt

red lentils + cinnamon + coriander + cumin

red lentils + coconut + garlic + ginger

red lentils + coriander + cumin

red lentils + garlic + onions

red lentils + lemon + *pasta* + rosemary

"**Red lentils** are very light. You can combine several different kinds of lentils — such as black, green, yellow, and chickpea lentils — and cook them together for a variety of colors and textures."
— HEMANT MATHUR, TULSI (NEW YORK CITY)

• LENTILS, YELLOW

Flavor: creamy in texture

Volume: quiet – moderate

asafoetida powder

chili powder

cumin

dals

Indian cuisine

oil, e.g., canola

onions

rice, e.g., basmati

salt

turmeric

"**Yellow lentils** are very light — they are also fast-cooking, with a soft, creamy texture. They can be simply boiled and seasoned with turmeric, chili powder, and salt. Or you can temper asafoetida powder by sautéing it in oil and adding cumin and onion to season the lentils."
— HEMANT MATHUR, TULSI (NEW YORK CITY)

• LETTUCES — IN GENERAL OR MIXED (see also specific LETTUCES, e.g., LETTUCE, BUTTER; LETTUCE, ROMAINE)

Season: spring – autumn

Flavor: slightly sweet/bitter

Volume: quiet – loud (depending on the type)

What it is: generic term for salad greens

Techniques: best served raw

Tips: Nutritionally, opt for butter, romaine, and other green and red lettuces. Beware fat-laden salad dressings. Consider using crisp whole lettuce leaves, in lieu of taco shells, for wrapping around fillings.

Botanical relatives: artichokes, chamomile, chicory, dandelion greens, endive, radicchio, salsify, tarragon

arugula

avocado

carrots

cashews

celery

CHEESE, e.g., blue, feta, Parmesan, pecorino

citrus, e.g., juice

cucumbers

eggs

fennel

garlic

ginger

greens, e.g., baby, other, salad

jícama

leeks

lemon, e.g., juice

lettuce wraps, e.g., around vegetables, firm tofu, etc.

mint

mushrooms, e.g., shiitake

mustard

Dishes

Sucrine Lettuce: Blue Hill Farm Yogurt, Hazelnuts, and Asparagus
— Blue Hill (New York City)

Greenhouse Head Lettuce: Homemade Yogurt, Peas, and Fava Beans
— Blue Hill (New York City)

Avocado Lettuce Salad with Ginger-Carrot Dressing
— Hangawi (New York City)

Spicy Thai Lettuce Wraps: Mango, Carrots, Cabbage, Cashews, Basil, Mint, Cilantro, Pea Shoots, Tamarind Sauce
— Pure Food and Wine (New York City)

OIL, e.g., hazelnut, **nut, olive,** peanut, walnut
olives, Greek
onions, e.g., spring
pears
peas
pepper, black
pine nuts
pomegranate seeds
radishes
rice
SALAD DRESSINGS, e.g., vinaigrettes
SALADS
salt
scallions
shallots
soups, e.g., lettuce, pea
tofu
tomatoes
vinaigrettes
vinegar, e.g., balsamic, cider, red wine
walnuts

"Not all salad is **lettuce**, but all lettuce is salad — so don't cook it."
— SIGN AT THE UNION SQUARE GREENMARKET IN NEW YORK CITY

LETTUCE, BIBB (aka LETTUCE, BUTTER; see LETTUCE, BUTTER)

LETTUCE, BOSTON (aka LETTUCE, BUTTER; see LETTUCE, BUTTER)

• LETTUCE, BUTTER (aka BIBB or BOSTON LETTUCE)

Flavor: sweet, with notes of butter, and a tender, slightly crunchy texture
Volume: quiet
Nutritional profile: 61% carbs / 25% protein / 14% fats

Calories: 10 per 1-cup serving
(chopped, raw)
Protein: 1 gram
Techniques: braise, grill, **raw**,
sauté

almonds
apples, e.g., green
avocado
basil
beans, e.g., black
bell peppers, e.g., red, roasted
bulgur, e.g., fine-grain
buttermilk
carrots
cauliflower
cayenne
celery
celery root
chayote
cheese, e.g., asiago, blue, feta,
    goat, Gorgonzola, Parmesan
chervil
chickpeas
chiles, e.g., red; chili paste and
    chili pepper flakes
chives
cilantro
cranberries, e.g., dried
crème fraîche
cucumbers
cumin
dill
eggs, soft-cooked
fennel
frisée
garlic
ginger
grapefruit
hazelnuts
herbs, delicate, e.g., chervil,
    chives, parsley, tarragon
honey
jícama
LEMON, e.g., juice, zest
lettuce wraps, e.g., around firm
    tofu, vegetables, etc.
lovage

mint
miso, e.g., light
mushrooms
mustard, e.g., Dijon
OIL, e.g., **OLIVE**, sesame
olives, e.g., black
onions, e.g., green, red
oranges and **blood oranges**
parsley
parsnips
pecans
pepper, black
persimmons
pistachios
pomegranate seeds
quinoa
radicchio
radishes
SALADS, e.g., green, tomato
sandwiches
scallions
seeds, e.g., pumpkin, sesame
shallots
squash, e.g., butternut
sugar snap peas
tangerines
tarragon
thyme
tofu, e.g., extra-firm
tomatoes and sun-dried tomatoes
vinaigrette, e.g., shallot
VINEGAR, e.g., balsamic,
    champagne, cider, red wine,
    sherry, white wine
walnuts
wraps, lettuce
yogurt

Dishes

Butter Lettuce with Feta and Scallions in a Soft-Cooked Egg Vinaigrette
— Calliope (New York City)

Bibb Salad with Maytag Blue Cheese, Crispy Shallots, Tomato, Truffle Vinaigrette
— Mayflower Inn & Spa (Washington, CT)

Boston Lettuce, Roasted Beet, Cashew Chèvre, Toasted Walnuts, Champagne Vinaigrette
— True Bistro (Somerville, MA)

Flavor Affinities
butter lettuce + almonds + jícama
    + orange
butter lettuce + avocado +
    grapefruit + pecans + radicchio
butter lettuce + chiles + orange +
    pecans
butter lettuce + fennel +
    grapefruit
butter lettuce + figs + goat cheese
    + tarragon
butter lettuce + Gorgonzola
    cheese + hazelnuts + lemon +
    olives

● LETTUCE, LAMB'S (aka CORN SALAD or MÂCHE)
Season: spring – summer
Flavor: sweet, with buttery,
floral, fruity, and/or nutty notes,
and a soft texture
Volume: very quiet – quiet
Techniques: raw, steam

almonds
apples, e.g., green
artichokes
arugula
basil
BEETS, e.g., roasted
celery
cheese, e.g., goat, Parmesan,
    ricotta salata
chervil
chives
citrus

eggs, e.g., poached
endive
fennel and **fennel seeds**
frisée
garlic
greens, other salad, e.g., mesclun
jícama
lemon, e.g., juice, zest
lettuce, Bibb
mint
mustard
oils, e.g., nut, olive, peanut,
   walnut
olives
orange, e.g., juice, zest
pears
pepper
radicchio
radishes
SALADS
salt
sandwiches
shallots
tarragon
tomatoes
vinaigrette
vinegar, e.g., balsamic,
   champagne, Pedro Ximénez
   sherry, sherry, wine
walnuts
yogurt

Flavor Affinities

lamb's lettuce + almonds + citrus
   + fennel
lamb's lettuce + apples +
   clementines + endive + walnuts
lamb's lettuce + beets + celery
lamb's lettuce + beets + ricotta
   salata
lamb's lettuce + garlic + yogurt

Dishes

Mesclun and Mâche Salad:
Spring Vegetables, Mustard
Vinaigrette, Crudités
— DANIEL (New York City)

● LETTUCE, ROMAINE

Season: spring – autumn
Flavor: bitter/slightly sweet,
with a crisp, crunchy texture
Volume: quiet
Nutritional profile: 67% carbs
/ 18% protein / 15% fats
Calories: 10 per 1-cup serving
(raw, shredded)
Protein: 1 gram
Techniques: braise, grill, raw,
sauté

Tips: To add a note of the sea
in Caesar salads, try nori strips,
or for a pungent salty note, try
capers.

almonds, e.g., sliced
apples
AVOCADO
basil
beans, black
beets
bell peppers, e.g., green, red
bread, e.g., croutons
buttermilk
capers
carrots
cayenne
celery

CHEESE, e.g., **blue, feta,**
   Gorgonzola, Monterey Jack,
   mozzarella, **PARMESAN**, queso
   fresco, Stilton
"cheese," nut, e.g., pinenut,
   pumpkin seed – macadamia
   "Parmesan"
chervil
chickpeas
chiles, e.g., jalapeño, serrano
chives
cilantro
corn, corn chips, and corn
   tortillas
croutons, e.g., whole-grain
CUCUMBERS
dill
eggs, e.g., boiled, hard-boiled,
   yolks
frisée
GARLIC
ginger
grapefruit
jícama
leeks
LEMON, e.g., juice, zest
lime, e.g., juice, zest
lovage
mangoes
mayonnaise, e.g., vegan

Flavor Affinities

romaine + almonds + avocado + carrots + smoked tofu + tomatoes
romaine + apples + celery + lime + raisins + walnuts
romaine + avocado + lime
romaine + avocado + pumpkin seeds
romaine + blue cheese + pears + walnuts
romaine + carrots + cucumbers + dill + feta cheese
romaine + chickpeas + **cucumbers** + feta cheese + **olives** + **red onions**
   + **tomatoes**
romaine + **dill** + garlic + lemon + **scallions**
romaine + **dill** + olive oil + red wine vinegar + **scallions**
romaine + Dijon mustard + lemon + olive oil + scallions
romaine + **feta cheese** + **tomatoes**
romaine + **garlic** + **lemon**
romaine + Gorgonzola cheese + walnuts
romaine + **lemon** + **Parmesan cheese**
romaine + pears + sherry vinegar + walnuts

miso, e.g., barley, white
mushrooms, e.g., shiitake
MUSTARD, e.g., creamy Dijon,
    powdered
nori
OIL, e.g., canola, OLIVE, sesame,
    vegetable
olives, e.g., kalamata, niçoise
ONIONS, e.g., green, red
oranges
parsley
pears
pecans
pepper, e.g., black, white
pistachios
pomegranates
potatoes, esp. new
raisins
salad dressings, e.g., Caesar,
    vinaigrette, yogurt
SALADS, e.g., CAESAR, chopped,
    Greek, green
salt, e.g., kosher, sea
sandwiches
scallions
seeds, e.g., pumpkin, sesame,
    sunflower
shallots
shiso
soy sauce

sprouts
tahini
tamari
tarragon
tempeh
thyme
tofu, e.g., silken, smoked, soft
TOMATOES and sun-dried
    tomatoes
umeboshi paste
VINEGAR, e.g., balsamic,
    champagne, cider, red wine,
    rice wine, sherry, tarragon,
    white balsamic
walnuts
watercress
Worcestershire sauce, vegetarian
yogurt

"Our popular 'raw taco'
substitutes a leaf of romaine
for a taco shell, and is filled
with sprouted and pureed
walnuts that have been seasoned
with jalapeño, cilantro, bell
peppers, and cayenne and served
with guacamole, cashew
'Parmesan' cheese, and fresh
scallions."
— AMI BEACH, G-ZEN (BRANFORD, CT)

Dishes

Chopped Romaine Salad with Smoked Tofu and Almonds
— Gobo (New York City)

Laughing Seed Salad: Romaine Lettuce, Spring Mix, Grated Carrots and Red Cabbage,
Cherry Tomatoes, Red Bell Peppers, Cucumbers, Red Onion, Fresh Corn, Blanched Broccoli,
Mung Bean Sprouts and Clover Sprouts, topped with Sunflower and Pumpkin Seeds
— Laughing Seed Café (Asheville, NC)

Insalata di Lattuga Romana: Baby Romaine Lettuce with Beets, Goat Cheese, Marcona
Almonds, and Citrus Vinaigrette
— Le Verdure (New York City)

Baby Romaine Salad: Olive, Mustard, Buttermilk, Lemon, Parmesan, Duck Yolk
— Rowland's Restaurant at Westglow (Blowing Rock, NC)

Grilled Romaine Heart, French Lentils, Roasted Tomatoes, Mustard, Croutons
— True Bistro (Somerville, MA)

● LIMES (e.g., JUICE, ZEST)

Flavor: bitter/sour/sweet, and a very juicy texture
Volume: moderate
Nutritional profile: 86% carbs / 8% protein / 6% fat
Calories: 20 per lime
Botanical relatives: grapefruit, kumquat, lemon, orange
Tip: Grind dried limes to make a powder that can be sprinkled on dishes like a spice.

almonds
apples
apricots
arugula
AVOCADOS
baked goods, e.g., pies, tarts
bananas
basil
bell peppers
berries, e.g., blackberries,
strawberries
beverages, e.g., limeade, margaritas,
    mojitos
broccoli
caramel
carrots
cheese, e.g., cotija
CHILES, e.g., chipotle, jalapeño,
    serrano; and chili powder
CILANTRO
COCONUT and COCONUT
    MILK
coriander
corn
cucumbers
cumin
drinks, e.g., margaritas
fruits, esp. tropical
garlic
ginger
graham crackers
grapes
guacamole

guavas
hoisin
honey
Indian cuisine
jícama
lemon
lemongrass
lettuces, e.g., romaine
lychees
mangoes
marinades
mayonnaise
melon, e.g., honeydew
Mexican cuisine
mint
mushrooms
mustard powder
noodles, e.g., Asian, rice
nuts, e.g., macadamia
oil, e.g., grapeseed, olive,
   sunflower seed
onions
orange
Pacific Rim cuisines
papayas
peanuts
pears
pies
pomegranates
puddings, e.g., rice
quinoa
raspberries
rice
rosemary
rum
salad dressings

salads, e.g., fruit
salsas
sauces, e.g., ponzu
scallions
sesame, e.g., oil
shallots
soups, e.g., noodle, Thai
Southeast Asian cuisines
soy sauce
squash, butternut
sugar, e.g., brown
tapioca
tarragon
tarts
tequila
Thai cuisine
tofu
tomatillos
tomatoes
Vietnamese cuisine
vinegar, e.g., champagne, rice,
   sherry
watermelon
yogurt

Flavor Affinities

lime + avocado + romaine
lime + chipotle chiles + corn
lime + cilantro + cumin
lime + cilantro + garlic + oil
lime + coconut + graham crackers
lime + ginger + honey
lime + ginger + mint
lime + lychees + mint
lime + mint + scallions
lime + mushrooms + sesame

Dishes

Key Lime Tart, Champagne Gelée, Almond Streusel, Toasted Meringue
— Green Zebra (Chicago)

Raw Key Lime Cheesecake: Made with Cashews, Avocado, and Fresh Limes in a Faux
Graham Cracker Crust
— Laughing Seed Café (Asheville, NC)

LIQUID SMOKE
Flavor: notes of meat and/or
smoke
Volume: moderate – loud
What it is: condensed smoke
in water — *not* an artificial
ingredient; comes in various
flavors, e.g., apple, hickory,
mesquite, pecan

baked beans
beans, e.g., black, navy, red
cabbage
casseroles
chili, vegetarian
dips
eggs
gravies
greens, e.g., collard, mustard
mushrooms
oil, olive
potatoes
sauces, e.g., barbecue
seitan
soups, e.g., *bean, split pea*
soy sauce
stews
stock, vegetable
tempeh, e.g., *tempeh bacon* or
sausage
tofu
veggie burgers

Flavor Affinities
liquid smoke + olive oil + soy
   sauce + vegetable stock

• LOTUS ROOT
Season: summer – winter
Flavor: slightly sweet, with
earthy notes of artichoke,
jícama, or water chestnut, and a
crunchy texture (similar to water
chestnuts)
Volume: quiet
Nutritional profile: 89% carbs
/ 10% protein / 1% fat

Calories: 60 per 10-slice serving (raw)
Protein: 2 grams
Techniques: bake, boil, candy, fry, grate, pickle, raw, roast, simmer, steam, stew, stir-fry
Botanical relative: water lilies

avocado
bean sprouts
beans, e.g., long
bell peppers
broccoli
cherries
chiles, e.g., jalapeño, and chili pepper flakes
Chinese cuisine
chips
cilantro
citrus
cloves
compotes, e.g., fruit
cucumbers
curries
fennel seeds
garlic
ginger
Indian cuisine
Japanese cuisine
leeks
LEMON, e.g., juice
lemongrass
lettuce, e.g., butter
lime, e.g., juice
lychees
macrobiotic cuisine
mangoes
miso
mushrooms, esp. Asian
noodles, Asian, e.g., rice
oil, e.g., olive, vegetable
okra
onions, e.g., spring
orange
pickles
pumpkin
radishes

rice, e.g., sweet
rice, fried
saffron
salads
salt, sea
sesame oil
snow peas
SOUPS, e.g., Asian
Southeast Asian cuisine
soy sauce
stews
STIR-FRIES
stock, vegetable
sugar
sugar snap peas
sunchokes
tamari
tempura
tofu
turmeric
vegetables, root
vinegar, e.g., rice, white wine
water chestnuts
watercress
wine, rice

Flavor Affinities
lotus root + ginger + lemon
lotus root + lemongrass + lime

LOVAGE
Season: spring – autumn
Flavor: sour, with musky notes of anise, basil, **celery**, lemon, **parsley**, pine, and/or yeast
Volume: moderate – **loud**
What it is: herb
Tips: Serve its hollow stem as a straw in a Bloody Mary or in tomato soup. Its seeds can be used like celery seeds.
Botanical relative and possible substitute: parsley

apples
baked goods, e.g., breads, pastries
beans, e.g., dried, green

bell peppers
British cuisine
bruschetta
butter
caraway seeds
carrots
casseroles
celery
chard
cheese, e.g., cream, Parmesan
chervil
chiles
chives
corn
cucumbers
dill
eggs, e.g., *frittatas*, hard-boiled
fennel
French cuisine
garlic and garlic scapes
greens
Italian cuisine
leeks
lemon, e.g., juice
lettuce
marjoram
mint
mushrooms
mustard
nettles, stinging
oil, olive
onions, e.g., sweet
oregano
parsley
pesto
pine nuts
POTATOES, e.g., mashed
radishes
rice
SALADS, e.g., carrot, egg, green
sandwiches, e.g., tea
sauces, e.g., tomato
sorrel
SOUPS, e.g., lentil, tomato
spinach
stews
stock, vegetable

stuffings
sugar snap peas
"tabbouleh"
tarragon
thyme
tomatoes and tomato juice
turnips
vegetables, esp. root
vinegar
zucchini

Flavor Affinities
lovage + garlic + oregano +
  tomato
lovage + potatoes + *soups* +
  turnips

LUNCH and DINNER
When you can't think of what to
make for lunch or dinner, start
here for ideas:

burritos, e.g., with beans, rice, and
  vegetables on whole-grain tortillas
casseroles, e.g., chilaquiles (baked
  tortilla chip casserole)
chili, vegetarian
crepes, vegetable, e.g., asparagus
Crock-Pot dishes
curries, e.g., Indian, Thai
eggs, e.g., frittatas, quiches
enchiladas
fajitas
falafel, e.g., on whole-grain pita,
  with cucumber, hummus, tomato
farrottos (farro made in the style of
  risotto), e.g., with vegetables
kebabs, e.g., mushrooms and
  vegetables
lasagna, e.g., with spinach, other
  vegetables, [tofu] ricotta, and
  tomato sauce
lettuce wraps, e.g., around grains,
  vegetables
mushrooms, e.g., portobello
  "steaks," with mashed potatoes
  and gravy

noodles, e.g., Asian, with sesame
sauce and vegetables
pastas, e.g., whole-grain, with
creamy (e.g., cashew-based) sauce
or tomato sauce, and vegetables
pilafs, e.g., wild rice
pizzas, e.g., whole-grain, with
tomato sauce and vegetables (and
optional cheese)
polentas, e.g., with mushrooms and/
or vegetables (and optional cheese)
risottos, e.g., with vegetables (and
optional cheese)
salads, e.g., bean, "Caesar,"
chickpea, fruit, grain, green,
pasta, potato, spinach, tofu (e.g.,
"tuna"), vegetable
sandwiches, e.g., on whole-grain
bread, pita, or tortilla; with
cheese, nut butter, or tofu and/
or fruits (e.g., apples, bananas)
or vegetables (e.g., avocado, bell
peppers, onions, tomatoes); or a
classic veg "Reuben"
seitan, e.g., with a sauce, a starch
(e.g., grains, potatoes), and
vegetables
soups, e.g., legume (e.g., bean, lentil,
pea), mushroom, or vegetable
spaghetti and "wheatballs," with
tomato sauce
spaghetti squash "pasta," e.g., with
tomato sauce
stews, e.g., grain, legume, vegetable
stir-fries, e.g., with brown rice, tofu,
and/or vegetables
stuffed (e.g., with grains) vegetables,
e.g., bell peppers, cabbage,
eggplant, mushrooms, squash,
tomatoes, zucchini
sushi, e.g., nori rolls
tacos, e.g., whole-grain tortillas
with beans, rice, salsa, vegetables
tempeh, e.g., with a sauce and
vegetables
tofu, e.g., grilled, with a sauce,
rice, and vegetables
tostadas

vegetables, e.g., steamed
veggie burgers
wheat berry "risotto," e.g., with
vegetables (and optional cheese)
wraps

● LYCHEES

Season: summer
Flavor: sweet; aromatic, with
notes of cherries and/or grapes,
and a juicy, jelly-like texture
Volume: quiet – moderate
Nutritional profile: 90% carbs
/ 6% fats / 4% protein
Calories: 125 per 1-cup serving
(raw)
Protein: 2 grams
Technique: raw
Tip: Do not eat the seeds, which
are toxic.

almonds
bell peppers
BERRIES, e.g., blackberries,
blueberries, raspberries,
strawberries
cheese, cream
cherries
chiles, e.g., jalapeño, serrano
Chinese cuisine
chocolate, white
cilantro
coconut and coconut milk
cream
desserts, e.g., fruit tarts
drinks, e.g., cocktails
garlic
gin
ginger
grapefruit
honey
ice cream
jícama
kiwi
lemon, e.g., juice
lemongrass
LIME, e.g., juice

mango
melon, e.g., honeydew
mint
nectarines
nuts
onions, e.g., green or red
oranges, e.g., mandarins,
tangerines
passion fruit
peaches
pears, e.g., Asian
pineapple
plums
puddings, e.g., bread, rice
rice
rose water
rum
sake
salads, fruit
salsas, fruit
sugar, e.g., brown, palm
vanilla
vodka
wine, e.g., plum, sparkling
yogurt

Flavor Affinities
lychees + coconut milk + rice
lychees + ginger + kiwi
lychees + ginger + lime
lychees + honey + lime

MACA, MACA POWDER, or MACA ROOT

Flavor: notes of butterscotch,
malt, and/or nuts
Volume: quiet – moderate
Tip: Use it to enhance the
creaminess of smoothies.

baked goods, e.g., breads, cookies,
muffins
bananas
berries, e.g., goji, raspberries,
strawberries
candy, e.g., chocolate truffles
cereals, hot breakfast, e.g., oatmeal

chia seeds

chocolate and cacao nibs

cinnamon

coconut and coconut water

coffee, espresso

dates

desserts, e.g., puddings

drinks, e.g., coffee-based

fruit, esp. tropical, e.g., mango, pineapple

maple syrup

milk, e.g., almond, coconut, hemp, rice

nuts, nut butters, and nut milks, e.g., almonds, macadamias

orange, e.g., juice

pancakes and waffles

smoothies

vanilla

Flavor Affinities

maca + almond butter + cacao

maca + almond butter + coconut milk + dates + vanilla

Dishes

I Am Free: Chia Seed Porridge with Hempseed Milk, Lucuma, Maca, Cinnamon, Maple Syrup, Goji Berries, and Seasonal Fruit
— Café Gratitude (Los Angeles)

Malted Chai Smoothie: Banana. Dates. Coconut Meat. Coconut Water. Cinnamon. Maca.
— M.A.K.E. (Santa Monica, CA)

Maca Magic Smoothie: Mango, Strawberry, Pineapple, Banana, Raspberry, Orange Juice, Coconut Milk, Maca Powder, Goji Berry
— Pomegranate Café (Phoenix)

MACARONI AND CHEESE

Tip: Many of the best vegan versions of mac-n-cheese incorporate whole-grain macaroni and some combination of chili pepper flakes + cornstarch + Dijon mustard + **garlic** + **milk (e.g., soy)** + **nutritional yeast** + oil (e.g., canola, soy) + **paprika** + parsley + **salt** (e.g., sea) + tamari + tofu

Dishes

Macaroni and Cheese
(Its creaminess is said to come from soy milk and tofu.)
— Woodland's Vegan Bistro, fka Everlasting Life Café (Washington, DC)

Mac & Shews
(calls for cashews + garlic + nutritional yeast + olive oil + sauerkraut)
— Isa Chandra Moskowitz

Spicy Cajun Mac 'n' Yease, Our Famous Vegan Mac and Cheese
(Its secret recipe is said to include chili pepper flakes + mustard + nutritional yeast + soy milk.)
— Plum Bistro (Seattle)

● MACE

Flavor: bitter/**sweet**; aromatic; with pungent notes of cloves, **nutmeg**, and/or pine
Volume: moderate – **loud** (and quieter than nutmeg, though similar in flavor)
What it is: spice
Botanical relative: nutmeg

apples

baked goods, e.g., cakes, cookies, muffins, pies

carrots

cheese and cheese dishes, esp. creamy

cherries

chocolate

chocolate, hot

chutneys

cream and milk

custards

doughnuts

drinks, e.g., eggnog, hot chocolate

fruits, e.g., dried, fresh

hot dogs, vegetarian

ice cream

lemon

maple syrup

nutmeg

nuts

oats

orange

puddings

pumpkin

purees, vegetable

raisins

rhubarb

salads, fruit

sauces, e.g., *béchamel, cream, onion*

soups, e.g., *clear, cream*

stuffings

sugar

sweet potatoes

vanilla

vegetables

walnuts

wine, e.g., *mulled wine*

MÂCHE (see LETTUCE, LAMB'S)

● MAMEY (aka MAMEY APPLE or MAMEY SAPOTE)

[MAH-may / MAH-may sah-POH-tay]

Season: spring – autumn
Flavor: sweet, with notes of almonds, amaretto, apricot, banana, caramel, honey, maraschino cherry, melon, nutmeg, pear, persimmon, pumpkin, sweet potato, and/ or vanilla, and a soft, creamy, melting texture
Volume: moderate
What it is: fruit
Nutritional profile: 89% carbs / 8% fats / 3% protein
Calories: 215 per mamey half serving
Protein: 2 grams
Techniques: raw, stew

Tips: Store at room temperature until fruit softens. Serve chilled for optimal flavor.

Possible substitute: mangoes

baked goods, e.g., breads, cakes, muffins, pies, tarts
beverages
buttermilk
Central American cuisines
citrus, e.g., kumquats, oranges
cloves
coulis
cream, e.g., whipped
Cuban cuisine
desserts, e.g., custards, mousses, puddings
ginger
greens, salad
honey
ice creams and sorbets
Mexican cuisine
milk and milkshakes
nutmeg
sake, e.g., dry
salads, e.g., fruit
smoothies
sugar, e.g., brown
vanilla
West Indies cuisine

MANDARINS (see ORANGES, MANDARIN)

● MANGOES

Season: spring – summer
Flavor: sweet/slightly sour, with notes of honey, peaches, and/or pineapple, and an extremely juicy texture
Volume: moderate – loud
Who says they're healthful: The Center for Science in the Public Interest's Nutrition Action includes mangoes on its "10 Best Foods" list.
Nutritional profile: 94% carbs / 3% protein / 3% fats
Calories: 110 per 1-cup serving (raw, sliced)
Protein: 1 gram
Techniques: grill, **raw**, roast
Botanical relatives: cashews, pistachios

almonds and almond milk
arugula
avocados
bananas
basil, Thai
BEANS, e.g., **BLACK**, cannellini
bell peppers, e.g., red, yellow
berries, e.g., **blackberries, blueberries, raspberries,** strawberries
beverages, e.g., juices, lassis, punch
cardamom
cashews
cayenne
chayote
chickpeas
CHILES, e.g., green, habanero, jalapeño, red, serrano, Thai
chocolate, white
chutneys
CILANTRO
cinnamon
cloves
COCONUT and coconut milk

coriander
corn
coulis
cream, crème fraîche, and ice cream
crepes
cucumbers
cumin
curry
desserts, e.g., cheesecake
endive
fennel
fenugreek
garlic
GINGER
ginkgo nuts
honey
Indian cuisine
jícama
Kaffir lime leaf
kiwi
lassis
lavender
lemon, e.g., juice
lettuce
*LIME, e.g., juice
lime, Kaffir
liqueurs, e.g., Kirsch
melon, e.g., cantaloupe
Mexican cuisine
milk, coconut
MINT
nectarines
noodles, Asian, e.g., soba
nuts
oil, e.g., canola, olive, peanut
ONIONS, e.g., green, **RED,** sweet
oranges and mandarin oranges, e.g., juice, zest
oregano
PAPAYAS
paprika, smoked
parsley
passion fruit
peaches
peanuts
pears

pineapple
plantains
puddings
quinoa
rhubarb
rice, e.g., sticky
rum
*salads, e.g., Asian noodle, **fruit**,*
  green, pasta, rice
SALSAS
salt
sauces
scallions
seaweed
sesame, e.g., oil, seeds
shallots
smoothies
snow peas
SORBETS

Dishes

Warm Apple Mango Cobbler with Cinnamon Oat Streusel and Fat-Free Vanilla Ice Cream
— The Golden Door Spa Café at The Boulders (Scottsdale, AZ)

Flavor Affinities

MANGO + avocado + CHILES + CILANTRO + LIME + ONIONS +
  vinegar
mango + bananas + honey + lime juice + orange juice
mango + **beans** + **cilantro + lime + onions**
mango + **bell peppers + cilantro + lime**
mango + blackberries + lime
mango + brown sugar + cinnamon + orange
mango + **cardamom + honey + yogurt**
mango + cashew + mint
MANGO + CHILES + CILANTRO + LIME + RED ONIONS
mango + chiles + cumin + garlic + **lime** + orange
mango + coconut + tapioca + white chocolate
mango + coconut + yogurt
mango + coconut milk + sticky rice
mango + fennel + lemon + rum
mango + honey + mint **+ yogurt**
mango + honey + orange juice + yogurt
mango + kiwi + papaya + pineapple
mango + lime + mint + orange + papaya
mango + lime + mint + red onions
mango + lime + raspberries + vanilla
mango + peach + raspberries

soups, e.g., fruit
spinach
star anise
stir-fries
sugar, e.g., brown, palm
sweet potatoes
tamarind
tapioca
tarts
tempeh
tofu
tomatillos
tomatoes
tortillas, e.g., whole-grain
tropical fruits
vanilla
vinegar, e.g., champagne, red
  wine, rice wine
wine, e.g., sparkling, sweet, and/

or white (e.g., Sauternes)
yogurt
yuzu

MANGOES, GREEN
(see also MANGOES)
What they are: unripe mangoes

Caribbean cuisines
chiles, e.g., green, Thai
chutneys
cilantro
curries
Filipino cuisine
ginger
lime, e.g., juice
mint
oil, e.g., sesame
onions, e.g., red
pickles
relishes
salads
sesame seeds
sugar, e.g., brown, palm
Thai cuisine

● MAPLE SYRUP
Flavor: SWEET/bitter, with
notes of caramel and/or honey,
and a syrupy texture
Volume: moderate – loud
Nutritional profile: 99% carbs
/ 1% fat
Calories: 50 per 1-tablespoon
serving

Tip: Grade-B syrup is darker in
color, less refined, and richer
in flavor and minerals.

allspice
apples
artichokes, Jerusalem
baked goods
bananas
beans, dried
berries, e.g., **blueberries**,
  raspberries, strawberries
bourbon

breakfast dishes, *e.g.*, *French toast, pancakes, waffles*
Brussels sprouts
butter
buttermilk
cardamom
carrots
chiles, e.g., jalapeño
cinnamon
citrus
cloves
cookies
corn
cornmeal
cranberries
figs
ginger
glazes
granola
lemon
mascarpone
miso
mustard, e.g., Dijon
nutmeg
NUTS, e.g., **ALMONDS**,

Flavor Affinities
maple syrup + acorn squash + butter + mustard
maple syrup + almonds + dried cranberries + oats + pumpkin seeds
maple syrup + blueberries + lemon
maple syrup + butternut squash + garlic
maple syrup + cinnamon + pecans + vanilla
maple syrup + mustard + pecans + seitan
maple syrup + pears + pecans
maple syrup + pecans + sweet potatoes

Dishes

Homestyle Quinoa Pancakes, Seasonal Fruit, Strawberry Butter, Gingered Maple Syrup
— Candle 79 (New York City)

Jalapeño Hush Puppies served with Maple Butter
— Dirt Candy (New York City)

Maple Harvest Salad: Arugula, Raisins, Walnuts, and Green Apple, served with Creamy Maple Vinaigrette
— Root (Allston, MA)

cashews, hazelnuts, macadamias, **PECANS**, walnuts
oats and oatmeal
oranges
pancakes
peaches
pears
pies, e.g., maple, pumpkin
poppy seeds
porridges
pumpkin
pumpkin seeds
raisins
rice
rum
rutabagas
seeds, sesame, e.g., black, white
squash, winter
sugar, e.g., brown
sweet potatoes
turnips
vanilla
waffles

"**Maple syrup** isn't technically raw, but it's the least-processed widely available sweetener, and it's vegan."
— AMI BEACH, G-ZEN (BRANFORD, CT)

"I especially love using **maple syrup** as a sweetener in autumn and winter. During other times of year, I'll use agave nectar, barley malt syrup, or organic cane."
— KATE JACOBY, VEDGE (PHILADELPHIA)

● MARJORAM
Season: summer – winter
Flavor: bitter/**sweet**; aromatic, with floral, pungent, and/or spicy notes of basil, oregano, and/or thyme
Volume: quiet (regular) – moderate/loud (wild)
What it is: herb
Tip: Add marjoram at the end of the cooking process.
Botanical relatives: basil, lavender, mint, oregano (which is louder), rosemary, sage, summer savory, thyme
Possible substitute: oregano

artichokes
basil
bay leaf
BEANS, e.g., dried, green, lima
beets
bell peppers
bouquets garnis
butter
cabbage
capers
carrots
cauliflower
cheese, e.g., cottage, cream, Fontina, fresh, goat, mozzarella, Parmesan
chiles, e.g., dried
corn

cumin
eggplant
eggs, e.g., *frittatas*, hard-boiled,
  omelets
European cuisines
fennel seeds
fiddlehead ferns
fines herbes
French cuisine
garlic
Greek cuisine
greens, e.g., beet
grilled dishes
Italian cuisine
lemon
marinades
MEDITERRANEAN CUISINES
mushrooms, e.g., wild
nuts
oil, e.g., olive
olives, e.g., green
onions
orange, e.g., juice
oregano
paprika
parsley
parsnips
pastas
pine nuts
pizzas
Portuguese cuisine
potatoes, e.g., new
ratatouille
rice
risotto
rosemary
salad dressings
salads, e.g., bean, green, pasta,
  tomato
sauces, e.g., barbecue, butter,
  marjoram, mushroom, pasta,
  tomato
soups, e.g., bean, onion, tomato,
  vegetable
spreads
squash, e.g., summer (esp.
  zucchini), winter (esp. butternut)

stews
stuffings
sugar snap peas
tarragon
thyme
TOMATOES and tomato sauces
vinegar, e.g., red wine
walnuts
wine

Flavor Affinities
marjoram + capers + green olives
  + parsley + pine nuts
marjoram + chiles + orange

● MASCARPONE
[mahs-kahr-POH-neh]
Flavor: sweet, with notes of
cream, and a smooth, soft, fluffy
texture
Volume: quiet
What it is: a fresh, soft Italian
"cheese" made from thick cream
Nutritional profile: 98% fat /
2% protein
Calories: 120 per 1-ounce
serving
Protein: 2 grams
Possible substitutes:
cream cheese (esp. whipped),
Neufchâtel, ricotta cheese (esp.
whipped)

Flavor Affinities
mascarpone + apples + cinnamon + maple syrup
mascarpone + apricots + pistachios
mascarpone + balsamic vinegar + cinnamon + maple syrup + pears
mascarpone + balsamic vinegar + strawberries
mascarpone + basil or sage + **pasta + walnuts**
mascarpone + beets + poppy seeds
mascarpone + chocolate + coffee + orange
mascarpone + cinnamon + Marsala + orange + pears + sugar
mascarpone + figs + ginger
mascarpone + Gorgonzola + polenta
mascarpone + mushrooms + pasta
mascarpone + oranges + vanilla
mascarpone + polenta + rosemary + walnuts

apples
apricots
artichokes
basil
beets
bell peppers, e.g., red, roasted
BERRIES, e.g., **blueberries,**
  raspberries, STRAWBERRIES
breakfast/brunch, e.g., French toast
chard
cheese, e.g., cream, Gorgonzola,
  Parmesan, Robiolo
chocolate, e.g., dark, white
cinnamon
cocoa
coffee and espresso
cream and whipped cream
dates
DESSERTS, e.g., cheesecakes,
  crepes, granitas, ice creams,
  parfaits, puddings, semifreddos,
  tarts, tiramisu
figs
fruit
garlic
honey, e.g., chestnut
Italian cuisine
lemon, e.g., juice, zest
lime, e.g., juice, zest
maple syrup
mint
mushrooms

nectarines

noodles

nuts, e.g., almonds, hazelnuts, pine nuts, pistachios, walnuts

oranges and blood oranges

pastas, e.g., *fettuccine, lasagna, linguini*

peaches

pears

peas

plums

polenta

poppy seeds

risottos

rosemary

sage

salads, e.g., *fruit*

sauces, e.g., *pasta*

soups, e.g., broccoli, butternut squash, mushroom, parsnip, pumpkin, spinach, tomato

spinach

spreads

sugar

TIRAMISU

tomatoes and sun-dried tomatoes

truffles, e.g., white

vanilla

vinegar, e.g., balsamic

wine, e.g., Marsala

zucchini

MATCHA POWDER

Flavor: bitter, with earthy vegetal notes

Volume: quiet – moderate

What it is: green tea powder

Nutritional profile: 67% protein, 33% carbs

Calories: 85 per ounce

Protein: 14 grams

agave nectar

avocado

baked goods, e.g., *cakes, cookies*

bananas

berries

beverages, e.g., *lattes*

cocoa

coconut water

desserts, e.g., *puddings*

ginger

honey

ice creams

mangoes

milk, nondairy, e.g., almond, rice, soy

pineapple

quinoa

salad dressings

smoothies

TEAS

Flavor Affinities

matcha powder + agave nectar + avocado + banana + (nondairy) milk

● MAYONNAISE

Tips: For a vegan (eggless) substitute, check out the longtime gold-standard Vegenaise vegan mayonnaise — or make your own. Wildwood also makes a zesty vegan garlic aioli (garlic "mayonnaise").

beans, e.g., green

bell peppers, e.g., red, roasted

capers

carrots

chiles, e.g., chipotle, green, red

corn, e.g., on the cob

eggs, e.g., hard-boiled

garlic

herbs, e.g., basil, chervil, chives, cilantro, dill, marjoram, parsley, **tarragon**

lemon

mustard, e.g., Dijon

orange, e.g., juice, zest

pickles

potatoes

salad dressings, e.g., *blue cheese, ranch*

salads, e.g., *egg, pasta, potato, vegetable*

sandwiches

sauces

scallions

slaws, e.g., cole

spices, e.g., cayenne, saffron

veggie burgers

MEDITERRANEAN CUISINES (see GREEK CUISINE, ITALIAN CUISINE — SOUTHERN, etc.)

"So much **Mediterranean food** is inherently vegan, which is why we refer to Crossroads as a Mediterranean restaurant. We don't use the word 'vegan' here. This way, the food is not seen as foreign to people who eat here. At Crossroads, people are not eating tofu or tempeh or seitan, whose textures are foreign to most people. While I like tempeh, you are not going to convince someone to go vegan if that is the first thing they try. People need familiar food that is transitional, and that will depend on the person. Our spanakopita or spiced chickpeas are dishes people are already acquainted with, and our risotto is the least threatening dish on the menu and something that people have already had."

—TAL RONNEN, CROSSROADS (LOS ANGELES)

MELON — IN GENERAL, or MIXED (see also MELON, CANTALOUPE; MELON, HONEYDEW; WATERMELON; etc.)

Season: summer – autumn

Flavor: sweet, with a juicy texture

Volume: quiet – moderate
Technique: raw
Botanical relatives:
cucumbers, pumpkins, squashes

arugula
bananas
basil
bell peppers
berries, e.g., blackberries,
    raspberries, **strawberries**
chiles
cilantro
coconut and coconut milk
cucumber
desserts
garlic
GINGER
granitas
grapes
honey
LEMON
lemongrass
LIME
mint
onions, e.g., red
oranges
pears
pepper, e.g., black, white
rum
salads, e.g., fruit
salsas
soups, fruit
Thai basil
tomatoes
vanilla
wine, e.g., **sparkling**, e.g.,
    Champagne, and/or **sweet**, e.g.,
    Moscato d'Asti, port
yogurt

Flavor Affinities
melon + berries + lemon
melon + chiles + cilantro + garlic
    + lime + onions
melon + honey + lime
melon + lime + mint

MELON, BITTER

Flavor: BITTER/sour, with notes
of **quinine**
Volume: loud
What it is: a fruit that is picked
green (unripe) and eaten as a
vegetable
Techniques: blanch, boil (sliced,
3 – 5 minutes), grill, pickle,
steam, stir-fry, stuff

Tips: To reduce bitterness, rub
raw slices with salt and let sit for
several minutes, or blanch slices
in boiling water 2 – 3 minutes.
Also, there's no need to peel —
the bumpy skin is edible.

Botanical relative: squash
Possible substitute: winter
melon

Asian cuisines
beans, e.g., black, fermented
    black
Cambodian cuisine
chiles, e.g., green, jalapeño, red
Chinese cuisine, esp. Cantonese
cilantro
coconut and coconut milk
coriander
cumin
curries
East Indian cuisine
eggs
garlic
ginger
ice creams
Indian cuisine
kamut
lemon
lime
miso
oil, e.g., canola, olive, peanut,
    sesame
onions
pickles
pomegranate seeds
poppy seeds

---

potatoes
rice
salt, e.g., sea
sesame, e.g., oil, paste, seeds
sorbets
soups
soy sauce
squash, e.g., kabocha
stir-fries
stuffed bitter melon
sugar, e.g., brown
tofu, e.g., firm
tomatoes
turmeric
vinegar, e.g., cider
yogurt

Flavor Affinities
bitter melon + garlic + soy sauce
bitter melon + honey + lemon
bitter melon + miso + tofu

● MELON, CANTALOUPE

Season: summer
Flavor: sweet, with a juicy
texture
Volume: quiet – **moderate**
Nutritional profile: 87% carbs
/ 8% protein / 5% fats
Calories: 60 per 1-cup serving
(raw, balls)
Protein: 1 gram
Botanical relatives:
cucumbers, pumpkin, squash

agave nectar
basil
BERRIES, e.g., **blackberries,
    blueberries**, raspberries
buttermilk
cheese, e.g., blue, cottage
chiles, e.g., jalapeño
cilantro
cinnamon
CITRUS, e.g., lemon, **LIME,
    orange**
cucumber

dates
figs
garlic
GINGER
honey
ices and granitas
lemongrass
mango
maple syrup
melon, other, e.g., honeydew
MINT
nectarines
nut butter, e.g., cashew
nutmeg
oil, olive
onions, red
papaya
peaches
PEPPER, e.g., black or white
raisins
raspberries
rice, brown
salads, e.g., fruit
salsas
salt, e.g., sea
sorbets
sorrel
SOUPS, FRUIT
vanilla
vinegar, e.g., balsamic
watermelon
wine, e.g., sparkling, sweet
YOGURT

Flavor Affinities

cantaloupe + agave nectar +
   ginger
cantaloupe + basil + black pepper
   + blue cheese

Dishes

Cantaloupe Sorbet with Anise Shortbread and Jasmine Consommé
— Charlie Trotter's (Chicago)

Chilled Melon Soup: Cantaloupe and Dried Chili Pepper, Pickled Carrots, Fried Shallots,
and Mint-Chive Oil
— Num Pang (New York City)

cantaloupe + ginger + lime +
   orange
cantaloupe + honey + vanilla +
   yogurt
cantaloupe + lemon + mint
cantaloupe + mango + papaya

● MELON, HONEYDEW

Season: summer
Flavor: sweet, with a juicy
texture
Volume: quiet – **moderate**
Nutritional profile: 92% carbs
/ 5% protein / 3% fats
Calories: 65 per 1-cup serving
(raw, balls)
Protein: 1 gram

arugula
basil
BERRIES, e.g., blackberries,
   blueberries, raspberries
beverages, e.g., fruit punch
cayenne
cinnamon
cucumbers
GINGER
honey
kiwi
LEMON, e.g., juice, zest
lemongrass
LIME
maple syrup
melon, other, e.g., cantaloupe
MINT
papaya
pepper, e.g., white
pomegranates
salads, e.g., fruit

salsas
salt
skewers, fruit
smoothies
sorbets
SOUPS, FRUIT
sugar
tofu
vanilla
vinegar, esp. fruit, e.g., apple,
   raspberry
wine, e.g., sparkling, sweet
yogurt

Flavor Affinities

honeydew melon + cayenne
   + lemon
honeydew melon + ginger +
   lemon + pomegranate
**HONEYDEW MELON
   (+ HONEY) + LEMON and/or
   LIME + MINT**

MELON, WINTER

Season: winter
Flavor: sweet, with notes of
zucchini, and a juicy melon-like
texture
Volume: quiet
What it is: Asian squash (not
technically a melon)
Techniques: braise, simmer,
steam
Possible substitute: bitter
melon

bamboo shoots
chili powder
Chinese cuisine
cilantro
coconut milk
garlic
ginger
Kaffir lime
lemongrass
mushrooms, e.g., shiitake
scallions
shallots

soups, e.g., *Chinese, winter melon*
stews
stir-fries

MESCLUN (see GREENS, MESCLUN)

MEXICAN CUISINE

achiote
avocados
bay leaf
BEANS, esp. black, pinto, red
burritos
canela
chalupas
chayote
cheese, e.g., cotija
chilaquiles
*CHILES, e.g., dried, fresh;** and
   chili powder
chocolate, Mexican
cilantro
cinnamon
citrus, e.g., lemon, lime, (bitter)
   orange
cloves
CORN
crema
cumin
enchiladas
epazote
fried dishes
garlic
gorditas
guacamole
lemon
lime, e.g., juice
masa harina, i.e., ground corn
   dough
milk, condensed
nuts
onions, e.g., white
orange, esp. bitter
oregano, Mexican
potatoes
quesadillas
refried beans
rice

saffron
salsas
scallions
seeds, e.g., pumpkin, sesame
soups, e.g., *tortilla*
SQUASH
tacos
tamales
tomatoes
tortillas, e.g., corn
tostadas
vanilla
vegetables
vinegar
wheat

"I've made an ice cream with all
the ingredients of a mole sauce,
such as the spices — but minus
the garlic and onions. I've also
made **Mexican** chocolate cake
with chipotle in the batter, served
with a vanilla and coconut sauce."
— ANGEL RAMOS, CANDLE 79
(NEW YORK CITY)

MIDDLE EASTERN CUISINES

beans, e.g., fava
bulgur wheat
cheese, e.g., feta
chickpeas
cinnamon
cloves
coriander
couscous
cumin
dill
eggplant
falafel
fruits, e.g., dried
garlic
ginger
honey
hummus
lemon, e.g., fresh, **preserved**
lentils
mint, e.g., dried

nutmeg
nuts, e.g., almonds, pine nuts,
   pistachios, walnuts
oil, olive
olives
onions
oregano
parsley
pepper, black
pita, e.g., whole-wheat
pomegranates
poppy seeds
raisins
ras el hanout
rice
roasted dishes
sesame, e.g., oil, sauce (tahini),
   seeds
sumac
tomatoes
yogurt
za'atar

Flavor Affinities
bulgur + mint + onions + parsley
chickpeas + garlic + lemon +
   tahini
eggplant + garlic + parsley +
   tahini

MILK, e.g., • WHOLE or • NONFAT — IN GENERAL

Tip: Vegans can use nondairy
milks (e.g., almond, hempseed, rice, soy, etc.) when baking or making French toast,
with breakfast cereals, and in
smoothies.

• MILK, ALMOND
Flavor: slightly sweet, with
notes of almonds, and a creamy
medium-to-full-bodied texture
Volume: moderate
Lactose-free: yes
Nutritional profile: 56% carbs
/ 42% fat / 7% protein

Calories: 60 per 1-cup serving
Protein: 1 gram
Tips: For a delicious vegan hot chocolate, melt bittersweet or semisweet chocolate, then blend with almond milk just until hot. Do not overheat, as almond milk will evaporate.
Brand: Blue Diamond Almond Breeze Unsweetened Original

agave nectar
baked goods, e.g., breads, cakes, cookies, muffins
cacao
cereals, breakfast
cinnamon

Dishes

Rodrigo's Rocket Fuel Smoothie: Almond Butter, Almond Milk, Raw Cacao, Banana, Chocolate Sunwarrior Protein, Cinnamon
— Pomegranate Café (Phoenix)

coffee
desserts, esp. creamy
dressings
drinks, creamy
French toast
fruit
mango
mint
nutmeg
oats and oatmeal
puddings
raspberries
sauces, e.g., dessert
smoothies
vanilla

Flavor Affinities

almond milk + agave nectar + cacao + vanilla

● MILK, COCONUT

Flavor: sweet, with notes of coconut, and a rich, creamy texture
Volume: moderate – loud
What it is: liquid from grated coconut
Lactose-free: yes
Nutritional profile: 91% fat / 5% carbs / 4% protein
Calories: 445 per 1-cup serving (canned)
Protein: 5 grams
Tips: Look for organic coconut milk in cartons (versus cans). The health-conscious can opt for light (both lighter in flavor and lower in fat) or unsweetened coconut milk. Condensed coconut milk can be used for desserts, sauces, and soups.

agar-agar
agave nectar
Asian cuisines
baked goods
bananas
basil

beans, e.g., **green**, kidney
beverages
brandy
broccoli
Caribbean cuisines
carrots
cashews
cauliflower
chard
chickpeas
chocolate
coconut and coconut oil
corn
CURRIES, e.g., Thai
custards
DESSERTS
eggplant
espresso
galangal
garlic
greens, e.g., bitter
Hawaiian cuisine
ICE CREAMS
Indian cuisine
Kaffir lime leaf
kuzu
Latin American cuisines
leeks
lemongrass
lentils
limes and key limes
mangoes
mushrooms
noodles, Asian, e.g., rice
onions, e.g., red
passion fruit
peanuts
peas
pineapple
plantains
potatoes
puddings, e.g., pumpkin, rice
pumpkin and pumpkin seeds
RICE, e.g., **brown**, **sticky**, wild
salad dressings
sauces
sesame seeds
smoothies

sorbets
SOUPS, e.g., bisque, carrot, mushroom, pea, potato, tomato
spinach
squash, winter, e.g., acorn, Hubbard
stews, e.g., Indian
sugar, e.g., brown
sugar snap peas
sweet potatoes
tapioca, pearl
tempeh
Thai basil
THAI CUISINE
tofu
vanilla
"whipped cream"
zucchini

Flavor Affinities

coconut milk + bananas + pearl tapioca + sesame seeds
coconut milk + carrots + lemongrass
coconut milk + cauliflower + potatoes + spinach
coconut milk + espresso + vanilla
coconut milk + galangal + lemongrass + noodles
coconut milk + Kaffir lime + peanuts
coconut milk + lime + peas + rice
coconut milk + lime + tapioca
coconut milk + sweet potatoes + wild rice

"We make our own **coconut milk** – based ice creams and use Irish moss to stabilize them. We'll even top them with 'whipped cream' from a siphon, which is also coconut milk-based. Coconut Bliss is a fantastic Oregon-based dairy-free 'ice cream' made with **coconut milk** and agave, which was recently sold to a dairy."
— AARON ADAMS, PORTOBELLO (PORTLAND, OR)

"We have a new vegan truck for selling burgers, and desserts like our Vegan Fat Boys, which are vegan brownies filled with **coconut milk**–based Coconut Bliss ice cream. The texture is very rich and creamy, not icy, and its flavor is not overpowering."
— MAKINI HOWELL, PLUM BISTRO (SEATTLE)

"We make our ice cream from a blend of **coconut milk** and soy milk, which prevents the flavor, texture, and color of either milk from interfering with that of the ice cream. The result is a very thick and creamy ice cream. . . . Our roast pumpkin ice cream is accented mostly by cinnamon, but also allspice, cloves, and nutmeg. . . . Coconut milk has such a high fat content that all you need to do is add a bit of powdered sugar and run it through a charged canister to have nice, thick whipped cream."
— KATE JACOBY, VEDGE (PHILADELPHIA)

"Our signature ice cream starts with **coconut cream**, organic unrefined cane sugar, agave, and a trace amount of plant-based stabilizers (guar and xanthan gum), and works well with exotic spicy and savory flavors, such as toasted pine nut and fennel, or Mexican chocolate with cayenne and cinnamon, or Thai chili peanut. Our nut-based flavors are made with an almond and cashew blend, and work best with more traditional flavors like caramel, chocolate, cookie, peanut butter, and vanilla. Our soft ice cream flavors are made with a soy base."
— DEENA JALAL, FOMU AND ROOT (ALLSTON, MA)

"**Coconut milk** is fantastic — it's saved our lives in being able to serve our vegan guests. We use it a lot in vegan desserts, like our coconut milk panna cotta. The mouthfeel is not the same as when making a dairy panna cotta, so you've got to use a bit more vanilla and sugar. And we've made mousses by putting a mixture of coconut milk and agar-agar through an iSi whipped cream dispenser."
— MARK LEVY, THE POINT (SARANAC LAKE, NY)

MILK, GOAT

Flavor: salty/sour/sweet
Volume: moderate – loud

Tips: Can be easier to digest given its lower level of lactose (4.1%) than cow's milk (4.7%) and the absence of cow's milk's main problem-causing protein (alpha SI casein). Sweeten and reduce over medium heat to make *cajeta* (a thick Mexican caramel sauce).

apples
butter
carrots and carrot juice
cheese
chocolate
cinnamon
confections, e.g., caramels, fudge
desserts, creamy, e.g., puddings
eggplant
eggs, e.g., *quiches*
honey
ice cream and gelato
pancakes
potatoes
smoothies
soups
sugar
vanilla
yogurt

• MILK, HEMP

Flavor: notes of nuts, and a creamy texture
Volume: quiet – moderate
What it is: milk made from hemp seeds
Lactose-free: yes

agave nectar
baked goods, e.g., cakes, muffins
breakfast dishes, e.g., pancakes, waffles
brown rice syrup
cashews
casseroles
cereals, breakfast, e.g. granola, oatmeal
chocolate
coffee
dates
dips
ice cream
lattes
maple syrup
puddings, e.g., chia seed
smoothies
soups, e.g., mushroom
vanilla

"We tested lots of different nondairy milks to come up with our recipe for a latte with the creamy richness of cow's milk, which is half **hemp milk** and half coconut milk, plus agave nectar as a sweetener, added to two shots of espresso. Either will be good on its own, but the fat from the coconut milk adds great richness, while the hemp milk adds a more understated nutty flavor, and together they foam up really well."
— CASSIE AND MARLENE TOLMAN, POMEGRANATE CAFÉ (PHOENIX)

• MILK, RICE

Flavor: sweet, with notes of rice, and a light-bodied texture
Volume: moderate
Lactose-free: yes

Tip: Given its sweetness, it works better in desserts than in savory dishes.

Brand: Rice Dream

baked goods, e.g., breads, cakes, cookies, muffins
bananas
cinnamon
desserts, e.g., creamy *(e.g., custards)*
horchata
"ice cream"
Latin American cuisine
Mexican cuisine
pastas, e.g., mac-n-cheese
puddings, e.g., banana, rice
raisins
sauces, e.g., béchamel
smoothies
sugar
vanilla

"**Rice milk** makes great custards and sauces. I'm using it to develop a vegan béchamel sauce."
— DIANE FORLEY, FLOURISH BAKING COMPANY (SCARSDALE, NY)

• MILK, SOY

Flavor: vegetal notes, and full-bodied
Volume: loud
Lactose-free: yes
Nutritional profile: 54% carbs / 27% fat / 19% protein
Calories: 165 per 12-ounce serving
Protein: 8 grams

Tips: Foams well, e.g., for cappuccinos and lattes. Consider vanilla-flavored soy milk for use in desserts and sweet beverages.
Brand: Silk

baked goods, e.g., breads, cakes, cookies, muffins
banana
chocolate
coffee and *coffee drinks, e.g., cappuccinos, lattes*
desserts, creamy (e.g., panna cotta)
gelatin
honey
lime, e.g., Kaffir
mangoes
mashed potatoes
puddings
raspberries
salad dressings
sauces, e.g., creamy, pasta
smoothies
tofu, e.g., silken
vanilla

Dishes

Vanilla – Kaffir Lime – Soy Milk Panna Cotta with Mango and Raspberries
— Charlie Trotter's Restaurant C at OneandOnly Palmilla (Los Cabos, Mexico)

• MILLET

[MILL-let]

Flavor: bitter/sweet, with notes of corn and/or nuts; chewy, crunchy, and/or fluffy in texture

Volume: quiet – moderate (toasted)

What it is: whole grain

Gluten-free: yes

Nutritional profile: 82% carbs / 11% protein / 7% fat

Calories: 210 per 1-cup serving (cooked)

Protein: 6 grams

Techniques: dry roast, marinate, pressure-cook, simmer, **steam**, toast

Timing: Simmer about 15 – 20 minutes (chewier) to 30 – 40 minutes (softer), until desired tenderness is reached.

Flavor Affinities

millet + agave nectar + almond milk + coconut milk

millet + almonds + cardamom + cinnamon + cumin + turmeric

millet + almonds + orange

millet + apricots + raisins

millet + black beans + sweet potatoes

millet + blueberries + fennel + hazelnuts

millet + cauliflower + *"mashed potatoes"*

millet + chickpeas + garlic + greens

millet + cilantro + lime + tomatoes

millet + dates + nuts

millet + garlic + mint + parsley

millet + ginger + winter squash

millet + honey + milk

millet + honey + nuts

millet + lemon + watercress

millet + orange + pecans

millet + peanuts + sweet potatoes

Dishes

Millet Salad: Beluga Lentils, Parsley, Roasted Zucchini, Cauliflower, Carrot, and Baby Turnips; served over Mesclun with a side of Creamy Cucumber Dressing
— Candle Cafe (New York City)

Ratio: 1: 2 – 3 (1 cup millet to 2 – 3 cups liquid. Use more liquid for softer texture; also, given its flavor neutrality, use vegetable stock instead of water.)

Tips: Toast before steaming to bring out its flavor. Marinate, or cook risotto-style: Sauté millet before adding liquid to simmer slowly.

Possible substitute: couscous

(NORTH) AFRICAN CUISINES

almonds

amaranth

apples, e.g., apple juice, applesauce

apricots, e.g., dried

arugula

Asian cuisines

avocado

baked goods, e.g., breads, muffins

basil

batters, e.g., pancake, waffle

bay leaf

BEANS, e.g., adzuki, **black**, broad, green, white

beets

bell peppers, red

berries, e.g., blueberries

"bowls"

broccoli

burdock

butter

cabbage

cardamom

CARROTS

casseroles

CAULIFLOWER

celery and celery root

CEREALS, HOT BREAKFAST

chard

cheese, e.g., cheddar, Jack, Parmesan, pecorino, ricotta

cherries

chervil

chickpeas

chiles, e.g., Anaheim, jalapeño

chili pepper sauce and chili powder

chives

cilantro

cinnamon

coconut

coriander

CORN

"couscous"

croquettes

CUMIN

currants

curry powder, curry spices, and *curries*

dals

dates

dill

eggplant

fennel

GARLIC

ginger

grains, **other,** e.g., bulgur, corn,
  oats, quinoa, rice
granola
greens, e.g., **bitter, mesclun, salad**
honey
(East) Indian cuisine
leeks
lemon, e.g., juice, zest
lentils
lime, e.g., juice
mango
maple syrup
milk, e.g., almond, other nondairy
millet cakes
mint
muffins
mushrooms, e.g., porcini,
  portobello
nuts, e.g., hazelnuts, **peanuts,**
  pecans, pine nuts
oats
OILS, e.g., canola, corn, **olive,**
  peanut, vegetable
ONIONS, e.g., green, spring,
  yellow
orange
oregano
PARSLEY
parsnips
peaches
peas
pepper, black
PILAFS
"POLENTAS"
porridges
puddings
pumpkin
raisins, e.g., golden
raspberries
rice, e.g., brown, long-grain
"risottos"
rosemary
saffron
salads, e.g., fruit, green
salt, sea
sandwiches, e.g., "sloppy Joes"
scallions
seeds, e.g., poppy, pumpkin,
  sesame, sunflower

sesame, e.g., oil, seeds
shallots
SOUPS
sour cream
soy sauce
SQUASH, e.g., acorn, butternut,
  kabocha, summer
stews (e.g., to thicken)
stir-fries
STOCK, e.g., corn, vegetable
stuffed mushrooms or vegetables,
  e.g., artichokes or onions
stuffings
sweet potatoes
"tabbouleh"
tamari
tarragon
tempeh
thyme
tomatillos
tomatoes, sun-dried
TOMATOES, tomato paste, and
  tomato sauce
turmeric
turnips
vanilla
vegetables, e.g., baby, sautéed
veggie burgers
vinegar, e.g., balsamic, red wine,
  umeboshi
walnuts
watercress
yams
yogurt
zucchini

"When I opened Verbena [in
1994], I would go to Kalustyan's
[the famed Manhattan spice
and specialty food store] and
buy unusual grains to serve.
Millet was never used at other
restaurants at the time. In
Verbena's review in *The New York
Times*, it was referred to as 'bird
seed.' So you see how much
times have changed!"
— DIANE FORLEY, FLOURISH BAKING
COMPANY (SCARSDALE, NY)

● MINT (typically
SPEARMINT)

Flavor: slightly sweet; aromatic,
with pungent notes of herbs and/
or lemon
Volume: quiet/moderate
(e.g., spearmint) – loud (e.g.,
peppermint)
Tips: Recipes that call for mint
typically mean spearmint (versus,
e.g., peppermint). Mint suggests
"false coolness," and adds a note
of freshness to dishes.
Botanical relatives: basil,
lavender, marjoram, oregano,
rosemary, sage, summer savory,
thyme

almonds
apples
artichokes
Asian cuisines
barley
basil
beans, e.g., black, fresh, green,
  white
bell peppers
berries, e.g., blueberries,
  raspberries, strawberries
BEVERAGES, e.g., juleps, lassis,
  lemonades, mojitos, teas
bourbon
Brussels sprouts
cabbage
cardamom
CARROTS
cashews
cheese, e.g., chèvre, feta, ricotta
chickpeas
CHILES, e.g., green, jalapeño
chives
CHOCOLATE, e.g., dark
chutneys
cilantro
citrus
coconut and coconut milk
coriander
couscous, e.g., Israeli, whole-
  wheat

cream
*CUCUMBERS
curries
desserts
dill
eggplant
endive
falafel
figs
frisée
fruits, e.g., dried, fresh
garlic
gin
ginger
grains
grapefruit
grapes and grape juice
ice cream
Indian cuisine
jícama
kale
LEMON
lemongrass
lentils
lettuce
LIME
lovage
lychees
mangoes, e.g., green
Mediterranean cuisines

MELON, e.g., honeydew
Middle Eastern cuisine
millet
mojitos
Moroccan cuisine
mushrooms, portobello
noodles, Asian, esp. rice
olives
onions
oranges and orange juice
papaya, e.g., green
parsley
pasta
peaches
pears
PEAS
"pestos"
pilafs
pineapple
pine nuts
pistachios
potatoes, e.g., new
quinoa
raitas
RICE
risotto
rum
SALADS, *e.g., bean, fruit, grain,*
green, Thai, vegetable
salsas

sauces, e.g., "chimichurri"
scallions
shallots
shoots, bean
soups
Southeast Asian cuisines
spinach
squash, e.g., acorn, butternut,
yellow
stuffings, e.g., grain
sugar, e.g., brown
TABBOULEH
TEAS, e.g., green, **mint, Moroccan**
TOMATOES
vegetables, e.g., marinated
Vietnamese cuisine
vinegar, e.g., balsamic, white
wine
watermelon
wheat berries
YOGURT
zucchini

Flavor Affinities

mint + artichokes + chiles
mint + balsamic vinegar + berries
mint + balsamic vinegar + peaches + ricotta
mint + barley + carrots + peas **mint** + basil + **cilantro** + **chiles** + **garlic**
+ lime
mint + bell peppers + chiles + garlic + papaya + pineapple
mint + cardamom + ginger + lemon
mint + **chiles** + **cilantro** + **garlic** + olive oil + vinegar
mint + chiles + lemon + shallots + sugar
mint + citrus + zucchini
MINT + CUCUMBER + YOGURT
mint + feta cheese + lentils
mint + feta cheese + peas + rice
mint + Israeli couscous + lime
mint + lemon + strawberries
mint + lime + lychees
mint + olive oil + white beans + white wine vinegar

MIRIN

Flavor: slightly sweet, with the texture of syrup
Volume: moderate
What it is: sweet Japanese rice wine used in cooking; contains about 13 – 14 percent alcohol and 40 – 50 percent sugar
Tip: Look for mirin labeled "hon-mirin honjozo" in health food stores; beware heavily sweetened versions in Asian markets, which often contain high-fructose corn syrup.

Asian cuisines
carrots
daikon
garlic
ginger
hiziki
JAPANESE CUISINE
macrobiotic cuisine
marinades
miso
sake

salad dressings
SAUCES, *e.g., dipping, teriyaki*
sesame oil
soups
SOY SAUCE
stews
stir-fries
sugar
tofu
vegetables, esp. sweet
vinegar, rice

Flavor Affinities

mirin + garlic + ginger + sesame
  oil + soy sauce

MISO — IN GENERAL (or MIXED MISOS), ORGANIC

[MEE-soh]

Flavor: sweet (light miso) and/
or salty (dark miso), with earthy/
savory notes of cocoa, coffee,
malt, nuts, and/or yeast

Volume: quiet (lighter miso,
e.g., white, yellow) – loud (darker
miso, e.g., red, brown)

What it is: Japanese fermented
soybean paste, available in
countless different varieties in
Japan — as many varieties as
there are types of cheese available
in the U.S.!

Nutritional profile: 55% carbs
/ 25% fat / 20% protein

Calories: 275 per ½-cup serving

Protein: 16 grams

Techniques: To protect miso's
nutritional value, never bring to
a boil.

Dishes

Miso Tortellini with Red Cabbage, Turnip Confit, and Ponzu
— Charlie Trotter's (Chicago)

Tips: Mix light and dark misos
for more complex flavors. Add
miso to mashed or pureed vegetables and use as a sauce. Also,
customize miso soup by the
season; for example, in *spring/
summer*, use light miso + basil
+ green beans, and in *autumn/
winter*, use dark miso + Brussels
sprouts + garlic.

asparagus
avocado
beans, e.g., adzuki, black, green,
  pinto
bok choy
Brussels sprouts
burdock
cabbage, e.g., Chinese, napa
CARROTS
chives
cilantro
daikon
dashi
dips, e.g., bean
dressings
dulse
edamame
eggplant
garlic
GINGER
glazes
gravies
greens, e.g., Asian, dandelion
hoisin
honey
JAPANESE CUISINE
kombu
leeks
lemon, e.g., juice, zest

lemongrass
lotus root
macrobiotic cuisine
maple syrup
*MARINADES
melon, bitter
millet
mint
mirin
MUSHROOMS, e.g., enoki,
  SHIITAKE, wild
mustard
NOODLES, ASIAN, e.g., ramen,
  rice, SOBA, udon
nori
oil, e.g., canola, sesame
onions, e.g., green, spring, white,
  yellow
orange, e.g., juice, zest
parsley
parsnips
peas
"pestos"
potatoes
pumpkin
radishes
rice, e.g., brown
sake
SALAD DRESSINGS
SAUCES
SCALLIONS
sea vegetables
sesame, e.g., oil, seeds
shiso
snow peas
SOUPS, e.g., kale, miso
soybeans
soy sauce
spinach
spreads
sprouts, bean
squash, e.g., kabocha
stews
stir-fries
stock, vegetable
sweet potatoes

tahini
tamari
TOFU
tomatoes
turnips
vegetables
vinegar, e.g., rice wine
WAKAME
walnuts
watercress

Flavor Affinities

miso + carrots + kale + kombu +
  shiitake mushrooms
miso + carrots + spinach + tofu
miso + ginger + lemongrass +
  soup
miso + ginger + scallions
miso + ginger + tofu
miso + kombu + onions +
  shiitake mushrooms
miso + mushrooms + scallions
miso + scallions + tofu + wakame
miso + sesame + tofu +
  watercress
miso + shiitake mushrooms +
  shiso
miso + shiitake mushrooms +
  watercress
miso + tofu + udon noodles

MISO, BROWN

Season: autumn – winter
Flavor: SALTY/*umami,* and rich
in texture

Volume: loud

basil
beer
garlic
GRAVIES
mushrooms
oil, grapeseed
onions
soups
tamari
thyme
tofu
tomato paste
wine, dry, e.g., sherry

MISO, DARK

Season: autumn – winter
Flavor: SALTY
Volume: moderate – loud
What it is: miso that has been
fermented for as long as three
years

beans, e.g., black, pinto
brown rice syrup
burdock
carrots
casseroles
chili, vegetarian
daikon
ginger
gravies
lentils
marinades

mirin
mustard
nuts
onions
parsley
sauces, e.g., red wine, tomato
sesame paste
SOUPS, e.g., carrot, dark or mixed
  miso, vegetable (esp. winter)
squash, winter
stews, e.g., vegetable
stir-fries, e.g., with root vegetables
tofu
tomatoes and tomato sauce
vegetables, root
vinegar, rice

MISO, LIGHT (aka SWEET MISO)

Season: spring – summer
Flavor: salty, sour, and/or sweet
Volume: quiet – moderate
What it is: miso that has been
fermented for one year or less

almonds
avocados
beans, e.g., green, pinto
chickpeas
corn, e.g., grilled
dill
dips, e.g., bean
garlic
ginger
gravies
honey
"hummus"
lemon, e.g., juice, zest
marinades
mirin
oil, e.g., canola
orange, e.g., juice,
  zest
parsley
potatoes, e.g., mashed
sake
salad dressings

M

sauces
sea vegetables
sesame, e.g., paste, seeds
soups, e.g., *"creamy"*
spreads
tofu
vinegar, rice wine
wine, rice

Flavor Affinities
light miso + almond butter +
 rice wine
light miso + garlic + lemon +
 parsley + sesame paste
light miso + honey + oil +
 vinegar
light miso + rice vinegar +
 sesame paste
light miso + sesame paste +
 vegetable stock
light miso + soy sauce + tofu

MISO, RED
Flavor: **salty**/sweet, with a rich
texture
Volume: moderate – loud
What it is: soybeans fermented
(longer than for light miso,
perhaps one to three years) with
mostly barley, until reddish-
brown

basil
beer
daikon
dashi
eggplant
garlic
ginger
glazes
gravies
heartier dishes
leeks
lemon, e.g., zest
marinades
mirin
mushrooms, e.g., shiitake
oil, grapeseed

onions
parsley
sake
scallions
sea vegetables, e.g., wakame
sesame, e.g., oil, paste, seeds
SOUPS, e.g., *richer*
sprouts, bean
stews
tahini
tamari
thyme
tofu
tomato paste
wine, dry, e.g., sherry
yuzu

MISO, WHITE (see also MISO, LIGHT)
Flavor: salty / slightly sweet
Volume: quieter
What it is: soybeans fermented
with rice

almonds and almond butter
carrots
dips, e.g., bean
marinades
mushrooms, e.g., portobello
mustard
oil, e.g., peanut, sesame
peanuts and peanut butter
potatoes, e.g., *mashed*
SALAD DRESSINGS
SAUCES, light-colored
scrambles, i.e., tofu
sesame, e.g., seeds
SOUPS, e.g., *miso*
stir-fries
tahini
tofu
vinegar, e.g., brown rice, rice

Flavor Affinities
white miso + carrots + sesame
 seeds
white miso + mustard + oil +
 tahini + vinegar

MISO, YELLOW (see also MISO, LIGHT)
Flavor: earthy notes
Volume: quieter
What it is: soybeans fermented
with mostly barley

glazes
marinades
salad dressings
sauces
SOUPS, miso
tofu

MIZUNA (see GREENS, MIZUNA)

● MOLASSES
Flavor: bitter (darkest) / **sweet**
(darkest) – **very sweet** (lightest),
with notes of brown sugar,
caramel, coffee, and/or smoke,
and a syrupy texture
Volume: moderately loud
(lightest) – very loud (darkest)
Tips: Molasses ranges from
mild (the lightest) to dark
to blackstrap (the darkest).
The darker the molasses, the
higher the nutrient content.
Try using it instead of maple
syrup to top whole-grain
pancakes and waffles.
Possible substitutes: barley
malt syrup, honey, maple syrup

baked beans
*BAKED GOODS, e.g., breads,
 cookies, gingerbread*
blueberries
cereals, e.g., hot breakfast
chili pepper flakes
cinnamon
cloves
coffee
garlic
GINGER
glazes

grains
lemon, e.g., juice
milk
nutmeg
oatmeal
orange, e.g., juice, zest
pears
sauces, e.g., barbecue, Thai barbecue
smoothies
squash, winter
sweet potatoes
tempeh
tofu
vanilla
walnuts

Flavor Affinities

molasses + chili pepper flakes +
   ginger
molasses + cinnamon + nutmeg
   + orange zest
molasses + garlic + ginger +
   orange
molasses +_ginger + lemon juice

MOROCCAN CUISINE
almonds
apricots
bell peppers, e.g., green
carrots
cayenne
chermoula
chickpeas
chiles
cilantro
cinnamon
coriander
couscous
cucumbers
cumin
dates
eggs
figs
fruits
garlic
ginger
harissa

honey
lemons, e.g., fresh, preserved
nuts
oil, olive
olives
onions
oranges
paprika
parsley
pepper
pine nuts
pistachios
raisins
ras el hanout
saffron
salads, e.g., carrot
sesame seeds
stews, aka **tagines***, vegetarian, e.g.,*
   carrot, chickpea, root vegetable
sugar
tomatoes
turmeric

MUNG BEANS (see BEANS, MUNG)

● MUSHROOMS — IN GENERAL
Flavor: earthy and/or woodsy
notes, and a meaty texture
Volume: quiet – moderate
What they are: fungi
Techniques: bake (6 – 8
minutes), broil, deep-fry, grill,
pan-roast, raw (e.g., in salads),
roast, sauté (3 – 4 minutes),
smoke, steam (5 minutes),
stew, stuff

Tips: Generally serve cooked.
Opt for Asian mushrooms
(e.g., maitake, shiitake), or wild
mushrooms (e.g., chanterelle,
morel), over common mush-
rooms (e.g., button, white) for
maximum health benefits.

almonds
artichokes
arugula
asparagus
avocado
bamboo shoots
BARLEY
basil
bay leaf
beans, e.g., navy, pinto, white
bok choy
BREAD CRUMBS, e.g., *panko,*
   whole-wheat
bread pudding, savory
Brussels sprouts
butter
cardamom
carrots
casseroles
cayenne
celery
chard
CHEESE, e.g., blue, feta, goat,
   Gruyère, Parmesan, ricotta salata
chervil
chickpeas
chiles
CHIVES
cilantro
cinnamon
coriander
cornmeal, e.g., to crust
cornstarch
cream
crepes
cumin
Czech cuisine
daikon
dashi
dill
eggplant
EGGS, *e.g., fried, frittatas, omelets,*
   quiches
endives
farro
fennel
*GARLIC

M

ginger
grains, whole
gravies, e.g., mushroom
honey
kale
leeks
LEMON, e.g., juice, zest
lemongrass
MARJORAM
mascarpone
"meatloaf," i.e., loaf made with mushrooms and nuts
milk, e.g., coconut
millet
mint
mirin
mizuna
mushrooms, other
mustard
noodles, e.g., egg, rice, udon
nutmeg
NUTS, e.g., **almonds**, hazelnuts, pecans, pine nuts, pistachios, **walnuts**

OIL, e.g., **OLIVE**, peanut, sesame, truffle (e.g., white), walnut
olives
ONIONS, e.g., green, white
orange
oregano
paprika
PARSLEY
PASTAS, e.g., pappardelle, ravioli
pâtés
peas
PEPPER, e.g., black, white
phyllo dough, whole-wheat
PIZZA
POLENTA
POTATOES
quinoa
rice and wild rice
risottos
ROSEMARY
sage
salads
salt, e.g., kosher, sea
sauces, e.g., mushroom

sauerkraut
savory
scallions
sesame, e.g., oil (esp. toasted), seeds
SHALLOTS
sorrel
SOUPS, e.g., mushroom, vegetable
sour cream
spinach
sprouts, e.g., sunflower
squash, e.g., butternut, winter
STOCK, e.g., mushroom, vegetable
stuffed mushrooms
stuffings
tahini
TARRAGON
THYME
tofu
tomatoes
turmeric
veggie burgers
vinegar, e.g., balsamic, sherry, white wine
watercress
WINE, e.g., dry red or white, dry sherry, Madeira
won tons
yogurt
zucchini

Flavor Affinities

mushrooms + arugula + pasta + peas
mushrooms + blue cheese + herbs + onions + walnuts
mushrooms + breadcrumbs + chives + **garlic + olive oil**
mushrooms + caraway seeds + dill + potatoes + sour cream
mushrooms + fennel + spinach + *stuffed*
mushrooms + garlic + ginger + scallions
mushrooms + garlic + leeks + **lemon** + walnuts
mushrooms + garlic + marjoram + mint + **parsley** + tomatoes
mushrooms + garlic + olive oil + parsley + rosemary + thyme
mushrooms + garlic + onions + thyme
mushrooms + garlic + onions + vegetable stock
mushrooms + goat cheese + rosemary
mushrooms + lemon + mustard
mushrooms + lemon juice + olive oil + Parmesan cheese + **thyme**
mushrooms + lemon juice + olive oil + parsley

Dishes

Roasted Mushroom Flat Bread with Tomato Jam, Roasted Mushrooms, Caramelized Onions, Fresh Almond Ricotta, and Frisée
— Crossroads (Los Angeles)

"If green vegetables are the king of Super Immunity, **mushrooms** are the queen. . . . White, cremini, portobello, oyster, maitake, and reishi mushrooms have all been shown to have anticancer effects."
— DR. JOEL FUHRMAN, IN *SUPER IMMUNITY*

"Bottom line, **mushrooms** are good medicine. Cook them well before eating them and enjoy a variety rather than any one specific type."
— DR. ANDREW WEIL, ON DRWEIL.COM

"Raw **mushrooms** are technically not supposed to be good for you. Also, the texture you get from them when they are cooked is much more exciting than when they are raw. So how do you give your mushrooms flavor without heat [as in raw cuisine]? You do it with citrus and salt because they will bring out a lot of flavor and enhance its texture. If you rub a mushroom with salt, the water comes out and the solids collapse and it becomes soft."

— AMANDA COHEN, DIRT CANDY (NEW YORK CITY)

"**Abalone mushrooms**, which are available in August and again in February through April in the Pacific Northwest, are incredibly meaty, meaty mushrooms. They're giant, about five inches in diameter. I'll slice them thick, score them, and poach them for an hour in butter, cognac, shallot, garlic, parsley, and thyme until they're soft, and serve them with candied pistachios."

— JON DUBOIS, GREEN ZEBRA (CHICAGO)

"I love **trumpet mushrooms**, which are milder in flavor and have the texture of scallops. They take marinades really well."

— MAKINI HOWELL, PLUM BISTRO (SEATTLE)

"I'll slice large **Trumpet Royale mushrooms** into scallops, whose great texture they resemble, although they're not as yielding or buttery. They can be woody, so I'll acidulate them with lemon juice, which makes them tender and lovely, and their residual sugar helps with their caramelization when I sauté them in garlic and olive oil."

— AARON ADAMS, PORTOBELLO (PORTLAND, OR)

MUSHROOMS, BLACK TRUMPET

Season: late summer – early winter
Flavor: aromatic, with earthy notes of butter, fruit, meat, and/or smoke, and a soft, rich and chewy texture
Volume: moderate – **loud**
Technique: sauté
Tip: Often sold dried, they can be rehydrated by soaking in hot water for 30 minutes.
Botanical relative: chanterelles
Possible substitute: truffles (Black trumpets are nicknamed "poor man's truffles.")

artichokes
butter
casseroles
cheese, e.g., Parmesan, Taleggio
eggs, e.g., *omelets*
garlic, e.g., green
horseradish
onions
parsley
pastas

Dishes

Artichoke and Green Garlic Soup with Black Trumpet Mushroom Crouton
— Chez Panisse (Berkeley, CA)

pizzas
potatoes
rice
sage
salads, e.g., bean
sauces, e.g., creamy
seitan
shallots
soups, e.g., butternut squash
squash, e.g., butternut
stir-fries
stock, vegetable
thyme
wine, e.g., dry, white

"I love the earthy, almost dirt-y, flavor of **black trumpet mushrooms**. A sauce of parsley, shallots, and white wine will help them to release their flavor — especially paired with seitan and roasted potatoes."
— JORGE PINEDA, CANDLE 79 (NEW YORK CITY)

● MUSHROOMS, BUTTON (aka WHITE MUSHROOMS)

Season: year-round
Flavor: slightly sweet, with earthy notes, and a tender texture
What they are: common, everyday mushrooms
Volume: very quiet (raw) – quiet/moderate (cooked)
Nutritional profile: 50% carbs / 37% protein / 13% fats
Calories: 15 per 1-cup serving (raw, sliced)
Protein: 2 grams

Techniques: bake, braise, broil, sauté, steam, stir-fry, stuff
Botanical relatives: cremini, enoki, and **portobello** mushrooms

barley
buckwheat
cheese, cream
chile pepper flakes
cilantro
coconut milk
curries
fennel
garlic
lemon, e.g., juice
miso, e.g., red
mushrooms, other, e.g., wild
noodles, e.g., egg
oil, olive
olives, e.g., Italian
paprika
parsley
rice, wild
salads, e.g., green, mushroom
sauces, e.g., mushroom
scallions
soups
sour cream
stews
stock, e.g., mushroom
stuffed mushrooms
tamari
yogurt

"People who don't like **white button mushrooms** probably haven't had them cooked well — which is seared on screamingly high heat. You want to caramelize them in some garlic and olive oil, seasoned with chili flakes and parsley."
— ERIC TUCKER, MILLENNIUM (SAN FRANCISCO)

MUSHROOMS, CHANTERELLE

Season: late spring – autumn
Flavor: slightly sweet/umami, with earthy notes of apricots, flowers, fruits, nuts, and/or pepper; and a chewy, meaty texture
Volume: quiet – moderate
Techniques: bake, braise, roast, sauté

Tips: Delicious both fresh and dried. The flavor quiets down during the cooking process. Do not overcook, or the mushrooms may become tough.

Botanical relative: black trumpet mushrooms

beans, e.g., shell
bread or toast
buckwheat
butter
celery root
chestnuts
corn
cream
EGGS, e.g., omelets, poached
fiddlehead ferns
GARLIC and black garlic
gravies
hazelnuts
herbs, e.g., chervil, chives, sage, thyme
leeks
lemon
mascarpone
millet
mushrooms, other, e.g., porcini
mustard
oils, e.g., hazelnut, **olive**, peanut
onions, e.g., red, white
oranges and orange liqueur
parsley
pastas
PEPPER, e.g., black, white
polenta

ramps
rice, e.g., Arborio, brown, wild
risottos
rosemary
salads
salt, e.g., kosher, sea
SAUCES, e.g., white
SHALLOTS
soups
squash, e.g., acorn, buttercup,
   butternut, delicata, spaghetti
stews
stir-fries
stock, e.g., mushroom, vegetable
tamari
tarragon
tempeh
thyme
vinegar, e.g., balsamic, cider,
   sherry, white wine
wine, dry white
wine, fortified, e.g., Madeira or
   Marsala

Flavor Affinities
chanterelles + celery root +
   wild rice
chanterelles + cream + parsley +
   shallots

MUSHROOMS, CHICKEN OF THE WOODS

Season: summer – autumn
Flavor: notes of **chicken**, crab,
lemon, lobster, and/or turkey,
with a chicken-like texture
Volume: quiet – moderate

Techniques: braise, broil, grill,
marinate, roast, sauté, simmer,
stir-fry

Tip: This is a species of mushroom different from hen of the woods.

artichokes, Jerusalem
butter
carrots
celery root
cheese, e.g., cream, Monterey
   Jack, Parmesan
cream
eggs
garlic
greens, salad
lemon, e.g., juice
mushrooms, other, e.g., button,
   shiitake
noodles
nuts
onions
orange
parsley
pastas
pepper, e.g., black, white
polenta
rice
risottos
rosemary
salt
sauces, e.g., pasta, teriyaki
shallots
stock, mushroom
tarragon
thyme
wine, e.g., dry white

• MUSHROOMS, CREMINI (aka CRIMINI or ITALIAN BROWN MUSHROOMS)

[krem-EE-nee]
Flavor: rich earthy, meaty notes,
and a firm, meaty texture
Volume: quiet – moderate
What they are: immature
portobello mushrooms
Nutritional profile: 60% carbs
/ 37% protein / 3% fat
Calories: 20 per 1-cup serving
(raw, sliced)
Protein: 2 grams
Techniques: broil, raw, sauté
Botanical relatives: button,
enoki, and **portobello** mushrooms

allspice
barley
bay leaf
beans, green
beans, white, e.g., cannellini
butter
cheese, e.g., Fontina, pecorino
chili pepper flakes
chives
cloves
cream
eggs, e.g., *frittatas, omelets, quiches*
garlic
gravies, e.g., mushroom
hazelnuts
Italian cuisine
lemon
lentils, French
maple syrup
marjoram
milk
MUSHROOMS, OTHER, e.g.,
   portobello, shiitake
oil, nut, e.g., hazelnut
oil, olive
onions
oregano
parsley
PASTAS, e.g., lasagna, ravioli

pâtés, e.g., walnut-mushroom
peas
pepper, black
pizzas
polenta
quinoa
rosemary
sage
salt
SAUCES, e.g., mushroom, tomato
shallots
SOUPS, e.g., mushroom barley
soy sauce
spinach
stews, e.g., bean
stir-fries
stock, e.g., mushroom, vegetable
stuffed mushrooms
stuffings, e.g., for ravioli
sweet potatoes
tarragon
THYME
tofu, e.g., scrambles
tomatoes and tomato sauce
veggie burgers
vinegar, e.g., balsamic
walnuts
wine, e.g., dry white
zucchini

Flavor Affinities

cremini mushrooms + cream +
tarragon
cremini mushrooms + eggs +
Fontina cheese
cremini mushrooms + lentils +
walnuts
cremini mushrooms + onions +
tempeh
cremini mushrooms + walnuts +
white beans

Dishes

Pesto-Stuffed Mushrooms: Cremini
Mushrooms stuffed with Pistachio Pesto
— 118 Degrees (California)

● MUSHROOMS, ENOKI (aka ENOKITAKE)

[enn-OH-kee or enn-oh-kee-TAH-kee]

Flavor: slightly sweet, with fruity (e.g., grape) notes, and a tender yet crisp/crunchy texture (and chewy when cooked)
Volume: quiet
Nutritional profile: 70% carbs / 23% protein / 7% fats
Calories: 30 per 1-cup serving (raw, sliced)
Protein: 2 grams
Techniques: deep-fry, raw, simmer, steam, stir-fry

Tip: Use these tiny long-stemmed mushrooms as garnishes.

Botanical relatives: button, cremini, and portobello mushrooms

apples
Asian cuisines
basil and Thai basil
beans, long
bell peppers, e.g., red
carrots
cayenne
cheese, Parmesan
chives
cucumbers
dill
garlic
ginger
hoisin
JAPANESE CUISINE
lemon, e.g., juice
lemongrass
miso

Dishes

Enoki Doki Hand Roll: Enoki, Shiitake, Portobello Mushroom, Cashew, Ginger, Romaine, Black Rice with Hot Pepper Paste
— Beyond Sushi (New York City)

mushrooms, other, e.g., portobello, shiitake, white
oil, olive
pepper, e.g., black, white
radishes
SALADS
salt
sandwiches
sauces
scallions
shallots
slaws
SOUPS, e.g., clear, miso
SOY SAUCE
spring rolls
stir-fries
stock, vegetable
sushi
tamari
tofu
vinegar
watercress

Flavor Affinities

enoki mushrooms + garlic + Parmesan cheese
enoki mushrooms + soy sauce + tofu + vegetable stock

MUSHROOMS, HEDGEHOG

Season: late summer – autumn
Flavor: slightly sweet, with earthy notes of fruit, nuts, pepper, and/or pine, and a semi-dry, firm, meaty texture
Volume: moderate (long-cooked) – loud (quick-cooked)
Techniques: braise, roast, sauté
Possible substitute: chanterelles

butter
casseroles
cheese, e.g., ricotta
cream
garlic
lemon
mascarpone
orange
parsley
pastas, e.g., fettuccine
pepper, black
pizzas
potatoes
shallots
wine, e.g., dry sherry

MUSHROOMS, HEN OF THE WOODS (aka MAITAKE MUSHROOMS)

Season: autumn
Flavor: umami, with rich, earthy notes of **chicken**, garlic, lobster, meat, and/or nuts, and a firm, meaty texture
Volume: quiet – moderate
Nutritional profile: 74% carbs / 21% protein / 5% fats
Calories: 30 per 1-cup serving (raw, diced)
Protein: 1 gram
Techniques: braise, grill, roast, sauté (about 5 minutes), simmer, stew

Tip: Soak in water or stock for 30 minutes before using.

Botanical relative: shiitake mushrooms

breadcrumbs
bruschettas
butter
celery root
cheese, pecorino
chiles, e.g., jalapeño
Chinese cuisine
cilantro
cornmeal

cream
dashi
fiddlehead ferns
garlic
grains
gravies
herbs
horseradish
hot sauce
Japanese cuisine
leeks
lemon juice
lentils, e.g., black
lime juice
Madeira
mascarpone
miso, white
mushrooms, other, e.g., oyster, shiitake
mustard
noodles, e.g., soba
oil, e.g., grapeseed, **olive**, truffle
onions and spring onions
orange, e.g., juice
PARSLEY
pastas
pâtés, mushroom
PEPPER, BLACK

pizzas
polenta
RICE
salads
salt, e.g., kosher
sauces, e.g., pasta
scallions
SESAME, e.g., oil, seeds
shallots
SOUPS
soy sauce
spinach
stews
stir-fries
stock, e.g., mushroom, vegetable
sweet potatoes
tamari
thyme
vinegar, e.g., balsamic, sherry
walnuts
wine, e.g., port
Worcestershire sauce, vegetarian

Flavor Affinities
hen of the woods mushrooms + celery root + mustard
hen of the woods mushrooms + garlic + greens + **olive oil**

Dishes

Hen + Egg: Hen of the Woods Mushroom, Soft Poached Egg, Beluga Lentils, Fresh Herbs
— The Acorn (Vancouver)

Hen of the Woods Mushroom Pâté, Vidalia Onion Marmalade, Herb Butter
— Green Zebra (Chicago)

Egg Yolk Gnocchi, Mushroom Brown Butter, Hen of the Woods
— Ink (Los Angeles)

Roasted Maitake and Asparagus, with Apple, Radish, Beets, Parsnip Puree
— Natural Selection (Portland, OR)

Roasted Maitake Mushroom with Crispy Sunchoke, English Peas, Creamy Horseradish
— Vedge (Philadelphia)

Tamari and Maple Roasted Maitake-Pecan Cream Tamale with Grilled Broccoli Raab, a Cardamom Mole Roja, and a Black Lemon Tequila Gastrique
—Sutra (Seattle)

hen of the woods mushrooms +
  garlic + olive oil + parsley + pasta
hen of the woods mushrooms
  + lemon juice + miso + tamari
hen of the woods mushrooms +
  parsley + rice

"We've been making our **Hen of the Woods mushroom** pâté for years now, and it tastes like wild, foraged maitakes. We sear them in olive oil with caramelized onions, shallots, garlic, thyme, mushroom stock, and port (like traditional pâté), and finish them with mascarpone and truffle oil. We use agar-agar to make a port gelée."

— JON DUBOIS, GREEN ZEBRA (CHICAGO)

"We serve a roasted **maitake mushroom** with celery root fritter and grilled leek rémoulade. We love the texture of the mushroom because it is a wedge, so you get the singed, frilly little edge of the mushroom along with the juicy succulent base."

— RICH LANDAU AND KATE JACOBY, VEDGE (PHILADELPHIA)

"**Maitake mushrooms** are massive umami bombs. When they're dried in the oven, they have a — dare I say — bacon-esque quality to them."

— ERIC TUCKER, MILLENNIUM (SAN FRANCISCO)

MUSHROOMS, LOBSTER

Season: summer – autumn
Flavor: salty/sweet, with notes of shellfish (e.g., **lobster!**), and a firm yet tender, chewy texture (not unlike lobster meat)
Volume: quiet
What they are: bright red-

orange fungi (not actually mushrooms)
Techniques: bake, braise, sauté, simmer, stir-fry

butter
cheese, e.g., pecorino
corn
cream
dill
eggs, e.g., *frittatas, omelets*
garlic
ginger
mushrooms, other, e.g., oyster
oil, olive
onions
pastas
rice
risottos
rosemary
salt
sauces, creamy
soups and bisques
stews
stir-fries
stock, mushroom or vegetable
stuffings
tarragon
terrines, mushroom
thyme
tofu
vinegar
zucchini and zucchini blossoms

Dishes

Pasta with Lobster Mushrooms, Squash, Pecorino, and Squash Blossom Butter
— FnB Restaurant (Scottsdale, AZ)

MUSHROOMS, MAITAKE (see MUSHROOMS, HEN OF THE WOODS)

MUSHROOMS, MATSUTAKE

Season: autumn – winter
Flavor: aromatic, with earthy notes of cinnamon, mint, nuts, pine, and/or spices, and a very firm, meaty texture
Volume: moderate – loud
Techniques: bake, braise, broil, en papillote, grill, marinate, sauté, steam, tempura-fry

Tips: Cook lightly. Beware drying the mushrooms, or slicing them too thinly, as their flavor may be lost.

apples
Asian cuisines
asparagus
bay leaf
bok choy
cabbage, e.g., savoy
carrots
celery and celery root
cheese, Parmesan
chervil
chiles, e.g., Thai
chives
cloves
custards
DASHI
eggs
frisée
garlic
ginger
gohan
honey
JAPANESE CUISINE
Kaffir lime
leeks
lemon, e.g., juice, zest
mâche
mirin
miso
mizuna
noodles, buckwheat
oil, olive
onions, white

orange, e.g., juice, zest
pepper, e.g., black, Szechuan
pine nuts
rice, e.g., short-grain
rosemary
sake
salt
scallions
shallots
soups
soy sauce
stir-fries
sugar
sukiyaki
tamari
thyme
vinegar, rice wine
wine, dry white

Flavor Affinities:

matsutake mushrooms + leeks
    + sake
matsutake mushrooms + soy
    sauce + vinegar

"There is nothing on the planet like **matsutake mushrooms**! You've got to treat them delicately. I've served them with housemade buckwheat noodles, or simply grilled over rice."
— ERIC TUCKER, MILLENNIUM (SAN FRANCISCO)

Dishes

Matsutake Sukiyaki Donburi: Matsutake Mushroom cooked with Konnyaku, Scallion, and Choji-Fu, served over Rice
— Kajitsu (New York City)

Matsutake Takiawase: Japanese Taro, Pumpkin-Fu, and Yuzu Zest on Top
— Kajitsu (New York City)

Braised Matsutake Mushrooms: Broccoli and Black Sesame Paste, Braising Jus infused with Yuzu
— Mélisse (Santa Monica, CA)

Grilled Matsutake Mushrooms with Miso Custard, Ginger, Soy, and Kaffir Lime
— The Point (Saranac Lake, NY)

"There may be no more prized ingredient in Japanese cuisine than **matsutake mushrooms**. They are as celebrated in Japan as truffles are in Italy or France. I love the texture of the mushroom, and will never forget a shockingly good version of a sukiyaki dish I tasted that featured them. But that dish was like a short-distance dash — and I like serving them cooked in a pot as a dobin mushi, which really celebrates their lasting flavor and is more like a long-distance marathon."
— RYOTA UESHIMA, KAJITSU (NEW YORK CITY)

MUSHROOMS, MOREL

Season: spring
Flavor: umami, with earthy and/or meaty notes of bacon, egg, nuts, and/or smoke, and a firm, chewy (esp. fresh) texture
Volume: quiet (lighter in color) – moderate (darker in color)
Techniques: boil, sauté, simmer, stew

Tip: Use morel mushrooms on their own, not mixed with other mushrooms.

Botanical relative: truffles

artichokes, Jerusalem
ASPARAGUS, e.g., green, white
beans, e.g., fava
breadcrumbs
butter
caraway seeds
carrots
celery root
chard
cheese, e.g., goat, **Parmesan**
chervil
chives
corn
CREAM
eggs, e.g., *frittatas*, poached
fennel seeds
fiddlehead ferns
French cuisine
GARLIC
greens, bitter
lamb's-quarter
lemon
nettles
oil, nut, e.g., hazelnut, peanut
oil, olive
onions, e.g., spring
parsley
PASTAS, e.g., gnocchi
peas
pepper, e.g., black, white
potatoes
rice
risottos
rosemary
saffron
salt
sauces, e.g., creamy
SHALLOTS
sour cream
spinach
stews
stock, e.g., mushroom, vegetable
tarragon
thyme
tomatoes
vinegar, e.g., champagne
watercress
wine, e.g., dry, sherry, white

M

Flavor Affinities

morel mushrooms + asparagus + chervil + fava beans

morel mushrooms + bitter greens + garlic + pasta

"**Morel mushrooms** are so decadent tasting — I'll cook them in Earth Balance with salt and pepper and serve them with a splash of champagne vinegar."
— MARK SHADLE, G-ZEN (BRANFORD, CT)

"You can find **morels** up in the Sierras in the springtime, when I'll pick them myself. The fat in cashew cream carries the flavor of the morels beautifully. I might serve them paired with peas in a pastry dough."
— ERIC TUCKER, MILLENNIUM (SAN FRANCISCO)

Dishes

Cavatelli, Morels, Peas, Ricotta, and Fresh Chiles
— ABC Kitchen (New York City)

One-Hour Poached Hen's Egg with Morel Mushrooms, Swiss Chard, and Liquorice
— Charlie Trotter's (Chicago)

Scaloppini with Marsala-Glazed Morel Mushrooms
— Crossroads (Los Angeles)

Foraged Morel Mushrooms, Fiddlehead Ferns, Hollandaise
— Green Zebra (Chicago)

Oregon Morel Risotto with Spring Peas, Baby Spinach, Asparagus, Shaved Pecorino
— Nora (Washington, DC)

Handrolled Potato Gnocchi and Morels with English Peas, Asparagus, Fiddlehead Ferns, Pea Shoots, Goat Ricotta
—Nora (Washington, DC)

MUSHROOMS, OYSTER

Season: autumn
Flavor: sweet and earthy, with notes of butter, oysters, pepper, and/or seafood, and a chewy, tender texture
Volume: quiet (cooked)
Nutritional profile: 60% carbs / 31% protein / 9% fats
Calories: 40 per 1-cup serving (raw, sliced)
Protein: 3 grams
Techniques: confit, deep-fry, roast, sauté, stew, stir-fry (Note: Do *not* eat raw.)

Tips: The cooking process lowers the volume of the flavor. Cook quickly, and do *not* overcook, lest you lose it all! Use as a substitute for oysters in bisques and other dishes.

artichokes (including Jerusalem)
arugula
Asian cuisines
asparagus
basil
bay leaf
beans, black
beans, fermented black
beans, green
bread crumbs
BUTTER
cabbage, e.g., red
carrots
celery
celery root
cheese, e.g., **Parmesan**, Swiss, Taleggio
chervil
chiles, e.g., chipotle, green, jalapeño
Chinese cuisine
chives
chowders
cider
cilantro
cinnamon

coconut and coconut milk
coriander
cornmeal
cream
crepes
cumin
curries, e.g., green
dashi
dill
eggplant, e.g., Japanese
eggs, e.g., *quiches, scrambled*
fennel
GARLIC
ginger
gratins
greens, e.g., Asian
horseradish
Japanese cuisine
kale
Korean cuisine
leeks
lemon, e.g., juice, zest
lemongrass
lettuce
lime
mint
mirin
MUSHROOMS, OTHER, e.g., button, enoki, lobster, shiitake
mustard, Dijon
noodles, e.g., rice, soba
nutmeg
NUTS, e.g., almonds, **hazelnuts,** peanuts, pecans, pine nuts, **walnuts**
OIL, e.g., canola, hazelnut, nut, **OLIVE,** pecan, sesame, walnut
ONIONS, e.g., red, yellow
oranges and orange juice
panko
PARSLEY
parsnips
PASTA, e.g., fettuccine, linguini, pappardelle, ravioli, tagliatelle
pesto
pizza
polenta
potatoes

Chef Colin Bedford of North Carolina's Fearrington House on Mushrooms

At the Fearrington House, we treat mushrooms very much like meat. We will take larger **king oyster** or **maitake** mushrooms and confit them whole in olive oil, or we will sous-vide them as that is another great technique to infuse flavor and to create layers of flavors. The flavors differ throughout the year. In March, we use thyme, garlic, and white wine, as the wine really brightens the flavor.

King Oysters are nice, big, fat mushrooms. We will confit them with garlic, bay leaf, and thyme. The ratio of stalk to cap is crazy — like 5 percent cap to 95 percent stalk, so we use the stalk for carpaccio, cooking the mushrooms at 85°C for one to one-and-a-half hours with lots of aromatics. Once they are cool, we slice them thin on a mandoline and lay them on the plate. With the dish, we add crosnes, which are like a really cool artichoke; sunchokes, roasted cippolini onions, and garlic chips for a crispy texture.

Maitake mushrooms are my favorite. They have a meaty quality and are so versatile. We will confit them whole. Sunchokes work really well with them, as does ginger, which gives it a warm, earthy tone — with fresh ginger adding heat, and candied ginger mellowing the flavor. I'll also use sherry vinegar, and a bit of maple syrup — we use Mikuni Wild Harvest's NOBLE maple syrup.

Chanterelles are another favorite. Thyme is one of my favorite pairings, as is sage; I will use one or the other. In the fall or winter, black garlic also works well with them: We will caramelize and puree the garlic, which has a kind of fermented quality that brings up sweetness, and from there we will add some Madeira and maple [syrup] for more flavor. Chanterelles are a mushroom that we don't cook to order. We like to cook them beforehand and stew them down with aromatics, butter, and just a pinch of white wine at the end to balance the flavors.

Matsutakes call for keeping it simple, so we don't mess around with them too much, and simply confit them. After they are cooked, we will score and then pan sear them so you get that contrasting texture.

Doubloons are smaller than shiitake mushrooms, but we treat them the same way.

Pickling Mushrooms with Colin Bedford

Beech mushrooms are perfect for pickling, as they are essentially sponges. A cremini would be too hard; you would just get little nuggets. When pickling mushrooms, the pickling solution will depend on the season, which will influence our choice of vinegar — for example:
- **Autumn:** madeira and sherry vinegars
- **Winter:** port wine, red wine, and raspberry vinegars
- **Spring:** lemon and chardonnay vinegars
- **Summer:** white balsamic and champagne vinegars

radicchio
rice, e.g., brown, jasmine
rosemary
sage
sake
salads, e.g., warm
salsify
SAUCES, e.g., cream, white
scallions
seitan
SHALLOTS
SOUPS , BISQUES and
CHOWDERS, e.g., mushroom
sour cream
soy sauce
spinach
squash, e.g., delicata, kabocha
stews
stir-fries
stock, e.g., mushroom, vegetable
sumac
tamarind
tarragon
tarts
tempura
teriyaki
THYME
TOFU
tomatoes
vegetables

vinegar, e.g., balsamic, cider,
rice wine
wine, e.g., rice, white
za'atar
zucchini

Flavor Affinities

oyster mushrooms + bay leaf +
olive oil + thyme
oyster mushrooms + cider +
cream + polenta + sage
oyster mushrooms + cream +
parsley + *pizza*
oyster mushrooms + fermented
black beans + ginger
oyster mushrooms + garlic +
lemon + parsley + pasta
oyster mushrooms + lemon +
mint + pasta + zucchini
oyster mushrooms + rosemary +
tomatoes

"The inspiration for my artichoke oysters dish [which is served with artichoke puree, crispy **oyster mushrooms**, yellow tomato béarnaise, and kelp caviar] came from peeling an artichoke one day. I was peeling the leaves and one fell on a plate on its back and it looked like an oyster shell. One of the things I love to do is re-create dishes I love that I miss being a vegan and dishes that are unexpected in a vegan diet. The inspiration was nature, and it turned into 'oysters Rockefeller.' "
—TAL RONNEN, CROSSROADS
(LOS ANGELES)

MUSHROOMS, POM POM

Flavor: notes of **crab**, lobster, and/or veal
Technique: sauté
Botanical relative: truffles

butter
mushrooms, other, e.g., maitake
oil, olive
onions
parsley
pastas
pepper, black
salt, sea
sauces
stews
stock, e.g., mushroom, vegetable
tarragon
tomatoes

● MUSHROOMS, PORCINI (aka BOLETES or CÈPES; see also MUSHROOMS, WILD)

Season: summer – autumn
Flavor: slightly sweet; aromatic, with earthy/pungent notes of meat, nuts, and/or smoke, and a rich, meaty texture
Volume: moderate – loud (and louder when dried)
Calories: 100 per 1-ounce serving (dried)
Protein: 7 grams
Techniques: bake, braise, grill, raw, roast, sauté, simmer, stew, stuff

Dishes

Artichoke Oysters: Artichoke Purée, Crispy Oyster Mushroom, Yellow Tomato Béarnaise, and Kelp Caviar (pictured on page 351)
— Crossroads (Los Angeles)

Sesame Cornmeal Crusted Oyster Mushrooms with Sweet and Spicy Apple-Pepper Jam, Shaved Onion, and Radish Salad
— Millennium (San Francisco)

Oyster Mushroom Fettuccine with Kale, Seitan, and Fresh Chives
— Plum Bistro (Seattle)

Cornmeal-Crusted Oyster Mushrooms, Horseradish-Dill Aioli, Aji Amarillo Chili Sauce
— True Bistro (Somerville, MA)

Tips: Often dried, which intensifies and enhances its flavor. Grind to a powder (e.g., in a spice grinder) and use to crust tofu before cooking, or use as a seasoning. To reconstitute, soak in hot water for 20 – 30 minutes before adding to dishes; the flavored water can be strained and added to sauces, soups, or stews.

almonds
artichokes
asparagus
BARLEY
basil
bay leaf
bread crumbs
bruschetta
butter
carpaccio, mushroom
carrots
casseroles
chard
cheese, e.g., goat, **Parmesan**, provolone, ricotta, Romano
chickpeas
chives
cloves
corn
cream
crostini
dill
dumplings, e.g., bread
eggplant
eggs, e.g., *frittatas, omelets*
endive, Belgian
escarole
figs
French cuisine

Dishes

Roasted Garlic Mashed Potatoes with Pinot Noir–Porcini Mushroom Sauce
— Greens Restaurant (San Francisco)

Porcini Bruschetta, with White Beans, Garlic, Fennel, Chèvre
— Natural Selection (Portland, OR)

GARLIC
grains
gravies
greens, bitter
Italian cuisine
leeks
lemon, e.g., juice
marjoram
mint
mushrooms, other, e.g., portobello
OIL, e.g., hazelnut, nut, **OLIVE**, **porcini**
onions, e.g., green, yellow
palm, hearts of
PARSLEY
PASTAS, e.g., fettuccine, gnocchi, lasagna
peanuts
peas
PEPPER, e.g., black, white
phyllo dough, whole-wheat
pilafs
pine nuts
polenta
potatoes
pumpkin
quinoa
rice
RISOTTOS
rosemary
sage
salads
salt, e.g., sea
sauces, e.g., mushroom, tomato
savory, e.g., summer
shallots
SOUPS
spinach
squash, e.g., winter

stews
stocks, e.g., mushroom, vegetable
stuffed peppers or zucchini
stuffings
tarts
tempeh
thyme
tomatoes and tomato paste
truffles, white
vinegar, e.g., **balsamic**, red wine, **sherry**, white balsamic
WINE, e.g., **dry red or white**, Madeira, or sherry

Flavor Affinities

porcini mushrooms + basil + garlic + olive oil + potatoes
porcini mushrooms + chard + chickpeas
porcini mushrooms + chives + lemon
porcini mushrooms + cream + potatoes
porcini mushrooms + garlic + lemon + olive oil + thyme

"**Porcini** are the godfather of wild mushrooms. They're big, giant, meaty, ultra-rich mushrooms that are really majestic to find when you're out foraging in the woods."
— ERIC TUCKER, MILLENNIUM (SAN FRANCISCO)

● MUSHROOMS, PORTOBELLO

Flavor: rich, earthy, meaty notes and texture
Volume: moderate – loud
Nutritional profile: 69% carbs / 25% fats / 6% protein
Calories: 45 per 1-cup serving (grilled, sliced)
Protein: 2 grams
Techniques: broil, **grill**, marinate, **roast**, sauté (about 15 minutes), sear, stuff

Botanical relatives: button, cremini, and enoki mushrooms

almonds
ARUGULA
asparagus
"bacon," i.e., made from smoked portobello mushrooms
barley, e.g., pearl
basil
beans, e.g., black, shell, white
BELL PEPPERS, e.g., green or red, esp. grilled or roasted
breadcrumbs
broccoli
bruschetta
buns, e.g., whole-grain "burger"
butter
cayenne
celery and celery leaves
chard, Swiss
CHEESE, e.g., cheddar, dry Jack, feta, **goat**, Gorgonzola, Gouda, manchego, **MOZZARELLA**, **PARMESAN**, provolone, ricotta, Swiss
chervil

chickpeas
chiles, e.g., chipotle, jalapeño; chili pepper flakes, chili powder
chives
cilantro
couscous, e.g., Israeli, whole-wheat
cream
crepes
dill
eggplant
eggs, e.g., *omelets*
endive, Belgian
escarole
fajitas
fennel
focaccia
GARLIC
ginger
gravies, e.g., mushroom
greens, e.g., bitter, salad
hazelnuts
herbs
Italian cuisine
leeks
lemon, e.g., juice
mâche

marjoram
millet
mint
mousses
mushrooms, other, e.g., cremini, porcini, shiitake, white
mustard
oil, e.g., canola, grapeseed, nut, **OLIVE**, truffle, walnut
ONIONS, e.g., green, red, white, yellow
orange, e.g., juice
oregano
paprika, smoked
parsley
parsnips
pasta, *e.g., fettuccine, lasagna, penne*
pâtés, e.g., mushroom, vegetable
pears
pepper, black
PESTO
pine nuts
pistachios
pizza
polenta
potatoes
quesadillas
rice, e.g., basmati, brown
rosemary
salads, e.g., mushroom
salt, sea
sandwiches, e.g., "French dip," panini, wraps
sauces
scallions
sesame, e.g., oil, seeds
shallots
soups
soy sauce
SPINACH
squash, summer
squash, winter, e.g., butternut
"steaks," mushroom
stews
stir-fries
stock, e.g., mushroom, vegetable
STUFFED MUSHROOMS

Flavor Affinities
portobellos + arugula + balsamic vinegar + mozzarella + rosemary
portobellos + arugula + mustard
portobellos + arugula + red bell peppers + white beans
portobellos + balsamic vinegar + garlic + olive oil + parsley
portobellos + barley + *soups* + thyme
portobellos + bell peppers + eggplant + goat cheese + *sandwiches*
portobellos + bell beppers + *pizza* + zucchini
portobellos + bitter greens + potatoes
portobellos + cilantro + garlic + ginger + jalapeño + soy sauce
portobellos + garlic + olive oil + Parmesan cheese + spinach
portobellos + garlic + soy sauce
portobellos + garlic + sun-dried tomatoes
portobellos + goat cheese + potatoes
portobellos + goat cheese + spinach
portobellos + mint + zucchini
portobellos + pesto + polenta
portobellos + polenta + rosemary
portobellos + spinach + tomatoes
portobellos + vinegar + walnut oil + walnuts

tacos
tamari
tarragon
thyme
tofu
tomatoes and tomato paste
TOMATOES, SUN-DRIED
tortillas
"veggie burgers"
VINEGAR, e.g., BALSAMIC, red
  wine, sherry
walnuts
watercress
wine, e.g., dry white or Madeira
zucchini

"I've made **portobello mushroom** 'bacon' by roasting portobellos that have been rubbed with smoked paprika, thyme, and shallots. When they're sliced thin, they've got layers of color from the infused spice mixture, and actually look like bacon."
— KEN LARSEN, TABLE VERTE
(NEW YORK CITY)

Dishes

Tuscan Portobello Sandwich: Grilled Portobello, Roasted Red Peppers, and Caramelized Onions, topped with Vegan Mozzarella and Spicy Mayo
— Blossom (New York City)

"French Dip Sandwich": Caramelized Onions, Swiss Cheese, and Portobello Mushrooms on Herbed Baguette with Roasted Garlic-Mushroom *Jus* and choice of Organic Wild Greens or Yam Fries
— Cafe Flora (Seattle)

Grilled Portobello Sandwich on Acme Focaccia with Grilled Peppers, Roasted Onions, Wagon Wheel, Basil Mayonnaise, and Arugula. Served with Fingerling Potatoes, Artichokes, Pickled Red Onions, Capers, and Champagne Dijon Vinaigrette
— Greens Restaurant (San Francisco)

Portobello Quesadilla: Marinated Mushrooms, Monterey Jack, Avocado, Caramelized Onion, and Poblano Cream
— Mii amo Café (Sedona, AZ)

Portabella Carpaccio, Garbanzo Tonatto, Fennel Mustard, and Crispy Capers
— Vedge (Philadelphia)

● **MUSHROOMS, SHIITAKE —**
DRIED and FRESH
[shee-TAH-kay]
Season: spring; autumn
Flavor: slightly sweet/*umami*; aromatic, with earthy, pungent notes of fruit, garlic, pine, smoke, steak, woods, and/or yeast, and a firm, chewy (esp. cooked), meaty texture
Volume: moderate (fresh) – loud (dried)
What they are: wild mushrooms
Nutritional profile: 90% carbs / 7% protein / 3% fats
Calories: 80 per 1-cup serving (cooked)
Protein: 2 grams
Techniques — fresh: bake, braise, broil, deep-fry, grill, roast (30 minutes), sauté (10 – 15 minutes), simmer, smoke, steam, stir-fry

Techniques — dried: Soak in boiling water 10 – 15 minutes, or overnight in cold water, to reconstitute; then cook as above. Strain, and add the nutritious soaking water to sauces, soups, or stews.
Botanical relative: hen of the woods mushrooms

arame
artichoke hearts
arugula
(EAST) ASIAN CUISINES
asparagus
avocado
bamboo shoots
basil and **Thai basil**
bay leaf
beans, e.g., adzuki, fermented black, green
beer and ale
bell peppers, e.g., green, red
bok choy
brandy
broccoli
burritos
butter
cabbage, e.g., Chinese or napa
carrots
casseroles
cayenne
celery
chard, e.g., Swiss
cheese, e.g., feta, goat, Parmesan
chiles, e.g., ancho, and chili pepper paste
Chinese cuisine
chives
coconut milk
daikon
dashi
dumplings, e.g., Asian, potstickers
eggplant
eggs, e.g., *omelets, quiches*
escarole
GARLIC

GINGER

GRAINS, e.g., **barley, brown rice,** buckwheat, kamut, kasha, **pearled barley,** quinoa, **rice,** wild rice

gravies

greens, e.g., mizuna

hazelnuts

honey

JAPANESE CUISINE

Kaffir lime leaves

kale

kombu

Korean cuisine

leeks

lemon, e.g., juice, zest

lemongrass

lettuce, e.g., romaine

lime

macrobiotic cuisine

marjoram

milk, dairy or nondairy, e.g., soy

mirin

Flavor Affinities

shiitake mushrooms + Asian noodles + sesame sauce + soy sauce

shiitake mushrooms + celery + onions + soy sauce

shiitake mushrooms + fermented black beans + rice vinegar + sesame oil + sriracha + tamari

shiitake mushrooms + garlic + soy sauce

shiitake mushrooms + ginger + mirin + sake + **soy sauce**

shiitake mushrooms + ginger + scallions

shiitake mushrooms + ginger + sesame + soy sauce

shiitake mushrooms + lemon juice + soy sauce

shiitake mushrooms + miso + sesame seeds

shiitake mushrooms + miso + shiso + soy sauce + tofu

shiitake mushrooms + olive oil + onions + *pizza* **+ rosemary + walnuts**

shiitake mushrooms + scallions + sweet potatoes

Dishes

Shiitake Salad: Marinated Shiitake Mushrooms, Julienne Carrots, Purple Beet, and Yellow Squash with Sweet Ginger Dressing
— 118 Degrees (California)

Shiitake Miso Soup: Served warm with Miso, Fresh Seaweeds, Shiitakes, and Scallions
—118 Degrees (California)

Farm Vegetable Dumplings with Miso Lemongrass Broth, Ginger, Scallions, Swiss Chard, and Shiitake Mushrooms
— The Lodge at Woodloch (Hawley, PA)

Pad Thai Sauté: Roasted Shiitake Mushrooms, Edamame, Napa Cabbage, Bean Sprouts, Broccolini, Tofu, Spicy Miso Vinaigrette
— Mii amo Café (Sedona, AZ)

Shiitake Mushrooms Roasted in a Garlic Rosemary Balsamic and Red Wine Sauce with Carrot Butter Pâté and Toasted Baguette Slices
— Sage's Cafe (Salt Lake City)

Shiitake and Tofu Lettuce Cups: Ginger, Soy, and Cashew
— True Food Kitchen (Phoenix)

MISO

MUSHROOMS, OTHER, e.g., button, cremini, maitake, oyster, porcini, portobello, wild

NOODLES, ASIAN, e.g., buckwheat, ramen, soba, udon

nori rolls (i.e., vegetarian sushi)

nuts, e.g., cashews, hazelnuts, pistachios, walnuts

OIL, e.g., grapeseed, hazelnut, **nut, OLIVE,** peanut, sesame

ONIONS, e.g., **caramelized, green, pickled, yellow**

parsley

pastas, e.g., fettuccine, linguini

pâtés, mushroom

pepper, black

pizza

polenta

ponzu sauce

rice

risotto

rosemary

sage

sake

salads, e.g., mushroom

salt, e.g., kosher

sauces, e.g., vegan XO

savory

scallions

seitan

sesame, e.g., oil, sauce, seeds

shallots

shiso

SOUPS, e.g., hot-and-sour, lentil, miso, noodle, vegetable

soybeans

SOY SAUCE

spinach

spring rolls

squash, e.g., winter

sriracha sauce

stews

STIR-FRIES

STOCKS, e.g., mushroom and/or vegetable

stuffings

sugar, e.g., brown

sugar snap peas
sushi
sweet potatoes
tacos
tamari
thyme
tofu
tofu scrambles
tomatoes, sun-dried
tomato paste and tomato sauce
turnip
veggie burgers
vinegar, e.g., **balsamic**, brown
  rice, rice, white wine
wine, e.g., Madeira, red
yuzu, e.g., juice, zest

"I'll sometimes want to serve
shiitake mushrooms in a non-
Asian cuisine context, such as
mixed with other mushrooms like
creminis and wrapped in pastry
dough in a Wellington-esque
dish."
— ERIC TUCKER, MILLENNIUM
(SAN FRANCISCO)

MUSHROOMS, WHITE (see MUSHROOMS, BUTTON)

MUSHROOMS, WILD — IN GENERAL, or MIXED (see also CHANTERELLE, HEN OF THE WOODS, MOREL, PORCINI, etc.)
Techniques: roast, stew

asparagus
barley
beans, e.g., cannellini
cheese, e.g., feta, goat, Gouda,
  Taleggio
crepes
crostini
eggs
enchiladas
flour, e.g., brown rice

garlic
garlic, green
herbs
leeks
mirin
nutmeg
OIL, e.g., OLIVE, truffle
onions, e.g., cipollini
parsley
pecans
pepper, black
phyllo dough
pilafs
pine nuts
pizza
rosemary
sage
salt
seitan
SHALLOTS
soy sauce
spinach
stews, e.g., mushroom
stock, vegetable
tamari
tarragon
tarts, e.g., mushroom
THYME
tofu, e.g., firm, smoked
wine, e.g., Madeira

Dishes

Wild Mushroom and Goat Cheese Strudel with Balsamic Reduction
— The Golden Door (Escondido, CA)

Wild Mushroom and Leek Tartlet with Gruyère and Thyme
— Greens Restaurant (San Francisco)

Wild Mushroom Ravioli with Grilled Matsutake and Chanterelle Mushrooms, Savoy Spinach, Spring Onions, Green Garlic, Pine Nuts, Herb Butter, Grana Padano
— Greens Restaurant (San Francisco)

Wild Mushroom Omelet with Quinoa, Sweet Onions, Baby Spinach, and White Cheddar
— The Lodge at Woodloch (Hawley, PA)

Wild Mushroom Risotto with Winter Squash, Black Truffle Butter
— Picholine (New York City)

Flavor Affinities

wild mushrooms + cannellini beans + parsley + truffle oil
wild mushrooms + eggs + pizza dough
wild mushrooms + feta cheese + phyllo dough + shallots + spinach
wild mushrooms + garlic + olive oil + shallots + thyme
wild mushrooms + goat cheese + herbs + shallots
wild mushrooms + Madeira + pecans

● **MUSTARD, e.g., DIJON (see also GREENS, MUSTARD; MUSTARD POWDER; MUSTARD SEEDS)**

Flavor: bitter; hot, with peppery, spicy notes
Volume: moderate – very loud

Tips: For most purposes, choose Dijon mustard (made with verjus instead of vinegar); other options include stone-ground and/or whole-grain mustard. Add mustard at the end of the cooking process.

Botanical relatives: broccoli, Brussels sprouts, collard greens, horseradish, kale, kohlrabi

agave nectar
arugula
asparagus
avocado
basil
beans, baked
beans, e.g., fava, **green**, pinto
black-eyed peas
BROCCOLI and CHINESE BROCCOLI
Brussels sprouts
cabbage
capers
casseroles
cauliflower
celery root
cheese
chives
cilantro
cream and crème fraîche
cucumbers
cumin
fennel
French cuisine, esp. Dijon mustard
fruits, e.g., mostardo
GARLIC
glazes
grains
greens, salad
honey
leeks
LEMON, e.g., juice, zest
lettuce
lime
maple syrup
marinades
marjoram
mayonnaise
mushrooms
oil, e.g., flaxseed, grapeseed, olive
parsley
pecans
pepper, e.g., black, green, white
potatoes

radishes
rice
SALAD DRESSINGS, e.g.,
  vinaigrettes
salads
sandwiches
SAUCES
sauerkraut
sausages, vegan
scallions
seitan
shallots
snow peas
sour cream
soy sauce
spinach
sugar, e.g., brown
tarragon
tempeh
thyme
verjus
VINEGAR, e.g., fig, raspberry, red
  wine, sherry, wine
wine, e.g., dry red
yogurt

Flavor Affinities

mustard + cabbage + potatoes
mustard + cilantro + lime +
  yogurt
mustard + maple syrup + oil +
  vinegar
mustard + maple syrup + pecans
  + tempeh

Dishes

Baby Lettuces with Dijon Cream, with
Figs, Pear, Pickled Carrots, Croutons,
and Spiced Pecans
— Natural Selection (Portland, OR)

MUSTARD POWDER (aka DRY MUSTARD)

Flavor: hot, pungent notes of
mustard

Volume: loud
What it is: ground mustard
seeds
  Tips: Use within six months,
  as it loses its potency. Mix with
  cold water (to maintain "loudness"; alternatively, use hot
  water to quiet the heat) to form
  a hot mustard paste; let stand
  10 – 15 minutes before using.
  Alternatively, mix with beer or
  white wine.
Brand: Colman's

beans, e.g., pinto
beer
cabbage
cheese, e.g., cheddar, Gruyere,
  Swiss
dips
herbs, e.g., oregano, tarragon
honey
lentils
maple syrup
mayonnaise
nutritional yeast
oil, e.g., olive
paprika
pastas, e.g., macaroni and cheese
popcorn
salad dressings
sauces, e.g., barbecue, hollandaise
slaws
spinach
split peas
tofu
vinegar

• MUSTARD SEEDS

Flavor: bitter; pungent
Volume: moderate (yellow) –
loud (brown)
Tips: Toast or sauté in a covered
pan to bring out their earthy
sweetness. Use black mustard
seeds in Indian curries.

African cuisines
American cuisine
Asian cuisines
butter and clarified butter
cauliflower
chickpeas
curries, e.g., Indian
European cuisines
Indian cuisines
lentils
marinades
mustard
pickles
rice
salad dressings
sauces
spinach
turmeric
vegetables, e.g., boiled
vinegar

NAMA-FU (see also recommendations for SEITAN)

Flavor: neutral, with a smooth,
chewy texture akin to dense
custard or scallops
What it is: fresh wheat gluten,
often made from wheat
gluten and mochi rice flour;
an important ingredient in
Japanese temple vegetarian
cuisine; the ancestor of seitan
Nutrional profile: mostly
protein, and nearly fat-free
Techniques: blanch, grill
  Tip: It is also available dried.

asparagus
confections
dashi
JAPANESE CUISINE
mirin
miso
mushrooms, e.g., black trumpet
oil, e.g., canola
palm, hearts of
sake

sauces
sea vegetables
sesame, e.g., oil, paste, seeds
shiso
soups, e.g., *miso, vegetable*
soy sauce
stews
sukiyaki
umeboshi plum paste
wasabi
water chestnuts

NATIVE AMERICAN CUISINE

BEANS (one of the "three sisters")
berries, e.g., cranberries, strawberries
bread, e.g., fry
chiles
chocolate
CORN (one of the "three sisters")
fruit, e.g., dried
garlic, e.g., wild
grains
honey
maple sugar
nuts
onions, e.g., wild
potatoes
seeds, e.g., pumpkin, sunflower
SQUASH (one of the "three sisters")
tomatoes

• NECTARINES (see also tips for PEACHES)

Season: summer
Flavor: sweet, with a juicy texture
Volume: quiet – **moderate**

Nutritional profile: 86% carbs / 8% protein / 6% fats
Calories: 65 per 1-cup serving (raw, sliced)
Protein: 2 grams

Techniques: bake, broil, grill, poach, raw, sauté

Tip: Opt for organic nectarines.

Botanical relatives: apricots, **peaches**, plums
Possible substitute: peaches

baked goods, e.g., breads, cakes
basil
BERRIES, e.g., blackberries, blueberries, RASPBERRIES, strawberries
brandy
butter
buttermilk
caramel
cereals, hot breakfast
cheese, e.g., blue, mozzarella
cherries
cinnamon
cloves
cream
desserts, e.g., crisps, fruit cobblers, shortcakes
figs
GINGER
greens, salad
hazelnuts
honey
ice creams
LEMON, e.g., juice
mangoes
maple syrup
mascarpone
melon, e.g., cantaloupe
mint
nutmeg
NUTS, e.g., ALMONDS, hazelnuts, **macadamias**
oats or oatmeal
oil, olive
orange
pancakes
peaches
pepper, black
pies
plums
relishes

rosemary
salads, e.g., *fruit and green*
salsas
sorbets
soups, e.g., *fruit*
SUGAR, e.g., brown
tarragon
VANILLA
vinegar, e.g., balsamic
wine, e.g., red or white, still or sparkling, e.g., Champagne
yogurt

Flavor Affinities
nectarines + almonds + caramel
nectarines + balsamic vinegar + basil
nectarines + caramel + ginger
nectarines + ginger + lemon

NETTLES (aka STINGING NETTLES)

Season: spring – summer
Flavor: bitter/sweet, with notes of meat (when cooked), spinach, and/or toast
Volume: loud
Techniques: blanch, boil, sauté
Tips: Beware: Use tongs to place nettles in your shopping bag. Blanch in boiling water to neutralize their sting. (Don't use cold water, which sets their bitterness.) Combine with miso or other, milder vegetables to neutralize nettles' strong flavor.
Possible substitute: spinach

almonds
(North) American cuisines
asparagus
basil
butter and brown butter
buttermilk
CHEESE, e.g., Parmesan, pecorino, **RICOTTA, ricotta salata**
chiles, e.g., red

chives
cream
crème fraîche
curries
eggs, e.g., *frittatas, poached*
European cuisines
fennel
French cuisine
garlic
Italian cuisine
kale
leeks
LEMON, e.g., juice
miso
mushrooms, e.g., morel
nuts
OIL, OLIVE
onions
PASTAS, e.g., gnocchi, manicotti,
ravioli
peas
pepper, black
pestos
pine nuts
pizzas
potatoes
rice, e.g., Arborio
risotto
sage
salt, e.g., sea
sauces
shallots
soufflés
SOUPS
STOCK, e.g., mushroom,
vegetable

Dishes

Pizzetta with Wild Nettles and Ricotta Salata
— Chez Panisse (Berkeley, CA)

Pearled Barley "Risotto," with Stinging Nettles, Shiitake Mushrooms, and
Pickled Mustard Seeds
— Green Zebra (Chicago)

Nettle and Red Chili Cappellettis, Brown Butter, Parmesan, Sage Flowers
— Verjus (Paris)

teas
vegetables, milder
walnuts
wine, e.g., dry white
yogurt

Flavor Affinities
nettles + basil + cheese + garlic +
lemon juice + olive oil + pine nuts
nettles + cream + eggs
nettles + leeks + potatoes

NIGELLA SEEDS
Flavor: slightly bitter and/or
pungent, with musty notes of
celery, cheese, mustard, nuts,
onions, oregano, pepper, and/or
smoke, and a crunchy texture
Volume: moderate
What they are: spice

allspice
*baked goods, e.g., breads and
flatbreads*
cardamom
chickpeas
cinnamon
coriander
cumin
curries
EGGPLANT
Egyptian cuisine
endive
FENNEL SEEDS
fenugreek
ginger

greens, e.g., turnip
Indian cuisines
legumes, e.g., lentils
Middle Eastern cuisines
mustard seeds
pepper, e.g., black
potatoes
pumpkin
rice, e.g., basmati
saffron
squash, e.g., butternut, Hubbard
sweet potatoes
Turkish cuisine
turmeric
vegetables, e.g., green
za'atar

Flavor Affinities
nigella seeds + cumin + fennel
seeds + fenugreek + mustard
seeds
nigella seeds + eggplant + fennel
seeds

"**Nigella** is my all-time favorite
spice. I'll even add it to my za'atar
spice blend, where it adds a
cheesy note that is hauntingly
beautiful."
— RICH LANDAU, VEDGE (PHILADELPHIA)

**NOODLES, ASIAN
(see NOODLES,
CELLOPHANE;
NOODLES, KELP;
NOODLES, RAMEN;
NOODLES, RICE;
NOODLES, RICE
VERMICELLI; NOODLES,
SOBA; NOODLES,
SOMEN; and NOODLES,
UDON)**
Tips: Many Asian noodles
should be soaked before cook-
ing. They can be served either
cold or hot. For the most nutri-
ents, opt for whole-grain noodles.

Flavor Affinities

Asian noodles + ginger + peanuts + rice vinegar

Asian noodles + kale + sesame oil + sesame seeds + soy sauce

Asian noodles + lime + peanuts

Asian noodles + mushrooms + napa cabbage

NOODLES, BEAN THREAD (see NOODLES, CELLOPHANE)

NOODLES, BUCKWHEAT (see NOODLES, SOBA)

NOODLES, CELLOPHANE (aka BEAN THREAD NOODLES, GLASS NOODLES, MUNG BEAN NOODLES)

Flavor: neutral, with a chewy texture

Volume: quiet

What they are: very thin mung bean flour noodles

Techniques: Soak (in hot water, until soft) first, and then cook until tender, about 8 – 15 minutes.

agave nectar
Asian cuisines
asparagus
bell peppers, e.g., red
bok choy
broccoli and Chinese broccoli
cabbage, e.g., Chinese, napa
carrots
chiles, e.g., jalapeño, Thai
cilantro
coconut milk

Dishes

Toasted Sesame Noodles, Housemade Kimchi, Braised Lotus Root, Chinese Mustard
— Green Zebra (Chicago)

cucumbers
curry powder and *curries*
dulse
eggplant, Asian
eggs, e.g., poached
garlic
ginger
Japanese cuisine
jícama
mirin
miso, e.g., yellow
MUSHROOMS, e.g., SHIITAKE
OIL, e.g., chili, peanut, **SESAME,** vegetable
onions
pea shoots
peanuts
pepper, e.g., black, Szechuan
sake
salads, e.g., noodle
scallions
sea vegetables, e.g., arame, hiziki, wakame
sesame, e.g., oil, seeds
soups, e.g., hot and sour
Southeast Asian cuisines
SOY SAUCE
spinach
spring rolls
stir-fries
stock, e.g., mushroom, vegetable
sugar
tamari
Thai cuisine
tofu, e.g., silken
vegetables
Vietnamese cuisine
vinegar, e.g., rice wine, white wine
watercress

Flavor Affinities

cellophane noodles + cabbage + carrots + seaweed + sesame

cellophane noodles + cilantro + cucumbers + garlic + ginger

cellophane noodles + cilantro + peanut oil + rice vinegar

cellophane noodles + shiitake mushrooms + spinach

NOODLES, CHINESE EGG

Flavor: notes of egg, and a rich, chewy texture

Volume: quiet – moderate

What they are: Chinese noodles made from egg and wheat

Possible substitute: egg-based pasta noodles

asparagus
bok choy
carrots
Chinese cuisine
chow mein
cilantro
curries
garlic
ginger
greens, Asian
lo mein
mushrooms, e.g., Asian
oil, e.g., chili, sesame
peanuts and peanut sauce
scallions
sesame, e.g., oil, sauce, seeds
soups
soy sauce
stir-fries
sugar, e.g., brown
vinegar, e.g., balsamic

NOODLES, GLASS (see NOODLES, CELLOPHANE)

NOODLES, GREEN TEA SOBA

Flavor: notes of green tea, and a chewy texture

Volume: quiet – moderate

What they are: soba noodles to which green tea has been added

Technique: Cover with boiling water for about 4 – 5 minutes.

cilantro
cucumbers
edamame
garlic
ginger
mushrooms, e.g., Asian, black trumpet, chanterelle, oyster, shiitake
nori
oil, sesame
peanuts
sauces, e.g., dipping
scallions
sesame seeds
soy sauce
spinach
vinegar, rice
wasabi

Flavor Affinities
green tea soba noodles + cucumbers + peanut sauce + scallions

NOODLES, KELP
Flavor: neutral, with a toothy (green) or crunchy (clear) texture
Volume: quiet (clear) – moderate (green)
What they are: noodles made from sea vegetables
What's healthful about them: virtually free of calories, carbohydrates, fat
Gluten-free: yes

agave nectar
almonds and almond butter
Asian cuisines
bell peppers
bok choy
"bowls"
cabbage
carrots
cashews and cashew butter
chiles, e.g., Thai
chili pepper flakes and chili powder
cilantro
cucumbers
garlic
greens, e.g., Asian, salad
lemon, e.g., juice
lime
miso
mushrooms, e.g., Asian, oyster
oil, e.g., olive, sesame
onions, e.g., green
orange
pad thai
raw cuisine
salads, e.g., green, noodle
sea vegetables
sesame, e.g., oil, sauce, seeds
shallots
shiso
snow peas
soups
soy sauce
spinach
stir-fries
tahini
tamari
tamarind paste
tomatoes
vegetables
zucchini

Flavor Affinities
kelp noodles + miso + orange + sea vegetables + sesame seeds
kelp noodles + miso + sesame seeds
kelp noodles + sesame + shiso + vegetables
kelp noodles + sesame sauce + spinach

NOODLES, MUNG BEAN (see NOODLES, CELLOPHANE)

NOODLES, RAMEN
What they are: baked or fried Chinese wheat noodles

bamboo shoots
bean sprouts
bok choy
carrots
chiles, e.g., dried
cilantro
corn
cucumbers
eggplant
EGGS, e.g., hard-boiled, poached
garlic
GINGER
greens, e.g., collard
honey
Japanese cuisine
kale
kombu
lemongrass
MISO
MUSHROOMS, e.g., Asian, shiitake, wood ear
nori
oil, e.g., canola, grapeseed, red chili, sesame
onions
peas

Dishes

Chilled Ramen Noodles and Vegetable Spring Roll: Japanese/Chinese Style Chilled Noodles with Cucumber, Avocado, Rikyu-Fu, Sesame, Tomato, Shishito Pepper, and Pak Choy, served with Spring Rolls
— Kajitsu (New York City)

pickles
salads
salt, e.g., kosher
SCALLIONS
sea vegetables
seitan
SOUPS
SOY SAUCE
sprouts, bean
stock, e.g., mushroom, vegetable
sugar
tamari
tofu
vegetables
vinegar, e.g., sherry
wine, rice

Flavor Affinities

ramen noodles + corn + garlic +
    green onions + miso
ramen noodles + ginger +
    scallions + soy sauce
ramen noodles + kale +
    mushrooms + red chili oil +
    seitan
ramen noodles + kale + shiitake
    mushrooms + soy sauce +
    vegetable stock

● NOODLES, RICE (aka RICE STICKS — or RICE VERMICELLI, which are thinner strands)

What they are: rice flour
noodles, typically flat like linguini
Nutritional profile: 95% carbs
/ 3% protein / 2% fats
Calories: 195 per 1-cup serving
(cooked)
Protein: 2 grams
Techniques: soak (in hot water,
until soft) — then stir-fry, if
desired
Tips: Using sufficient oil during the cooking process (e.g.,
stir-frying) keeps noodles from
sticking together. Opt for brown
rice noodles.

almonds
Asian cuisines
basil and Thai basil
beans, e.g., green
bell peppers, e.g., red
bok choy
broccoli
cabbage, e.g., purple, savoy
carrots
cashews
cauliflower
cayenne
chiles, e.g., jalapeño, serrano,
    Thai; chili pepper paste and
    chili pepper sauce
CILANTRO
coconut
cucumber
eggplant
eggs
five-spice powder
GARLIC
ginger
greens, e.g., mustard
hoisin sauce

Flavor Affinities

rice noodles + almonds + ginger + lime + papaya + savoy cabbage
rice noodles + basil + walnuts
rice noodles + bean sprouts + garlic + lime + peanuts + scallions +
    tamarind + tofu
rice noodles + bok choy + shiitake mushrooms
rice noodles + broccoli + hoisin + peanuts + tofu
rice noodles + carrots + cucumbers + lettuce + oil + scallions
rice noodles + chiles + garlic + ginger + tofu
rice noodles + cilantro + parsley + sesame oil + soy sauce
rice noodles + coconut + eggplant + mustard greens + shiitake
    mushrooms
rice noodles + garlic + miso + sesame seeds
rice noodles + mint + zucchini

Dishes

Crispy Rice Noodles, Baby Bok Choy, Miso Glazed Turnips, Lotus Root, Cashews
— Green Zebra (Chicago)

Tofu Pad Thai: Rice Noodles, Julienne Vegetables, Thai Coconut Peanut Sauce
— The Lodge at Woodloch (Hawley, PA)

Indonesian cuisine
kimchi
lettuce, e.g., romaine
LIME, e.g., juice
maple syrup
mint
miso
mushrooms, e.g., Asian, shiitake
nori, e.g., strips
oil, e.g., olive, peanut, scallion,
    sesame
onions, e.g., red
PAD THAI, VEGETARIAN
parsley
PEANUTS
ponzu sauce
salads, e.g., green, noodle
sauces, e.g., sriracha
scallions
SESAME, e.g., oil, paste, seeds
shallots
Singapore cuisine
soups
SOY SAUCE
SPROUTS, e.g., mung bean

STIR-FRIES
stock, vegetable
sugar, e.g., brown, palm
tamari
TAMARIND
tempeh
Thai cuisine
TOFU, e.g., extra-firm, smoked
tomatoes, e.g., cherry
vegetables, esp. crisp, green
Vietnamese cuisine
vinegar, e.g., balsamic or rice
walnuts
water chestnuts
watercress
zucchini

NOODLES, SHIRATAKI and TOFU SHIRATAKI

Flavor: bland in flavor, with notes of the ocean (e.g., fish or seafood), and the chewiness of pasta (tofu versions)
Volume: quiet – moderate
What they are: These low-calorie noodles are made from a type of yam (and sometimes tofu, which makes them closer in flavor and texture to typical pasta).
What's healthful about them: virtually free of calories

Tip: Rinse noodles well (three or more times) to reduce any fishy aromas or flavors.

bell peppers, e.g., red
bok choy
coconut milk
curries, esp. Thai
curry paste and curry spices
garlic
ginger
lime, e.g., juice
miso
pad thai
salads, e.g., noodle, vegetable
sauces, e.g., creamy
scallions

soups
soy sauce
stir-fries
stock, vegetable
tofu, e.g., grilled, smoked

Flavor Affinities
shirataki noodles + coconut milk + curry spices + tofu
shirataki noodles + vegetable stock + lime juice

NOODLES, SOBA — WHOLE-GRAIN

What they are: buckwheat and wheat-based noodles
Nutritional profile: 82% carbs / 17% protein / 1% fats
Calories: 115 per 1-cup serving (cooked)
Protein: 6 grams

Tips: Remove starch after cooking by rinsing in cold water. Serve noodles cold during warmer seasons and hot during colder seasons.

asparagus
avocado
basil and Thai basil
beans, e.g., green
beans, fermented black
BELL PEPPERS, e.g., red, yellow
broccoli, broccolini, and broccoli rabe
Brussels sprouts
CABBAGE, e.g., napa, red, savoy
CARROTS
cashews
celery
chard

chiles, e.g., jalapeño, and **chili pepper flakes**
CILANTRO
coconut milk
corn
cucumber
daikon
dashi
dips, e.g., hot broths
edamame
eggplant
GARLIC
GINGER
greens, salad
hoisin sauce
Japanese cuisine
Kaffir lime leaves
kale
kombu
lemon, e.g., juice
lettuce, e.g., romaine
lime
lotus root
mirin
MISO, e.g., red
MUSHROOMS, e.g., enoki, portobello, shiitake, wild
nori
OIL, e.g., canola, corn, grapeseed, olive, peanut, **SESAME**
onions, red
orange, e.g., juice
peanuts and peanut sauce
peas
pea shoots
pickled cabbage, e.g., red
plums and plum sauce
radishes, e.g., icicle
sake
SALADS, e.g., Asian, chilled noodle
SCALLIONS

Dishes

Shirataki Noodle Stir-Fry: Sweet Chili Marinated Tofu, Wok-Fried Zucchini, Lotus Root, and Edamame
— The Lodge at Woodloch (Hawley, PA)

sea vegetables, e.g., arame, dulse, hiziki, wakame
SESAME, e.g., oil, paste, seeds
snow peas
SOUPS, e.g., coconut, miso
SOY SAUCE
SPINACH
sprouts, e.g., alfalfa, buckwheat, mung bean, sunflower
stir-fries
stock, e.g., vegetable

sugar, e.g., brown
sugar snap peas
sushi, noodle
sweet potatoes
TAHINI
TAMARI, e.g., low-sodium
tempeh
teriyaki sauce
TOFU, e.g., firm, silken, smoked
tomatoes, e.g., cherry or grape, and tomato paste

VINEGAR, e.g., apple cider, balsamic, RICE WINE, white wine
wasabi
water chestnuts
watercress
wine, e.g., dry sherry
wraps, e.g., in rice paper

Flavor Affinities

soba noodles + avocado + carrots + cashews + cilantro + peanuts + tofu
soba noodles + broccoli + cabbage + carrots + lotus root + snow peas
soba noodles + cashews + enoki and shiitake mushrooms + romaine + wraps
soba noodles + chili pepper flakes + garlic + scallions + sesame oil/seeds + tamari
soba noodles + cilantro + lime + peanut sauce + scallions
soba noodles + cucumbers + feta cheese + lemon + parsley
soba noodles + daikon + dashi + nori + scallions + soy sauce + wasabi
soba noodles + dry sherry + kombu + tamari
soba noodles + garlic + ginger + cilantro + scallions
soba noodles + garlic + ginger + hiziki + miso
soba noodles + garlic + ginger + peanuts + red cabbage
soba noodles + garlic + ginger + rice vinegar + tamari
soba noodles + garlic + sesame paste + soy sauce
soba noodles + ginger + seaweed + shiitake mushrooms + soy sauce
soba noodles + greens + lime + sesame oil + soy sauce + tofu
soba noodles + orange + sesame + tofu

Dishes

Dashi and Noodles: Bowl of traditional Japanese Broth made with Shiitake Mushrooms, Kombu, Fresh Ginger, and Shoyu, served warm over Soba Noodles
— Angelica Kitchen (New York City)

Nutty Buddy: Buckwheat Noodles, Cashews, Carrots, Cilantro, Jalapeño Peanut Butter, Avocado, Sesame Oil, Tofu, Romaine
— Beyond Sushi (New York City)

Cold Soba Salad: Soba Noodles, Julienne Vegetables, Cucumbers, Cilantro, Sesame Seeds, Peanuts, Peanut Dressing
— Real Food Daily (Los Angeles)

Buckwheat Noodles tossed in a Sesame Vinaigrette, served on a bed of Mixed Greens and topped with Tahini Dressing, Seasonal Vegetables, and Cumin-Sesame Blackened Tempeh
— Sage's Cafe (Salt Lake City)

"During a kaiseki menu, you want to make a certain impact with the very first course, and to make sure the main course itself is outstanding. But the courses before and after the main course should be toned down, to enhance its impact. I would serve something very simple and delicious before the main course, like soba noodles."
— RYOTA UESHIMA, KAJITSU (NEW YORK CITY)

• NOODLES, SOMEN

Season: spring – summer, when they are typically served cold
Flavor: neutral, with a light, smooth texture
Volume: quiet
What they are: very thin whole-wheat noodles
Nutritional profile: 87% carbs / 12% protein / 1% fats
Calories: 230 per 1-cup serving (cooked)
Protein: 7 grams
Timing: Boil until tender, about 2 minutes.

Tip: Remove starch after cooking by rinsing in cold water.

bell peppers
carrots
celery
cilantro
cucumber
edamame
garlic

ginger
Japanese cuisine
Korean cuisine
lime
palm, hearts of
papaya
parsnips
peanuts and peanut sauce
salads, e.g., noodle
sauces, dipping
scallions
shiso
soups, e.g., cold or hot
soy sauce
turnips
vinegar, e.g., rice

NOODLES, UDON

Flavor: neutral, with a soft, slippery texture
Volume: quiet
What they are: thick (flat or round) noodles made from wheat
Timing: Cook until tender, about 1–3 minutes (fresh noodles) or 5–7 minutes (dried noodles).
Tip: Remove starch after cooking by rinsing in cold water.
Possible substitute: linguini

agave nectar
almonds
beans, green
bell peppers, e.g., red, yellow
bok choy
broccoli cabbage, e.g., napa
carrots
celery

Dishes

Chilled Somen Noodles, Hawaiian Hearts of Palm, Papaya, Edamame, Shiso, Ginger-Soy
— Green Zebra (Chicago)

Chilled Somen Noodles with Sesame Sauce and Inari Sushi: Japanese Extra-Thin Noodles with Sesame, Umeboshi, Chive, Myoga, and Pak Choy, served with Inari Sushi
— Kajitsu (New York City)

chili paste and chili pepper flakes
cilantro
coconut milk
cold sesame noodles
cucumbers
daikon
dashi
eggs
garlic
GINGER
hoisin
honey
Japanese cuisine
kombu
lemon, e.g., juice
maple syrup
mirin
miso
MUSHROOMS, e.g., Asian, button, cremini, oyster, **shiitake**
nori
oil, e.g., olive, sesame
onions
peanuts, peanut butter, and peanut sauce
radishes
sake
SALADS, e.g., Asian, chilled noodle
sauces, dipping
scallions
SESAME, e.g., oil, paste, sauce, seeds
snow peas
soups, e.g., coconut milk–based
SOY SAUCE
squash, e.g., kabocha
stir-fries
stock, e.g., mushroom, vegetable

sugar snap peas
tahini
tamari
tempura
TOFU, e.g., baked, extra-firm
vegetables
vinegar, rice
wasabi
watercress

Flavor Affinities

udon noodles + almonds + ginger + mushrooms + scallions
udon noodles + bok choy + miso + shiitake mushrooms
udon noodles + chili paste + garlic + peanut butter + rice vinegar + soy sauce
udon noodles + dashi + kombu + soy sauce
udon noodles + garlic + rice vinegar + scallions + soy sauce + tahini
udon noodles + ginger + mushrooms + tofu
udon noodles + mirin + mushroom stock + soy sauce + watercress
udon noodles + peanut sauce + snow peas
udon noodles + rice vinegar + snow peas + soy sauce

NORI (aka LAVER)

[NOR-ee]
Flavor: salty, with notes of the sea, and the texture of handmade paper
Volume: quiet (as is) – moderate (after toasting)
What it is: dried and pressed sheets of seaweed, typically used to wrap sushi, hand rolls, and nori (aka maki) rolls
What's healthful about it: easy to digest; higher in protein than any other seaweed

Nutritional profile: 53% carbs / 40% protein / 7% fats

Calories: 1 calorie per sheet

Tips: Lightly toast the dried seaweed sheet before using, by waving it over an open flame on your stovetop, which enhances its flavor and texture. At traditional sushi restaurants, vegetarian options typically include white or brown short-grain sticky rice rolls filled with avocado and/or cucumber. However, New York City's Beyond Sushi features iron-rich six-grain rice — a delicious medley of rye berries, barley, pearl barley, brown rice, red rice, and black rice.

arugula, e.g., micro
asparagus
AVOCADO
barley, e.g., hulled, pearled
beans, e.g., haricots verts
bell peppers, red
burdock
carrots
chayote
chili pepper flakes
cilantro
CUCUMBER
daikon
eggs, e.g., *omelets*
ginger, pickled
GRAINS, WHOLE, e.g., brown
   rice, hulled barley, pearl barley,
   quinoa, rye berries

greens, dandelion
Japanese cuisine
kiwi
kombu
macrobiotic cuisine
mango
mirin
miso
MUSHROOMS, e.g., enoki,
   shiitake
noodles, e.g., soba, udon
NORI ROLLS
onions
popcorn
RICE, esp. **black**, **brown**,
   Japanese, red, **short-grain**,
   sticky, **sushi**, white
rice balls

rye berries

SALADS, e.g., bean, grain, green

salt, sea

scallions

sea vegetables

SESAME SEEDS, *e.g., white*

shiso

snow peas

SOUPS

SOY SAUCE

spinach

sprouts, e.g., alfalfa

stews

SUSHI, VEGETARIAN

sweet potato

tamari

tempeh

teriyaki sauce

tofu

umeboshi and umeboshi paste

vegetables

VINEGAR, *e.g., brown rice, rice wine*

wakame

WASABI

"Toast **nori**, then grind it, and use the nori powder as a seasoning to add an ocean-esque quality to dishes like fried mushrooms."

— ERIC TUCKER, MILLENNIUM (SAN FRANCISCO)

Flavor Affinities

Nori roll combinations = nori + sticky rice + any of the groups listed below:

alfalfa sprouts + avocado + sweet potato

almonds + spinach + tofu

avocado + carrots + cucumbers

avocado + chayote + chiles + cilantro

avocado + cucumber + mango

avocado + pickled ginger + shiitake mushrooms

cucumber + daikon + umeboshi paste

cucumber + shiitake mushrooms + spinach

cucumber + tofu + wasabi

mushrooms + teriyaki sauce + tofu

• NUTMEG

Season: autumn – winter

Flavor: bitter/**sweet**, with spicy notes of cloves and/or mace

Volume: moderate – **loud**

Botanical relative: mace

> **Tips:** Add nutmeg toward the end of the cooking process. Use in moderation, as it is high in saturated fat.

apples

BAKED GOODS, e.g., biscuits, cakes, cookies, pastries, pies

bananas

carrots

cereals, hot breakfast

cheese, *e.g., cheddar, Gruyère, pecorino, ricotta*

CHEESE DISHES, e.g., fondues, soufflés

chocolate

cinnamon

cloves

coconut milk

cream and milk

desserts, e.g., cheesecake, custards, puddings

drinks, esp. cream- or milk-based, e.g., eggnogs

eggs and *egg dishes, e.g., quiches*

French cuisine

fruit, e.g., dried, fresh

---

ginger

greens, bitter, e.g., sautéed

ice cream

Indian cuisine

Italian cuisine, e.g., sauces

lemon

lemongrass

mace

milk

mushrooms

noodle dishes, e.g., macaroni and cheese

pastas

potatoes, *e.g., mashed*

puddings, e.g., rice

pumpkin

quatre épices

rice

sauces, e.g., barbecue, béchamel, cheese, cream, pasta, tomato

soups, e.g., cream

SPINACH

squash, e.g., winter

stews, e.g., vegetable

sweet potatoes

vanilla

yams

"When I visited France, I noticed that every house I visited smelled of **nutmeg**! I use fresh whole nutmeg in my potatoes Dauphinois. I will also add nutmeg to the yam I make with cinnamon, bay leaf, thyme, and few other ingredients. I will also add it to potatoes, cream, garlic, and thyme. It even works with sautéed spinach and greens as balance to the bitterness."

— KEN LARSEN, TABLE VERTE (NEW YORK CITY)

NUTRITIONAL YEAST (aka affectionately as NOOCH)

Flavor: savory/*umami*, with rich notes of **CHEESE** (esp.

untoasted), chicken stock (esp. toasted), and/or nuts
Volume: quiet – moderate
What it is: yellowish flaky deactivated yeast (Note: It is *not* the same as brewer's yeast.)
Calories: 30 per 1-tablespoon serving
Protein: 4 grams
Brand: Red Star

almonds
arrowroot
artichokes
barley
beans
bread, garlic
breadings
broccoli
cashews, raw
casseroles
chard
cheeses, nondairy, e.g., nut
dips
dressings
garlic, e.g., fresh, powder
gravies
hummus
kelp powder
lemon, e.g., juice
macaroni
milk, nondairy
mustard, e.g., Dijon
nuts, raw, e.g., cashews, macadamia
oil, e.g., grapeseed, olive
onion, e.g., powder
paprika
pastas
pepper, black
pizza
POPCORN
potatoes, e.g., baked
rice
salad dressings
salads
salt, e.g., sea
SAUCES, e.g., "cheese-y"

sesame seeds
soups
spinach
spreads
stews
stocks, vegetable
tamari
thyme
tofu, e.g., *scrambles*
turmeric
vegetables

Flavor Affinities
nutritional yeast + Dijon mustard + garlic + nondairy milk
nutritional yeast + garlic + lemon **+ mustard**
nutritional yeast + garlic + onion + sesame seeds
nutritional yeast + pasta + soy milk
nutritional yeast + tofu + turmeric

"I will go old school when I make gravy, and start with a roux before adding aromatics like garlic and onion. The two big flavor components I also add are tamari instead of salt and **toasted nutritional yeast** to give it that poultry-like flavor."
— DAVE ANDERSON, MADDY'S AND FORMERLY MADELEINE BISTRO (LOS ANGELES)

NUTS (see also ALMONDS, CASHEWS, PEANUTS, WALNUTS, etc.)

NUTS, BRAZIL
Flavor: nutty, with tropical (e.g., coconut, macadamia) notes, and a very rich texture
Volume: moderate
Calories: 185 per 1-ounce serving
Protein: 4 grams

Tip: Avoid too-high levels of selenium (which can be toxic) by not eating more than two Brazil nuts per day.

apples
baked goods, e.g., cakes, cookies, pies
cereals, hot breakfast
chocolate
dates
desserts
figs
nuts, mixed
piecrusts
raisins
salads
smoothies
snacks
stuffings
trail mix

● NUTS, MACADAMIA
Flavor: salty (esp. if salted) / slightly sweet, with notes of butter, and a rich, creamy/crunchy texture
Volume: moderate – loud
Nutritional profile: 88% fat / 8% carbs / 4% protein
Calories: 205 per 1-ounce serving
Protein: 2 grams

almonds
baked goods, e.g., breads, cookies, muffins
bananas
broccoli
cabbage
chiles, e.g., chipotle
CHOCOLATE, e.g., DARK, white
cinnamon
coconut and coconut milk
coffee
desserts
fruits, dried, e.g., cranberries
garlic
ginger

grapes
HAWAIIAN CUISINE
hazelnuts
honey
ice cream
kiwi
lemon
lime
mangoes
nectarines
oats and oatmeal
orange
pancakes
papaya
pears
pestos
pineapple
rice, e.g., basmati, wild
rum
salads
salsas, e.g., pineapple
sauces, e.g., chocolate, nut
soups
spreads
starfruit
stir-fries
strawberries
sugar, brown
tangerines
vanilla

Flavor Affinities
macadamia nuts + chocolate + coffee
macadamia nuts + coconut + white chocolate

● OATMEAL and OATS

Flavor: slightly sweet, with notes of nuts, and a chewy and/or creamy texture (when cooked)
Volume: quiet
What it is: whole grain
Nutritional profile: 70% carbs / 15% protein / 15% fats
Calories: 110 per 1-ounce serving (uncooked)
Protein: 5 grams

Techniques: boil, simmer
Timing: Cook Scottish oats about 10 minutes, or old-fashioned (aka rolled) oats about 10 – 15 minutes, covered; steel-cut oats will cook in about 30 minutes, although cooking time can be cut by presoaking.
Ratio: 1: 2 – 3 (1 cup oats to 2 – 3 cups liquid, e.g., almond milk or water)
Tips: To make a creamier oatmeal, use Scottish oats and/or substitute milk (e.g., almond) for some or all of the water. For chewier oatmeal, opt for steel-cut oats. In-between? You might prefer good old-fashioned rolled oats. Whole oat groats can be used in savory dishes, such as pilafs.

Flavor Affinities
OATS + ALMONDS + CINNAMON + fruit (e.g., blueberries, cherries) **+ MAPLE SYRUP**
oats + almond milk + dates + sunflower seeds
OATS + ALMONDS + cashews + **CINNAMON + MAPLE SYRUP** + vanilla
oats + almonds + cinnamon + yogurt
oats + almonds + honey + raisins
oats + almonds + kombu + sunflower seeds
oats + apples + brown sugar + **cinnamon + raisins**
oats + apples + cheddar cheese
oats + apples + cinnamon + dates
oats + apples + cinnamon + honey + raisins
oats + apples + honey + *muffins*
oats + apples/pears + maple syrup
OATS + bananas + **CINNAMON + MAPLE SYRUP**
oats + bananas + maple syrup + nuts (e.g., hazelnuts)
oats + brown sugar + nuts + raisins
oats + cinnamon + figs + honey + vanilla
OATS + CINNAMON + MAPLE SYRUP
oats + cranberries + nuts (e.g., hazelnuts, walnuts)
oats + ginger + plums
oats + honey + miso + walnuts
oats + honey + nuts + raisins
oats + pecans + sweet potatoes + vanilla

ALMONDS
APPLES and APPLE JUICE
apricots, e.g., **dried**
BAKED GOODS, e.g., biscuits, breads, cakes, COOKIES, muffins, quick breads
bananas
berries, e.g., **blueberries**, raspberries
breading, e.g., for seitan
butter
buttermilk
cardamom
cashews
celery
CEREALS, HOT BREAKFAST
cheese, e.g., Parmesan
CINNAMON
coconut
cream
DESSERTS, e.g., fruit crisps and crumbles

dill
fennel seeds
FRUITS, DRIED, e.g., cherries,
 cranberries, currants, dates,
 figs, peaches, plums, RAISINS
ginger
GRANOLA
HONEY
Irish cuisine
juice, fruit, e.g., apple, pear
kefir
MAPLE SYRUP
"meatballs" or "meatloaf,"
 vegetarian
milk, dairy or nondairy, e.g.,
 almond, coconut, hemp, rice, soy
molasses
muesli
nutmeg
NUTS, e.g., **ALMONDS**, cashews,
 hazelnuts, macadamias,
 peanuts, **pecans**, pistachios,
 walnuts
★OATMEAL
oil, e.g., coconut, flaxseed,
 safflower, sesame
orange, e.g., juice, zest
pancakes and waffles
parsley
peaches
pears
PLUMS
RAISINS
sage
salt, sea
Scottish cuisine
SEEDS, e.g., flax, pumpkin,
 sesame, **sunflower**
soups, e.g., Irish, Scottish, or as a
 thickener, to make creamier
stock, vegetable
sugar, e.g., brown
trail mix
vanilla
veggie burgers
yogurt

• OIL — IN GENERAL

Virtually all oils have about 120 calories per 1-tablespoon serving, and are high in fats and low in nutrients.

Tips: Select an oil based on its intended purpose, e.g., finishing dishes (e.g., extra-virgin olive, flavored), or low-, medium-, or high-temperature (e.g., grapeseed, peanut, safflower) cooking. Always opt for unrefined and less processed oils (e.g., "expeller-pressed" or "cold pressed"), which are free of chemicals and solvents, and choose organic corn and soybean oils.

• OIL, ACORN SQUASH SEED

Flavor: earthy notes of brown butter, chestnuts, spice, squash, and/or toasted walnuts, and a rich texture
Volume: moderate
Tip: Use for medium-temperature cooking (e.g., sautéing).
Brand: Stony Brook

Brussels sprouts
casseroles
cheeses, e.g., soft
marinades
salads
soups, e.g., winter
squash, esp. winter, e.g., acorn, butternut
vegetables, e.g., roasted, sautéed

• OIL, ALMOND

Flavor: notes of almonds
Volume: quiet – moderate
Techniques: bake, raw
Tip: Use for medium- (e.g., baking, sautéing) to high-temperature (e.g., frying) cooking.
Brand: La Tourangelle

almonds
asparagus
baked goods
Chinese cuisine
dressings
Indian cuisine
lettuce, e.g., romaine
mustard
pastas
salad dressings, e.g., vinaigrettes
salads
sauces
sautéed dishes
stir-fries
vegetables
vinegar, e.g., champagne

• OIL, ARGAN

Flavor: notes of cream, fruit, and/or **nuts**, with a creamy texture
Volume: quieter (untoasted) – louder (toasted)
Tip: Use only for finishing dishes, not for cooking.
Possible substitutes: almond oil, hazelnut oil

almonds and almond paste
basil
bell peppers, e.g., red, roasted
cheese, e.g., blue, goat
chickpeas
chocolate
couscous
cream
cucumbers
desserts
dips
eggs, e.g., *fried, scrambled*
honey
hummus

Dishes

Creamless Cream of Pea Soup with Crispy Burrata and Argan Oil
— Mélisse (Santa Monica, CA)

lemon, e.g., juice
lentils
Moroccan cuisine
pastas
pestos
pine nuts
rice
salad dressings and salads
sauces
sesame, e.g., paste, seeds
soups, e.g., bean, cucumber, lentil, pea, potato, vegetable
stews, e.g., tagines
sweet potatoes
tomatoes
vegetables, e.g., grilled
verjus
vinegar, e.g., apple cider, champagne
yogurt
za'atar
zucchini

Flavor Affinities
argan oil + almonds + honey
argan oil + honey + yogurt
argan oil + lentils + tomatoes

• OIL, AVOCADO

Flavor: rich, with notes of avocado and/or butter
Volume: quiet
Techniques: emulsify, fry, grill, raw, roast, sauté, stir-fry
Tip: Use for medium- (e.g., baking, sautéing) to high-temperature (e.g., frying, stir-frying) cooking.

avocado
cilantro
eggs, e.g., *fried eggs*

fruit, e.g., citrus
grapefruit
lemon, e.g., juice, zest
lime, e.g., juice, zest
melon
orange, e.g., juice, zest
pestos
salad dressings
salads
vegetables, e.g., grilled, roasted
vinegar, e.g., fruit, sherry,
    tarragon
yogurt

Flavor Affinities
avocado oil + cilantro + lime juice
    + yogurt

● OIL, CAMELINA SEED
Flavor: notes of asparagus,
broccoli, cauliflower, greens, nuts,
and/or seeds
Volume: moderate – loud
Techniques: bake, sauté, stir-fry
Tip: stays fresher longer than
flaxseed oil

asparagus
baked goods, e.g., muffins, quick
    breads
cabbage
carrots
cereals, hot breakfast
cheese, e.g., Parmesan
chickpeas
dill
dips, e.g., baba ghanoush, hummus
eggplant
eggs, e.g., *quiche*
garlic, e.g., green
granola
honey
kale
lemon, e.g., caramelized
marinades
mustard, e.g., Dijon
pastas, e.g., primavera
pepper, black

pestos
pilafs
rice
salad dressings
salads
sauces, oil-based
slaws, e.g., Asian, cole
smoothies
vegetables, e.g., roasted
vinegar, e.g., apple cider, balsamic
zucchini

"**Camelina seed oil** has a really
interesting, strong, seed-y flavor.
I'll combine it with caramelized
lemon and green garlic."
— JOSIAH CITRIN, MÉLISSE
(SANTA MONICA, CA)

● OIL, CANOLA
Flavor: neutral
Volume: quiet
What it is: rapeseed oil from
CANada (which is where it gets
its name)
Techniques: bake, **fry**, sauté
Tips: Use *only organic, expeller-*
pressed canola oil, as many
canola oils are made from GMO
seeds; otherwise, opt for another
oil altogether. Use as fresh as
possible, and check regularly
for rancidity (as it goes rancid
quickly). Canola oil can be used
for medium- (e.g., baking) to
high-temperature (e.g., frying)
cooking. Use with boldly flavored dishes that would obscure
the flavor of more expensive oils.

Asian cuisines
baked goods, e.g., *muffins, quick*
    breads
chiles
curries, e.g., Asian
dips
dressings
Mexican cuisine

pancakes
salad dressings
salads
sauces
soups
spicy dishes
stews

● OIL, CHILI
What it is: vegetable (e.g.,
peanut) oil infused with chiles
Tip: Add at the end of the cooking process, to finish a dish and
add heat.

Asian cuisines
cabbage, e.g., Chinese, napa
cilantro
garlic
ginger
mangoes
noodles, Asian
oil, sesame
peanuts
salad dressings
sauces, e.g., dipping, peanut
shallots
soy sauce
sugar, e.g., brown
sweet potatoes
tatsoi
vinegar, e.g., red wine, rice wine

Flavor Affinities
chili oil + rice vinegar + sesame
    oil + soy sauce + sugar

● OIL, COCONUT
Flavor: notes of coconut, cream,
nuts, and/or vanilla, with a rich,
creamy texture
Volume: quiet – moderate
Technique: fry (as it has a high
smoke point)
Tip: Opt for virgin, non-hydro-
genated coconut oil.
Brand: Omega

agave nectar

almonds and almond butter

Asian cuisines

baked goods, e.g., cakes, cookies

chocolate and cocoa powder

coconut

confections, e.g., truffles

coriander

curries

desserts, e.g., raw

doughnuts

garlic

ginger

greens, e.g., bitter

"ice creams"

icings

Indian cuisine

lime

nutmeg

oatmeal

onions

popcorn

scallions

Southeast Asian cuisines

stir-fries

sweet potatoes

Flavor Affinities

coconut oil + almonds + cocoa
  powder + coconut

coconut oil + coriander + ginger

"I'll blend **coconut oil** with cacao powder to make raw truffles, while I use coconut butter in raw desserts."

— AMI BEACH, G-ZEN (BRANFORD, CT)

"The choice of oil in baking is important. For cookies I will use canola, grapeseed, or **coconut oil**. The coconut oil is used in our doughnuts and cakes as well, but you have to be careful so that the flavor does not become overpowering."

— FERNANDA CAPOBIANCO,
VEGAN DIVAS (NEW YORK CITY)

"**Coconut oil** is a liquid when it's at 72°F and up, and a solid with the texture of butter or shortening at temperatures below 72°F. When we make biscuits, we'll use solid coconut oil and cut it into the dough, which results in a layering effect and flakier biscuits. We'll also cut solid coconut oil into our pancake batter, where it has a leavening effect that makes our pancakes light and fluffy — more so than with canola oil."

— DEENA JALAL, FOMU AND ROOT
(ALLSTON, MA)

● OIL, FLAXSEED

What's healthful about it:

omega-3 fatty acids

Tips: Flaxseeds are said to be even higher in lignans than flaxseed oil is. Heating flaxseed oil destroys its nutrients. Store in the refrigerator.

artichokes

bell peppers, e.g., roasted red

bread

cereals, breakfast

herbs

lemon

mustard, Dijon

popcorn

porridges

rice

SALAD DRESSINGS

salads

sauces

smoothies

spreads

vinegar, apple cider

Flavor Affinities

flaxseed oil + apple cider vinegar
  + lemon juice

flaxseed oil + herbs + red wine
  vinegar

● OIL, GRAPESEED

Flavor: neutral, with delicate notes of fruit, grapes, and/or nuts

Volume: very quiet

Tips: Use for high-temperature cooking, e.g., sautéing. Buy only cold-pressed oil.

Possible substitutes: butter, canola oil

citrus

coconut

herbs

marinades

mayonnaises

oils, other, e.g., nut, olive

SALAD DRESSINGS, e.g.,
  vinaigrettes

salads

sauces, oil-based

sautéed dishes

vinegar

"The flavor of olive oil can sometimes be overpowering, so I will often use **grapeseed oil** — which has a nice, neutral flavor — in a ratio of two parts grapeseed oil to one part olive oil."

— JOSIAH CITRIN, MÉLISSE (SANTA
MONICA, CA)

● OIL, HAZELNUT

Flavor: notes of hazelnuts

Volume: moderate – loud

Tips: Use for low- to medium-temperature cooking (e.g., baking, sautéing), or as a finishing oil. Use caution when cooking, as hazelnut oil burns easily. Store in the refrigerator, and use within a few months after opening.

apples

artichokes

baked goods

beans, e.g., green

berries, e.g., blackberries, raspberries
bread
broccoli
cheese, e.g., fresh
chicory
citrus juices
desserts, e.g., confections, cookies
dips
dressings
endive
figs
garlic
greens, e.g., bitter, dandelion
hazelnuts
lemon, e.g., juice
mustard, e.g., Dijon
oils, other quieter
pastas
pears
persimmons
potatoes
rice, e.g., wild
SALAD DRESSINGS, e.g., vinaigrettes
salads
sauces
shallots
spinach
tomatoes
VINEGAR, e.g., apple cider, balsamic, champagne, fruit, sherry, tarragon

"**Hazelnut oil** with either artichokes or endives is a nice combination."
— JOSIAH CITRIN, MÉLISSE (SANTA MONICA, CA)

● OIL, HEMP
Flavor: notes of nuts and, um, marijuana; with a creamy texture
Volume: mild – moderate/loud
What's healthful about it:
omega-3s

Tips: Refrigerate, and use quickly. Do not heat.

garlic
grains, e.g., oats, quinoa
honey
lemon, e.g., juice
mustard, e.g., Dijon
oils, other quieter
pestos
popcorn
salad dressings
salads
sauces
smoothies
soups, e.g., avocado, cold
vegetables
vinegar, e.g., balsamic

● OIL, LEMON
Flavor: notes of lemon
Volume: loud

artichokes
arugula
asparagus
baked goods, e.g., pastries
beans, green
beets
broccoli and broccolini
carrots
cheese, e.g., goat
chili pepper flakes
fennel
garlic
olives, black
parsley
pastas
pepper, e.g., black
rosemary
salad dressings, e.g., lemon vinaigrettes
salads
thyme

OIL, NUT (see OIL, ALMOND; OIL, HAZELNUT; OIL, PISTACHIO; OIL, WALNUT)

● OIL, OLIVE
Flavor: earthy notes of fruit and/ or olives, with a rich texture
Volume: quieter (e.g., lighter-colored virgin) – louder (e.g., deeper-colored extra-virgin)
Techniques: bake, fry, raw, sauté (on low heat)

Tips: Use raw, or warm only to low temperatures. Opt for lighter, quieter virgin (aka "pure") oil for baking, frying, grilling, roasting, and sautéing, and darker, louder extra-virgin oil for dressing salads or drizzling on bruschetta or pizza. For salad dressings, the typical ratio is one part vinegar to three or four parts extra-virgin olive oil, but those looking to lower the fat in their diets (not to mention calories) should consider using less oil.

almonds
arugula
baked goods, esp. Italian, e.g., cakes, cookies, piecrusts
basil
beans, e.g., cannellini, white
beets
bread and breadcrumbs
bruschetta
capers
cheese, e.g., mozzarella, Parmesan, pecorino
chickpeas
chiles
citrus
coriander
cornmeal

cumin
dressings
eggplant
eggs, e.g., fried
fennel
French cuisine, e.g., Provençal
GARLIC
greens, bitter and salad
herbs, e.g., fresh
hummus
Italian cuisine
LEMONS, e.g., juice, zest
limes, e.g., juice, zest
marinades
mayonnaises
Mediterranean cuisines
Middle Eastern cuisines
Moroccan cuisine
mushrooms, e.g., portobello
mustard, e.g., Dijon
oils, other, e.g., hazelnut, walnut
olives
onions
oranges, e.g., juice, zest
parsley
pastas
pepper, black
pesto
pine nuts
pizzas
potatoes
rosemary
salad dressings, e.g., *vinaigrettes*
salads, e.g., bean, green, panzanella,
   pasta, potato
salt
sauces, e.g., cold
sautéed dishes
soups
Spanish cuisine
thyme
tomatoes
vegetables
vinegar, e.g., balsamic,
   champagne, fruit, red wine,
   sherry, white wine
walnuts

Flavor Affinities
olive oil + basil + chili pepper
   flakes + garlic + tomatoes
olive oil + basil + garlic +
   Parmesan cheese + pine nuts
olive oil + garlic + parsley
olive oil + garlic + red wine
   vinegar
olive oil + salt + vegetables

"I can sum up in two words the
difference between vegetarian
cooking in the 1970s vs. today:
olive oil. Back then, it was
common to mask dishes with the
richness of butter and cream.
Olive oil lets more of the flavor
shine through, particularly dishes
made with garlic and herbs."
— MOLLIE KATZEN, AUTHOR

"One you've fallen in love with
the flavor of **extra-virgin olive oil,**
there's no place to go after that.
I'll only use it to finish dishes. For
high-heat cooking, I use canola,
grapeseed, or safflower oil—or
some combination thereof."
— RICH LANDAU, VEDGE (PHILADELPHIA)

● **OIL, PEANUT**
Flavor: neutral (regular) – nutty
(roasted)
Volume: quiet (regular) –
moderate/loud (roasted)
Techniques: deep-fry, fry, grill,
raw, roast, sauté, **stir-fry**

Tips: Use regular, unroasted
peanut oil for high-temperature
cooking. Given the severity of
peanut allergies, make sure to
let guests know when it is used
in a dish.

Brand: Loriva roasted peanut oil

ASIAN CUISINES
baked goods

Chinese cuisine
curries
fried dishes
fruits
garlic
ginger
lentils
noodles, e.g., Asian
pasta
peanuts
salad dressings, e.g., Asian, fruit
salads, e.g., fruit
sauces, e.g., peanut
scallions
sesame, e.g., oil, seeds
soy sauce
STIR-FRIES
tofu
vinegar, e.g., balsamic, malt

Flavor Affinities
peanut oil + ginger + scallions +
   soy sauce

● **OIL, PINE NUT**
Flavor: neutral, with notes of
pine nuts and/or pine resin
Volume: quiet

basil
broccoli and broccoli rabe
chard
cheese, e.g., Parmesan
chili pepper flakes
garlic
parsley
pastas
pestos
pine nuts
rice
sauces
soy sauce
spinach
stuffings
thyme
tomatoes
vinegar, e.g., rice, wine

● OIL, PISTACHIO

Flavor: notes of pistachios
Volume: quiet – moderate
Tip: Use for medium-temperature cooking (e.g., baking, sautéing).

apples
asparagus
avocado
baked goods, e.g., breads
beets
cheese, e.g., goat
dips
dressings
garlic
grapes
lettuce
mayonnaise
orange
pastas
pears
pestos
pistachios
salad dressings
salads
sauces
tomatoes
vinegar, e.g., balsamic, red wine, tarragon
zucchini and zucchini blossoms

Flavor Affinities
pistachio oil + orange + pistachios

● OIL, PUMPKIN SEED

Flavor: notes of nuts, and a very rich texture
Volume: quieter (untoasted) – louder (toasted)
What's healthful about it: omega-3 fatty acids
Tips: Do not cook with pumpkin seed oil. Use it to drizzle on finished dishes.

American cuisine
Austrian cuisine
avocados
baked goods, e.g., pastries
citrus
corn
Croatian cuisine
desserts
dips
dressings
ice cream, e.g., vanilla
Indian cuisine
maple syrup
marinades
Mexican cuisine
mustard, e.g., Dijon
oils, other quieter, e.g., vegetable
pastas
pumpkin
pumpkin seeds
rice
salads
sauces
Slovenian cuisine
soups
squash, e.g., winter
vegetables
vinegar, e.g., apple cider, balsamic, rice wine

OIL, RAPESEED (see OIL, CANOLA)

● OIL, RED PALM

Flavor: pungent notes of smoke, with a texture that is a cross between that of oil and tomato paste
Volume: moderate – loud
What it is: oil pressed from palm *fruit* (not to be confused with palm *kernel* oil)
Brand: Jungle Products

(West) African cuisine
baked goods, e.g., muffins
bananas
chiles

chili, vegetarian
cilantro
coconut
couscous
curries
eggs and egg dishes
garlic
ginger
lemon
lime
macaroni and cheese (for yellow/ orange color)
oils, other, e.g., canola, coconut, neutral
onions
pastas, homemade (for yellow/ orange color)
plantains
popcorn
rice
salad dressings
sauces, e.g., tomato
soups, e.g., pumpkin
tomatoes and tomato sauce
vegetables, e.g., roasted, sautéed

● OIL, SAFFLOWER

Flavor: neutral, sometimes with notes of nuts, and a rich texture
Volume: quiet
Tips: Use for deep-frying, sautéing, stir-frying. Choose the high-oleic versions as well as those processed without chemicals.
Botanical relatives: the sunflower family, e.g., Jerusalem artichokes, salsify
Brands: Loriva, Spectrum

artichokes, Jerusalem
baked goods
chicory
curries
granola
lettuces
noodles, e.g., Asian

salad dressings
salads
salsify
stir-fries

● OIL, SESAME

Flavor: aromatic, with notes of nuts, and a rich texture
Volume: moderate (light) – **loud** (dark)
What it is: oil pressed from sesame seeds

> **Tips:** Use light sesame oil for low- to medium-heat cooking (e.g., baking, sautéing), and dark (roasted or toasted) sesame oil primarily drizzled on as a seasoning, to finish raw or cooked dishes. Buy sesame oil fresh, and use within one year.

ASIAN CUISINES
baked goods
beans, e.g., green
Chinese cuisine
dips and dipping sauces
dressings
garlic
ginger
grains
greens
Japanese cuisine
Korean cuisine
lemon, e.g., juice
lime, e.g., juice
MARINADES
mirin
miso
mustard, e.g., Dijon
noodles, e.g., Asian
oil, other, e.g., canola, olive, sunflower
orange
pastas
pumpkin
SALAD DRESSINGS, e.g., Asian
salads, e.g., Asian, green, noodle
SAUCES

SEEDS, SESAME
soups, e.g., miso
SOY SAUCE
STIR-FRIES
sugar snap peas
tamari
tofu
vinegar, e.g., apple cider, rice

Flavor Affinities
sesame oil + garlic + ginger + mirin + soy sauce

● OIL, SUNFLOWER SEED

Flavor: notes of nuts
Volume: quiet – moderate

> **Tips:** Use for medium- (e.g., baking, sautéing) to high-temperature cooking (e.g., frying, stir-frying). Use sparingly, if at all, as sunflower seed oil is often highly refined and processed, as well as high in unhealthful omega-6 fatty acids. If you do use it, look for the high-oleic version and/or Loriva brand.

salad dressings
salads, e.g., green, spinach
sauces
sprouts, sunflower
sunflower seeds
vinegar, e.g., apple cider, red wine

● OIL, TRUFFLE — IN GENERAL (i.e., BLACK or WHITE)

Flavor: umami
Volume: moderate – loud

> **Tips:** Truffle oil can be drizzled on top of dishes; it is not suitable for cooking. Look for oils with visible truffle bits in the oil, e.g., those produced by Urbani.

cheese
eggs
leeks
mushrooms, e.g., chanterelle, portobello
pastas
potatoes
risottos
salad dressings

● OIL, TRUFFLE — BLACK

Flavor: umami
Volume: loud

eggs
French cuisine
marinades
mushrooms
potatoes
salads

● OIL, TRUFFLE — OREGON

Flavor: umami
What it is: oil made from Oregon-foraged truffles

mushrooms, e.g., wild
pastas, esp. creamy
pizzas
popcorn
potatoes, e.g., baked, mashed
risottos
sauces, e.g., creamy

● OIL, TRUFFLE — WHITE

Flavor: umami
Volume: loud

artichokes
asparagus
eggs, e.g., scrambled
Italian cuisine
marinades
mushrooms, e.g., porcini

pastas, e.g., *fettuccine, gnocchi*
potatoes
risottos

Flavor Affinities
white truffle oil + mushrooms +
    risotto

● OIL, VEGETABLE

Tip: Skip the formerly ubiquitous generically named "vegetable oil" in favor of an oil with a specific name, so you can be quite sure what you're getting.

● OIL, WALNUT

Flavor: earthy notes of walnuts, and a rich texture
Volume: moderate – loud
What's healthful about it:
omega-3 fatty acids
Tips: Drizzle on dishes before serving. Use for low-heat to medium-high-heat cooking (e.g., baking, sautéing).

apples
artichokes, Jerusalem
arugula
asparagus
baked goods, e.g., *breads, scones*
beets
breads
celery and celery leaves
cheese, e.g., blue
chicory
citrus, e.g., juices
dips
endive
escarole
fennel
figs
frisée
garlic
grapes
greens, e.g., bitter, dandelion, salad
ice cream
lemon, e.g., juice

lentils
mustard, Dijon
oil, other quieter, e.g., olive
parsley
pastas
peaches
pears
pepper, black
persimmons
pomegranates
radicchio
SALAD DRESSINGS, e.g.,
    vinaigrettes
salads, e.g., grain, green
sauces
shallots
tomatoes
vegetables, e.g., grilled
VINEGAR, e.g., **balsamic**,
    champagne, cider, **red wine**,
    sherry, tarragon, white wine
WALNUTS

Dishes

Ensalada Clasica: Bayless Garden Greens, La Nogalera Walnut Oil, Fresh Lime, Toasted Walnuts and Chile Threads
— Topolobampo (Chicago)

Flavor Affinities
walnut oil + blue cheese + celery
    + pears + walnuts

OIL SUBSTITUTES

Tips: When baking sweets (e.g., cakes, cookies, cupcakes, muffins, etc.), substitute 1 cup of fruit puree for each cup of oil called for in the recipe. You can use applesauce or other fruit purees (e.g., banana, prune, pumpkin), and even pureed black beans in dark-colored baked goods such as brownies and chocolate cakes. Substitute vegetable stock for oil when sautéing garlic, onions, or other vegetables.

CHOOSE YOUR OIL

Cooking Methods	Best Types of Oil
No heat	almond, avocado, flaxseed, hazelnut, pumpkin, safflower, sunflower, walnut
Low-heat cooking methods (e.g., baking, sautéing)	coconut, corn, olive, peanut, sesame
Medium-heat cooking methods (e.g., higher-heat baking, sautéing)	canola, grapeseed, safflower
High-heat cooking methods (e.g., frying, stir-frying)	canola, corn, peanut, safflower, sunflower

• OKRA

Season: summer – autumn
Flavor: bitter/sour, with notes of artichoke, asparagus, and/or eggplant, and a sometimes slightly slimy texture
Volume: moderate – loud
Nutritional profile: 71% carbs / 21% protein / 8% fats
Calories: 20 per ½-cup serving (boiled)
Protein: 1 gram
Techniques: bake, blanch, boil, braise, bread, deep-fry, fry, grill, marinate, pickle, pressure-cook, sauté, simmer, steam, stew

Tips: To minimize okra's potential sliminess, blanch it in salt water before shocking it in ice water. Do not cook in brass, copper, or iron pans, or okra will turn black.

African cuisine
apricots, dried
BASIL
beans, e.g., green
bell peppers, e.g., green, red, yellow
bulgur
butter
Caribbean cuisine
cayenne
celery
chickpeas
chiles, chili pepper flakes, chili pepper sauce, and chili powder
cilantro
cinnamon
coconut
coriander
CORN and cornmeal
CREOLE CUISINE

Dishes

Wood Oven Roasted Okra and Shishitos, with Sesame-Garlic Crumbs
— ABC Kitchen (New York City)

cucumbers
cumin
CURRIES
curry powder
dill
eggplant
Ethiopian cuisine
fennel
garam masala
GARLIC
GINGER
grits
GUMBOS
honey
Indian cuisine
LEMON, e.g., juice
lime
Mediterranean cuisines
Middle Eastern cuisines
mint
mushrooms
mustard seeds
nutmeg
OIL, e.g., grapeseed, OLIVE, sesame
ONIONS, e.g., green, **red**
orange
PARSLEY
pepper, black
plantains
potatoes
ratatouille
RICE, e.g., long-grain
salads
salt, e.g., kosher
SAUCES, e.g., hot (e.g., Tabasco), TOMATO
SOUPS
Southern (U.S.) cuisine
STEWS
sweet potatoes
thyme
*TOMATOES

turmeric
vinegar
yogurt

Flavor Affinities
okra + beans + rice
okra + bell peppers + curry powder + red onions
okra + black pepper + lemon juice
okra + corn + tomatoes
okra + cornmeal + olive oil + onions
okra + garlic + ginger + tomatoes
okra + ginger + tomatoes
okra + potatoes + *stews* + tomatoes

"**Okra,** when stewed with cinnamon, dried apricots, lemon juice, and tomatoes, releases its thick viscosity into the sauce, uniting this irresistible combination."
— DIANE FORLEY, FLOURISH BAKING COMPANY (SCARSDALE, NY)

• OLIVES — IN GENERAL, or MIXED

Flavor: bitter, **salty**, and/or sour
Volume: quiet/moderate – loud (depending on the type)
Nutritional profile: 88% fat / 10% carbs / 2% protein (and high in sodium)
Calories: 4 per olive

almonds
artichokes, e.g., globe, Jerusalem
arugula
asparagus
avocados
baked goods, e.g., breads, focaccia
basil
bay leaf
beans, e.g., black, cannellini, fava, green
bell peppers, esp. roasted
breads
CAPERS

caponata
cauliflower
chard, Swiss
CHEESE, e.g., **feta**, kasseri,
  Parmesan
chickpeas
chiles, e.g., jalapeño, and chili
  pepper flakes
cilantro
citrus
coriander
couscous
cumin
dips
eggplant
eggs, e.g., *deviled, frittatas,* hard-
  boiled, soft-boiled
endive
fennel
figs
GARLIC
grains
Greek cuisine
greens, e.g., salad
herbs
hummus
kale
leeks
LEMON, e.g., juice, zest
mayonnaise
Mediterranean cuisines
Moroccan cuisine
muffulettas
mushrooms
nuts
OIL, OLIVE
onions, e.g., red
ORANGE, e.g., juice, zest
oregano
paprika
parsley
PASTAS, e.g., linguini, spaghetti
pepper, e.g., black, white
pesto
pine nuts
PIZZA
polenta
potatoes, e.g., new

Flavor Affinities

olives + arugula + figs + Parmesan cheese
olives + asparagus + basil
olives + basil + tofu + tomatoes
olives + beets + feta cheese
olives + beets + olives + orange
olives + capers + garlic + onions + oregano + tomatoes
olives + capers + lemon juice + olive oil
olives + capers + tomatoes
olives + chili pepper flakes + garlic + lemon + rosemary
olives + fennel + orange
olives + feta cheese + garlic + spinach
olives + garlic + lemon + rosemary
olives + herbs + lemon
olives + orange + parsley + pine nuts
olives + pasta + pine nuts + tomatoes

Provençal cuisine
rice
risottos
ROSEMARY
SALADS, e.g., bean, chopped,
 grain, Greek, niçoise, pasta
salsas
salt, e.g., kosher, sea
sandwiches
SAUCES, e.g., pasta, puttanesca
 (vegetarian)
spinach
spreads
TAPENADES
thyme
TOMATOES and sun-dried
 tomatoes
vegetables, roasted
vinegar, e.g., red wine, sherry
walnuts
zucchini

OLIVES, KALAMATA

[kah-lah-MAH-tah]
Flavor: salty, with notes of fruit
and/or wine, and a rich, meaty
texture
Volume: loud
What they are: black or dark
purple Greek olives cured in a
salted vinegar brine

artichoke hearts
basil
bell peppers
capers
caponata
cardoons
chard, Swiss
cheese, e.g., feta
chickpeas
chili pepper flakes
cucumbers
cumin
GARLIC
GREEK CUISINE
herbs
leeks

lemon, e.g., juice, zest
miso
mushrooms
mustard, Dijon
OIL, OLIVE
onions
orange, e.g., zest
oregano
paprika
parsley
pasta, e.g., linguini, penne, rigatoni
pastes, olive
pepper, black
pizza
polenta
potatoes, e.g., red
rosemary
salad dressings
salads, *e.g., Greek, spinach*
salt, sea
sauces, e.g., pasta, puttanesca
scallions
spinach
spreads
tapenades
tofu, e.g., extra-firm, soft
tomatoes and tomato sauce
tomatoes, sun-dried
vinegar, e.g., red wine
wine, dry

Flavor Affinities

kalamata olives + artichoke hearts
 + sun-dried tomatoes
kalamata olives + basil + capers
kalamata olives + bell peppers
 + cucumbers + feta cheese +
 tomatoes
kalamata olives + capers + pasta +
 tomatoes
kalamata olives + chili pepper
 flakes + garlic + lemon + olive
 oil + orange + oregano
kalamata olives + Dijon mustard
 + garlic + lemon
kalamata olives + garlic +
 rosemary

OLIVES, MANZANILLA (aka SPANISH OLIVES)

Flavor: salty, with notes of nuts
(esp. almonds) and/or smoke,
and a firm, rich, meaty texture
Volume: moderate – loud
What they are: smallish green
brine-cured Spanish olives

almonds, e.g., Spanish
cocktails, e.g., martinis
garlic
oil, olive
pimento
pizza
salads
Spanish cuisine

OLIVES, NIÇOISE

Flavor: sour, with nutty notes,
and a rich texture
Volume: quiet – moderate
What they are: small black
olives from southern France
Possible substitute: kalamata
olives

beans, e.g., green, white
French cuisine, esp. Provençal
herbs
lemon, e.g., juice, zest
lettuce, e.g., romaine
onions
oranges, e.g., blood
pastes, olive
potatoes
rosemary
salads, e.g., niçoise, vegetable
salt
tapenades
thyme

OLIVES, PICHOLINE

Flavor: notes of anise and/or
nuts, and a crisp texture
Volume: moderate
What they are: green olives
from the south of France

artichokes
avocadoes
bay leaf
chickpeas
citrus, e.g., lemon, orange
fennel
French cuisine, esp. Provençal
garlic
lemon
mustard
oil, olive
onions, e.g., red
orange
salads, e.g., egg, fennel, green
thyme
vinegar

• ONIONS — IN GENERAL, or MIXED

Season: year-round, esp. autumn
Flavor: sweet (and sweeter, when caramelized), with pungent notes
Volume: quieter (cooked) – louder (raw)
What they are: vegetables
Nutritional profile: 90% carbs (high in sugars) / 8% protein / 2% fats
Calories: 65 per 1-cup serving (raw)
Protein: 2 grams
Techniques: bake (60 – 90 minutes), boil, braise, broil, caramelize, deep-fry, fry, grill,

Dishes

Red Wine Braised Heirloom Onions: Arrowleaf Spinach, Broccolini, Cauliflower "Florettes," Meyer Lemon, and Preserved Horseradish
— Per Se (New York City)

Onion Pie: Cranberry, Radish Chow-Chow, Bourbon Glaze
— Rowland's at Westglow (Blowing Rock, NC)

French Onion Soup au Gratin: Caramelized Onions, Croutons, Swiss au Gratin in Veggie Stock
— Table Verte (New York City)

pickle, pressure-cook, roast, sauté, steam, stir-fry
Tips: Onions increase appetite and pair well with virtually all savory foods.
Botanical relatives: asparagus, chives, garlic, leeks, shallots

APPLES, e.g., cider, fruit, juice
arame
arugula
avocado
barley and pearl barley
basil
bay leaf
BEANS, e.g., black, green, kidney, pinto, white
beets
bell peppers
black-eyed peas
breadcrumbs
breads, e.g., focaccia
butter
caramelized onions
cardamom
CARROTS
casseroles
cauliflower
cayenne
CELERY
celery seeds
chard
CHEESE, e.g., blue, **cheddar**, chèvre, Comté, Emmentaler, feta, goat, Gouda, **GRUYÈRE**,

nondairy, **Parmesan**, pecorino, **Swiss**
chestnuts
chickpeas
chiles
chili, vegetarian
cinnamon
cloves
compotes
confit
coriander
corn
couscous
cream
crème fraîche
croutons
curries
curry powder
dates
dill
dips
eggplant
EGGS, e.g., *frittatas*, hard-boiled, *omelets, quiches*
fennel and fennel seeds
figs
French cuisine, e.g., soups, tarts
frisée
GARLIC
grains, whole
gravies
greens, e.g., bitter (e.g., collard) or salad
honey
kale
lemon, e.g., juice, zest
LENTILS
Madeira
marjoram
milk
mint
miso
MUSHROOMS, e.g., porcini
mustard, Dijon
nutmeg
OIL, e.g., OLIVE
olives
oregano

PARSLEY
parsnips
pastas, e.g., ziti
PEPPER, e.g., black, white
pies
pine nuts
pizza
polenta
poppy seeds
potatoes
pumpkin
quinoa
raisins
relishes
RICE, e.g., Arborio, brown, **wild**
risottos
ROSEMARY
sage
salad dressings
SALADS
salt, e.g., kosher, sea
sandwiches
sauces
savory
shallots
sherry

sorrel
SOUPS, e.g., onion, vegetable
soy sauce
spinach
squash, e.g., spaghetti
stews
STOCKS, e.g., vegetable
stuffed onions, e.g., with cheese, herbs, and/or rice
sugar (i.e., a pinch)
sumac
sweet potatoes
tahini
tamari
tarts, onion
THYME
TOMATOES and tomato paste
vegetables, e.g., root
veggie burgers
VINEGAR, e.g., balsamic, **red wine**, sherry, tarragon, white balsamic
walnuts
WINE, e.g., dry red or white
yogurt
zucchini

Flavor Affinities
onions + arugula + chèvre cheese + figs
onions + avocado + garlic + *salads*
onions + bell peppers + potatoes
onions + bitter greens + soy sauce
onions + black pepper + nutmeg + Swiss cheese
onions + black pepper + oil + tomato paste + vegetable stock
onions + blue cheese + walnuts
*ONIONS + CARROTS + CELERY
onions + cheese + croutons + garlic + vegetable stock
onions + cream + Dijon mustard
onions + feta cheese + olives
onions + garlic + mint + white balsamic vinegar
onions + lemon + parsley
onions + parsley + tamari
onions + rosemary + vinegar
onions + thyme + vinegar

ONIONS, CIPOLLINI
Flavor: sweet
Techniques: glaze, grill, roast

bay leaf
cinnamon
honey
Italian cuisine
kebabs
oil, olive
onions, other
pastas
raisins
rosemary
sage
salads
sauces
shallots
stock, vegetable
sugar, e.g., brown
thyme
vinegar, e.g., balsamic, champagne, sherry
wine, dry red

ONIONS, GREEN (see SCALLIONS)

ONIONS, PEARL
Flavor: sweet
Volume: quiet

breadcrumbs
Brussels sprouts
burdock
carrots
casseroles
cream
garlic
grains, e.g., barley, couscous
gratins
kebabs
lentils
mushrooms, e.g., porcini, portobello
oil, e.g., olive
parsley
pasta

potatoes
rice
rosemary
salads
sauces
shallots
soups, e.g., mushroom
spinach
stews
stock, e.g., mushroom, vegetable
tempeh
vinegar, e.g., balsamic

Flavor Affinities
pearl onions + cream + spinach

ONIONS, RED
(see also ONIONS)
Flavor: slightly sweet,
with a firmer, drier texture
than that of yellow onions
Volume: quiet
Techniques: can be eaten raw, as
in salads — otherwise: grill, roast
Tip: The quiet flavor of red
onions works well with fruits as
well as quieter and/or sweeter
vegetables and legumes, not to
mention served raw in salads
and salsas or on sandwiches
and veggie burgers.

avocado
beans, e.g., black
beets
carrots
cauliflower
celery
cheese, e.g., blue, feta, goat, Jack,
Parmesan
chickpeas
cilantro
eggs, e.g., *frittatas*
fennel
fruits, e.g., apples, mangoes,
melons, oranges, papayas,
peaches, pineapple
garlic

ginger
honey
jícama
lemon, e.g., juice
lime, e.g., juice, zest
maple syrup
miso, e.g., dark or red
mushrooms, e.g., portobello
OIL, OLIVE
olives
onion rings
orange, e.g., juice, zest
parsley
pepper, black
pizza
potatoes
quesadillas
SALADS, *e.g., green, potato, tomato*
SALSAS, *e.g., fruit, tomato*
salt, e.g., kosher, sea
soups
squash, winter, e.g., butternut
stock, vegetable
sweet potatoes
thyme
tomatoes
veggie burgers
VINEGAR, e.g., balsamic, red
wine, rice wine, sherry, white
wine
wine, e.g., dry red

Flavor Affinities
red onions + balsamic vinegar +
olive oil
red onions + basil + tomatoes
red onions + chiles + cilantro +
olive oil + vinegar
red onions + chiles + corn + garlic
+ lime + tomatoes
red onions + corn + tomatoes
red onions + cranberries + ginger
+ orange
red onions + feta cheese + pine nuts

red onions + jícama + orange
red onions + lemon + olive oil
+ Parmesan cheese + parsley +
salads
red onions + lime + mint
red onions + miso + vegetable
stock
red onions + red wine vinegar +
thyme

● ONIONS, SPRING
(see also SCALLIONS)
Tip: *Spring onions* refers to
both **green onions** (small and
mild) and **scallions** (smaller and
milder), which are immature
onions. They can typically be
used interchangeably.

ONIONS, VIDALIA
Season: spring – summer
Flavor: sweet – very sweet, with
a juicy texture
Volume: quiet – moderate
What they are: Georgia's "state
vegetable," famed as the world's
sweetest onions

basil
breadcrumbs
cheese, e.g., blue, goat, Parmesan
garlic
mustard, Dijon
oil, olive
pepper, black
pine nuts
salt
sauces
stuffed onions
thyme
vinegar, e.g., balsamic, red wine
wine, dry white
zucchini

Dishes

Potato, Spring Onion, and Celeriac Soup, with Pear, Celery, Lemon, and Chives
— Natural Selection (Portland, OR)

C

● ORANGES, ● ORANGE JUICE, and ORANGE ZEST

Season: year-round, esp. winter
Flavor: sour/**sweet**, with a very juicy texture
Volume: moderate – loud
Nutritional profile: 91% carbs / 7% protein / 2% fats
Calories: 65 per medium orange
Protein: 1 gram
Techniques: poach, raw

Tips: Buy organic oranges. Lemon brightens the flavor of orange.

Botanical relatives: grapefruit, kumquats, lemons, limes
Possible substitutes:
clementines, mandarins, tangerines

anise seeds
apples
apricots
Armagnac
arugula
Asian cuisines
asparagus
avocados
BAKED GOODS, e.g., cakes, muffins, quick breads, scones, tarts
bananas
barley, e.g., pearl
basil
beans, e.g., black, white
BEETS
berries, e.g., **blueberries**, raspberries, **strawberries**
beverages, e.g., juices, sangrias, smoothies
brandy
broccoli and broccolini
bulgur
cabbage, e.g., red
cardamom
CARROTS
celery root

cereals, hot breakfast
cheese, e.g., cream, **feta**, goat
chickpeas
chili pepper flakes
chiles, e.g., chipotle
Chinese cuisine (native ingredient)
chives
CHOCOLATE, e.g., dark, white
cilantro
CINNAMON
citrus fruits, other, e.g., grapefruit, **lemon**, lime
cloves
coconut
compotes
coriander
couscous
CRANBERRIES
cream

Flavor Affinities
oranges + almonds + Bibb lettuce + jícama
oranges + almonds + dates + figs
oranges + arugula + hazelnuts
oranges + asparagus + couscous
oranges + avocados + beets
oranges + avocados + black beans + red onions
oranges + balsamic vinegar + beets + fennel
oranges + barley + fennel + radishes
oranges + black beans + quinoa
oranges + carrots + ginger
oranges + cashews + rice
oranges + chickpeas + couscous + fennel
oranges + chili pepper flakes + garlic + ginger + soy sauce
oranges + cilantro + jícama
oranges + cinnamon + honey + pears
oranges + cranberries + pears
oranges + dandelion greens + pine nuts
oranges + fennel + olives
oranges + fennel + parsley
oranges + fennel + walnuts
oranges + fennel + watercress + white beans
oranges + feta cheese + spinach
oranges + ginger + rice wine vinegar
oranges + goat cheese + pomegranates + walnuts
oranges + honey + rosemary
oranges + pecans + radicchio
oranges + sesame + spinach

cumin
daikon
DATES
desserts, e.g., puddings
endive
escarole
FENNEL
figs
fruit, dried and fresh
garlic
GINGER
greens, e.g., dandelion, salad
"gremolata"
HONEY
horseradish
jícama
kiwi
lettuce, e.g., Bibb

liqueurs, orange, e.g., Cointreau, Grand Marnier
mangoes
maple syrup
marinades
marmalade
mascarpone
mesclun
millet
mint
miso
mushrooms, e.g., shiitake, wild
mustard, Dijon
noodles, Asian
NUTS, e.g., ALMONDS, cashews, hazelnuts, peanuts, PECANS, pine nuts, pistachios, WALNUTS
oil, e.g., olive, sunflower seed
OLIVES, e.g., black, kalamata
onions, e.g., green, red, Vidalia
oranges, blood
papayas
parsley
parsnips
pears
pepper, black
pineapple
plums
pomegranates
pumpkin
quinoa
radicchio
radishes
rhubarb
rice and wild rice
rosemary
rutabagas
sage
salad dressings
salads, e.g., avocado, carrot, fruit, green
sauces
scallions
seitan
sesame, e.g., oil, seeds
shallots
smoothies, e.g., berry, pineapple
snow peas

soups, e.g., fruit
sorbets
soy sauce
spinach
squash, e.g., butternut
star anise
starfruit
stir-fries
sugar, e.g., brown
sweet potatoes
tamari
tofu
turnips
vanilla
vinegar, e.g., balsamic, champagne, cider, red wine, rice wine, sherry, white wine
watercress
wine, e.g., red
yams
yogurt

● ORANGES, BLOOD
(see also ORANGES)
Season: winter – spring
Flavor: sour/sweet, with notes of raspberries
Volume: moderate

almonds
arugula
avocado
beets
beverages, e.g., juices, mimosas
Brussels sprouts
caramel
cheese, e.g., blue, feta, goat
chicory
chiles
chocolate, e.g., white
cilantro
cinnamon
citrus, other, e.g., limes, regular oranges
cloves
cream
desserts, e.g., fruit tarts
endive

FENNEL
grains, e.g., quinoa
grapefruit
greens, salad
honey
ices/granitas
jícama
kiwi
kumquats
lemon
lettuce, e.g., romaine
mangoes
mint
oil, e.g., olive
olives, e.g., black
onions, red
papaya
pomegranates
poppy seeds
radishes, e.g., black
salad dressings
SALADS, e.g., fruit, green
salsas
sauces
spinach
sugar, e.g., brown
tangerines
thyme
vanilla
vinegar, e.g., balsamic, milder
walnuts
watercress
wine, sparkling, e.g., Champagne

Flavor Affinities
blood oranges + arugula + beets + walnuts
blood oranges + black olives + fennel + lemon juice + olive oil

● ORANGES, MANDARIN
Season: autumn – spring
Flavor: sweet/sour, with notes of orange, and a very juicy texture
Volume: moderate
What they are: Clementines and tangerines are varieties of

mandarins, which are a smaller variety of oranges.

Nutritional profile: 90% carbs / 5% protein / 5% fat
Calories: 50 per medium-sized mandarin (raw)
Protein: 1 gram
Techniques: broil, raw
Botanical relatives and possible substitutes:
clementines, oranges, tangerines

agave nectar
almonds
bananas
basil
berries
caramel
cashews
cheesecake
chili paste
Chinese cuisine
chives
chocolate, dark
cilantro
coconut
compotes
cranberries
cream
ginger
greens, salad
hazelnuts
hoisin sauce
ice creams
jícama
kumquats
lemon, e.g., juice

Dishes

Pasticcini with Caramel and Clementine Ice Creams, Toasted Hazelnuts, and Bittersweet Chocolate
— Chez Panisse (Berkeley, CA)

Enlightened Asian Salad: Sweet Clementines, Organic Edamame, and Sliced Almonds grace an invigorating blend of Organic Spring Mix, Red Cabbage, Carrots, Cucumbers, and Tomatoes; paired with our Sesame-Ginger Vinaigrette
— Wildflower (Millville, NJ)

lettuce, e.g., romaine
lime
mangoes
mint
nutmeg
oil, e.g., flaxseed, olive
onions, e.g., red
orange, e.g., zest
parsley
peaches
pears
pecans
pepper, black
rice
salad dressings
SALADS, e.g., fruit, green, spinach
salsas
sauces
shallots
sorbets
spinach
strawberries
sugar, e.g., brown
tarts
tomatoes
vinegar, e.g., champagne, sherry
yogurt

Flavor Affinities

mandarins + cilantro + lime + onions + tomatoes

● OREGANO

Flavor: bitter (esp. Greek oregano) / slightly sweet (esp. Italian oregano), with pungent

floral, herbal, lemon, and/or marjoram notes
Volume: moderate (Italian < Greek) – loud (Mexican)
Tips: Add dried oregano at the beginning of cooking, fresh at the end. Oregano can have great variability, i.e., from milder to hotter and spicier. Italian oregano is sweeter (and quieter) than Greek or Mexican oregano.
Botanical relatives: basil, lavender, marjoram, mint, rosemary, sage, summer savory, thyme

basil
BEANS, dried, e.g., black, white
bell peppers, red and yellow, esp. roasted
capers
cayenne
cheeses, e.g., feta, soft, white
chickpeas
chiles, e.g., red
chili, vegetarian
cilantro
citrus, e.g., lemon, orange
corn
cumin
EGGPLANT
eggs, e.g., *omelets*
endive
fennel
garlic
grains
Greek cuisine
Italian cuisine
kebabs
*LEMON, e.g., juice, zest
marinades
marjoram
MEDITERRANEAN CUISINES
Mexican cuisine
Middle Eastern cuisines
mushrooms
mustard, Dijon
oil, olive

olives
onions
orange
PASTA
pepper, black
PIZZA
potatoes
rice
salad dressings
SALADS, e.g., Greek
salt, sea
SAUCES, esp. pasta, PIZZA,
    tomato
scallions
soups, e.g., minestrone, spinach,
    tomato, yogurt
Southwest (American) cuisine
squash, summer
squash, winter
stews
stuffings
tahini
TOMATOES and TOMATO
    SAUCE
vegetables, e.g., roasted, stir-fried,
    summer
zucchini

Flavor Affinities

oregano + cannellini beans +
    zucchini

oregano + feta cheese + *salads* +
    tomatoes

oregano + **garlic** + **lemon** + *salad*
    dressings

oregano + lemon juice + olive oil
    + *marinades*

OREGANO, MEXICAN

Flavor: bitter, with pungent
floral, herbal, lemon, and/or
marjoram notes
Volume: loud
Tip: Add at the beginning of
cooking.
Possible substitute: epazote

---

beans, e.g., black
burritos
Central American cuisines
chiles, e.g., green
chili, vegetarian
chili powder
cumin
empanadas
enchiladas
garlic
MEXICAN CUISINE
onions
paprika
salsas
sauces
soups
Southwest (American) cuisine
spicy dishes
stews, vegetable
tacos
Tex-Mex cuisine

ORGANIC PRODUCE

Tip: Opt for organic produce
whenever possible — and definitely when you buy one of the
Environmental Working Group
(EWG)'s so-called "Dirty Dozen
Plus" fruits or vegetables, which
are those most affected by chemical contamination, i.e., **apples,
bell peppers, celery, cherry
tomatoes, chili peppers, collard
greens, cucumbers, grapes, kale,
nectarines (imported), peaches,
potatoes, spinach, strawberries,**
and **summer squash.**

    The EWG notes that "[t]he
health benefits of a diet rich in
fruits and vegetables outweigh
the risks of pesticide exposure.
Use EWG's *Shopper's Guide to Pes-
ticides™* to reduce your exposures
as much as possible, but **eating
conventionally-grown produce is
far better than not eating fruits
and vegetables at all.**"

ORZO (see PASTA, ORZO)

● PALM, HEARTS OF (aka HEARTS OF PALM)

Flavors: slightly sweet, with
earthy notes of artichoke hearts,
bamboo shoots, and/or nuts, and
a tender and flaky yet firm texture
Volume: quiet
What they are: the hearts of the
stems of the Sabal palmetto tree
Nutritional profile: 59% carbs
/ 22% protein / 19% fats
Calories: 40 per 1-cup serving
(canned)
Protein: 4 grams
Techniques: blanch, grill,
marinate, raw, sauté, sear, steam,
stew, stir-fry
Tip: Substitute for seafood
(e.g., crab) in texture, or white
asparagus in flavor.

almonds, e.g., marcona
artichokes and artichoke hearts
arugula
asparagus
AVOCADO
bell peppers
breadcrumbs
cabbage, red
carrots
cashews
cayenne
celery
Central American cuisines
cheese, e.g., manchego
cilantro
corn
Costa Rican cuisine
"CRABCAKES"
dips
garlic
grains, whole
herbs
jícama

P

Dishes

Coconut Garlic Soup with Japanese Wood Grilled Hawaiian Hearts of Palm
— Bouley Restaurant (New York City)

Salad of Boston Bibb, Red Watercress, Fresh Hawaiian Hearts of Palm, Julienne of Royal Trumpet Mushrooms
— Bouley Restaurant (New York City)

"Crab Cakes": Hearts of Palm / Apples / Beets / Horseradish Cream (pictured above)
— Crossroads (Los Angeles)

Curried Wild Rice and Hawaiian Hearts of Palm: Sea Bean Tempura, Myoga Shavings
— DANIEL (New York City)

Hearts of Palm — Vadouvan Ravioli: Eggplant Caponata, Young Cilantro Leaves
— DANIEL (New York City)

Ensalada de Palmitos: Romaine, Tomatoes, Hearts of Palm, Avocado, Toasted Almond Vinaigrette, and Manchego Shavings
— El Parador Café (New York City)

Hawaiian Hearts of Palm with Tangerines, Pea Shoots, Cucumber, Tamarind Vinaigrette
— Nora (Washington, DC)

Hawaiian Hearts of Palm, Lemongrass Corn Purée, Lomi Tomatoes, Pickled Corn
— Vedge (Philadelphia)

Flavor Affinities

hearts of palm + almonds + avocado + manchego cheese + romaine + tomatoes
hearts of palm + asparagus + basil + shiitake mushrooms
hearts of palm + avocado + black olives + pine nuts + tomatoes
hearts of palm + avocado + mango
hearts of palm + avocado + orange
hearts of palm + cayenne + salt
hearts of palm + chickpeas + tomatoes
hearts of palm + cilantro + jícama + lemon + orange
hearts of palm + garlic + herbs + lime + olive oil
hearts of palm + mayonnaise + mustard + nori + Old Bay seasoning + *"crabcakes"*

---

kelp
Latin American cuisines
LEMON, e.g., juice, zest
lemongrass
lentils
lettuce, e.g., romaine
LIME, e.g., juice, zest
mango
mayonnaise
mushrooms, e.g., shiitake
mustard, e.g., Dijon
noodles, Asian, e.g., somen
oil, e.g., olive, vegetable
Old Bay seasoning
onions, e.g., green, red
oranges and blood oranges
oregano
papaya
parsley
pepper, black
pineapple
SALADS, e.g., green, noodle
salt
scallions
soups
South American cuisines
spinach
spreads
sprouts
stock, vegetable
tacos
tangerines
thyme
TOMATOES, e.g., cherry, grape
vinaigrette
vinegar, e.g., balsamic

• PALM SHORTENING

Flavor: neutral
Volume: quiet
What it is: fat
Technique: deep-fry
Brands: Spectrum Organics, or another non-hydrogenated, organic, sustainable shortening produced by small-scale farmers

certified by ProForest, which ensures that the palm oil is sustainably harvested and meets strict social, environmental, and technical criteria

baked goods, e.g., cakes, cookies, crumbles, piecrusts
desserts
fries, e.g., French
icings

"I'll use **palm shortening** to make an icing with vegan powdered sugar and a little soy milk. If I want aroma, I'll add some orange flower or rose water."

— AARON WOO, NATURAL SELECTION (PORTLAND, OR)

● PAPAYA (i.e., RED)

Season: summer – autumn
Flavor: **sweet**/sour, with musky notes of melon, and a soft, juicy texture (when ripe)
Volume: quiet – moderate
Nutritional profile: 92% carbs / 5% protein / 3% fats
Calories: 55 per 1-cup serving (raw, cubed)
Protein: 1 gram
Techniques: bake, grill, raw, sauté

Tip: Avoid using with gelatin, as the fruit's enzymes interfere with its setting.

agave nectar
arugula
AVOCADOS
bananas
beans, e.g., black
bell peppers, red, esp. roasted
berries, e.g., raspberries, **strawberries**
Caribbean cuisines
carrots
cayenne

cheese, e.g., Mexican
CHILES, e.g., ancho, jalapeño, and chili pepper sauce
chutneys
CILANTRO
cinnamon
CITRUS, e.g., grapefruit, LEMON, *LIME
coconut
cucumbers
cumin
curries
daikon
garlic
GINGER
grapefruit
greens, salad
honey
ice creams
jams
jícama
kiwi
lavender
lemongrass
lettuce
MANGO
marinades

Flavor Affinities

papaya + banana + honey
papaya + bananas + mangos + vanilla + yogurt
papaya + bananas + oranges
papaya + bell peppers + cilantro + lime + onions
papaya + cayenne + cilantro + **lime**
papaya + cayenne + greens + jicama + lemon + **lime**
papaya + chiles + cilantro + ginger
papaya + chiles + mango + mint + pineapple
papaya + cilantro + mango + scallions
papaya + coconut + rice
papaya + ginger + lime
papaya + ginger + mango + orange
papaya + honey + mint + yogurt
papaya + jícama + orange + red onions
papaya + kiwi + mango + pineapple
papaya + lime + mango + **mint** + orange
papaya + lime + mint
papaya + passion fruit + raspberries
papaya + strawberries + yogurt

melon, e.g., cantaloupe, honeydew
MINT
nutmeg
nuts, e.g., almonds, cashews, macadamia nuts, peanuts
oil, olive
ONIONS, RED
orange, e.g., fruit, juice, zest
passion fruit
peaches
pineapple
rice
salad dressings
SALADS, e.g., fruit
SALSAS
salt
scallions
shallots
SMOOTHIES
sorbets
soy sauce
spinach
sprouts, mung bean
sugar, e.g., brown
summer rolls
tofu

tomatoes

tortillas, corn

vanilla

vinegar, e.g., rice wine, tarragon

yogurt

● PAPAYA, GREEN (UNRIPE)

Flavor: slightly sweet, with a firm, crunchy, yet watery (apple- or cucumber-like) texture

Volume: very quiet

Technique: shred

Tip: Green (unripe) papayas are typically eaten as vegetables, while ripe papayas are eaten as fruit.

basil, Thai

beans, green

carrots

chiles, e.g., fresh red, and chili pepper paste

cucumbers

garlic

ginger

lettuce, e.g., Boston, butter

LIME, e.g., juice

mint

onions, red

PEANUTS

SALADS, e.g., Thai

soy sauce

sugar, e.g., brown, palm

tamari

tamarind

Thai cuisine

tomatoes, e.g., cherry

vinegar, rice

Flavor Affinities

green papaya + chili pepper + garlic + **lime + peanuts**

green papaya + green beans + lime + peanuts + tomatoes

green papaya + lime + peanuts + Thai basil

● PAPRIKA (see also PAPRIKA, SMOKED)

Flavor: bitter / slightly sweet (and sometimes hot, depending on variety), with earthy/fruity/pungent notes

Volume: quiet (e.g., sweet paprika) – loud (e.g., hot or smoked paprika)

What it is: finely ground dried capsicums (hot peppers)

Tips: Hungarian paprika is typically sun-dried and sweet. Try Spanish **smoked paprika** (aka pimenton), which has been smoked over fire, to add notes of smokiness to dishes.

Botanical relatives: bell peppers, chiles, eggplant, gooseberries, potatoes, tomatillos, tomatoes

beans, black

cayenne

cheese

chiles and chili powder

chili, vegetarian

cilantro

coriander

corn

cumin

deviled eggs

Eastern European cuisines, e.g., Hungarian

EGGS, e.g., hard-boiled, *omelets*

garlic

goulash, vegetarian

Hungarian cuisine

lemon

lime

marinades

mushrooms, e.g., stuffed

onions

Dishes

Crispy Chickpeas, Smoked Paprika, and Lemon
— FnB Restaurant (Scottsdale, AZ)

orange

oregano

pecans

pepper, black

potatoes

purees

rice

salad dressings

salads, e.g., macaroni, potato

sauces, e.g., cream, tomato

sauerkraut

soups

sour cream

Southwestern (U.S.) cuisine

Spanish cuisine, **esp. smoked paprika**

spreads

stews

stroganoff, e.g., mushroom

sweet potatoes

Texas cuisine

tomatoes

turmeric

vegetables

vinegar, e.g., balsamic, sherry

Flavor Affinities

paprika + mushrooms + sour cream

● PAPRIKA, SMOKED (aka PIMENTON or PIMENTON DE LA VERA)

Flavor: bitter / slightly sweet (and sometimes hot, depending on variety), with notes of meat and/or smoke

Volume: moderate – loud

Tip: Release the flavors of smoked paprika by heating in hot oil very briefly before adding to liquids or sauces.

almonds
avocados
bell peppers, e.g., red, roasted
casseroles
chickpeas
coriander
cumin
eggplant
eggs, e.g., *baked, deviled,* hard-boiled, *scrambled*
garlic
greens, e.g., collard
hummus
kale
legumes, e.g., **beans** (e.g., black, kidney, white), black-eyed peas, **chickpeas**, lentils, split peas
lemon, e.g., juice
mushrooms, e.g., portobello
nuts
oil, olive
onions
orange
paella, e.g., mushroom, vegetarian
pastas
potatoes
rice
root vegetables, e.g., carrots, rutabagas
salad dressings
salt, sea
sauces, e.g., *romesco, tomato, yogurt*
sausage, vegan chorizo (e.g., seitan + olive oil + smoked paprika)
seitan
SOUPS, e.g., *bean, chickpea, kale, lentil, split pea, tomato, vegetable, winter squash*
sour cream
Spanish cuisine
stews
stock, vegetable
sweet potatoes
tahini
tempeh bacon
tomatoes
yogurt

Flavor Affinities
smoked paprika + garlic + olive oil + seitan

PAPRIKA, SPANISH (see PAPRIKA, SMOKED)

● PARSLEY, generally ITALIAN (aka FLAT-LEAF PARSLEY)

Flavor: sweet, with astringent, earthy notes of celery, herbs, lemon, and/or pepper
Volume: **quiet** (curly) – quiet/ moderate (flat-leaf or Italian)
Techniques: fresh, sauté
Tips: Parsley is best served fresh (not dried). Use to enhance the flavor of other herbs and spices. Add toward the end of the cooking process. Chew on a sprig to freshen your breath. Don't forget that the stems have a lot of flavor — Noma chef René Redzepi sautés them in the winter, deeming them "incredible."
Botanical relatives: anise, caraway, **carrots, celery, celery root,** chervil, coriander, cumin, **dill, fennel, parsley root,** parsnips

almonds
apples
artichokes
avocados
baba ghanoush
barley
basil
bay leaf
beans, e.g., black, green
beets
bell peppers, red
bouquets garnis
breadcrumbs
bulgur
butter

cabbage
CAPERS
CARROTS
cauliflower
celery root
cheese, e.g., kasseri, Parmesan
chervil
chickpeas
chiles and chili pepper flakes
chimichurri sauce
chives
cilantro
corn
couscous
cucumbers
cumin
dips
eggplant
EGGS, e.g., **hard-boiled,** *omelets*
endive
fennel and fennel seeds
fines herbes
GARLIC
ginger
gravies
greens, salad
herbs, other
hummus
legumes
LEMON, e.g., juice, zest
lentils
lovage
marjoram
Mediterranean cuisines
Middle Eastern cuisines
MINT
Moroccan cuisine
mushrooms
noodles
OIL, OLIVE
olives
onions
orange, e.g., juice, zest
parsnips
PASTAS, e.g., *fettuccine, linguini, penne, spaghetti*
peas
pepper, black

pestos
pine nuts
pizza
POTATOES
radishes
rice
rosemary
salad dressings
SALADS, e.g., egg, green, parsley,
  pasta, potato, rice, tabbouleh
salsas, e.g., verde
salt, sea
sandwiches
SAUCES, e.g., chimichurri, parsley,
  pasta
savory
scallions
SHALLOTS
sorrel
SOUPS, e.g., bean, carrot, onion
spinach
squash, e.g., summer, winter
  (e.g., butternut)
stews
STOCKS, e.g., vegetable
stuffings
sumac
sweet potatoes
TABBOULEH, or Middle Eastern
  parsley salad with bulgur
tarragon
thyme
tomatoes and sun-dried tomatoes
vinegar, e.g., balsamic, red wine,
  sherry
walnuts
zucchini

Flavor Affinities

parsley + artichokes + garlic
parsley + breadcrumbs + butter +
  garlic + shallots
parsley + bulgur + lemon + mint
  + tomatoes
PARSLEY + CAPERS + garlic +
  LEMON + olive oil
parsley + chili pepper flakes +
  garlic + olive oil + vinegar

PARSLEY + GARLIC + *gremolata*
  + LEMON
PARSLEY + GARLIC + LEMON +
  mint + olive oil + walnuts

"I love **parsley** as a flavor. Parsley risotto is amazing, and its color is as vibrant as its flavor. There is more to parsley than just the leaf; I use the stems and roots as well. The stems add good texture, and I use them to add crunch to soups. As for the root, which has an herbaceousness similar to parsnips, I like to roast and puree them for soups as well. . . . People also need to remember that there is more than flat-leaf parsley out there. I am a fan of curly parsley, which is often overlooked and has an intense, almost celery-like flavor. There was a time in America when you couldn't serve a plate without the orange wedge and curly parsley."
— CHRISTOPHER BATES, HOTEL FAUCHÈRE (MILFORD, PA)

PARSLEY ROOT

Season: winter
Flavor: aromatic, with earthy notes of carrots, celery, celery root, parsley, and/or parsnips
Volume: moderate – loud
What it is: root vegetable
Techniques: boil, braise, grate, mash, puree, roast, sauté, steam, stew

Dishes

Dairy-Free Garlic and Almond Soup, Parsley Root, and Parsley Purée with Shiitake Mushrooms
— Bouley Restaurant (New York City)

Parsley Root Puree with Sunchoke Fricassee: Hedgehog Mushrooms, Verjus-Pickled Celery, Cocoa Bean Shavings
— DANIEL (New York City)

Botanical relatives: anise, caraway, **carrots, celery, celery root,** chervil, **dill, fennel, parsley,** parsnips
Possible substitutes: carrots, celery root, parsnips, turnips

apples
bay leaf
beans, e.g., cannellini, white
butter
caraway seeds
carrots
cauliflower
celery
cheese, e.g., Parmesan
chestnuts
cream
crème fraîche
European cuisines, esp. Central and
  Eastern
fennel
garlic
gratins
hash
hazelnuts
lemon, e.g., juice
maple syrup
mashed potatoes
mushrooms, e.g., chanterelle,
  hedgehog
oil, olive
ONIONS
orange, e.g., zest
PARSLEY
pepper, black
pilafs
POTATOES

purees, *e.g.*, *parsnip, potato*
rémoulades
sage
salads
salt, e.g., kosher
sauces, e.g., chimichurri
shallots
slaws
SOUPS, *e.g., celery root, potato*
squash, e.g., butternut
stews, e.g., vegetable
stock, vegetable
thyme
truffles, e.g., black
turnips
vegetables, other root
vinegar, e.g., champagne
watercress
wine, dry white

Flavor Affinities
parsley root + garlic + olive oil

• PARSNIPS

Season: autumn – spring
Flavor: sweet, with earthy notes of celery, herbs, and/or nuts, and a smooth, starchy potato-like texture (when cooked)
Volume: moderate – **loud**
What they are: root vegetables resembling pale carrots
Nutritional profile: 91% carbs / 5% protein / 4% fats
Calories: 55 per ½-cup serving (boiled, sliced)
Protein: 1 gram
Techniques: bake, blanch, boil, braise, deep-fry, fry, grate, grill, mash, pressure-cook, puree, **roast**, sauté, simmer (15 – 20 minutes), steam

Tip: Select young, tender parsnips for optimal flavor and texture.

Botanical relatives: anise, caraway, **carrots**, **celery**, **celery root**, chervil, **dill**, **fennel**, **parsley**, **parsley root**

allspice
anise seeds
APPLES, apple cider, and apple juice
baked goods, *e.g.*, *breads, cakes, muffins, pies*
basil
bay leaf
beans
BREADCRUMBS
BUTTER and brown butter
capers
caramel
cardamom
CARROTS
celery, celery leaves, and celery seeds
celery root
chayote
CHEESE, e.g., cream, Parmesan
chervil
chips, parsnip
CHIVES
cilantro
CINNAMON
cloves
coconut
coriander
couscous
CREAM
crème fraîche
cumin
CURRY, e.g., powder, spices, and *curries*

dates
desserts, *e.g.*, *cakes, custards*
dill
eggs
fennel
GARLIC
ghee
GINGER
gratins
greens, bitter, e.g., dandelion, mustard
hash browns
HONEY
horseradish
"hummus"
kale
LEEKS
LEMON, e.g., juice, zest
lentils
lettuce
lime, e.g., juice, zest
mace
MAPLE SYRUP
marjoram
mayonnaise
milk, dairy or nondairy, e.g., almond, rice, soy
mint
miso
MUSHROOMS, e.g., porcini, portobello, shiitake
MUSTARD, e.g., Dijon, whole-grain
NUTMEG

Dishes

Potato Parsnip Croquette, Okanagan Apple, House-Smoked Aged Cheddar, Pale Ale Sauce
— The Acorn (Vancouver)

Confit Parsnip with Savoy Cabbage, Sautéed King Oyster Mushroom, Caramelized Onion
— DANIEL (New York City)

Parsnip Soup with Coconut, Lime, and Mint
— Jean-Georges (New York City)

Charred Parsnips with Garlic, Spanish Almonds, Smoked Tofu, Thyme, and Lemon
— Plum Bistro (Seattle)

P

nuts, e.g., **almonds**, hazelnuts, pecans, **walnuts**

OILS, e.g., flaxseed, grapeseed, hazelnut, **OLIVE**, peanut, sesame, sunflower, walnut

ONIONS, e.g., pearl, red, yellow

ORANGE, e.g., juice, zest

pancakes

paprika

PARSLEY

pasta, e.g., gnocchi, ravioli

pears

PEPPER, e.g., black, white

POTATOES

pumpkin

PUREES, e.g., carrot, parsnip, potato, pumpkin

rice and "root rice" (a raw alternative to rice)

root vegetables, other, e.g.,

carrots, celery root, rutabagas, turnips

ROSEMARY

rutabaga

sage

SALADS, e.g., parsnip, vegetable

SALT, SEA

savory

scallions

sesame, e.g., oil, seeds

shallots

slaws

sorrel

SOUPS and BISQUES, e.g., cream, lentil, parsnip, potato, winter vegetable

sour cream

squash, winter

star anise

STEWS

STOCK, vegetable

sugar, e.g., brown

sweet potatoes

tarragon

THYME

tofu, e.g., silken

turmeric

turnips

vanilla

VEGETABLES, other root

vinegar, e.g., **balsamic**, **cider**, rice, **sherry**, white wine

wine, e.g., dry red

yogurt

"I've made **parsnip** jam by seasoning it with vanilla and rice wine vinegar."
— MARK LEVY, THE POINT (SARANAC LAKE, NY)

"If I'm serving a smooth pureed **parsnip** soup, I'll layer other parsnip flavors into the dish — for example, both cooked and raw parsnips, fried parsnip chips, and a confited parsnip 'butter.' I'll keep working to think of new ways to get more parsnip flavor into the dish one more time — like taking the parsnip oil from confited parsnips and reemulsifying it back into the soup. All together, the flavor becomes so much more impactful."
— AARON WOO, NATURAL SELECTION (PORTLAND, OR)

• PASSION FRUIT

Flavor: sweet/sour, with notes of guava, honey, jasmine, and/or vanilla, and gel-like flesh filled with crunchy seeds

Volume: moderate – loud

Nutritional profile: 86% carbs / 8% protein / 6% fats

Calories: 230 per 1-cup serving (raw)

Flavor Affinities

parsnips + allspice + almonds + cinnamon + vanilla

parsnips + almonds + honey + sage

parsnips + apples + cinnamon + pecans

parsnips + apples + sweet potatoes

parsnips + black pepper + butter

parsnips + caramel + cream cheese + walnuts

parsnips + carrots + dill + potatoes

parsnips + carrots + rutabagas + **sweet potatoes**

parsnips + celery root + potatoes

parsnips + chestnuts + mushrooms + Parmesan cheese

parsnips + cinnamon + cloves + ginger + nutmeg

parsnips + coconut + lime + mint

parsnips + coriander + cumin + ginger

parsnips + cumin + orange

parsnips + curry + yogurt

parsnips + garlic + onions + tomatoes

parsnips + ginger + orange juice/zest

parsnips + honey + rosemary

parsnips + honey + sesame oil/seeds + soy sauce

parsnips + leeks + lemon + parsley + potatoes

parsnips + lentils + root vegetables

parsnips + maple syrup + pecans

parsnips + maple syrup + thyme

parsnips + potatoes + pumpkin

parsnips + potatoes + shiitake mushrooms

Dishes

Baked Alaska: Coconut Ice Cream and Passion Fruit Caramel
— Oleana (Cambridge, MA)

Passion Fruit Tart, Shortbread Crust, Cascabel Coconut Caramel
— True Bistro (Somerville, MA)

Protein: 5 grams
Techniques: bake, cook, puree, raw

> **Tip:** The seeds are edible.

agave nectar
apples
bananas
basil
cakes
caramel
chiles, chipotle
chocolate, e.g., dark, white
cinnamon
citrus, e.g., grapefruit, lemon, **orange**
COCONUT and COCONUT MILK
cream
desserts, e.g., filled, frozen, panna cottas, puddings (e.g., rice), sorbets, tarts
fruit, other tropical
ginger
honey
ice cream
kiwi
lemongrass
lime
mangoes
marinades
melon, e.g., cantaloupe
meringue
mint
nuts, e.g., almonds, cashews, hazelnuts, macadamia, peanuts, pistachios
papayas
pineapple
plums
raspberries
rum

salad dressings
salads, fruit
sauces
smoothies
STRAWBERRIES
sugar, e.g., brown
vanilla
vinegar, e.g., white wine
wine, e.g., sparkling (e.g., Champagne)
yogurt

Flavor Affinities

passion fruit + almonds + brown sugar + cinnamon
passion fruit + cashews + coconut + white chocolate
passion fruit + chocolate + hazelnuts
passion fruit + coconut + lemongrass
passion fruit + coconut + pistachios
passion fruit + cream + strawberries
passion fruit + honey + strawberries + yogurt
passion fruit + mint + strawberries

• PASTA — WHOLE-GRAIN, IN GENERAL

What it is: whole-grain product (refined)
Nutritional profile: 81% carbs / 15% protein / 4% fats
Calories: 175 per 1-cup serving (whole-wheat spaghetti, cooked)
Protein: 7 grams

> **Tips:** There are more whole-grain varieties than ever, including brown rice, buckwheat, corn, oat, quinoa, rice, spelt, whole-wheat, etc. Experiment with various shapes, e.g., penne, rotini, shells, etc.

Dishes

Spaghetti and Wheatballs, with Truffle-Tomato Sauce, Roasted Garlic, Sautéed Spinach, and Cashew Parmesan (pictured above)
— Candle Café West (New York City)

Butternut Squash Ravioli with Sweet Onion Puree and Smoked Farmers Cheese, Cranberry, Pecan, Cinnamon, and Kale
— The Fearrington House (Fearrington Village, NC)

Fava Bean Agnolotti with Ramps, Pecorino Froth, and Pistou
— Picholine (New York City)

Talking with Chef Chris Eddy of Winvian about Cooking for Vegetarians

One of my favorite dishes of 2013 was a simple vegetarian pappardelle dish I was served at Winvian, a unique Connecticut resort that houses eighteen individually designed cottages, including a helicopter and a treehouse. It featured a green sauce, along with sautéed cauliflower, mushrooms, and onions, and a very light dusting of grated cheese on top. The creamy sauce turned out to be a steamed broccoli puree made in a Vitamix with a bit of ice ("to cool the broccoli as quickly as possible," according to chef Chris Eddy), some clear vegetable stock ("so as not to interfere with the beautiful green color"), a hint of heat in the form of either cayenne or chili pepper flakes ("always — it's a 'calling card' that leaves an impression even after you've finished eating"), and just a touch of brown butter ("to add an amazing dimension to the sauce"). It's based on a "ridiculously simple" technique Eddy learned while working with Chef Alain Ducasse and, I can attest, it's ridiculously delicious.

Eddy says the technique works just as well with other vegetables — whether cabbage, carrots, cauliflower, celery root, or parsnips — and if added richness is desired, one could substitute cream for some of the clear vegetable stock ("although its whiteness fades the bright colors"), though the dish is creamy and rich even without added cream.

While Eddy characterizes Winvian's customers as about 35 to 40 percent pescetarian, he and chef de cuisine Patrick Espinoza and their kitchen team spent a month eating vegetarian during the summer of 2013, just for the experience of putting themselves into the shoes of the significant portion of Winvian's clientele ("about 7 or 8 percent of our customers") who eat vegetarian. Why? "Number one, we love vegetables," Eddy admits. But out of compassion for Winvian's vegetarian customers, "We wanted to 'feel their pain.' We came to understand their frustration [at other restaurants] of only being offered the same dishes again and again — whether eggplant Parmesan, or risotto, or a salad — when they went out to dine." In addition to prompting Eddy and his team to come up with an ever-changing array of dishes like the incredible pappardelle I fell in love with, their month-long vegetarian experiment had an added bonus: a number of Eddy's cooks discovered that they felt healthier and sometimes less irritable.

"Now, we like to go all out for our vegetarian guests, and give them something special," says Eddy. Mission accomplished.

Possible substitutes: spiralized vegetables (e.g., zucchini) instead of linguini, spaghetti, etc.; sliced vegetables (e.g., eggplant, summer squash, sweet potato) instead of lasagna noodles

"There are entire regions of Italy that make **pasta** without eggs. Gnocchi is made without eggs in Liguria [so it's naturally vegan]. I don't use eggs in my ravioli dough — I use tapioca flour. I sometimes stuff ravioli with thick cashew cream, or kale, or a vegetable puree. I've served English pea ravioli with morels, mint, lemon zest, and sweated shallots."

— AARON ADAMS, PORTOBELLO (PORTLAND, OR)

"**Pastas** are a good way to get people to try a vegan dish in a vegan restaurant. Pizzas, too. They're a friendly entry point that can help to pull people in, and when they're served with ingredients like heirloom tomatoes or pestos, they're not intimidating."

— MAKINI HOWELL, PLUM BISTRO (SEATTLE)

● PEACHES

Season: summer
Flavor: sweet/sour, with a soft, juicy texture
Volume: quiet – moderate
Nutritional profile: 87% carbs / 8% protein / 5% fats
Calories: 70 per large peach
Protein: 2 grams
Techniques: bake, broil, grill, poach, puree, raw, roast, sauté

Tips: Opt for organic peaches. The lighter (i.e., whiter) the skin, the sweeter the peach; the darker (i.e., yellower) the skin, the more acidic the peach.

Botanical relatives: apples, apricots, blackberries, cherries, pears, plums, quinces, raspberries, strawberries

Possible substitute: nectarines

allspice
apples and apple juice
apricots, e.g., dried, fresh, pureed
arugula
baked goods, e.g., pies, scones
basil
BERRIES, e.g., **blackberries, BLUEBERRIES, RASPBERRIES, strawberries**
butter

Dishes

Peaches: Ginger Cake, Fromage Blanc Sorbet, and Pine Nuts
— Blue Hill (New York City)

Baby Roma Tomato and White Peach Salad, Peterson's Greens, Basil, and Balsamic-Honey
— Cal-a-Vie (Vista, CA)

Arugula and Peach Salad with Parmesan, Lemon and Vanilla Dressing, Truffle, Celery, Sesame Seeds, Fennel
— Fearrington House (Fearrington Village, NC)

"Rupert": "Demi-Sec" Peaches, Walnut Tapenade, Pearl Onions, and Watercress
— The French Laundry (Yountville, CA)

Peach Trifle: Lemon Verbena Panna Cotta, KandJ Orchard Peaches, and Champagne Granite
— The French Laundry (Yountville, CA)

Grilled Haloumi Cheese and Peaches with Chard Rib Salad, Sundried Olive, and Sweet Pepper Broth
— Oleana (Cambridge, MA)

P

buttermilk
caramel
cardamom
cheese, e.g., blue, burrata, cream,
    goat, halloumi, mozzarella,
    ricotta, ricotta salata
chiles, e.g., chipotle, serrano
chocolate
chutneys
cilantro
CINNAMON
cloves
coconut
compotes
coriander
*****CREAM** and crème fraîche
cress, e.g., pepper
currants
DESSERTS, e.g., cobblers, crisps,
    crumbles, Melba, pies

endive
fennel
GINGER
grains, whole, e.g., quinoa, wheat
    berries
grapes
greens, salad, e.g., baby chard
hazelnuts
HONEY
ice cream
kefir
lavender
LEMON, e.g., juice, zest
lemongrass
LEMON VERBENA
lime
lychees
mangoes
MAPLE SYRUP
mascarpone

MINT
nutmeg
NUTS, e.g., **ALMONDS**,
    cashews, macadamias,
    PECANS, **pistachios**, walnuts
oats and oatmeal
oil, olive
onions, red
ORANGE, e.g., juice, liqueur, zest
pepper, black
pomegranates
pumpkin seeds
radishes
rosemary
rum
saffron
salads, e.g., fruit, grain, green
salsas
salt, sea
scallions
sherry
smoothies
sorbets
soups, e.g., cold and/or fruit
sour cream
Southern (U.S.) cuisine
spirits, e.g., bourbon, brandy,
    cognac, Cointreau, Kirsch
STONE FRUITS, OTHER, e.g.,
    cherries, nectarines, plums
SUGAR, e.g., brown, maple
tarragon
VANILLA
VINEGAR, e.g., apple cider,
    balsamic, champagne, rice, wine
watercress
whiskey
wine, red or white; fruity,
    sparkling, and/or sweet, e.g.,
    Champagne, Prosecco,
    Sauternes
yogurt
yuzu

Flavor Affinities

peaches + almonds + cinnamon + yogurt
peaches + almonds + lemon + olive oil + saffron
peaches + balsamic vinegar + endive + maple syrup + olive oil +
    watercress
peaches + balsamic vinegar + mint + ricotta
peaches + basil + mozzarella cheese
peaches + berries + lemon
PEACHES + BLUEBERRIES + LEMON + maple syrup
peaches + blue cheese + hazelnuts
peaches + cashew cream + balsamic vinegar
peaches + cherries + balsamic vinegar
peaches + chiles + coriander + **ginger + lime** + vinegar
peaches + cilantro + **ginger + lime**
peaches + cinnamon + honey + lemon + yogurt
peaches + cream + lemon verbena + raspberries
peaches + fennel + lemon
peaches + ginger + honey + **lemon** + lemongrass
peaches + ginger + lemon
peaches + honey + lemon + yogurt
peaches + honey + **nuts** (e.g., almonds, pecans) + **oatmeal/oats**
peaches + mangoes + raspberries
peaches + maple syrup + **nuts** (e.g., almonds, walnuts) + orange juice
    + ricotta
peaches + maple syrup + orange + vanilla
peaches + mascarpone + strawberries + vanilla
peaches + pistachios + vanilla

"The flavor of **peaches** takes me
to the South, so I like pairing
them with pecans and whiskey."
— KATE JACOBY, VEDGE (PHILADELPHIA)

"We'll make a vegan **Peach**
Melba — leveraging the winning
combination of peaches with
raspberries and almonds — by
replacing the vanilla ice cream
with a coconut milk sorbet."
— MARK LEVY, THE POINT (SARANAC
LAKE, NY)

● PEANUTS and PEANUT BUTTER

Flavor: salty and/or sweet, with
astringent notes of nuts
Volume: moderate – loud
What they are: legumes
Nutritional profile: 73% fat /
16% protein / 11% carbs
Calories: 160 per 1-ounce
serving of peanuts
Protein: 7 grams
Calories: 190 per 2-tablespoon
serving of peanut butter
Protein: 8 grams
Techniques: boil, stew

Tips: Opt for all-natural peanut butter containing only peanuts and salt (check the label).
Because of the severity of peanut
allergies, be sure to alert guests
to any dishes you serve that
contain peanuts.

Botanical relatives: beans,
lentils, peas

African cuisines
agave nectar
apples
American cuisine
Asian cuisines
baked goods, e.g., cookies, muffins
bananas
basil, Thai
beans, green
bell peppers, e.g., red
bran, e.g., oat, wheat
broccoli
cabbage, e.g., green, napa
candy

carrots
cayenne
CHILES, e.g., serrano; chili oil,
chili paste, chili pepper flakes,
chili sauce
Chinese cuisine
CHOCOLATE, e.g., dark, milk
CILANTRO
cinnamon
cloves
**COCONUT and COCONUT
MILK**
cucumbers
cumin
curries
desserts
dips and dipping sauces
fruit, dried
GARLIC
GINGER
granola

grapes
greens, bitter, e.g., collard,
mustard
greens, salad, e.g., arugula
honey
lemongrass
lime, e.g., juice, zest
mangoes
mint
NOODLES, esp. Asian, e.g.,
Chinese egg, **rice, soba, udon**
nuts, other
oats and oatmeal
OILS, e.g., olive, **peanut, sesame,**
vegetable
onions, red
orange, e.g., juice
pad thai
paprika
pastas

Flavor Affinities

peanuts + apples + raisins
peanuts + Asian noodles + broccoli + hoisin sauce + tofu
peanuts + bananas + chocolate
peanuts + bran + honey + vanilla
peanuts + brown rice vinegar + chiles + cilantro + coconut milk + **garlic**
+ **ginger** + mint + *sauce* + **soy sauce**
peanuts + brown sugar + *dipping sauce* + rice wine vinegar + soy sauce
peanuts + chiles + cilantro + **garlic + soy sauce** + vinegar
peanuts + chiles + coconut milk + scallions
peanuts + chiles + lime
peanuts + chili paste + coconut milk + lemongrass
peanuts + chili paste + lemongrass + tamarind
peanuts + chili paste + rice wine vinegar + sesame paste + soy sauce
peanuts + coconut + curry
peanuts + garlic **+ ginger + soy sauce** + tahini + vinegar
peanuts + ginger + scallions + **soy sauce**
peanuts + ginger + sesame seeds
peanuts + rice wine vinegar + sesame oil + soy sauce + whole-wheat
spaghetti

Dishes

Rennie's Peanut-Kale Salad: Hearty Kale, Carrots, Butternut Squash, Red Peppers, and
Peanut-Cider Marinade
— Seva (Ann Arbor, MI)

pepper, black
pesto
potatoes
pumpkin
raisins
rice
salad dressings, e.g., Thai
SALADS, e.g., cabbage, noodle, Thai
salt
sandwiches
satays
SAUCES, e.g., peanut, vegetable
scallions
seeds, e.g., sesame, sunflower
sesame, e.g., paste, seeds
smoothies
SOUPS, e.g., peanut, sweet potato
Southeast Asian cuisines
SOY SAUCE
spinach
stews
stir-fries
sugar, e.g., brown
sweet potatoes
tahini
tamari
tamarind and tamarind juice
tempeh
Thai cuisine
TOFU
tomatoes
trail mix
turmeric
vanilla
Vietnamese cuisine
VINEGAR, e.g., apple cider, brown rice, red wine, RICE WINE

● PEARS — IN GENERAL
Season: autumn – winter
Flavor: sweet, with subtle notes of citrus, custard, honey, nuts, Sauternes, and/or vanilla, and a crisp, juicy, and/or soft texture (when ripe)
Volume: quiet – moderate
What they are: fruit

Nutritional profile: 96% carbs (high in sugars) / 2% protein / 2% fats
Calories: 105 per one medium pear (raw)
Protein: 1 gram
Techniques: bake, braise, grill, pickle, **poach**, puree, raw, roast, sauté, stew
Botanical relatives: apples, apricots, blackberries, cherries, peaches, plums, quinces, raspberries, strawberries

agave nectar
allspice
anise seeds
APPLES, apple cider, and apple juice
ARUGULA
baked goods, e.g., cakes, pies, tarts
bananas

blackberries
bourbon
brandy, e.g., pear
butter
cabbage, e.g., red, white
CARAMEL
cardamom
cashew cream
celery
CHEESE, e.g., **BLUE** (e.g., Cabrales, Gorgonzola, Roquefort, Stilton), Brie, cream, **feta**, **goat**, Gruyère, halloumi, **Parmesan**, pecorino, ricotta
cherries, e.g., dried, fresh
chestnuts
chicory
chives
CHOCOLATE (esp. dark) and cocoa
CINNAMON
citrus

Dishes

Citrus and Spice Cake: Poached Pear, Mascarpone Mousse, Ginger Gelato
— Boulud Sud (New York City)

CityZen Fruit Plate: Ginger Poached Pear, Pomegranate, Mission Fig, Butternut Squash, and Concord Grape Sorbet
— CityZen (Washington, DC)

Grilled Frog Hollow Warren Pear with Watercress, Point Reyes Original Blue, Hazelnuts, Golden Balsamic, and Arbequina Olive Oil
— Greens Restaurant (San Francisco)

Pears and Fall Greens Salad with Shaved Fennel, Red Onion and Radish, Rosemary Candied Pecans, and Pear-Miso Dressing
— Millennium (San Francisco)

Walnut Pear Shortcake with Spiced White Chocolate Filling, Gingerbread Ice Cream, and Cinnamon Anglaise
— Millennium (San Francisco)

Curly Cress and Pear Salad: Dried Figs, Chèvre, Orange Flower Honey, Raisin Croutons
— Natural Selection (Portland, OR)

Pear Salad with Mâche, Miner's Lettuce, Chickweed, Toasted Hazelnuts, and Truffle Vinaigrette
— Portobello (Portland, OR)

cloves
CRANBERRIES
cream and crème fraîche
currants, e.g., black
dates
DESSERTS, e.g., crisps, crumbles,
  ice creams, sorbets, tarts
endive
fennel and fennel seeds
figs
fruits, dried
GINGER
gingerbread
grapefruit
GREENS, BITTER OR SALAD,
  e.g., baby, mesclun
HONEY

juniper berries
LEMON, e.g., juice, zest
lettuces, e.g., butter, romaine
lime
MAPLE SYRUP
mascarpone
mint
molasses
nutmeg
NUTS, e.g., **ALMONDS,**
  hazelnuts, PECANS, pistachios,
  walnuts
oats and oatmeal
oils, e.g., grapeseed, olive
onions, e.g., red
ORANGE, e.g., juice, zest
pancakes

parsley
parsnips
passion fruit
pepper, black
persimmons
phyllo dough
pineapple
pizzas
plums, dried
poached pears
pomegranates
quinces
radicchio
raisins
raspberries
rémoulade
rhubarb
rosemary
SALADS, e.g., fruit, green, spinach
salt, sea
sauces, e.g., dessert
shallots
smoothies
soups

Flavor Affinities

pears + agave nectar + lemon + strawberries
pears + allspice + black pepper + maple syrup + red wine
pears + almonds + chicory
pears + almonds + figs
pears + arugula + balsamic vinegar + blue cheese + fennel + olive oil
pears + pomegranate seeds + shallots
pears + balsamic vinegar + cinnamon + maple syrup
pears + blue cheese + fennel
pears + butter lettuce + honey
pears + caramel + peanuts
pears + cardamom + white wine
pears + cayenne + ginger + soy sauce
PEARS + CHEESE (e.g., blue, goat, Parmesan) + **NUTS** (e.g.,
  hazelnuts, pecans, walnuts)
pears + cherries + ginger
pears + cinnamon + cranberries + oats
pears + cinnamon + lemon juice + **maple syrup** + red wine
pears + cranberries + hazelnuts
pears + cranberries + orange
pears + cranberries + pecans + vanilla
pears + cream + molasses
pears + fennel + fennel seeds + ginger
pears + feta cheese + red onions + salad greens
pears + ginger + orange
pears + ginger + pecans
pears + goat cheese + hazelnuts
pears + Gorgonzola cheese + pecans + spinach
pears + hazelnuts + raspberries
pears + honey + maple syrup + orange + Parmesan cheese + pears

sour cream
SPINACH
squash, winter, e.g., butternut
star anise
stews, esp. dried pears
sugar, e.g., brown
tarragon
thyme
trail mixes, esp. dried pears
VANILLA
VINEGAR, e.g., balsamic, cider, fruit, raspberry, rice, sherry, white balsamic
WATERCRESS
WINE, RED or WHITE — dry or sweet, e.g., port
yogurt

● **PEAS (aka ENGLISH PEAS, GARDEN PEAS, or GREEN PEAS; see also BLACK-EYED PEAS and PEAS, SPLIT)**

Season: spring – summer
Flavor: slightly sweet, with a soft, starchy texture
Volume: quiet – moderate
What they are: legumes (however, nutritionally, often considered a starchy vegetable)
Nutritional profile: 73% carbs / 23% protein / 4% fats
Calories: 120 per 1-cup serving (raw)
Protein: 8 grams
Techniques: blanch, boil (2 – 3 minutes), braise, poach, puree, sauté, simmer (2 – 3 minutes), steam, stir-fry (2 – 3 minutes)
Tip: Try frozen peas, which maintain their freshness and nutritional value.
Botanical relatives: beans, lentils, peanuts

allspice
almonds
artichokes
ASPARAGUS
avocados
barley
BASIL
bay leaf
beans, fava
breadcrumbs
bulgur
butter
buttermilk
cabbage
cardamom
CARROTS
cashews
casseroles
cauliflower
celery
cheese, e.g., feta, goat, mozzarella, **Parmesan,** ricotta
chervil
chiles, e.g., green, red
chives
cilantro

coconut milk
coriander
couscous
cream and crème fraîche
cucumbers
CURRIES, esp. green
curry powder
dill
eggs
fennel
garam masala
GARLIC, e.g., green, white
ghee
GINGER
grapefruit
greens, bitter
"guacamole"
"hummus"
Kaffir lime leaf
LEEKS
LEMON, e.g., juice, zest
lemongrass
LETTUCE, e.g., butter
lime
marjoram
mayonnaise

Flavor Affinities
peas + almonds + grapefruit + thyme
peas + artichokes + oregano + snap peas
peas + arugula + potatoes
peas + buttermilk + mint + olive oil + scallions
peas + carrots + mushrooms
peas + chiles + yogurt
peas + chili powder + mint
peas + cilantro + coconut
peas + coconut + coriander
peas + dill + mint
peas + garlic + mint + spinach
peas + ginger + sesame oil
peas + lime + mint + paprika
peas + mint + mushrooms + rhubarb
peas + mint + ricotta
peas + mint + risotto
peas + mushrooms + pasta
peas + mushrooms + peanut oil + soy sauce
peas + pasta + ricotta cheese

MINT
MUSHROOMS, e.g., morel, oyster, shiitake, wild
noodles
nutmeg
OILS, e.g., OLIVE, peanut, sesame, sunflower
ONIONS, e.g., green, pearl, red, spring, white, yellow
oregano
paellas, vegetarian
PARSLEY
PASTAS, e.g., fettuccine, fusilli, penne
pepper, e.g., black, green
pesto
POTATOES, e.g., new
quinoa
RICE, e.g., brown
RISOTTOS
rosemary
saffron
sage
SALADS, e.g., pasta, vegetable
salt, e.g., kosher, sea
sauces
savory
scallions
sesame, e.g., oil, seeds
shallots
snow peas
sorrel
SOUPS, e.g., pea, spinach, vegetable
sour cream

soy sauce
spelt
spinach
squash, e.g., butternut, delicata
stews
stir-fries
stock, e.g., vegetable
sugar snap peas
tarragon
thyme
tofu, e.g., silken
tomatoes
turmeric
turnips
vinegar
yogurt

"With some vegetables there is a real need for speed [i.e., getting them from the garden to the table], and corn and peas are the greatest examples. Fresh **peas** are the world's greatest. I love risotto or pasta with fresh peas."
— CHRISTOPHER BATES, HOTEL FAUCHÈRE (MILFORD, PA)

"There is nothing better than English **peas** or snap peas that are really sweet. I like to make a pea and radish salad with pea tendrils, pea shoots, and a bright lemon olive oil dressing."
— ANNIE SOMERVILLE, GREENS RESTAURANT (SAN FRANCISCO)

Dishes

Chilled Pea Soup: Braised Romaine Lettuce, Ricotta Cheese, Lemon Zest
— Café Boulud (New York City)

Garden Salad: Pea, Tarragon, Morel Crouton, Local Organic Vegetables
— Rowland's Restaurant at Westglow (Blowing Rock, NC)

Farmers Market Salad: English Peas, Artichoke, Lemon, Mint, and Manchego
— True Food Kitchen (Santa Monica, CA)

PEAS, SNAP (see SUGAR SNAP PEAS)

PEAS, SNOW (see SNOW PEAS)

● PEAS, SPLIT

Flavor: slightly sweet, with earthy notes, and a soft, creamy, luscious texture
Volume: quiet (e.g., yellow) – moderate (e.g., green)
What they are: peas that have been dried and split
Nutritional profile: 72% carbs / 25% protein / 3% fats
Calories: 335 per 1-cup serving (raw)
Protein: 24 grams
Technique: puree
Timing: Boil then simmer split peas about 30 – 60 minutes (or longer, for yellow split peas), until tender. No need to pre-soak.

Tip: Do **not** pressure-cook, as split peas foam, which can clog the valve and cause the cooker to explode(!).

P

barley
basil
BAY LEAF
bell peppers, e.g., red
CARROTS
celery
chili pepper flakes and chili powder
chives
cilantro
croutons, e.g., whole-grain
cumin
curries
curry powder and curry spices
dals
dill
dips
dulse
GARLIC

ginger
greens, salad
herbs
kale
leeks
lemon, e.g., juice
marjoram
mint
OIL, OLIVE
ONIONS, e.g., green, red, white,
  yellow
oregano
paprika, smoked
PARSLEY
pastas
peas, fresh
PEPPER, e.g., black, white
pesto
potatoes
purees
purslane
rice, e.g., basmati, brown
rosemary
salads
salt, sea
sauces
savory
sorrel
SOUPS, e.g., SPLIT PEA
soy sauce
spices
spinach
spreads
stews
STOCK, VEGETABLE
tarragon
THYME
tofu, smoked
tomatoes and tomato paste
turmeric
vegetables, root
veggie burgers (e.g., with rice)
vinegar, e.g., red wine, white
  wine

Flavor Affinities
split peas + dill + garlic
split peas + potatoes + *soup*

**PEA SHOOTS (see
SHOOTS, PEA)**

**PEAS, SUGAR SNAP (see
SUGAR SNAP PEAS)**

● **PECANS**
Season: autumn
Flavor: bitter/sweet, with notes
of butter and/or nuts, and a rich
texture
Volume: quiet – moderate
Nutritional profile: 87% fats /
8% carbs / 5% protein
Calories: 375 per ½-cup serving
(chopped)
Protein: 5 grams
**Botanical relative and
possible substitute:** walnuts

almonds
*(Native and North) American
  cuisines*
APPLES
asparagus
*BAKED GOODS, e.g., breads,
  cakes, cookies, pastries, pies,
  scones*
bananas
berries, e.g., blueberries
bourbon
brown rice syrup
Brussels sprouts
butter, e.g., brown
cabbage, red
caramel
casseroles
cayenne
celery
*cereals, breakfast, e.g., **granola***
cheese, e.g., blue, goat, ricotta
cherries, esp. dried
chili powder
chocolate
cinnamon
clementines
CRANBERRIES, DRIED
cream

---

dates
DESSERTS
endive
figs
garlic
ginger
grains, whole, e.g., amaranth,
  spelt
granola
grapes
greens, bitter
honey, e.g., raw
ice cream, e.g., butter pecan
kale
lemon, e.g., juice
lentils
lettuce, e.g., romaine
MAPLE SYRUP
molasses
muesli
MUSHROOMS, e.g., shiitake,
  wild
mustard
nutmeg
nuts
oats
ORANGES
pancakes
paprika
parsley
pâtés
peaches
PEARS
PIES, e.g., pecan, sweet potato
pilafs
pineapple
pizzas
pomegranate seeds
popcorn
puddings
PUMPKIN
purees, vegetable
radicchio
raisins
RICE, e.g., brown, red, **WILD**
salads
salsify
salt, sea

seitan
soups, e.g., butternut squash
Southern (U.S.) cuisine
spinach
SQUASH, WINTER, e.g.,
 butternut
stuffings
sugar, e.g., brown, maple
sumac
SWEET POTATOES
tamari
tarts
vanilla
veggie burgers
waffles
wheat germ
yogurt

Flavor Affinities
pecans + apples + butternut
 squash
pecans + apples + romaine
pecans + asparagus + lemon +
 wild rice
pecans + brown rice + shiitake
 mushrooms
pecans + butter + caramel + salt
pecans + cayenne/chili powder +
 cinnamon + salt + sugar
pecans + dates + vanilla
pecans + dried cranberries +
 wild rice
pecans + oranges + radicchio
pecans + pears + spinach

PEPITAS (see SEEDS, PUMPKIN)

● PEPPER, BLACK

Flavor: hot (and sometimes
sweet); aromatic, with pungent
notes of cloves, lemon, and/
or wood
Volume: moderate – loud

Tips: Look for tellicherry black
peppercorns, which are often
regarded as the best in the world
for their rich, complex flavor.
Pepper suggests "false heat,"
and also stimulates the appetite.
Always use freshly ground black
pepper from a pepper mill for
optimal flavor. Add at the very
last minute before serving.

allspice
(North) American cuisine
apricots
baked goods, e.g., spice cakes
basil
berries
Cajun cuisine
cardamom
cheese
cherries
cinnamon
cloves
coconut milk
coriander
Creole cuisine
cumin
eggs
European cuisines
fruit, fresh, e.g., berries,
 pineapple
garlic
ginger
gravies
Indian cuisine
lemon, e.g., juice
lentils
lime, e.g., juice
marinades
nutmeg
nuts
oil, olive
olives
onions
parsley
pickles
potatoes

pumpkin
rosemary
salad dressings
salads
SALT
sauces, e.g., black pepper
soups
Southeast Asian cuisine
Southern (U.S.) cuisine
stocks
strawberries
thyme
tomatoes
turmeric
vegetables
vinegar, e.g., cider

"I think **black pepper** and the
whole rainbow of peppercorns
are among the most underrated
spices in the kitchen. Peppercorns are truly berries — they are
sweet, fruity, and spicy — so a
great pepper adds a lot of flavor.
I've served cauliflower crusted
with pepper, and the pepper
helped the cauliflower sing on the
plate."
— RICH LANDAU, VEDGE (PHILADELPHIA)

PEPPER, ESPELETTE
Flavor: hot, with notes of the
ocean, peaches, pepper, and/or
smoke
Volume: quiet/moderate – loud
What it is: paste or powder
made from dried chiles from
the Basque region of France and
Spain
Possible substitutes: (milder)
cayenne, (hot) paprika

almonds
Basque cuisine
bell peppers
breads
cheese, e.g., French, Spanish

chocolate
drinks, e.g., Bloody Marys
eggs
garlic
honey
mayonnaise
oil, olive
onions
parsley
potatoes

PEPPER, SZECHUAN
Flavor: sour/hot, with pungent
notes of anise
Volume: loud
Tips: Dry-roast for a few
minutes before grinding. Add at
the end of the cooking process.
Botanical relatives: NOT black
pepper

Asian cuisines
beans, e.g., black
chiles
Chinese cuisine
citrus fruit, e.g., lemon, lime,
   orange
deep-fried dishes
five-spice powder
garlic
ginger
Indian cuisine
Japanese cuisine
mushrooms
noodles, Asian
onions
salt
scallions
sesame, e.g., oil, seeds
soups
soy sauce
star anise
stir-fries

● PEPPER, WHITE
Flavor: hot, with wine-like notes
Volume: moderate – loud (and
quieter than black pepper)

Tips: Use white pepper when
you don't want to see black
flecks in your dish, and/or when
you want a milder pepper than
black pepper. Add at the end of
the cooking process. Look for
Sarawak white peppercorns.

allspice
Asian cuisines
cloves
coriander
eggs, e.g., *quiches, scrambled*
European cuisines
ginger
gravies, e.g., white
Japanese cuisine
lemongrass
macaroni and cheese
mashed potatoes
nutmeg
pastas
potatoes
salad dressings, e.g., clear
sauces, e.g., white
soups, e.g., cream, light-colored,
   white
Southeast Asian cuisines
stocks
Thai cuisine
white and light-colored foods

● PEPPERMINT
Flavor: slightly sweet
Volume: very loud
What it is: herb

apples
baked goods, e.g., *brownies, cakes,*
   cookies, esp. as icing
berries, e.g., strawberries
chiles
CHOCOLATE and cocoa
cilantro
cucumbers
desserts, esp. chocolate
drinks
ice cream

mangoes
salads, e.g., *spinach*
sauces
smoothies
sorbets
stews
TEAS
vanilla
yogurt

PEPPER SAUCE (see HOT PEPPER SAUCE)

PEPPERS, BELL (see BELL PEPPERS)

PEPPERS, CHILE (see CHILES)

● PEPPERS, PIQUILLO
Flavor: hot
Volume: moderate – loud
Techniques: roast, stuff

aioli
almonds
artichokes
asparagus
beans, white
bread
CHEESE, e.g., GOAT, manchego,
   mozzarella
chickpeas
chocolate, dark
eggs
garlic
lemon
mushrooms
oil, olive
olives
onions
orange
"paella," vegetarian
paprika, e.g., smoked, Spanish
parsley
pepper, black
potatoes
rice, e.g., bomba

salads
salt
soups
Spanish cuisine
spreads
stews
stuffed piquillo peppers, *e.g., with
goat cheese or white beans*
sugar
tomatoes
vinegar, e.g., sherry

Flavor Affinities
piquillo peppers + goat cheese +
mushrooms

PEPPERS, SWEET (see BELL PEPPERS — RED and YELLOW)

● PERSIMMONS

Season: autumn – winter
Flavor: sweet/sour, with apricot
and/or spicy notes
Volume: moderate – loud
Nutritional profile: 95% carbs
(high in sugars) / 3% fats / 2%
protein
Calories: 35 per persimmon
(raw)
Techniques: bake (esp.
Hachiya), broil, freeze, puree,
raw, roast

> **Tips:** Generally allow (Hachiya)
> persimmons to become very
> soft (and sweet) before using.
> However, smaller, sweeter
> (Fuyu) persimmons should be
> enjoyed while still firm and crisp.

agave nectar
avocados
*BAKED GOODS, e.g., breads,
cakes, cookies, muffins, pies, quick
breads* (esp. Hachiya)
bananas
barley

brandy
caramel
cheese, e.g., creamy, feta, goat
cherries, e.g., dried or fresh
CINNAMON
cloves
cranberries
CREAM
custards
daikon
endive, Belgian
escarole
figs
frisée
ginger
graham crackers
grapefruit
grapes, e.g., red
greens, salad
honey
ice cream
jams

kiwi
leeks
LEMON, e.g., juice
lettuces, e.g., butter, mixed
lime
maple syrup
mushrooms, wild
nutmeg
NUTS, e.g., almonds, hazelnuts,
pecans, walnuts
oil, e.g., grapeseed, hazelnut,
olive, walnut
onions, e.g., Bermuda, red
oranges and orange juice
parsnips
pears and Asian pears
pepper, black
pineapple
pomegranates
puddings (esp. Hachiya)
radicchio
radishes

Flavor Affinities

persimmons + allspice + cinnamon + ginger
persimmons + almonds + goat cheese
persimmons + avocado + grapefruit + onions
persimmons + cranberries + maple syrup
persimmons + feta or goat cheese + hazelnuts + lettuces
persimmons + ginger + lemon juice + orange juice
persimmons + greens + olive oil + orange juice + pears + pecans +
sherry vinegar
persimmons + lemon + sesame + soy sauce
persimmons + lemon + vanilla + walnuts
persimmons + maple syrup + pecans
persimmons + pomegranates + walnuts
persimmons + vanilla + yogurt

Dishes

Hachiya Persimmon Pudding with Cognac Cream
— Chez Panisse (Berkeley, CA)

"Glace à la Vanille": Steamed Persimmon Pudding, Candied Walnuts,
and Lemon-Vanilla Syrup
— Per Se (New York City)

raisins
rice, e.g., Arborio, wild
rum
SALADS (esp. Fuyu)
salt, e.g., sea
sauces, e.g., dessert
sesame, e.g., paste, seeds
shallots
smoothies
sorbets
soups
soy sauce
stock, vegetable
sugar, e.g., brown
sweet potatoes
tofu and tofu paste
turnips
vanilla
vinegar, e.g., rice, sherry
watercress
yams
yogurt
yuzu

"My personal preference is to serve fruit only at the end of a meal, but **persimmons** are an exception: They are not too sweet, and not too overwhelming in flavor, so they are easy to use at other points in a meal. I've served a mid-menu dish of chilled persimmon with tofu paste, and I also think sesame paste accents it well."
— RYOTA UESHIMA, KAJITSU (NEW YORK CITY)

PHYLLO, WHOLE-WHEAT

What it is: paper-thin sheets made of flour and water
Nutritional profile: 73% carbs / 18% fats / 9% protein
Calories: 60 per sheet
Protein: 1 gram

Tips: Opt for organic whole wheat versions. Coconut or grapeseed oil can be substituted for melted butter when preparing vegan dishes made with phyllo dough.

apples
baklava
butter, esp. melted
cheese, e.g., goat, ricotta
figs
Greek cuisine
honey
Middle Eastern cuisines
mushrooms
nuts
oil, e.g., coconut, grapeseed
pears
phyllo triangles
spanakopita
spinach
strudels
vegetables, roasted

Flavor Affinities

phyllo + feta + **garlic** + onions + ricotta + **spinach**
phyllo + **garlic** + lemon + mushrooms + nutmeg + **spinach** + tofu
phyllo + goat cheese + honey

Dishes

Apple Baklava: Mulled Wine Roasted Apples, Pistachio Baklava, Ginger Syrup, Pistachio-Nutmeg Ice Cream
— Millennium (San Francisco)

PIECRUSTS, VEGAN

Tip: Think creatively when coming up with healthful, delicious vegan piecrusts based on ground fruits, nuts, spices, and more. You can press a crust based on one of the following combinations into your next pie plate:
almond milk + almonds + oat flour + oil
applesauce + coconut + graham cracker crumbs + pecans
brown rice syrup + cinnamon + coconut oil + oats + pecans
coconut + dates + vanilla + walnuts
dates + graham cracker crumbs (+ orange juice)

PIMENTON (see also PAPRIKA, SMOKED)

Flavor: bitter/sweet; sometimes hot and/or smoky
Volume: ranges from quiet (dulce, or sweet) to moderate (agridulce, or bittersweet) to loud (picante, or hot)
What it is: Spanish paprika
Tip: Look for pimenton labeled "de la Vera," or "from La Vera," in Extremadura, which is considered to be the best quality.

● PINEAPPLE

Season: winter
Flavor: sour/**sweet**, with a juicy texture
Volume: moderate
Nutritional profile: 94% carbs (high in sugars) / 4% protein / 2% fats
Calories: 85 per 1-cup serving (raw, chunks)
Protein: 1 gram
Techniques: bake, broil (at 500°F, about 3 – 5 minutes), grill, poach, raw, roast, sauté

agave nectar
apricots
avocados
baked goods, e.g., cakes (esp. pineapple upside-down)
BANANAS
basil
beans, black
beets
bell peppers, red
berries, e.g., blueberries, **raspberries, strawberries**
butter
caramel
Caribbean cuisines
cashews
cheese, e.g., ricotta
chiles, e.g., chipotle, jalapeño, red, serrano
chili powder
chocolate, e.g., dark, white
chutneys
CILANTRO
cinnamon
cloves
COCONUT and COCONUT MILK
cream and ice cream
cucumbers
curries and curry powder/spices
drinks, e.g., piña coladas
fruit, other tropical
garlic
ginger
grapefruit
Hawaiian cuisine
honey
jícama
kiwi
kumquats
lavender
lemon, e.g., juice, zest
lemongrass
LIME, e.g., juice, zest

liqueurs, e.g., brandy, Cointreau, Grand Marnier, Kirsch, orange
mangoes
maple syrup
melon
mint
molasses
mushrooms, portobello
nutmeg
nuts, e.g., **almonds**, hazelnuts, macadamia, peanuts,

pistachios, walnuts
oil, e.g., grapeseed, olive
onions, e.g., red
orange, e.g., juice, zest
palm, hearts of
papayas
parsnips
passion fruit
pepper, e.g., black, Szechuan
raisins
RICE, e.g., brown

Flavor Affinities

pineapple + almonds + vanilla
pineapple + apple + brown sugar + ginger + orange juice + soy sauce
pineapple + banana + brown sugar
pineapple + banana + lemon + red onions + *salsas*
pineapple + black beans + cucumbers + *salsas*
pineapple + brown sugar + ginger + lime (+ oats + walnuts)
pineapple + brown sugar + honey + **rum + vanilla**
pineapple + brown sugar + lime
pineapple + carrots + cinnamon + raisins
pineapple + chiles + cilantro + garlic + lime + red onions
pineapple + chiles + lime + mint + tomatoes
pineapple + chiles + lime + red onions
pineapple + cilantro + lime
pineapple + cinnamon + curry + star anise
pineapple + coconut + brown sugar
pineapple + coconut + ginger + rum
pineapple + coconut + passion fruit + white chocolate
pineapple + coconut + rum
pineapple + coconut + yogurt
pineapple + ginger + maple syrup
pineapple + honey + mint + yogurt
pineapple + kiwi + mango + papaya
pineapple + *lassi* + star anise + yogurt
pineapple + lime + mint
pineapple + peanuts + yams

Dishes

Grilled Pineapple Crisp: Pineapple baked with Ginger, Lime, and Brown Sugar and a Crisp Walnut-Oat Topping
— Great Sage (Clarksville, MD)

Annana Epice, Roti, Couli de Mures: Roast Smoked Chipotle Spiced Pineapple with a touch of Sea Salt, Coconut Sorbet, and a Blackberry Sauce
— Table Verte (New York City)

rosemary
rum, e.g., white
sage
salad dressings
salads, e.g., fruit
SALSAS
salt, e.g., kosher
sauces, e.g., teriyaki
scallions
seeds, e.g., pumpkin, sunflower
seitan
skewers, fruit
SMOOTHIES
sorbets
soups
sour cream
spirits, e.g., gin, **RUM**
star anise
stews, e.g., vegetable
stir-fries
SUGAR, e.g., BROWN
sweet potatoes
tempeh
tofu
tomatoes
VANILLA
Vietnamese cuisine
vinegar, e.g., apple cider, red
   wine, rice, white wine
YOGURT

"All Jamaicans grow up eating
pineapple chicken. I love making
[vegan] pineapple stew, sautéing
vegetables with pineapple, white
rum, and brown sugar, with a
dash of either apple cider or red
wine vinegar, so that the stew is
sweet and spicy and tangy."
— SHAWAIN WHYTE, CAFÉ BLOSSOM
(NEW YORK CITY)

● PINE NUTS (aka PIGNOLI)

Flavor: slightly sweet, with notes
of butter and/or pine resin, and a
rich, soft texture

Volume: moderate – loud
Nutritional profile: 85% fats /
8% carbs / 7% protein
Calories: 190 per 1-ounce
serving
Protein: 4 grams
What they are: seeds of certain
kinds of pine trees
Techniques: raw, roast, toast

(North) African cuisine
anise
apples
apricots
arugula
asparagus
baked goods, e.g., cookies
BASIL
beans, green
beets
bell peppers, e.g., red
breadcrumbs
BROCCOLI
broccoli rabe
carrots
chard, Swiss
CHEESE, e.g., feta, goat,
   mozzarella, **PARMESAN, ricotta**
chickpeas
couscous
cranberries, dried
currants, e.g., dried
desserts
eggplant
endive
escarole
fennel
GARLIC
GRAINS, WHOLE, e.g., bulgur,
   couscous, millet, quinoa, spelt,
   wheat berries
GREENS, BITTER, e.g., beet,
   collard
greens, salad
Italian cuisine, esp. southern
kale
lemon, e.g., juice
lettuce, e.g., romaine

maple syrup
mascarpone
(Eastern) Mediterranean cuisines
Mexican cuisine
Middle Eastern cuisines
nuts, other, e.g., almonds, pistachios, walnuts
oil, nut, e.g., pine nut, walnut
olive oil
olives
onions
oranges, e.g., blood
parsley
PASTAS: fettuccine, orzo, penne, ravioli, spaghetti
*PESTOS
pilafs
potatoes, e.g., new
radicchio
RAISINS
rice
"ricotta," pine nut
risottos
rosemary
saffron
sage
SALADS, e.g., fruit, green, pasta, spinach
sauces
soups
SPINACH
squash, e.g., summer, winter
stuffed grape leaves
sweet potatoes
tahini
tangerines
tofu, e.g., silken
TOMATOES and sun-dried tomatoes
Turkish cuisine
vanilla
vegetables, e.g., roasted
watercress
wheat berries
zucchini

Flavor Affinities

pine nuts + basil + garlic + olive oil + Parmesan cheese
pine nuts + beets + mascarpone
pine nuts + bitter greens + raisins
pine nuts + broccoli + pasta
pine nuts + couscous + lemon
pine nuts + currants + rice
pine nuts + garlic + green beans
pine nuts + garlic + spinach
pine nuts + goat cheese + pesto + sun-dried tomatoes
pine nuts + olives + oranges + parsley
pine nuts + olives + pasta + tomatoes

● PISTACHIOS

Flavor: notes of butter and nuts, and a rich texture
Volume: moderate
What they are: nuts
Nutritional profile: 67% fats / 20% carbs / 13% protein
Calories: 345 per ½-cup serving (raw)
Protein: 12 grams
Techniques: raw, roast
Botanical relatives: cashews, mangoes, sumac

almonds
APRICOTS, e.g., dried
arugula
asparagus
avocados
BAKED GOODS, e.g., BAKLAVA, cakes, cookies, muffins, quick breads
basil
beets
biryani

Dishes

Braised Baby Beets: Endive, Green Celery, Blue Cheese, Pistachios, Raspberry Vinaigrette
— Glenmere Mansion (Chester, NY)

broccoli
Brussels sprouts
bulgur
CARDAMOM
carrots
celery
cheese, e.g., blue, goat, Gorgonzola, Parmesan, ricotta, Taleggio
cherries
chili powder
chocolate, e.g., dark, white
coconut
cornmeal
couscous
cranberries
currants
curries and curry powder/spices
dates
desserts
dips
eggplant
endive
FIGS
fruit, dried
garlic
ginger
granola
grapefruit grapes
honey
ICE CREAM
Italian cuisine
lemon
lentils
lime, e.g., juice, zest
mangoes
maple syrup
Mediterranean cuisines
Middle Eastern cuisines
mint
oatmeal and oats
ORANGE

PASTAS
pâtés
peaches
"PESTOS"
phyllo dough
pilafs
pineapple
pine nuts
pomegranate
puddings
quinces
quinoa
rhubarb
rice, esp. wild
rice puddings
rose water
saffron
salads, e.g., grain
salt, e.g., sea
sauces
smoothies
squash, e.g., butternut
sugar, e.g., maple
sumac
tahini
tomatoes
Turkish cuisine
vanilla
vegetables

Flavor Affinities
pistachios + almonds + rose water
pistachios + apricots + dates
pistachios + basil + mint
pistachios + Brussels sprouts + olive oil + vinegar
pistachios + cardamom + orange
pistachios + cardamom + *puddings* + rice + rose water
pistachios + chili powder + garlic powder + onion powder
pistachios + citrus + mango
pistachios + dried fruit (e.g., apricots, cherries) + **grains** (couscous, quinoa)
pistachios + garlic + orange
pistachios + goat cheese + grapes
pistachios + goat cheese + tomatoes
pistachios + pine nuts + rice + saffron
pistachios + rhubarb + yogurt
pistachios + strawberries + yogurt

vinegar, e.g., raspberry
walnuts
watercress
watermelon
YOGURT

● PLANTAINS — IN GENERAL, or MIXED

Flavor: range from savory and starchy (green) to slightly sweet and firm (yellow/brown) to sweet and creamy (black), with fruity (banana-like) notes
Volume: quiet/moderate (green) – moderate (yellow, black)
What they are: fruit
Nutritional profile: 97% carbs (high in sugars) / 2% protein / 1% fats
Calories: 235 per 1-cup serving (cooked, mashed)
Protein: 2 grams
Techniques: bake (at 350°F, 45 – 60 minutes), boil (25 – 40 minutes), broil, deep-fry, grill, mash, raw (*only* when all black), sauté, simmer, steam (about 10 minutes)

Tips: Serve as a starchy vegetable. When adding to soups or stews, add during the last 10 minutes of the cooking process.

Botanical relative: bananas

African cuisine
almonds
BEANS, BLACK
bell peppers
butter
Caribbean cuisine
Central American cuisine
cheese, e.g., blue, goat
chiles, chili pepper flakes, and chili pepper sauce
cinnamon
coconut and coconut milk
Cuban cuisine
fruit, tropical, e.g., papaya, **pineapple**
ginger
Latin American cuisines
lemon
LIME, e.g., juice
oils, e.g., coconut, olive, vegetable
onions, e.g., red, yellow
rice, e.g., jasmine

PLANTAINS, GREEN

Flavor: neutral, with a starchy texture
Volume: quiet – moderate
Techniques: bake, boil, deep-fry, fry, mash, sauté, stew

Tip: Look for green plantains without any yellow.

African cuisine
beans, e.g., black, pinto
butter
cardamom
Caribbean cuisine
Central American cuisine
cheese, e.g., queso fresco

chickpeas
chiles and chili powder
chips, plantain
cilantro
cinnamon
cloves
coconut and coconut cream
coriander
cumin
curry
fruits, tropical
garam masala
garlic
ginger
lime, e.g., juice
Mexican cuisine
molasses
mole sauces
oils, e.g., achiote, almond, **olive**,
   vegetable
olives
onions, e.g., red
paprika
pepper, black
Puerto Rican cuisine
rice
salsa
salt, e.g., kosher
scallions
shallots
soups
STEWS
thyme
TOSTONES
yogurt

Flavor Affinities
green plantains + garlic + thyme

PLANTAINS, SWEET (e.g., BROWN or YELLOW)

Flavor: sweet, with notes of banana, and a soft, creamy yet firm texture
Volume: moderate

Techniques: bake, boil, deep-fry, grill, mash, pan-fry, sauté

African cuisine
allspice
beans, black
bell peppers, e.g., green
butter
Central American cuisine
chocolate
cilantro
cinnamon
cloves
coconut milk
Cuban cuisine
desserts, e.g., puddings
fruits, tropical
garlic
ginger
honey
lemon
lime
Mexican cuisine
molasses
oil, olive
onions, red
orange
pepper, black
raisins
rice, e.g., brown
rum, esp. dark
salt
scallions
soups
star anise
stews, vegetable
sugar, e.g., brown

Dishes

Black Bean and Plantain Tamales: Corn Husk-Steamed Tamales studded with Black Beans and Sweet Plantains. Red Guajillo Chile Sauce, Sour Cream, Queso Añejo, Arugula Salad
— Frontera Grill (Chicago)

Flavor Affinities
sweet plantains + bell peppers + black beans + cilantro + rice + scallions

• PLUMS

Season: summer – autumn
Flavor: **sweet** and/or sour, with astringent notes of cherries, citrus, and/or honey, and a very juicy texture
Volume: quiet – moderate
Nutritional profile: 90% carbs (high in sugars) / 5% protein / 5% fats
Calories: 30 per plum
Techniques: bake, poach, raw, stew
Botanical relatives: almonds, apples, apricots, blackberries, cherries, peaches, pears, quinces, raspberries, strawberries

allspice
anise hyssop
apples and apple juice
apricots
arugula
bananas
bay leaf
beans, e.g., black
bell peppers, e.g., red
blackberries
butter
caramel
cardamom
cheeses, e.g., blue, cream, feta, goat, manouri, soft

P

cherries
chiles, e.g., jalapeño, and chili
    powder
chocolate
chutneys
cilantro
CINNAMON
cloves
compotes, fruit
coriander
cream and crème fraîche
custard
dates
DESSERTS, e.g., cobblers, crisps,
    crumbles, pies, tarts
garlic
GINGER
grapefruit
HONEY, e.g., acacia, clover
Kirsch
LEMON, e.g., juice, zest
lime
liqueurs, e.g., brandy (e.g., plum)
maple syrup
mascarpone
mint
molasses
nectarines
nutmeg
NUTS, e.g., ALMONDS,
    hazelnuts, pecans, walnuts
oatmeal and oats
oil, olive
onions, red
ORANGE, e.g., juice, liqueur, zest
parsley
passion fruit
peaches
pears
pepper, e.g., black
ponzu
port
raspberries
rhubarb
sage
SALADS, e.g., fruit, green, spinach
salsas, e.g., plum

salt
sauces, e.g., plum
sesame, e.g., seeds
shallots
sorbets
star anise
strawberries
SUGAR, e.g., brown
VANILLA
VINEGAR, e.g., balsamic,
    champagne, red wine, umeboshi
walnuts
wine, e.g., red, sweet, white
yogurt

Flavor Affinities
plums + almonds + cinnamon +
    orange
plums + almonds + honey +
    mascarpone
plums + barley + goat milk +
    honey
plums + brown sugar + oats
plums + chiles + garlic + ginger
    + lemon
plums + cinnamon + honey
plums + cinnamon + orange
plums + garlic + honey + olive oil
    + red onions + vinegar
plums + ginger + orange
plums + honey + orange + vanilla
plums + maple syrup + orange

───────────────────────

● **PLUMS, DRIED (aka
PRUNES) and DRIED
PLUM PUREE**
Flavor: sweet, with notes of
raisins, and a sticky, chewy
texture
Volume: moderate
Nutritional profile: 96% carbs
/ 3% protein / 1% fats
Calories: 210 per ½-cup serving
(pitted dried plums)
Protein: 2 grams
Techniques: poach, raw

Tip: Substitute puree of dried
plums for fat or oil in baking.

ALMONDS
apples
apricots
BAKED GOODS, e.g., breads,
    cakes, muffins
bananas
caramel
cheese, e.g., blue, Brie, cream,
    feta, goat, ricotta
chestnuts
CHOCOLATE, e.g., dark
CINNAMON
cloves
coffee
compotes
cornmeal
cream
crème fraîche
crisps
currants
desserts, e.g., cobblers
granola
hazelnuts
honey
ice cream
jams and preserves
LEMON
LIQUEURS, e.g., *ARMAGNAC,
    brandy (e.g., apple, pear),
cognac
mascarpone
nuts
oatmeal and oats
ORANGE, e.g., juice, zest
pancakes
pears
pecans
pistachios
poppy seeds
porridges
puddings, e.g., bread
raisins
salads
snacks

squash, winter, e.g., acorn
star anise
stews
sugar, e.g., brown
vanilla
vinegar, balsamic
WALNUTS
wine, e.g., fruity red (e.g.,
Beaujolais), port (e.g., tawny),
sweet white (e.g., Muscat,
Sauternes)
yogurt

Flavor Affinities
dried plums + apples + cinnamon
+ raisins
dried plums + brown sugar +
red wine
dried plums + caramel + pecans
dried plums + cinnamon +
orange

PLUMS, UMEBOSHI and UMEBOSHI PLUM PASTE (see UMEBOSHI PLUMS)

POLENTA (see CORNMEAL, from which polenta is made)

POMEGRANATE MOLASSES

Volume: loud (and louder than
fresh pomegranate seeds)

allspice
arugula
bananas
beans
bell peppers
beverages
bulgur
cardamom
carrots
cheese, e.g., goat
chickpeas

chiles
cinnamon
cloves
cumin
desserts
dips
drinks
eggplant
garlic
ginger
glazes
grapefruit
lemon, e.g., juice
lentils
marinades
Middle Eastern cuisines
mustard and mustard seeds
oil, olive
pears
pilafs
SALAD DRESSINGS
salads
sauces
sorbets
spinach
stews, e.g., lentil
Turkish cuisine
vegetables, esp. root
vinegar, e.g., balsamic
walnuts

• POMEGRANATES and • POMEGRANATE JUICE (see also POMEGRANATE MOLASSES)

Season: autumn
Flavor: sour/sweet, with notes
of cranberries, and juicy, crunchy
seeds (when fresh)
Volume: moderate (fresh seeds)
Nutritional profile: 81% carbs
/ 12% fats / 7% protein
Calories: 75 per ½-cup serving
(fresh seeds)
Protein: 1 gram
Techniques: juice, raw

Tips: While the season for
fresh pomegranates is short, the
fruit freezes well (e.g., whole,
in a zip-locked plastic bag). Just
thaw, cut open, and remove
the delicious, juicy seeds to add
to smoothies and other dishes,
all year long.

agave nectar
allspice
almonds
apples
arugula
avocado
bananas
barley
beans
bell peppers
bulgur
cardamom
carrots
cheese, e.g., cream, **goat**
cherries, e.g., dried, fresh
chickpeas
chiles, e.g., poblano
chocolate
cinnamon
cloves
coconut
couscous
cranberries, e.g., dried, fresh
cucumbers
cumin
curries
desserts, e.g., fruit cobblers and
crisps, ices, sorbets
dips
drinks
eggplant
endive
figs
frisée
garlic
ginger
glazes
grains

P

granita
grapefruit
greens, salad
honey
legumes
LEMON, e.g., juice
lentils, e.g., red
lime
maple syrup
marinades
Mediterranean cuisines
melon, e.g., bitter
Middle Eastern cuisines
mint
mustard and mustard seeds
oil, olive
olives, e.g., green
onions, e.g., red
ORANGES and orange juice, e.g.,
   blood, navel
parsley
pears
pecans
pilafs
pine nuts
pistachios
quinces
quinoa
rice
SALAD DRESSINGS
SALADS, e.g., cucumber, fruit, green
sauces
smoothies
SORBETS
soups, esp. autumn

Dishes

Jerk Pomegranate Molasses Seitan Steak
with Fresh Fennel, Candied Orange,
and Rose Petals, served on a bed of
Wild Rice
— Plum Bistro (Seattle)

Pomegranate Kiwi Pancakes with
Whipped Pomegranate Molasses Butter
and Crème Fraîche
— Plum Bistro (Seattle)

spinach
squash, winter, e.g., butternut,
   delicata
stews, e.g., lentil
sugar, e.g., brown
sumac
sweet potatoes
tahini
thyme
tomatoes
Turkish cuisine
vegetables, esp. root
vinegar, e.g., balsamic, sherry,
   red/white wine
WALNUTS
watermelon
wheat berries
yogurt
yuzu, e.g., juice

Flavor Affinities

pomegranates + apples +
   butternut squash + walnuts
pomegranates + arugula + endive
pomegranates + balsamic vinegar
   + pine nuts + spinach
pomegranates + bell peppers +
   chiles + cumin + lemon +
   walnuts
pomegranates + cucumbers +
   garlic + mint
pomegranates + goat cheese +
   orange + walnuts
pomegranates + grapefruit +
   greens + red onions
pomegranates + lemon + sugar
pomegranates + orange + yuzu

POMELO (see recommendations for GRAPEFRUIT)

Season: winter
Flavor: sour/sweet, with
grapefruit notes (although
milder, sweeter, and juicier than
grapefruit)
Volume: loud
What it is: citrus fruit

● POPCORN, e.g., air-popped

What it is: whole grain
What's healthful about it:
high in fiber, low in calories
(when air-popped)

Tips: Opt for organic popcorn,
as non-organic popcorn is on
the USDA's top 10 list of foods
contaminated with toxic chemicals and pesticides. Spritz with
a little soy sauce for flavor and
saltiness — or with a little olive
oil and a sprinkle of cheesy-
tasting nutritional yeast for a
dose of vitamin B12.

Washington Post food editor Joe
Yonan, author of *Eat Your Vegetables*, created his own version
of the addictive herbed popcorn
produced by Seventh-day Adventist vegetarian restaurant Little
Lad's, which features oil-popped
popcorn seasoned with nutritional yeast, dried oregano, dried
dill, dried thyme, crushed red
pepper flakes, and an optional
shake of fine sea salt.

almonds
caramel
cayenne
cheese, e.g., cheddar, Parmesan
chili pepper flakes
cinnamon
coconut, e.g., oil, sugar
coriander
cumin
curry powder
dill, dried
dulse
garlic and garlic powder
gomashio
herbs, esp. dried
honey
lemon
nutritional yeast
oil, e.g., coconut, grapeseed,

peanut
oil, truffle
onion powder
oregano, dried
parsley
peanut butter and peanuts
pecans
rosemary
sage
salt, sea
sesame seeds
soy sauce
sugar, brown
tamari
thyme
turmeric
vanilla

Flavor Affinities
popcorn + almonds + honey
popcorn + brown sugar +
cinnamon

POPPY SEEDS (see SEEDS, POPPY)

POSOLE (see HOMINY)

• POTATOES — IN GENERAL, WITH SKIN

Season: year-round, esp. summer – winter
Flavor: neutral, with earthy notes, and a starchy texture
Volume: quiet
What they are: vegetable — starchy
Nutritional profile: 93% carbs / 6% protein / 1% fats
Calories: 70 per ½-cup serving (boiled)
Protein: 1 gram
Techniques: bake (whole, wrapped in foil, at 400°F, about 50 – 60 minutes), boil (note: use the leftover, nutritious water for sauces, soups), deep-fry, fry, grill, mash (esp. older, starchier

potatoes), puree, roast (quartered, 20 – 40 minutes at 400°F), sauté, steam, stuff

Tips: Opt for organic potatoes. Leave the skins on for extra flavor, texture, and nutrition. Scrub well before cooking. Boil potatoes whole, not cut, so they don't absorb water. Before baking potatoes, poke with a fork several times so steam can escape. Potatoes are America's favorite vegetable (especially as French fries!), but don't forget the importance of enjoying a wide variety of vegetables to ensure yourself the benefits of an equally wide variety of nutrients.

Botanical relatives: bell peppers, chiles, eggplant, gooseberries, tomatillos, tomatoes
Possible substitutes for mashed potatoes: mashed white beans, millet, pureed cauliflower

arugula
asparagus
baked goods, e.g., breads, cakes
basil
bay leaf
beans, e.g., fava, **green**
bell peppers, e.g., green and/or roasted
broccoli
BUTTER
buttermilk
cabbage, e.g., savoy
capers
caraway seeds
cardamom
carrots
cashews
casseroles
cauliflower
cayenne
celery, **CELERY ROOT**, and

celery seeds
chard
CHEESE, e.g., Asiago, blue, **cheddar**, Fontina, **goat**, Gouda, **Gruyère**, Jack, manchego, mozzarella, **Parmesan**, pecorino, Swiss
chervil
chicory
chickpeas
chiles, e.g., chipotle
CHIVES and garlic chives
cilantro
cinnamon
cloves
coconut and coconut cream
coriander
corn
cream
crème fraîche
cumin
curry powder and spices
curries
dill
eggplant
EGGS, e.g., *frittatas*, hard-boiled, *omelets, quiches, tortillas*
fennel
fenugreek
French cuisine
garam masala
GARLIC
ginger
grains, whole, e.g., quinoa, spelt
gratins
greens, e.g., collard, mustard, salad, winter
horseradish
Indian cuisine
kale
lavender
LEEKS
lemon, e.g., juice, **zest**
lentils
lovage
marjoram
mayonnaise
milk, dairy or nondairy (e.g., rice, soy)

mint
MUSHROOMS, e.g., **morel**,
  porcini, portobello, **wild**
mustard, e.g., Dijon, oil, seeds
nutmeg
OIL, e.g., canola, chili, **OLIVE**,
  peanut, vegetable
okra
olives, e.g., black, green
ONIONS, e.g., **green**, red,
  Spanish, Vidalia, yellow

oregano
paprika
PARSLEY, esp. **flat-leaf**, and
  parsley root
parsnips
pasta, e.g., gnocchi
peas
peas, split
PEPPER, e.g., **BLACK**, white
pesto
pine nuts

Flavor Affinities

potatoes + black olives + lemon + sun-dried tomatoes
potatoes + buttermilk + chocolate + cinnamon + vanilla
potatoes + butternut squash + sage
potatoes + cauliflower + leeks
potatoes + celery root + parsnips
potatoes + cheddar cheese + chiles + corn
potatoes + chipotle chiles + garlic
potatoes + cilantro + coconut
potatoes + cream + garlic + thyme
potatoes + crème fraîche + dill
potatoes + fennel + garlic + leeks
potatoes + fennel + lemon + yogurt
potatoes + garlic + herbs (e.g., oregano, rosemary, sage)
potatoes + garlic + lemon + olive oil + **parsley** + vinegar
potatoes + garlic + lemon zest + parsley + rosemary + thyme
POTATOES + GARLIC + OLIVE OIL
potatoes + garlic + olive oil + walnuts
potatoes + Gruyère cheese + winter squash
potatoes + herbs (e.g., oregano, rosemary, thyme) + **lemon**
potatoes + leeks + nutmeg + onions + **parsley**

Dishes

Pierogis: Pan Seared, filled with Potato and Caramelized Onion, Cashew Sour Cream, Scallions

— Blossoming Lotus (Portland, OR)

Tomato-stuffed Russet Potato: Glazed Chanterelles, Romanesco Purée, Scallion Oil

—DANIEL (New York City)

Nichol's Farm Confit Potato Salad, Goat's Feta, Kalamata Olive, Shaved Onion, Oregano

— Green Zebra (Chicago)

Potato "Mille-Feuille" with Carrots, Salsify, and a Parsley Vinaigrette

— Picholine (New York City)

potato cakes / potato pancakes
ramps
ROSEMARY
rutabagas
saffron
SAGE
SALADS, e.g., egg, green, potato
  (cold or hot)
SALT, e.g., kosher, sea, smoked
savory
scallions
shallots
skordalia
SORREL
SOUPS, e.g., leek, potato, sorrel,
  vegetable
sour cream
spinach
squash, winter, e.g., butternut,
  delicata
stews
stock, vegetable
stuffed baked potatoes / twice-baked
  potatoes
sweet potatoes
tahini
tarragon
THYME
tomatoes
truffles, e.g., black, white
turmeric
turnips
vegetables, root
vinegar, e.g., champagne, sherry,
  white wine
walnuts
watercress
wine, e.g., dry white
yogurt

POTATOES, BLUE (or PURPLE)
Season: year-round, esp.
summer – mid-winter
Flavor: neutral, with earthy
notes of nuts, and a dry, floury,
starchy texture
Volume: quiet

What's healthful about them:
antioxidants
Techniques: bake, boil, fry, grill, mash, roast, steam

Tips: Keep the nutritious skins on when cooking. Lemon juice enhances the brightness of their color while accenting their flavor.

artichokes
beans
butter
cheese, e.g., cheddar, cotija
chiles, e.g., poblano
chips
chives
cilantro
corn
cream
garlic
greens, e.g., salad
lemon, e.g., juice

mashed potatoes
oil, e.g., chive, olive
paprika, e.g., smoked
parsley
Peruvian cuisine
salads, e.g., green, potato
salt, e.g., sea
shallots
soups, e.g., potato, vegetable
thyme
vinegar, e.g., apple cider, red wine

"While I was first attracted to **purple potatoes** for their beautiful color, I love them for their flavor, which is nuttier and with more body than your typical Russet or yellow potato. I serve them smashed with any herb, some salt and pepper, and a little lemon juice or zest — or smashed and served with pesto tofu."
— MAKINI HOWELL, PLUM BISTRO (SEATTLE)

POTATOES, FINGERLING
Flavor: slightly sweet, with rich, earthy notes of butter and/or nuts, and a firm, waxy texture
Volume: quiet
Techniques: braise, oven-roast, pan-fry, roast

beans, green
butter
capers
cashew cream
chervil
chiles, e.g., jalapeño
chives
cream
dulse
eggs, e.g., *frittatas*
fines herbes
garlic
horseradish
mayonnaise

P

oil, olive
paprika, smoked
parsley
pepper, black
pizzas
rosemary
sage
salads, e.g., green, green bean,
*   potato*
salt, e.g., sea
shallots
soups and chowders, e.g., corn
tarragon
Worcestershire sauce,
   vegetarian

POTATOES, HIGH-STARCH (e.g., IDAHO, RUSSET)

Tip: High-starch potatoes leave a creamy white liquid on the knife when cut; the greater the residue, the higher the level of starch.

Techniques: bake, fry, **mash**

POTATOES, LOW-STARCH (e.g., NEW)

boiled potatoes
gratins
salads, potato

POTATOES, NEW (aka RED POTATOES)

Season: spring – summer
Flavor: slightly sweet, with a moist, creamy texture
Volume: quiet
What they are: freshly harvested potatoes of the season
Techniques: boil, mash, roast, salt-bake, steam (Avoid frying.)

capers
carrots
cashews, e.g., ground raw

chives
cream
dill
garlic
gratins
herbs
horseradish
leeks
lemon, e.g., juice
mint
mustard, e.g., Dijon
oil, olive
paprika
parsley
pepper, e.g., black, white
rosemary
saffron
salads, e.g., green, potato
salt, e.g., sea
savory
scallions
shallots
soups and bisques
sour cream
stews
stock, vegetable
tarragon
thyme
vinegar, e.g., apple cider
walnuts
yogurt

Flavor Affinities

new potatoes + chives + lemon + olive oil
new potatoes + cider vinegar + **dill** + horseradish + **olive oil**
new potatoes + dill + *mash* + **olive oil** + parsley + soy milk
new potatoes + garlic + lemon + mustard
new potatoes + garlic + shallots + tarragon + vinegar
new potatoes + horseradish + mustard + scallions + yogurt

POTATOES, RED (see POTATOES, NEW)

POTATOES, RUSSET

Flavor: slightly sweet, with earthy notes, and dry, crumbly/fluffy texture with a thick, chewy skin
Volume: quiet
Techniques: bake, fry, **mash,** roast

Tip: As they don't hold their shape well, russets are not recommended for casseroles or salads.

baked "fries"
baked potatoes
chives
gnocchi
mashed potatoes
sour cream

POTATOES, SWEET (see SWEET POTATOES)

POTATOES, THICK-SKINNED (e.g., IDAHO, RUSSET)

Techniques: bake, fry

POTATOES, THIN-SKINNED (e.g., NEW POTATOES, WHITE POTATOES)

Techniques: boil, pressure-cook, steam

POTATOES, WHITE

Flavor: neutral, with a thin skin
Volume: quiet
Techniques: boil, fry, mash, steam

casseroles
mashed potatoes with skins
salads, e.g., potato
soups
stews

POTATOES, YELLOW (e.g., YUKON GOLD)

Flavor: slightly sweet, with notes of butter, and a rich texture
Volume: quiet
What they are: versatile, all-purpose, medium-starch potatoes
Techniques: bake (whole, 60 minutes at 400°F), boil, grill, mash, roast (quartered, 20 – 40 minutes at 400°F)

apples
baked potatoes
chives
mashed potatoes
roasted potatoes
sage
salads, e.g., potato
sour cream

PRESSURE-COOKING

Tip: Cooks foods 50 – 70 percent faster than traditional methods — which is especially helpful when it comes to slow-cooking foods such as **dried beans** and **grains**.

"I love **pressure-cooking** beans and grains, not only because it's faster but because it makes them more digestible. Chickpeas that would normally take hours and hours of boiling will be done in 60 minutes in a pressure-cooker. The only beans I won't pressure-cook are white beans, because it makes them too mushy for our arugula salad that features them. And you shouldn't pressure-cook split peas or soybeans because they foam, which can clog the mechanism and make it explode — something I unfortunately learned the hard way after just painting my kitchen. . . . Brown rice can pressure-cook in just 40 minutes, and only needs a 1:2 rice-to-liquid ratio, because you don't need much liquid when pressure-cooking."

— PAM BROWN, GARDEN CAFÉ ON THE GREEN (WOODSTOCK, NY)

PRUNES and PRUNE PUREE (see PLUMS, DRIED)

PULSES (see also specific BEANS, CHICKPEAS, specific LENTILS; PEAS, SPLIT)

What they are: legumes
Protein: up to 9 grams per ½-cup serving
Tips: A half-cup of cooked pulses is equivalent to one serving of vegetables and the protein in two ounces of meat. For more information, visit the website cookingwithpulses.com.

African cuisines
Australian cuisine
Indian cuisines
Mediterranean cuisines
Middle Eastern cuisines
South American cuisines

"With up to 9 grams of protein per half-cup serving, **pulses** offer a low-fat or fat-free alternative to animal proteins. Pulses improve the protein quality of cereal grains, by adding a complimentary amino acid profile. **Due to the high nutrient density, pulses can be considered both a protein and a vegetable.**"

— COOKINGWITHPULSES.COM

• PUMPKIN (see also SQUASH, WINTER)

Season: autumn
Flavor: sweet, with earthy notes of sweet potatoes, and a dense, fibrous texture
Volume: quiet – moderate
What it is: Technically, pumpkins are a hard-rind (i.e., winter) squash.
Nutritional profile: 88% carbs / 9% protein / 3% fats
Calories: 50 per 1-cup serving (cooked, mashed)
Protein: 2 grams
Techniques: bake (at 350 – 400°F, 45 – 60 minutes), boil, grill, mash, puree, roast (at 350°F for 60 minutes), steam
Tip: For ease of use, consider canned pumpkin.
Botanical relatives: cucumbers, melons, squashes
Possible substitutes: carrots, winter squash

ALLSPICE
almonds
American cuisine
APPLES, apple cider, and apple juice
baked baby pumpkins
BAKED GOODS, e.g., bread puddings, breads, cookies, muffins, pies, quick breads, scones
basil
BAY LEAF
BEANS, e.g., Anasazi, black, **cannellini**, kidney, lima, pinto, **white**
brandy
breadcrumbs
butter and brown butter
caramel
cardamom
carrots
cashews
cayenne
celery
CHEESE, e.g., blue, **cream**, Emmental, **feta**, Fontina,

goat, **GRUYÈRE**, mozzarella,
PARMESAN, pecorino, ricotta,
Romano, soft, Swiss, vegan
cheesecake
chestnuts
chickpeas
CHILES, e.g., ancho, chipotle,
green, guajillo, habanero,
orange, red, Scotch bonnet
chili pepper flakes
chives
chocolate, e.g., dark, white
cilantro
CINNAMON
CLOVES
COCONUT and COCONUT MILK
cognac
coriander
corn
couscous
cranberries, e.g., dried, and
cranberry juice
cream

cumin
curries **and curry leaves, paste,**
powder
custards
desserts, e.g., cheesecakes, pies
fennel and fennel seeds
frisée
garam masala
GARLIC
GINGER
graham cracker crumbs
gratins
greens
hazelnuts
honey
leeks
lemon, e.g., juice, zest
lemongrass
lime, e.g., juice, zest
mace
MAPLE SYRUP
milk, dairy or nondairy, e.g.,
coconut, soy

millet
mint
mirin
miso, e.g., light
molasses
mushrooms, e.g., shiitake,
wood ear
mustard and mustard seeds
NUTMEG
nuts
oats and oatmeal
OILS, e.g., **nut**, **olive**, peanut,
pumpkin seed, sesame,
sunflower, vegetable, walnut
ONIONS, e.g., red, white
ORANGE, e.g., juice, zest
pancakes and waffles
paprika
parsley
parsnips
PASTAS, e.g., cannelloni, gnocchi,
orzo, ravioli, tortellini
peanuts

Flavor Affinities

pumpkin + allspice + **cinnamon** + **ginger** + **orange** + vanilla
pumpkin + almonds + raisins
pumpkin + apples + cilantro + curry + leeks
pumpkin + balsamic vinegar + Parmesan cheese + sage
pumpkin + black sesame + corn + spinach
pumpkin + breadcrumbs + garlic + parsley
pumpkin + brown sugar + **cinnamon** + **cloves** + **ginger** + **nutmeg** +
orange + walnuts
pumpkin + cardamom + **cinnamon** + **cloves**
pumpkin + chickpeas + cilantro + garlic + ginger + lemongrass
pumpkin + chiles + garlic + orange + rosemary
pumpkin + **cinnamon** + **cloves** + coconut milk + **ginger** + **nutmeg** +
vanilla
pumpkin + **cinnamon** + **ginger** + maple syrup + pecans
pumpkin + **cinnamon** + **ginger** + oatmeal + raisins
PUMPKIN + **CINNAMON** + **MAPLE SYRUP**
pumpkin + coconut milk + curry paste
pumpkin + cranberries + orange
pumpkin + cream cheese + graham cracker crumbs + orange
pumpkin + garlic + olive oil + rosemary + thyme
pumpkin + nutmeg Parmesan cheese
pumpkin + oats + sage + walnuts
pumpkin + onions + sage + *soups* + soy milk

pears
PECANS
pepper, e.g., **black**, white
PIES
pineapple
pine nuts
pistachios
plantains
plums, dried
potatoes
puddings
PUMPKIN SEEDS

quinces
radicchio
raisins
RICE, e.g., Arborio, brown,
long-grain
rice, wild
rice syrup *risottos*
rosemary
rum
SAGE
salt, e.g., kosher, sea
sesame seeds, e.g., black

soufflés
SOUPS, e.g., pumpkin, winter
vegetable
Southeast Asian cuisines
soy sauce
spinach
stews
stock, vegetable
stuffed mini-pumpkins
SUGAR, e.g., brown
tarragon
thyme
tofu, e.g., firm
TOMATOES, e.g., paste, sauce,
sun-dried
vanilla
vegetables, root
vinegar, e.g., balsamic,
champagne
WALNUTS
wine, white
yogurt
zucchini

Dishes

Pumpkin Mousse with Cranberries and Candied Pecans
— Angelica Kitchen (New York City)

Pumpkin Cinnamon Roll: Housemade Jumbo Cinnamon Roll with Pumpkin and Pecans
— Blossoming Lotus (Portland, OR)

Griddled Pumpkin Bread: Ginger Purée, Pumpkin Jam, and Oatmeal Sherbet
— CityZen (Washington, DC)

Pumpkin Enchiladas: Pumpkin, Black Beans, Roasted Corn, Cilantro, and Chiles wrapped
in Corn Tortillas, topped with Cilantro "Sour Cream" and Mole, over Spanish Quinoa
— Great Sage (Clarksville, MD)

Pumpkin Coconut Bisque with Pumpkin Seeds
— The Lodge at Woodloch (Hawley, PA)

Tamale: Pumpkin and Roasted Jalapeño Tamale with Pumpkin Seed Mole
— Mana Food Bar (Chicago)

Pumpkin Custard: Spiced Whipped Cream, Candied Pumpkin Seeds, Caramel Sauce,
Ginger Molasses Cookies
— Millennium (San Francisco)

"Seminole" Pumpkin Roasted with Vadouvan and Hibiscus, Braised Borage, "Delfino"
Cilantro
— Oxheart (Houston)

Pumpkin Pancakes with Whipped Maple Butter, Maple Syrup, Pumpkin Seeds, Brown
Sugar, and Raisins
— Plum Bistro (Seattle)

Pumpkin Sage Ravioli with Roasted Fennel Cream Sauce, Maple Smoked Tofu,
and Pumpkin
— Plum Bistro (Seattle)

Pumpkin Cheesecake, Pecan Crust, Bourbon, and Brown Sugar Cream
— True Bistro (Somerville, MA)

PUMPKIN SEEDS (see SEEDS, PUMPKIN)

• PURSLANE (aka VERDOLAGA)

Season: summer –
early autumn
Flavor: bitter/salty/**sour**, with
notes of cucumber, lemon,
pepper, sorrel, and/or tomato,
and a crunchy, juicy texture
Volume: very quiet / quiet
(raw) – moderate (cooked)
What it is: herb/green
Nutritional profile: 71% carbs /
20% protein / 9% fats
Calories: 20 per 1-cup serving
(cooked)
Protein: 2 grams
Techniques: raw, sauté, steam
Tips: Can cook like spinach.
Bitterness increases during
cooking, so cook only lightly.

P

arugula
basil
beans, e.g., green, pinto
beets
bell peppers
bread, e.g., pita
Brussels sprouts
butter
buttermilk
carrots
cheese, e.g., feta, goat, Jack, mozzarella
chickpeas
chiles, e.g., green, jalapeño
chives
cilantro
CITRUS
couscous, Israeli
cream
cucumbers
dill
dips
eggplant
eggs, e.g., *frittatas*
garlic
grapefruit
hazelnuts
honey
kale, e.g., baby
lemon
lentils, e.g., beluga
lettuce, e.g., romaine
Mexican cuisine
mint
mustard, Dijon
noodles, rice
oil, olive
olives

onions, e.g., cipollini, green, red, white
oranges
parsley
pepper, black
pistachios
potatoes
Provençal (French) cuisine
radishes
salad dressings
*SALADS, e.g., bread, chopped, cucumber, egg, fattoush, green, **potato**, vegetable*
salsas
salt, sea
sandwiches
scallions
shallots
sorrel
soups, e.g., Bonne Femme
sour cream
squash, e.g., delicata, summer
stock, vegetable
sumac
tahini
tarragon
tomatillos
TOMATOES
vinegar, e.g., rice
yogurt
zucchini

Flavor Affinities

purslane + basil + croutons + cucumbers + olive oil + onions + tomatoes + vinegar
purslane + basil + goat cheese + scallions + tomatoes
purslane + feta cheese + tomatoes

purslane + garlic + nutmeg + onion + potatoes + sorrel
purslane + garlic + yogurt
purslane + romaine + scallions

"**Purslane** is one of those ingredients that people will taste and ask, 'What is that?' I enjoy it in the summertime raw in salads, or lightly sautéed — but be aware that it cooks down a lot."
— ANGEL RAMOS, CANDLE 79 (NEW YORK CITY)

QUELITES (see LAMB'S-QUARTER)

● QUINCES

Season: autumn
Flavor: sour, with notes of apples, flowers, and/or pears, and a very hard texture
Volume: quiet – moderate
Nutritional profile: 97% carbs / 2% protein / 1% fat
Calories: 50 per medium quince (raw)
Techniques: bake, poach (e.g., in simple syrup and/or wine), stew

Tips: Never serve raw. Remove skin before serving. High in pectin (a gelling agent), quinces can substitute for powdered pectin in certain preparations.

Botanical relatives: almonds, apples, apricots, blackberries, cherries, peaches, pears, plums, raspberries, strawberries

Dishes

Mâche and Purslane Salad with Roasted Delicata Squash, Cipollini Onions, Brussels Sprouts, Chickpeas, Radish, and Sunflower Seeds, tossed with a Creamy Tarragon Dressing
— Candle 79 (New York City)

Dishes

Sticky Toffee Pudding: Quince, Amaretto, and Honey
— Mélisse (Santa Monica, CA)

*APPLES and APPLE JUICE

baked goods, e.g., cakes, crisps, pies
butter
CHEESE, e.g., blue, cream, goat,
    Gorgonzola, manchego, ricotta,
    soft, Spanish, esp. with quince
    paste
cherries, dried tart
chicory
chili pepper flakes
chutneys
cilantro
CINNAMON
compotes
coriander
cream
crème fraîche
crepes
cumin
desserts, e.g., apple or pear: crisps,
    crumbles, tarts
ginger
honey
lemon, e.g., juice
maple syrup
nutmeg
nuts, e.g., almonds, pecans,
    pistachios, walnuts
oil, e.g., nut, walnut
orange
pancakes
paste, aka membrillo
*PEARS
pies and tarts, e.g., apple, pear
pomegranates and pomegranate
    molasses
preserves/jams
puddings, e.g., bread, rice
raspberries
salads, e.g., green
SUGAR, e.g., BROWN
vanilla
vinegar, e.g., balsamic,
    champagne, rice
wine, e.g., sweet, white
yogurt

Flavor Affinities

quince + apples + cinnamon
quince + blue cheese + greens
    + sherry vinegar + walnut oil
    + walnuts
quince + cinnamon + ginger +
    pancakes

● QUINOA
[KEEN-wah]
Flavor: bitter/slightly sweet,
with earthy notes of couscous,
grass, herbs, millet, **nuts**, and/
or sesame, and a light and fluffy
(when cooked), slightly crunchy
texture
Volume: quiet – moderate
What it is: often thought of
as a whole grain, even though
it's the fruit of an herb, not
a grain
What's healthful about it:
Most quinoa contains 15 – 20%
protein (higher than the
typical 14% of wheat, 9 – 11%
of millet, and 7 – 8% of rice),
and is richer in calcium than
milk.
Gluten-free: yes
Nutritional profile: 71% carbs /
15% protein / 14% fat
Calories: 220 per 1-cup serving
(cooked)
Protein: 8 grams
Techniques: boil, simmer,
steam, toast
Timing: Cooks in 10 – 15
(white) to 20 (red) to 30 (black)
minutes.
Ratio: 1: 1½ – 2 (1 cup quinoa to
1½ – 2 cups liquid, e.g.,
stock, water)

Tips: Quinoa must be rinsed
very well before cooking, to
remove all traces of bitterness
(and "suds" from the rinse
water). Toast first before using
in dishes to enhance its flavor.
For enhanced flavor and texture,
try sautéing for 5 minutes before
adding liquid — and/or substituting vegetable stock or juice,
or fruit juice (e.g., orange or
passion fruit), for some or all of
the water. Fluff with a fork after
cooking to separate the grains
(and remember that black and
red quinoa won't stick together
as much as white). Quinoa
doesn't get mushy, even when
overcooked.

Botanical relatives: amaranth,
beets, chard, lambs'-quarter,
spinach

almonds and almond milk
arugula
avocados
baked goods, multigrain, e.g.,
    breads, muffins
basil
BEANS, e.g., adzuki, **BLACK**,
    fava, green, kidney, lima, navy,
    pinto, **white**
beets
bell peppers, esp. red or yellow
carrots
celery
cereals, hot breakfast
chard, Swiss
CHEESE, esp. FETA, goat,
    Parmesan, ricotta salata
chiles, e.g., chipotle, green
chives
cilantro
CITRUS, e.g., lemon, lime,
    orange, i.e., juice, zest
CORN
cucumbers
cumin

Dishes

Quinoa with Snow Peas, Sugar Snaps, and Ginger
— ABC Kitchen (New York City)

Veggie Burger: Butternut Squash and Quinoa Patty, Roasted Red Peppers, Avocado, Lettuce, Tomato, Mayo on a Semolina Bun
— Blossom (New York City)

Homestyle Quinoa Pancakes with Seasonal Fruit, Strawberry Butter, and Gingered Maple Syrup
— Candle 79 (New York City)

Tempeh Vegetable Tamale with Quinoa Pilaf, Sautéed Spinach, Pumpkin Seeds, Chocolate Mole Sauce, Guacamole, Sour Cream, and Mango Salsa
— Candle 79 (New York City)

Red Quinoa: Pan-Roasted Fresh Artichoke Hearts and Fava Beans / Light Tomato Broth
— Crossroads (Los Angeles)

Quinoa Salad with Fennel, Avocado, and Grapefruit
— Lake Austin Spa Resort (Austin, TX)

Quinoa and Wakame Salad with Sesame Ginger Vinaigrette
— The Lodge at Woodloch (Hawley, PA)

Quinoa and Baby Greens Salad, Pomegranate, Candied Walnuts, Dried Cranberries
— Madeleine Bistro (Los Angeles)

Quinoa: Toasted Grain, Currants, Almonds, Mint, and Tangerine
— Mana Food Bar (Chicago)

Quinoa with Crushed Pistachio and Za'atar (i.e., herbs, salt, sesame, sumac)
— Oleana (Cambridge, MA)

Gluten-Free Quinoa Johnny Cake with Banana, Maple Syrup, and Greek Yogurt
— True Food Kitchen (Phoenix)

Quinoa Tabbouleh Salad with Watercress, Beet, Pomegranate, Lemon, and Cold-Pressed Olive Oil
— True Food Kitchen (Santa Monica, CA)

endive
fruit, dried, e.g., apricots, cranberries, currants, raisins
garlic
grains, other, e.g., quieter-flavored
greens, e.g., beet, collard
kale
Mexican cuisine, e.g., enchiladas, fajitas, salsas

mint
mushrooms, esp. cremini, shiitake
NUTS, esp. almonds, **cashews**, peanuts, **PECANS**, pine nuts (esp. toasted), pistachios, walnuts
OIL, e.g., **OLIVE**, walnut
ONIONS, e.g., green, red, spring, white, yellow

oregano
parsley
pilafs
pineapple
pomegranate seeds
SALADS, e.g., grain, green
salt, esp. sea
scallions
soups, e.g., cucumber
South American cuisines
SPINACH
squash, esp. winter, e.g., acorn, butternut
stews
stock, e.g., mushroom, vegetable
stuffed vegetables, e.g., bell peppers, tomatoes, zucchini
stuffings
"sushi," e.g., maki rolls stuffed with quinoa
"tabbouleh"
TOMATOES, e.g., cherry, **red**, sun-dried
veggie burgers
vinegar, e.g., balsamic, champagne, red wine, rice, sherry, umeboshi
yogurt
zucchini

Flavor Affinities
quinoa + almond milk + cinnamon + nuts
quinoa + bell peppers + carrots + parsley + rice vinegar + sesame oil/seeds
quinoa + black beans + cumin
quinoa + black beans + mango
quinoa + cashews + pineapple
quinoa + cucumbers + feta cheese + parsley + **tomatoes**
quinoa + cucumbers + lemon + mint + **parsley**
QUINOA + DILL + LEMON JUICE + zucchini

"Eating plain white **quinoa** can be like eating bird food. What I like to do is mix it with red and black quinoa, which gives you great flavor and texture with some nuttiness and chew to it."

— CHARLEEN BADMAN, FnB RESTAURANT (SCOTTSDALE, AZ)

"I love **quinoa**. I especially like making quinoa tabbolueh. I add onions, tomatoes, cucumber, parsley, lemon, and salt. You don't have to cook it that long and it absorbs all the flavors."

— AMANDA COHEN, DIRT CANDY (NEW YORK CITY)

"Every ingredient in our dishes is there for a reason — either flavor, texture, and/or its health benefit. **Quinoa** is kind of our 'house grain' because of all of the above — it's great in salads, and golden quinoa is one of two key ingredients [along with black beans] in our signature Root veggie burger. Our burgers are also made with pureed carrots, garlic, onions, and breadcrumbs seasoned with black pepper and paprika before shaping into patties. To achieve their meaty texture, they're cooked twice — the first time slowly on low heat on the grill, and the second time seared on high heat to crisp it."

— DEENA JALAL, FOMU AND ROOT (ALLSTON, MA)

● RADICCHIO

[rod-EEK-ee-oh]

Season: year-round, esp. summer – winter

Flavor: bitter, with earthy notes, and crisp/crunchy and firm in texture

Volume: moderate – loud

Nutritional profile: 76% carbs / 15% protein / 9% fats

Calories: 10 per 1-cup serving (raw, shredded)

Protein: 1 gram

Techniques: bake, **braise**, broil, **grill**, julienne, oven-grill, **raw**, roast, **sauté**, sear, steam, stir-fry

Tip: Cooking radicchio (and, cookbook author Marcella Hazan says, slicing it thinly on the diagonal) brings out its sweetness.

Botanical relatives: artichokes, chamomile, chicory, dandelion greens, endive, lettuces (e.g., Bibb, iceberg, romaine), salsify, tarragon

apples
arugula
basil
bay leaf
BEANS, e.g., cannellini, white
beets
breadcrumbs
butter
cabbage, e.g., savoy
capers
carrots
CHEESE, e.g., pungent: Asiago, blue (**Gorgonzola**, Roquefort, Stilton), feta, Fontina, goat, Gruyère, **mozzarella**, **PARMESAN**, pecorino, ricotta, Taleggio
chickpeas
chicory
chili pepper flakes
chives
citrus
eggs, e.g., hard-boiled, *omelets*
endive
escarole

FENNEL and fennel seeds
figs
frisée
fruit, dried, e.g., cherries, cranberries, raisins
fruit, tree, e.g., apples, pears
GARLIC
grains
grapefruit
gratins
greens, e.g., dandelion, **other salad,** winter
hazelnuts
honey
horseradish
ITALIAN CUISINE
lemon, e.g., juice, zest
lettuce
lime, e.g., juice, zest
mango
MUSHROOMS, e.g., porcini, shiitake, wild
mustard, e.g., Dijon
OIL, e.g., corn, hazelnut, **nut, OLIVE,** peanut, pumpkin seed, walnut
onions, e.g., red
orange, e.g., juice, zest
parsley, e.g., flat-leaf
PASTAS, e.g., lasagna, orecchiette, penne, spaghetti
pears
pecans
pepper, e.g., black, white
pine nuts
pistachios
pizza
polenta
potatoes
pumpkin
radishes
rice, e.g., Arborio, wild
RISOTTOS
rosemary
sage
SALADS, **e.g., grain, mixed green, tricolore** (radicchio + arugula + endive)

salt, e.g., sea
shallots
soups
soy sauce
spinach
squash, winter
stews
stock, e.g., mushroom, vegetable
tamari
thyme

tomatoes
VINEGAR, e.g., BALSAMIC, cider, fruit, **red wine**, **sherry**
WALNUTS
watercress
wine, e.g., dry white
Worcestershire sauce, vegan

Flavor Affinities

radicchio + apples + fennel
radicchio + arugula + endive
radicchio + balsamic vinegar + garlic + **olive oil**
radicchio + balsamic vinegar + mushrooms + **Parmesan cheese** + *risotto*
radicchio + beets + blue cheese + walnut oil + walnuts
radicchio + blue cheese + walnut oil + walnuts
radicchio + breadcrumbs + hard-boiled egg + parsley
radicchio + breadcrumbs + Parmesan cheese
RADICCHIO + CHEESE (e.g., Asiago, blue, goat) + **FRUIT** (e.g., dried cranberries, oranges, pears) + **NUTS** (e.g., hazelnuts, pecans, pine nuts, walnuts)
radicchio + fennel + olive oil + orange + pear
radicchio + fennel + olive oil + red wine vinegar
radicchio + frisée + mustard + nuts + pears + red wine vinegar
radicchio + garlic + olive oil + Parmesan cheese + white beans
radicchio + garlic + olive oil + vinegar
radicchio + garlic + parsley + pasta + ricotta cheese
radicchio + Gorgonzola cheese + mushrooms
radicchio + lemon + pasta

Dishes

Radicchio Salad with Mozzarella, Mango, and Basil
— Eleven Madison Park (New York City)

Roasted Beet Salad with Radicchio Slaw, Blue Cheese Dressing, and Toasted Walnuts
— Marché (Eugene, OR)

Grilled Radicchio Salad with Cinnamon-Roasted Carrots, Pomegranate, Farro, Toasted Pistachio, Preserved Lemon Vinaigrette, Tahini, Black Olive-Urfa Chili Oil, and Fresh Herbs
— Millennium (San Francisco)

● RADISHES — IN GENERAL (see also DAIKON)

Season: spring – summer
Flavor: slightly sweet/hot, with pungent notes of nuts and pepper, and a crunchy (raw) or creamy (cooked) texture
Volume: moderate (cooked) – loud (raw)
Nutritional profile: 83% carbs / 12% protein / 5% fats
Calories: 20 per 1-cup serving (raw, sliced)
Protein: 1 gram
Techniques: braise, grate, **raw** (best served raw), roast, sauté, shave (e.g., into noodles), steam
Botanical relatives: broccoli, Brussels sprouts, cabbage, cauliflower, collard greens, horseradish, kale, kohlrabi, land cress, rutabagas, turnips, watercress

almonds
arugula
asparagus
avocados
basil
beans, e.g., **fava**, green, white
beets
bell peppers, e.g., green
bread, e.g., crusty whole-grain (e.g., rye, wheat)
BUTTER
cabbage
capers
carrots
cayenne
celery
celery salt
cheese, e.g., **blue**, **cream**, dry Jack, **feta**, goat, Gouda, Gruyère, manchego, Parmesan, ricotta
chervil
chickpeas
chives

cilantro
cream
cucumbers
curry powder
dill
edamame
eggs, hard-boiled
European cuisines, e.g., French,
German
fennel
garlic
grains, whole, e.g., barley, brown
rice, quinoa
greens, e.g., radish, salad
hummus
LEMON, e.g., juice, zest
lettuce, e.g., iceberg, romaine
lime, e.g., juice, zest
lovage
mâche
marjoram
mesclun
MINT
mushrooms
mustard
oil, e.g., **olive**, pistachio, sesame,
walnut
olives, e.g., black
onions, e.g., red
ORANGES and blood oranges,
e.g., juice, zest
oregano

parsley, e.g., flat-leaf
pears
pecans
pepper, black
pistachios
purslane
radish sprouts
rosemary
salad dressings, esp. cheese-,
lemon-, or vinegar-based, e.g.,
vinaigrettes
SALADS, e.g., bean, grain, green,
potato, radish, vegetable
SALT, e.g., *fleur de sel*, **sea**,
smoked
scallions
sesame, e.g., oil, seeds
shallots
snow peas
soups, e.g., gazpacho, vegetable
soy sauce
spring rolls, e.g., Vietnamese
sugar snap peas
tamari
thyme

Dishes

Fancy Radishes: Roasted, Raw, and
Pickled, Smoked Tamari, Avocado,
Shishito

— Vedge (Philadelphia)

Flavor Affinities
radishes + avocados + lettuce
RADISHES + bread + BUTTER + SALT
radishes + cabbage + celery salt + onions
radishes + carrots + cayenne + lime juice + salt + *slaws*
radishes + chives + cream cheese + sour cream
radishes + cilantro + lime + olive oil
radishes + cucumbers + dill
radishes + cucumbers + endive + mustard
radishes + dill + salt + vinegar + yogurt
radishes + escarole + lemon + orange
radishes + garlic + yogurt
radishes + lemon + pistachios
radishes + mint + orange
radishes + rice wine vinegar + sesame oil + soy sauce

turnips
VINEGAR, e.g., cider, rice wine,
white wine
watercress
yogurt

RADISHES, BLACK
Season: winter – spring
Flavor: notes of horseradish,
with a firm, crisp texture
Volume: loud
Techniques: grate, pickle, raw,
roast, sauté, stew, stir-fry

Tips: Peel before eating. Grate
into soups and stews.

almonds
apples
beans, e.g., mung, pinto
bell peppers, e.g., red
chili pepper flakes
chips
chives
cilantro
garlic
ginger
greens
honey
lemon
mint
mirin
oil, e.g., **olive**, sesame
onions, e.g., **red**
oranges, blood
parsley
parsnips
pepper, e.g., black
potatoes
salads, e.g., green, potato
salt, e.g., sea
shallots
shiso
soups
squash, e.g., butternut
stews
sweet potatoes
vinegar, rice
walnuts

R

"I love the strong flavor of **black radishes,** especially with sesame oil and mirin — [the latter's] sweetness tames [the former's] bitterness."
— RICH LANDAU, VEDGE (PHILADELPHIA)

RADISHES, DAIKON (see DAIKON)

RADISHES, WATERMELON

Season: autumn – spring
Flavor: slightly sweet, with notes of jícama and/or pepper, and a firm, crunchy texture
Volume: quiet – moderate
Techniques: grate, marinate, pickle, raw, sauté, shave, slice
Factoid: Watermelon radishes are named for their green skin and pink/red flesh.

apples, e.g., green
arugula
asparagus
avocado
butter and brown butter
buttermilk
carrots
cayenne
celery
cheese, e.g., blue, chèvre, feta, goat, Gouda, Parmesan, ricotta salata
chives
cilantro
CITRUS, e.g., lemon, lime
crème fraîche
cucumbers
dill
eggs, e.g., hard-boiled
fennel
figs

frisée
GARLIC
jícama
kale
leeks
lemon
lime
mayonnaise
mint
mustard, e.g., Dijon
noodles, Asian, e.g., soba, udon
nuts, e.g., hazelnuts, pistachios, walnuts
oil, e.g., **olive,** sesame
olives, e.g., green
onions, white
orange, e.g., juice
parsnips
peas
pepper, black
pomegranate seeds
pumpkin seeds
quinoa
salads, e.g., citrus, grain, green, three-bean
salt, sea
sesame seeds
soy sauce
spinach
strawberries
sugar
sugar snap peas
tarragon
vinegar, e.g., apple cider, balsamic, rice, white balsamic, white wine
watercress
watermelon

Flavor Affinities

watermelon radishes + avocados + pumpkin seeds + salad greens
watermelon radishes + citrus segments + salad greens

Dishes

Wild Arugula Salad with Watermelon Radishes and Kimchi Dressing
— Dirt Candy (New York City)

"I'll slice **watermelon radishes** so that they cook through — they turn so red they look almost bloody. I toss them in butter, and add them to parsnip dishes, or salads. I'll also pickle them to make kimchi."
— AMANDA COHEN, DIRT CANDY (NEW YORK CITY)

"**Watermelon radishes** are as wonderful for their color as they are for their flavor. They grate well, they slice on the mandoline well, and they even hold well, with a good shelf life."
— MARK LEVY, THE POINT (SARANAC LAKE, NY)

"People eat with their eyes first — so food should always look beautiful at the table. **Watermelon radishes** are beautiful, and their color and flavor enhance everything from citrus salads to grain salads to spring rolls."
— ANNIE SOMERVILLE, GREENS RESTAURANT (SAN FRANCISCO)

• RAISINS

Flavor: sweet – very sweet, with a chewy texture
Volume: moderate
Nutritional profile: 95% carbs / 3% protein / 2% fats
Calories: 120 per ¼-cup serving (seeded)
Protein: 1 gram
Techniques: bake, raw, steam, stew
Tip: Opt for organic, sun-dried raisins; sun-drying helps maintain the nutrients.

allspice
almonds
anise
apples

apricots, e.g., dried
BAKED GOODS, e.g., breads,
  cookies, fruitcakes, muffins, scones
bananas
barley, pearl
brandy
broccoli rabe
butter
buttermilk
cabbage
caramel
cardamom
CARROTS
celery root
cereals, cold or hot breakfast
chard, e.g., Swiss
cheese, e.g., goat, ricotta
chestnuts
chickpeas
chocolate, e.g., dark, white
cinnamon
cloves
cognac
compotes
corn
couscous
crème fraîche
currants
custard
dates
desserts
escarole
fruit, other dried, e.g., figs
garlic
ginger
granola
greens, e.g., collard
hazelnuts
honey
ice cream, e.g., rum
Indian cuisine
Italian cuisine, esp. Venetian
kale

lemon, e.g., juice, zest
liqueurs, e.g., nut
maple syrup
mascarpone
Moroccan cuisine
nutmeg
nuts
OATS and OATMEAL
onions, e.g., sweet
orange, e.g., juice, zest
parsley
pasta, e.g., orzo
peanuts
pears
pecans
pineapples
pine nuts
pistachios
plums, dried
puddings, e.g., bread, rice
pumpkin
pumpkin seeds
quinces
quinoa
rice, e.g., basmati
RUM
salads, e.g. carrot, Waldorf
sauces, e.g., mole
snacks
sour cream
Southern Comfort
spinach
squash, e.g., acorn
stews
stuffings
sugar, e.g., brown
sunflower seeds
sweet potatoes
tagines
trail mix
vanilla
walnuts
whiskey

Dishes

Pumpkin Raisin French Toast with Local Maple Syrup
— The Lodge at Woodloch (Hawley, PA)

wine, e.g., red, sweet, white
yogurt

Flavor Affinities
raisins + almonds / almond milk
  + cinnamon + grains (e.g., rice,
  pearled barley)
raisins + brown sugar + **oats**
raisins + cardamom + rice
raisins + carrots + **cinnamon +**
  lemon + **quinoa**
raisins + carrots + cumin
raisins + carrots + flaxseed oil
  + tamari + umeboshi vinegar
raisins + carrots + pine nuts
raisins + carrots + walnuts
raisins + cinnamon + grains (e.g.,
  couscous, oats, pearled barley,
  quinoa)
raisins + couscous + lemon
raisins + orange + rum

RAMPS

Season: spring – summer
Flavor: slightly sweet; aromatic,
with pungent notes of garlic and/
or onion
Volume: quiet – moderate
What they are: wild leeks
Techniques: blanch, braise,
grill, parboil, pickle, raw, simmer,
stew
Tip: Flavor becomes sweeter
with cooking.
Botanical relatives: leeks, lily

(North) American cuisine
ASPARAGUS
beans, fava
breadcrumbs
butter
carrots
cayenne
chard
cheese, e.g., burrata, goat,
  mozzarella, **Parmesan**
chiles, e.g., jalapeño
cream

EGGS, e.g., *custards, frittatas, omelets, quiches,* scrambled
fiddlehead ferns
garlic
gratins
greens
hazelnuts
lemon, e.g., zest
lentils
lovage
mascarpone
MUSHROOMS, WILD, e.g., morel
mustard, e.g., Dijon
nettles
oil, nut, e.g., walnut
oil, olive
onions, spring
oranges
parsley
pasta, e.g., fettuccine, linguini, spaghetti
peas
pepper, black
"pestos"
polenta
potatoes, e.g., new
rice, e.g., Arborio
risottos
shallots

soups, e.g., asparagus
soy sauce
spinach
stews
stock, e.g., vegetable
sunflower seeds
tarragon
thyme
tomatoes
vinegar, e.g., balsamic, sherry, wine
walnuts
wine, dry white
yogurt

Flavor Affinities
ramps + asparagus + eggs + morels
ramps + asparagus + lemon + mint + pasta
ramps + asparagus + **Parmesan cheese + risotto**
ramps + burrata cheese + garlic + tomatoes
ramps + garlic + jalapeño + pasta
ramps + mascarpone + polenta
ramps + olive oil + Parmesan cheese + *"pestos"* + walnuts
ramps + pasta + tomatoes

Dishes

Spaghetti: Spring Ramps, Roasted Mushrooms, Asparagus, Herb Butter, Parmigiano
— Glenmere Mansion (Chester, New York)

Wild Ramp Risotto, Navel Orange, Ramp Pesto, Sunflower Seeds, Grilled Bitter Greens
— Green Zebra (Chicago)

Linguini Pasta: Ramp and Walnut Pesto, Slow-Cooked Egg, English Peas, Morels, Parmesan Cheese
— Plume (Washington, DC)

● RASPBERRIES
Season: summer
Flavor: sweet/sour, with a delicate, juicy texture
Volume: quiet – moderate

Nutritional profile: 82% carbs / 10% fat / 8% protein
Calories: 65 per 1-cup serving (raw)
Protein: 1 gram

Botanical relatives: almonds, apples, apricots, blackberries, cherries, peaches, pears, plums, quinces, strawberries

ALMONDS
apples
apricots
baked goods, e.g., breads, muffins, scones
bananas
BERRIES, other, e.g., blackberries, blueberries, strawberries
beverages
buttermilk
cheese, e.g., Brie, cream, goat, ricotta
CHOCOLATE, e.g., dark
***CHOCOLATE, WHITE**
cinnamon
citrus fruits
cloves
coulis
CREAM
crème anglaise and crème fraîche
DESSERTS*, e.g., crepes, crisps, crumbles, custards*
figs
ginger
graham crackers
grapefruit
grapes
hazelnuts
honey
ice cream
LEMON, e.g., juice, zest
lime, e.g., juice, zest
liqueurs, e.g., berry, brandy, cognac, Cointreau, framboise, Grand Marnier, Kirsch, rum (esp. dark), tequila
mangoes
maple syrup
mascarpone
melons, e.g., honeydew
meringue
milk

mint
nectarines
nuts, e.g., macadamia
oats and oatmeal
oil, e.g., olive, walnut
orange, e.g., juice, zest
pancakes
papaya
PEACHES
pears
pecans
pepper, black
pineapple
pine nuts
pistachios
plums
poppy seeds
preserves
quince
rhubarb
salad dressings, e.g., vinaigrettes
salads, *e.g., fruit, green*
sauces
smoothies
sorbets
sour cream
star anise
sugar, e.g., brown
tangerine
vanilla
verbena
vinegar, e.g., balsamic, red wine,
   sherry
watermelon
wine, e.g., red, sparkling (e.g.,
   Champagne), sweet (e.g.,
   Moscato d'Asti)
YOGURT

Flavor Affinities
raspberries + apricots + mint
raspberries + brown sugar +
   cinnamon + oats
raspberries + (honey +) **lemon +**
   yogurt
raspberries + mango + peaches
raspberries + mint + pistachios

● RHUBARB

Season: spring – summer
Flavor: very sour, with notes of
lemon, and a crisp (raw) or tender
(cooked) texture
Volume: loud
What it is: a vegetable
(technically) that is more often
eaten as a fruit
Nutritional profile: 78% carbs
/ 14% protein / 8% fats
Calories: 25 per 1-cup serving
(raw, diced)
Protein: 1 gram
Techniques: bake, poach, puree,
sauté, stew

Tip: Never eat rhubarb leaves,
which are poisonous.

ALMONDS and almond-flavored
   cookies or cream
ANGELICA
APPLES and apple juice
apricots
BAKED GOODS, e.g., cakes, pies,
   tarts
bananas
BERRIES, e.g., blackberries,
   blueberries, STRAWBERRIES

butter
buttermilk
caramel
cardamom
celery
cheese, e.g., blue, cream, goat,
   ricotta
cherries
chutneys
CINNAMON
citrus
cloves
coconut cream and coconut milk
compotes, fruit
cream
crème fraîche
crème de cassis
DESSERTS, e.g., cobblers, crisps,
   crumbles, custards, fools
drinks, esp. sparkling
elderflower syrup
fruit
GINGER
grapefruit, e.g., juice, zest
hazelnuts
HONEY
ice creams
lemons and Meyer lemons, e.g.,
   juice, zest
lime, e.g., juice, zest
mangoes
maple syrup
milk, e.g., goat's
mint
nutmeg
oats and oatmeal
ORANGE, e.g., juice, zest
peaches
pepper, e.g., black, pink
pineapple, e.g. fruit, juice
pistachios
plums
polenta
pomegranates
puddings, e.g., tapioca
raisins
raspberries and raspberry juice
rose water

Dishes

Raspberries: Goat's Milk Cheesecake and Pistachios
— Blue Hill (New York City)

White Chocolate Pots de Crème: Raspberry, Ginger, Almond Brittle
— Natural Selection (Portland, OR)

salads

sauces

soups, *e.g., rhubarb, strawberry, sweet-and-sour*

sorbets

sour cream

spinach

star anise

stews

*STRAWBERRIES

SUGAR, e.g., brown

VANILLA

vinegar, *e.g., balsamic, fruit, sherry*

wine, *e.g., red; sparkling, e.g., Champagne; sweet*

YOGURT, *e.g., sheep's milk*

Flavor Affinities

rhubarb + almonds + apples + maple syrup + raspberries

rhubarb + almonds + ginger + maple syrup

RHUBARB (+ ALMONDS+ OATS) + ORANGE + STRAWBERRIES + VANILLA

rhubarb + almonds + vanilla

Dishes

Rhubarb: Steamed Goat's Milk Cheesecake and Yogurt Sorbet

— Blue Hill (New York City)

Chilled Fall Rhubarb Soup: Santa Barbara Organic Strawberries, Buckwheat Gelato

— Bouley (New York City)

Strawberry and Rhubarb Panna Cotta: Almond Crumble, Vanilla Chantilly, Mimosa Sorbet

— Café Boulud (New York City)

Strawberry-Rhubarb Crumb Pie

— Candle Cafe (New York City)

Rhubarb Slow-Cooked with Celery and Sheep's Milk Yogurt Sorbet

— Eleven Madison Park (New York City)

Strawberry Rhubarb Crumble, with Lemon and Basil Sorbet

— Natural Selection (Portland, OR)

rhubarb + apples + cinnamon + cloves + orange

rhubarb + apples + pomegranates

rhubarb + brown sugar + ginger + vanilla

rhubarb + cloves + honey + orange

rhubarb + fennel + goat cheese + hazelnuts + watercress

rhubarb + ginger + strawberries

rhubarb + lemon + strawberries

rhubarb + mangoes + oranges

RICE — IN GENERAL

Flavor: slightly sweet

Volume: quiet

What it is: grain

Gluten-free: yes

Nutritional profile: 92% carbs / 7% protein / 1% fat

Calories: 120 per ½-cup of white rice (medium-grain, cooked)

Protein: 2 grams

Techniques: boil, steam

Tip: The darker the rice, the greater the nutrients (i.e., ● black > ● brown > ● white).

amaranth

American cuisine, esp. Southern and Southwestern

anise seeds

ASIAN CUISINES

basil

bay leaf

BEANS, e.g., black

bell peppers, e.g., red, roasted, *stuffed*

beverages, e.g., horchata

biryani

broccoli

butter

cabbage, stuffed

cardamom

Caribbean cuisines

R

carrots

casseroles

cayenne

cheese, Swiss

chervil

chili powder and chili sauce

Chinese cuisine

chives

cilantro

cinnamon

cloves

COCONUT and COCONUT MILK

cream

cumin

curry powder and *curries*

custard

dill

eggplant

fennel

fruit, dried, e.g., apricots, plums, raisins

garlic

ginger

greens, Asian

Indian cuisine

Italian cuisine

Japanese cuisine

Korean cuisine

leeks

legumes, e.g., lentils

lemon, e.g., juice, zest

lemon thyme

lemongrass

marjoram

Mexican cuisine

Middle Eastern cuisines

milk

mushrooms

nutmeg

nuts, e.g., almonds, pecans, pine nuts, pistachios, walnuts

onions

oranges

oregano, e.g., Mexican

paellas

paprika

parsley

peas

pilafs

pineapples

plantains

puddings

pumpkin

raisins

rhubarb

SAFFRON

sage

salt

savory

sea vegetables

soups

soy sauce

Spanish cuisine

squash, summer

stock, vegetable

stuffed mushrooms or vegetables, *e.g., bell peppers, eggplants, tomatoes*

sugar, e.g., brown

tamari

tarragon

terrines, vegetable

thyme

tomatoes

turmeric

vanilla

vegetables, e.g., spring

vinegar, rice

yogurt

Dishes

Breakfast Rice Porridge: Brown Sugar, Apples, Almonds, Cranberries, and Spices mixed with a Blend of Rice, served with Lowfat Yogurt

— Canyon Ranch Grill (Las Vegas)

Flavor Affinities

rice + almonds or almond milk + caradamom + cinnamon (+ fruit, e.g., apples) + **sweetener** (brown sugar, honey, maple syrup)

rice + carrots + leeks/onions + parsley + *pilafs*

rice + cilantro + garlic + Mexican oregano + tomatoes

rice + cinnamon + milk (+ raisins) + vanilla

rice + coconut + lemon

rice + coconut + raisins

rice + feta cheese + mint

● RICE, ARBORIO (aka RISOTTO)

Flavor: neutral, with a firm chalky center and a starchy, creamy surface (when cooked)

Volume: quiet

Techniques: Sauté rice in butter or oil until white. Stir while gradually adding hot/boiling liquid (e.g., vegetable stock) and simmering, about 20 minutes.

Ratio: 1: 3 – 3½ (1 cup rice to 3 – 3½ cups cooking liquid, e.g., juice, stock, water, and/or wine)

Tips: Let the seasons inspire your risotto pairings, e.g., basil and tomato in summer, wild mushrooms in autumn. Try the same flavor pairings with "risottos" made from other grains, e.g., barley, farro. Look for brown Arborio rice, which is higher in nutrients.

Possible substitutes: baldo rice, carnaroli rice (which, while less widely available, makes the creamiest — and arguably the best — risotto), vialone nano rice

artichokes

arugula

ASPARAGUS

basil
beans, e.g., fava, green
beer, e.g., IPA
beets
bell peppers
butter
carrots
cauliflower
celery
chard, Swiss
CHEESE, e.g., blue, feta, Fontina, goat, **PARMESAN**, pecorino, ricotta, Taleggio
chiles, e.g., red
chives
corn
fennel
fiddlehead ferns
garlic
garlic, green
greens, e.g., beet

(NORTHERN) ITALIAN CUISINE

juice, vegetable, e.g., cauliflower

kale
leeks
LEMON, e.g., juice, zest
lemon thyme
lime, e.g., juice, zest
maple syrup
mascarpone
mint
MUSHROOMS, e.g., button, chanterelle, cremini, morels, oyster, porcini, shiitake, wild
mustard seeds
nettles
nutmeg
oil, olive
onions, e.g., spring, yellow
paellas
PARSLEY
PEAS
pepper, e.g., black, white
pesto
pine nuts
puddings, rice
radicchio
***RISOTTOS**
risotto cakes
SAFFRON
sage
salt, kosher
scallions
shallots
sorrel
spinach
squash, summer or winter, e.g., butternut
STOCK, e.g., mushroom or vegetable
tarragon
thyme
tomatoes
tomatoes, sun-dried
truffles, white
vanilla
vermouth
vinegar, balsamic
WINE, e.g., dry red or white
zucchini
zucchini blossoms

Flavor Affinities

risotto + apples + cinnamon + maple syrup
risotto + artichokes + cheese (e.g., ricotta) + fava beans
RISOTTO + ASPARAGUS + LEMON + peas
risotto + asparagus + mint + ricotta
risotto + asparagus + morel mushrooms + Parmesan cheese
risotto + basil + eggplant + **tomatoes**
risotto + basil + green vegetables (e.g., asparagus, peas) + **saffron**
risotto + basil + tomatoes + zucchini
risotto + beets + dill + fennel
risotto + blue cheese + sage + walnuts
risotto + butternut squash + chanterelles + saffron
risotto + butternut squash + chard + **kale** + mushrooms
risotto + carrots + garlic + lemon + thyme
risotto + cheese (e.g., Gorgonzola, Parmesan) + pumpkin + sage
risotto + coconut milk + lemon + vanilla
risotto + eggplant + mint + tomatoes
risotto + feta cheese + garlic + mushrooms + spinach
risotto + green vegetables (e.g., peas, spinach) + mushrooms (e.g., porcini)
risotto + lemon thyme + morels + peas + spring onions
risotto + morel mushrooms + spring garlic + spring onions
risotto + peas + pesto + tomatoes
risotto + *pesto* + sun-dried tomatoes + zucchini
risotto + pine nuts + raisins + spinach

Dishes

Roasted Artichoke Risotto with Basil Pesto
— The Lodge at Woodloch (Hawley, PA)

Winter Harvest Risotto with Butternut Squash, Cranberries, Shallots, Pumpkin Seeds, and Port Wine Sauce
— The Lodge at Woodloch (Hawley, PA)

R

RICE, BASMATI, and BROWN BASMATI RICE

Flavor: slightly sweet; aromatic, with notes of nuts, popcorn, smoke, and/or toast, and a firm, slightly chewy texture
Volume: quiet – moderate
What it is: aged long-grain rice
Techniques: boil, simmer (about 2 minutes), steam
Timing: Simmer, covered, about 20 (white) to 40 (brown) minutes.
Ratio: 1: 1½ (white) – 2 (brown) (1 cup rice to 1½ – 2 cups cooking liquid)

Tips: Rinse basmati rice before using. Soak it for 10 minutes before cooking in enough water to "reach your first knuckle," according to Hemant Mathur of Tulsi.

Brand: Falak

ALMONDS
apricots, e.g., dried
basil
bay leaf
beans, e.g., fava, mung
bell peppers, esp. red
biryani
butter
buttermilk
CARDAMOM, e.g., black, green
carrots
cashews
cauliflower
cherries, dried
chervil
chickpeas
chiles, esp. dried red
chives
cilantro
cinnamon
cloves
coconut and coconut milk
cumin
currants
CURRIES, e.g., Indian

dates
dill
fennel seeds
garam masala
garlic
ghee
ginger
honey
INDIAN CUISINE
lemon, e.g., juice, zest
lime
mangoes
mascarpone
milk
mint
mustard seeds, e.g., black
oil, e.g., canola, olive, safflower
onions, e.g., green, red, yellow
orange, e.g., juice, zest
Pakistani cuisine
parsley
pasta, e.g., orzo
peas
pilafs
pine nuts
pistachios
puddings, rice
raisins, e.g., golden
saffron
salads, e.g., rice
salt, e.g., kosher, sea
scallions
seeds, pumpkin
soups
squash, winter, e.g., acorn
stock, vegetable

Flavor Affinities
basmati rice + almonds + honey + orange + vanilla
basmati rice + bay leaf + cardamom + cloves + cumin
basmati rice + cardamom + cinnamon + dates + garlic + **ginger**
basmati rice + cardamom + cinnamon + ginger + vanilla
basmati rice + cardamom + milk + orange + raisins + **vanilla**
basmati rice + cumin + fennel seeds + saffron
basmati rice + cumin + ghee + mung beans + mustard + turmeric
BASMATIC RICE + DRIED FRUIT (e.g., apricots, dates, raisins) + NUTS (e.g., almonds, cashews, pine nuts)
basmati rice + fennel seeds + orange

strawberries
stuffings
sugar, e.g., brown
tarragon
turmeric
vanilla

● RICE, BLACK (aka FORBIDDEN RICE)

Flavor: slightly sweet, with notes of mushrooms and/or nuts
Volume: quiet – moderate
What's healthful about it: antioxidants; even more nutritious than brown rice
Ratio: 1:2 (1 cup rice to 2 cups cooking liquid, e.g., stock, water)
Factoid: In ancient China, black rice was called "forbidden rice" because only nobles were allowed to eat it.

anise seeds
Asian cuisines
avocados
bananas
basil
beets
bell peppers, e.g., red, yellow
bok choy
cabbage, e.g., red
carrots
cashews
celery
cheese, e.g., Parmesan
chickpeas

chiles, e.g., chipotle, jalapeño
Chinese cuisine
chives
cilantro
cinnamon
COCONUT and coconut butter/
   cream/**milk**
desserts
garlic
ginger
greens, e.g., collard
kimchi
lettuces
lime
mangoes
maple syrup
milk, dairy or nondairy, e.g.,
   almond, **coconut**, hemp,
   rice, soy
mirin
mushrooms, porcini
nutmeg
nuts, e.g., cashews, peanuts
oil, e.g., olive, peanut, sesame
onions, e.g., red
onions, green
orange, e.g., juice, zest
peanuts
peas
pepper, black
pilafs
PUDDINGS, *e.g., rice*
pumpkin seeds
risottos
salads, e.g., rice
salt
scallions
Southeast Asian cuisines
soy sauce
soybeans, green
spinach
star anise
stir-fries
stock, vegetable
sugar, brown, palm
sushi
tempeh
Thai cuisine

tofu
vanilla
wine, white

Flavor Affinities
black rice + almond milk +
   cinnamon + vanilla
black rice + coconut/coconut
   cream/coconut milk + fruit
   (e.g., banana, mango) +
   sweetener (e.g., brown sugar,
   maple syrup, palm sugar)
black rice + ginger + star anise
black rice + kimchi + scallions
black rice + sesame oil +
   soy sauce

RICE, BOMBA (see also SPANISH CUISINE)

Tip: Bomba rice absorbs
30 percent more liquid than
other rices.

asparagus
garlic
mushrooms
oil, olive
olives, e.g., green
onions, yellow
PAELLAS
paprika, e.g., smoked, sweet
parsley
saffron
Spanish cuisine
stock, vegetable
tomatoes
wine, dry white

● RICE, BROWN — IN GENERAL

Flavor: nutty, with a chewy
texture
Volume: quiet – moderate
What it is: whole grain
Nutritional profile: 87% carbs
/ 7% protein / 6% fat
Calories: 220 per 1-cup serving
(medium-grain, cooked)

Protein: 5 grams
Timing: Cook at a low boil,
covered, for about 30 – 50
minutes, until tender.
Ratio: 1:2 (1 cup brown rice to
2 cups of cooking liquid)
Tips: Because brown rice takes
so long to cook, make sure you
cook extra. You can freeze the
leftovers, then reheat the frozen
rice in about 10 minutes on the
stove. If you're short on time,
quick brown rice cooks in about
10 – 15 minutes.
Brand: Lundberg Organic

basil
bay leaf
bell peppers, e.g., red
bibimbap
broccoli and broccoli rabe
burdock
cabbage, e.g., green, savoy,
   stuffed
carrots
cayenne
cereals, hot breakfast, e.g., with
   fruit and nuts
chili, vegetarian
cilantro
coriander
cucumbers
edamame
eggs
fennel seeds
fried rice
garlic
GINGER
GRAINS, other whole, e.g.,
   barley, buckwheat, farro,
   millet, oats, rye, wheat berries,
   wild rice
greens
kale
LEGUMES, e.g., adzuki or black
   beans, chickpeas, lentils
lemon, e.g., juice, zest
lime

R

macrobiotic cuisine
"meatballs" (e.g., brown rice +
   onion + parsley + walnuts)
miso
MUSHROOMS, e.g., shiitake
nuts, e.g., almonds, walnuts
oil, e.g., canola, olive, sesame
onions, e.g., green, red
PARSLEY
peas
pilafs
puddings
raisins
"risottos"

salads, e.g., grain
scallions
sea vegetables, e.g., hiziki, kombu
seitan
sesame seeds, e.g., black, and
   sesame paste
soups, e.g., tomato
SOY SAUCE
SPINACH
sprouts, e.g., bean, pea
squash, e.g., butternut
stir-fries
stock, vegetable

sweeteners, e.g., mirin, brown
   sugar
tahini
tamari
tarragon
thyme
TOFU and tofu skin
turmeric
vegetables, esp. root
veggie burgers
vinegar, e.g., brown, umeboshi
walnuts
watercress

RICE, BROWN — BASMATI (see RICE, BASMATI)

RICE, BROWN — JASMINE (see RICE, JASMINE)

• RICE, BROWN — LONG-GRAIN

Flavor: earthy, with a fluffy texture and separate grains
Timing: Simmer, covered, for 40 – 50 minutes.
Ratio: 1:2 (1 cup rice to 2 cups cooking liquid, e.g., broth, water)

casseroles
pilafs
salads
soups
stir-fries
stuffings

• RICE, BROWN — SHORT-GRAIN

Flavor: nutty, with a creamy, soft yet chewy and sticky texture
Timing: Simmer, covered, for 40 – 50 minutes.
Ratio: 1:2 (i.e., 1 cup rice to 2 cups cooking liquid, e.g., broth, water)

Flavor Affinities

brown rice + almonds + cinnamon + fruit (e.g., blueberries, raisins) +
   maple syrup + vanilla
brown rice + black beans + garlic + kale + tahini
brown rice + broccoli + tofu
brown rice + brown sugar + dried plums + orange zest
brown rice + butternut squash + garlic
brown rice + cilantro + garlic + lime + onions
brown rice + edamame + ginger
brown rice + ginger + leeks + peas
brown rice + ginger + miso + tofu + vegetables
brown rice + kale + scallions
brown rice + lemon + tahini + vegetables
brown rice + lentils + spinach
brown rice + mushrooms + spinach + tofu
brown rice + sage + root vegetables
brown rice + sesame + shiitake mushrooms + tofu

Dishes

Vegetable Stir-Fry: Wok-Sautéed String Beans, Broccoli Florets, Zucchini, Cremini
Mushrooms, Bell Pepper, and Baby Bok Choy with Organic Tamari Brown Rice
— Josie's (New York City)

Bi Bim Bop: Hot Pepper Miso and Vegetables over Brown Rice and Sunny Side Up Egg
— Mana Food Bar (Chicago)

Cilantro-Peanut Stir Fry: Stir-Fried Broccoli, Red and Yellow Peppers, Mushrooms, Mung
Sprouts, Carrots, and Green Onions with a Spicy Cilantro-Peanut-Ginger-Lime Sauce, over
Organic Brown Rice, topped with Roasted Peanuts
— Seva (Ann Arbor, MI)

Teriyaki Brown Rice Bowl, Asian Vegetable, Sesame, and Avocado (+ Optional Tofu)
— True Food Kitchen (Santa Monica)

croquettes
desserts
paella
puddings
rice balls or rice croquettes
risotto
salads, e.g., grain, green
sushi, *nori rolls*
VEGGIE BURGERS

RICE, CARNAROLI (aka RISOTTO; see recommendations for RICE, ARBORIO)

What it is: rice with a slightly larger grain than Arborio rice grains

● RICE, JASMINE (see also THAI CUISINE)

Flavor: aromatic, with notes of flowers, nuts, popcorn, and/or toast, and a soft texture
Volume: moderate
What it is: long-grain rice
Timing: 15 – 20 minutes
Ratio: 1:1½ (1 cup rice to 1½ cups cooking liquid, e.g., broth, water)

bay leaf
cashews
cilantro
coconut and coconut milk
cranberries, dried
curries
dates
desserts
fennel seeds
garlic
ginger
grapes
lemon, e.g., juice, zest
lemongrass
melon, e.g., cantaloupe
milk, coconut
orange, e.g., juice
peanuts

pecans
pesto
pilafs
plantains
salads
seitan
THAI CUISINE
tofu
walnuts
yogurt

Flavor Affinities

jasmine rice + coconut + lemon

RICE, LONG-GRAIN (see also RICE, BASMATI and RICE, JASMINE)

Tip: "Long-grain" refers to grains that are at least three times as long as they are wide. Opt for brown long-grain rice, which is higher in fiber than white rice, for more nutrients.

curries
fried rice
pilafs
salads
stews
stir-fries

RICE, SHORT-GRAIN (see also RICE, ARBORIO and RICE, SUSHI)

Tips: "Short-grain" refers to grains that are less than twice as long as they are wide. Opt for brown short-grain rice, which is higher in fiber than white rice, for more nutrients.

"bowls," Japanese
cereal, hot breakfast
puddings, e.g., rice
risottos
sushi, vegetarian, e.g., nori rolls

RICE, STICKY

Flavor: sweet, with a sticky texture that makes it easier to eat with chopsticks
Volume: quiet
Tip: Soak sticky rice overnight before steaming.
Techniques: boil, then steam
Ratio: 1:1⅓ (1 cup sticky rice to 1⅓ cups cooking liquid, e.g., stock, water)
Brand: Nishiki

Asian cuisines
banana leaves
bananas
bibimbap
carrots
coconut and coconut milk
cucumber
desserts, Asian
gomashio
Japanese cuisine
kimchi
Korean cuisine
mango
mushrooms, shiitake
oil, e.g., grapeseed, sesame
pineapple
scallions
sprouts, mung bean
strawberries
sugar, e.g., brown
sushi
Thai cuisine
vanilla
zucchini

Flavor Affinities

sticky rice + coconut milk + mango

RICE, SUSHI

What it is: short-grain rice with a sticky texture
Techniques: boil, steam
Ratio: 1:1½ (1 cup sushi rice

to 1½ cups cooking liquid, e.g., stock, water)

Tips: Consider using sticky brown sushi rice to get more nutrients. Instead of using ordinary sushi rice, Beyond Sushi in New York City uses a delicious six-grain combination of (hull-less) barley, (pearl) barley, black rice, (short-grain) brown rice, red rice, and rye berries in its nori rolls and vegan sushi.

sushi

Flavor Affinities
sushi rice + rice vinegar + sugar

● **RICE, WILD**
Season: autumn
Flavor: bitter/sweet, with complex earthy/savory notes of grass and/or **NUTS**, and a very chewy texture
Volume: moderate – loud
What it is: considered a whole grain, even though it is technically a seed (of aquatic grass) and not in the botanical grain family
What's healthful about it: twice the fiber and protein of brown rice
Gluten-free: yes
Nutritional profile: 83% carbs / 14% protein / 3% fats
Calories: 170 per 1-cup serving (cooked)
Protein: 7 grams
Techniques: pressure-cook (20 – 25 minutes), simmer (covered, 35 – 60 minutes), steam
Ratio: 1: 3 – 4 (1 cup wild rice to 3 – 4 cups cooking liquid)
Tips: Rinse wild rice thoroughly before cooking. Combine with other rice(s) to lessen its chewiness.

Factoid: It is the only native North American grain.

almonds
AMERICAN CUISINE
apples, apple cider, and apple juice
artichoke hearts
asparagus
baked goods, e.g., breads, cakes
bay leaf
beans, e.g., green, white
bell peppers, e.g., red, yellow
bulgur
butter
cardamom
carrots
casseroles
celery
celery leaves and celery seeds
celery root
cheese, e.g., blue, feta, goat
chives
cinnamon
corn
crepes
dates
dill
eggs, e.g., *frittatas, omelets*

Flavor Affinities
wild rice + beets + orange
wild rice + bread crumbs + celery + dried cranberries + herbs + onions + *stuffings*
wild rice + brown rice + nuts
wild rice + cider vinegar + walnut oil
wild rice + cinnamon + orange zest
wild rice + dates + pecans
wild rice + dried cherries + pine nuts
wild rice + feta cheese + lemon + mint
WILD RICE + FRUIT (e.g., apples, dates, dried cherries or cranberries, raisins) + NUTS (e.g., almonds, pecans, pine nuts, walnuts)
wild rice + garlic + spinach
wild rice + ginger + pineapple
wild rice + green onions + hazelnuts
wild rice + kabocha squash + sage
wild rice + pine nuts + shiitake mushrooms + spinach
wild rice + scallions + walnuts

FRUIT, DRIED, e.g., cherries, CRANBERRIES
GARLIC
ghee
grains, other, e.g., barley, rice
greens, e.g., collard
hazelnuts
leeks
LEMON, e.g., juice, zest
maple syrup
Midwestern American cuisine
MUSHROOMS, e.g., chanterelle, cremini, morel, porcini, shiitake, white
mustard
Native American cuisine
nuts, e.g., macadamia
OIL, e.g., hazelnut, **olive**, walnut
ONIONS, e.g., green, red, white, yellow
orange, e.g., juice, zest
oregano
pancakes and waffles
parsley
pecans
pepper, black
pilafs
PINE NUTS
pumpkin

raisins

RICES, OTHER, e.g., basmati, **brown**, long-grain brown, red

sage

salads, e.g., wild rice

salt, e.g., kosher, sea

scallions

seeds, e.g., sunflower

shallots

soups, e.g., mushroom

sour cream

soy sauce

spinach

squash, summer and winter, e.g., acorn, butternut, kabocha

stock, vegetable

stuffings, e.g., cabbage, mushrooms, peppers, pumpkins, squash

tamari

tangerines

tarragon

thyme

vinegar, e.g., champagne, red wine, white balsamic, white wine

WALNUTS

watercress

wine, dry white

zucchini

RICOTTA (see CHEESE, RICOTTA)

What it is: While not technically a cheese, ricotta is commonly referred to as such and so is listed under "Cheese."

RISOTTO (see recommendations for RICE, ARBORIO)

ROMAINE (see LETTUCE, ROMAINE)

ROOT VEGETABLES — IN GENERAL, or MIXED (see also BEETS, CARROTS, PARSNIPS, RUTABAGAS, SWEET POTATOES, TURNIPS, etc.)

"I'll confit **root vegetables** — like carrots, celery root, parsley root, and parsnips — that have been shaved thin on a mandoline in olive oil with herbs, spices, and citrus for six to eight hours in an 85°F oven, which breaks down their cell wall structure. As they become tender, their water is replaced with fat. I strain and puree them, which creates the texture of room-temperature butter. Because this 'root vegetable butter' has the same qualities as butter or soft cheese, I can use it in similar ways, such as on canapés or to bind other ingredients."

— AARON WOO, NATURAL SELECTION (PORTLAND, OR)

● ROSEMARY

Season: winter (when rosemary is milder; it is stronger in summer)

Flavor: bitter/slightly sweet; aromatic; with notes of camphor, lemon, mint, pepper, pine, sage, smoke, and/or wood

Volume: moderately loud (winter) – loud (summer)

Technique: grill

Tip: Add early in the cooking process.

Botanical relatives: basil, lavender, marjoram, mint, oregano, sage, summer savory, thyme

apples

apricots

asparagus

BAKED GOODS, e.g., breads, cakes, cookies, focaccia, scones, shortbread

barley

bay leaf

BEANS, e.g., **cannellini, dried, fava**, green, **white**

beets

bell peppers

bouquet garni

bread crumbs

breads

Brussels sprouts

butter

cabbage, e.g., savoy

carrots

cauliflower

celery

cheese, e.g., cheddar, chèvre, cream, feta, goat, **Parmesan**, ricotta

chives

citrus

cream

desserts

eggplant

eggs and egg *dishes*

fennel and fennel seeds

figs

French cuisine, esp. Provençal

fruit, e.g., poached

***GARLIC**

gin

grains

grapefruit

grapes

grilled dishes, e.g., vegetables

herbes de Provence

honey

Italian cuisine

kebobs, vegetable

lavender

leeks

LEMON, e.g., juice, zest

lentils

lime

lovage

marinades

marjoram

Mediterranean cuisines

milk

mint

mushrooms, e.g., morel, oyster, porcini, portobello, shiitake

oil, olive

olives
onions
orange, e.g., juice, zest
oregano
parsley
parsnips
pastas, e.g., orzo
pears
peas, e.g., split
pepper, black
pine nuts
pizza
polenta
POTATOES
pumpkin
quinoa
radicchio
rice, e.g., Arborio
risotto
sage
salad dressings
salads, *e.g., bean, fruit*
SAUCES, e.g., barbecue, cream,
   pasta, tomato
savory
scallions
shallots
sherry
SOUPS, e.g., bean, minestrone,
   tomato
spinach
squash, summer and winter, e.g.,
   acorn, butternut
stews
stock, vegetable
strawberries
stuffings
sweet potatoes
thyme
tofu
TOMATOES, tomato juice, and
   tomato sauce
vegetables, esp. grilled, kebabs,
   roasted
vinegar, e.g., balsamic, red wine
wine
yogurt
zucchini

Flavor Affinities
rosemary + balsamic vinegar +
   shallots
rosemary + balsamic vinegar +
   spinach
rosemary + butter + lemon
rosemary + feta cheese + spinach
rosemary + garlic + lemon + olive
   oil + white beans
ROSEMARY + GARLIC + OLIVE
   OIL + POTATOES
rosemary + honey + orange
rosemary + lemon + tofu
rosemary + lemon + white beans
rosemary + mushrooms + thyme
rosemary + onions + potatoes
rosemary + oregano + thyme
rosemary + Parmesan cheese +
   polenta
rosemary + Parmesan cheese +
   tomatoes + white beans

"Anytime you combine **rosemary**
and thyme, you've got instant
Thanksgiving! Their soulful, dark,
rich flavors will enhance
anything, from a bag of chips to a
mushroom dish. But rosemary is
very pungent, so you only need a
little. I won't add rosemary to a
soup: by the time rosemary turns
gray, it's given everything it has to
give, and you want it out of there
anyway. Instead, I'll use a
rosemary branch to stir the soup
and infuse the flavor."

— RICH LANDAU, VEDGE (PHILADELPHIA)

● RUTABAGAS

Season: autumn – spring
Flavor: sweet/sometimes bitter,
with sometimes sharp, peppery,
and/or pungent notes of cabbage,
nuts, and/or turnips, and a crisp
texture
Volume: moderate (esp.
cooked) – loud (esp. raw)
What they are: root vegetables

Nutritional profile: 86% carbs
/ 9% protein / 5% fats
Calories: 70 per 1-cup serving
(cooked, cubed)
Protein: 2 grams
Techniques: bake (at 350°F
for 50 – 60 minutes), blanch,
boil, braise, deep-fry, grate,
hash, julienne, marinate, mash,
pressure-cook, puree, roast, sauté,
shred, steam (10 – 15 minutes),
stew, stir-fry

Tips: Do not undercook. The
longer it cooks, the sweeter
the flavor, but do *not* overcook.
Add a touch of sweetness (e.g.,
sugar) to counteract bitterness.
Puree with quieter vegetables,
e.g., potatoes.

Botanical relatives: broccoli,
Brussels sprouts, cabbage,
cauliflower, collard greens,
horseradish, kale, kohlrabi,
land cress, radishes, turnips,
watercress
Possible substitute: turnips

agave nectar
allspice
almonds
APPLES, apple cider, and
   apple juice
artichokes, Jerusalem
baked goods, e.g., pies, tarts
barley
basil
bay leaf
beets
bok choy
broccoli
butter
caraway seeds
cardamom
CARROTS
casseroles
cayenne
celery
celery root

cheese, e.g., blue, cream, goat, **Gruyère**, Parmesan
chestnuts
chives
cinnamon
coconut milk
coriander
cream
cumin
dill
eggs, e.g., frittatas
farro
fennel and fennel seeds
garlic
ginger
greens, e.g., bitter, collard, dandelion
hash, e.g., served with eggs
hazelnuts
herbes de Provence
honey
horseradish
kale
leeks
lemon, e.g., juice
lentils
lime
mace
maple syrup
marjoram
mint
miso
mushrooms, wild
mustard
nutmeg
nuts, e.g., peanuts, pistachios
OIL, e.g., hazelnut, nut, **olive**, sunflower, vegetable
onions, e.g., red, yellow
orange, e.g., juice, zest

oregano
paprika, e.g., smoked
PARSLEY
parsley root
parsnips
pears
pepper, e.g., black, white
POTATOES, e.g., MASHED
purees
quinoa
raisins
rosemary
saffron
sage
salads
salt, sea
savory
scallions
Scottish cuisine
SOUPS, e.g., rutabaga
sour cream
squash, winter, e.g., butternut
star anise
stews
stir-fries
stock, e.g., root vegetable, vegetable
sugar, e.g., brown
Swedish cuisine
sweet potatoes
tarragon
THYME
tofu
tomatoes
TURNIPS
vanilla
vegetables, root
vinegar, e.g., balsamic, cider, malt, sherry
watercress

Dishes

Glazed Chestnuts Rutabaga-Mace Puree, Wild Mushrooms Fricassee with Horseradish
— DANIEL (New York City)

Roasted Rutabaga Salad, Grilled Trumpet Mushrooms, Charred Onion, Pistachio
— Vedge (Philadelphia)

Flavor Affinities

rutabaga + apples + carrots + onions + sweet potatoes
rutabaga + apples + maple syrup
rutabaga + broccoli + carrots
rutabaga + caraway seeds + garlic
rutabaga + carrots + (fried) egg + parsnips + **potatoes**
rutabaga + carrots + mustard + parsley + **potatoes**
rutabaga + carrots + nutmeg + **potatoes**
rutabaga + cheese + potatoes
rutabaga + celery + onions
rutabaga + coconut milk + lime
rutabaga + leeks + turnips
rutabaga + parsnips + potatoes
rutabaga + potatoes + rosemary + thyme

"**Rutabagas** are one of those vegetables that are a hard-sell on a menu. I probably wouldn't put a rutabaga gratin on Greens' menu, but I'd tuck it into a dish as one of several ingredients [e.g., in a hash] — or perhaps not even mention that it was there."
— ANNIE SOMERVILLE, GREENS RESTAURANT (SAN FRANCISCO)

● RYE BERRIES (aka WHOLE RYE)

Flavor: sweet/sour, with notes of rye and walnuts, and a firm, *very* chewy texture
Volume: moderate – loud
What they are: whole grain
What's healthful about them: a lower glycemic index than wheat and other grains; promote feeling full quickly
Gluten-free: no
Nutritional profile: 81% carbs / 13% protein / 6% fats
Calories: 150 per ¼-cup serving (dry)
Protein: 6 grams

R

Techniques: simmer (covered, about 60 minutes), steam
Ratio: 1:3 (1 cup rye berries to 3 cups cooking liquid)
Tips: Rinse rye berries well. Soak overnight. Use in blends with other less chewy grains.
Botanical relatives: barley, corn, spelt, triticale, wheat
Possible substitutes: triticale, wheat berries

anise
apples
baked goods, e.g., breads
beans, e.g., black, kidney
beets
bell peppers, e.g., red
***breads**, e.g., pumpernickel, rye*
cabbage, red
CARAWAY SEEDS
carrots
casseroles
celery
cereals, hot breakfast
cheese, e.g., goat, Gruyère, halloumi
chervil
chickpeas
chili, vegetarian
cinnamon
corn
dates
(Northern) European cuisines
fennel
garlic
GRAINS, OTHER, less chewy, e.g., barley, **brown rice**, quinoa
honey
leeks
lentils, e.g., red

maple syrup
molasses
mustard, e.g., Dijon
Northern European cuisines
nuts, e.g., pecans, walnuts
oil, e.g., olive, sesame, walnut
onions, e.g., caramelized, red
orange, e.g., zest
parsley
parsnips
peas
pilafs
potatoes
raisins
"risottos"
Russian cuisine
sage
***salads**, e.g., grain*
sauerkraut
Scandinavian cuisines
***soups**, e.g., borscht*
stews
stock, vegetable
stuffings
sugar, brown
sunflower seeds
thyme
tomatoes
vegetables
vinegar, e.g., apple cider, balsamic

Flavor Affinities

rye berries + apples + brown sugar + caraway seeds + red cabbage
rye berries + apples + cinnamon + raisins
rye berries + caraway seeds + carrots + celery + olive oil + onions + soy sauce
rye berries + raisins + walnuts

Dishes

Rye Spaetzle, Kraut, Smoked Caramelized Onion, Caraway, Stout Foam
— Green Zebra (Chicago)

• SAFFRON

Flavor: bitter/sour/sweet, with earthy/pungent notes of honey
Volume: quieter (yellow) – louder (orange, red)
Tips: Add later in the cooking process; saffron is activated by the heat of cooking. This bright yellow/orange-hued spice is used for its color as well as its flavor. A little saffron goes a very long way — never add more than is necessary.

***baked goods**, e.g., breads, cakes, scones*
basil
bell peppers, e.g., roasted
biryani
butter
cardamom
cayenne
chard
chives
cinnamon
couscous
curries
desserts
eggplant
fennel
garlic
ginger
(Northern) Indian cuisine
lemon, e.g., juice, zest
marjoram
mayonnaise
Mediterranean cuisines
Moroccan cuisine
nuts, e.g., almonds, pistachios
oil, olive
orange, e.g., juice, zest
***PAELLA**, vegetarian*
parsley
***pasta**, e.g., linguini*
pepper, e.g., black
pilafs
potatoes
puddings, rice

Dishes

Saffron Cheesecake: Rhubarb Ice Cream, Basil Gel, Black Olive-Pistachio Crumble
— Vedge (Philadelphia)

raisins
*RICE
*RISOTTOS
rose water
salad dressings
sauces, e.g., cream, tomato
shallots
soups
Spanish cuisine
stews, e.g., bean, vegetable
tomatoes
yogurt
zucchini

Flavor Affinities
saffron + cardamom + rose water
saffron + Parmesan cheese +
    risotto

● SAGE
Season: autumn (savory) –
spring (minty)
Flavor: bitter/sour/sweet, with
astringent/musty/pungent/
rich/spicy notes of camphor,
eucalyptus, flowers, herbs, lemon,
mint, and/or pine
Volume: moderate – **loud**
What it is: herb
> **Tip:** Add near the end of the
> cooking process.

Botanical relatives: basil,
lavender, marjoram, mint,
oregano, rosemary, summer
savory, thyme

artichokes
asparagus
baked goods, e.g., biscuits, corn
    bread, focaccia
BEANS — in general, and e.g.,
    borlotti, **dried**, pinto, **WHITE**
bread and bread crumbs

butter and brown butter
casseroles
CHEESE, e.g., Brie, cheddar, feta,
    Fontina, Gruyère, **Parmesan**,
    ricotta
chestnuts
corn
cornmeal, e.g., as *corn bread*
eggplant
eggs, e.g., *frittatas*, scrambled
fennel
GARLIC and garlic scapes
ghee
grains
gravies
juniper berries
leeks
lemon
lentils
marjoram
Mediterranean cuisines
mint
mushrooms, e.g., wild
OIL, OLIVE
ONIONS, e.g., yellow
parsley
PASTA, e.g., gnocchi, lasagna,
    orecchiette, spaghetti
peas, e.g., green, split
pepper, black
"pestos"
pine nuts
pizza
POTATOES
pumpkin
rice
ricotta, e.g., baked
risotto
rosemary
rutabaga
salads, e.g., bean, herb
sauces
savory

SOUPS, e.g., butternut squash,
    lentil, pumpkin, sweet potato,
    white bean
SQUASH, WINTER, e.g., acorn,
    butternut
stews
stock, vegetable
STUFFINGS
thyme
tomatoes
vegetables, e.g., root
vinegar
walnuts

Flavor Affinities
sage + bread crumbs + olive oil
sage + butter + lemon +
    Parmesan cheese + *pasta*
sage + butternut squash +
    walnuts
sage + cheese + tomatoes
sage + garlic + olive oil + parsley
    + winter squash
sage + garlic + potatoes
sage + garlic + white beans
sage + walnuts + *pesto*

SALAD DRESSINGS

Flavor Affinities
almonds + dill + garlic + lemon
    juice + tahini
apple cider vinegar + chives +
    garlic + lemon juice + olive oil +
    parsley + tahini + tamari
apple cider vinegar + **cilantro** +
    garlic + **lime juice/zest** +
    olive oil
apple cider vinegar + maple syrup
    + mustard
apple cider vinegar + onions +
    poppy seeds + tahini
avocado + cayenne + garlic +
    lemon juice + olive oil + parsley
avocado + cucumber + dill +
    lemon juice + maple syrup
BALSAMIC VINEGAR + BASIL
    + GARLIC + MUSTARD +
    OLIVE OIL

The Secret to Loving Salads: A Great Salad Dressing

One of the most healthful and flavorful changes you can make to your diet is to eat more vegetables — a *lot* more vegetables. At least half of them should be eaten raw, such as in salads. Keeping things flavorful through mastering a compelling array of salad dressings is a worthwhile pursuit.

Don't undo the good you've done by using typical oil-laden dressings, which clock in at nearly 120 calories per tablespoon (like pure fat itself). Below are some ways to cut calories and fat without eliminating flavor:

Ratio: The standard radio is 1:3 or 1:4 (1 part vinegar to 3 or 4 parts oil), but consider minimizing (if not eliminating) oil in salad dressings.

Tips: Always start the process of making salad dressing with the vinegar and/or citrus (e.g., lemon, lime, orange) juice and seasonings (e.g., citrus zest, herbs; minced garlic, onions, or shallots; spices), and slowly whisk in any oil. If too much oil is added, the flavor balance will be lost. For more Omega-3s, consider substituting flaxseed or walnut oil for part of the extra-virgin olive oil. With citrus vinaigrettes, use a lighter vinegar, e.g., champagne, rice, or sherry. Those looking to minimize or eliminate oil can base salad dressings on other liquids or pastes, such as buttermilk, fruit juice, kefir, nut butters, tahini, vegetable juice or stock, vinegar, yogurt, and/or water — or even pureed fruit, silken tofu, or vegetables (e.g., avocados). To make vegetarian dressings creamier, add a little cream cheese, fresh goat cheese, kefir, mascarpone, or ricotta; vegans can blend with nutritional yeast or silken tofu.

Not only great for salads, the combinations listed in this section can also be used for dips, dipping sauces, marinades, sautés, or stir-fries — or drizzled over hot vegetables, Asian noodles, or pastas.

[Balsamic Vinaigrette] **BALSAMIC VINEGAR + DIJON MUSTARD + GARLIC + OLIVE OIL** [+ basil + lemon juice]

BALSAMIC VINEGAR + DIJON MUSTARD + GARLIC + ginger + maple syrup

BALSAMIC VINEGAR + DIJON MUSTARD + GARLIC + honey + tofu (e.g., silken)

["Green Goddess"] basil + celery + dill + garlic + green onions + mayonnaise

BASIL + LEMON JUICE

black sesame + garlic + sesame oil + wasabi

BUTTERMILK + CHIVES

buttermilk + cider vinegar + dill + garlic + shallots

["Ranch"] buttermilk + garlic + herbs [e.g., chives, cilantro, parsley] + lime + mayonnaise + salt

buttermilk + horseradish

["Caesar"] capers + garlic + lemon juice + miso + olive oil

CARROT + dill + **GINGER**

CARROT + garlic + **GINGER** + onions + (cider) vinegar

CARROT + GINGER + miso

champagne vinegar + honey + canola oil

chickpea + garlic + lemon juice + mustard + (balsamic) vinegar

["Green Goddess"] chives + parsley + tarragon vinegar + tofu

Talking with Charleen Badman of FnB in Scottsdale about Making a Great Salad

For a great salad, you need the elements of crunch, sweetness, savoriness, and fattiness.

- **Crunch:** "For crunch in a salad, I can use a variety of things beyond nuts. I like to use things in the onion family — for example, julienning and salting onions, and frying them in olive oil. Leeks and shallots both crisp up well and can be used as a garnish. I also like using puffed rice to add texture."

- **Sweetness:** "Sweetness can be added with fresh fruits, like apples or pears; dried fruits like raisins; or even sweet vegetables like corn or tomatoes."

- **Savoriness:** "Adding some spice is also a great way to enhance a salad. You can do it with some chili pepper or even raw fresh ginger, which tastes great with rutabaga."

- **Fattiness:** "To add fat, there are many options. You can select a fatty vegetable, like an avocado. You can use a mayonnaise turned into aioli. Cheese is good in dressings, as are infused olive oils."

CILANTRO + cumin + **LIME**

cilantro + garlic + ginger + ponzu + sesame

cilantro + garlic + olive oil + red wine vinegar + roasted tomato

CILANTRO + honey + **LIME**

CILANTRO + LIME + garlic + olive oil + sherry vinegar

citrus + soy sauce

[Asian Peanut] coconut milk + curry paste + ginger + peanut butter + soy sauce

[Cucumber Dill] cucumber + dill + lemon juice + onion + silken tofu

cumin + lime juice

["Caesar"] **Dijon mustard + garlic + lemon juice + olive oil** + Parmesan cheese + **red wine vinegar** + (vegetarian) Worcestershire sauce

Dijon mustard + garlic + lemon juice + olive oil + Vegenaise + vinegar

DIJON MUSTARD + LEMON JUICE + OLIVE OIL + orange juice + soy sauce

DIJON MUSTARD + LEMON JUICE + OLIVE OIL + shallots

Dijon mustard + red wine vinegar + shallots + walnut oil

["Ranch"] dill + garlic + lemon juice + onion + parsley + Vegenaise + vinegar

dill + garlic + mustard

dill + tahini + tofu

feta + garlic + oregano

garlic + ginger + lemon juice + parsley + sesame oil

garlic + ginger + miso + orange

garlic + ginger + olive oil + rice vinegar + sesame oil + tamari

garlic + ginger + peanuts + rice vinegar + soy sauce

GARLIC + hemp seed + honey + **LEMON JUICE + TAHINI**

["Ranch"] garlic + herbs + onions + soy milk + Vegenaise

garlic + lemon juice + mustard + tarragon

garlic + lemon juice + olive oil + tamari

garlic + lemon juice + orange juice

[Lemon Tahini] **GARLIC + LEMON JUICE** + sesame oil + **TAHINI** + tamari

garlic + lemon juice + nori + **olive oil** + soy sauce + tofu

[Greek] **garlic + lemon juice + olive oil** + crumbled feta or extra-firm tofu

GARLIC + LEMON JUICE + TAHINI + tamari + umeboshi plum vinegar

garlic + mustard + rice vinegar

garlic + olive oil + **red wine vinegar**

garlic + sesame paste/seeds + wasabi

GINGER + honey + **MISO** + rice vinegar

GINGER + LEMON JUICE + oil + tahini + tamari

GINGER + lemongrass + maple syrup + orange juice + rice vinegar + **SESAME OIL**

ginger + lime + mango

[Citrus Vinaigrette] **ginger + lime** + orange juice + vinegar

[Asian Sesame] **GINGER** + maple syrup + orange juice + rice vinegar + **SESAME OIL**

GINGER + MISO + mustard + sesame oil + tahini + tamari + (cider) vinegar

GINGER + MISO + sesame

ginger + peanut butter/oil + soy sauce

GINGER + SESAME

GINGER + SESAME + soy sauce

ginger + tahini

["Green Goddess"] **green onions** + olive oil + **parsley** + shallots + **white wine vinegar**

[Italian] herbs (basil, oregano) + olive oil + vinegar

green onions + parsley + tahini + **vinegar**

honey + peanut oil + white **wine vinegar**

honey + poppy seeds + red **wine vinegar**

["Thousand Island"] ketchup + onion + chopped pickle relish + silken tofu or Vegenaise

lemon juice + maple + **mustard + tamari**

lemon juice + mustard + nutritional yeast + **tamari** + vinegar

[Greek] lemon juice + oregano + thyme + (red wine) vinegar + crumbled feta or extra-firm tofu

[Japanese Ponzu] lemon juice + rice vinegar + sesame oil + soy sauce

lemon juice + tahini

lemon juice + mustard + olive oil + walnut oil

lime juice + (garlic + ginger + honey) + sesame seeds

lime juice + mint + rice wine

lime juice + miso + peanut oil

[Maple Mustard] maple syrup + mustard + (balsamic) vinegar

[Middle Eastern] chickpeas + garlic + lemon juice + vinegar

mirin + miso + soy sauce + (brown rice) vinegar

[Japanese Miso] miso + mustard + (rice wine) vinegar

miso + orange

miso + sesame oil

mustard + olive oil + parsley + **tarragon**

olive oil + orange juice + sherry vinegar + walnut oil

olive oil + red wine vinegar + shallots

orange + saffron + tahini

orange + sesame oil + soy sauce

PARSLEY + SCALLIONS + TAHINI + umeboshi purée

sesame oil/paste/seeds + soy sauce

SHALLOTS + SHERRY VINEGAR + walnut oil

"Every dish needs a vibrant quality about it. In a leafy green **salad**, when you toss it and serve it, it doesn't have the leaves all upside down so their backs are to someone. I call it 'fluffy and lofty' — the greens twins — that make the salad inviting. If you list a bunch of ingredients in the salad, don't hide them all at the bottom. Make sure the stand-out ingredients stand out. And don't go cheap: three extra cherry tomatoes is not going to break the bank. You want a person to feel that you care every step of the way."

— ANNIE SOMERVILLE, GREENS RESTAURANT (SAN FRANCISCO)

● SALSIFY

Season: autumn – winter

Flavor: slightly sweet, with notes of artichoke hearts, asparagus (esp. white), coconut (esp. black salsify), Jerusalem artichokes, nuts, and/or **oysters**

Volume: moderate

What it is: root vegetable

Nutritional profile: 87% carbs / 11% protein / 2% fats

Calories: 95 per 1-cup serving (boiled)

Protein: 4 grams

Techniques: bake, blanch, boil (about 10 – 20 minutes), braise (about 45 minutes), fry, glaze, mash, pan-roast, poach, puree, raw, roast, sauté, simmer, **steam**, stew

Tips: Remove inedible peel. Soak in lemon water to avoid browning. Cook until very tender.

Botanical relatives: artichokes, chamomile, chicory, dandelion greens, endive, lettuces (e.g., Bibb, iceberg, romaine), radicchio, tarragon

anise

apples

artichokes

artichokes, Jerusalem

bell peppers, e.g., red

bread crumbs

burdock

butter and brown butter

carrots

cayenne

celery

celery root

chard, e.g., Swiss

cheese, e.g., Parmesan, sheep's milk

chervil

chives

coriander

cream

crème fraîche
currants
eggs
endive, Belgian
fennel
garlic
ghee
grains, e.g., pearled barley,
    quinoa, rice
gratins
hashes
hazelnuts
herbs
leeks
LEMON, e.g., juice
lovage
mushrooms, e.g., button, oyster,
    morel, wild
mustard, Dijon
nuts, e.g., almonds, **pecans**, pine
    nuts, walnuts
OIL, e.g., **olive**, pecan, safflower,
    sunflower, walnut
onions
onions, green
orange, e.g., juice, zest
PARSLEY
parsnips
pasta, e.g., fettuccine
pepper, black
polenta
pomegranates
potatoes
purees
quince
risottos
sage
salad dressings, e.g., vinaigrettes
salads
salt, e.g., kosher, truffle

Dishes

Smoked Salsify Risotto, Grilled Treviso, Orange Supreme, Fresh Dill
— Green Zebra (Chicago)

Caramelized Salsify "Potage": Watercress Glaze, Sultanas, and Madeira Mousseline
— Per Se (New York City)

sauces, e.g., hollandaise
scallions
SHALLOTS
sorrel
SOUPS, e.g., salsify, vegetable
stews
stock, e.g., mushroom, vegetable
thyme
tomatoes
truffles, black
vinegar, e.g., champagne, white
    wine
wine, white
yogurt

Flavor Affinities

salsify + apples + hazelnuts
salsify + bread crumbs + eggs +
    Parmesan cheese
salsify + chervil + chives
salsify + lemon + parsley +
    shallots

● SALT — IN GENERAL

"Because of my French training,
fleur de sel is one of the salts I
rely on most. Its flavor is perfect
with tomatoes. I'll use **Malden sea
salt**, which has lots of notes of the
ocean, for dishes like roasted root
vegetables. **Sel gris**, which often
comes in blue bottles, is strong,
and not as fine as other salts. I
have nothing against **kosher salt**,
but its flavor is just not what I'm
used to working with."
— JOSIAH CITRIN, MÉLISSE
(SANTA MONICA)

SALT, BLACK

Flavor: salty; pungent with notes
of eggs and/or sulphur
Volume: very loud
What it is: pinkish-gray Indian
mineral salt

Tips: Look for Indian kala
namak. Adds a boiled egg
flavor to vegan dishes (e.g., tofu
scrambles, "egg salads" made
with tofu). Caution: A little goes
a long way! Grind it fine to use
in the smallest doses.

apples
bananas
chats
chili pepper flakes
chutneys
cucumbers
fruits
honey
Indian cuisine
kiwi
lemon, e.g., juice
oranges
pickles
raitas
salad, vegan "egg"
sauces, e.g., "cheese"
tofu, e.g., *omelets, scrambles*
tomatoes
yogurt

Flavor Affinities

black salt + chili pepper flakes +
    honey + lemon juice
black salt + cucumbers +
    tomatoes + yogurt

SALT, HIMALAYAN

"**Himalayan salt** is the only
seasoning I use with any
regularity. It definitely helps to
bring the flavor out of virtually
anything — especially raw food."
— AMI BEACH, G-ZEN (BRANFORD, CT)

SALT, KOSHER

Volume: loud

Tip: Use kosher salt as an everyday salt for bolder-flavored or heavier dishes.

SALT, SEA

Volume: moderate

Tip: Use sea salt as an everyday salt for most dishes, especially to flavor dishes that are served cold.

SALT, SMOKED

Flavor: salty, with notes of smoke

beans
lentils
potatoes, e.g., baked

SALT, TRUFFLE

Flavor: salty, with earthy notes of truffles

Tip: Add just before serving.

celery root
eggs and egg dishes
popcorn
potatoes
risottos
salads
vegetables, e.g., root

SALTINESS

Tip: Adding salt to a dish diminishes the effects of bitter, sour, and sweet flavors. Below are some ways to add saltiness to a dish.

Bragg Liquid Aminos
Herbamare, an organic herb and salt blend
salt, e.g., kosher, sea, smoked, truffle
sea vegetables, e.g., dulse
soy sauce
tamari, organic wheat-free

"I've seasoned with sea vegetables like dulse to add minerals as well as **saltiness**."
— DIANE FORLEY, FLOURISH BAKING COMPANY (SCARSDALE, NY)

● SAUERKRAUT

Flavor: salty, **sour** and/or sweet, with a crunchy (fresher) or soft (older) texture
Volume: moderate – **loud**
What it is: fermented/pickled shredded cabbage
What's healthful about it: live enzymes, probiotics
Nutritional profile: 80% carbs / 16% protein / 4% fat
Calories: 30 per 1-cup serving
Protein: 1 gram
Technique: braise

apples and apple cider
"bacon"
bay leaf
bread, e.g., rye
caraway seeds
carrots
casseroles
cheese, e.g., Swiss
chestnuts
dill
Eastern European cuisine
fennel seeds
garlic
juniper berries
mushrooms, e.g., porcini
noodles, e.g., egg
oil, e.g., grapeseed
onions
pepper, black
potatoes
rosemary
salad dressing, e.g., Thousand Island
salt
sandwiches, e.g., "Reuben," "sausage"
sausages, vegan

savory, winter
shallots
sour cream
stews
sugar, brown
tempeh
vinegar, e.g., cider, white wine
wine, dry to off-dry white, e.g., Alsatian Riesling

Flavor Affinities

sauerkraut + apples + caraway seeds

● SAVORY

Season: year-round, esp. summer (summer savory) and winter (winter savory)
Flavor: bitter, with earthy/herbaceous notes of mint, **pepper**, and/or thyme
Volume: moderately loud (summer savory) – loud (winter savory)

Tips: Use each type of savory in the season when it's available; each naturally complements seasonal produce. However, one can almost always be used in place of the other. Winter savory is more biting and pungent than summer, so use less. Add at the end of the cooking process.

Botanical relatives: basil, lavender, marjoram, mint, oregano, rosemary, sage, thyme
Possible substitute: thyme

basil
bay leaf
*BEANS, DRIED, e.g., cannellini, white (esp. winter savory)
BEANS, FRESH, e.g., fava, green, lima (esp. summer savory)
beets
bell peppers
black-eyed peas
bouquets garnis

Brussels sprouts
cabbage
cassoulets, vegetarian
cauliflower
celery
cheese, e.g., cottage, cream, goat,
   Parmesan, and *cheese dishes*
chestnuts
chives
cumin
eggplant
eggs, e.g., *omelets*, scrambled
European cuisines
fatty foods
fennel
fines herbes
French cuisine, esp. Provençal
garlic
German cuisine
gravies
herbes de Provence
herbs, other, e.g., as a blending
   herb
Italian cuisine
kale
lavender
legumes
lemon
lentils
marjoram
Mediterranean cuisines
mint
mushrooms, e.g., porcini
nutmeg
oil, olive
olives
onions
oregano
paprika
parsley
pâtés
peas
polenta
potatoes
rice
rosemary
sage
salad dressings, e.g., vinaigrettes

salads, e.g., bean, potato
sauces, e.g., gravies, tomato sauces
seitan
shallots
soups, e.g., *bean, split pea, tomato-
   based*
squash, summer
stews
stock, vegetable
stuffings
tarragon
thyme
tomatoes and tomato sauces
vegetables, esp. root, e.g., turnips
vinegar, e.g., red wine, sherry
wine, red
zucchini

Flavor Affinities

savory + bay leaf + dried beans +
   onions
summer savory + artichoke hearts
   + fava beans + olive oil
summer savory + garlic +
   green beans
winter savory + eggs + onions
   + parsley
winter savory + garlic + tomatoes
   + *sauces*

• SCALLIONS (aka GREEN ONIONS or SPRING ONIONS)

Season: spring (scallions) –
summer (green onions)
Flavor: pungent notes of onions,
with a tender texture
Volume: quiet/moderate
(scallions) – moderate/loud
(green onions)
What they are: baby onions
that mature into green onions
(Immature scallions and green
onions are both often referred to
as spring onions and can be used
interchangeably.)
Nutritional profile: 81% carbs
/ 14% protein / 5% fats

Calories: 35 per 1-cup serving
(raw, chopped)
Protein: 2 grams
Techniques: braise, broil, grill,
pickle, poach, raw, sauté, simmer,
stir-fry
Botanical relative: onions

artichokes
Asian cuisines
asparagus
basil
bay leaf
beans, e.g., black, fava, white
bell peppers
bok choy
broccoli
butter
carrots
cheese, e.g., cheddar, cream, goat,
   mild, Parmesan
chiles
Chinese cuisine
cilantro
cinnamon
cloves
corn
couscous
cream
crudités, esp. milder scallions
cucumbers
curry powder/spices and *curries*
daikon
dill
dumplings, Asian
eggplant, e.g., Japanese
EGGS, e.g., *omelets, quiches*
fennel
garlic
ginger
grains, whole, e.g., couscous
gravies
greens, e.g., bitter
honey
Japanese cuisine
Korean cuisine
leeks
lemon, e.g., juice

lemongrass
lima beans
lime
mangoes
marinades
milk, coconut
mint
miso
mushrooms
mustard, e.g., Dijon, and mustard
    seeds
NOODLES, ASIAN, e.g., soba
nutmeg
oil, e.g., olive, peanut, sesame
oranges
oregano
pancakes, scallion
papayas
paprika
parsley
pastas
peanuts
pepper, e.g., black, white
pineapple
POTATOES, e.g., baked, mashed
rice, e.g., black, brown, sushi,
    wild
risottos
rosemary
sage
salad dressings
SALADS, *e.g., asparagus, corn,*
    noodle, potato, tomato, zucchini
salsas
salt, e.g., kosher
sandwiches
sauces
scallion pancakes
sesame oil
SOUPS, *e.g., gazpacho, mushroom,*
    noodle
Southeast Asian cuisines
soy sauce
squash
stir-fries
stock, e.g., vegetable
sugar
tabbouleh

Thai cuisine
thyme
tofu
tomatoes
vegetables
vinegar, e.g., balsamic,
    champagne, cider, rice,
    white wine
walnuts
watermelon
zucchini

Flavor Affinities

scallions + black beans + corn +
    tomatoes
scallions + garlic + ginger
scallions + ginger + soba noodles
scallions + mint + zucchini
scallions + sesame oil + soy sauce

SCRAMBLES (see TOFU, SCRAMBLED)

SEA BEANS (aka GLASSWORT or SAMPHIRE)

Season: spring – summer
Flavor: salty/sour, with notes
of apples (green), asparagus,
the ocean, and/or spinach, and
a crisp, crunchy texture (when
fresh)
Volume: moderate
What they are: marsh plants

Dishes

Seaweed Salad: Mixed Baby Greens, Laver, Sea Lettuce, Dulse Flakes, Avocado, and
Cucumber tossed in Miso Dressing
— 118 Degrees (California)

Raw Sea Vegetable and Avocado Salad with Satsuma Mandarin, Marinated Shiitake
Mushroom, Shredded Daikon and Carrot, Citrus-Ginger Vinaigrette, Wasabi Cream, and
Chile-Toasted Cashews
— Millennium (San Francisco)

Sea Cake: Butternut Squash, Yam and Sea Vegetable Croquette, Pesto, Sweet Chili Aioli
— Real Food Daily (Los Angeles)

Techniques: blanch, deep-fry,
pickle, raw, sauté, steam, stir-fry
(Note: Cook quickly to retain its
crispness.)
Botanical relatives: *not* sea
vegetables

avocados
cayenne
chiles, e.g., red
dill
garlic
ginger
lemon, e.g., juice
lime, e.g., juice
mushrooms, e.g., shiitake
oil, e.g., olive
pepper, black
salads
stir-fries
tempura
vinegar, e.g., balsamic, rice wine,
white wine

SEA VEGETABLES (see also ARAME, DULSE, HIZIKI, KOMBU, NORI, WAKAME)

Flavor: salty, with notes of the
sea
Volume: range from quieter
(e.g., arame, wakame) – louder
(e.g., hiziki)

What's healthful about them:
very high in essential and trace minerals

Tips: Kept in a cool, dry area, sea vegetables store beautifully. Soak dried sea vegetables in cold water for 5+ minutes to reconstitute before cooking (and to reduce sodium). Serve either cold or hot.

"If you dry **sea lettuce**, it tastes just like black truffles — it's an umami bomb! You can find sea lettuce along the San Mateo coast, and harvest it in the wintertime — just dry it and grind it to a powder to use to season sea vegetable salads or onigiri."
— ERIC TUCKER, MILLENNIUM (SAN FRANCISCO)

SEASONALITY (see AUTUMN, SPRING, SUMMER, WINTER)

"Live in each **season** as it passes: Breathe the air, drink the drink, taste the fruit, and resign yourself to the influences of each."
— HENRY DAVID THOREAU

SEAWEED (see SEA VEGETABLES, ARAME, DULSE, HIZIKI, KELP, NORI, WAKAME)

SEEDS, CARAWAY (see CARAWAY SEEDS)

SEEDS, CHIA (see CHIA SEEDS)

SEEDS, FLAX (see FLAXSEEDS)

SEEDS, HEMP
Flavor: slightly sweet, with notes of **nuts**, pine nuts, sesame seeds, **sunflower seeds**, and/or vanilla, and a buttery, creamy texture
Volume: quiet – moderate
What's healthful about them: omega-3 fatty acids
Botanical relative: marijuana (but without the same psychoactive properties, sorry)
Brand: Nutiva

almonds
avocados
BAKED GOODS, e.g., breads, cookies, muffins, piecrusts, quick breads
beans, white, e.g., cannellini
bell peppers
berries
blackberries
cabbage
carrots
cashews and cashew butter
CEREALS, breakfast, e.g., muesli
celery root
cheese, e.g., cottage
chili, vegetarian
chocolate
cilantro
dips
eggs, e.g., *omelets*
grains, whole
granola
lemon, e.g., juice
lime, e.g., juice
mushrooms, e.g., portobello
noodles, e.g., soba
oatmeal
oil, e.g., hemp
onions, green
PESTOS
pilafs
popcorn
rice
salad dressings
SALADS, e.g., green

smoothies
soups
spreads, e.g., chickpea
squash, winter, e.g., acorn, butternut
stir-fries
trail mixes
vegetables
veggie burgers
vinegar, white wine
walnuts
watercress
yogurt

• SEEDS, POPPY
Flavor: slightly sweet, with notes of nuts or smoke, and a rich, crunchy texture
Volume: quiet
Tip: Toast poppy seeds to heighten their flavor.

almonds
apples
Asian cuisines
BAKED GOODS, e.g., bagels, biscuits, breads, cakes, cookies, pastries, rolls
beans, e.g., green
blueberries
butter
buttermilk
cabbage
candies
carrots
cauliflower
cheese, e.g., ricotta
cinnamon
cloves
cream
curry powder
desserts
dips, e.g., cheese
eggplant
eggs and *egg dishes*
(Central) European cuisines
fruits
ginger

S

honey
Indian cuisine
LEMON, e.g., juice, zest
lentils
Mediterranean cuisines
Middle Eastern cuisines
noodles
nutmeg
onions, e.g., sweet
oranges and blood oranges, e.g.,
    juice, zest
pastas, e.g., pappardelle
potatoes, e.g., boiled
plums, dried
rice
Russian cuisine
SALAD DRESSINGS, esp. creamy,
    e.g., for fruit or green salads
salads, e.g., fruit, pasta
sauces, e.g., cream
sesame seeds
slaws, e.g., cole
soups
sour cream
spinach
strawberries
sugar
tomatoes
Turkish cuisine
vanilla
vegetables
walnuts
zucchini

Flavor Affinities

poppy seeds + blueberries +
    lemon
poppy seeds + lemon + vanilla

● SEEDS, PUMPKIN

Season: autumn
Flavor: sweet, with notes of

Dishes

Pumpkin Seed-Crusted Seitan with Quinoa, Corn Pilaf, Sautéed Lobster Mushrooms,
Broccoli, Leeks, and a Smoky Tomato-Chipotle Sauce with Radish Salad
— Candle 79 (New York City)

Brazil nuts and/or coconut, and
a chewy (when raw) or crunchy
(when toasted) texture
Volume: quiet
Nutritional profile: 71% fat /
16% protein / 13% carbs
Calories: 150 per 1-ounce
serving (dried)
Protein: 7 grams
Techniques: bake (at 250°F
about 60 – 90 minutes), boil,
raw, roast (at 350 for 15 – 20
minutes), toast

Tips: Rinse seeds, then soak in
salted water for a few hours. Let
dry before toasting. You can also
roast other winter squash seeds
in the same way as pumpkin
seeds.

Possible substitute: sunflower
seeds

American cuisine
***baked goods**, e.g., breads, cakes,*
    cookies, muffins
beans, e.g., black, green
breadings
caramel
cayenne
cheese, e.g., goat, quesos
chiles, e.g., chipotle, dried ancho,
    green, jalapeño
chili powder, e.g., chipotle
cilantro
cinnamon
coriander
corn
cranberries, dried
cumin
curry powder
enchiladas
garlic

grains, whole, e.g., farro, millet,
    wheat berries
granola
hazelnuts
lemon, e.g., juice
lime, e.g., juice
maple syrup
masa
"mayonnaise," vegan
MEXICAN CUISINE
moles
muesli
oatmeal
OIL, e.g., **corn**, olive, peanut,
    pumpkin seed, safflower,
    sunflower, vegetable
pestos
pumpkin
quinoa
raisins
rice, e.g., wild
salad dressings
***salads**, e.g., green, noodle, pasta*
salsas
SALT, e.g., kosher, sea
SAUCES, e.g., mole, pumpkin seed
seitan
***soups**, e.g., butternut squash,*
    pumpkin
South American cuisines
Southwestern (U.S.) cuisine
soy sauce
spinach
spreads
squash, e.g., butternut
stews
sugar, e.g., brown
tamales
tamari
tofu, e.g., in *scrambles*
tomatillos
tomatoes and sun-dried
    tomatoes
trail mixes
veggie burgers
yams

Flavor Affinities

pumpkin seeds + cayenne +
  curry powder
**pumpkin seeds + cayenne + olive
  oil** + sea salt
pumpkin seeds + chiles + cilantro
  + lime + *salsa*
pumpkin seeds + chiles + garlic
  + *salsa*
pumpkin seeds + chili powder +
  garlic + **lime** + salt + sugar
pumpkin seeds + ginger + tamari

"I like to fry **pumpkin seeds** and
treat them like nuts for our guests
with nut allergies."
— JON DUBOIS, GREEN ZEBRA (CHICAGO)

SEEDS, SESAME (see SESAME SEEDS)

● SEEDS, SUNFLOWER

Season: autumn
Flavor: notes of nuts
Volume: quiet – moderate

Dishes

Warm Sunflower Seed Soup, Burnt Onion, Puffed Rices and Grains, Pumpkin Seeds,
Black Tea
— Oxheart (Houston)

Nutritional profile: 74% fat /
14% carbs / 12% protein
Calories: 165 per 1-ounce
serving (dried)
Protein: 6 grams
Techniques: raw, roast, sprout,
toast
Tips: To enhance flavor, toast
before using. Check out sunflower seed butter as an alternative to peanut butter.
Possible substitute: pumpkin
seeds

apricots
*BAKED GOODS, e.g., breads,
  cookies, muffins, piecrusts*
beans, green
casseroles

cereals, e.g., hot breakfast
cranberries, dried
desserts
fruit
GRAINS, WHOLE, e.g., kasha,
  millet, oats, **quinoa**, long-grain
  rice, wheat berries
GRANOLA
honey
leeks
lemon
lentils
molasses
muesli
nutritional yeast
nuts, e.g., almonds, hazelnuts
pancakes
pastas
pâtés

SUNFLOWER MILLET FLAX – $4

pestos
raisins
"risottos"
SALADS, *e.g., green*
seeds, other, e.g., flax, pumpkin
soups
Southwestern (U.S.) cuisine
spreads
stuffings
tamari
tofu, esp. silken
tomatoes, sun-dried
trail bars and mixes
veggie burgers
yogurt

Flavor Affinities
sunflower seeds + basil + garlic +
　olive oil + pasta
sunflower seeds + flaxseeds +
　millet
sunflower seeds + lentils + onions
　+ *pâtés*
sunflower seeds + quinoa +
　raisins

"I've cooked **sunflower seeds**
risotto-style in an onion fennel
broth, accenting the dish with
sunflower-seed puree and toasted
whole sunflower seeds."
— JON DUBOIS, GREEN ZEBRA (CHICAGO)

● **SEITAN (see also tips
for NAMA-FU)**
[SAY-tahn]
Flavor: neutral, with a meaty
(e.g., chicken cutlet-like) texture
Volume: quiet
What it is: a meat substitute
made from wheat gluten,
nicknamed "wheat meat"
Nutritional profile: 81%
protein / 15% carbs / 4% fat
Calories: 105 calories per
1-ounce serving (vital wheat
gluten)

Protein: 21 grams
Techniques: bake, barbecue, fry,
grill, marinate, pan-sear, sauté,
sear, steam, stew, stir-fry

Tips: For peak flavor, be sure to
marinate the seitan for at least a
few hours. Add texture through
seasoned crusts, e.g., herbs,
panko. Use seitan "scraps" for
sauces, soups, taco fillings.
Seitan also freezes well.

　You can easily make your
own seitan from scratch with
vital wheat gluten, seasoning
it to taste (e.g., as you would
making your own chorizo or
gyros). However, if you're just
getting started, you might try
one of Arrowhead Mills's quick
mixes or a Knox Mountain mix.
You can also find commercially
prepared seitan from national
brands like Lightlife and White-
Wave, or local producers like
The Bridge (Middleton, CT).

Possible substitutes: tempeh,
extra-firm or super-firm tofu

Flavor Affinities
seitan + balsamic vinegar + ginger + maple syrup
seitan + basil + ginger + sesame + snow peas
seitan + bell peppers + "cheese" + onions
seitan + bell peppers + coconut milk + curry + **onions**
seitan + capers + garlic + lemon + parsley + shallots + white wine
seitan + capers + garlic + lemon + spinach
seitan + cayenne + fennel + garlic + paprika + *"Italian sausage"*
seitan + chickpeas + fennel + olives
seitan + citrus + herbs
seitan + daikon + ponzu + soy sauce + yuzu
seitan + eggplant + lemon + tahini
SEITAN + GARLIC + GINGER + kombu + soy sauce/tamari
seitan + garlic + lime + oregano
seitan + garlic + oregano + rosemary
seitan + maple + mustard + pecans
seitan + Marsala wine + shallots + thyme
seitan + miso + shiitake mushrooms + tamari
seitan + mushrooms + spinach + wine
seitan + olive oil + smoked paprika + *"chorizo sausage"*

Asian cuisines
barbecue sauce
basil and Thai basil
bay leaf
beans, e.g., black, green, pinto,
　red
bell peppers
Bragg Liquid Aminos
broccoli and broccoli rabe
burdock
CAPERS and caper berries
carrots
"chicken" (+ chicken-flavored
　vegetarian stock)
chickpeas
chiles, e.g., jalapeño
chili pepper flakes and chili
　powder
Chinese cuisine
citrus
coconut
cornmeal (e.g., as a crust)
curry powder and **curries**
daikon
eggplant
fajitas

Dishes

Seitan Scallopini: Seitan Cutlets in a White Wine-Lemon-Caper Sauce, served with Mashed Potatoes and Kale
— Blossom (New York City)

Seitan Skewers with Chimichurri Citrus-Herb Sauce
— Candle Café (New York City)

Scallopini with Marsala-Glazed Morel Mushrooms (pictured above)
— Crossroads (Los Angeles)

All Veggie Meatloaf: Organic Lentil, Seitan, Shiitake Mushrooms, and Sweet Potato Loaf with Miso Gravy and Wok-Sautéed Greens
— Josie's (New York City)

Barbeque Seitan with Mushroom Sage Cornbread Stuffing and Seared Collard Greens
— Karyn's on Green (Chicago)

Seitan and Waffles with Caramelized Onions, Ancho Chili-Maple Redux, Watercress and Creamy Caesar, and Candied Walnuts
— Plant (Asheville, NC)

Barbecued Seitan: Molasses-Mustard Glazed Seitan, Crispy Fried Polenta Tots, and Slow-Cooked Collard Greens
— Portobello (Portland, OR)

The Club (Sandwich): Crispy Seitan, Tempeh Bacon, Avocado, Lettuce, Tomato, and Vegenaise on Sourdough Bread
— Real Food Daily (Los Angeles)

Blackened Seitan, Creamy Grits, Melted Collards, Smoked Onion, and Chili Vinegar
— True Bistro (Somerville, MA)

fennel
GARLIC
GINGER
"gyros," esp. when served with pita and tzatziki sauce
herbs and *herbes de Provence*
hoisin sauce
Japanese cuisine
kombu
leeks
LEMON
lemongrass
lentils
macrobiotic cuisine
maple syrup
miso, e.g., white
MUSHROOMS, e.g., chanterelle, shiitake, wild
mustard, e.g., Dijon
noodles, e.g., rice
nori
nutritional yeast
oil, e.g., olive, sesame
olives
ONIONS, e.g., red, white
oregano
paprika, smoked
parsley
pastas
peanuts and peanut butter
PECANS
pepper, black
"piccata"
pilafs
pine nuts
polenta
ponzu
pumpkin seeds
rice, e.g., brown
rosemary
sage
salt, sea
sandwiches, e.g., club (with crisp tempeh "bacon"), Philly "cheesesteak," "Reuben"
"sausage," e.g., chorizo, Italian
"schnitzel"
sea vegetables

"Tofu, tempeh, and seitan are the holy trinity of vegetarianism. **Seitan** is my favorite because of its versatility."
— JOY PIERSON, CANDLE 79 (NEW YORK CITY)

"I love serving **seitan** with a crunchy crust, such as crushed cashews, pumpkin or sunflower seeds, or even quinoa. Instead of egg wash, we'll dip the seitan in a vegan mixture of water, lemon juice, garlic, and nutritional yeast before crusting and sautéing."
— ANGEL RAMOS, CANDLE 79 (NEW YORK CITY)

"I don't know of any other vegetarian restaurant that offered a vegetarian Reuben sandwich before we did. Ours is made with a **seitan**-based pastrami 'wheat meat,' a little sauerkraut, spicy mustard, Thousand Island dressing, and Vegenaise on oversized Jewish rye bread, which you can get with either Swiss cheese, vegan cheese, or — my favorite — cottage-style tofu, which is mashed tofu seasoned with garlic, chives, and onions. I've probably eaten two hundred of them over the past ten years. In the beginning, we used to make our Reubens with vegetarian bacon bits, which softened on the sandwich, which was spread with a layer of Vegenaise. But the seitan version is more authentic."
— BOB GOLDBERG, FOLLOW YOUR HEART (CANOGA PARK, CA)

sesame seeds
shallots
shepherd's pie
skewers
snow peas
soups
SOY SAUCE
spinach
sprouts, bean
stews
stir-fries
STOCK, e.g., mushroom, vegetable
stroganoff, e.g., mushroom
sweet potatoes
tahini
TAMARI
tamarind
thyme
tofu
tomatoes and tomato paste
tomatoes, sun-dried
turmeric

umeboshi plum sauce
vinegar, balsamic
wakame
walnuts
wine, e.g., dry red or white, Marsala, port
Worcestershire sauce, vegan
yuzu

SESAME OIL (see OIL, SESAME)

● SESAME SEEDS — IN GENERAL (aka GOMA)

Flavor: slightly sweet, with notes of butter, milk, and/or nuts (e.g., almonds), and a rich texture
Volume: quiet (white seeds) – moderate (dark seeds)
Nutritional profile: 73% fats / 16% carbs / 11% protein
Calories: 160 per 1-ounce serving (dried)
Protein: 5 grams
Techniques: raw, roast
Tips: Toast to bring out their flavor. Use ground or whole.

ASIAN CUISINES, esp. black sesame seeds
asparagus
avocado
BAKED GOODS, e.g., bagels, breads, breadsticks, cakes, cookies, corn bread, crackers, pastries, piecrusts
bananas
basil
beans, e.g., green
berries
broccoli
brown rice syrup
burdock
cabbage
carrots
casseroles
chickpeas
chili, e.g., pepper flakes, oil
Chinese cuisine, esp. black sesame seeds
cilantro
citrus, e.g., lemon, lime
cucumber
daikon
dates
desserts, e.g., cakes, cookies, puddings
dressings
falafel
fruit
garlic
GINGER
gomashio (sesame seeds + salt, in an 8:1 ratio)
grains, whole, e.g., barley, couscous, millet, quinoa, rice
granola
gravies
greens, bitter, salad

halvah
honey
Indian cuisine
Japanese cuisine, esp. black sesame
  seeds
kuzu
maple syrup
MIDDLE EASTERN CUISINE
mirin
miso
mushrooms, e.g., shiitake
NOODLES, ESP. ASIAN, e.g.,
  soba
nori
"pesto"
RICE, e.g., sticky
salad dressings
salads, e.g., fruit, green, pasta
salt, e.g., sea
sauces, e.g., mole, tahini
scallions
seeds, other, e.g., flax, hemp, poppy

seitan
sesame, e.g., butter, oil, paste
shallots
shiso, e.g., red
snow peas
soups
soy sauce
spinach
spreads
stir-fries
sugar snap peas
sumac
sushi, e.g., nori rolls
tahini
tamari
thyme
TOFU
tomatoes
trail mixes
vegetables
vinegar, rice
za'atar

Flavor Affinities
sesame seeds + avocado + greens
  + tomatoes
sesame seeds + bananas +
  coconut
sesame seeds + chili pepper
  flakes + hemp seeds + nori +
  poppy seeds
sesame seeds + ginger + honey
  + lime
sesame seeds + lemon + **za'atar**
sesame seeds + nori + shiso
sesame seeds + sumac + thyme

• SHALLOTS
Season: summer – autumn
Flavor: slightly sweet, with
complex notes of garlic and/or
onions
Volume: **quiet** – moderate
Nutritional profile: 89% carbs
/ 10% protein / 1% fat

S

Calories: 10 per 1-tablespoon
serving (raw, chopped)
Techniques: bake, blanch, boil,
braise, deep-fry, fry, grill, pickle,
raw, roast, sauté, stew, stir-fry,
toast

Tip: Shallots are quieter than
garlic or onions.

Botanical relatives: asparagus,
chives, garlic, leeks, onions
Possible substitute: onions

Asian cuisines
asparagus
avocados
basil
bay leaf
beans, green
beets
Brussels sprouts
butter
carrots
cheese, e.g., Roquefort
chiles
Chinese cuisines
chives
CITRUS, e.g., grapefruit, lemon,
   lime, orange
coconut milk
corn
cream
curries
dips
eggplant
eggs, e.g., *omelets*
endive
European cuisines, e.g., French,
   Italian
fennel
French cuisine, esp. northern
fruit
galangal
garlic
ginger
grains, whole, e.g., barley, bulgur,
   kasha, **rice**

gravies
greens, bitter, e.g., turnips
honey
legumes, e.g., lentils
lemongrass
lemon, e.g., juice, zest
lentils, e.g., yellow
lettuce
lime
marinades
Mediterranean cuisines
miso
MUSHROOMS, e.g., shiitake
mustard, e.g., Dijon
noodles, e.g., Asian, stir-fried
oil, e.g., grapeseed, hazelnut,
   olive, walnut
orange
papaya
parsley
parsnips
pastas
peanuts
pepper, black
POTATOES
raisins
rosemary
sage
SALAD DRESSINGS, esp.
   vinaigrettes
SALADS
salt, sea
*SAUCES, e.g., **butter**, French*
soups
SOUTHEAST ASIAN CUISINES
squash, e.g., butternut
stews
stock, vegetable
sugar, e.g., brown

Dishes

Pan-Fried Shishito Peppers with Parmesan, Sesame, and Miso
—Girl & the Goat (Chicago)

tarragon
thyme
tofu
tomatoes
vegetables, e.g., root, e.g., turnips
VINEGAR, e.g., balsamic, brown
   rice, champagne, cider, red
   wine, **sherry**, white wine
WINE, e.g., dry red or white
Worcestershire sauce, vegan
zucchini

Flavor Affinities

shallots + chiles + ginger +
   lemongrass
shallots + herbs + lemon juice +
   mustard
shallots + lemon juice
   + Roquefort cheese + vegan
   Worcestershire sauce + yogurt

SHISHITO PEPPERS

Flavor: sweet/hot, with notes of
citrus
Volume: quiet (for peppers)
What they are: small green
Asian peppers
Techniques: grill, roast, sauté,
stuff

Asian cuisines
cheese, e.g., blue, goat, Parmesan
chili pepper flakes
eggs, e.g., *omelets*, scrambled
lemon
miso
oil, e.g., canola, olive, sesame
pickled peppers
salt, e.g., sea

sesame, e.g., seeds, oil
soy sauce
stir-fries
stuffed shishito peppers

Flavor Affinities
shishito peppers + chili pepper
  flakes + lemon + soy sauce

SHISO LEAF (aka JAPANESE BASIL or PERILLA)

Flavor: slightly sour; aromatic,
with notes of anise, basil,
cinnamon (esp. green), fennel,
lemon, licorice, **mint**, pepper,
and/or sage
Volume: quieter (red) –
moderate/louder (green)

Tip: This Japanese herb comes
in green (typical) and red (more
astringent, with notes of anise,
flowers, and mint).

Techniques: blanch, raw, steam,
tempura-fry
Botanical relatives: basil,
mint
Possible substitute: mint

avocado
beets
cabbage, e.g., napa
corn
cucumbers
daikon
edamame
garlic
ginger, e.g., pickled
grains, whole, e.g., bulgur, rice
grapefruit
JAPANESE CUISINE
Korean cuisine
lime, e.g., juice
melons
mirin
miso, e.g., white

mushrooms, e.g., shiitake
NOODLES, ASIAN, e.g., soba,
  somen
nori rolls (e.g., avocado +
  cucumber)
oil, e.g., olive, peanut, sesame
onions
peaches
rice, e.g., brown, sushi
sake
salads, e.g., pasta
scallions
seeds, e.g., pumpkin, **sesame**
snow peas
soups, e.g., noodle
soy sauce
spring rolls
stir-fries
sushi, vegetarian
tamari
tempura
TOFU, e.g., served chilled
umeboshi plums and plum paste
vinegar, e.g., balsamic, rice

Flavor Affinities
shiso leaf + avocado + cucumber
  + nori + sushi rice
shiso leaf + garlic + oil + soy
  sauce + vinegar
shiso leaf + ginger + lime
shiso leaf + ginger + tamari

SHOOTS, PEA

Season: spring
Flavor: sweet, with notes of
peas, and a crispy/crunchy
texture
Volume: quiet
What they are: pea sprouts
before they grow into baby pea
greens
Calories: 30 per 1-cup serving
(raw)
Protein: 2 grams
Techniques: raw, or very lightly
cooked; sauté, steam, stir-fry

Tips: Cook only briefly, if at all
(e.g., quickly sauté in olive oil
and garlic). Add to dishes at the
end of the cooking process or
just before serving.

Asian cuisines
avocado
basil
cheese, e.g., feta, goat, Parmesan
chervil
Chinese cuisine
chives
corn
dill
eggs, e.g., scrambled
endive, Belgian
GARLIC
ginger
grapefruit
kale
lemon, e.g., juice
mango
mushrooms, e.g., chanterelle,
  cremini
noodles, Asian
nori rolls
OIL, e.g., flax, **OLIVE**, roasted
  peanut, sesame
orange
pastas
pears
radishes
risottos
SALADS
salt, e.g., sea
sandwiches
seeds, e.g., sesame
shallots
soups
Southeast Asian cuisines
sprouts, e.g., sunflower
stir-fries
stock, vegetable
strawberries
sugar
vinegar, e.g., rice wine
wheat berries

Flavor Affinities

pea shoots + garlic + ginger + sesame oil

pea shoots + garlic + mushrooms + olive oil + *pasta* + Parmesan cheese

pea shoots + lemon + olive oil + radishes

SHOOTS, SUNFLOWER

Flavor: notes of lemon and nuts, and a crisp texture
Volume: quiet – moderate
What they are: sunflower sprouts before they grow into sunflower baby greens
Techniques: raw, sauté (very briefly!)

apples
avocado
cheese, e.g., goat, Parmesan
garlic
lemon
oil, olive
pepper, black
pestos
salads
salt, sea
sunflower seeds
yogurt

SLOW-COOKED

Season: autumn – winter
Tips: These herbs and flavorings taste better with longer cooking. For the opposite of slow-cooked, see **freshness.**

cumin
garlic
ginger
horseradish
onions
oregano
rosemary
shallots
thyme

SMOKING

Tips: It doesn't take more than 30 – 60 seconds in a smoker to add a smoked flavor to many foods. You definitely *don't* want to *over*smoke foods, which makes them bitter and leaves an unpleasant brownish coating. Experiment with various woods for different flavors, but you'll typically want to lean toward lighter woods like apple and cherry (which are sweeter), or perhaps oak and pecan (which are a bit louder), rather than hickory, maple, and mesquite (which are much more pronounced and can easily overwhelm fruits and vegetables).

Brand: Nordic Ware and other companies for small stovetop/grilltop smokers

Dishes

Smoked Broccoli Dogs, Broccoli Kraut, Salt, and Vinegar Broccoli Rabe
— Dirt Candy (New York City)

Lady Duck Farm Egg, Smoked Potato Purée, Parsley, and Country Sourdough
— Green Zebra (Chicago)

"I like **smoked flavors** and smoke lots of different fruits and vegetables. Smoked lettuce has the flavor of a grilled hamburger. It's comical how convincing it can be: Customers have accused us of putting bacon into our smoked potato puree dish, which evokes bacon and eggs. We'll smoke garlic or onions and puree them for sauces — or to add a bacony note to pasta alla carbonara. Customers automatically expect raisins to taste dry, chewy, and sweet — but serving them raisins that have been pickled then smoked will make them think again."
— JON DUBOIS, GREEN ZEBRA (CHICAGO)

"Sometimes I'll add a little tequila to a black bean sauce to give it a unique **smoky** flavor — a sauce that would be delicious with chile-grilled seitan with collard greens and sweet plantains."
— ANGEL RAMOS, CANDLE 79 (NEW YORK CITY)

SMOOTHIES (see also JUICES)

What they are: differentiated from juices in that they contain fiber, which makes them creamy and more nutritious.
Tips: When in doubt, add a banana for texture and flavor; they combine well with many other fruits and even vegetables. For richer-tasting smoothies, use frozen fruit.

"**Smoothies** made with tropical fruits will hide the flavor of strong greens. One of our most popular smoothies is the Island Green, which is made with coconut, coconut water, cucumber, kale, mango, pineapple, spinach, and strawberries."
— CASSIE AND MARLENE TOLMAN, POMEGRANATE CAFÉ (PHOENIX)

"The seasons are an inspiration to all of us here. One autumn, I came up with an ideal seasonal treat: a sweet potato **smoothie** flavored with maple syrup, almond milk, cinnamon, and nutmeg. Every fall, we bring it back!"

— MARK DOSKOW, EXECUTIVE DIRECTOR, CANDLE 79 (NEW YORK CITY)

SNACKS

Tips: When you're craving a snack, reach for one of the healthier veg options below instead of the standard American snacks of salty or sweet processed foods. For example, if you're craving chocolate, don't snack on candy bars or even chocolate chips — try cacao nibs.

apples (e.g., with cheese or nut butter) and applesauce
baba ghanoush
bagel, whole grain, e.g., with nut butter
bananas
berries
bread, whole grain, e.g., with nut butter or other *spread*
cacao nibs
carrot sticks
chips, e.g., baked tortilla
crudités, e.g., with dip
dips, e.g., artichoke, bean, lentil, spinach
edamame, e.g., dry-roasted, fresh
eggs, e.g., deviled, hard-boiled
fruit, e.g., dried or fresh, e.g., apples, bananas, clementines, pears
graham crackers (whole grain), e.g., with nut butter
granola or granola bar
grapes, e.g., frozen
guacamole

hummus with raw veggies and/or whole-grain pita
melon
nuts and nut butters, e.g., almond, peanut
olives
peanuts
pesto, e.g., with whole-grain bread or vegetables
pickles and pickled vegetables
pita bread, whole grain
popcorn, e.g., with nutritional yeast
rice cakes
salsas, e.g., with baked chips
seeds, e.g., pumpkin, sunflower, esp. toasted
smoothies
soups, e.g., vegetable, with whole-grain bread or crackers
spreads, e.g., bean, sun-dried tomato
tortilla chips, baked, e.g., with salsa
trail mix
vegetables, raw, e.g., carrots, celery, cucumber slices, e.g., with *dips*
yogurt, e.g., fresh, frozen

Flavor Affinities

almond butter + apple slices (or whole-grain bread) + raw honey (one of Chef Matthew Kenney's favorite snacks)

SNAP PEAS (see SUGAR SNAP PEAS)

● SNOW PEAS (aka CHINESE PEA PODS) (see also SUGAR SNAP PEAS)

Season: spring, autumn

Dishes

Pesto Linguini with Lemon Zest, Sun-Dried Tomato, and Snow Peas
— Rancho La Puerta (Mexico)

Flavor: sweet, with a crisp, crunchy yet tender texture
Volume: moderate
Nutritional profile: 73% carbs / 23% protein / 4% fats
Calories: 40 per 1-cup serving (raw, chopped)
Protein: 3 grams
Techniques: blanch, boil (2 – 3 minutes), raw, sauté, simmer, steam, stir-fry (2 – 3 minutes)
Tip: Cook only briefly – just 3 or 4 minutes.
Botanical relatives: peas, sugar snap peas

Asian cuisines
bamboo shoots
bean sprouts
bell peppers, e.g., red
bok choy
broccoli
butter
cabbage, e.g., napa
carrots
cashews
cauliflower
celery
chiles, chili paste, and chili sauce
Chinese cuisine
cilantro
coconut and coconut milk
curries, **curry paste, and curry powder**
five-spice powder
GARLIC
GINGER
herbs
hoisin sauce
kale
lemon
lemongrass

lime
mint
mirin
miso
mushrooms, e.g., Asian, oyster, portobello, wild
mustard
NOODLES, ESP. ASIAN, e.g., ramen or udon
OIL, e.g., canola, **peanut, sesame**
onions, e.g., green, red
orange, e.g., juice, zest
pad thai
peanuts and peanut sauce
peas
pepper, e.g., black, Szechuan
ponzu sauce
radishes
rice, e.g., basmati, brown, wild
SALADS, e.g., Asian, bean, grain, noodle
salt
SCALLIONS
SESAME, E.G., OIL, seeds
slaws, e.g., Asian
soups
Southeast Asian cuisines
SOY SAUCE
sprouts, bean
squash, summer
STIR-FRIES
stock, vegetable
sugar, e.g., brown
sugar snap peas
tarragon
Thai cuisine
TOFU
vinaigrette
vinegar, rice
water chestnuts
Worcestershire sauce, vegetarian
zucchini

Flavor Affinities
snow peas + Asian noodles + lime + peanut sauce
snow peas + Asian noodles + mirin

snow peas + bell peppers + curry powder + scallions + tofu
snow peas + carrots + ginger
snow peas + carrots + honey + orange
snow peas + chiles + ginger + lemongrass
snow peas + coconut milk + garlic + lime
snow peas + garlic + ginger
snow peas + garlic + peanut oil + pepper
snow peas + ginger + scallions

● SORGHUM (aka JOWAR and MILO)

Flavor: slightly sweet, with nutty notes, and the appearance of Israeli couscous; very chewy
Volume: quiet – moderate
What it is: whole grain
Gluten-free: yes
Nutritional profile: 89% carbs / 8% fat / 3% protein
Calories: 165 per ¼-cup serving
Protein: 5 grams
Techniques: pop (like popcorn), simmer (50 – 60 minutes), steam
Ratio: 1:3 (1 cup sorghum to 3 cups cooking liquid, e.g., water or stock)

African cuisines
avocado
bay leaf
carrots
cereals, hot
cayenne
cheese, e.g., feta, Parmesan
chili powder
chives
coconut milk
cucumbers
curry powder
garlic
ginger
Indian cuisine
khichuri

lemon, e.g., juice, zest
lentils
mirin
miso
oil, olive
onions, e.g., green, spring
orange
oregano
parsley
pepper, black
pilafs
pine nuts
popped sorghum (like popcorn)
porridges, e.g., savory or sweet
raisins
rosemary
salads, e.g., grain
salt, sea
sesame, e.g., oil, seeds
soups
soy sauce
stock, e.g., vegetable
tahini
thyme
vegetables
vinegar, rice

SORREL

[SOR-ell]
Season: spring – autumn
Flavor: bitter/**very sour**/sweet, with astringent notes of lemon and/or spinach, and a soft texture
Volume: moderate (younger and/or cultivated) – loud (older and/or wild)
Techniques: raw, simmer, wilt
Botanical relative: buckwheat

asparagus
basil
beans, e.g., green, lima, white
beets
bell peppers
bread crumbs
butter
carrots
celery

celery root
chard
cheese, e.g., goat, Gruyère,
    Parmesan, ricotta
chervil
chives
cream
crème fraîche
cucumbers
cumin
curry powder
custards
dill
EGGS, *e.g., frittatas,* hard-cooked,
    omelets, poached, *quiches*
European cuisines
French cuisine
garlic
grains, whole
gratins
greens, e.g., beet, salad
leeks
lemon, e.g., juice, zest
lentils, e.g., green
lovage
mint
mushrooms, e.g., porcini, wild
mustard
nettles
nutmeg
OILS, e.g., hazelnut, **olive,** walnut
olives
ONIONS, e.g., red, yellow
onions, spring
parsley
pastas

peas, split
peas, e.g., spring
pepper, e.g., black, white
pine nuts
POTATOES
purees
purslane
ramps
rice
risottos
SALADS, E.G., GRAIN, GREEN
    (esp. young sorrel)
salt, e.g., **sea**
sandwiches
SAUCES, e.g., cream, sorrel, white
shallots
SOUPS, e.g., cream, lentil, potato,
    sorrel
sour cream
SPINACH
stock, e.g., mushroom, vegetable
tarragon
thyme
tomatoes
vegetables, esp. green, grilled,
    root
vinegar, e.g., balsamic, red wine,
    sherry
wine, dry white
yogurt

Flavor Affinities
sorrel + asparagus + risotto
sorrel + chives + garlic + yogurt
sorrel + garlic + mushrooms
sorrel + garlic + yogurt

Dishes

Turnip and Potato Soup with Sorrel
— Chez Panisse Café (Berkeley)

Barigoule Consommé en Gelée: Heirloom Sorrel, Toasted Pine Nuts, and Castelvetrano
Olives
— Per Se (New York City)

Strawberry-Sorrel Bread Pudding with Beet Root Jam and Sorrel Bon Bon
— Vedge (Philadelphia)

sorrel + mushroom stock + red
    onions + *sauces*
sorrel + garlic + nutmeg + onion
    + potatoes + purslane
sorrel + potatoes + spring onions
    + *soups*
sorrel + tomatoes + white beans
    + *soups*

● SOUR CREAM
Flavor: sour, with a creamy
texture
Volume: moderate – loud
Tips: Use fresh, or cook at low
temperatures only. Try ● fat-free
or dairy-free (e.g., cashew or
tofu) sour cream.
Vegan Brand: Tofutti non-
hydrogenated Better Than Sour
Cream

baked goods, e.g., cakes, cookies
beans, black
beets
blintzes
chiles, e.g., chipotle
cilantro
corn
cucumbers
desserts
dill
dips
European cuisines, esp. Eastern,
    Northern
fajitas
fruit
horseradish
lemon, e.g., juice
lime, e.g., juice
Mexican cuisine
mustard, e.g., Dijon
noodles
pancakes, savory, e.g., corn, griddle
paprika
pepper, e.g., black
potatoes, e.g., baked
Russian cuisine

salad dressings
salads
salsa
sauces
scallions
Scandinavian cuisines
soups, *e.g., beet, borscht, broccoli,*
carrot, mushroom, pumpkin,
sweet potato
sugar, e.g., brown
toppings
vanilla
vegetables

Flavor Affinities
sour cream + chili powder +
cilantro + garlic + honey + salt
sour cream + mustard +
vegetable stock

SOURNESS

Tips: Sourness tends to
sharpen other flavors. In small
amounts, sour notes enhance
bitterness; in large amounts,
they suppress bitterness. Examples of sour foods are below:

apples, tart, e.g., Granny Smith,
winesap
blackberries
buttermilk
caraway seeds
cheese, sour, e.g., chèvre and
other goat cheeses, cream
cherries, sour
citrus
cloves
coriander
cornichons
cranberries
cream of tartar
crème fraîche
currants
fermented foods
fruits, e.g., sour, unripe
galangal
ginger

grapefruit
grapes, green
Kaffir lime
kiwi
kumquats
lemon, e.g., juice, zest
lemon, preserved
lemongrass
lime, e.g., juice, zest
milk, e.g., goat
miso
mushrooms, e.g., enoki
orange, e.g., juice, zest
pickled foods
plums, esp. unripe
ponzu
quince
rhubarb
rose hips
sauces, e.g., reduced wine
sauerkraut
sorrel
sour cream
soy sauce
sumac
tamarind
tomatoes, esp. green
verjus
vinegars
whey
wine, dry
yogurt
yuzu

SOUTH AMERICAN CUISINE
beans, e.g., black
bell peppers
cheese, e.g., queso fresco
chiles
corn
fruit, tropical
maca
potatoes
quinoa
squash
yuca

SOUTHWESTERN (U.S.) CUISINE
What it is: an amalgam of
Mexican, Native American, and
Spanish influences

avocados
BEANS, e.g., black, red
bell peppers
cactus
cayenne
chayote
cheese, e.g., cotija, queso fresco
chiles, e.g., anaheim, ancho,
chipotle, jalapeño, poblano,
serrano; and chili powder
chocolate
cilantro
cinnamon
CORN
cumin
garlic
jícama
lime
masa
mushrooms
nuts
onions
oregano, Mexican
posole
pumpkin seeds
rice
scallions
squash
tomatillos
tortillas
squash

Flavor Affinities
bell peppers + black beans +
brown rice + butternut squash
+ cilantro + scallions

• SOYBEANS (see also EDAMAME, which are green soybeans)
Flavor: neutral, with notes of
beans and/or grass

Volume: quiet
Nutritional profile: 43% fat / 33% protein / 24% carbs
Calories: 300 per 1-cup serving (boiled)
Protein: 29 grams
Timing: Cook presoaked dried soybeans about 3 – 4 hours. **Do not** pressure-cook, as soybeans foam, which can clog the valve and cause the cooker to explode.
Tips: Buy only organic (non-GMO) soybeans. Look for black soybeans, which have more flavor.

baked beans
bay leaf
cardamom
carrots
casseroles
cayenne
celery
chiles, e.g., chipotle, and chili powder
chili, vegetarian
cilantro
coriander
cumin
garlic
ginger
grains, e.g., barley, millet
honey
"hummus"
lemon, e.g., juice
mint
molasses
mushrooms
natto
nut butter, e.g., almond, cashew, peanut, walnut
oats
oil, e.g., peanut, sesame, sunflower
onions
peanuts
salads, e.g., grain, green
scallions

sesame seeds
soups, e.g., minestrone, vegetable
soy sauce
spinach
squash, e.g., kabocha
star anise
stews
tahini
tamari
tamarind
tempeh
veggie burgers
vinegar
wasabi

Flavor Affinities
soybeans + cilantro + mint + spinach
soybeans + nut butter + soy sauce

SOY SAUCE, NATURALLY FERMENTED (see also TAMARI)
Flavor: salty, with notes of caramel and/or toast
Volume: moderate – loud
What it is: brewed soybeans, sea salt, water, and wheat
Nutritional profile: 58% carbs / 41% protein / 1% fat (and very high in sodium)
Calories: 10 per 1-tablespoon serving
Protein: 1 gram
Tips: Add at the end of the cooking process or to finish a dish. Look for raw (unpasteurized) soy sauce. Japanese soy sauce tends to be slightly sweeter and louder than Chinese soy sauce. Those watching their sodium intake can opt for low-sodium soy sauce.
Brands: Nama Shoyu or San-J
Possible substitutes: Bragg Liquid Aminos, tamari

Asian cuisines

basil, Thai
chiles
Chinese cuisine
citrus
dumplings, e.g., Asian
eggplant
garlic
ginger
greens
honey
Japanese cuisine
marinades
mirin
molasses
mushrooms, e.g., portobello, shiitake
mustard and mustard paste
noodles, Asian, e.g., *pad thai*
oil, e.g., **sesame**, vegetable
onions
rice
salad dressings
sauces and dipping sauces
sesame, e.g., oil, seeds
soups
stir-fries
sugar
sushi, vegetarian
tamarind
tempeh
tofu
vinegar, rice

Flavor Affinities
soy sauce + brown rice + nori + sesame seeds
soy sauce + brown rice vinegar + chili sauce + lime + sesame oil
soy sauce + chiles + garlic
soy sauce + chiles + garlic + **ginger** + honey + mirin + **scallions** + sesame oil + vinegar
soy sauce + **garlic** + **ginger** + mirin + sesame oil
soy sauce + **ginger** + **scallions**
soy sauce + **ginger** + **sesame**
soy sauce + tamarind + tofu
soy sauce + Thai basil + tofu

SOY SAUCE, THAI (aka LIGHT, THIN, or WHITE SOY SAUCE)

Flavor: salty, with a thin, watery texture
Volume: moderate

> **Tip:** Use instead of fermented fish sauce in Southeast Asian dishes.

Brand: Healthy Boy

marinades
noodles, e.g., Asian, rice
sauces, e.g., dipping
Southeast Asian cuisines
stir-fries
Thai cuisine
tofu
Vietnamese cuisine

SPANISH CUISINE

almonds
bay leaf
bread
custards
eggs
garlic
hazelnuts
lemon
oil, olive
olives
onions
orange
paprika, e.g., smoked, sweet
parsley
peppers, esp. guindilla, piquillo (esp. roasted)
pimenton
pine nuts
pomegranates
rice, e.g., bomba
roasted dishes
saffron
soups
stews
thyme
tomatoes

tortillas (crustless quiches filled with potatoes and/or vegetables)
vanilla
vinegar, sherry
walnuts
wine, e.g., sherry

● SPELT BERRIES

Flavor: slightly sweet, with notes of barley and/or nuts, and a dense, firm, chewy texture
Volume: quiet – moderate/loud
What they are: whole grain (Note: spelt is *not* the same as farro, which is a much faster-cooking grain.)
What's healthful about them: higher in **protein** than wheat and some other grains
Gluten-free: no
Nutritional profile: 78% carbs / 16% protein / 6% fats
Calories: 250 per 1-cup serving (cooked)
Protein: 11 grams
Techniques: marinate, simmer, steam
Timing: If a richer flavor is desired, toast grains first. Rinse grains, presoak for 8 hours, and then simmer about 30 – 60 minutes, covered, until tender.
Ratio: 1:2 (chewy) – 1:3 (soft) (1 cup spelt to 2 – 3 cups cooking liquid, e.g., water, stock)
Botanical relatives: barley, corn, rye, triticale, wheat
Possible substitute: wheat berries

allspice
apples
artichokes, Jerusalem
avocado
baked goods, e.g., breads, cakes, muffins
basil
beans, e.g., green, **white**
Brussels sprouts
butter
buttermilk
casseroles
celery
cereals, e.g., hot breakfast
cheese, e.g., feta, goat, Parmesan
chickpeas
chili, vegetarian
chives
cilantro
cinnamon
cumin
currants
dill
dolmas
escarole
European cuisines, e.g., Austrian, German, Swiss
fennel
French cuisine, e.g., southern
garlic
ginger
grains, other, e.g., brown rice
kale
kefir
lemon, e.g., juice, zest
lentils, e.g., black, green
lovage
marjoram
Mediterranean cuisines

Dishes

Warm Marinated Artichoke and Spelt Salad with Shaved Fennel and Red Onion, Escarole and Bitter Greens, Olive and Currant Vinaigrette, and Pink Peppercorn Aioli
— Millennium (San Francisco)

mushrooms, e.g., black trumpet

nuts, e.g., almonds, hazelnuts, pecans, walnuts

oil, e.g., nut, **olive**, sesame

onions, e.g., caramelized, red

pancakes

parsley

pastas

pepper, black

pilafs

pine nuts

pizza dough

"risottos"

salads, e.g., *grain*, *green*

salt, e.g., sea

soups, e.g., *minestrone*, *vegetable*

squash, e.g., winter

stews

strawberries

stuffings, e.g., grape leaves, vegetables

"tabbouleh"

tarragon

tempeh

thyme

tofu

turnips

vinegar, e.g., balsamic

walnuts

za'atar

Flavor Affinities

spelt berries + apples + pine nuts + *salads*

spelt berries + balsamic vinegar + nuts (or tofu) + olive oil + raw vegetables

spelt berries + caramelized onions + lentils

spelt berries + cornmeal + *pizza dough*

spelt berries + currants + walnuts

● SPINACH

Season: year-round, but especially spring – **autumn**

Flavor: **bitter**/slightly sweet, with a soft texture

Volume: quieter (when young) – louder (when older)

What it is: vegetable – green

Nutritional profile: 59% carbs / 32% protein / 9% fats

Calories: 40 per 1-cup serving (boiled)

Protein: 5 grams

Techniques: blanch, boil, raw, sauté, steam (2 – 3 minutes), stir-fry, wilt

Tips: Opt for organic spinach. Use as fresh as possible.

Botanical relatives: beets, quinoa, Swiss chard

Possible substitute: Swiss chard

allspice

apples

artichokes, e.g., globe, hearts, Jerusalem

arugula

asparagus

avocado

basil

beans, e.g., adzuki, black, cannellini, green, mung

beets

bell peppers, e.g., red, roasted

bread crumbs, e.g., whole grain

broccoli

burritos

butter

calzones

capers

cardamom

carrots

casseroles

cauliflower

cayenne

CHEESE, e.g., blue, cheddar, cottage, Emmental, **FETA**, Fontina, **GOAT**, Gorgonzola, **Gruyère**, paneer, **PARMESAN**, pecorino, **RICOTTA**, ricotta salata, Swiss

chervil

CHICKPEAS

chicory

chiles, e.g., green, jalapeño, serrano; and **chili pepper flakes**

chives

cilantro

cloves

coconut milk

coriander

CREAM

creamed spinach

crepes

cumin

curry powder/spices, and *curries*

dill

dips

eggplant

EGGS, e.g., *Florentine*, *frittatas*, hard-boiled, *omelets*, poached, *quiches*, soft-boiled, *soufflés*

falafel

figs

fruit, dried, e.g., cranberries, **raisins**

GARLIC

GINGER

gomashio

grains, e.g., barley, bulgur, **quinoa**

gratins

Greek cuisine

horseradish

Indian cuisine

Italian cuisine

Japanese cuisine

leeks

LEMON, e.g., juice, zest

lemongrass

LENTILS

lime, e.g., zest

lovage

mace

marjoram

Mediterranean cuisines

milk

mint

mirin

Dishes

Spinach, Mushroom, and Pine Nut Ravioli in Cashew Cream
— Blossom (New York City)

Spinach and Mushroom Salad with Warm Caramelized Onion and Mustard Vinaigrette
— Canyon Ranch (Lenox, MA)

Creamed Spinach-Filled Crepe, Oyster Mushrooms, Confit Artichoke, Parmesan
— Green Zebra (Chicago)

Star Route Wilted Spinach Salad with Chicory, Red Dandelion, Feta, Croutons, Red Onions, Gaeta Olives, Garlic, Mint, Sherry Vinegar, and Hot Olive Oil
— Greens Restaurant (San Francisco)

Spinach Falafel with Tahini, Yogurt, Beets, and Crinkled Cress
— Oleana (Cambridge, MA)

Spinach Crepe with Pesto, Pear, Ricotta, and Arugula
— Plum Bistro (Seattle)

Organic Spinach Salad: Cauliflower, Radish, Verjus, Morel Aioli, Westglow Nasturtium Vinaigrette
— Rowland's Restaurant at Westglow (Blowing Rock, NC)

Warmed Spinach tossed into a Balsamic Emulsification topped with Seasonal Grilled Fruit, Seasonal Vegetables, and Pure Maple Candied Walnuts
— Sage's Cafe (Salt Lake City)

Spinach Enchiladas: Spinach, Onions, Garlic, Mushrooms, and Cheese baked in Organic Corn Tortillas, with Spicy Sour Cream Sauce
— Seva (Ann Arbor)

---

miso, e.g., white
*MUSHROOMS, e.g., button, chanterelle, cremini, porcini, portabello, shiitake, wild
mustard, e.g., Dijon, dry
noodles, e.g., soba, udon
*NUTMEG
NUTS and nut butters, e.g., almonds, cashews, hazelnuts, pecans, pine nuts, pistachios, WALNUTS
OIL, e.g., almond, grapeseed, hazelnut, OLIVE, peanut, sesame, walnut
olives, e.g., kalamata
ONIONS, e.g., caramelized, red, sweet, yellow
orange, e.g., juice

oregano
parsley
PASTA, e.g., cannelloni, gnocchi, gnudi, lasagna, manicotti, ravioli, shells
pears
peas
peas, split
pepper, e.g., black, white
"pestos"
PHYLLO DOUGH, e.g., spelt, whole-wheat
pies
pilafs
PIZZA
polenta
POTATOES
purees
quesadillas

quinoa
raisins
ramps
RICE, esp. basmati, black, brown
risottos
rosemary
sage
salad dressings, e.g., creamy, hot
SALADS, e.g., green, mushroom, pasta, spinach
salt, e.g., sea
sandwiches
scallions
seeds, e.g., pumpkin, sesame, sunflower
sesame, e.g., oil, seeds
shallots
smoothies
sorrel
soufflés
SOUPS, e.g., mushroom, spinach, vegetable, yogurt
soy sauce
spanakopita / spinach pie
spreads
sprouts, e.g., mung bean, sunflower
squash, e.g., delicata, summer
stews
stir-fries
stock, e.g., vegetable
sugar (just a pinch)
sweet potatoes
tahini
tamari
tangerines
tarragon
thyme
TOFU, e.g., raw, silken, smoked
TOMATOES and TOMATO SAUCE
vegetables
veggie burgers
VINEGAR, e.g., balsamic, brown rice, cider, red wine, rice, sherry, white wine
YOGURT
yuzu, e.g., juice, zest
zucchini

Flavor Affinities

spinach + almonds + chanterelle mushrooms + lemon

spinach + artichoke hearts + feta cheese + *pizza*

spinach + avocado + grapefruit + **red onions**

spinach + beets + fennel + **orange + walnuts**

spinach + carrots + ginger + *salads*

spinach + carrots + orange + sesame (oil and seeds)

SPINACH + CHEESE + fruit (e.g., apples, pears, strawberries) + **NUTS**

SPINACH + CHEESE (e.g., blue, feta, goat) + **NUTS** (e.g., almonds, walnuts)

spinach + chili pepper flakes + garlic + olive oil + vinegar

spinach + chili pepper flakes + lemon

spinach + citrus + pomegranate + onion + walnuts

spinach + Dijon mustard + dried cherries + maple syrup + pecans

spinach + dried cranberries + goat cheese + hazelnuts + pears

spinach + dill + feta cheese

spinach + fennel + orange + red onions

spinach + feta cheese + garlic + lemon + nuts

spinach + feta cheese + orange + walnut oil

spinach + feta cheese + *pasta*

SPINACH + FRUIT + NUTS

spinach + garlic + ginger + peanut oil + soy sauce

spinach + garlic + goat cheese + herbs + *phyllo dough* + ricotta + walnuts

spinach + garlic + lemon + olive oil + Parmesan cheese + parsley

spinach + garlic + mushrooms + tofu

spinach + garlic + olive oil + pine nuts

spinach + garlic + rosemary

spinach + garlic + sesame

spinach + ginger + onions + orange + sesame

spinach + ginger + peanut butter + peanut oil + soy sauce

spinach + goat cheese + lemon + olive oil/olives

spinach + lemon + tahini

spinach + miso + sesame seeds + soy sauce + tahini

spinach + mushrooms + nutmeg + ricotta

SPINACH + NUTS (e.g., **pine nuts, walnuts**) + **RAISINS**

spinach + pumpkin seeds + wild rice

spinach + shiitake mushrooms + soba noodles

"Zucchini 'noodles' are soft and pliable — especially if blanched in lemon juice, which gives them a soft 'cooked' texture — making them the #1 raw pasta option. While using a **spiralizer** produces a more realistic noodle, using a mandoline is fine if you're pressed for time."

— AMI BEACH, G-ZEN (BRANFORD, CT)

Dishes

Housemade Coconut Curry, Jícama Noodles, Garlic Chives, Ube, Roasted Shiitake

— Green Zebra (Chicago)

"I'll use a **spiralizer** to make 'noodles' like vermicelli from raw kohlrabi or zucchini or other vegetables. Just massage them with a little oil and salt, and in just one minute, the noodles are no longer crunchy but chewy."

— AMANDA COHEN, DIRT CANDY (NEW YORK CITY)

"**Spiralized** jícama looks like pho noodles. I'll add them to a vegetarian pho [Vietnamese noodle soup], or a mushroom curry made with roasted shiitakes and purple sweet potatoes, with the red curry sauce poured tableside."

— JON DUBOIS, GREEN ZEBRA (CHICAGO)

SPRING

Weather: typically warm
Techniques: pan-roast and other stovetop methods

artichokes, esp. baby (peak: March – April)
artichokes, Jerusalem (peak: autumn/**spring**)
arugula (peak: spring/summer)
asparagus, e.g., green, purple, white (peak: April)
avocados (peak: spring/summer)
bamboo shoots (peak: spring/ summer)
beans, fava (peak: April – June)
beets
blueberries (peak: spring/ summer)
borage
boysenberries (peak: spring/ summer)
carrots
cauliflower (peak: March)
chard, Swiss
cherries
chervil
chicory
chives, esp. garlic
cilantro (peak: spring/summer)
cucumbers (peak: spring/summer)
currants, red
dill (peak: spring/summer)
endive, e.g., Belgian, curly
escarole
fennel, esp. baby
fennel pollen (peak: spring/ summer)
fiddlehead ferns
FRESHNESS, i.e., ingredients that are raw or only lightly cooked

garlic, e.g., green (peak: March), spring
greens, e.g., collard, dandelion (peak: May – June), mizuna, mustard, salad, spring
jícama (peak: winter/spring)
leeks
lemons
lemons, Meyer
lettuces, e.g., lamb's, oak leaf, romaine, spring
lighter dishes
limes, key
loquats
mâche
mangoes (peak: spring/summer)
mint
miso, light
mushrooms, e.g., chanterelle, **morel** (peak: April), shiitake
nettles (peak: spring/summer)
noodles, e.g., somen
onions, e.g., spring, Vidalia (peak: May)
oranges, e.g., blood (peak: winter/ spring)
oranges, navel (peak: March)
peas, e.g., English, spring, sweet (peak: May)
potatoes, new
radishes
ramps (peak: May)
rhubarb (peak: April)
scallions
shoots, e.g., garlic, pea
snow peas (peak: spring; autumn)
sorrel (peak: May)
soufflés
spinach
sprouts, e.g., daikon

strawberries
sugar snap peas (peak: spring)
tea, green, esp. early
tomatillos (peak: spring/summer)
tomatoes, heirloom
wakame (peak: winter/spring)
watercress (peak: spring/ summer)
zucchini blossoms

"When I see ramps come in, I know there is light at the end of the tunnel — and that I will not be using squash and potatoes much longer! I look forward to **spring**'s asparagus and morels, which grow in the Midwest. When June hits, it is strawberry season."
— JON DUBOIS, GREEN ZEBRA (CHICAGO)

"In the **spring**, asparagus is the first thing to roll in, then the peas, followed by the fava beans. We are lucky and spoiled here at Greens because we get great produce all year and we know it. It would be hard to do what we do anywhere else!"
— ANNIE SOMERVILLE, GREENS RESTAURANT (SAN FRANCISCO)

● SPROUTS — IN GENERAL, or MIXED

What they are: edible shoots of germinated beans, grains, or seeds (typically crunchy)
What's healthful about them: many more nutrients than the nonsprouted versions
Techniques: raw, or *very* lightly cooked, e.g., steamed
Tip: Always buy sprouts from a trusted source, e.g., a respected farmers' market provider, especially if you choose to eat them raw.

Dishes

Mixed Sprout Salad: A refreshing toss of Snow Pea Shoots, Sunflower Sprouts and Seeds, and Mint, mixed with Cabbage, Daikon, Carrots, and Watercress in a Cool Mint Vinaigrette. Adorned with Toasted Peanuts and Sprouts of Onion and Daikon
— Angelica Kitchen (New York City)

apples and apple juice

avocado

breads, whole-grain, e.g., whole-wheat

cabbage, e.g., green, red

carrots

cheese, e.g., blue, cottage, Monterey Jack

citrus

cucumbers

garlic

greens, e.g., mesclun, salad

lemon, e.g., juice, zest

lettuce, e.g., romaine

mint

oil, e.g., olive

onions

parsley

radishes

raisins

SALADS, e.g., egg, green

SANDWICHES

sesame seeds

soy sauce

tahini

tomatoes

vinegar, e.g., balsamic, rice

Flavor Affinities

sprouts + avocado + *bread* + carrots + cucumber + onions + tahini

---

● SPROUTS, ALFALFA

Flavor: slightly sweet, with nutty notes

Volume: quiet

Tips: Cook very quickly, or else they turn to mush. Beware possible toxins in raw alfalfa sprouts.

avocados

beans, e.g., pinto

bell peppers, e.g., orange, red

bread, e.g., whole-grain

cabbage

cilantro

dill

eggs, e.g., *omelets*

ginger

honey

lemon, e.g., juice

lime

mango

miso

nori rolls

onions, e.g., green, red

oranges

raisins

rice paper wrappers

salads

SANDWICHES, e.g., grilled cheese, wraps

sesame, e.g., oil, seeds

slaws

smoothies

soups

sprouts, other, e.g., radish

stir-fries

sunflower seeds

tofu

tortillas, e.g., whole-grain

vinegar, rice

walnuts

watercress

wraps

Flavor Affinities

alfalfa sprouts + avocado + lime + mango

alfalfa sprouts + honey + lemon

SPROUTS, BEAN (see SPROUTS, MUNG BEAN)

SPROUTS, BROCCOLI

Flavor: neutral, with notes of broccoli

Volume: quiet

Calories: 20 calories per 1-cup serving

Protein: 3 grams

Techniques: raw, steam, stir-fry

Tip: Cook quickly, if at all, to preserve nutrients.

beets

carrots

cheese, e.g., Havarti, Muenster

salads, e.g., green

sandwiches, e.g., veggie burgers

sprouts, other, e.g., clover

stir-fries

tahini

SPROUTS, BUCKWHEAT

Techniques: Better served raw.

batters, e.g., pancake, waffle

carrots

lemon

salads, e.g., green

sandwiches, e.g., cheese

seeds, e.g., sesame

shoots, e.g., pea

sprouts, other, e.g., alfalfa

tahini

SPROUTS, CHICKPEA

Tips: Cook lightly, and never eat raw.

hummus

stir-fries

SPROUTS, CLOVER

Flavor: slightly sweet

Volume: quiet

cole slaws

eggs, e.g., *omelets*

onions

salads

sandwiches, e.g., peanut butter

sprouts, other, e.g., broccoli

stir-fries

SPROUTS, DAIKON (see also SPROUTS, RADISH)

Season: spring – summer

Flavor: bitter

Volume: quiet

Technique: raw

Japanese cuisine
salads
sushi

SPROUTS, LEAFY (see ALFALFA SPROUTS and CLOVER SPROUTS)

• SPROUTS, LENTIL

Flavor: slightly sweet, with earthy notes of bell pepper, celery and/or nuts
Volume: moderate
Nutritional profile: 75% carbs / 21% protein / 4% fat
Calories: 80 per 1-cup serving (raw)
Protein: 7 grams
Techniques: steam (Note: never raw)
Possible substitutes: celery, green bell pepper

arugula
beans
butter
drinks, e.g., juices, smoothies
ginger
greens, salad
honey
lemons
onions
oranges
peas
rice
salads, e.g., green, potato
sandwiches
seeds, e.g., sunflower
soups, e.g., sprouted lentil
soy sauce
stews
stir-fries
vinegar

• SPROUTS, MUNG BEAN

Flavor: slightly sweet, with notes of spring peas, and a crisp, crunchy, juicy texture

Volume: quiet
Nutritional profile: 70% carbs / 25% protein / 5% fat
Calories: 30 per 1-cup serving (raw)
Protein: 3 grams
Techniques: sauté, steam, stir-fry (just 30 seconds, to maintain sprouts' crispy texture) (Note: never raw)
Factoid: the most-consumed sprout worldwide

Asian cuisines
beans, e.g., black
bell peppers, e.g., red
bok choy
butter
cabbage, e.g., napa
carrots
celery
cheeses, soft
chickpeas
chiles, e.g., red
Chinese cuisine
cumin seeds
curry powder
dips
drinks, e.g., juices, smoothies
egg rolls
eggs
garlic
ginger
greens, e.g., salad
hoisin sauce
hummus
Indian cuisine
kimchi
Korean cuisine
lemon, e.g., juice
lentils
lo mein
miso
moo shu vegetables
mushrooms, e.g., shiitake
mustard
mustard seeds
noodles, Asian, e.g., rice, rice vermicelli, udon

oil, e.g., grapeseed, peanut, sesame
onions, e.g., red
pad thai
parsley
peanuts and peanut butter
peas
quinoa
radishes
rice
rice paper wrappers
SALADS, e.g., Asian, potato, vegetable
salt, e.g., sea
sandwiches
sesame, e.g., oil, seeds
slaws, e.g., Asian
soups, e.g., miso
soy sauce
spinach
spring rolls, i.e., fried
sprouts, other, e.g., adzuki, lentil
stews
STIR-FRIES
stock, vegetable
sugar
summer rolls, i.e., not fried
Thai cuisine
tofu
vegetables
Vietnamese cuisine
vinegar, e.g., rice
watercress

Flavor Affinities
bean sprouts + *miso soup* + tofu
bean sprouts + red bell peppers + shiitake mushrooms
bean sprouts + rice vinegar + salt + sugar + sesame oil/seeds

• SPROUTS, PEA

Flavor: notes of fresh peas, and a starchy texture
Nutritional profile: 78% carbs / 17% protein / 5% fat
Calories: 150 per 1-cup serving (raw)
Protein: 11 grams

S

dips
garlic
mustard
oil, e.g., sesame, vegetable
rice
salads
soups, e.g., cold, pea
soy sauce
stir-fries
tarragon
tofu

• SPROUTS, RADISH (see also SPROUTS, DAIKON)

Flavor: slightly sour/hot, with spicy notes of pepper and/or radishes
Volume: moderate – loud

avocado
bread, whole-wheat
cheeses, soft
dips
eggs, e.g., *omelets*
greens, salad
oil, nut (e.g., walnut), olive
onions, e.g., red
salad, egg
SANDWICHES, e.g., egg salad, wraps
shallots
slaws
stir-fries
sushi, vegetarian
vinegar, e.g., red wine

SPROUTS, SUNFLOWER SEED

Flavor: bitter/sweet, with earthy notes of sunflower seeds, and a crisp texture
Volume: quiet

avocado
basil
cheese, e.g., feta
citrus, e.g., grapefruit, orange

dill
garlic
kale
lemon, e.g., juice
oil, e.g., sunflower
parsley
pea shoots
salads
sandwiches, *e.g., wraps*
scallions
seeds, e.g., sesame, sunflower
shallots
smoothies
spinach
sushi, vegetarian
tomatoes
vinegar, red wine

SQUASH (see SQUASH, SUMMER; SQUASH, WINTER; ZUCCHINI, and other specific varieties of squash)

Tips: Spaghetti squash is named for its spaghetti-like strands, which you can toss with sauce and serve just like pasta. But consider slicing summer squash (e.g., yellow squash, zucchini) into julienne strips on a mandoline, or spiralizing it, and serving in the same manner.

• SQUASH, ACORN (see also SQUASH, WINTER)

Season: autumn – winter
Flavor: slightly sweet, with notes of black pepper and/or nuts
Volume: quiet – **moderate**
Nutritional profile: 93% carbs / 5% protein / 2% fat
Calories: 85 per 1-cup serving (boiled, mashed)
Protein: 2 grams
Techniques: bake (e.g., at 350°F – 375°F for 45 minutes), braise, mash, pressure-cook

(3 – 8 minutes), roast, steam (10 – 12 minutes), stuff
Tips: Choose larger, heavier acorn squash. The texture is not good for pureeing.

ACORN SQUASH, STUFFED

allspice
almonds
APPLES
apricots, e.g., dried
beans, e.g., anasazi, fava, kidney
bell peppers, e.g., red
bread crumbs and bread stuffings,
e.g., whole-grain
bulgur
butter and brown butter
celery
chard, Swiss
cheese, e.g., **Parmesan**, Swiss
CINNAMON
cloves
coconut and coconut milk
corn
cranberries, e.g., dried
currants
curry powder
fennel
garlic
ghee
ginger
hazelnuts
honey
kale
lemon, e.g., juice
liqueur, e.g., amaretto, Grand Marnier
MAPLE SYRUP
mint
miso
mushrooms, e.g., chanterelle
nutmeg
olive oil
onions
orange, e.g., juice, zest
parsley, flat-leaf
pears
pecans

PEPPER, e.g., black, white
pilafs
pine nuts
pistachios
plums, dried
quinoa
raisins
RICE (e.g., **wild**) and *rice stuffing*
sage
salt, sea
savory
scallions
soups
soy sauce
stews
SUGAR, BROWN
sweetener, esp. evaporated cane
   juice
tamari
vanilla
vinegar, e.g., cider

Flavor Affinities

acorn squash + apples + curry
   powder
acorn squash + apples + maple
   syrup
acorn squash + cinnamon +
   olive oil
acorn squash + corn + potatoes
acorn squash + cranberries +
   orange
acorn squash + ginger + maple
   syrup + soy sauce
acorn squash + pecans + quinoa

SQUASH, BUTTERCUP (see also SQUASH, WINTER)

Flavor: sweet – very sweet, with
notes of chestnuts, honey, and/
or sweet potato, and a somewhat
dry texture (akin to that of sweet
potatoes)
Volume: quiet – moderate
Techniques: bake, braise, puree,
roast (for 30 – 45 minutes at
400°F), steam

almonds
arugula
***baked goods**, e.g., muffins, pies*
bell peppers
butter and brown butter
casseroles
cheese, e.g., feta, Taleggio
chiles and chili powder
cilantro
coconut milk
cumin
curries
garlic
ginger
gratins
hominy
honey
leeks
lemon, e.g., juice
lemongrass
oil, e.g., chili, corn, peanut
onions, e.g., red
parsnips
***pasta**, e.g., gnocchi, ravioli*
peanuts
pears
pepper, black
purees
sage
shallots
SOUPS, e.g., minestrone, squash
soy sauce
spinach
squash, other winter, e.g.,
   butternut
stews
stock, vegetable
tamari
yogurt, e.g., Greek

Flavor Affinities

buttercup squash + bell peppers
   + chiles + coconut milk + curry
   paste + peanuts
buttercup squash + ginger +
   pears

● SQUASH, BUTTERNUT (see also SQUASH, WINTER)

Season: autumn – winter
Flavor: sweet, with notes of
butter, fruit, nuts, and/or **sweet
potatoes**, and creamy in texture
Volume: moderate
Techniques: bake, braise, mash,
puree, roast, simmer, sauté,
steam, tempura-fry
Who says it's healthful:
The Center for Science in the
Public Interest's *Nutrition Action*
includes butternut squash on its
"10 Best Foods" list.
Nutritional profile: 93% carbs
/ 5% protein / 2% fats
Calories: 85 per 1-cup serving
(baked, cubed)
Protein: 2 grams
Possible substitutes:
pumpkin, sweet potatoes, yams

allspice
apples, e.g., fruit, juice
artichokes, Jerusalem
arugula
baked goods, e.g., muffins
barley
basil
bay leaf
BEANS, e.g., adzuki, lima, pinto,
   white
berries, e.g., blackberries,
   blueberries
butter and brown butter
cabbage, savoy
cardamom
carrots
casseroles
cauliflower
cayenne
celery
celery root
CHEESE, e.g., Asiago,
   Camembert, **cheddar**, cream,

Fontina, goat, **PARMESAN**,
pecorino, **ricotta**, Romano
chestnuts
chickpeas
CHILES, e.g., ancho, chipotle,
jalapeño; **chili pepper flakes;**
chili pepper sauce
chives
cilantro
CINNAMON
cloves
coconut and **coconut milk**
coriander
corn
couscous
cranberries
cream
cumin
curry powder and *CURRIES*
dates
eggs
fennel
GARLIC

GINGER
grains, whole, e.g., bulgur, farro,
millet, quinoa
gratins
greens
honey
kale
leeks
lemon, e.g., juice, zest
lemongrass
LIME, e.g., juice, zest
MAPLE SYRUP
marjoram
milk, dairy or nondairy, e.g.,
cashew
miso, e.g., white
MUSHROOMS, e.g., black
trumpet, chanterelle, wild
NUTMEG
NUTS, e.g., **almonds**, hazelnuts,
peanuts, **pecans**, pine nuts,
pistachios, **walnuts**

OIL, e.g., canola, grapeseed,
OLIVE, pumpkin seed, walnut
ONIONS, e.g., green, red,
yellow
orange, e.g., juice, zest
oregano
paprika, smoked
parsley, flat-leaf
pasta, e.g., gnocchi, lasagna, ravioli
pears and Japanese pears
pepper, e.g., black, white
pizza
pomegranate seeds
PUMPKIN SEEDS
purees
raisins
rice, e.g., Arborio
RISOTTOS
rosemary
saffron
SAGE
salt, e.g., sea
savory
sesame seeds, e.g., black, white
shallots
shiso
SOUPS and bisques
spinach
star anise
stews
STOCK, e.g., mushroom or
vegetable
succotash
sugar, e.g., brown
sunflower seeds
tahini
tamari
tarragon
tarts
thyme
tofu
tomatoes
vanilla
VINEGAR, e.g., **balsamic,** cider,
red wine, sherry
wine, e.g., dry white
yogurt
za'atar

Dishes

Butternut Squash Risotto with Toasted Almonds and Toasted Sage
— Gobo (New York City)

Soft Tacos: Corn Tortillas with Roasted Butternut Squash, Poblano Chiles, Peppers,
Grilled Onions, Rancho Gordo Beans, Cheddar, Cilantro, Napa Cabbage, Avocado,
Tomatillo Salsa, and Crème Fraîche
— Greens Restaurant (San Francisco)

Butternut Squash Filled Ravioli, Olive Oil, Garlic, Lemon, Sage Leaves, and Ricotta Salata
Cheese
— Mana Food Bar (Chicago)

Butternut Squash and Apple Salad with Endives, Ricotta Cranberries, Pecans, and Balsamic
— Plum Bistro (Seattle)

Butternut Risotto: Toasted Pistachio, Brussels Sprouts, Pumpkin Seed Oil, Crispy Shallots,
and Sage
— Portobello (Portland, OR)

Enchiladas Calabaza: Butternut Squash, Cream Cheese and Green Onions with Chiles,
Cumin, and a hint of Cinnamon, baked in Organic Corn Tortillas, topped with Spicy
Tomato Sauce and Cheese
— Seva (Ann Arbor, MI)

Flavor Affinities

butternut squash + allspice + **cinnamon** + cloves + **maple syrup** + vanilla

butternut squash + almond butter + cinnamon + garlic + ginger

butternut squash + almonds + cumin + raisins

butternut squash + apples + **cinnamon** + ginger + **maple syrup** + walnuts

butternut squash + apples + cheese + honey

butternut squash + apples + curry powder

butternut squash + apples + **nuts** (e.g., pecans, walnuts)

butternut squash + balsamic vinegar + mushrooms + *pasta*

butternut squash + bananas + cilantro + coconut milk + lime

butternut squash + brown butter + pine nuts + sage + *pasta*

butternut squash + chanterelle mushrooms + risotto + saffron

butternut squash + chickpeas + couscous

butternut squash + chiles + lime

butternut squash + cilantro + curry powder + lime + yogurt

butternut squash + **citrus** (e.g., lime, orange) (+ garlic) + **ginger**

butternut squash + coconut milk + lemongrass

butternut squash + curry + peas + tofu

butternut squash + **fruit** (e.g., cranberries, dates) + **nuts** (e.g., pecans, pistachios)

butternut squash + ginger + tamari + tofu

butternut squash + hominy + red beans

butternut squash + maple syrup + walnut oil

butternut squash + **onions** + *pasta* + pecans + **sage**

butternut squash + orange + sage

butternut squash + Parmesan cheese + pumpkin seeds

butternut squash + quinoa + walnuts

butternut squash + rosemary + tomatoes + white beans

butternut squash + **sage** + **walnuts**

"We've juiced **butternut squash** to add color and flavor to risotto. I don't like the mouthfeel that results from drying and powdering the [leftover] mulch to flavor dishes. But I've made a **butternut squash** chutney out of adding the juice back to the mulch and seasoning it with cardamom, garlic, star anise, sugar, and vinegar."

— MARK LEVY, THE POINT (SARANAC LAKE, NY)

SQUASH, CROOKNECK (see also SQUASH, SUMMER)

Techniques: grill, raw, sauté

basil

bay leaf

chiles, e.g., jalapeño

cilantro

curry powder

marjoram

milk, e.g., nondairy (almond, coconut, rice)

mint

oil, e.g., olive, vegetable

onions

oregano

parsley

pepper, black

sage

salt

scallions

soups, e.g., squash

thyme

SQUASH, DELICATA (see also SQUASH, WINTER)

Season: winter

Flavor: sweet, with notes of butter, corn, and/or **sweet potatoes**, and a creamy, firm texture

Volume: quiet – moderate

Techniques: bake (at 350°F for 45 minutes), grill, roast, **sauté**, steam

Tip: Its thin skin can be easily peeled or even eaten.

allspice

anise

apples, apple cider, and apple juice

beans, e.g., black, cannellini, cranberry, white

beets

bread crumbs

butter

cayenne

celery

cheese, e.g., feta, mozzarella, Parmesan, smoked mozzarella

chiles, e.g., chipotle, jalapeño

cilantro

cinnamon

cloves

cranberries, dried

cream

cumin

dates

fennel

fennel seeds

garlic

honey

kale

lime, e.g., juice

maple syrup

mint

mushrooms, e.g., cremini, oyster, shiitake

mustard, Dijon

nutmeg

NUTS, e.g., **almonds**, hazelnuts, pine nuts, **pistachios**, walnuts

oil, **olive**

ONIONS, e.g., red, yellow

orange, e.g., juice

parsley

pepper, e.g., white

pizzas

pomegranate seeds

potatoes, e.g., fingerling

quinoa

rice, brown

rosemary

sage

seeds, e.g., sesame

soy sauce

squash, stuffed

stock, vegetable

sugar, brown

tahini

THYME

tomatoes

vinegar, apple cider or balsamic

yogurt

Flavor Affinities

delicata squash + apple cider/ **apples** + **herbs** (e.g., rosemary, **sage**) + walnuts

delicata squash + beets + feta cheese + mint

delicata squash + black pepper + garlic + olive oil + Parmesan cheese + pasta

delicata squash + brown sugar + soy sauce

delicata squash + chipotle chiles + lime

delicata squash + garlic + sage

delicata squash + honey + sage

delicata squash + orange + thyme

● **SQUASH, HUBBARD (see also SQUASH, WINTER)**

Flavor: neutral, with a watery texture

Volume: quiet

Techniques: bake, boil, mash, puree, roast

Possible substitute: pumpkin

allspice

almonds

baked goods, e.g., pies

bay leaf

beans, e.g., lima

carrots

cayenne

chives

cinnamon

curry spices, e.g., coriander, cumin

fennel

garlic

hazelnuts

leeks

lemon, e.g., juice

maple syrup

molasses

nutmeg

oil, e.g., olive

pancakes

pepper, black

purees

risottos

rosemary

sage

salt

soups

squash, stuffed

sugar, brown

tamari

SQUASH, KABOCHA (see also SQUASH, WINTER)

[kah-BOH-chah]

Season: summer – winter

Flavor: sweet with notes of honey, nuts, pumpkin, and/or sweet potatoes; dry and starchy yet creamy, custardy, and smooth in texture (when cooked)

Volume: moderate – loud

Techniques: bake (20 – 25 minutes at 400° F), boil, braise, deep-fry, mash, **puree**, pressure-cook, roast, simmer (20 – 25 minutes), steam

Tip: This is a quick-cooking squash with an edible skin.

almonds

apples

basil and Thai basil

bay leaf

beans, e.g., adzuki, cranberry, green, kidney, mung

butter

cayenne

celery root

chard

cheese, e.g., Parmesan, ricotta

chestnuts

chiles, e.g., chipotle

chili pepper flakes and chili powder

cilantro

cinnamon

coconut and coconut milk

coriander

couscous

cranberries, dried

cream

crème fraîche

cumin

currants

curry paste, powder, and spices, and *curries, e.g., Thai*

desserts

fennel and fennel seeds

GARLIC

GINGER

grains, whole, e.g., millet

greens, winter, e.g., mustard

hazelnuts

honey

Japanese cuisine

Kaffir lime leaves

kale

leeks

lemon, e.g., juice

lemongrass
lettuce, e.g., Bibb
lime, e.g., juice, zest
maple syrup
melon, bitter
mirin
miso, e.g., white
mushrooms, e.g., black trumpet,
    oyster
noodles, udon
nutmeg
oils, e.g., canola, olive, sesame
ONIONS, e.g., red, sweet, yellow
orange, e.g., juice, zest
paprika, e.g., hot, smoked
pastas, e.g., lasagna
pears
pecans
pepper, e.g., black
pies
pomegrantes
puddings
pumpkin seeds
purees
radicchio
raisins
rice, e.g., basmati and/or brown
rice, wild
rosemary
sage
sake
salt, sea
scallions

Dishes

Blended Essence of Butternut and Kabocha Squash, Smoked Paprika
— Brushstroke (New York City)

Kabocha Squash Curry: Bok Choy, Quinoa, Bulgur, and Pumpkin Seeds
— Gramercy Tavern (New York City)

Kabocha Pumpkin Soup with Soy Whip Cream and Mixed Greens Salad
(with Dried Persimmon in Sesame Soy Sauce and Lemon Dressing)
— Hangawi (New York City)

Kabocha Squash Agnolotti with Pomegranate, Black Trumpet Mushrooms,
Walnut Crumble
— Mélisse (Santa Monica)

shiso
SOUPS, e.g., vegetable
soybeans, e.g., black
soy sauce
stews
stock, vegetable
sugar
tamari
tempura, vegetable
tofu
tomatoes, e.g., green or red
umeboshi paste
vinegar, e.g., apple cider,
    balsamic, brown rice
walnuts
yuzu, e.g., juice, zest

Flavor Affinities

kabocha squash + brown rice +
    shiso + tofu
kabocha squash + brown rice
    vinegar + mirin + miso +
    tamari + umeboshi paste
kabocha squash + cinnamon +
    maple syrup
kabocha squash + coconut milk +
    curry spices
kabocha squash + coconut milk +
    Kaffir lime leaves + lemongrass
kabocha squash + garlic + ginger
    + sesame oil + soy sauce
kabocha squash + ginger + maple
    syrup + **soy sauce**

kabocha squash + hazelnuts +
    thyme
kabocha squash + kale + tamari
kabocha squash + mirin +
    scallions + soy sauce
kabocha squash + sage + wild rice

SQUASH, PATTYPAN (see also SQUASH, SUMMER)

Season: summer – early autumn
Flavor: notes of butter, cucumber, nuts, and/or **zucchini**, with a firm, tender texture
Volume: quiet
Techniques: bake, sauté, steam, stuff (**Note:** Cook small pattypan whole.)

Tip: As pattypan tastes similar to zucchini, use it in similar ways.

allspice
apples
asparagus
bread crumbs, e.g., whole-wheat
capers
cheese, e.g., goat, Gruyère,
    manchego, Parmesan, ricotta
chili pepper flakes
chives
corn
eggplant
eggs
garlic
leeks
lemon
mushrooms, e.g., chanterelle
nutmeg
oils, e.g., **olive**, walnut
onions, e.g., red
parsley
PATTYPAN SQUASH, STUFFED
pecans
pepper, e.g., black
pesto
rosemary
sage
salt, e.g., kosher

soups, e.g., *squash*
stock, vegetable
thyme
tomatoes
zucchini

Flavor Affinities

pattypan squash + asparagus +
mushrooms + onions + walnut oil
pattypan squash + bread crumbs
+ garlic
pattypan squash + corn + onions

• SQUASH, SPAGHETTI

Season: late summer – winter
Flavor: slightly sweet, with the
texture of crunchy (if stringy)
spaghetti
Volume: quiet – moderate
Nutritional profile: 86% carbs
/ 8% fats / 6% protein
Calories: 45 per 1-cup serving
(boiled or baked)
Protein: 1 gram
Techniques: bake (at 350°F
about 30 – 90 minutes), boil
(about 30 – 60 minutes), roast
(at 400°F for 15 – 20 minutes),
sauté, steam (20 – 45 minutes,
until tender)

Tips: Spaghetti squash is
named after the appearance of
its cooked flesh, whose strands
resemble the pasta. You can
bake it whole (as some insist
on), after puncturing it in a
few places to allow steam to
escape, or halved (as Andrew
taught me). Use a fork to pull off
strands of cooked squash. Toss
or top with sauce and serve like
spaghetti. Although spaghetti
squash can be found as early as
late summer, look to pairing tips
for *winter* squash, which its flavor more closely resembles.

basil
bay leaf
beans, e.g., black, kidney
bell peppers, e.g., red
bok choy
broccoli
bulgur
butter and brown butter
carrots
casseroles
chard
CHEESE, e.g., Gruyère,
mozzarella, **PARMESAN**
chiles, dried; and chili pepper
flakes
cilantro
cinnamon
eggs
fennel
GARLIC
ginger
gratins
hazelnuts
lentils
"meatballs"
mushrooms, e.g., button,
chanterelle, oyster, porcini
nutmeg
oil, e.g., corn, flaxseed, **olive**,
peanut, sesame
ONIONS
oregano
parsley
parsnips
"PASTA"
pepper, black
pesto
pistachios
rosemary
sage
salads
salt
sauces, e.g., pasta, tomato

"sausage," vegan
scallions
soy sauce
sugar, brown
thyme
tomatillos
TOMATOES, TOMATO PASTE,
and TOMATO SAUCE
vinegar, e.g., balsamic, rice,
sherry, wine
walnuts
zucchini

Flavor Affinities

spaghetti squash + balsamic
vinegar + kidney beans
spaghetti squash + basil + garlic
spaghetti squash + basil +
tomatoes
spaghetti squash + brown butter
+ hazelnuts
spaghetti squash + garlic +
tomatoes
spaghetti squash + mozzarella
cheese + tomatoes
spaghetti squash + mushrooms +
onions

• SQUASH, SUMMER
(see also CHAYOTE;
SQUASH, CROOKNECK;
SQUASH, PATTY PAN;
and ZUCCHINI)

Season: summer
Flavor: slightly bitter/sweet,
with earthy notes of butter,
cucumber, and/or nuts, and a
tender, juicy texture
Volume: very quiet – quiet/
moderate
What it is: vegetable
Nutritional profile: 73% carbs
/ 18% protein / 9% fats

Dishes

Spaghetti Squash Casserole with Fresh Mozzarella, Organic Tomato, and Zucchini
— True Food Kitchen (Santa Monica)

Calories: 20 per 1-cup serving (sliced, raw)

Protein: 1 gram

Techniques: bake (at 375°F about 20 minutes), boil, braise, deep-fry, grate, **grill**, marinate, mash, pressure cook (whole, 2 – 3 minutes), raw, **roast**, **sauté**, steam (5 – 10 minutes), stir-fry (2 – 3 minutes), stuff

Tips: Opt for organic summer squash. Eat the peel, too, which is a great source of fiber.

Botanical relatives: winter squashes

allspice
arugula
baked goods, e.g., muffins, quick breads
BASIL
beans, e.g., cannellini, white
bell peppers, e.g., green, red
bread crumbs
butter
capers
carrots
chard, Swiss
CHEESE, e.g., Asiago, cheddar, feta, **goat**, Gruyère, Monterey Jack, mozzarella, **PARMESAN**, **pecorino**, provolone, ricotta, ricotta salata, Swiss
chiles, e.g., dried, fresh, jalapeño, red, green; chili pepper flakes and chili powder
chives
cilantro
cinnamon
coriander
corn
curry, e.g., powder, spices
DILL
eggplant
eggs, e.g., *frittatas, omelets*
enchiladas
escarole
escarole
fennel seeds

GARLIC
ginger
grains, whole, e.g., bulgur
greens, e.g., mustard, turnip
LEMON, e.g., juice, zest
marjoram
mint
mustard, e.g., Dijon, and mustard seeds
nutmeg
OIL, e.g., canola, OLIVE
olives
onions, e.g., red
oregano
paprika
PARSLEY
pasta, e.g., lasagna, linguini, orzo, rigatoni
pepper, black
pesto
pine nuts
ratatouille
rice
risotto
ROSEMARY
saffron
sage
salads, e.g., green, pasta
salt, e.g., sea
savory
scallions
shallots
soups, e.g., squash
stews, e.g., vegetable
stock, e.g., vegetable
sunflower seeds
tarragon
thyme
TOMATOES and TOMATO SAUCE
tomatoes, sun-dried
vegetables, root, e.g., parsnips, turnips
VINEGAR, **e.g., balsamic**, cider, **red wine**, rice wine, **white wine**
walnuts
yogurt
zucchini blossoms

Flavor Affinities
summer squash + basil + tomato
summer squash + cheese + eggs + *frittata* +scallions
summer squash + cilantro + escarole + scallions
summer squash + eggs + *frittata* + goat cheese
summer squash + garlic + olive oil
summer squash + garlic + parsley
summer squash + lemon + rosemary
summer squash + mint + thyme
summer squash + pecorino cheese + truffles

● SQUASH, WINTER — IN GENERAL, OR MIXED SQUASHES (see also PUMPKIN; SQUASH, ACORN; SQUASH, BUTTERCUP; SQUASH, BUTTERNUT; SQUASH, DELICATA; SQUASH, HUBBARD; SQUASH, KABOCHA)

Season: autumn – winter

Volume: moderate

What it is: starchy vegetable

Techniques: bake (at 375°F for 30 – 45 minutes), boil (6 – 10 minutes, in small pieces), braise, grill, mash, pressure-cook, puree, roast, sauté, simmer, steam (15 – 40 minutes), stew, stuff

Botanical relatives: cucumbers, melons, pumpkins

Possible substitutes: carrots, pumpkin

allspice
anise seeds
APPLES, e.g., cider, fruit, juice
baked goods, e.g., breads, cakes, cookies, muffins, pies
basil
beans, white

S

bell peppers, e.g., red
bread crumbs, e.g., whole-grain
burritos
butter and brown butter
cardamom
carrots
cashews
casseroles
cauliflower
cayenne
celery
CHEESE, e.g., blue, cheddar, feta,
  Fontina, Gorgonzola, **Gruyère**,
  mozzarella, **Parmesan**,
  pecorino, ricotta, ricotta salata,
  Romano, Roncal
chestnuts
chiles, e.g., dried, jalapeño,
  red; chili pepper flakes and chili
  powder
cider
cilantro
CINNAMON
citrus, e.g., juice, zest
cloves
coconut, e.g., butter, fruit, milk
coriander
cornmeal
cranberries, e.g., dried
cream
cumin
curry, e.g., paste, powder, spices
dates
eggs, e.g., poached
fennel seeds
figs and fig syrup
GARLIC
ghee
GINGER
grains, whole, e.g., farro, spelt
gratins
greens, e.g., mesclun, mustard
honey
leeks
lemon, e.g., juice
lemongrass
licorice
lime

mace
maple syrup
marjoram
mint
mirin
miso, e.g., white
molasses
mousses
mushrooms, e.g., chanterelle,
  wild
noodles, e.g., udon
NUTMEG
NUTS, e.g., hazelnuts,
  macadamia, pecans, walnuts
OIL, e.g., **OLIVE**, safflower,
  sesame, sunflower
ONIONS, e.g., green, RED

Flavor Affinities

winter squash + apples + cinnamon + ginger + pecans
winter squash + bread crumbs + cheese
winter squash + brown butter + cheese (e.g., Gruyere, Parmesan,
  ricotta salata) + **sage**
winter squash + cashews + cilantro + coconut + curry powder +
  sesame seeds
winter squash + cinnamon + cloves + ginger + nutmeg
winter squash + cranberries + mustard greens + nutmeg + ricotta
winter squash + cranberries + pecans
winter squash + dill + sour cream
winter squash + garlic + leeks + olive oil + sage
winter squash + honey + lemon juice
winter squash + lime juice + soy sauce
winter squash + parsley + rosemary + sage + thyme

oranges, e.g., juice
pancakes
paprika
parsley
parsnips
***pastas*, e.g., ravioli**
pears
PECANS
pepper, e.g., black
pies
pine nuts
pineapples
pistachios
potatoes
puddings
purees
quince

Dishes

Winter Luxury Squash and Ginger Soup with Pear Compote, Crème Fraîche, Chives
— Greens Restaurant (San Francisco)

Chipotle-Glazed Roasted Winter Squash with Sage-Scented Risotto, Hazelnut Nogada
Sauce, and Fried Sage
— Millennium (San Francisco)

Roasted Winter Squash, Tempeh-Kale Stuffing, Brandied Applesauce,
Rye Breadcrumbs
— True Bistro (Somerville, MA)

Autumn Squash Pierogies, Chanterelles, Madeira, Hazelnut Picada
— Vedge (Philadelphia)

radicchio
raisins
radicchio
rice, e.g., brown, wild
risottos
rosemary
rum
SAGE
savory
scallions
seeds, e.g., flax, pumpkin, sesame
   (e.g., black)
shallots
soufflés
SOUPS, e.g., squash, winter
   vegetable
soy sauce
spreads
squash, other winter
squash, stuffed
stews
stock, vegetable
SUGAR, BROWN
tahini
tarragon
thyme
tofu
turmeric
vanilla
vinegar, e.g., balsamic, sherry
WALNUTS

SQUASH, YELLOW (see SQUASH, SUMMER)

SRIRACHA (aka CHILI GARLIC SAUCE)

Flavor: bitter/sour/hot, with a smooth texture
Volume: loud
What it is: Thai hot sauce: chili paste + garlic + salt + sugar + vinegar

Tip: Huy Fong does not include fish sauce or shrimp paste, while other brands may.

Possible substitutes: veg Asian chili garlic sauce or Malaysian sambal oelek

Asian cuisines
carrots
cashews
celery
chickpeas
chili, vegetarian
fried rice
garlic
ginger
mushrooms
noodles, Asian, e.g., rice
onions, e.g., green, white
rice, e.g., jasmine
sesame, e.g., oil, seeds
soy sauce
stir-fries
stock, vegetable
Thai cuisine
tofu
tomatoes

STAR ANISE

Flavor: bitter/sweet, aromatic, with pungent notes of anise, licorice, and/or spices
Volume: moderate – loud

Tips: Star anise is slightly more bitter than anise seeds, to which it is not related. Add at the beginning of the cooking process.

Possible substitute: anise seeds

Asian cuisines
baked goods
bay leaf
berries, e.g., blackberries
chiles
CHINESE CUISINE
chocolate, e.g., milk
cinnamon
citrus
curries
curry leaves and curry powder
five-spice powder
ginger
greens, e.g., mizuna

ice creams
Malaysian cuisine
marinades
mint
noodles, Asian
orange
pears, e.g., poached
pepper, black
plums
rose water
salad dressings
sauces, e.g., barbecue
sorbets
soups
soy sauce
stews
stir-fries
sugar, e.g., brown
teas
Vietnamese cuisine, e.g., pho

Dishes

Blackberry and Star Anise Sorbet with Rosemary Sable: Hazelnut, Lemon, Crab Apple, Brown Sugar
— Fearrington House (Fearrington Village, NC)

• STAR FRUIT (aka CARAMBOLA)

Flavor: sour and/or sweet, with notes of apples, citrus, and/or tropical fruit, and a crisp, juicy texture
Volume: moderate
Nutritional profile: 80% carbs / 11% protein / 9% fat
Calories: 40 per 1-cup serving (raw)
Protein: 1 gram

Tips: Look for browning edges to get the sweetest fruit. The star-shaped slices are so pretty it's hard to recommend serving them in smoothies, but some do!

agave nectar
cardamom
chili powder
chutneys
desserts, e.g., tarts (when fully ripe)
honey
Indian cuisine
kiwi
lemon, e.g., juice, zest
lime, e.g., juice, zest
mango
mint
orange
papayas
salads, *e.g., fruit, green*
salsas
salt
smoothies
Southeast Asian cuisines
stir-fries
strawberries
Thai cuisine

STOCK, "BEEF"

Brand: Better Than Bouillon's "No Beef Vegan Base," beef-flavored bouillon

STOCK, "CHICKEN"

Brand: Better Than Bouillon's "No Chicken Vegan Base," chicken-flavored bouillon

STOCK, MUSHROOM

Tip: Use a mushroom stock (made from several of the ingredients below) as an earthier, bolder alternative to vegetable stock in many heartier dishes, such as mushroom-based pastas, risottos, sauces, and soups.

bay leaf
carrots
celery
fennel
garlic
leeks

marjoram
MUSHROOMS, e.g., dried or fresh; mixed, porcini, shiitake, white
oil, olive
onions, e.g., yellow
oregano
parsley
pepper, black
rosemary
salt
tamari
thyme
wine, e.g., marsala

STOCK, VEGETABLE (see also DASHI)

Tips: Vegetable stock is a great staple to have on hand as a base for grains, legumes, marinades, rices, risottos, sauces, or soups. It's easy to make by simmering your favorite combination of several of the vegetables and seasonings below with water. To make a louder version, roast the vegetables first. As a low-fat substitute, use vegetable stock instead of oil when sautéing or stir-frying foods.

basil
bay leaf
beans, black (fermented)
cabbage
carrots
celery
cilantro
garlic
kombu
leeks
lemongrass
marjoram
mirepoix (carrots + celery + onions)
mushrooms, e.g., shiitake, white
oil, olive
onions, e.g., yellow
oregano

parsley
parsnips
pepper, black
potatoes
rosemary
sage
salt, kosher or sea
savory
thyme
water
wine, dry white

"The foundation of my **vegetable stock** is about 60 percent onions, 25 percent celery, and 15 percent carrots. I'll often add garlic and portobello or shiitake mushrooms and stems."
— AARON ADAMS, PORTOBELLO (PORTLAND, OR)

• STRAWBERRIES

Season: spring – summer
Flavor: sweet/sour, and a delicate texture
Volume: quiet – moderate
Nutritional profile: 85% carbs / 8% fats / 7% protein
Calories: 50 per 1-cup serving (raw, halved)
Protein: 1 gram
Techniques: puree, raw, **sauté**
Tips: Opt for organic strawberries. Adding sugar enhances strawberry flavor, as does adding an acid such as citrus juice or vinegar.
Botanical relatives: almonds, apples, apricots, blackberries, cherries, peaches, pears, plums, quinces, raspberries

agave nectar
almonds
apples
apricots
arugula
bananas

BASIL
bell peppers
BERRIES, OTHER, e.g.,
   blackberries, blueberries,
   raspberries
buttermilk
caramel
cheese, e.g., burrata, cream, feta,
   goat, mozzarella, **ricotta**, ricotta
   salata, sheep's milk
chocolate, e.g., dark
cinnamon
coconut
CREAM
crème fraîche
cucumber
DESSERTS, e.g., cobblers,
   crumbles, custards, **ICE CREAMS,**
   pies, *puddings,* **sorbets,** *strawberry*
   shortcake, **tarts**
drinks, e.g., sparkling water,
   sparkling wine
fennel
figs
ginger
grapefruit
granitas
guava
hazelnuts
honey
jams
kiwi
LEMON, e.g., juice
lime, e.g., juice
liqueurs, e.g., Cointreau, curaçao,
   framboise, Grand Marnier, Kirsch
lychees
mango
maple syrup
mascarpone
melon, e.g., cantaloupe
milk, almond
mint
nuts
oats and oatmeal
oil, olive
orange, e.g., juice, zest
pancakes

Dishes

Strawberry Honey Shortcake, Strawberry Sorbet, Buttermilk Lemon Sorbet
— ABC Kitchen (New York City)

Strawberry Almond Cake: Almond Bavarois, Strawberry Gelée, Toasted Almond Ice Cream
— Café Boulud (New York City)

Strawberry Gazpacho with Basil, Black Pepper, and Olive Oil
— Eleven Madison Park (New York City)

Frais de Bois Vacherin with Lemon Parfait and Basil
— Eleven Madison Park (New York City)

Strawberry White Balsamic Salad with Spring Mix, Toasted Sunflower Seeds, Blue Cheese Crumbles, Dried Cranberries
— The Golden Door Spa Café at The Boulders (Scottsdale, AZ)

Local Leaf Lettuces and Belgian Endive with Local Strawberries, Ashed Goat Cheese, Tarragon Vinaigrette
— Nora (Washington, DC)

Strawberry Chopped Salad: Snap Pea, Fennel, Goat Cheese, Walnut and Balsamic Vinaigrette
— True Food Kitchen (Phoenix)

passion fruit
peaches
pecans
PEPPER, e.g., black, tellicherry
pineapple
pine nuts
pistachios
***RHUBARB**
salads, e.g., fruit, green
sauces, e.g., dessert
shortcakes
SMOOTHIES
sorbets
soups, e.g., fruit, "gazpacho"
sour cream
spinach
SUGAR, e.g., brown,
 confectioners'
tarts
thyme
tofu, silken
tomatoes
VANILLA
VINEGAR, E.G., *BALSAMIC,
 esp. aged; red wine
walnuts
watermelon

Flavor Affinities
strawberries + almonds + lemon
strawberries + arugula + balsamic vinegar + pine nuts + ricotta
strawberries + balsamic vinegar + basil + burrata cheese
strawberries + balsamic vinegar + spinach + walnuts
strawberries + balsamic vinegar + tellicherry pepper
strawberries + basil + balsamic vinegar
strawberries + basil + Grand Marnier
strawberries + basil + lemon + mint
strawberries + brown sugar + cinnamon + oatmeal
strawberries + cream cheese + lemon
STRAWBERRIES + GINGER + MAPLE SYRUP + RHUBARB
strawberries + honey + lime
strawberries + lemon + ricotta
strawberries + maple syrup + thyme
strawberries + mascarpone + passion fruit + vanilla
strawberries + pistachios + yogurt
strawberries + rhubarb + vanilla
strawberries + ricotta salata + walnuts

wine, e.g., Beaujolais, Marsala, port, rose, sherry, sparkling (e.g., Champagne), sweet
yogurt

"I know it's boring, but the classic combination of **strawberries** and cream or vanilla ice cream is something you simply can't improve on. Together, they have perfect flavor and texture."
— AMANDA COHEN, DIRT CANDY (NEW YORK CITY)

● **SUCANAT**

Flavor: sweet
Volume: moderate
What it is: a sweetener (SUgar CAne NATural) made from sugar cane juice that has been evaporated and granulated
Possible substitutes: Can substitute for regular (or muscovado) sugar in equal amounts, especially in baked goods.

● **SUGAR, BROWN — DARK**

Flavor: sweet, with deep notes of molasses
Factoid: Dark brown sugar is 6.5 percent molasses.

● **SUGAR, BROWN — LIGHT**

Flavor: sweet, with light caramel notes
Factoid: Light brown sugar is 3.5 percent molasses.

● **SUGAR, DATE**

Flavor: sweet, with notes of dates
Volume: moderate
What it is: ground dehydrated dates

● **SUGAR, MAPLE**

Flavor: sweet, with notes of maple

● **SUGAR, MUSCOVADO**

Flavor: sweet, with earthy molasses notes
Volume: moderate – loud

● **SUGAR, ORGANIC CANE**

Brand: Rapadura

● **SUGAR, PALM**

Flavor: sweet, with notes of caramel and/or maple syrup
Volume: quieter (paler) – louder (darker)
Technique: grate
Possible substitute: light brown sugar
Brand: Big Tree Farms Organic Coconut Palm Sugar

baked goods, e.g., cookies
bananas

beans, adzuki
chiles
chocolate
**COCONUT and COCONUT
  MILK**
coffee
cream
curries, Thai
custards
desserts
fruits
Indonesian cuisine
jackfruit
lime
Malaysian cuisine
mango
maple syrup
pad thai
papaya, green
puddings
pumpkin
rice, sticky
salads, e.g., fruit
sauces
Southeast Asian cuisines
Thai cuisine
water chestnuts

• SUGAR SNAP PEAS (aka SNAP PEAS)

Season: spring
Flavor: sweet, with notes of peas and snow peas, and a crisp, crunchy texture
Volume: quiet – moderate
Nutritional profile: 68% carbs / 27% protein / 5% fats
Calories: 70 per 1-cup serving (cooked)
Protein: 5 grams
Techniques: blanch, boil, braise (add at the last minute), raw, **sauté**, simmer, **steam** (2 – 3 minutes), **stir-fry**
Tip: To retain crispness, cook only briefly.

asparagus
basil
bell peppers, e.g., yellow
broccoli
butter and brown butter
carrots
cashews
cauliflower
cheese, e.g., Parmesan
chervil
chiles
chives
cilantro
coconut milk
cumin
curry powder
curries

dill
dips
fennel
garlic and garlic scapes
ginger
grains, whole
horseradish
LEMONS, e.g., juice, zest
lettuce
lotus root
marjoram
MINT
miso
MUSHROOMS, e.g., portobello, shiitake
mustard, Dijon
noodles, Asian, e.g., soba

Dishes

Snap Pea Salad: Goat's Milk Yogurt, Cucumber, and Radish
— Gramercy Tavern (New York City)

Spring Chopped Salad with Snap Peas, Strawberries, Walnuts, Goat Cheese, and Balsamic Vinaigrette
— True Food Kitchen (Santa Monica)

S

OILS, e.g., canola, corn, grapeseed, **OLIVE**, **SESAME**
onions, e.g., green, **red**
parsley
pastas
peanuts and peanut sauce
peas
pepper, black
pine nuts
pistachios
radishes
rice
sage
salads, e.g., grain, noodle, pasta
salt, e.g., kosher
scallions
sesame, e.g., oil, seeds
shallots
snow peas
soups
soy sauce
stews
stir-fries
stock, vegetable
sugar
tarragon
thyme
tofu
vinegar, e.g., red wine
water chestnuts
yogurt

Flavor Affinities
sugar snap peas + basil + garlic scapes
sugar snap peas + basil + *stir-fries* + tofu
sugar snap peas + chiles + garlic + lemon
sugar snap peas + cumin + thyme
sugar snap peas + dill + olive oil + scallions
sugar snap peas + garlic + lemon zest + *pasta*
sugar snap peas + garlic + mushrooms
sugar snap peas + garlic + pine nuts
sugar snap peas + ginger + sesame oil
sugar snap peas + lemon + mint
sugar snap peas + mustard + olive oil + vinegar
sugar snap peas + *noodles/pasta* + peanut sauce + soy sauce
sugar snap peas + sesame oil + sesame seeds

SUMAC
[SOO-mack]
Flavor: bitter/salty/**sour**/sweet, with astringent fruity and/or lemony notes
Volume: quiet – moderate
What it is: a tart-flavored spice

Tip: Add to foods over which you might otherwise squeeze lemon juice or grate lemon zest.

(North) African cuisines
avocados
beans, e.g., white
beets
bell peppers
breads, e.g., pita
cheese, e.g., feta
chickpeas
chiles and chili powder
cilantro
coriander
cucumbers
cumin
dips
drinks, e.g., "lemonade"
dukkah (Egyptian spice blend of almonds + coriander + cumin + salt + sesame seeds + sumac)
eggplant
eggs, e.g., boiled

falafel
fennel
garlic
ginger
grains, whole, e.g., farro, quinoa
HUMMUS
Iranian cuisine
kebabs
Lebanese cuisine
lemon, e.g., juice
lentils, e.g., red
marinades
mayonnaise
(Eastern) Mediterranean cuisine
MIDDLE EASTERN CUISINES
mint
Moroccan cuisine
oil, olive
ONIONS, e.g., raw
orange
oregano
parsley
pepper, black
pilafs
pine nuts
pomegranates
purslane
rice
salad dressings, e.g., tahini
SALADS, *e.g., chickpea, cucumber, fattoush, tomato*
salt
sauces
sesame seeds
sour cream
stews
sugar snap peas
Syrian cuisine
tahini
THYME
tomatoes
Turkish cuisine
vegetables
walnuts
yogurt
za'atar
zucchini

Flavor Affinities

sumac + bell peppers + garlic + lemon + onions + tomatoes

sumac + chickpeas + coriander + cumin

sumac + cucumbers + feta cheese + lemon + mint + parsley + tomatoes

sumac + dates + feta cheese + parsley

sumac + feta cheese + whole grains + zucchini

sumac + garlic + lemon

sumac + oregano + **sesame seeds + thyme** (aka *za'atar*)

SUMMER

Weather: typically hot
Techniques: barbecue, grill, marinate, raw, sauté

anise hyssop
apricots (peak: June)
arugula (peak: spring/summer)
avocados (peak: spring/summer)
bamboo shoots (peak: spring/ summer)
basil (peak: summer)
beans, e.g., cranberry, fava, **green**, lima
bell peppers, e.g., red or yellow (peak: summer/autumn)
berries (peak: spring/summer)
blackberries (peak: June)
blueberries (peak: July)
boiled dishes
bok choy (peak: summer/ autumn)
boysenberries (peak: June)
callaloo
celery (peak: summer/autumn)
chard (peak: summer/autumn)
cherries
chickpeas, fresh
chiles, e.g., poblano
chilled dishes and beverages
cilantro (peak: spring/summer)

corn (peak: July – August)
cucumbers (peak: August)
currants, black
dill (peak: spring/summer)
edamame
eggplant
elderberries and elderflower
escarole (peak: summer/autumn)
fennel pollen (peak: spring/
summer)
figs (peak: August)
flowers, edible
FRESHNESS
garlic (peak: August)
goji berries (peak: summer/
autumn)
grapes (peak: summer/autumn)
greens, e.g., beet, leafy, mizuna
grilled dishes
grilling
guavas (peak: summer/autumn)
herbs, cooling, e.g., basil, cilantro,
dill, fennel, licorice, marjoram,
mint
horseradish (peak: summer/
autumn)
huckleberries
ice cream
ices and granitas
jackfruit
kohlrabi (peak: summer/autumn)
lamb's-quarter
lettuce, e.g., green leaf, lamb's,
red leaf
limes (peak: June)
loquats
lychees
mangoes (peak: spring/summer)
melons, e.g., cantaloupe (peak:
August)
miso, light
mushrooms, e.g., chicken of the
woods, hedgehog, lobster, porcini
nectarines (peak: July)
nettles (peak: spring/summer)
noodles, e.g., chilled, somen
okra (peak: August)

onions (peak: August)
onions, green
onions, red (peak: July), Vidalia
(peak: June)
papalo
papayas (peak: summer/autumn)
peaches (peak: July – August)
pears, Bartlett (peak: August)
peas (peak: spring/summer)
picnics
plums (peak: August)
potatoes, e.g., new (peak: spring/
summer)
puddings, summer
purslane
raspberries (peak: June – August)
raw foods (e.g., salads)
SALADS, e.g., fruit, green, pasta
salsas, fresh
savory, summer
sea beans
shallots (peak: summer/autumn)
slaws
snow peas (peak: June – July)
sorbets
soups, chilled, e.g., fruit, gazpacho
spices, cooking, e.g., peppercorns,
white; turmeric
sprouts, daikon (peak: spring/
summer)
SQUASH, SUMMER, e.g.,
pattypan, yellow, zucchini
steamed dishes
stone fruits, e.g., peaches, plums
strawberries (peak: spring/
summer)
summer rolls
tarragon
thyme
tomatillos (peak: August)
TOMATOES
vegetables, green leafy
watercress
WATERMELON
**ZUCCHINI and ZUCCHINI
BLOSSOMS** (peak: July)

"**Summer** is the easiest time of
the year to cook because there is
so much out there. It is all the
flavors people wish they could eat
year-round: fruit, tomatoes, and
corn."

— JON DUBOIS, GREEN ZEBRA (CHICAGO)

SUNCHOKES
(see ARTICHOKES, JERUSALEM)

SUNFLOWER SEEDS (see SEEDS, SUNFLOWER)

SUNFLOWER SHOOTS (see SHOOTS, SUNFLOWER)

SUSHI, VEGETARIAN (see NORI and NORI ROLLS)

● SWEET POTATOES

Season: autumn – winter
Flavor: slightly sweet – sweet,
with notes of chestnuts,
pumpkin, and/or vanilla, and a
soft texture (when cooked)
Volume: moderate – loud
What they are: starchy
vegetable
Who says they're healthful:
The Center for Science in the
Public Interest's *Nutrition Action*
lists sweet potatoes on its "10 Best
Foods" list and as "a nutritional
All-Star — one of the best
vegetables you can eat."
Nutritional profile: 93% carbs
/ 6% protein / 1% fats
Calories: 180 per 1-cup serving
(baked)
Protein: 4 grams
Techniques: bake (whole, after
pricking skins, at 400°F about

40 – 60+ minutes), boil (about 25 – 40 minutes), broil, candy, deep-fry, fry, grill (or wrap in foil and place in coals), **mash**, pressure-cook (3 – 7 minutes), puree, **roast**, sauté, simmer, steam (slices, about 20 minutes)
Possible substitutes: carrots, pumpkin, winter squash, yams

agave nectar
allspice
APPLES, apple cider, apple juice, and applesauce
apricots
arugula
*baked goods, e.g., biscuits, breads, cakes, cookies, muffins, **pies***
bananas
basil and Thai basil
bay leaf
BEANS, e.g., BLACK, green
beans, green
BELL PEPPERS, e.g., green, red, yellow
bourbon
burritos
butter and brown butter
caramel
cardamom
carrots
casseroles
cauliflower
cayenne
celery
chard, Swiss
cheese, e.g., blue, feta, Fontina, goat, Parmesan, Stilton, Taleggio
chickpeas
CHILES, e.g., chipotle, green, jalapeño, poblano
chili, e.g., flakes, paste, powder
chips, vegetable
chocolate
CILANTRO
CINNAMON
cloves

COCONUT, e.g., butter, cream, milk
coriander
corn
cranberries, e.g., dried, juice
cream
crème fraîche
croutons, whole-grain
cumin
curries
curry, e.g., powder, spices
custards
desserts, e.g., custards, pies, puddings
eggs
fennel

figs
fruit, dried
garam masala
GARLIC
ghee (clarified butter)
GINGER
grains, whole, e.g., barley, couscous, **millet**, oats
gratins
greens, e.g., collard, mustard, salad
hash
hoisin sauce
honey
Indian cuisine
Italian cuisine

Dishes

Flourish Vegetable Pot Pie: Two Potato Mash with Carrots and Celery, Sweet Potatoes, Russet Potatoes Organic Rice Milk, Extra-Virgin Olive Oil, and Sea Salt
— Flourish Baking Company (Scarsdale, NY)

Maple Pecan Sweet Potato: Organic Baked Sweet Potato topped with Spicy Chipotle Cashew Cream and Sweet Candied Maple Pecans
— Follow Your Heart (Canoga Park, CA)

Poached Eggs with Black Bean and Sweet Potato Hash, Roasted Chili Sauce
— The Lodge at Woodloch (Hawley, PA)

Potato Pancake: Sweet and White Potatoes, with Apple Cranberry Chutney and Crema
— Mana Food Bar (Chicago)

Sweet Potato Tamale: Smoky Pecan and Poblano Chile Filling, Black Bean Chocolate Mole, Winter Greens and Caramelized Onions, Avocado, Pickled Onion-Nopales Salsa, Spicy Pumpkin Seed Emulsion
— Millennium (San Francisco)

Sweet Potato Quesadilla: Sweet Potato, Sautéed Onion, and Kale, served with a Creamy Thyme Sauce
— Root (Allston, MA)

House Made Ravioli, Sweet Potato and Galangal Filling, Lemongrass Coconut Cream
— True Bistro (Somerville, MA)

Wood Grilled Sweet Potato Paté, Grain Mustard, Jerk Cashews, Toast
— Vedge (Philadelphia)

Sweet Potato Turnover with Sweet Kraut and Cream, Melted Figs, Smoked Maple Ice Cream, Walnut Streusel
— Vedge (Philadelphia)

Japanese cuisine
KALE
lemon, e.g., juice, zest
lemongrass
lentils, e.g., red
LIME, e.g., juice, zest
MAPLE SYRUP
marjoram
milk, e.g., almond, cashew, coconut
mirin
miso, e.g., sweet, white

molasses
mushrooms, e.g., shiitake
mustard, e.g., Dijon
NUTMEG
**NUTS, nut butters, and nut
  milks, e.g., almonds, peanuts,
  PECANS, WALNUTS**
OIL, e.g., grapeseed, hazelnut,
  nut, **OLIVE, peanut, sesame,**
  walnut
ONIONS, e.g., **red**, white, **spring,**

sweet, yellow
ORANGES, e.g., juice, zest
oregano
pancakes, e.g., sweet potato
paprika, e.g., sweet, smoked
PARSLEY
parsnips
pasta, e.g., gnocchi, lasagna, ravioli
pâtés
pears
pepper, e.g., black, white
pineapple
poppy seeds
potatoes, white
pumpkin seeds
purees
quesadillas
quinoa
radicchio
raisins
rice, e.g., brown
ROSEMARY
rum
sage
salads
salsa
salt, e.g., kosher, sea, smoked
savory
scallions
seeds, e.g., sesame, sunflower
SESAME, e.g., oil, paste, seeds
shallots
shepherd's pie
soufflés
*SOUPS, e.g., black bean, sweet
  potato, tomato*
sour cream
SOY SAUCE
spinach
stews
stock, vegetable
SUGAR, BROWN
tamari
tempeh
tempura
thyme
tofu, e.g., smoked
tomatoes

Flavor Affinities

SWEET POTATOES + allspice + **CINNAMON** + ginger + maple syrup
  + **NUTMEG** (+ vanilla)
sweet potatoes + almond milk + cinnamon + maple syrup + nutmeg
  (+ vanilla)
sweet potatoes + almonds + almond milk + apples
sweet potatoes + apples + ginger
sweet potatoes + avocado + black beans + chiles
sweet potatoes + balsamic vinegar + kale + sage
sweet potatoes + bell peppers + garlic + *hash* **+ onions**
sweet potatoes + black beans + cilantro + mango + *salsa*
sweet potatoes + black beans + *salsa* **+** *tortillas*
sweet potatoes + bourbon + brown sugar + pecans
sweet potatoes + brown butter + sage
sweet potatoes + brown sugar + cinnamon + vanilla
sweet potatoes + brown sugar + citrus (e.g., lemon/lime/orange juice)
sweet potatoes + brown sugar + ginger
sweet potatoes + chiles + ginger + **lime** + salt
sweet potatoes + chiles + honey
sweet potatoes + chocolate + cinnamon + nuts + vanilla
sweet potatoes + cilantro + lime + onions + vinegar
sweet potatoes + coconut milk + curry spices
sweet potatoes + garlic + herbs (e.g., rosemary, sage, thyme)
sweet potatoes + ginger + honey + sesame + **soy sauce**
SWEET POTATOES + GINGER + LIME + pears
sweet potatoes + ginger + miso
sweet potatoes + ginger + orange + yogurt
sweet potatoes + ginger + peanuts
sweet potatoes + ginger + sesame oil/seeds
sweet potatoes + greens + quinoa
sweet potatoes + honey + lime
sweet potatoes + lime + salt
SWEET POTATOES + MAPLE SYRUP + PECANS
sweet potatoes + molasses + sesame seeds
sweet potatoes + nuts + raisins
SWEET POTATOES + SESAME OIL/SEEDS + SOY SAUCE

tortillas
turmeric
turnips
vanilla
VINEGAR, e.g., BALSAMIC, red
wine, rice wine, **sherry**
waffles, sweet potato
watercress
yogurt

SWEETNESS / SWEETENERS

Tips: The colder the food or the drink, the less the perception of sweetness. Sweetness tends to round out flavors, while acidity sharpens them. There are lots of ways to add it to a dish other than with refined white sugar: Below are some examples.

agave nectar, e.g., raw
apple juice and applesauce
barley malt syrup
brown rice syrup
cane juice, evaporated
cinnamon
coconut nectar
coconut sugar
dates and date sugar
fruit, fresh, e.g., bananas
fruit, dried, e.g., dates, raisins
fruit juice, esp. concentrated, e.g.,
    fruit syrup
fruit preserves and jams
honey, e.g., raw
maple sugar
maple syrup
mirin
molasses
nutmeg
rice syrup
stevia
sucanat, which is an acronym for
    sugar cane natural
sugar, e.g., brown, coconut, date,
    maple, muscovado, organic,
    palm, raw, turbinado
vanilla

SYRUP, RICE (see BROWN RICE SYRUP)

SZECHUAN PEPPER (see PEPPER, SZECHUAN)

● TAHINI

[tah-HEE-nee]
Flavor: sweet and/or salty, nutty, with a creamy texture
Volume: moderate
What it is: sesame butter, made from ground sesame seeds
Nutritional profile: 70% fat / 19% carbs / 11% protein
Calories: 90 per 1-tablespoon serving
Protein: 3 grams
Tip: Opt for tahini made from raw, stone-ground kernels.
Possible substitute: smokier Chinese sesame paste (in Asian dishes)

(North) African cuisines
Asian cuisines
asparagus
baba ghanoush
baked goods, e.g., breads
beans, e.g., black, cannellini,
    green, white
beets
bok choy
cabbage
carrots
cashews
cauliflower
CHICKPEAS
cilantro
couscous, Israeli
cumin
dips
eggplant
falafel
fruit
garlic
ginger
Greek cuisine
greens, e.g., salad

halvah
honey
*****HUMMUS**
icings, e.g., for cakes, cupcakes
LEMON, e.g., juice
lime
MIDDLE EASTERN CUISINES
milk, nondairy, e.g., almond, rice,
    soy
miso
mushrooms, e.g., shiitake
noodles, Asian, e.g., chilled, soba
nuts, e.g., macadamia
oil, e.g., sesame
onions, e.g., yellow
orange
pine nuts
potatoes
pumpkin
purees, e.g., carrots, potatoes, sweet
    potatoes
quinoa
SALAD DRESSINGS
salads, e.g., fattoush, fruit, legume
sandwiches
sauces
SESAME, e.g., oil, seeds
smoothies
snow peas
soups
soy sauce
spinach
SPREADS
squash, butternut
stews
stock, vegetable
sumac
sweet potatoes
tamari
tempeh
tofu
vanilla
vinegar, e.g., balsamic or rice
wine
walnuts
yogurt
za'atar
zucchini

Flavor Affinities

tahini + carrots + ginger

TAHINI + CHICKPEAS +
  GARLIC + LEMON JUICE +
  OLIVE OIL

tahini + chickpeas + Israeli
  couscous

TAHINI + GARLIC + LEMON +
  sesame oil + tamari

tahini + garlic + yogurt

tahini + lemon juice + soba
  noodles

tahini + lemon juice + yogurt

tahini + noodles + sesame oil +
  soy sauce + rice wine vinegar

● TAMARI

[tah-MAHR-ee]

Flavor: salty/sweet/umami, with
meaty notes

Volume: moderate

> **Tips:** Tamari tends to be
> sweeter (and more complex in
> flavor) than Chinese soy sauce,
> which tends to be saltier. Add
> to food during or after cooking.
> Opt for low-sodium versions.

Asian cuisines
baked dishes
casseroles
dips and dipping sauces
ginger
greens, Asian
grilled dishes
honey
marinades
mushrooms
onions, e.g., green
peanuts
pumpkin seeds
roasted dishes
salad dressings
SAUCES
sesame, e.g., seeds
soups
stews
stir-fries

sunflower seeds
sushi, e.g., nori rolls
tofu
tomatoes and tomato sauce
vinegar, rice
walnuts

Flavor Affinities

tamari + honey + rice vinegar +
  sesame seeds

"**Tamari**, which is basically
fermented salt, is great for
marinades. I don't tend to drizzle
it onto food directly, because it's
too easy to oversalt."
— MARK SHADLE, G-ZEN (BRANFORD, CT)

● TAMARIND and TAMARIND PASTE

Flavor: very sour/slightly sweet,
with pungent notes of apricots,
brown sugar, dates, dried plums,
and/or molasses

Volume: moderate – very loud

What it is: tropical fruit pulp

apricots
Asian cuisines
bananas
beans
beverages, fruit
black-eyed peas
Caribbean cuisines
carrots
cashews
cauliflower
chard, Swiss
chickpeas
chiles, e.g., jalapeño, Thai
chili powder
CHUTNEYS

cilantro
citrus, e.g., grapefruit, lemon,
  lime, orange, tangerine
coconut and coconut milk
coriander
cumin
**curry leaves, curry powder, curry
  spices, and *curries***
dates
*desserts, frozen, e.g., granitas,
  sorbets*
eggplant, Japanese
GARLIC
GINGER
grains
grapefruit
INDIAN CUISINE
Latin American cuisines
legumes
lemon
lemongrass
lentils, e.g., red
lime, e.g., juice, zest
maple syrup
marinades
Mediterranean cuisines
Mexican cuisine
Middle Eastern cuisines
mint
molasses
mushrooms
mustard and mustard seeds
noodles, Asian, e.g., rice
oil, e.g., grapeseed
oranges
pad thai
peanuts
potatoes, e.g., new
rice, e.g., basmati, jasmine
salad dressings
***salads**, e.g., noodle, Thai*

Dishes

Tamarind Scented Banana Split, Chocolate Marshmallow, Tamarind-Coriander Mousse,
and Banana-Crème Fraîche Sherbet
— Per Se (New York City)

sauces, e.g., *barbecue, sweet-and-sour, tomato*

scallions

shallots

sorbets

SOUPS, e.g., *hot-and-sour, lentil, vegetable*

soy sauce

star anise

stir-fries

sugar, e.g., brown, palm, white

sweet potatoes

tamari

tangerines

Thai cuisine

tofu

tomatoes and tomato paste

turmeric

vanilla

vegetables

vinegar, e.g., apple cider, brown rice

walnuts

yogurt

zucchini

Flavor Affinities

tamarind + cashews + tofu + tomatoes

tamarind + curry spices + peanuts + sweet potatoes

tamarind + garlic + ginger

● TANGERINES (see ORANGES, MANDARIN)

● TAPIOCA (see also FLOUR, TAPIOCA)

Flavor: neutral, with small, firm "pearls"

Dishes

Coconut and Vanilla Tapioca Pudding, with Huckleberry, Blood Orange, and Tangerine
— Natural Selection (Portland, OR)

Vanilla and Coconut Tapioca Pudding, with Apricot, Raspberry, Almonds, and White Chocolate
— Natural Selection (Portland, OR)

Volume: very quiet

What it is: pearls made from starch from the cassava plant; used as a thickening agent because, unlike cornstarch, it thickens without having to boil

Nutritional profile: 100% carbs

Tip: Soak for a few hours before using.

almonds

apples

bananas

chocolate

coconut and COCONUT MILK

DESSERTS, e.g., *fruit cobblers, crisps, pies, tarts*

eggs

fruits

ginger

Malaysian cuisine

mango

maple syrup

melon, e.g., honeydew

milk

nuts

puddings

sesame seeds, e.g., toasted

sugar, e.g., brown

VANILLA

Vietnamese cuisine

yuzu

Flavor Affinities

tapioca + bananas + coconut milk + ginger

tapioca + bananas + coconut milk + vanilla

"Our **tapioca** puddings are so popular that it's hard to take them off our menu. Coconut milk is a source of both flavor and richness [as opposed to rice milk, which is thin and has no flavor, or soy milk, which can taste chalky]. We thicken the pudding with agar-agar, which doesn't mask flavors, unlike cornstarch. We like to accent it with fruit in both raw and cooked form, such as fresh cherries with a cherry sauce or gel."

— AARON WOO, NATURAL SELECTION (PORTLAND, OR)

● TARO (aka TARO ROOT)

Flavor: earthy notes of nuts, potatoes, water chestnuts, and/or yeast, and a soft, flaky, starchy (and sometimes slippery) texture

Volume: quiet

What it is: starchy vegetable (tuber)

Nutritional profile: 98% carbs / 1% fat / 1% protein

Calories: 190 per 1-cup serving (cooked)

Protein: 1 gram

Techniques: bake, boil, braise, fry, grate, grind, mash, puree, sauté, simmer, steam, stew (Note: *never* raw!)

Possible substitute: potatoes

(West) African cuisines

Asian cuisines

Caribbean cuisines

Chinese cuisine

chips

coconut milk

curries

garlic

Hawaiian cuisine

honey

Japanese cuisine

"mashed potatoes"
milk, coconut
mushrooms, e.g., Asian, dried
"nests"
onions
pancakes, savory
POI
scallions
sesame, e.g., seeds
SOUPS
soy sauce
squash, e.g., kabocha
STEWS
sweet potatoes
taro leaves

Flavor Affinities
taro + chiles + coconut milk
taro + honey + sesame

● TARRAGON
[TEHR-ah-gon]
Season: summer
Flavor: bitter/sour/**sweet**;
aromatic, with pungent notes of
anise, basil, fennel, herbs, lemon,
licorice, mint, and/or pine
Volume: loud

> **Tips:** Add at the end of the
> cooking process. Unlike other
> herbs, fresh tarragon is louder
> than dried.

Botanical relatives: artichokes,
chamomile, chicory, dandelion
greens, endive, lettuces (e.g.,
Bibb, iceberg, romaine),
radicchio, salsify

anise
apples
apricots
artichokes
ASPARAGUS
beans, e.g., dried, fresh, green,
    lima, white
beets
bouquets garnis
broccoli

butter, e.g., flavored
capers
carrots
cauliflower
celery seeds
celery root
cheese, e.g., goat, ricotta
chervil
chives
citrus, e.g., grapefruit, lemon,
    lime
corn
cream
dairy products, e.g., butter, cream
dill
dips
EGGS, e.g., hard-boiled, *omelets,*
    quiches
fennel and fennel seeds
FINES HERBES (i.e., tarragon +
    chervil + chives + parsley)
French cuisine
frisée
garlic
GRAINS, WHOLE, e.g., barley,
    brown rice, **bulgur**, wheat berries
grapefruit
greens, bitter
herbes de Provence
leeks
LEMON, e.g., juice, zest
lemony herbs, e.g., balm, thyme,
    verbena
lentils
lime
lovage
marinades
marjoram
MAYONNAISE
melon
mint
mushrooms
mustard, e.g., Dijon
oil, e.g., canola, hazelnut, olive,
    walnut
onions
orange, e.g., juice, zest
paprika

PARSLEY and parsley root
pasta
peaches
peas, e.g., English
pepper, e.g., black, green, pink
potatoes
radishes
rice
SALAD DRESSINGS, e.g.,
    vinaigrettes
SALADS, e.g., egg, fruit, grain,
    green, pasta, potato
salsify
SAUCES, esp. classic French, e.g.,
    béarnaise, hollandaise; creamy,
    tartar
shallots
sorrel
SOUPS, e.g., cream-based,
    mushroom, white bean
spinach
stock, vegetable
stuffings
sugar snap peas
tofu
TOMATOES
vegetables
VINEGAR, e.g., champagne, red
    wine, sherry, white wine
walnuts
zucchini

Flavor Affinities
tarragon + anise + celery seeds
tarragon + bulgur + lentils +
    walnuts
tarragon + Dijon mustard +
    lemon juice
tarragon + Dijon mustard + red
    wine vinegar
tarragon + green beans +
    tomatoes
tarragon + green vegetables
    (asparagus, green peas) +
    lemon + olive oil
tarragon + sesame + soy sauce
tarragon + shallots + wine

"**Tarragon** instantly transports me to the French countryside with its herby, licorice-y flavor. I love it in spring with light dishes like green vegetables such as asparagus or English peas, with a little olive oil and lemon."

— RICH LANDAU, VEDGE (PHILADELPHIA)

● TATSOI (aka TAT SOI)
[taht-SOY]

Flavor: bitter/sour/sweet, with notes of bok choy, cabbage, minerals, **mustard**, nuts, and/or spinach, and a thick, crunchy/chewy texture

Volume: quiet – moderate

What it is: Asian green leafy vegetable

Calories: 35 calories per 1-cup serving (raw)

Protein: 3 grams

Techniques: braise, raw (esp. young), sauté, steam (about 10 minutes)

Tips: Rinse thoroughly. Serve raw or lightly cooked.

Botanical relatives: broccoli, mustard

Possible substitute: spinach

chives
cucumbers
edamame
garlic
ginger
greens, other, e.g., bok choy, mizuna
mangoes
mushrooms, e.g., shiitake
noodles, Asian, e.g., soba
oil, e.g., grapeseed, olive
onions, green
peanuts and peanut sauce
SALADS
scallions
sea vegetables, e.g., kombu, wakame

SESAME, e.g., oil, seeds
shallots
soups
soy sauce and **tamari**
stews
stir-fries
tahini
tofu, e.g., baked
vinegar, e.g., rice wine

Flavor Affinities

tatsoi + garlic + ginger + shallots

tatsoi + garlic + ginger + soy sauce

tatsoi + garlic + olive oil

tatsoi + ginger + sesame oil + soy sauce

tatsoi + rice wine vinegar + sesame oil/seeds

tatsoi + sesame oil + soy sauce + tahini + vinegar

• TEFF

Flavor: slightly sweet, with notes of hazelnuts, malt, and/or molasses, and extremely tiny grains
Volume: quiet – moderate
What it is: whole grain
Gluten-free: yes
Nutritional profile: 80% carbs / 14% protein / 6% fat
Calories: 105 per 1-ounce serving (uncooked)
Protein: 4 grams
Techniques: dry-roast, sauté, simmer
Timing: Presoak; toast grains before cooking; cook about 15 – 20 minutes, covered.
Ratio: 1:4 (1 cup teff to 4 cups cooking liquid)

Tip: Due to its tiny size, teff is always a whole grain.

(North) African cuisine
allspice
baked goods, e.g., breads, cookies
casseroles
cayenne
CEREALS, hot breakfast
chives
cinnamon
dates
ETHIOPIAN CUISINE
grains, other larger, e.g., barley, millet, rice
gravies
INJERA
maple syrup
milk
nuts, e.g., pecans, walnuts
onions
pancakes
parsley
pilafs
raisins
scallions
soups
stews
stuffings
thyme
vegetables

Flavor Affinities
teff + maple syrup + milk

• TEMPEH

[TEM-pay]
Flavor: slightly sweet/bitter, with earthy notes of **mushrooms, nuts,** smoke, and/or **yeast,** and a firm, chewy, meaty texture
Volume: moderate – loud
What it is: soybeans that have been fermented with a grain or grains (e.g., rice, barley, millet) and formed into cakes; weightier than tofu
Nutritional profile: 47% fats / 33% protein / 20% carbs
Calories: 160 per ½-cup serving
Protein: 15 grams
Techniques: bake (at 350°F about 30 minutes), braise, broil (4 – 5 minutes per side), fry, grate, grill (4 – 5 minutes per side), pan-fry (10 minutes), roast, sauté, steam, stir-fry (Note: Be sure to cook *thoroughly*.)

Tips: Steam for 10 minutes to calm tempeh's bitterness. After steaming, make sure to properly **marinate** (at least 30 minutes) and season for optimal flavor.

Brands: Lightlife, Soyboy, Surata, WestSoy, Wildwood (Look for organic versions.)

agave nectar
"bacon," tempeh
barbecue sauce
basil, Thai
bay leaf
beans, e.g., black, green, pinto
bell peppers, e.g., roasted
burritos
cabbage, e.g., green
carrots
casseroles
celery
celery root
chard
cheese, e.g., cheddar, Swiss
chiles, e.g., chipotle, jalapeño
CHILI, VEGETARIAN
chili pepper flakes
cilantro
cinnamon
COCONUT and COCONUT MILK
coriander
cumin
curries
curry powder and *curries*
fennel, e.g., pureed
five-spice powder
GARLIC
GINGER
grains, whole, e.g., millet
gravies, mushroom
greens, e.g., collard
hoisin sauce
honey
INDONESIAN CUISINE
kale
kebabs
kombu
lemon, e.g., juice
lemongrass
lettuce
lime, e.g., juice
liquid smoke
macrobiotic cuisine
maple syrup
mango
mirin
miso
molasses
mushrooms, e.g., porcini, portobello, shiitake
mustard
noodles, e.g., soba

OILS, e.g., canola, **OLIVE**,
  peanut, safflower, sesame,
  sunflower
onions, e.g., red, yellow
orange
oregano
paprika, e.g., smoked, sweet
parsley

Flavor Affinities

tempeh + avocado + black beans + mushrooms + *tortillas*

tempeh + avocado + *burrito* or *chili* or *tacos* + chipotle chiles + tomatoes

tempeh + black beans + orange

tempeh + caraway seeds + cumin

tempeh + chiles + cilantro

tempeh + chiles + citrus (e.g., lemon, orange)

tempeh + chiles + coconut + **ginger** + lemongrass + peanuts

tempeh + chiles + ginger + lemon + soy sauce

tempeh + cilantro + scallions + sesame seeds

tempeh + cilantro + tomatoes

tempeh + coconut milk + collard greens + curry + sweet potato

tempeh + coriander + cumin + ginger

TEMPEH + GARLIC + GINGER + SOY SAUCE

tempeh + garlic + lemon + parsley + shallots + white wine

tempeh + garlic + onion + tamari + vinegar

tempeh + garlic + orange + soy sauce

tempeh + lemon + mushrooms + shallots

tempeh + maple syrup + mustard

tempeh + *Russian dressing* + sauerkraut + Swiss cheese + *sandwiches*

"Tofu, tempeh, and seitan are the holy trinity of vegetarianism. . . .
Tempeh is my favorite because it has the most nutrients."
— BART POTENZA, COFOUNDER, CANDLE 79 (NEW YORK CITY)

"I prefer **soy tempeh** in the summertime, because it pairs well with
lighter flavors like citrus, lemon, and white wine. When the weather
cools down in the fall, I prefer **multigrain tempeh** because its earthier
flavor pairs better with the season's richer flavors of mushrooms
and spices like cinnamon. I really like Surata [brand] tempeh's texture
and flavor."
— MAKINI HOWELL, PLUM BISTRO (SEATTLE)

"I prefer **tempeh** to tofu or seitan because it is heartier and stands up
to flavorful sauces like mole the best."
— ANGEL RAMOS, CANDLE 79 (NEW YORK CITY)

pastas
PEANUTS and PEANUT SAUCE
peas
RICE, e.g., brown or jasmine
salad dressing, *e.g.*, *Russian,*
  Thousand Island
salads, *e.g.*, "chicken" (e.g., + carrots
  + celery + mayonnaise), *taco*

salt, sea
SANDWICHES, *e.g.*, "Reuben,"
  TBLT, *wraps*
sauces, *e.g.*, *pasta*
sauerkraut
scallions
scrambles, tempeh
sesame, e.g., oil, paste, seeds
shallots
"sloppy Joes"
smoke, liquid
soups
SOY SAUCE
sriracha sauce
star anise
stews, *e.g.*, *vegetable*
stir-fries
stock, vegetable
sugar, e.g., brown
sweet potatoes
tacos
TAMARI
tamarind
thyme
tomatoes, tomato paste, and
  tomato sauce
umeboshi plum sauce
veggie burgers
vinegar, e.g., apple cider,
  balsamic, brown rice, Chinese
  black, rice
wine, e.g., dry red or white
Worcestershire sauce, vegan

THAI CHILI PASTE, VEGETARIAN

What it is: dried Thai chiles +
galangal + garlic + kaffir lime leaf
+ lemongrass + salt + shallots +
soybean oil + sugar (e.g., palm) +
tamarind

bamboo shoots
beans, green
bell peppers
broccoli

T

Dishes

Tempeh Reuben Sandwich: Our version of this classic features Baked Marinated Tempeh, seasoned with Caraway and Cumin, Tofu Russian Dressing, Sauerkraut, and Lettuce, served on choice of Mixed Grain or Spelt Bread
— Angelica Kitchen (New York City)

Feijoadinha with Smokey Tempeh (a lighter version of feijoada, the Brazilian national dish): Stew of Smoky Roasted Tempeh, Black Beans, Chayote Squash, and Sweet Potatoes in an Orange-Lime Broth
— Blossom (New York City)

Maple Mustard Tempeh Sandwich on Grilled Spelt Bread with Roasted Garlic Aioli, Kale, Tomato, and Onion
— Cinnamon Snail Food Truck (Red Bank, NJ; New York City)

Tempeh and Root Hash: Roasted Sweet Potatoes, Parsnips, and Butternut tossed with Baked Tempeh, Sausage, Red Onions, and Spinach over Creamy Grits with Sautéed Farm Mizuna and Béarnaise
— Laughing Seed Café (Asheville, NC)

Black Garlic and Miso Glazed Tempeh: Kim Chee Fried Bhutanese Red Rice, Snap Peas and Edamame, Watercress-Chrysanthemum Green Salad with Yuzu-Ginger Vinaigrette, Toasted Peanuts, Spicy Pickled Thai Chile, and Fuyu Persimmon Relish
— Millennium (San Francisco)

Creole Tempeh with Blackening Spice Maple Glaze, Creole Pepper and Tomato Stew, Garlic Mashed Sweet Potatoes, Sautéed Kale with Caramelized Onions and Sea Vegetable, Dijon Cream
— Millennium (San Francisco)

Maryland Tempeh Cakes: Freshly Caught Native Tempeh Blended with Red Onion, Peppers, Herbs, and Spices, Seared Hot and Crisp, Served with a Chipotle Rémoulade
— Native Foods (multiple locations)

Ginger Fire Stir-Fry: Seasonal Vegetables, Grilled Tempeh, Udon Noodles, Sesame-Miso Broth
— Plant (Asheville, NC)

Thai Tempeh Salad: Mixed Lettuces and Herbs, Carrots, Avocado, Red Onion and Radish, Cucumber, and Peanut-Lime Dressing
— Plant (Asheville, NC)

Maple Grilled Tempeh with Charred Brussels Sprouts and Turnip Mash
— Plum Bistro (Seattle)

Andy's Favorite "TLT": Tempeh, Lettuce, Tomato, Avocado, Mayo, and Whole-Grain Bread
— True Food Kitchen (Santa Monica)

cabbage
carrots
coconut milk
curries, Thai vegetable
eggplant
lemongrass
lime, e.g., juice
mushrooms
noodles, Asian
onions
peanuts
pineapple
rice, e.g., jasmine
soups, e.g., spicy/sour, Thai
tamari
tofu
tomatoes
zucchini

THAI CUISINE

Tips: Authentic Thai cuisine strives for a balance of hot, salty, sour, and sweet. Be aware that Thai fish sauce is such a prevalent seasoning that it is sometimes part of "vegetarian" dishes at Thai restaurants.

bamboo shoots
bananas
BASIL, THAI
bell peppers
CHILES, e.g., serrano, **THAI**
chili paste, esp. Thai
chili powder
chili sauce
cilantro
COCONUT and COCONUT MILK
coriander
cumin
CURRIES
CURRY PASTE, THAI
eggplant, Asian
garlic
ginger
herbs, fresh
Kaffir lime leaves

lemongrass
lime
mangoes, e.g., green
mint
noodles, e.g., Asian, rice
pad thai
papaya, e.g., green
peanuts
pineapple
relishes
rice, e.g., jasmine
salads
salt
soups
soy sauce
spices
squash, winter
sugar
tamarind
tofu
turmeric
vegetables

THANKSGIVING

"If you ask people what they love about **Thanksgiving** food, the answer is usually what we think of as the 'sides.' It's all about the herbs and spices; the sage in the stuffing and the ginger in the squash; the thyme in the gravy and the pepper in the potatoes. There are so many ways to build satisfying flavors for the holiday table. I love a nice centerpiece of course, perhaps a pot pie or a lentil roast, but I think that making sure that all of the familiar flavors are present is the most important part of the holiday table."

— ISA CHANDRA MOSKOWITZ, AUTHOR OF *ISA DOES IT* AND *VEGANOMICON*

Thanksgiving Dishes

Butternut Squash Gnocchi with Pumpkin Seed-Crusted Tofu Medallions
— Candle Café (New York City)

Veggie Turkey, Faux Beef Wellington, and Pumpkin Ravioli
— The Chicago Diner (Chicago)

Thanksgiving Preview: Herb-Crusted Seitan, Rustic Mashed Potatoes, Pan Gravy, Sourdough-Sage Stuffing, Coconut Whipped Yams, and Cranberry Relish
— Madeleine Bistro (Los Angeles)

THICKENING AGENTS

When you can't or don't want to rely on butter and cream to thicken dishes, consider these options:

agar-agar (although this works better as a gelatin substitute)
arrowroot powder
cornstarch
kudzu root (aka kuzu)

● THYME

Season: summer
Flavor: bitter/sweet; aromatic, with earthy/pungent notes of caraway, cloves, flowers, herbs, lemon, mint, orange, and/or pine
Volume: moderate – loud
Tips: Opt for fresh rather than dried thyme. Add at the end of the cooking process to retain flavor. Lemon thyme has more citrus notes than regular thyme.
Botanical relatives: basil, lavender, marjoram, mint, oregano, rosemary, sage, summer savory
Possible substitute: oregano

apples
basil
baked goods, e.g., biscotti, biscuits, cookies
bay leaf
beans, dried, e.g., black, kidney, pinto

beans, green
beets
bell peppers
BOUQUETS GARNIS
bread puddings, savory
breads
Brussels sprouts
Caribbean cuisine
Cajun cuisine
carrots
casseroles
chard
CHEESE, e.g., blue, cheddar, fresh, **goat**, ricotta
chives
chowders
CITRUS, e.g., **lemon**, orange
corn
Creole cuisine
eggplant
eggs, e.g., *omelets*
European cuisines
fennel
French cuisine
garlic
gratins
Greek cuisine
greens, salad, e.g., mesclun
gumbos
herbes de Provence
Italian cuisine
Jamaican cuisine, e.g., jerk dishes
leeks
LEMON
lettuce, e.g., romaine
lovage

T

marinades
marjoram
Mediterranean cuisines
Middle Eastern cuisines
MUSHROOMS and wild
mushrooms, e.g., cremini
mustard
oil, olive
ONIONS
orange, e.g., zest
oregano
parsley
pastas
pears
peas
peas, split
pepper, black
polenta
potatoes
quinoa
rosemary
salad dressings, e.g., vinaigrettes
salads, e.g., pasta
sauces, e.g., barbecue, cheese, cream,
pasta, red wine, tomato
savory
sesame seeds
SOUPS, e.g., broths, chowders,
creamy, gumbos, vegetable
spinach
squash, summer and winter, e.g.,
butternut, delicata
STEWS, e.g., mushroom, vegetable
stocks, vegetable
stuffings
sumac
tofu
TOMATOES and tomato sauce
vegetables, e.g., root, winter
zucchini

Flavor Affinities
thyme + garlic + lemon + olive oil
thyme + goat cheese + olive oil
thyme + onions + spinach
thyme + sesame seeds + sumac
(za'atar)

TOFU — IN GENERAL
[TOH-foo]
Flavor: neutral, ranging from
delicate to firm in texture
Volume: quiet
What it is: bean curd made
from soybeans
Nutritional profile: 50% fats /
38% protein / 12% carbs (raw, firm)
Calories: 185 per ½-cup serving
(raw, firm)
Protein: 20 grams (raw, firm)
Techniques: bake (at 350°F
for 15 minutes per side), blanch
(esp. before long simmering),
boil (10 minutes), braise,
broil, crumble, cube, freeze
(after defrosting, chewiness
is enhanced), fry, grill (4 – 5
minutes per side), marinate, pan-
sear, puree, roast, sauté, slice,
simmer (20 minutes), stir-fry,
tempura-fry, toast

Tips: Its flavor neutrality is a
boon, as tofu readily absorbs the
flavors with which it is cooked.
Tofu is solidified using nigari or
lemon juice, so flavors that pair
well with lemon often work beautifully. Rinse tofu in cold water
before using, and drain well to
better allow tofu to absorb seasonings. You can press out the excess
water from tofu by using paper
towels and heavy books or cans,
but frequent tofu cooks might
consider investing in a tofu press
(e.g., TofuXpress).

Brands: The Bridge
(Middletown, CT), Fresh Tofu
(Allentown, PA), Island Spring
(Vashon Island, WA)

Asian cuisines
asparagus
avocado
basil
beans, e.g., black, green, pinto

bell peppers, e.g., red
black bean paste, e.g., fermented
bok choy
"bowls," e.g., grains/veggies/
dressings
broccoli and broccoli rabe
burdock root
cabbage, e.g., Chinese, napa
carrots
cashews
celery
chard
"cheesecakes"
chiles, e.g., ancho, chipotle; chili
paste and chili pepper flakes
chili, vegetarian
Chinese cuisine
cilantro
cinnamon
coconut and coconut milk
cornmeal, e.g., to crust
cumin
curries
curry powder
daikon
dashi
desserts, e.g., creamy
dill
dips
dressings
eggplant
five-spice powder
GARLIC
GINGER
grains, whole, e.g., millet
greens, e.g., Asian, collard
hiziki
hoisin
honey
Japanese cuisine
kale
kebabs
Korean cuisine
leeks
LEMON, e.g., juice, zest
lemongrass
lime, e.g., juice, zest
maple syrup

Dishes

Tofu Scramble: Fresh Tofu sautéed with Onion, Mushrooms, Spinach, Tomatoes, and Soy Sausage
— Blossom (New York City)

Breakfast Tofudilla: Southwest Seasoned Tofu with Black Bean Chili, Avocado, and Tomatoes, served with Jalapeño Cucumber Relish
— Canyon Ranch Café (Las Vegas)

Crispy, Silken Tofu with Georgia Peaches, Red Curry, and Pea Blossoms
— Charlie Trotter's (Chicago)

Tofu Schnitzel: Lightly Breaded Pan-Fried Tofu with a Citrus Glaze, served with Sweet and Sour Purple Onion, Caramelized Carrots, and House Made Spinach Spaetzle sautéed in Extra-Virgin Olive Oil with Arugula and Shallots
— Laughing Seed Café (Asheville, NC)

Ma Po Tofu: Spicy Eggplant, Tofu, Chinese Black Beans and Red Chili Paste, over Brown Rice
— Mana Food Bar (Chicago)

Ranchero Skillet: Tofu with Soy Chorizo, Avocado, Cheese, Spinach Tortilla, Salsa, Tepary Beans (pictured at right)
— Pomegranate Café (Phoenix)

Tofu Bruschetta: Slices of 7-Grain Bread topped with Fresh Basil Walnut Pesto, Baked Tofu, Tomato, and Almond Sprinkles
— Sage's Cafe (Salt Lake City)

mayonnaise and Vegenaise
mint
mirin
MISO
MUSHROOMS, e.g., SHIITAKE
mustard
NOODLES, esp. Asian, e.g.,
   buckwheat, rice, soba, udon
nori
oil, e.g., olive, peanut, sesame
onions, e.g., green, red, spring,
   yellow
orange, e.g., juice, zest
pad thai
PEANUTS and PEANUT SAUCE
pepper, black
plum sauce
pumpkin and pumpkin seeds
quinoa

RICE, e.g., black, brown
rosemary
salad dressings
salads, e.g., green, mock egg,
   vegetable
salt, sea
sandwiches
satays
sauces, e.g., peanut
scallions
sea vegetables, e.g., dulse, hiziki
scrambles, tofu
SESAME, e.g., oil, sauce, seeds
shiso
skewers
snap peas
snow peas
soups, e.g., "creamy," miso
SOY SAUCE

SPINACH
spreads, e.g., pureed tofu
spring rolls
squash, e.g., butternut, kabocha
star anise
STIR-FRIES
stock, e.g., vegetable
sugar, e.g., brown
TAMARI
Thai cuisine
tomatoes
umeboshi plum sauce
veggie burgers
VINEGAR, e.g., balsamic,
   brown rice, Chinese black, rice,
umeboshi
walnuts
watercress
wine
zucchini

Flavor Affinities

tofu + asparagus + cashews + shiitake mushrooms

tofu + asparagus + sesame

tofu + avocado + brown/sushi rice + nori

tofu + balsamic vinegar + basil + lemon + soy sauce

tofu + black bean paste + mushrooms

tofu + black beans + tomatoes + zucchini

tofu + bok choy + garlic + sesame

tofu + butter + lemon + white wine

tofu + butternut squash + curry + peas

tofu + celery + dill + *mock egg salad* + pickle + red onions + *Vegenaise*

tofu + chiles + garlic + ginger

tofu + cilantro + garlic + mushrooms + peanuts + soy sauce

tofu + coconut milk + curry + peanuts

tofu + coconut milk + ginger + lemongrass

tofu + daikon + ginger + mirin + soy sauce

tofu + garlic + ginger + honey + mustard + **soy sauce**

TOFU + GARLIC + GINGER + RICE VINEGAR + SESAME OIL + SOY SAUCE

tofu + garlic + herbs + miso + onions

tofu + garlic + *kebabs* **+ lemon** + rosemary

tofu + garlic + lemon + soy sauce

tofu + garlic + mint

tofu + garlic + mushrooms + spinach

tofu + ginger + honey + peanut butter + sesame oil

tofu + ginger + miso

tofu + ginger + orange

tofu + ginger + parsley + soy sauce

tofu + ginger + peanuts

tofu + ginger + rice + soy

tofu + ginger + scallions + tamari

tofu + herbs (e.g., mint, parsley, rosemary) **+ lemon**

tofu + kale + miso + sesame seeds + walnuts

tofu + kombu + miso + shiitake mushrooms + wakame

tofu + lemon + miso + **parsley** + sesame

tofu + maple syrup + tamari

tofu + miso + shiitake mushrooms + shiso + soy sauce

tofu + mushroom + spinach

tofu + pumpkin + tomatoes

tofu + pumpkin seeds + *tortillas*

tofu + snap peas + soba noodles

● TOFU, FIRM or EXTRA-FIRM

Flavor: neutral, with a texture that is denser and heartier than silken, yet moister than super-firm tofu

Volume: quiet

Nutritional profile: 54% fat / 38% protein / 8% carbs

Calories: 85 per ⅕-block serving (extra-firm)

Protein: 9 grams (extra-firm)

Techniques: bake, crumble, deep-fry, fry, grate (esp. extra-firm), grill, marinate, pan-fry, roast, sauté, scramble, stir-fry

Tips: Marinate overnight or for as long as several days. For a chewier texture, freeze firm or extra-firm tofu for 24+ hours, then thaw, and squeeze out water in tofu before marinating; the texture can approximate that of ground beef or chicken in dishes such as vegetarian chili or tacos. Crumble and season (e.g., with basil, garlic, lemon juice, nutritional yeast, oregano, salt) extra-firm tofu to make a vegan ricotta cheese substitute that can be used in pastas and on pizzas.

basil

bell peppers, e.g., green, red

Bragg Liquid Aminos

brochettes

"cheesecakes"

chiles, e.g., jalapeño; and chili pepper sauce

cilantro

coconut milk

curries

"frittatas"

GARLIC

ginger

greens, e.g., bitter, watercress

hoisin sauce

honey

lemon, e.g., juice

maple syrup

marjoram

"meatballs"

mushrooms, e.g., porcini or shiitake

mustard, e.g., Dijon

nutritional yeast

OIL, e.g., grapeseed, **olive, sesame**

onions, e.g., red

orange, e.g., zest

oregano

parsley

pepper, black

rice, e.g., brown, long-grain, wild

"ricotta," tofu

rosemary

salads, e.g., "egg," green

salt, e.g., sea

sandwiches

sauces, e.g., barbecue, peanut

scallions

"scrambles"

sesame seeds, e.g., black, white

shallots

SOY SAUCE

spinach

steaks, tofu

stir-fries

stock, e.g., vegetable

sugar, e.g., brown

tamari

thyme

tomatoes, e.g., cherry

vegetables, e.g., broccoli, eggplant, zucchini

vinegar, e.g., apple cider, brown rice, red wine, sherry

watercress

Flavor Affinities

(extra-)**firm tofu + basil** + cashews + garlic + **lemon + olive oil**

(extra-)**firm tofu + basil** + garlic + **lemon** + nutritional yeast + **olive oil**

(extra-)firm tofu + bell peppers + *brochettes* + mushrooms + onions

(extra-)firm tofu + capers + lemon + watercress

(extra-)firm tofu + hoisin sauce + sesame oil + sesame seeds + soy sauce

(extra-)firm tofu + honey + soy sauce

(extra-)firm tofu + lemon + sesame oil + soy sauce

"I like **extra-firm tofu** with tapenade and tomatoes. If you put extra-firm tofu through your food processor, it will come out the texture of ricotta cheese, and you can use it that way in lasagnas and other pasta dishes."

— FERNANDA CAPOBIANCO, VEGAN DIVAS (NEW YORK CITY)

TOFU, FROZEN

Tips: Freezing firm or extra-firm tofu changes its texture. Once thawed and cooked, it has a chewy, meaty texture. Cubed, it approximates the texture of meat. Crumbled, it approximates the texture of ground beef.

casseroles

pastas

pizzas

sauces, e.g., tomato

stews

TOFU, JAPANESE

Tip: Use when you're looking for the softest texture.

TOFU, SCRAMBLED

Tips: Substitute crumbled firm or extra-firm tofu for scrambled eggs as a base to mix in vegetables and seasonings, e.g., avocados, bell peppers, black beans, cilantro, garlic, mushrooms, onions, parsley, scallions, spinach, tempeh bacon, tomatoes, or vegan sausage. Achieve the yellow hue of scrambled eggs via nutritional yeast or turmeric.

● TOFU, SILKEN

Flavor: slightly sweet, with a creamy, moist, smooth, custard-like texture

Volume: quiet

Tips: Puree into sauces and soups to give them a creamy texture. Blend silken tofu with agave nectar and/or maple syrup plus vanilla for a vegan topping to enjoy on French toast, pancakes, or waffles — or on desserts. Do not substitute silken for regular tofu, or vice versa; use the type specified by the particular recipe.

Brand: Mori-Nu Silken Tofu

agave nectar

cheesecake

desserts

dips

dressings, *e.g., creamy*

maple syrup

"mayonnaise"

mousses

pastas, e.g., lasagna

puddings

raitas

salad dressings

sauces, esp. creamy, *e.g., alfredo*

smoothies

soups, e.g., creamy, potato

"sour cream"

vanilla

T

Flavor Affinities

silken tofu + cilantro + lime + mint + miso

silken tofu + cucumbers + lemon + mint + sugar

silken tofu + ginger + scallions + soy sauce

TOFU SKIN (aka YUBA)

Flavor: slightly sweet, with notes of custard, meat, and/or nuts, with a chewy, tender, custard-like/noodle-like texture
Volume: quiet
What it is: soymilk skin
Techniques: red-braise, sauté (for crispness)

avocado
cabbage, e.g., napa
carrots
chiles, e.g., dried red, and chili pepper flakes
cilantro
cinnamon
cloves
coconut milk
curry powder and spices
dashi
ginger
Japanese cuisine
lemongrass
mirin
miso
mushrooms, e.g., shiitake
mustard
mock "seafood" salad
oil, e.g., sesame
onions
orange, e.g., zest
rice, e.g., sushi
salt
sauces, e.g., dipping, peanut
scallions
sesame, e.g., oil, seeds
shiso
soups, e.g., curry

soy sauce
soybeans, black
star anise
stir-fries
stock, e.g., dashi, mushroom, vegetable
sushi and rolls
Thai chili paste
tofu skin "noodles," sliced long and served with dipping sauce
Vietnamese cuisine
vinegar, e.g., rice wine
wasabi
wine, rice, e.g., sake
zucchini

Flavor Affinities

tofu skin + chiles + orange zest + salt + sesame seeds

tofu skin + rice + **soy sauce + wasabi**

TOFU, SMOKED

Flavor: slightly salty, with notes of bacon, ham, and/or **smoke**, and a firm, meaty texture
Volume: quieter (slightly smoked) – louder (strongly smoked)
Calories: 170 per 100-gram serving
Protein: 25 grams
Techniques: fry, grill

Tips: Substitute for bacon, paneer (in Indian cuisine), smoked meat, or tuna in dishes. If smoking it yourself, use extra-firm tofu.

Dishes

Wilted Spinach, Smoked Tofu, Pecans, Cranberries, Red Onion, Balsamic Vinegar
— True Bistro (Somerville, MA)

BLT: House-Smoked Tofu, Boston Lettuce, Fresh Tomato, Ciabatta Roll
— True Bistro (Somerville, MA)

Salt Roasted Gold Beets, Avocado, Smoked Tofu, Rye, Capers, Creamy Cucumber
— Vedge (Philadelphia)

almonds
apples and apple cider
arame
artichokes
asparagus
avocado
basil
beans, e.g., black or kidney
beets
bell peppers
breads, whole-grain
cabbage
carrots
cauliflower
cayenne
chard
cilantro
citrus, e.g., lemon, lime, orange
coconut
corn
cucumbers
daikon
dips, e.g., spinach
edamame
eggplant, e.g., Japanese
garlic
grains, e.g., rye berries
greens, e.g., Asian, mustard, salad
Kaffir lime
kale
lentils
lettuce, e.g., romaine
lime
mint
mirin
miso, e.g., white

mushrooms, e.g., enoki, oyster, portobello, shiitake
noodles, Asian, e.g., rice, soba, udon
oil, e.g., olive, sesame
onions, e.g., red
PAD THAI
parsley
pastas, e.g., carbonara
pears
pesto
quinoa
rice, e.g., basmati, jasmine, wild
salads, e.g., Asian, cobb, mushroom, noodle, pasta, **spinach**
sandwiches, e.g., *AvocadoLT, "BLT"*
scallions
sesame, e.g., oil, sauce, seeds
snow peas
soups, e.g., corn, lentil, miso, vegetable
soy sauce
spinach
spring rolls
sprouts, e.g., daikon radish
squash, winter, e.g., butternut
stews
stir-fries
stock, vegetable
sugar snap peas
thyme
tomatoes
tomatoes, sun-dried
veggie burgers
vinegar, balsamic
walnuts
watercress

Flavor Affinities
smoked tofu + almonds + **avocado** + **romaine** + *salads* + **tomatoes**
smoked tofu + balsamic vinegar + mushrooms + olive oil + spinach
smoked tofu + basil + butternut squash + miso + soba noodles
smoked tofu + basil + pesto + sun-dried tomatoes
smoked tofu + beans + garlic + onions

"**Tofu** is so versatile! You can use it as a savory element to make a mousse or a veggie burger. If you marinate it, you can use it like a cheese and add it to salads. I add soy milk and silken tofu to polenta, then serve it with broccoli rabe. I like to marinate tofu with turmeric or with raw onion, sherry vinegar, red or green pepper, and soy sauce. Easiest of all is marinating a whole block of tofu in miso, then baking it for 20 minutes — it comes out with such a great flavor, and is even better with some brown rice and broccoli rabe."
— FERNANDA CAPOBIANCO, VEGAN DIVAS (NEW YORK CITY)

"Island Spring is the Cadillac of **tofu**. It takes time to develop a great product, and theirs is dense and flavorful and absorbs other flavors well. . . . I like to grill my tofu before marinating it, because citrus tears apart the fiber and makes it impossible to char afterward. Marinating grilled tofu pushes the flavor of the char and the marinade into the tofu."
— MAKINI HOWELL, PLUM BISTRO (SEATTLE)

"Our spin on tuna with wasabi is spicy grilled **tofu** taken in a Korean direction with gochujang, which is the paste used in bibambap. The gochujang is a little sharp, so we add bean paste for a sweet balance that is turned into a glaze to finish the tofu."
— RICH LANDAU AND KATE JACOBY, VEDGE (PHILADELPHIA)

"We season Wildwood organic sprouted **tofu** for our Ranchero Skillet with chipotle powder, curry powder, nutritional yeast, salt, and turmeric." (pictured on page 511)
— CASSIE TOLMAN, POMEGRANATE CAFÉ (PHOENIX)

smoked tofu + *bread* + edamame + red onions + watercress
smoked tofu + *pasta* + spinach

"I make my own **smoked tofu** after marinating tofu in tamari, sesame oil, and agave [nectar] and baking it. It doesn't need more than 45 to 60 minutes in the smoker. I've added smoked tofu to spinach salad with orange-miso dressing."
— ERIC TUCKER, MILLENNIUM (SAN FRANCISCO)

TOFU, SOFT
Tips: Soft tofu is halfway between firm and silken tofu. Crumble to use.

"cottage cheese"
"cream cheese"
dips
pastas, e.g., lasagna, manicotti
"ricotta"
salad dressings
sauces
scrambles
smoothies
soups

• TOFU, SUPER-FIRM
Flavor: neutral, with a very dense, meaty texture akin to that of chicken, crab, or fish
Techniques: bake, fry, grate, grill, marinate, roast, shred, simmer, smoke

Nutritional profile: 46% fat / 41% protein / 13% carbs
Calories: 100 per one 80-gram serving
Protein: 10 grams
> **Tips:** Often labeled "high protein" tofu. Opt for this version when there's no time for pressing, as it requires only draining.

Brands: Wildwood

"chicken nuggets"
"crabcakes"
"jerky"
kebobs
ma po tofu, vegetarian
"panir" in Indian dishes, e.g., curries, tikka masalas
"quiches"
smoked tofu
stir-fries

● TOMATILLOS

[toh-mah-TEE-yohz]
Season: spring – summer
Flavor: sour/sweet, with notes of fruits (e.g., lemons, plums), herbs, and green tomatoes
Volume: moderate – loud
Nutritional profile: 66% carbs / 27% fats / 7% protein
Calories: 20 per ½-cup serving (diced, raw)
Protein: 1 gram
Techniques: grill, puree, raw
> **Tip:** Balance their sourness with salt and sweetness.

Botanical relatives: bell peppers, chiles, eggplant, gooseberries (which share a similar husk), potatoes, tomatoes

AVOCADOS
basil
bell peppers, e.g., green
chilaquiles
CHILES, e.g., ancho, chipotle, green, guajillo, jalapeño, poblano, serrano
CILANTRO
corn
cucumbers
cumin
eggs and *egg dishes, e.g., huevos rancheros*
enchiladas
epazote
GARLIC
guacamole
jícama
lettuce, e.g., romaine
LIME, e.g., juice
mangoes
Mexican cuisine
mint
oil, olive
ONIONS, e.g., red, white, yellow
oregano
polenta
posole
pumpkin seeds
quinoa
salad dressings
salads
SALSAS, e.g., green, esp. salsa verde
salt, sea
sauces, e.g., enchilada
scallions
soups, e.g., cold, green gazpacho
Southwestern (U.S.) cuisine
stock, vegetable
tacos
Tex-Mex cuisine
thyme
tomatoes, e.g., cherry
tortillas, e.g., corn
vinegar, e.g., red wine

Flavor Affinities
tomatillos + avocados + lime
tomatillos + avocados + pumpkin seeds
tomatillos + bell peppers + chiles + onions
TOMATILLOS + CHILES (e.g., jalapeños) + CILANTRO + onions
TOMATILLOS + CHILES + CILANTRO + garlic + red onions + vinegar
tomatillos + chiles + cilantro + mango
tomatillos + chiles + corn **+ lime**
tomatillos + chiles + lime + mint
tomatillos + cilantro + garlic + green bell peppers + onions
tomatillos + cilantro + garlic + lime + olive oil
tomatillos + cilantro + lime
tomatillos + jalapeños + lime + onions

• TOMATOES, TOMATO JUICE, TOMATO PASTE, and TOMATO SAUCE

Season: summer – autumn
Flavor: sweet/sour
Volume: moderate
What they are: technically a fruit; generally considered a vegetable nutritionally
Nutritional profile: 79% carbs / 12% protein / 9% fats
Calories: 35 per 1-cup serving (chopped, raw)
Protein: 2 grams
Techniques: bake, broil, confit, fry, grill, juice, puree, raw, roast, sauté, stew, stuff, sun-dry
Botanical relatives: bell peppers, chiles, eggplant, gooseberries, potatoes, tomatillos
Brands: When fresh tomatoes are out of season or when you otherwise need them, look for Muir Glen (fire-roasted) or San Marzano canned tomatoes.

almonds
artichokes
arugula
asparagus
avocados
barley
***BASIL**
bay leaf
BEANS, e.g., black, borlotti, cannellini, cranberry, dried, fava, **green**, kidney, mung, pinto, red, **white**
beets
BELL PEPPERS, e.g., green, red, esp. roasted
breads (e.g., focaccia) and bread crumbs
bruschetta
butter
capers
caraway seeds
casseroles

Dishes

Heirloom Tomato Salad: Grilled Melon, Cucumbers, and Tomato Water
— Blue Hill (New York City)

Heirloom Tomato Salad: Opal Basil, White Balsamic, Burrata Cheese
— Café Boulud (New York City)

Sweet Pickled Baby Tomatoes with Iced Tomato Water: Parmesan, Cucumber, Eggplant, Celery
— Fearrington House (Fearrington Village, NC)

Heirloom Tomato Lasagna, Pistachio Pesto, Red Pepper Marinara, Pine Nut Ricotta
— M.A.K.E. (Santa Monica, CA)

cauliflower
cayenne
celery and celery seeds
chard, e.g., Swiss
CHEESE, e.g., blue, Cabrales, **cheddar**, cottage, **FETA, GOAT**, Gorgonzola, Gruyère, **MOZZARELLA, PARMESAN**, pecorino, **ricotta**, ricotta salata
chervil
chickpeas
CHILES, e.g., jalapeño; chili pepper flakes and chili pepper sauce
chili, vegetarian
CHIVES
chutneys
cilantro
cinnamon
coriander
corn
couscous
cream
CUCUMBERS
cumin
curries
dill
EGGPLANT
eggs, e.g., *frittatas, omelets*
enchiladas
fennel
French cuisine
GARLIC
gazpacho

ginger
grains, whole, e.g., barley, bulgur, farro
gratins
greens, e.g., baby, salad
gumbos
Italian cuisine
leeks
legumes
lemon, e.g., juice
lemon thyme
lentils
lettuce, e.g., romaine
lime
lovage
marjoram
Mexican cuisine
mint
mushrooms, e.g., porcini or portobello
nutmeg
OIL, OLIVE
olives, e.g., black, green
ONIONS, e.g., red, sweet, yellow
orange and orange juice
OREGANO
paprika, e.g., hot, smoked, sweet
PARSLEY, flat-leaf
parsnips
PASTAS
pepper, e.g., black, white
pesto
pizza
polenta

	Flavor Affinities
potatoes	tomatoes + avocados + chiles + cilantro + garlic + scallions + vinegar
pumpkin	
purees	**tomatoes + balsamic vinegar + basil** + garlic + olive oil + *sauces*
quinoa	**tomatoes + balsamic vinegar + basil** + mozzarella
ratatouille	tomatoes + basil + cashews + **goat cheese** + olive oil + watermelon
relishes	**TOMATOES + BASIL + MOZZARELLA CHEESE**
rice, e.g., black, brown	**tomatoes + basil + olive oil**
risottos	**tomatoes + basil + Parmesan cheese**
rosemary	**tomatoes + bell peppers + cucumbers + olive oil + onions + vinegar**
saffron	tomatoes + chiles + cilantro + garlic + lime + onions
sage	tomatoes + chiles + garlic + oil + onions + *salsas* + salt
salad dressings, e.g., vinaigrettes	tomatoes + chipotle chiles + cilantro + lime
SALADS, e.g., bean, bread (e.g., panzanella), grain, green, spinach, tomato	tomatoes + cucumbers + garlic + green bell peppers
	tomatoes + feta cheese + marjoram
	tomatoes + garlic + oregano
salsas, e.g., pico de gallo	tomatoes + lemon + mint
salt, e.g., kosher, **sea**, smoked	tomatoes + *pesto* + pine nuts + ricotta
sandwiches	tomatoes + sesame oil + shiso + tofu

SAUCES, e.g., marinara, pasta, pizza, tomato
savory
scallions
seitan
shallots
shiso
snap peas
SOUPS, e.g gazpacho, tomato, vegetable
sour cream
soy sauce
Spanish cuisine
spinach
squash, e.g., summer
stews
stocks, e.g., vegetable
sugar (just a pinch)
tabbouleh
tamari
tamarind
tarragon
tarts
THYME
tofu
tomatoes, stuffed, e.g., with rice
turmeric
VINEGAR, e.g., balsamic, red wine, rice, sherry, or wine
watermelon
wheat berries
Worcestershire sauce, vegan
yogurt
ZUCCHINI

"The best way to treat **tomatoes** is to never wash them because they get waterlogged — and never refrigerate them because they get mealy and grainy."
— CHRISTOPHER BATES, HOTEL FAUCHÈRE (MILFORD, PA)

TOMATOES, GREEN
Techniques: fry, grill

bell peppers
cheese, e.g., burrata, feta, **Parmesan**

chives
corn
cornmeal
dill
eggs, e.g., *frittatas*
mustard
oil, e.g., olive, vegetable
onions, e.g., red
parsley
pepper, black
salsas
salt, e.g., sea
savory
scallions
soups
tomatoes, fried green

Flavor Affinities
green tomatoes + burrata cheese + mustard + olive oil

● TOMATOES, SUN-DRIED (or OVEN-DRIED TOMATOES)
Flavor: salty/slightly sweet, with intense tomato notes, and a chewy texture
Volume: loud – very loud
Tip: To soften, soak in boiling water for 60 seconds before draining and cooling.
Brand: Mediterranean Organic

almonds
artichokes and artichoke hearts
arugula
asparagus
BASIL
bay leaf
beans, e.g., white
bell peppers
bread, e.g., whole-wheat
capers

Dishes

Fried Green Tomatoes with Green Goddess Dressing and Feta
— FnB (Scottsdale, AZ)

cashews
casseroles
CHEESE, e.g., **chèvre**, feta, **goat**, mozzarella, Parmesan, ricotta
chickpeas
chiles, e.g., jalapeño, red
chili pepper flakes
dips
EGGS, e.g., *frittatas, omelets*
enchiladas
GARLIC
harissa
hazelnuts
hummus
Italian cuisine
kale
lemon, e.g., juice, zest
lime, e.g., juice, zest
Mediterranean cuisines
OLIVE OIL
olives, e.g., black, kalamata
onions, e.g., red
orange, e.g., zest
oregano
parsley
PASTAS, e.g., cannelloni, linguini
pepper, black
pesto
pine nuts
PIZZA
polenta
potatoes
risottos
rosemary
salads, e.g., bean, grain, green, potato
salt, sea
sandwiches, e.g., cheese, panini
SAUCES, e.g., pasta, tomato
scallions
shallots
soups
spinach

spreads
stews
stuffings
tapenades
thyme
tofu
tomato paste
tomatoes, fresh
tortillas
vinegar, e.g., balsamic, rice wine
walnuts
wine, e.g., dry white

Flavor Affinities
sun-dried tomatoes + artichokes +
  feta cheese
**SUN-DRIED TOMATOES +
  BASIL + GARLIC + OLIVE OIL**
**sun-dried tomatoes + basil +
  herbs** (e.g., rosemary, thyme)
  + olive oil
sun-dried tomatoes + capers +
  garlic + goat cheese + oregano
sun-dried tomatoes + goat cheese
  + *pesto* + pine nuts
sun-dried tomatoes + olive oil +
  oregano + red onions

TRAIL MIX and TRAIL BARS

Tips: Use only unsalted raw
nuts and unsweetened organic
fruit. If nuts are roasted, opt
for dry roasted rather than oil
roasted.

"We make [trail] bars that combine
unsulfured dried fruits, nuts, and
spices to sweeten and spice a tasty
blend of organic whole grains.
Our top flavors are based on
apricot, cashew, and turmeric;
almond, cacao, and coconut; date,
ginger, and sesame seeds; and
cinnamon, prune, and walnut."
— DIANE FORLEY, FLOURISH BAKING
COMPANY (SCARSDALE, NY)

● TRITICALE
[trit-ih-KAY-lee]
Flavor: slightly sweet, with earthy
notes of nuts, and a chewy texture
Volume: moderate – loud
What it is: whole grain (a hybrid
of rye and wheat)
Gluten: yes
Nutritional profile: 82% carbs
/ 13% protein / 5% fats
Calories: 325 per ½-cup serving
Protein: 12 grams
Techniques: pressure-cook,
simmer (30-40 minutes), toast
Timing: Cook presoaked triticale
about 15 – 20 minutes, covered.
Botanical relatives: barley,
corn, rye, spelt, wheat
Possible substitutes: rye
berries, wheat berries

baked goods, e.g., biscuits, breads
basil
casseroles
cereals, e.g., muesli
chard
cheese, e.g., Parmesan
chives
cilantro
cinnamon
dates
dill
garlic
ginger
greens
mushrooms, e.g., cremini,
  shiitake
mustard, e.g., Dijon
oil, e.g., nut, olive, sesame,
  walnut
onions
oregano
pancakes
parsley
peanuts
pepper, black
pilafs
porridges

raisins
sage
salads, grain
scallions
squash, winter, e.g., butternut
stock, vegetable
thyme
vinegar, e.g., balsamic, sherry

Flavor Affinities
triticale + cilantro + garlic +
  ginger + peanuts + scallions +
  sesame oil
triticale + garlic + mushrooms
  + olive oil + Parmesan cheese +
  parsley + vinegar

TRUFFLES, AUSTRALIAN
Season: winter (in Australia, so
they're shipped to North America
June – September)
Flavor: umami
Volume: moderate – **loud**
What they are: black truffles
that have been cultivated in
Australia since 1999
Tip: Use like other black
truffles (see below).

"**Australian black truffles** are
already the equal of other [e.g.,
French] black truffles in terms of
aroma and flavor and continue
to develop a stronger, longer-
lasting flavor every year. Plus, it's
fun to use truffles in the summer
[which is Australia's winter] —
their earthiness is an amazing
complement to the sweetness of
corn agnolotti."
— JOSIAH CITRIN, MÉLISSE
(SANTA MONICA)

TRUFFLES, BLACK
Season: autumn – **winter**
Flavor: aromatic, with earthy
notes of cheese, chocolate,
mushrooms, and/or smoke

Volume: moderate – **loud**

Tips: Shave on top of dishes to finish them. Allow truffles to permeate ingredients (e.g., rice) for 24+ hours before serving.

Botanical relative: mushrooms

celery root
cheese, e.g., Castelmagno
chives
cream
EGGS, e.g., scrambled
FRENCH CUISINE
leeks
Madeira
mushrooms, e.g., black, morel, porcini
oil, nut, e.g., pecan, walnut
pastas
potatoes
sauces
soups
stock, vegetable

TRUFFLES, PACIFIC NORTHWEST (esp. OREGON)

Flavor: aromatic
Volume: quieter – louder
Botanical relatives: European truffles

butter
celery root
cheese, e.g., goat, smoked gouda
eggs
leeks, esp. with black truffles
nuts, esp. hazelnuts
pastas, esp. with white truffles
potatoes, esp. with white truffles
risottos
salads, esp. with white truffles
vegetables, root, esp. with white truffles

"**Oregon white truffles** are at least as good as their Italian cousins."
— JAMES BEARD (1983)

TRUFFLES, WHITE

Season: autumn
Flavor: aromatic, with earthy notes
Volume: moderate – very loud

Tips: Consider storing truffles in a closed jar of rice to capture their aroma and flavor. Do *not* cook — shave over finished dishes at the last possible moment.

Botanical relatives:
mushrooms

butter
cheese, e.g., Fontina, Parmesan
eggs, esp. *scrambled*
fonduta
ITALIAN CUISINE
mushrooms, e.g., porcini
oil, olive
parsley
PASTAS, e.g., fettuccine
polenta
potatoes
rice, e.g., Arborio
RISOTTOS

Flavor Affinities

white truffles + eggs + *fonduta* + Fontina cheese + milk
white truffles + Parmesan cheese + potatoes

"I never saw anyone use **white truffles** in a traditional Japanese restaurant in Kyoto. But I love seeing how popular they are here, and I am already planning to feature them on our seasonal menu in November. Last November, I served deep-fried sushi rolls flavored with miyoga ginger, with shaved truffles on top."
— RYOTA UESHIMA, KAJITSU (NEW YORK CITY)

TURKISH CUISINE

Techniques: fry, grill, roast

artichokes
beans, e.g., fava, green
bell peppers
bulgur
carrots
cheese, e.g., feta, goat, sheep's milk, white
chickpeas
chiles and chili pepper flakes
cinnamon
cloves
cucumbers
cumin
dill
EGGPLANT
garlic
grape leaves
honey
lemon
lentils, e.g., red
mint
nutmeg
nuts, e.g., almonds, pistachios, walnuts
oil, olive
olives
onions
oregano, e.g., dried
paprika
parsley
pepper, black
phyllo dough
pistachios
pita bread
pomegranates
rice
rose water
sesame seeds
spinach
sumac
tahini
TOMATOES and tomato paste
walnuts
yogurt
zucchini

T

Flavor Affinities

bulgur + mint

dill + garlic + lemon + scallions

dill + yogurt + zucchini

eggplant + garlic + onions + parsley + tomatoes

● TURMERIC (see also CURRY POWDER, which contains turmeric)

[TER-mer-ic]

Flavor: bitter/sweet, with earthy/pungent notes of ginger, orange, and/or pepper

Volume: moderate – loud

> **Tip:** Used to add its characteristic yellow/orange color to curries, mustard, tofu scrambles, and other foods as much as its flavor.

Botanical relative: ginger

carrots

CAULIFLOWER

chickpeas

chiles

cilantro

cinnamon

cloves

coconut and coconut milk

coriander

cumin

CURRIES, e.g., Indian, Thai (esp. red, yellow)

*****CURRY LEAF** and *CURRY POWDER*

dals

eggs, e.g., *deviled eggs, egg salads, omelets*

fruit, dried, e.g., cranberries, currants, raisins

garlic

ginger

grains, e.g., quinoa

greens, stewed

INDIAN CUISINE

kohlrabi

lemon, e.g., juice

lemongrass

lentils

lime

Middle Eastern cuisines

Moroccan cuisine

mustard** and **mustard seeds

noodles, e.g., Asian, rice

oil, olive

okra

onions

peanuts

peas

pepper, black

pickles

pistachios

potatoes

raisins

RICE, e.g., basmati, brown

salad dressings

salads, e.g., egg

sauces

scallions

shallots

SOUPS, e.g., carrot, sweet potato

Southeast Asian cuisines

spinach

STEWS

stir-fries

sugar, brown

sweet potatoes

tagines

tamarind

Thai cuisine

tofu

tofu scrambles (for yellow color)

vegetables, esp. root

yogurt

Flavor Affinities

turmeric + basmati rice + dried fruit + garlic + lemon + pistachios + scallions

turmeric + black pepper + lemon juice + olive oil

turmeric + carrots + chickpeas + cinnamon + couscous + saffron + zucchini

turmeric + cilantro + cumin + garlic + onion + paprika + parsley + pepper

turmeric + coriander + cumin

● TURNIPS (see also GREENS, TURNIP)

Season: autumn – winter

Flavor: sweet (esp. in autumn/ winter), with pungent notes of cabbage, mustard, nuts, and/ or pepper

Volume: moderate (e.g., younger and/or cooked) – loud (e.g., older and/or raw)

What they are: root vegetable

Nutritional profile: 88% carbs / 9% protein / 3% fats

Calories: 35 per 1-cup serving (cooked, cubed)

Protein: 1 gram

Techniques: bake (at 400°F for about 40 minutes for sliced turnips, and 60 – 90 minutes for whole), boil (about 10 – 15 minutes), braise, broil, deep-fry, glaze, grate, mash (esp. with potatoes), pickle, pressure-cook (2 – 8 minutes), puree, raw, roast, sauté, simmer, steam (5 – 20 minutes, depending on whether sliced or whole), stew, stir-fry, stuff, tempura-fry

> **Tips:** Peel before using. Cook only until tender; do not overcook.

Botanical relatives: broccoli, Brussels sprouts, cabbage, cauliflower, collard greens, horseradish, kale, kohlrabi, land cress, mustard, radishes, rutabagas, watercress

Possible substitute: Can substitute for rutabagas in many dishes; see also tips for rutabagas.

allspice
almonds
anise seeds
apples and apple cider
apricots, dried
basil
bay leaf
bread and bread crumbs, *e.g.,*
whole-grain
broccoli and broccoli rabe
butter
cabbage
caraway seeds
CARROTS
celery, celery leaves, and celery
root
cheese, e.g., blue, cheddar,
Gorgonzola, Gouda, **Gruyère**,
Parmesan
chili pepper flakes
chives
cilantro
cinnamon
citrus, e.g., zest
couscous
cream
curry powder
dill
French cuisine
GARLIC

ghee
ginger
gratins
GREENS, e.g., TURNIP
honey
kale
kohlrabi
leeks
lemon, e.g., juice, zest
lentils
maple syrup
mascarpone
"mashed potatoes"
mirin
miso, e.g., white
mushrooms, e.g., porcini,
portobello
mustard, e.g., Dijon, and mustard
powder
nutmeg
oil, e.g., grapeseed, nut, **olive**,
sunflower, vegetable, walnut
ONIONS, e.g., green, white,
yellow
orange, e.g., juice, zest
PARSLEY
parsnips
pears
peas
pecans

pepper, e.g., **black**, white
pine nuts
poppy seeds
POTATOES and new potatoes
pumpkin
purees
radishes
rosemary
rutabagas
salads, *e.g., grated*
salt, e.g., kosher, rock, **sea**
savory
sesame seeds, e.g., black, white
shiso
SOUPS, *e.g., creamy, minestrone,*
potato, turnip
soy sauce
squash, winter, e.g., acorn,
butternut
star anise
stews
stir-fries
stock, vegetable
sugar, e.g., brown
sweet potatoes
tarragon
THYME and lemon thyme
tofu
tomatoes
vegetables, root, esp. roasted
vinaigrette
VINEGAR, e.g., balsamic or white
balsamic, red wine, rice, sherry,
white wine
walnuts
watercress
wine, e.g., red, sherry
yogurt

Flavor Affinities

turnips + almonds + balsamic vinegar
turnips + basil + black pepper + lemon
turnips + caraway seeds + carrots
turnips + carrots + greens
turnips + carrots + lentils
turnips + carrots + potatoes
turnips + garlic + leeks + rutabagas + thyme
turnips + ginger + orange + rosemary
turnips + greens + lemon + pine nuts
turnips + *gratins* + Gruyère cheese + thyme
turnips + leeks + miso
turnips + maple syrup + parsley
turnips + mirin + miso + scallions + sesame seeds
turnips + *pasta* + turnip greens
turnips + potatoes + rutabagas
turnips + potatoes + tarragon + tomatoes

UMAMI

Flavor: savory, or savory
and salty
Umami-rich vegetarian foods
include these:

aged foods, e.g., cheese
bean pastes, fermented
beer

broccoli
caramelized dishes
carrots, caramelized
cheese, aged, e.g., blue, Gruyère,
    Parmesan, Roquefort
*fermented foods and beverages
    (e.g., miso, tamari, wine)*
grapefruit
grapes
grilled dishes
ketchup
miso
mushrooms, e.g., dried,
    matsutake, shiitake
nutritional yeast
onions, caramelized
potatoes
ripe foods
roasted dishes
sauerkraut
sea vegetables, e.g., dried, kombu
soybeans, e.g., fermented
soy sauce
stock, mushroom
sweet potatoes
tamari
tea, green
tempeh
tofu
tomatoes and tomato sauce, and
    sun-dried tomatoes
truffles
umeboshi plums and plum paste
vinegar, e.g., balsamic, sherry,
    umeboshi
walnuts
wine

UMEBOSHI, UMEBOSHI PASTE (aka PICKLED PLUM PUREE), and UMEBOSHI PLUMS (see also VINEGAR, UMEBOSHI PLUM)

[oo-meh-BOH-shee]
Flavor: sour/very salty/sweet/
umami, with complex fruity notes
Volume: moderate – very loud

What it is: Japanese "plum"
fermented with salt and shiso
Botanical relative: apricots
(not plums)
Brands: Eden Foods, Emperor's
Kitchen (plum paste)

agave nectar
avocado
basil
beans, e.g., kidney
BROCCOLI
cabbage, e.g., napa
cauliflower
celery
chives
cilantro
CORN, e.g., corn on the cob
cucumbers
curries, e.g., Thai
daikon
dips
dressings
frisée
garlic
ginger
grains
greens, e.g., collard
Japanese cuisine
jícama
lemon, e.g., juice
lentils
lettuces, e.g., romaine
lime, e.g., juice
macrobiotic cuisine
marinades
mayonnaise
mirin
mushrooms
mustard, Dijon
noodles, Asian, e.g., soba
nori and *NORI ROLLS*
oil, e.g., olive, peanut, sesame
parsley
pecans
RICE, e.g., short-grain brown,
    sushi, white
RICE BALLS

*SALAD DRESSINGS, e.g., Caesar,
    green*
SALADS, e.g., Caesar, green
SAUCES
scallions
sesame, e.g., paste, seeds, sauce
SHISO
snow peas
soups
sour cream
spreads
stir-fries
sugar
tamari
tempeh
TOFU, e.g., extra-firm
vegetables, e.g., sautéed
vinegar, rice
walnuts

Flavor Affinities

umeboshi + agave nectar + garlic
    + mustard + olive oil + *salad
    dressing*
umeboshi + broccoli + rice +
    scallions + tofu
umeboshi + lentils + walnuts
**umeboshi + nori + rice + rice
    vinegar** + scallions + walnuts
umeboshi + nori + rice + rice
    vinegar + shiso
umeboshi + olive oil + parsley +
    rice + sesame seeds
umeboshi + olive oil + rice
    vinegar + sugar + tamari

VANILLA
Flavor: bitter/slightly sweet;
aromatic, with rich notes of
cream and hints of smoke
Volume: quiet
Botanical relative: orchids
(which are inedible)

apples
apricots
*BAKED GOODS, e.g., cakes,
    cookies*

bananas
beans, e.g., green
beets
berries, e.g., raspberries,
   strawberries
beverages, e.g., eggnogs
brandy
butter
cardamom
cheesecake
cherries
chiles
CHOCOLATE
cinnamon, e.g., Ceylon
cloves
coffee
cream
DESSERTS, e.g., custards, *ICE
   CREAM
eggs
French toast
FRUITS, e.g., poached
ginger
honey
lemon, e.g., juice, zest
maple syrup
milk
nutmeg
nuts, e.g., **almonds**, cashews
oats and oatmeal
peaches
pears
pepper, black
puddings, e.g., avocado, bread, chia
   seed, rice
pumpkin
raspberries
rice, e.g., basmati, jasmine
salads, fruit
*sauces, e.g., **butter**, **cream**, **dessert***
smoothies
soups, e.g., fruit
spices, other
strawberries
sugar, e.g., brown
teas
tofu

tomatoes
vegetables, sweet, e.g., corn, peas
vodka
wine
yogurt

Flavor Affinities
vanilla + almond milk + almonds
   + maple syrup + rice
vanilla + apples + cinnamon
vanilla + apples + lemon
vanilla + chocolate + cinnamon
vanilla + honey + pears + yogurt

"The combination of **vanilla** with
Ceylon cinnamon is potent and
delicious."
— AMI BEACH, G-ZEN (BRANFORD, CT)

VEGETABLES, ROOT (see ROOT VEGETABLES)

VEGGIE BURGERS

There are almost as many
versions of veggie burgers as
there are vegetarian chefs! Play
with your favorite combination
of whole grains, legumes,
mushrooms, nuts, seeds, and/or
vegetables to come up with your
own.

"I developed a **veggie burger** from
brown rice, chickpeas, lentils,
and mushrooms for a restaurant
project outside Mélisse — but I've
used the same combination as a
'sausage' in a bean and portobello
mushroom cassoulet. There's no
casing — the broken rice serves
as the binder, and I wrap it in
plastic wrap and steam it before
finishing it in a pan to give it a
crust."
— JOSIAH CITRIN, MÉLISSE
(SANTA MONICA)

"We serve three different **veggie
burgers**. My favorite is the Follow
Your Heart burger, which is a
meatlike soy-based patty. My
second favorite is the Nut Burger
Supreme, which is based on nuts
and vegetables and topped with
lettuce, rennetless cheddar
cheese, tomatoes, mushrooms,
onions, sauerkraut, Vegenaise,
and carrot shreds. It's not a
cohesive patty, but more like a
pâté, that's been heated on the
grill so that it squeezes out as you
take a bite. We also offer a Multi-
Grain Mushroom burger, which
is somewhat similar in texture to
the nutburger and based on
brown rice, wheat berries, barley,
lentils, mushrooms, and herbs."
— BOB GOLDBERG, FOLLOW YOUR
HEART (LOS ANGELES)

V

Dishes

118 Bristol Sliders: Marinated Portobello Mushrooms, Tomato, Spinach, Garlic Crème Sauce, and Basil Aioli on a Buckwheat Bun
— 118 Degrees (California)

Loaded Southwest Vegetarian Burger: Spicy Veggie Burger Patty Home-made with Fresh Vegetables, Certified Gluten-Free Oats and Pumpkin Seeds, served on a Whole-Wheat Roll with Avocado and Pico de Gallo
— Canyon Ranch (Lenox, MA)

Homemade Southwestern Black Bean and Roasted Sweet Potato Burger on Toasted Bun with Guacamole and Salsa
— Garden Café (Woodstock, NY)

Green Lentil and Butternut Squash Burger: Pumpkin Seed-Crusted Vegetable Burger Made with Green Lentils, Butternut Squash, Quinoa, Green Cabbage, Caramelized Onion, Carrot, and Spices
— Great Sage (Clarksville, MD)

Mana Slider: Brown Rice and Mushroom Burger, with Spicy Mayo
— Mana Food Bar (Chicago)

Millet and Quinoa Burger with Orange Slices, Cilantro, Fried Shallots, Mint Pesto, and Beet-Root Chips
— Plum Bistro (Seattle)

Oven Broiled Lentil Burger with Tomatoes, Charred Beet Leaves, Fried Shallots, Dill Aioli, and Yam Chips
— Plum Bistro (Seattle)

Fresh Herb Grilled Seitan Steak Burger with Charred Beet Leaves, Shaved Carrots, Fried Shallots, and Winter Squash Chips
— Plum Bistro (Seattle)

Buffalo Portobello Burger: Deep Fried Panko-Coated Portobello, Dipped in Buffalo Hot Sauce, with Vegan Ranch, Grilled Onions, Cucumber, Mixed Greens, and French Fries
— Plum Bistro (Seattle)

House-Made Beet Burger, Fresh-baked Rosemary Focaccia Bun, Carrot Aioli, Arugula, Red Onions and Tomato Confit, with or without Cashew Cheese
— Portobello (Portland, OR)

Root Burger: House-made Black Bean and Quinoa Burger with Boston Lettuce, Tomato, Crispy Onions, and Garlic Aioli, served with side of Dressed Greens or Herbed Fries
— Root (Allston, MA)

VERJUS
[vair-ZHOO]
Flavor: sour/sweet, often with notes of fruit
Volume: varies, from quiet to moderate-loud
What it is: juice from unripe (i.e., low-sugar, high-acid) red or white grapes

Tips: Substitute white verjus for citrus (e.g., lemon, lime) and red verjus for red wine vinegar when looking to add a quieter acid to a dish or when looking to pair the dish with wine (as it's more wine-friendly than vinegar). In general, opt for white verjus with quieter or lighter ingredients, and earthy red verjus with louder or darker ingredients. Look for verjus from American wineries coast to coast, e.g., Navarro (CA) to Wölffer Estate (NY), as well as the French producer Roland.

apples
arugula
beets
cheese, e.g., Parmesan
desserts
drinks, e.g., cocktails
French cuisine
fruit
grapes
greens, salad
herbs
icy desserts, e.g., granitas, sorbets, esp. fruit-flavored
kiwi
lettuces, butter
marinades
mustards
oil, e.g., olive
peaches
pears
salad dressings

salads, e.g., fruit, green

sauces

soups, e.g., fruit, gazpacho

stews

thyme

Flavor Affinities

verjus + apples + grapes

verjus + arugula + olive oil +
Parmesan cheese

verjus + beets + olive oil + thyme

verjus + garlic + olive oil +
shallots

verjus + pears + salad greens

VIETNAMESE CUISINE

bananas

basil, Thai

chiles

cilantro

coconut milk

cucumbers

curry powder and curry spices

dill

garlic

ginger

lemon

lemongrass

lettuce

lime

milk, e.g., sweetened condensed
(e.g., in coffee)

mint

noodles, e.g., rice

peanuts

raw dishes

rice, e.g., jasmine

rolls, e.g., spring, summer

salads, e.g., rice noodle

scallions

shallots

spring rolls

sprouts, bean

star anise

sugar

summer rolls

tapioca, pearl

vinegar, rice

Flavor Affinities

cabbage + cashews + rice noodles
+ salad greens + tofu

VINEGAR — IN GENERAL (see also specific vinegars)

Flavor: ranges from slightly to very sour

Volume: ranges from quieter – louder

Nutritional profile: virtually 100% carbs

Calories: 25 (cider, wine) – 100 (balsamic) per ½ cup

Tip: Can act as a flavor enhancer to many dishes

Possible substitutes: lemon juice, lime juice, tamarind paste, verjus, wine

"I love fancy **vinegars**! I will use a few drops of champagne or sherry vinegar to finish a dish."
— MOLLIE KATZEN, BESTSELLING AUTHOR OF COOKBOOKS SUCH AS *THE HEART OF THE PLATE*

• VINEGAR, APPLE CIDER (aka VINEGAR, CIDER)

Flavor: sour/slightly sweet, with fruity notes of apple and/or honey

Volume: quiet – moderate-loud

What it is: made from fermented apple juice

Tip: Opt for unfiltered, organic cider vinegar.

apples and apple juice

baked goods

black-eyed peas

chutneys

cucumbers

fruits

grains, whole

herbs, e.g., dill

marinades

oils, e.g., olive, peanut, sunflower

peaches

pears

peas

plums

SALAD DRESSINGS

SALADS, e.g., fruit, green, pasta, vegetable

salt, sea

slaws

soups, e.g., borscht

vegetables, esp. steamed

vegetables, pickled

• VINEGAR, BALSAMIC

Flavor: sour/sweet, with great complexity, and a rich, slightly syrupy texture

Volume: moderate – loud

Tips: The best is aged, and expensive — but worth every penny. Balsamic vinegar can be used without oil as a low-fat dressing. Add it at the end of cooking (never boil!), or use it to finish a dish just before serving, especially when you want a sweet, low-acid vinegar. Opt for white balsamic vinegar (e.g., with grapeseed oil) when a lighter flavor (or color) is desired.

Possible substitutes: none or, in a pinch, perhaps sherry vinegar

beets

butter, brown

cakes

cheese, e.g., goat, mozzarella, Parmesan, ricotta

cherries

citrus fruits

desserts, fruit

V

eggplant
fennel
figs
fruits
garlic
greens, e.g., bitter, braised
ice cream
(Northern) ITALIAN CUISINE
kale, e.g., braised
marinades
mustard, e.g., Dijon, dry, seeds
OIL, OLIVE, esp. extra-virgin
onions, esp. caramelized
orange
pasta
pepper, e.g., black or white
salad dressings
salads
salt, e.g., kosher
scallions
seitan
shallots
soups
*****STRAWBERRIES**
sugar
*****TOMATOES**
vegetables
vinegars, other, e.g., stronger, e.g.,
  red wine, sherry

Flavor Affinities
balsamic vinegar + beets + fennel
  + orange
balsamic vinegar + garlic + olive
  oil + scallions
**balsamic vinegar + honey
  + mascarpone/ricotta +
  strawberries**

"I use **white balsamic vinegar**
whenever I want to bring a little
sweetness to a dish, such as bitter
greens or braised kale."
— JOSIAH CITRIN, MÉLISSE
(SANTA MONICA)

VINEGAR, BANYULS
Flavor: sour/sweet, with
complex notes of berries, ginger,
honey, nuts (almonds, walnuts),
plums, and/or vanilla, and a rich
texture
Volume: quiet – moderate
What it is: made from Grenache
grapes used in making Banyuls
dessert wine
Possible substitutes: red wine
vinegar (e.g., in deglazing), sherry
vinegar

barley
beans
cheese, e.g., blue, goat
chickpeas
French cuisine, esp. Provençal
greens, salad, e.g., frisée
lentils, e.g., black, French, green
marinades
oil, e.g., hazelnut, olive, walnut
ragoûts
salad dressings, e.g., vinaigrettes
salads, e.g., frisée, green
salt, sea
sauces
walnuts

VINEGAR, BEER
Flavor: sour, with notes of malt
Volume: moderate – loud

cheese, esp. soft, e.g., burrata
oil, e.g., olive
salads
vegetables
watercress

Dishes

Sorbello Farms Organic Field Greens with Banyuls Vinaigrette
— Picholine (New York City)

VINEGAR, BROWN RICE (aka CHINESE BLACK VINEGAR)
Flavor: sour to very sour/sweet,
with complex notes of fruit, **smoke**,
and/or Worcestershire sauce
Volume: moderate – loud
Tip: Think of it as the balsamic
vinegar of Asia.
Possible substitute: balsamic
vinegar

Asian cuisines
bean paste, fermented
Chinese cuisine
condiments
garlic
grains
Japanese cuisine
marinades
mushrooms, e.g., portobello,
  smoked
noodles, Asian
oil, e.g., sesame
rice, e.g., sushi
salad dressings
salads
*sauces, e.g., dipping, sweet-and-sour,
  vegan XO*
soups, e.g., rice-based
soy sauce
sriracha
stews
stir-fries
sugar
sushi, vegetarian
tamari
vegetables, e.g., grilled
zucchini, e.g., grilled

Flavor Affinities

Chinese black vinegar + Asian
noodles + soy sauce

"We like using **black vinegar** in
our Chinese dishes, because the
flavor is really interesting. We
created a grilled zucchini hors
d'oeuvre that was marinated in
sesame oil and black vinegar,
then we upped the flavor with a
mushroom XO sauce."

— RICH LANDAU AND KATE JACOBY,
VEDGE (PHILADELPHIA)

VINEGAR, CHAMPAGNE

Flavor: sour, with crisp notes of
grapes, and light-bodied
Volume: quiet – moderate (and
one of the quietest vinegars
available)
Tip: As one of the most delicate
vinegars, it is mild enough to
be used without oil as a salad
dressing.
Possible substitutes: cider vinegar, rice vinegar, white wine vinegar (although none are as quiet)

berries, e.g., raspberries,
strawberries
citrus, e.g., grapefruit, lemon,
lime, orange, tangerine;
juice, zest
fruit, esp. berries, citrus, and
stone fruit
greens, salad, esp. lighter
herbs, e.g., lemon thyme
honey
lettuces, e.g., butter
oil, e.g., nut, olive, truffle
orange, e.g., juice, zest
salad dressings
salads, e.g., fruit, "quieter"
sauces
vegetables, "quieter"

VINEGAR, CIDER (see VINEGAR, APPLE CIDER)

VINEGAR, COCONUT

Flavor: sour, with notes of yeast
Volume: moderate – loud

curries
Filipino cuisine
rice
Southeast Asian cuisines
stir-fries

VINEGAR, QUINCE

Flavor: **sour**/sweet, with notes of
apples, pears, and/or quince
Possible substitute: apple
cider vinegar

apples
artichokes, Jerusalem
baked goods, e.g., pastries
berries, e.g., strawberries
cabbage, e.g., braised
celery root
cheese, e.g., hard
chestnuts
citrus, e.g., orange
fruit, fresh
melon
oil, e.g., olive, pine nut, pistachio
onions
pears
pineapple
pine nuts
pistachios
pumpkins
quince
salads, e.g., green
sauces

● VINEGAR, RED WINE (see also VINEGAR, WINE – IN GENERAL)

Flavor: sour – very sour
Volume: moderate (e.g.,
young) – loud (e.g., aged)

Tip: Red wine vinegar can stand
up to spices and stronger herbs.
Possible substitutes: balsamic
vinegar, sherry vinegar, white
wine vinegar

chard, Swiss
cold dishes
French cuisine
garlic
greens, e.g., dandelion, salad,
stronger
kale
lemon, e.g., juice
marinades
mushrooms
mustard, Dijon
oils, e.g., nut, **olive** (esp.
extra-virgin)
pepper, black
***salad dressings**, e.g., vinaigrettes*
salads
sauces
shallots
soups
spinach
stews
vegetables, root

Flavor Affinities

red wine vinegar + black pepper +
garlic + mustard + **olive oil**

VINEGAR, RICE (WINE)

Flavor: slightly sour/slightly
sweet
Volume: quiet (e.g., white) –
moderate (e.g., brown)
What it is: vinegar made from
fermented rice (and not rice wine,
despite its common moniker)
Tip: Mild enough to be used
without oil as a salad dressing.
Possible substitutes: apple
cider vinegar (+ sweetener),
champagne vinegar, white wine
vinegar

V

Asian cuisines
bamboo shoots
burdock
cabbage, e.g., Chinese, napa
carrots
chiles and chili pepper flakes
chili, vegetarian
Chinese cuisine
citrus, e.g., grapefruit, lemon,
   lime, orange, tangerine; juice,
   zest
cloves
cucumbers
daikon
fruit
garlic
ginger
grains, whole
JAPANESE CUISINE
Korean cuisine
lime, e.g., juice
lotus root
mirin
mushrooms
noodles, Asian
oils, e.g., peanut, **sesame**
pickled vegetables, Asian
RICE, e.g., sushi
salad dressings
*SALADS, e.g., **Asian**, cucumber,*
   fruit, green, noodle
SAUCES, e.g., dipping, ponzu
soups
SOY SAUCE
stews, e.g., Asian
stir-fries
sugar
sushi
tamari
turnips
vegetables, e.g., lighter
Vietnamese cuisine
yuzu

Flavor Affinities
rice vinegar + Asian noodles +
   ginger

rice vinegar + chili pepper flakes
   + sugar + tamari
rice vinegar + ginger + soy sauce
rice vinegar + lime juice +
   soy sauce
rice vinegar + mirin + soy sauce
   + yuzu
rice vinegar + salt + sugar
rice vinegar + sesame oil +
   soy sauce

VINEGAR, SHERRY
Flavor: sour/sweet, with
complex notes of caramel,
flowers, grapes, and/or nuts, with
a smooth texture
Volume: moderate – loud
Possible substitutes: balsamic
vinegar, red wine vinegar, rice
vinegar

beans
beets
butter
cheese, e.g., blue, mozzarella
citrus, e.g., grapefruit, lemon,
   lime, orange, tangerine;
   juice, zest
eggs, e.g., *frittatas*, hard-boiled,
   tortillas
fennel
garlic
grains
greens, bitter
herbs
lemon, e.g., juice, zest
marinades
mustard, e.g., Dijon
OILS, e.g., nut, olive, walnut
onions
orange, e.g., juice, zest
potatoes
radicchio
salad dressings, e.g., sherry
   vinaigrette
SALADS, e.g., fruit, vegetable
salt

sauces, e.g., butter
soups, e.g., gazpacho
SPANISH CUISINE
tomatoes
vinegar, other, e.g., balsamic, red
wine, white wine
walnuts

"A good **sherry vinegar** makes
your mouth water in a way that
not even a white wine vinegar or
balsamic vinegar can. I love using
it with extra-virgin olive oil, and
for marinades."
— RICH LANDAU, VEDGE (PHILADELPHIA)

VINEGAR, UMEBOSHI PLUM (or UME PLUM)
Flavor: sour/salty, with fruity
notes of lemon
Volume: moderate
Tip: While not technically a
vinegar, umeboshi brine may be
substituted for vinegar and salt
as an instant flavor enhancer.

beans
beets
DIPS
grains
greens
marinades
miso
pickles
SALAD DRESSINGS
sauces, fresh and cooked
shiso leaf
soups, e.g., miso
stews
vegetables, e.g., steamed

VINEGAR, WHITE WINE
Flavor: sour/sweet
Volume: quiet – moderate
Tip: Opt for white wine vinegar
for lighter-colored foods (e.g.,
cauliflower), as red wine vinegar
may affect their color.

Possible substitutes:
champagne vinegar, cider vinegar, rice wine vinegar

berries
cauliflower
citrus, e.g., juice, zest
dill
French cuisine
lighter-colored foods
marinades
melons
mustard, Dijon
oil, e.g., olive, safflower,
  sunflower
peaches
pepper, e.g., black, white
SALAD DRESSINGS, e.g.,
  vinaigrettes
salads
SAUCES, e.g., bearnaise,
  hollandaise
shallots
soups
stews
tarragon
vegetables, e.g., grilled

VINEGAR, WINE — IN GENERAL

Flavor: sour, with notes of fruit (e.g., grapes)
Volume: quiet – moderate
Tip: Opt for high-quality, unpasteurized red or white wine vinegar.
Possible substitute: cider vinegar

berries
fruit
marinades
melon
salad dressings
salads
salsas
sauces
stews

VITAMIX

What it is: a high-performance blender that is the price of a used car, with a motor that's just as powerful as one
Tips: Consider making this investment — it's truly more than a blender! Just a sampling of what you can make: batters, dips, doughs, dressings, flours (i.e., by grinding grains), juices, milks, nut butters, purees (e.g., vegetables), salad dressings, sauces and dipping sauces, smoothies, soups, sorbets, and spreads.

"Four kitchen tools I would never want to be without are my **Vitamix**, spiralizer, dehydrator, and deep fryer."
— AMANDA COHEN, DIRT CANDY (NEW YORK CITY)

● WAKAME (FRESH and DRIED)

Season: winter – spring
Flavor: salty/sweet/umami, with notes of the sea, and a slippery, chewy texture
Volume: quiet – moderate
What it is: sea vegetable
Nutritional profile: 72% carbs / 16% protein / 12% fats
Calories: 5 per 2-tablespoon serving (raw)
Tips: Rinse first, then soak in cool water (just a few minutes for fresh, and 20 – 30+ minutes for dried) before using. Note that dried wakame may expand tenfold or more upon being reconstituted. Cook only briefly, about 5 minutes. Add to dishes shortly before serving.
Brand: Eden Foods

agave nectar
Asian cuisines
beans
bok choy
carrots
cayenne
chiles, e.g., jalapeño, and chili
  pepper flakes
Chinese cuisine
CUCUMBERS
daikon
garlic
ginger
gomashio
grains
greens, e.g., collard, dandelion,
  mustard
Japanese cuisine
kale
legumes
lemon, e.g., juice
lentils
lime, e.g., juice
macrobiotic cuisine
miso
noodles, e.g., ramen, soba
oil, e.g., olive, **sesame**
onions, e.g., green, red
orange, e.g., juice
patés, e.g., nut
potatoes
radishes
rice, e.g., brown, short-grain
SALADS, e.g., cucumber, green
salt, sea
scallions
seeds, e.g., pumpkin, **sesame**
slaws
*SOUPS, e.g., cold, **miso**, winter*
soy sauce
spring rolls
squash, winter, e.g., butternut
stews
stir-fries
stocks, vegetable
tamari
tempeh

W

Dishes

Soba-Wakame Rolls in Togarashi Aioli and Maple Teriyaki
— Cal-a-Vie (Vista, CA)

tofu
vegetables
vinegar, e.g., rice wine

Flavor Affinities
wakame + cucumbers + orange
wakame + cucumbers + rice
   vinegar + sesame seeds + tamari
wakame + lemon juice + sesame
   oil + soy sauce
wakame + sea salt + sesame seeds

"The first time I ever cooked
wakame, I just dumped the whole
bag in a pot, covered it with water,
turned it on to boil, and left the
kitchen. I didn't know that
seaweed expands seven times its
size — so I was shocked to return
to find it heaving over the pot and
my stove like a monster!"
— PAM BROWN, GARDEN CAFÉ
(WOODSTOCK, NY)

● WALNUTS
Season: autumn
Flavor: slightly sweet to
bitter, with earthy notes of
butter, cream, and/or nuts (and
astringent notes from the skins),
and a rich, crunchy texture
Volume: quiet – moderate
What's healthful about them:
omega-3 fatty acids
Nutritional profile: 83% fats /
9% carbs / 8% protein
Calories: 185 per 1-ounce
serving
Protein: 4 grams
  Tip: Opt for black, dried walnuts.
Botanical relatives: other tree
nuts

APPLES
apricots, e.g., dried
artichokes and artichoke hearts
arugula
BAKED GOODS, e.g., breads,
  cakes, cookies, muffins, pastries,
  tarts
baklava
bananas
basil
beans, e.g., fava, green, white
BEETS
bell peppers, red, esp. roasted
berries, e.g., blueberries
butter
cabbage
caramel
carrots

celery and celery root
cereals, hot
chard
CHEESE, e.g., BLUE,
  Camembert, cheddar, cream,
  feta, **GOAT**, **Gorgonzola**,
  Monterey Jack, manchego,
  Parmesan, pecorino, **ricotta**,
  Roquefort, sheep's milk, Stilton
cherries, e.g., dried, sour
CHOCOLATE, e.g., dark, milk,
  white
cinnamon
coconut
coffee
couscous
cranberries
cream
cucumbers
cumin
currants
dates
desserts, e.g., fruit crisps

eggplant
endive, Belgian
fennel
FIGS
frisée
fruits, e.g., dried, fresh
garlic
grains, whole, e.g., amaranth,
    barley, bulgur, oats, quinoa,
    spelt berries, wheat berries
granola
grapefruit
grapes
Greek cuisine
GREENS, e.g., beet, bitter, salad
HONEY
ice cream
kumquats
leeks
lemon, e.g., juice, zest
lettuce, e.g., romaine
maple syrup
mascarpone
miso, sweet white
molasses
muesli
muffins
mushrooms, e.g., porcini
nutmeg
nuts, other, e.g., cashews,
    hazelnuts
oats and oatmeal
oil, e.g., olive, walnut
olives, e.g., green
onions
ORANGE, e.g., juice, zest
pancakes
parsley
parsnips
pastas, e.g., bowtie, cannelloni, orzo,
    pappardelle
pastries
pâtés
peaches
PEARS
pestos
phyllo dough
pizzas

plums, e.g., dried, fresh
pomegranates and pomegranate
    molasses
pumpkin
quinces
quinoa
RAISINS
rice, e.g., brown, wild
SALADS, e.g., Waldorf
salt, e.g., sea
sage
sauces, e.g., tomato, walnut
seeds, e.g., hemp, pumpkin
snacks
soups
spelt berries
spinach

Flavor Affinities

walnuts + apples + beets + *salads*
walnuts + apples + cinnamon
walnuts + apples + wheat berries
walnuts + artichoke hearts + couscous
walnuts + arugula + beets + feta cheese
walnuts + arugula + *pesto*
walnuts + basil + eggplant
walnuts + beets + spinach
walnuts + (roasted) bell peppers + garlic + parsley + *pasta*
walnuts + blue cheese + endive
walnuts + blue cheese + onions
walnuts + bread crumbs + garlic + olive oil + Parmesan cheese
walnuts + bread crumbs + pomegranate molasses + roasted (bell)
    peppers
walnuts + butternut squash + sage
walnuts + carrots + raisins
WALNUTS + CHEESE (e.g., blue, goat, Parmesan) + **FRUIT**
    (e.g., apples, dates, figs, pears)
walnuts + cranberries + ginger + **orange** + vanilla
walnuts + dill + dulse + lemon
walnuts + endive + Roquefort cheese
walnuts + figs + honey + yogurt
walnuts + figs + frisée + Gorgonzola cheese + walnut oil
walnuts + garlic + *pasta* + raisins
walnuts + garlic + tamari
walnuts + goat cheese + honey
walnuts + mascarpone + *pasta* + sage
walnuts + molasses + vanilla
walnuts + mushrooms + thyme

squash, e.g., summer, winter
stuffings
sugar
sweet potatoes
tabbouleh
tapenade
thyme
tomatoes and sun-dried tomatoes
trail mix
vanilla
vinegar, sherry
wine, sweet, e.g., Madeira, port,
    sherry
YOGURT
zucchini

W

● WASABI

[wah-SAH-bee]

Flavor: very hot/slightly sweet, with pungent notes of horseradish and/or nuts

Volume: very loud

What it is: Japanese horseradish

Nutritional profile: 83% carbs / 12% protein / 5% fat

Tips: Add toward the end of cooking, or serve with chilled foods.

Botanical relative: cabbage

Asian cuisines
avocados
cold dishes
eggs, hard-boiled
ginger
JAPANESE CUISINE
marinades
mayonnaise
noodles, e.g., soba
nori rolls
potatoes
rice, e.g., sticky
salad dressings
sauces
sesame, e.g., oil, seeds
SOY SAUCE
sugar, e.g., brown
SUSHI
tahini
tamari
tempura
tofu
vinegar, brown rice

"Shojin cuisine [developed in Zen Buddhist monastaries] prohibits garlic, which has a strong, long-lasting flavor that can overpower other flavors, even affecting the flavor of the next course — or the next day! **Wasabi** is also strong, but its flavor evaporates quickly."
— RYOTA UESHIMA, KAJITSU (NEW YORK CITY)

● WATER CHESTNUTS

Season: year-round

Flavor: slightly sweet, with notes of apples and/or Jerusalem artichokes, and a crunchy, juicy texture

Volume: quiet

Nutritional profile: 95% carbs / 4% protein / 1% fat

Calories: 60 per ½-cup serving (sliced, raw)

Protein: 1 gram

Techniques: bake, boil, braise, deep-fry, fry, raw, sauté, steam, stir-fry

Tip: If using canned water chestnuts for convenience, blanch in boiling water before using.

Asian cuisines
bamboo shoots
beans, fermented black
beans, green
bell peppers, e.g., red
bok choy
broccoli
Brussels sprouts
cabbage, e.g., red
carrots
celery
chiles, dried
Chinese cuisine
cilantro
corn
dumplings
edamame
GARLIC
GINGER
hoisin sauce
leeks
lettuce, e.g., Bibb
lettuce wraps
mint
MUSHROOMS, e.g., Chinese, dried, oyster, shiitake
noodles, Asian
nuts, e.g., macadamia
oil, e.g., olive, peanut, sesame, vegetable
onions, red
orange, e.g., juice
parsley
peanuts and peanut sauce
peas
pineapple
pine nuts
rice, brown
salads, e.g., fruit, noodle, rice, vegetable
scallions
sesame, e.g., oil, seeds
snow peas
soups, e.g., winter melon
SOY SAUCE
spring rolls
sriracha
stews
STIR-FRIES
stock, vegetable
sugar
sugar snap peas
TOFU, e.g., extra-firm
vegetables
vinegar, e.g., balsamic, rice
watercress
wine, rice

Flavor Affinities

water chestnuts + Asian noodles + peanut sauce

water chestnuts + shiitake mushrooms + sugar snap peas

● WATERCRESS (see also LAND CRESS)

Season: late spring – summer

Flavor: bitter, ranging from mild to hot, with pungent notes of mustard and/or pepper, and a delicate yet crunchy texture

Volume: moderate – loud

What it is: green leafy vegetable

Nutritional profile: 51% protein / 41% carbs / 8% fats

Calories: 5 per 1-cup serving (chopped, raw)

Protein: 1 gram

Techniques: Although watercress can be quickly steamed or stir-fried (which brings out its sweetness), it is best served raw.

Botanical relatives: broccoli, Brussels sprouts, cabbage, cauliflower, collard greens, horseradish, kale, kohlrabi, land cress, mustard, radishes, rutabagas, turnips, watercress

Flavor Affinities

watercress + almonds + balsamic vinegar + strawberries

watercress + apples + beets

watercress + asparagus + poached egg

watercress + avocado + grapefruit

watercress + beets + cheese (e.g., goat, pecorino) + walnuts

watercress + beets + egg salad

watercress + beets + mustard

watercress + blood orange + ricotta

watercress + celery + radishes + walnut oil

WATERCRESS + CHEESE (e.g., blue, pecorino) **+ FRUIT** (e.g., apples) **+ NUTS** (e.g., almonds, walnuts)

watercress + chives + cream cheese + **parsley** + *tea sandwiches*

watercress + cucumbers + mint + red onions

watercress + Dijon mustard + olive oil + red wine vinegar

watercress + fennel + orange

watercress + garlic + miso + sesame oil

watercress + garlic + onions + potatoes + thyme

watercress + goat cheese + tomatoes

watercress + leeks + potatoes

watercress + onions + potatoes + vegetable stock

Dishes

Well-Cultured Salad: Mélange of Seasonal Greens and Watercress tossed with Homemade Kimchee, Nori Strips, Toasted Sesame Seeds, and Extra Virgin Olive Oil, with garnish of Radish Slices
— Angelica Kitchen (New York City)

Watercress Salad with Apple, Celery Root, Cheddar, Grapefruit, and Honey
— Artisans Restaurant at Lake Placid Lodge (Lake Placid, NY)

almonds

apples

asparagus

avocado

beans, e.g., fermented black, white

BEETS

bell peppers, esp. red

butter

buttermilk

carrots

CHEESE, e.g., blue, cheddar, cottage, cream, feta, goat, Gruyère, Monterey Jack, pecorino, ricotta, ricotta salata, sheep's milk, white

chicory

chiles, e.g., jalapeño

Chinese cuisine

chives

cilantro

citrus

cream

cucumbers

currants

dill

EGGS, e.g., fried, *frittatas*, hard-boiled, *omelets*, poached, scrambled

endive

fennel

garlic

ginger

grains, whole

grapefruit

greens, milder salad

honey

horseradish

jícama

leeks

LEMON, e.g., juice

lettuce, e.g., butter, romaine

lime

mascarpone

mayonnaise

mint

MUSHROOMS, e.g., button, enoki, portobello

MUSTARD, e.g., Dijon, grainy

OILS, e.g., canola, grapeseed, olive, peanut, sesame, vegetable, walnut

olives

onions, e.g., red

ORANGE, e.g., blood, sections

parsley

parsnips

pastas

peaches

pears

peas

pepper, e.g., black, white
pineapple
pistachios
pomegranates
POTATOES
radicchio
radishes
raspberries
rice
SALADS, e.g., bean, egg, green,
    potato, watercress
salt, e.g., kosher, sea
SANDWICHES, e.g., egg salad,
    grilled cheese, tea
sauces
sesame, e.g., seeds
shallots
SOUPS, e.g., barley, creamy, miso,
    mushroom, potato
sour cream
soy sauce
stews
stir-fries
stock, vegetable
strawberries
tamari
tangerines
thyme
tofu
TOMATOES
tomatoes, sun-dried
Vietnamese cuisine
vinaigrette
VINEGAR, e.g., balsamic,
    champagne, red wine, rice
    wine, sherry, white balsamic,
    white wine
walnuts
wine, e.g., dry white, rice
yogurt
yuca

● WATERMELON

Season: late summer
Flavor: very sweet, with a very
juicy texture

Volume: quiet – moderate
Nutritional profile: 89% carbs
/ 7% protein / 4% fats
Calories: 45 per 1-cup serving
(raw, balls)
Protein: 1 gram
Techniques: grill, raw

Tips: Try roasting the seeds, or
pickling the rind, both of which
are edible.

Flavor Affinities

watermelon + agave nectar + lemon juice
watermelon + almonds + basil + lime + oranges
watermelon + arugula + black pepper + pistachios
watermelon + arugula + cucumber + feta cheese + red onions
watermelon + arugula + walnuts
watermelon + balsamic vinegar + basil + tomatoes
watermelon + basil + feta cheese + vinegar (e.g., white balsamic)
watermelon + cantaloupe + mint
watermelon + cucumbers + red onions
watermelon + fennel + feta cheese
watermelon + feta cheese + lime + mint
watermelon + feta cheese + olive oil + red onion + vinegar
    (e.g., white wine)
watermelon + ginger + mint
watermelon + goat cheese + tomatoes
watermelon + jalapeño + lime
watermelon + jalapeño + olive oil + sherry vinegar + tomatoes
watermelon + lemon/lime + mint + strawberries
watermelon + lime + poppy seeds
watermelon + raspberry vinegar + red onions

agave nectar
agua fresca
almonds
arugula, e.g., baby
basil
berries, e.g., blackberries,
    blueberries, **raspberries**,
    strawberries
CHEESE, e.g., blue, FETA, goat,
    ricotta salata

Dishes

Watermelon Ricotta Salad: Tatsui and Spinach Leaves, Watermelon, Cashew Ricotta
Salata, Fennel Oil, Vanilla, and Black Pepper
— The Butcher's Daughter (New York City)

Watermelon and Anise Hyssop Salad: Kaffir Lime, Avocado, Pickled Ginger
— DANIEL (New York City)

Watermelon Goat Cheese Salad: Candied White Balsamic Vinegar and Arugula Sprouts
— Mii amo Café (Sedona, AZ)

Watermelon Salad, Spicy Kisir, Farm Lettuce, and Mint
— Oleana (Boston)

chiles, e.g., jalapeño
chili powder
cilantro
cranberries
cucumbers
desserts
drinks, e.g., agua fresca
fennel
granitas, ices, sorbets
honey
jícama
lemon, e.g., juice, zest
LIME, e.g., juice, zest
maple syrup
melon, other, e.g., cantaloupe
MINT
oil, e.g., avocado, canola, grapeseed, **olive**
onions, e.g., green, red
orange, e.g., juice
parsley
pepper, black
pistachios
poppy seeds
rosemary
salads, e.g., fruit
salsas, fruit
salt, e.g., kosher, sea
scallions
sesame seeds, black
shallots
sorbets
soups, e.g., fruit, "gazpacho," watermelon
sugar
TOMATOES
vanilla
vinegar, e.g., balsamic (black or white), raspberry, red wine, rice wine, sherry
yogurt

● WHEAT BERRIES (see also BULGUR)

Flavor: slightly sweet, nutty, with a very chewy texture
Volume: quiet
What it is: whole grain

Gluten-free: no
Nutritional profile: 83% carbs / 14% protein / 3% fats
Calories: 165 per ¼ cup uncooked (which yields ½ cup cooked)
Protein: 6 grams
Timing: Cook until tender, about 1 hour (if presoaked) to 2 hours.
Ratio: 1:3 (1 cup wheat berries to 3 cups cooking liquid)

> **Tips:** Seek out hard red wheat berries for highest protein content (15%). Toast before soaking or cooking to achieve an even nuttier flavor. Sprout wheat berries and add to salads.

Botanical relatives: barley, corn, kamut, rye, spelt, triticale
Possible substitutes: rye berries, spelt, triticale

apples
artichoke hearts
asparagus
baked goods, e.g., breads
bay leaf
beans, e.g., black, white

bell peppers
breads
carrots
casseroles
cereals, hot breakfast
celery
chard, Swiss
cheese, e.g., cheddar, feta, goat, manchego, Parmesan, pecorino
chickpeas
chiles, e.g., green, jalapeño
chili, vegetarian (e.g., with beans)
cilantro
citrus
cloves
coriander
corn
cumin
curry powder
dill
eggplant
eggs, e.g., poached
fennel
figs
GARLIC
garlic chives
ginger
grains, other, e.g, barley, rice
kale

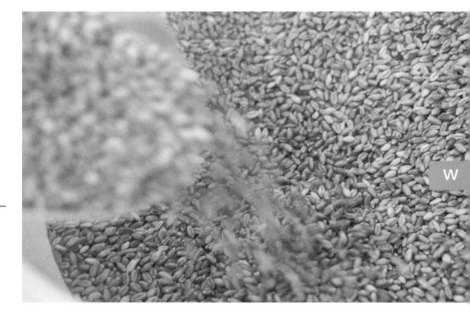

lemon, e.g., juice, zest
lentils
lime
milk
MUSHROOMS, e.g., shiitake, wild
NUTS, e.g., almonds, cashews,
    pine nuts, **walnuts**
oil, e.g., olive, sesame
ONIONS, e.g., red, yellow
parsley
peaches
peas
pepper, black
pilafs
pomegranate molasses
pumpkin seeds
quinoa
raisins
ramps
RICE, e.g., basmati, brown, wild
"RISOTTOS"
rosemary
sage
SALADS, e.g., grain, green
salt, e.g., sea
scallions
shallots
soups
spinach
sprouts, e.g., bean
STEWS, e.g., vegetable
STOCK, e.g., mushroom,
vegetable
stuffings, e.g., mushroom
sugar, e.g., brown
tamari
tarragon
thyme
tofu
tomatoes
tomatoes, sun-dried
turmeric
turnips
vegetables, esp. root
vinaigrette
vinegar, e.g., balsamic, cider,
    sherry
wine, e.g., dry white

yams
yogurt
zucchini

Flavor Affinities

wheat berries + apples + raisins +
    walnuts
wheat berries + asparagus +
    cheese + mushrooms + *risottos*
wheat berries + black beans +
    cilantro + garlic + lime
wheat berries + carrots + cumin
wheat berries + carrots + scallions
    + sesame oil + sprouts + tamari
wheat berries + celery +
    mushrooms + sage + thyme
wheat berries + feta cheese +
    lemon + pine nuts + spinach
wheat berries + peaches + yogurt

WHOLE FOODS

Refers to foods as they appear
in nature — that is, whole
(not processed, skinned, etc.).
Examples: fruits, grains, legumes,
mushrooms, nuts, seeds,
vegetables

WHOLE GRAINS (see GRAINS, WHOLE)

WILD RICE (see RICE, WILD)

WINE

(See sidebar.)

Sommelier Pascaline Lepeltier of Rouge Tomate in New York City on Pairing Wine with Vegetarian and Vegan Dishes

Although we are not a vegetarian restaurant, the cuisine here is
vegetable-focused. With meatless dishes, there is an incredible
spectrum of aromas, tastes, and textures — from raw fennel to
tomato-based dishes to grains and mushrooms. But with vegetables,
60 percent of the time, you're talking about pairing with a white
wine. To simplify things, think **seasonally:**

- **Spring / Summer:** When there are lots of green vegetables — such
  as spring asparagus, fava beans, and peas — you'll want to reach
  for aromatic wines with high acid, such as Sauvignon Blanc, Grüner
  Veltliner, dry Muscat, and Riesling. In summertime, you can add
  high-acid wines such as Assyrtiko, Muscadet (which is great with
  asparagus and artichokes, which are often wine killers),
  and Vouvray.
- **Autumn / Winter:** When there are lots of root vegetables — such
  as turnips and parsnips — you'll want to turn to wines with more
  richness and oxidation, such as white wines from the Rhone,
  including Viognier and Roussanne/Marsanne blends. Chardonnay
  with some malolactic and some oak and [slate-grown] Chenin
  will work here, too. I love Fiano from Italy at this time of year, or
  Pinot Grigio or wines from Friuli that have been made with some
  skin contact.

When you do want a red wine with vegetable dishes, we're talking about a higher-acid, lower-tannin red wine, such as a lighter-bodied Pinot Noir, Gamay (e.g., Beaujolais), or Grenache.

When I pair wines with dishes, I think about two primary things: (1) **Texture:** How a dish is built — (is it soft, crunchy, chewy, or melting in your mouth?), and (2) **Flavor:** Taste (is it sweet, sour, salty, bitter, umami?) plus Aroma.

When pairing with raw vegetables, there is typically a dressing of some kind — often lemon- or vinegar-based — to complement the crisp, bright, fresh flavors in the wine.

There are two main schools of thought: (1) Have the wine parallel a dish, so that it mimics it; or (2) have the wine balance the dish, so the wine brings something to the pairing. A few examples:

- **Green salad with herbs.** This is always on the menu and is slightly bitter with a lemon vinaigrette, which gives an overall impression of freshness. So I'm looking for a fresh-tasting wine. Sauvignon Blanc is the obvious choice — but I like to play with different types. I've turned to Sauvignon Gris from Burgundy, which is more aromatic yet has the green notes of a Sauvignon Blanc plus the minerality of a Chablis. If you're looking for a more adventurous or funky choice, I might turn to a dry Jurançon — a Manseng without oak, with a clean, herbal component.
- **Carrot salad with honey.** This salad has a touch of sweetness from the carrots, which are roasted and poached and accented with honey, and has a very soft texture, so it's almost melting in your mouth. The wine should have at least a hint of sweetness. I'm crazy about Chenin (Blanc), which can be slightly oily in texture while high in acid. Vouvray (which is made from Chenin Blanc) has a slightly vegetal character when it is young, and a touch of chamomile-like freshness, which is perfect with this.
- **Beet salad with pineapple.** This is perfect with rosé, especially a Grenache-based rosé, which has a strawberry aspect and a sweeter and earthier profile. I've also paired this salad with a white wine from the Douro region of Portugal, made from Rabigato grapes. It's rich and slightly off-dry, and similar to a Grenache Blanc, with its earthy tea and jasmine notes.
- **Potato/nettle soup.** Because the base is potato, the soup is starchy and the texture is thick — plus it's paired with an egg, which adds its own richness. So here, I want a wine that is rich and full-bodied, so higher in alcohol, to give the mouthfeel I'm looking for. I turn to a Juhfark from Hungary, which is similar to a Roussanne, but more aromatic and flinty.

WINTER

Weather: typically cold
Techniques: bake, braise, glaze, roast, simmer, slow-cook

allspice
apples
artichokes, Jerusalem
baked dishes
bananas
beans, e.g., dried, pinto, white
beets
braised dishes
broccoli (peak: February)
Brussels sprouts (peak: December)
buckwheat
cabbage, e.g., red, savoy
cardoons (peak: autumn/winter)
casseroles
cauliflower (peak: autumn/winter)
celery root
chayote
cheese, Vacherin Mont d'Or
chestnuts (peak: autumn/winter)
chicories
chocolate
cinnamon
citrus
clementines
coconut
cranberries (peak: autumn/winter)
daikon (peak: autumn/winter)
dates (peak: December)
endive, Belgian
escarole
fennel (peak: autumn/winter)
flour, heavier, e.g., buckwheat
frisée
grains, heavy
grapefruit (peak: February)
gratins
greens, bitter, e.g., mustard, turnip
herbs, dried
hot dishes

W

jícama (peak: winter/spring)
kale
kasha
kumquats (peak: autumn/winter)
leeks
lemons (peak: January)
lemons, Meyer
lentils (peak: autumn/winter)
limes
mâche
maple syrup
melon, winter
miso, dark
mushrooms, e.g., matsutake, wild
noodles, soba, esp. served hot
nutmeg
nuts
oils, nut
onions, e.g., pearl
oranges, e.g., blood
oranges, mandarin (peak:
   January)
parsley root
parsnips
passion fruit
pears (peak: December)
plantains
pomelo
potatoes, esp. baked
pressure-cooked dishes
radicchio
radishes, e.g., black (peak: winter/
   spring)
ragoûts
roasted dishes
root vegetables, e.g., carrots,
   celery root, parsnips, rutabagas,
   sweet potatoes, turnips
rosemary
rutabagas
sage
salsify (peak: autumn/winter)
savory, winter
SLOW-COOKED
soups, hot
spices, warming
squash, winter, e.g., acorn,
   buttercup, butternut, delicata

stews
sweet potatoes (peak: December)
tangerines (peak: January)
todok
truffles, e.g., black
turnips (peak: December)
ugli fruit (peak: winter/spring)
wakame (peak: winter/spring)
water chestnuts (peak: February)
yams (peak: December)

WORCESTERSHIRE SAUCE
Vegan Brands: Annie's, Edward & Sons' The Wizard's (organic)

YAMS
Flavor: slightly sweet, with notes of sweet potato, and a starchy texture
Volume: moderate

What they are: starchy
vegetable
Nutritional profile: 95% carbs
/ 4% protein / 1% fats
Calories: 160 per 1-cup serving
(boiled, cubed)
Protein: 2 grams
Techniques: bake (40 minutes),
boil (10 – 20 minutes), mash,
puree, roast, steam, stew (Note:
never raw)
Factoids: Yams are *not* botanical
relatives of sweet potatoes. Sweet
potatoes are more closely related
to morning glories than they are
to yams.
Possible substitutes: carrots,
pumpkin, sweet potatoes, winter
squash

African cuisine
agave nectar
allspice
almonds
apples
apricots, e.g., dried, fresh
Asian cuisine, and sometimes called
   "the potato of Asia"
bananas
cardamom
Caribbean cuisine
carrots
cayenne
chestnuts
chiles rellenos
chili pepper flakes and chili
   powder
chips

cilantro
CINNAMON
cloves
COCONUT and COCONUT
   MILK
coriander
crème fraîche
cumin
currants
curry powder and curry spices
eggs
GARLIC
ginger
gratins
greens, bitter, e.g., mustard
honey
kale
LEMON, e.g., juice, zest
lime, e.g., juice
maple syrup
milk, e.g., coconut, rice
millet
mustard and mustard seeds
North African cuisines
nutmeg
oil, e.g., canola, corn, grapeseed,
   olive, peanut, sesame
onions
ORANGE, e.g., juice, zest
oregano
parsnips
pasta, e.g., gnocchi
peanuts and peanut butter
peas, green
pepper, black
pistachios
plantains, e.g., green
potatoes
puddings

quesadillas
rice, brown
sage
salads
salt, kosher or sea
seeds, e.g., pumpkin, sesame,
   sunflower
sesame, e.g., oil, seeds
shallots
SOUPS, e.g., kale, peanut, yam
soy sauce
stews
tamari
tamarind, e.g., paste
tangerine
tempeh
thyme
tomatoes and tomato paste
turmeric
veggie burgers
yogurt

Flavor Affinities
yams + bananas + cinnamon +
   honey + orange juice
yams + cinnamon + orange
yams + coconut milk + garlic +
   nutmeg + thyme
yams + coconut + ginger + maple
yams + garlic + sage
yams + garlic + thyme
yams + honey + lime
yams + sesame seeds + tahini

YEAST, NUTRITIONAL (see NUTRITIONAL YEAST)

YOGURT
Flavor: sour, with a thick,
creamy texture
Volume: moderate – loud
Nutritional profile: 53% carbs
(high in sugars) / 44% protein /
3% fat (skim, plain)
Calories: 140 per 1-cup serving
(skim, plain)
Protein: 13 grams

Dishes

Slow Roasted Garnet Yam: Cherry Belle Radishes, Hadley Orchards' Medjool Dates,
Broccolini, Marcona Almonds, and Madras Curry
— Per Se (New York City)

Homemade Yam Chips with Fresh Thyme and Garlic Oil
— Plum Bistro (Seattle)

Y

Tips: Consider opting for plain (i.e., unflavored), ● skim, or ● low-fat yogurt, or nondairy (e.g., soy) yogurt. Freeze partially and serve as a semifreddo; drizzle with maple syrup, and/or top with fresh fruit, such as berries.

almonds
apples
apricots
avocados
bananas
barley
basil
beans, e.g., fava, **lima**, white
beets
berries, in general or mixed
blueberries
carrots
cayenne
celery
cereals, breakfast, esp.
  GRANOLA, MUESLI
cheese, e.g., feta, goat
cherries
chervil
chickpeas
chives
cilantro
coconut
coriander
CUCUMBERS
cumin
DILL
dips
drinks
EGGPLANT
fennel
figs
fruit, dried
GARLIC
ginger
grains, whole, e.g., bulgur, oats,
  spelt
Greek cuisine
greens, e.g., dandelion
hazelnuts

Dishes

Yogurt and Berries: Vanilla Greek Yogurt with Fresh Seasonal Berries, Granola, Honey
— The Golden Door Spa Café at The Boulders (Scottsdale, AZ)

Yogurt Parfait: Buckwheat, Hemp Seed, and Dried Fruit Granola with Fresh Blueberries
— Pure Food and Wine (New York City)

Lemon-Ginger Low-Fat Frozen Yogurt, Fresh Berries
— True Food Kitchen (Santa Monica)

Flavor Affinities

yogurt + balsamic vinegar + strawberries
yogurt + basil + Dijon mustard + olive oil + sherry vinegar
yogurt + beets + cucumbers
yogurt + beets + walnuts
yogurt + berries (e.g., blueberries) + **sweetener** (e.g., honey, maple syrup)
yogurt + cardamom + vanilla
yogurt + chickpeas + spinach
yogurt + chiles + dill + lemon + scallions
yogurt + cilantro (+ cumin) + **lime**
yogurt + coriander + cumin + garlic + ginger
YOGURT + CUCUMBERS + CUMIN + MINT
YOGURT + CUCUMBERS + GARLIC
YOGURT + CUCUMBERS + GARLIC + LEMON + MINT + parsley + tahini + white wine vinegar
yogurt + cucumbers + onions
yogurt + dill + feta cheese + garlic
yogurt + eggplant + garlic + walnuts
yogurt + fennel + leeks *soups*
yogurt + figs + honey + walnuts
yogurt + garlic + mint + *raitas*
yogurt + garlic + lemon + olive oil + oregano + spinach
yogurt + ginger + plums
yogurt + herbs (e.g., oregano, thyme) + lemon
yogurt + honey + lavender + mint
yogurt + honey + vanilla + walnuts
yogurt + lemon + thyme
yogurt + maple syrup + walnuts
yogurt + orange + walnuts
yogurt + pistachios + strawberries
yogurt + pomegranate seeds + walnuts

herbs, in general or mixed
honey
horseradish
Indian cuisine

lamb's lettuce
lassis, e.g., *mango*
lavender
Lebanese cuisine

LEMON, e.g., juice
lentils
lime, e.g., juice
mango
maple syrup
marinades
Middle Eastern cuisines
MINT
mushrooms
mustard, e.g., Dijon, seeds
nuts
oats
oil, olive
onions, e.g., yellow
orange, e.g., juice, zest
oregano
papaya
paprika
parsley
peaches
peas
pecans
pineapple
pistachios
plantains
pomegranate seeds
potatoes
radishes
raisins
RAITAS
raspberries
rhubarb
rice
salad dressings, e.g., green goddess
salads
salt
SAUCES, e.g., raita, tzatziki,
  yogurt
scallions
smoothies
SOUPS, e.g., cucumber
sorrel
spinach
spreads
squash, butternut
strawberries
sugar, e.g., brown
tahini

tamarind
tempeh
thyme
tomatoes
Turkish cuisine
vanilla
vinegar, e.g., balsamic, red wine,
  sherry, wine
WALNUTS
watercress
yogurt, e.g., frozen or semi-frozen
za'atar
zucchini

YUBA (see TOFU SKIN)

● YUCA (aka CASSAVA)
[YOO-kah]
Flavor: slightly sweet, with starchy notes of tapioca, and a crisp texture (similar to that of potatoes)
Volume: quiet
What it is: root vegetable, made from cassava
Nutritional profile: 97% carbs / 2% protein / 1% fat
Calories: 330 per 1-cup serving (raw)
Protein: 3 grams
Techniques: bake, boil (20 – 30 minutes), fry, grate, mash, puree, roast, sauté, simmer (20+ minutes), stew (Note: Never eat it raw, as raw yuca can be toxic.)

Tip: Cook like potatoes, to which yucas are similar.

Botanical relative: tapioca

Asian cuisines
baked goods, e.g., breads
beans, e.g., kidney
bell peppers, e.g., roasted
beans, black
butter
cakes, yuca
chayote

chiles, e.g., jalapeño, serrano; and chili pepper flakes
chips, yuca
CILANTRO
COCONUT, coconut cream, and coconut milk
corn
curry powder
custard
Dominican cuisine
fries, yuca
GARLIC
ginger
Indian cuisine
Latin American cuisines
LIME, e.g., juice
Mexican cuisine
noodles
oil, e.g., olive, vegetable
onions
orange
oregano
parsley
plantains
salt, e.g., sea
shepherd's pie
soups, e.g., corn
South American cuisines
Southwestern (U.S.) cuisine
spinach
stews
sweet potatoes
tarragon
Thai cuisine
thyme
tortillas, e.g., corn, whole-wheat
vinegar, e.g., red wine, white wine

Flavor Affinities
yuca + bell pepper + chiles + garlic + lime + olive oil
yuca + chiles + citrus (e.g., lime, orange)
YUCA + CILANTRO + LIME

YUCCA (see YUCA)

YUZU

Season: autumn – spring
Flavor: sour; aromatic, with citrus (grapefruit, lemon, lime, orange) notes
Volume: moderate – loud (and louder than lemon juice)
What it is: Japanese citrus fruit
What's healthful about it: contains three times the vitamin C of lemons

> **Tip:** Use like other citrus fruit, i.e., for both its juice and zest.

Asian cuisines
bananas
beverages, e.g., cocktails, juices, lemonades/limeades
cheese, cream
chiles, e.g., green, red
daikon
desserts
Japanese cuisine
Korean cuisine
marinades
mirin
miso
oil, e.g., canola, grapeseed, olive, vegetable
orange, e.g., juice
pomegranates
PONZU SAUCE
salad dressings
salt
sauces, e.g., mayonnaises, mignonettes
sea vegetables
SESAME, e.g., SEEDS
shiso
sorbet
Southeast Asian cuisines
soy sauce
sugar
tapioca
vinegar, e.g., rice

Flavor Affinities
yuzu + bananas + chocolate + sesame
yuzu + chiles + salt
yuzu + pomegranates + sorbet
yuzu + sea vegetables + sesame seeds

ZA'ATAR (the herb; see also ZA'ATAR, the spice blend)

[zah-TAHR]
Flavor: pungent, aromatic, with notes of marjoram, oregano, and/or thyme
Volume: moderate – loud
What it is: a family of herbs that has been called "the king of herbs" and "one of the world's greatest seasonings" by some chefs.

dips
hummus
Mediterranean cuisines
Middle Eastern cuisines
oil, olive
olives
sesame seeds
soups
sumac

ZA'ATAR (the spice blend; see also ZA'ATAR, the herb)

[zah-TAHR]
Flavor: sour (tangy), with notes of herbs and nuts, and a coarse texture
Volume: moderate
What it is: a blend of dried herbs and spices used in the Middle East and North Africa that may include some or all of the following: black pepper + coriander + cumin + fennel seeds + hyssop + **marjoram** or **oregano** + mint + parsley + sage + **SALT** + savory + *SESAME SEEDS* + *SUMAC* + *THYME*

beans, e.g., black, fava, white
BREADS, e.g., WHOLE-GRAIN FLATBREADS, PITA
cauliflower
cheese, e.g., labneh
chickpeas
cucumbers, e.g., sliced
dips, e.g., for bread
eggplant
eggs
falafel
fennel
garlic
hummus
kebabs
Lebanese cuisine
lentils
lime, e.g., juice
Mediterranean cuisines
MIDDLE EASTERN CUISINES
mint
North African cuisine
OLIVE OIL
olives, e.g., black
onions
pasta
peas
pistachios
pizza
potatoes, e.g., baked, fried, steamed
quinoa
rice
rosemary
saffron
salads
sandwiches
tomatoes
vegetables, e.g., grilled
yogurt, e.g., greek
zucchini

Flavor Affinities
za'atar + feta cheese + olive oil + yogurt

Dishes

Tasting of Fennel with Zaatar: Saffron-Tomato Relish, Garbanzo Bean
— DANIEL (New York City)

za'atar + olive oil + pine nuts + yogurt

za'atar + olive oil + pistachios + quinoa

"I make my own **za'atar spice mix** with marjoram, sesame seeds, sumac, oregano, and thyme, which I'll dry out on sheet trays. I'll use it as an accent on cornmeal flatbread with onion and rosemary — or as a good garnish for falafel. You can also add mint and sprinkle on fava beans."

— CHARLEEN BADMAN, FnB (SCOTTSDALE, AZ)

● ZUCCHINI (see also SQUASH, SUMMER)

Season: summer

Flavor: sweet, with notes of butter, cream, cucumber, and/or nuts, and a soft, tender texture

Volume: quiet – moderate

Nutritional profile: 73% carbs / 18% protein / 9% fats

Calories: 20 per 1-cup serving (chopped, raw)

Protein: 2 grams

Techniques: bake, boil, broil, deep-fry, fry, grate, grill, marinate, pan-roast, raw, sauté, shave (e.g., on mandoline, into pappardelle), spiralize, steam, stir-fry, stuff

Tips: Shave raw zucchini thinly lengthwise on a mandoline for salads or to use as "pasta." Eat the peel, too, which is an excellent source of fiber.

Botanical relatives: squash, summer and winter

almonds
apples
artichokes
arugula
asparagus
baked goods, e.g., *breads, cakes, muffins, quick breads*
BASIL and Thai basil
beans, e.g., fava, green, kidney
bell peppers, e.g., green, red, esp. roasted
bread crumbs
bulgur
butter
capers

"carpaccio"
carrots
cayenne
CHEESE, e.g., cheddar,
  FETA, Fontina, goat, Gruyère,
  mozzarella, PARMESAN,
  pecorino, **RICOTTA,** ricotta
  salata, Romano, sheep's milk,
  Swiss
chervil
chickpeas
chiles, e.g., ancho, green,
  poblano; chili pepper flakes and
  chili powder
chips, vegetable
chives
cilantro
cinnamon
citrus
coconut milk
corn
couscous
curry powder and *curries*
DILL
eggplant
eggs, e.g., *frittatas, omelets,*
  quiches, scrambled
GARLIC
ginger
gratins
hazelnuts
"lasagna," made with zucchini
  strips instead of noodles
leeks
LEMON, e.g., juice, zest
lime, e.g., juice, zest
marjoram
mascarpone
millet
MINT
mushrooms, e.g., cremini
noodles, Asian, e.g., kelp, rice
nutmeg
OILS, e.g., grapeseed, hazelnut,
  OLIVE, pecan, sunflower,
  walnut
olives, e.g., black
onions

orange, e.g., fruit, juice
oregano
parsley
PASTA, e.g., farfalle, fettuccine,
  lasagna, linguini,
  orecchiette, penne, rigatoni
pecans
pepper, e.g., black, white
pesto
pilafs
PINE NUTS
pistachios
pizza
polenta

potatoes
pumpkin
quinoa
raisins
ratatouille
rice, e.g., brown
risottos
rosemary
sage
salads, e.g., raw zucchini
salt, e.g., kosher, sea
sauces
SOUPS, *e.g., potato, tomato,*
  vegetable, zucchini

Flavor Affinities

zucchini + arugula + lemon + olive oil + **Parmesan cheese**
zucchini + balsamic vinegar + eggplant + tomatoes
zucchini + basil + capers + olives
zucchini + basil + garlic + olive oil + **Parmesan** + pistachios
zucchini + basil + lemon + ricotta cheese
zucchini + basil + nuts (e.g., almonds, pine nuts, pistachios) +
  Parmesan cheese
zucchini + basil + *risotto* + tomatoes
zucchini + bell peppers + eggplant + garlic + parsley
zucchini + chiles + cilantro + corn + garlic + tomatoes
zucchini + chili pepper flakes + marjoram + yogurt
zucchini + cinnamon + nutmeg + nuts + raisins + vanilla
zucchini + citrus + mint
zucchini + coconut + curry + tofu
zucchini + coconut + ginger
zucchini + dill + **feta cheese** + lemon + **mint**
zucchini + feta cheese + garlic + parsley
ZUCCHINI + GARLIC + LEMON
zucchini + garlic + lemon + mascarpone + nutmeg + parsley + *pasta*
zucchini + garlic + mint + olive oil + vinegar
ZUCCHINI + GARLIC + OLIVE OIL + oregano + **Parmesan cheese** +
  tomatoes
zucchini + ginger + orange + tofu
ZUCCHINI + LEMON (+ mint) + PARMESAN CHEESE
zucchini + lemon + mint + pine nuts + yogurt
zucchini + lemon + olive oil + ricotta + thyme
zucchini + lemon + olives + oregano
zucchini + marjoram + ricotta cheese + tomatoes
zucchini + mint + rice noodles
zucchini + mushrooms + polenta
zucchini + nutmeg + Parmesan cheese + parsley
zucchini + pine nuts + raisins + rice

spinach

stews

stir-fries

tagines

tahini

tamari

tapenade

tarragon

tempura

thyme

tofu

TOMATOES and sun-dried tomatoes

vanilla

veggie burgers (e.g., zucchini + almonds)

vinegar, e.g., balsamic, champagne, red wine, sherry, white wine

walnuts

yogurt

zucchini blossoms

zucchini, stuffed, e.g., with couscous, mushrooms, pine nuts, raisins, rice, ricotta

"**Zucchini** shaved on a mandoline into pappardelle, and marinated in lime juice, olive oil, and salt, makes a very silky vegetable pasta. If it's grilled when raw, it cooks unevenly and tends to turn to mush — but if you roast it first to al dente, and just flash it on the grill, it helps it maintain its integrity."

— RICH LANDAU, VEDGE (PHILADELPHIA)

Dishes

Zucchini Cake with Cream Cheese Frosting and Candied Limes

— ABC Kitchen (New York City)

Raw Zucchini Rolatini: Basil Cashew Cheese Filling, Chive Oil Sesame Sunflower Sprouts, Avocado

— Blossom (New York City)

Raw Pesto Linguini: Ribbons of Raw Zucchini, Walnut-Basil Pesto, Marinated Mushrooms, Cherry Tomatoes, and Cashew Ricotta

— The Butcher's Daughter (New York City)

Live Zucchini Enchiladas: Cashew Cheese, Spinach, Guacamole, Chipotle-Tomato Sauce, Cashew Sour Cream, Pumpkin Seeds, Baby Romaine, Cucumber-Tomato Salsa

— Candle 79 (New York City)

Tostadas de Frijol y Calabaza: Smashed White Beans and Roasted Zucchini on a Fried Tortilla with Green Cabbage, Jalapeno Relish, Crema, and Cilantro

— El Parador Café (New York City)

Flourish Veggie Roast Vegetable Pot Pie with Roasted Zucchini, Red Bell Peppers, Onions, and Eggplant stewed with Tomato, Spinach, Garlic, and Fresh Basil

— Flourish Baking Company (Scarsdale, NY)

Zucchini Pappardelle: Squash Blossom Tempura filled with Tofu Ricotta, Basil Pesto, Preserved Tomato

— Plume (Washington, DC)

ZUCCHINI BLOSSOMS

Season: summer

Flavor: notes of zucchini, with a very delicate texture

Volume: quiet

Techniques: bake, braise, deep-fry, fry, poach, sauté, steam, stew, stuff

basil

beans

beets, e.g., yellow

bell peppers, e.g., red, yellow

bread crumbs

capers

celery

CHEESE, e.g., feta, **goat, mozzarella, PARMESAN, RICOTTA,** sheep's milk, soft

chiles, e.g., poblano

chives

cilantro

corn

dill

EGGS, e.g., *frittatas, omelets*

epazote

French cuisine

GARLIC

grains

gratins

herbs

Italian cuisine

lemon

marjoram

Mediterranean cuisines

Mexican cuisine, e.g., *quesadillas, soups*

mint

nutmeg

OIL, OLIVE

olives, e.g., French, Italian

onions, e.g., white

orange, e.g., juice, zest

oregano

parsley

pastas, e.g., *fettuccine, gnocchi, linguini, pappardelle*

pepper, black
pine nuts
potatoes, new
rice
risottos
sage
salads
salt, e.g., sea
sauces
scallions
shallots
soups
Southwestern (U.S.) cuisine
spinach
squash, summer
stock, vegetable
STUFFED ZUCCHINI
  BLOSSOMS, e.g., fried
tempura
thyme
tomatoes *and* **tomato sauce**
zucchini

Flavor Affinities
zucchini blossoms + basil + garlic
  + olive oil
zucchini blossoms + feta cheese
  + mint
zucchini blossoms + goat cheese
  + pine nuts
zucchini blossoms + ricotta +
  sage

"I love serving **zucchini blossoms**
with pastas, especially linguini or
pappardelle. Their flavors pair
beautifully with fresh tomatoes,
basil, and zucchini, not to
mention cashew cheeses."
— ANGEL RAMOS, CANDLE 79
(NEW YORK CITY)

Dishes

Zucchini Flowers bursting with Softened Buckwheat; Purees of Roasted Sweet Potato,
 Onion
— Brushstroke (New York City)

Cornmeal-Crusted Zucchini Blossoms with Heirloom Tomatoes, Balsamic Reduction,
Watercress Salad with a Spicy Jalapeno-Lime Vinaigrette
— Candle 79 (New York City)

ACKNOWLEDGMENTS

"[The Flavor Bible] is a resource tool that I turn to time and time again."
— ANGELA LIDDON, BLOGGER AND AUTHOR OF *THE OH SHE GLOWS COOKBOOK*

"[The Flavor Bible is] one of my three favorite non-cookbook books."
— ROBIN ROBERTSON, AUTHOR OF MORE THAN TWENTY COOKBOOKS, INCLUDING *VEGAN PLANET*

"If you look on any professional chef's bookshelf, chances are that Page and Dornenburg's books are going to be there, battered and bruised, coffee stained and taped together at the spine. Why this place of pride? Because these books contain the most useful culinary lists ever assembled."
— MICHAEL NATKIN, BLOGGER AND AUTHOR OF *HERBIVORACIOUS*

I am grateful for the warm support of the countless vegetarian and vegan writers whose appreciation of our work provided invaluable encouragement along this path.

I am grateful to all the chefs, restaurateurs, fellow authors, and other experts I interviewed, who were unfailingly generous in sharing their time and insights. Candle 79 co-owners Joy Pierson and Bart Potenza are so warm and welcoming that I felt as if I'd known them forever upon our first meeting, and Joy — a nutritionist by training — became an especially valuable sounding board.

I am grateful for the awe-inspiring work of three authors whose work has influenced me greatly. I am enormously grateful to Dr. T. Colin Campbell for making his Center for Nutrition Studies' extraordinary certificate program in plant-based nutrition available through Cornell University; I found it nothing short of life-changing. I am grateful to Dr. Neal Barnard, whose articulate arguments helped me discover what I myself believe. And I am grateful to Dr. Joel Fuhrman for being responsible for my "seeing the light" about nutrient density, a concept that has helped me make more healthful food choices every day since.

My husband, Andrew (to whom I'm grateful for his extraordinarily beautiful photographs, and more), joins me in expressing gratitude to our family members and to new and old friends who were incredible sources of love, support, and friendship, especially Rosario Acquista, Ivan Askwith, Steve Beckta, Kristen Bell, Bill Bratton, Brian Burry, Susan Bulkeley Butler, John Carter, Ilene Cavagnuolo, Howard Childs, Maureen Cunningham, Julia D'Amico, Blake Davis, Julia Davis, Susan Davis, Laura Day, Samson Day, Susan Dey, Deborah Domanski, Jill Eikenberry, Ashley Garrett, Michael Gelb, Marketa Irglova, Alan Jones, my nutrition-obsessed bff Rikki Klieman, Brendan Milburn, Jody Oberfelder, Kelley Olson, Scott Olson, Cynthia Penney, Jeff

Penney, Lynn Pike, Deborah Pines, Caroline Pires, Juergen Riehm, Stuart Rockefeller, Stephen Schiff, Tony Schwartz, Leslie Scott, Michael Tucker, Jane Umanoff, and Valerie Vigoda. Cynthia Penney provided invaluable editorial feedback, and we must also thank Shauna James Ahern, Joan Green, Tami Hardeman, Cameron Karger, Ellie Krieger, Teresa Schlanger, and Janos Wilder for their kindnesses.

I will be forever grateful to everyone on the extended Little, Brown team — with special, heartfelt thanks to my editor Michael Sand — who shared my passion for this book and for making it as good, true, and beautiful as possible, and who offered moral or other support along the way, including Reagan Arthur, Judy Clain, Nicole Dewey, Heather Fain, Peggy Freudenthal, Cathy Gruhn, Keith Hayes, Denise LaCongo, Garrett McGrath, Michael Pietsch, Kathryn Rogers, Andrea Shallcross, Rebecca Westall, and Jean Wilcox.

KAREN PAGE

PHOTOGRAPHER'S ACKNOWLEDGMENTS

I am grateful to the author of this book for giving me my big break as a photographer. I am also grateful to her for writing such an epic book and giving me the opportunity to create images to help bring it to life, providing the countless hours of encouragement and support that I needed to accomplish this mission, and being the greatest wife on the planet all along the way. With all the love in the universe, I thank you, Karen.

I am grateful to the farmers who pour their hearts and souls into creating produce all across the country — from the North Fork of Long Island to the heartland of Chicago to the California coast — produce so beautiful that it was a privilege to photograph it. My very favorite is the Union Square Greenmarket in New York City (GrowNYC.org), with which — after buying the vast majority of the produce we've eaten over the past two years there — I have come to feel a sacred bond. Special thanks to Bobolink Dairy and Jonathan White; Bodhitree Farm and Nevia No; Greener Pastures; Lani's Farm; Lucky Dog Farm and Richard Giles; Keith's Farm; Migliorelli Farm; Queens County Farm Museum and Keha McIlwaine and Karen Jarman; S & S O Produce Farms; Violet Hill Farm; Windfall Farms; and W. Rogowski Farm and Andrzej Kurosz.

I am grateful to all of the restaurants that inspired me by creating beautiful plant-based dishes, including Betony, Candle 79 and both Candle Cafes, Café Gratitude, Cookbook, Crossroads, Dirt Candy, Dovetail, Downtown, Eleven Madison Park, FnB, Glenmere Mansion, Hotel Fauchère, The Inn at Little Washington (and Rachel Hayden), Kajitsu, Mélisse, Narcissa, Per Se, Picholine, The Point, Pomegranate Café, Rouge Tomate, Suenos, Table Verte, Tulsi, and Vedge.

I am grateful to Little, Brown editor Michael Sand for his keen eye and invaluable input on the photography for this book.

Finally, I am grateful to my talented photographer friend Howard ("I will be in Japan, but call me if you have a question") Childs for never failing to offer encouragement, time, and advice.

ANDREW DORNENBURG

ABOUT THE EXPERTS

Aaron Adams is the chef-owner of Portobello Vegan Trattoria in Portland, Oregon. portobellopdx.com

Dave Anderson is the chef-owner of Maddy's (opened 2013), and the former chef-owner of Madeleine Bistro (2005–2013), in Los Angeles. maddysla.com

Charleen Badman is the vegetarian chef-owner of the vegetable-centric restaurant FnB in Scottsdale, Arizona. fnbrestaurant.com

Dr. Neal Barnard is the founder of the Physicians Committee for Responsible Medicine, based in Washington, DC. pcrm.org

Christopher Bates, MS, was the executive chef and general manager of the vegetable-driven Delmonico Room at the Hotel Fauchère in Milford, Pennsylvania. hotelfauchere.com / elementwinery.com

Ami Beach is the raw chef and co-owner with her husband, chef Mark Shadle, of G-Zen in Branford, Connecticut. g-zen.com

Colin Bedford is the executive chef of the Fearrington House Restaurant in Fearrington Village, North Carolina. fearrington.com

Terrance Brennan is the chef-owner of Picholine in New York City, which has offered a vegetarian tasting menu since 2008. picholinenyc.com

Pam Brown is the chef-owner of Garden Café on the Green in Woodstock, New York. woodstockgardencafe.com

Fernanda Capobianco is the chef-owner of Vegan Divas in New York City. vegandivasnyc.com

Josiah Citrin is the chef-owner of Mélisse in Santa Monica, California, which has offered a vegetarian tasting menu since its opening. melisse.com

Amanda Cohen is the chef-owner of the restaurant Dirt Candy in New York City. dirtcandynyc.com

Jon DuBois is the chef de cuisine of Green Zebra in Chicago. greenzebrachicago.com

Chris Eddy is the executive chef of Winvian in Morris, Connecticut. winvian.com

Diane Forley is the chef and co-owner with her husband, Chef Michael Otsuka, of Flourish Baking Company in Scarsdale, New York. www.flourishbakingcompany.com

Bob Goldberg is one of four founders and co-owner (with Paul Lewin) of Follow Your Heart, one of Los Angeles' first vegetarian restaurants and the originator of Vegenaise. followyourheart.com

Gael Greene has been one of America's leading restaurant critics for more than four decades. insatiable-critic.com

Makini Howell is the chef-owner of Plum Bistro in Seattle. plumbistro.com

Kate Jacoby is the pastry chef and co-owner with her husband, chef Rich Landau, of Vedge in Philadelphia. vedgerestaurant.com

Deena Jalal is the co-owner (with her husband, Hin Tang) of FoMu: Alternative Ice Cream and Root: Inspired Food and Juicery in Allston, Massachusetts, just outside Boston. fomuicecream.com / rootboston.com

Mollie Katzen is the bestselling vegetarian cookbook author — and one of the bestselling cookbook authors — of all time. molliekatzen.com

Matthew Kenney is the chef-owner of M.A.K.E. in Los Angeles. matthewkenneycuisine.com

Rich Landau is the chef and co-owner with his wife, pastry chef Kate Jacoby, of Vedge in Philadelphia. vedgerestaurant.com

Ken Larsen was the executive chef of Table Verte, New York City's first French vegetarian restaurant. He and his sous chef, Matt Roth, now operate Simply Home, a vegetarian catering company. simplyhomenyc.com

Mark Levy is the executive chef of The Point in Saranac Lake, New York. thepointsaranac.com

Pascaline Lepeltier, MS, is the sommelier of Rouge Tomate in New York City. www.rougetomatenyc.com

Deborah Madison is the founding chef of Greens Restaurant in San Francisco and one of America's bestselling vegetarian cookbook authors. deborahmadison.com

Gaby Martinez is the general manager and mixologist of Candle 79 in New York City. candle79.com

Hemant Mathur is the chef-owner of Tulsi in New York City. tulsinyc.com

Selma Miriam is the founder and chef of Bloodroot in Bridgeport, Connecticut. bloodroot.com

Adam Mosher is the co-chef of the Lodge at Woodloch in Hawley, Pennsylvania. thelodgeatwoodloch.com

Isa Chandra Moskowitz, whose books include *Isa Does It* and *Veganomicon,* is one of America's bestselling vegan cookbook authors and is based in Omaha. theppk.com

Andres Padilla is the chef of Rick and Deann Bayless's restaurant Topolobampo in Chicago. fronterafiesta.com/restaurants

Joy Pierson is a nutritionist and a co-owner of Candle 79 in New York City. candle79.com

Jorge Pineda is the pastry chef and kitchen manager of Candle 79 in New York City. candle79.com

Bart Potenza is the founder and a co-owner of Candle 79 in New York City. candle79.com

Angel Ramos is the executive chef of Candle 79 in New York City. candle79.com

Tal Ronnen is the chef-owner of Crossroads in Los Angeles. crossroadskitchen.com

Suvir Saran was the executive chef of Devi in New York City and is the chef-owner of a forthcoming Indian restaurant in San Francisco. suvir.com

Chad Sarno leads the Plant-Based Professional Certification Course at Rouxbe.com and is co-author with Kris Carr of the bestseller *Crazy Sexy Kitchen*. chadsarno.com

Mark Shadle is the chef and co-owner, with his wife, raw chef Ami Beach, of G-Zen in Branford, Connecticut. g-zen.com

Bryce Shuman is the executive chef of Betony in New York City. betony-nyc.com

Annie Somerville is the executive chef of Greens Restaurant in San Francisco. greensrestaurant.com

Cassie Tolman (with her mother, Marlene Tolman) is the co-chef and co-owner of Pomegranate Café in Phoenix. pomegranatecafe.com

Marlene Tolman (with her daughter, Cassie Tolman) is the co-chef and co-owner of Pomegranate Café in Phoenix. pomegranatecafe.com

Eric Tucker is the executive chef of Millennium in San Francisco. millenniumrestaurant.com

Ryota Ueshima is the executive chef of Kajitsu in New York City. kajitsunyc.com

Shawain Whyte is the executive chef of Café Blossom in New York City's Greenwich Village. blossomnyc.com / cafecarmine.php

Aaron Woo is the chef-owner of Natural Selection in Portland, Oregon. naturalselectionpdx.com

ABOUT THE AUTHOR

Karen Page is a two-time James Beard Award–winning author whose books include *The Flavor Bible,* which was named one of the year's best cookbooks on both *Today* and *Good Morning America,* one of the 100 best cookbooks of the last twenty-five years by *Cooking Light,* and one of the ten best cookbooks in the world of the past century by *Forbes.* The former *Washington Post* wine columnist is also the author of *What to Drink with What You Eat,* which was named the IACP Cookbook of the Year and Georges Duboeuf Wine Book of the Year. She lives with her husband, author and photographer Andrew Dornenburg, in New York City.

ABOUT THE PHOTOGRAPHER

Former restaurant chef **Andrew Dornenburg** grew up in San Francisco with a grandmother who had her own darkroom, and he inherited her love of photography and, later, his family's camera equipment, which fueled his early experimentation. The culmination of a lifelong dream to unite his love of food with his passion for creating beautiful images, this is his first book as a photographer.

"The fact is that healthful eating consistently emphasizes the same foods: vegetables, fruits, beans, legumes, nuts, seeds, and whole grains."
—DR. DAVID KATZ, IN *DISEASE-PROOF: THE REMARKABLE TRUTH ABOUT WHAT MAKES US WELL* (2013)

"Seven of the top ten causes of death in 2010 were chronic diseases [such as heart disease, stroke, cancer, diabetes, obesity. Health risk behaviors that cause chronic diseases include poor nutrition.] . . . In 2011, more than one third (36%) of adolescents said they ate fruit less than once a day, and 38% said they ate vegetables less than once a day. In addition, 38% of adults said they ate fruit less than once a day, and 23% said they ate vegetables less than once a day."
— NATIONAL CENTER FOR CHRONIC DISEASE PREVENTION AND HEALTH PROMOTION (2014)

"It takes kids about twelve exposures to a taste to begin to like it. So it takes a while for them to get used to the idea that broccoli actually tastes good — and to admit that it does."
— DR. MEHMET OZ, WHO HAS SAID ON OPRAH.COM THAT HE EATS VEGETARIAN AT HOME WITH HIS WIFE, LISA (A VEGETARIAN SINCE AGE 15)

NOELLE, DAUGHTER OF TOM AND JILL STEVENSON, GROWERS OF EXQUISITE BERRIES AT OYSTERPONDS FARM ON THE NORTH FORK OF LONG ISLAND